14⁹⁵

Trees and Shrubs
For
Pacific Northwest Gardens

A native specimen of the western dogwood (*Cornus nuttallii*) flowering in Seattle in late April. Photo by E. F. Marten.

JOHN A. GRANT AND CAROL L. GRANT

Trees and Shrubs For Pacific Northwest Gardens

Second Edition

Revised by
Marvin E. Black, Brian O. Mulligan,
Joseph A. Witt and Jean G. Witt

TIMBER PRESS
Portland, Oregon

ISBN 0-88192-145-9
Printed in The United States of America

TIMBER PRESS, INC.
9999 S.W. Wilshire
Portland, Oregon 97225

Library of Congress Cataloging-in-Publication Data

Grant, John A. (John Alexander), 1913-
    Trees and shrubs for Pacific Northwest gardens / John A. Grant and
Carol L. Grant. -- 2nd ed. / revised by Marvin E. Black ... [et al.]
      p.   cm.
    Bibliography: p.
    Includes index.
    ISBN 0-88192-145-9
    1. Ornamental trees--Northwest, Pacific. 2. Ornamental shrubs-
-Northwest, Pacific. 3. Landscape gardening--Northwest, Pacific.
I. Grant, Carol L. (Carol Longabaugh). 1906-   . II. Black, Marvin
E.   III. Title.
SB435.52.N6G73   1989
635.9'76'09795--dc20
                                                89-31343
                                                   CIP

Contents

To Joe and Marvin

————————————

Foreword

The need for this book became increasingly apparent when I started to write on garden design for this region. I soon came to the conclusion that a book on design would have little value unless there was an easily available source of information about plant materials—the material from which a garden design is made.

The preparation of this volume has involved not only a great deal of research but a tremendous amount of checking and editing to make sure that it was as nearly complete and comprehensive as possible within its given boundaries. To Carol Grant, my wife, goes the credit for much of the hard work, the typing and re-typing, the checking and re-checking, the constant revision and refinement, that has made the book what it is in form, style, and content. It would have been impossible without her enthusiasm, combined with her executive and organizing ability, for the book to have assumed either the proportions or the degree of completeness which it has now reached. In addition to this, she has brought to the work a fresh viewpoint, and, in particular, is responsible for seeing that this book on plant material was not top-heavy with design. A much clearer statement of horticultural facts and practices has resulted from our combined viewpoints.

I want also to express my deepest appreciation to all those who have given me encouragement and convinced me of the need for this book, as well as to those who have taken part in the actual labour of its execution.

J. A. G.

Preface to the Second Edition

Forty-five years ago when the first edition of this book was published it filled a real need for information on plants and their cultivation in our gardens here in the Pacific Northwest; in the subsequent 4½ decades it has fully lived up to its authors' purposes, as its continuing popularity attests.

In the interim Northwesterners have become increasingly aware of the favored status in the gardening world which our geographical location and climate give us, and interest in gardening and plants of all kinds has never been higher. Not only have the numbers of our gardens increased as our population has grown, but the quality and variety of available plant materials has greatly expanded; it has probably doubled or more so within this time frame, as has the number of nurseries growing and distributing plants.

The purpose of this second edition, therefore, is to acquaint another generation of the gardening public with this great volume of suitable and useful plant material, to the end that more of it will come into common use and our Northwest gardens will become even more beautiful and varied in the future.

We wish to express our particular appreciation to those persons who have assisted us at various stages of this work with special texts or suggestions, especially to Mr. Bob Badger, Miss Sharon Collman, Mr. A. L. Jacobson, Mr. Edward Lewis, and Mr. Ted van Veen. Also to numerous other friends who answered questions and contributed ideas. Mr. and Mrs. John Grant have read and approved the revised text, with some welcome additions.

B. O. M. and J. G. W.

CHAPTER I

Introduction

The Pacific Northwest has a climate all its own. Its gardening needs are unique. In 1943, when the original edition of this book was published, no comprehensive book had been written about garden plants for this region. By this region we mean the natural geographic and climatic unit which includes southwestern British Columbia, western Washington, western Oregon, northwestern California, and by extension, eastern Washington and Oregon. Books written for the eastern United States or for California are of little practical value to gardeners of the Pacific Northwest, and publications which cover the United States as a whole do not deal adequately with our local problems.

The wealth of garden literature written for the British Isles has been for many years the main source of practical information for gardeners of the Pacific Northwest because the climate is quite similar. It continues to be of great help. However, the weather patterns are not identical, particularly our drier summers, and some modification of the information is necessary. Further, we have marked local variations which need careful consideration.

Our aim is to provide Northwest gardeners with information on the best trees and shrubs for use in our region, in keeping with the three criteria set forth in the original edition, while incorporating the results of 45 additional years of growing and testing woody plant materials under Northwest conditions.

First, all plants described should be available in nurseries either in this country or Canada, and primarily from nurseries on the Pacific Coast. Some of the species and varieties are still uncommon in the trade, but usually can be found with a little searching. The latter are usually superior or recent new selections still in the process of distribution. The *Annotated Checklist of Woody Ornamental Plants of California, Oregon, and Washington,* authored by Dr. E. McClintock and Prof. A. T. Leiser and published by the University of California, February 1979, is a useful sourcebook for plants in cultivation in this region.

Second, the plants listed are normally hardy in the area. They are classified by hardiness zone according to the system of the Arnold Arboretum. See Map, facing page. These zones are fully described in the chapter "Water, Wind, and Weather." Some plants are listed with the qualification that they require protected locations, or that they have not yet been thoroughly tested. Apart from these exceptions, all plants included here may be regarded as hardy to the zone indicated, *under good cultural conditions.*

Third, all materials recommended are plants of reasonably sound garden constitution. Plants which are difficult to grow and thus more suitable for the specialist have been omitted or dismissed with a brief appraisal. It will certainly be possible to find a few omissions of worthwhile items. Those listed form a comprehensive group of trees and shrubs which in our opinion are the best and most suitable species and varieties for the gardens of our region. From it anyone can make his own choices with confidence.

In the years since World War II our region has experienced a tremendous upsurge of interest in gardens and gardening. The amount of available plant material of woody species alone has probably doubled in that length of time, with new introductions appearing in the trade every year. Yet as individual gardeners, we have only begun to draw upon this tremendous store of outstanding ornamentals. Part of the purpose of this book is to help us develop more interesting and unusual gardens than we have had in the past. As the demand for quality plants increases nurserymen are responding with an ever greater variety.

The role of public gardens in this horticultural burgeoning has been very important. Our arboreta and botanic gardens are constantly acquiring and testing new plants from all over the world, then introducing them to the nursery trade and to the public. Among the gardens engaged in this activity are the Washington Park Arboretum in Seattle, the Rhododendron Species Foundation in Federal Way, the University of British Columbia Botanic Garden and VanDusen Gardens in Vancouver, B.C., the Carl S. English Gardens at the Hiram M. Chittenden Locks in Seattle, and the Berry Botanic Garden in Portland. The new Center for Urban Horticulture at the University of Washington, under Professor H. B. Tukey Jr., is fast becoming a leader in this field. Many of these organizations sponsor plant sales for their members and for the general public, at which rare and little-known plant materials are introduced.

Also instrumental in the increased development and availability of plant materials are the specialty plant societies such as the American Rock Garden Society, the American Rhododendron Society, the American Rose Society, the American Holly Society, the American Bamboo Society, the American Heather Society and others.

In addition to the specialty plant societies, there has been a rise in the number of large and small nurseries in our region. Many of the large

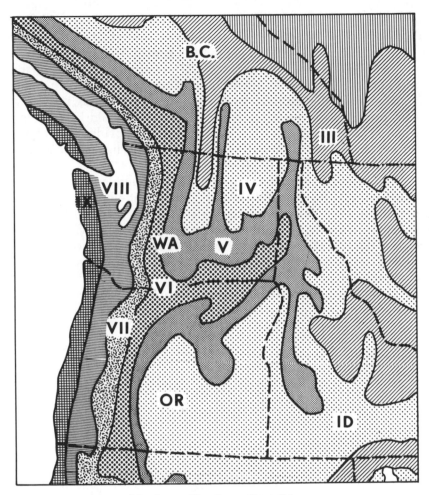

Northwest Hardiness Zone Map
Adapted from map by the Arnold Arboretum, Harvard University.

nurseries carry a wide selection of woody plants. Small specialty nurseries deal in a more limited range of plants, often those which are hard to find in the general trade. Some of these, and others scattered across the country, sell by mail order, a convenient method of obtaining small plants and groundcovers which may not be available locally.

This book is intended to be of use to amateur gardeners, both beginners and those who are more advanced—those who have always gardened in the Northwest and want to expand the range of plants they grow, and those who have recently come to our region from other parts of the United States or abroad, and need to know why things are done differently here, and how to do them. Both the introductory chapters and the introductions to the various classes of plant material should be read before seeking information on an individual plant, so that each gardener is aware of his own garden conditions before making his choices. The book must be studied as a whole in order to get the full benefit from its contents.

Following the descriptive chapters, lists of plants for varying circumstances or sets of conditions are included. They involve a certain amount of repetition of material already given in the body of the book, but they are meant primarily for quick reference. These lists should be of help to anyone looking for a certain type of plant to fit specific cultural conditions. Also they should greatly simplify the problem of selection for the beginner with a limited knowledge of plants.

In conclusion, we wish to repeat that this is intended to be a practical handbook for the Pacific Northwest, and we have attempted to present all our material from this perspective. In some cases it is hard to say just where the line should be drawn between a plant for the specialist and one which is not too exacting for the average gardener. In most cases, the deciding factors have been the value of the plant for its visual effect, its sound constitution, and its hardiness. In short, the selection of plant material has been made from the viewpoint of those who have had actual experience in growing woody plants in the Pacific Northwest.

CHAPTER II

Garden Fundamentals

Most gardeners in the Pacific Northwest, whether born here or transplanted from other regions, are well aware of the favored status our climate confers upon our gardens. However, many of us are still not aware of the tremendous wealth of plant material which can be grown here. The number and variety of trees and shrubs which will thrive here has probably more than doubled since the first edition of this book was published 40 years ago. Whether one seeks a floral display in the spring, the brilliance of colored fruits and foliage in the autumn, or the year-around beauty of broad-leaved or coniferous evergreens, variations in color, pattern and texture are endless, providing an exciting field for discovery.

This book is written not only for the gardener who loves the beauty of individual plants and therefore grows a collection of specimens, but also for the gardener who, loving the individual plant, wants to combine it with others in a pleasing design. But perhaps most of all it is written for those who work with plants just for the joy of working with growing things—those who have a real feeling for the plants they grow—those who are inspired by the upward reach of a tree's bare branches in winter, or the deep, lush green of shade-loving plants growing by a cool north wall, or the aromatic foliage of rosemary and lavender basking on a hot, dry bank. The love and understanding of growing things is something which comes only from working with the plants. As Kipling says:

> And when your back stops aching and your hands begin to harden,
> You will find yourself a partner in the Glory of the Garden,
> *And the Glory of the Garden, it shall never pass away!*

The gardener must be familiar with plant material to understand how it should be used in garden design. In fact, this knowledge is the basis of a sound design. For instance, if you have a hot, sunny bank to plant, you should be familiar with the materials which thrive under those conditions. The same thing applies to a moist, boggy area. In practice, you most often have to deal with situations in between these two extremes, but even so, you will need an understanding of the plants which are suited to the various exposures and conditions of light, moisture, and soil type which even a small garden presents.

There is no question that the Pacific Northwest is one of the finest garden spots on the whole continent. Even so, there are methods and techniques of gardening which are peculiar to our region. And though gardening here may be easier than elsewhere, it remains an endeavor that requires a certain amount of skill. There are several vitally important subjects in which every gardener needs to be thoroughly grounded.

Adequate preparation of the soil is of prime importance. While the vigorous and rapid-growing conifers, English laurel, privets, holly, and so forth, may grow satisfactorily with little or no preliminary working of their site, the majority of really choice shrubs do not thrive, and may in fact prove disappointing unless properly provided for in advance.

It is much sounder policy to prepare the ground thoroughly before planting any trees or shrubs than it is to set them out hastily and then attempt to make up for it by subsequent irregular fertilization. Beds for shrubs should be prepared and fertilized to a depth of 18 inches at the very least. Skimping on the initial preparation of the soil is false economy.

Once you have provided for your plants with a properly cultivated site you have gone a long way toward protecting them from both diseases and insect pests. A plant growing under ideal conditions is much less subject to attack from disease; and even if it is attacked by insect pests, it will not be nearly so likely to sustain serious injury. Maintaining healthy plants depends much more on providing them with the best possible growing conditions than on constantly spraying after troubles begin.

Ours is an area where summer irrigation is necessary for most plants. This matter is dealt with in detail in a later chapter, as is pruning.

The gardener in his planning needs especially to consider the rate of growth and ultimate size of the plants he/she intends to use. A plant like *Kalmia latifolia,* the Mountain Laurel, may be so slow growing as to be considered a relatively small shrub—6–8 feet tall at the very most—whereas it will ultimately (that is to say in 50–60 years or more!) occasionally reach three or four times that size. In the average garden, it is neither practical nor desirable to leave enough space for such shrubs to reach their ultimate size. In memorial plantings around churches, cemetery chapels, and other public buildings—plantings of a long-term permanent nature—it is necessary to make proper allowance for the mature sizes of individual shrubs. For the private garden, the homeowner can choose between planting for an immediate effect of maturity, or accomplishing the same result over a period of several years.

The once-common practice here of using large conifers in foundation plantings without regard for their eventual size has left current homeowners with a dilemma—they can either let the trees grow unhampered (which in extreme cases means losing light, air, and view) or they can lop them back repeatedly, a process to which conifers do not take kindly and which in any event makes the true plant lover cringe. A more sensible third alternative is simply to remove the unsuitable species altogether and begin again with shrubs which can be depended upon not to outgrow their position.

The rate of growth of the plant is often a measure of its quality. Fast-growing trees and shrubs are usually inexpensive because they can be propagated easily and reach a marketable size quickly. Large plants of this sort can be purchased for the same price as small specimens of choicer plants, which if properly selected, will never outgrow their position. Although the smaller plant may take a number of years to be fully effective, it will constantly increase in value and beauty. Materials which fill a given space immediately but which must be cut back periodically to keep them within bounds, deteriorate and diminish in value, and are often shortlived. Therefore it is wise not only to obtain plant materials of the best quality, but also to be willing to wait a reasonable length of time for them to reach their full beauty. You will then be able to enjoy them for a period of many years.

In our region, as elsewhere, ornamental native plants should always be considered a basic part of the garden; they should not be classified as cheap plant material in any sense of the word. Such shrubs as *Mahonia aquifolium,* the Tall Oregon Grape; *Vaccinium ovatum,* the Evergreen Huckleberry; and *Gaultheria shallon,* Salal, are beautiful and desirable garden plants. The horticultural merits of these and other Northwest species have been appreciated by keen plantsmen overseas for many years, but "natives" have not been fully recognized nor especially popular in our own gardens until recently. The idea dies hard that because they are easily collected locally (a questionable practice) they are less desirable than exotic species, but their value in the garden should not be underrated even though they may be relatively inexpensive.

Today's plants are much more accurately labeled than formerly, and fewer long-obsolete names are encountered. Reputable nurserymen strive to keep their stocks correctly labeled and to keep abreast of the occasional name changes made by botanists. The gardener asking for a plant by its botanical name is generally able to find it, and to be reasonably well assured that he is getting what he asks for.

Beginners frequently want only the common names for plants, but as they deal with a wider range of materials they soon come to realize that botanical names are actually simpler and more accurate. They provide a reliable system of identification besides having the advantage of international usage. Common names tend to be misleading, since the same name may be applied to quite different plants in different parts of the United States, or to one plant in Britain and still another in North America. Plants such as *Rhododendron,* with many hundreds of species worldwide, have no

English names individually, and it is more logical to call them by their Latin specific names than to coin common names for them.

Botanical names serve a purpose. Many are descriptive of the plants, or commemorate their place of origin, or the person who first collected them. *Nana* means dwarf, *grandiflora* means with large flowers, *latifolia* means broad foliage, and so on. *Yunnanensis* and *sikkimensis,* tell us that a plant has come from the Chinese province of Yunnan, or the Himalayan state of Sikkim; *chinensis* means from China, *japonica* from Japan. There are many other descriptive words such as *viridis,* meaning green; *foetidus,* stinking; *hirsutus,* hairy. Botanists' names appear in either the genus, such as *Linnaea,* Twin-Flower, named for the great Swedish father of botany Linnaeus; or the species name, such as *lewisii,* or *clarkei* named for the intrepid explorers of the Louisiana purchase, Meriweather Lewis and William Clarke; or *douglasii,* for David Douglas, sent out from England to explore the flora of the Pacific Northwest in the 1820s.

Pronunciation of botanical names need not overawe the "plain dirt" gardener, particularly if he keeps in mind that even botanists do not agree that any one pronunciation is the "right" one. The important thing is not how a name is pronounced, but whether others understand what plant is being discussed. As a partial guideline, in this book the accented syllable is indicated for each name at the beginning of its descriptive paragraph.

Plant materials are discussed according to their function as design elements. The various types fall naturally into a number of distinct groups, each having a definite function in the garden scheme. We will deal solely with plants of woody growth habit, as opposed to herbaceous plants with no permanent woody stems. From the standpoint of garden design, the most important distinction—not always clear-cut—is between trees and shrubs. Each of these in turn is divided further into those with deciduous leaves and those which are evergreen. Conifers—cone bearers—whether trees or shrubs, are treated in a single chapter. Additional chapters deal with scandent shrubs such as climbing roses and *Hydrangea petiolaris,* and woody vines such as *Clematis* and *Wisteria.* Palms, yuccas, and bamboos are distinct enough in form to rate a separate discussion. In each chapter the genera and species are described with the conditions required, and typical uses are suggested.

One of the differences between this book and those written for the eastern part of the United States is that it includes a much larger section on broad-leaved evergreen shrubs. West of the Cascades we are fortunate in being able to grow a wide variety of these plants. Because of their year-around effect they have become basic to garden design in this area. Small conifers and deciduous shrubs take their place east of the mountains.

CHAPTER III

Water, Wind and Weather

TOPOGRAPHY

The unusually mild climate of the Pacific Northwest is due in part to the nearness of the great water mass of the Pacific Ocean, but more particularly to its warm currents. Consequently this region is far warmer than the eastern coast of the continent in the same latitude. A glance at the Zone map on page 11 will show you this striking comparison. Notice how these winter temperature zones run almost east and west on the Atlantic Coast and practically north and south on the Pacific Coast, where they coincide with the main topographical divisions of the land. Note also that the main trend is broken in several places. There are five natural north-south subdivisions—the seacoast, the east and west slopes of the coastal mountain ranges, a wide interior lowland extending from the Strait of Georgia through Puget Sound to the Siskiyou Mountains in southern Oregon, and the western slope of the Cascades. Most of the coastline which faces the full pounding of the Pacific is wild and picturesque—bold, rugged bluffs of rock broken at intervals with sandy beaches. In southwestern Oregon the Cascades are connected by the lower Siskiyou Mountains with the rugged masses of the Coast Range, which diminish as they approach the mouth of the Columbia River. North of the Columbia the hills again build up to the dramatic masses of the Olympic Mountains, whose spectacular peaks with their heads in the eternal snows cast their rain shadow over the whole Puget Sound area. Again the mountain chain is broken, this time by the deep gorge of the Strait of Juan de Fuca, but the peaks reappear to form the backbone of Vancouver Island. The strait carries the warming ocean influence into the Puget Sound area.

The two great rivers of this region, the Fraser and the Columbia, cut deeply through the Cascade Mountains and also produce a marked effect on the climate. They expose the adjacent areas west of the Cascades to the extremes of the interior continental climate with its hotter summers and colder winters accompanied by drying winds. This interruption of the natural north-south land division causes many variations in weather and in the plant materials which will grow in the great valley of the Columbia.

PRECIPITATION

The climate of the Pacific Northwest is sadly misunderstood. Considering that everyone depends upon the weather for a safe subject of conversation, it is amazing how few of the facts are known even to gardeners who have every reason to observe the weather. Most of us have been completely convinced that we have a dark, dank climate, that the Pacific Northwest is dripping wet for the greater part of the year—which is far from the truth! The most important characteristic of Pacific Northwest climate is its marked division into wet and dry seasons. Over eighty percent of the annual rainfall occurs between October and April.

A brief dry spell accompanied by warm drying winds usually occurs sometime between early April and the beginning of June. If it lasts for more than two weeks (and it occasionally lasts for as many as six), most gardeners are caught unawares. The majority of trees and shrubs are making their new growth at this time of year, and broad-leaved evergreens need more moisture than at any other time.

The average annual rainfall varies enormously within comparatively short distances. It reaches a total of 260 inches a year on the west coast of Vancouver Island, and about 140 inches a year on the western slopes of the Olympic Mountains. Only a few miles to the east, in the rain shadow of the Olympics, the amazingly low average of 15 inches has been recorded for Sequim, Washington—the same as that of Los Angeles, California! Other annual averages in this section are: Victoria, B.C., 28 inches; Seattle, Washington, 36 inches; Portland, Oregon, 45 inches. Local variations are very noticeable. Two gardens as little as four or five miles apart may show a striking difference in rainfall, and accurate information about local variations (microclimates) is usually not readily available. A study of plant material to be found in any given section may give an indication of moisture conditions. Wherever Madroña (*Arbutus menziesii*) appears in association with Greasewood (*Ceanothus velutinus*) and Manzanita (*Arctostaphylos columbiana*), the soil is dry and well drained, and precipitation is relatively low. A thriving stand of Western Hemlock (*Tsuga heterophylla*), Western Red Cedar (*Thuja plicata*) or Sitka Spruce (*Picea sitchensis*), is a clear indication that there is ample soil moisture.

The amount of rainfall in your particular locality will have a direct bearing on your gardening. You can offset lack of rainfall by copious summer watering, or better still, you can choose plants which will thrive with little or no watering even in the driest sections of this region. You cannot successfully grow drought-tolerant trees and shrubs where there is heavy precipitation without special soil preparation and attention to site selection.

WINTER TEMPERATURE

Winter cold is more restrictive than rainfall in its effect on choice of plant material. You will see from the map on page 11 that the Pacific Northwest west of the Cascades includes three zones—7, 8, and 9. These numbers are given directly after the plant names in the text. This general division into zones is very helpful in determining the approximate hardiness of plant material, and the best reference books and many nursery catalogs now give this information. The word "hardiness" as used in this book means strictly the resistance of plants to winter cold. It does not refer to the vigor of their growth, but simply the degree of cold they can stand. Many other factors beside winter temperatures determine hardiness, including soil conditions, moisture, humidity, air drainage, wind and exposure—all of which will be discussed.

All plants listed as hardy to zone 7 will be found reliably so throughout this region under correct cultural conditions, and most of them will have an ample margin of hardiness. Plants listed for zone 8 are well worth trying in sheltered gardens throughout the region, while zone 9 plants may be tried in unusually favored gardens, against south or west walls or fences. You will find that the majority of broad-leaved evergreens, which make up so large a part of the garden plants of this region, are drawn from zones 6, 7, and 8.

Current North American horticultural books list these hardiness zones in their discussions of plants. However, Sunset's *New Western Garden Book* uses more detailed hardiness zones.

SUMMER TEMPERATURES

There are smaller differences between summer and winter temperatures in the Pacific Northwest than in most other parts of North America. On the seacoast there is less temperature fluctuation, and more in the main interior valleys, this being most marked in the vicinity of the Columbia river. Throughout most of the area, however, the summers are much cooler and winters much warmer than in the eastern states. As a result many trees and shrubs from cold-winter, warm-summer areas do not behave as they do in their home ranges. They start growth earlier in the spring and continue later into the autumn. Many shrubs which require some shade in the east do better here in full sun. We also find that those species which are grown for their fruits, either decorative or edible, may not produce as well.

HUMIDITY

During much of the year the humidity of the area is quite high, a factor favoring most broad-leaved evergreens. During the summer drought period, however, daytime humidity may become very low and newly transplanted plants will suffer if not given some protection from sun and wind. Fortunately humidity usually rises during the evening. Even in winter, we may experience short periods when humidity becomes dangerously low for plants. This usually occurs when a continental air mass from northern Canada crosses the Cascades from the northeast. The triad of low temperature, low humidity and strong northeast winds will cause severe injury to many evergreen plants.

WIND

West, southwest or southerly winds prevail throughout this region except at certain periods of the year. As might be expected, the greatest force of these winds is felt on the seacoast and lessens considerably by the time it reaches the inland valleys. Winds which blow strongly off the continent from the north and east, usually for short periods, bring extremes of temperature during midsummer and the middle of winter. At either season this wind may prove damaging to garden plants.

A bitter cold spell accompanied by drying winds may occur at the end of December or the beginning of January. Fortunately, most plants have hardened off and are prepared for this so that damage to the garden is lessened.

In 1985 a cold mass of air came suddenly in early November, while plants were still growing, and wrought havoc with a wide range of species including native trees and shrubs. Such events are rare, fortunately, but early-winter cold spells with drying winds may be expected any year and the wise gardener must be prepared to give shelter—either temporary or long term—from such winds. Snow, which may or may not precede these cold spells, offers excellent protection for those specimens which it covers, but does nothing for broad-leaved plants rising above it. Also, it is more common for a snowstorm to follow the cold, when its protection comes too late.

In summer, hot drying winds are particularly bad in the vicinity of the Columbia river valley. The utmost precautions should be taken to provide shelter for gardens in a situation exposed to the full blast of these seasonal winds. This can be accomplished by shelter-belt planting in larger areas, and in smaller gardens by hedges, fences or walls.

Shelter from summer wind should also be considered an essential feature of every Northwest garden planned for outdoor living. During the warm dry spells the wind is usually from the north, and while pleasant during the day may be too chilly for the evening hours. The cooler south winds may also make the garden unpleasant in the evening. Some shelter should be planned as protection from both these directions.

Some wind-resistant shrubs are not, however, cold resistant. *Cistus,* which are broad-leaved evergreen shrubs from the Mediterranean region, and some of the escallonias from South America are especially fine for seaside planting, cheerfully taking the full brunt of the prevailing southerly or westerly winds, but they must be completely shielded from the cold north or northeast winds.

Drafts are sometimes a serious menace to plantings in city gardens. Wind may form curious eddies, which can cause plants to suffer, especially in narrow spaces between tall buildings. Drafts can frequently be eliminated by a heavy planting of wind-resistant shrubs, or by the construction of walls or fences. It is better to moderate the force of the air by having it pass through a screen of plants or fence pickets rather than to block it with a solid barrier.

EXPOSURE

The question of exposure is of vital importance in its effect on plants of doubtful hardiness. A shrub which may periodically be harmed by frosts when placed with an eastern exposure may well be unscathed if given a westerly exposure. Shrubs which flower in winter or early spring frequently have their blossoms nipped by even a light frost if they are exposed to the early morning sun. More injury is caused by rapid thawing than by actual freezing. Consequently a shrub which is exposed to the early morning sun is much more likely to be damaged than one which can thaw out before the sun strikes it.

In planning the planting around a building it is well to know the effect of different exposures on the cultural requirements of shrubs. East and northeast exposures may be considered equivalent to partial shade. Southern exposure against a wall is an especially warm situation due to direct sunlight and also to that reflected from the wall. A western exposure is much hotter than an eastern one for the simple reason that in the early morning it takes the sun a little while to dispel the dew and warm the atmosphere. Any situation may be modified by the shade cast from neighboring buildings or from nearby trees. The amount of heat on each aspect of the building should be carefully considered and the planting planned accordingly. Contrary to common opinion, the north side of a house is not difficult to treat, especially if there is plenty of indirect light. It is only when this indirect light is cut off that a northern exposure will be at all difficult.

AIR DRAINAGE

Air drainage is a vital consideration for the gardener. Stop and think of some of the physical characteristics of air. Like water, it is fluid; it can be still like water in a pond, or it can be violently agitated. Also, it follows the line of least resistance, flowing through a natural channel or gap. Cold air sinks, and like water, drains to the lowest level. The fact that gardens in low-lying sections are frequently subjected to severe frosts is entirely a matter of poor air drainage.

Air drainage on a large scale follows the flow of large rivers. The Columbia river drains a large area which is exposed to continental winter cold and brings with it to the coast a heavy flow of cold air. This explains why Longview, Washington; Portland, Oregon; and Vancouver, Washington, experience somewhat colder low temperatures than those recorded for other lowland places in our area.

Proper air drainage is a problem to be considered on a smaller scale in every individual garden. Sluggish movement of cold air is as harmful as sluggish movement of water through the soil. Be sure that cold air can drain rapidly from any area in which you want to cultivate plants. Frosts that occur in late spring or early fall are those that do the most damage to plants, and they are the ones which can be greatly lessened, if it is possible to get sufficient air drainage. Many plants which are completely hardy during their dormant season may be blasted by a sharp frost as they start into growth in the spring or before they are hardened off in the fall. Blossoms on many early-flowering shrubs are also likely to be damaged by frost where the air drainage is inadequate.

When choosing a garden site, always give the foregoing careful consideration, to avoid being saddled with these problems. Of course, it is not always possible to find a site which is ideal in every respect. However, you can usually improve conditions or choose your plant materials so as to reduce frost damage to a minimum.

The effect of air drainage will perhaps be most easily explained by a few examples. A little garden was situated in a gently sloping ravine which at one time was crossed by a trestle bridge located below the garden. Later the trestle was replaced by an earth fill, and the effect on that garden was drastic. As late as the middle of June it was visited with killing frosts, whereas previously nothing had ever suffered damage after the middle of April. Virtually nothing can be done to eliminate the frost in a discouraging case like this except the possibility of installing a large culvert through the fill.

In some cases, gardens in low-lying areas where air drainage is barely adequate to prevent serious frosts, have suffered startlingly increased damage after being enclosed by a hedge or fence. Placement of buildings is also sometimes unfortunate in this respect. Large groups of buildings may block the mouth of a small valley or swale when they could just as well have been sited to avoid obstructing cold-air drainage.

Again, streams and rivers invariably bring an air-drainage problem. One piece of property had a stream running through a heavily wooded area at the base of a steep slope. A space on both sides of the stream was cleared for a house and a small garden. To protect this area as much as possible, it was necessary to plant the upper boundaries very heavily to deflect the cold air. The lower boundaries were left open to permit the cold air to drain away. The garden, left unprotected in the clearing, would have formed a cold-air pocket, had this not been done. Not many gardeners are lucky enough to have a stream to plant, and consequently this type of problem seldom occurs.

In rare instances land contours may have to be modified to prevent cold air from collecting in a hollow, but air drainage usually can be controlled by careful planting with densely growing conifers and the most frost-resistant broad-leaved evergreens.

In the Puget Sound region, both large and small saucerlike depressions are common. Although the soil in these depressions is frequently very fertile, no gardener, tempted by that consideration, should overlook the serious menace of complete lack of air drainage. In such cases, when it is impossible to have adequate air drainage, you must confine your selection of plant material to the trees and shrubs least likely to be damaged by late and early frosts. Of course, if you become too exasperated by the conditions imposed upon you by inadequate air drainage, there is always the alternative of selling the property to someone else who is not such a keen gardener!

CHAPTER IV

Plant Geography

The golden rule for selecting plant material for your garden is to start with those plants native to this region which are best suited to your particular set of cultural conditions; then combine with them plants which grow under similar climatic and cultural conditions in other parts of the world. Having briefly analysed the climatic conditions of the Pacific Northwest, we are ready to look to other geographical units throughout the world where similar or comparable conditions exist. It is fascinating as you go around your garden to realize that this *Pieris* grows wild in moist Asian woodland; that this little rhododendron comes from the high mountains of western China where it grows in sheets in the alpine meadows, acres at a time perhaps, like our native "heathers" and the true heathers of Europe; or this *Cistus,* basking in the sun, is found perched on hot cliffs overlooking the blue waters of the Mediterranean.

Of all the places in the world upon which we draw to supplement our native plants in stocking our gardens, probably the most famous for its great wealth of plant materials is that vast territory designated as western China. This huge area, combined with northern Burma, Assam and eastern Tibet, has been a treasure house for plant explorers during the present century. Within the last 75 years plants from western China have found a very large place in our gardens, and we in the Pacific Northwest are especially fortunate in being able to grow most of the finest importations from that region.

We are indebted to a great number of adventurous plant collectors who have brought back so much of the beauty of western China and established it in both Europe and America. Ernest H. Wilson collected many valuable new plants from this prolific region on several expeditions from 1898 onwards. "Chinese Wilson" wrote several books about garden plants from the Orient which make very informative reading. Reginald Farrer, author of *The English Rock Garden,* made the final corrections in the manuscript of that famous work while wintering in the Chinese province of Kansu. Two of his most fascinating books, *The Rainbow Bridge* and *On the*

Eaves of the World, both deal with the absorbing story of his travels in that part of the world. Other well-known plant explorers include George Forrest, the Abbe Delavay, Robert Fortune, Frank Kingdon-Ward, and more recently Frank Ludlow and George Sherriff in the eastern Himalayas. Since access to interior China has again become possible, in the the last few years we have seen a number of officially sponsored expeditions as well as private ones going there with the purpose of introducing fresh plant material to our botanical/horticultural institutions as well as our gardens.

The climate of this part of Asia is actually quite distinct from our own. It, too, is divided into a wet and dry season, but in the reverse order to ours. There the winters are cold and dry and the summers warm and moist. The peak of the wet season is in June. The conditions of a warm, moist summer are closely approximated in watered gardens here in the Pacific Northwest. There the summer moisture is carried by the monsoons, the warm, rain-bearing trade winds blowing in from the Indian Ocean. Just as the coastal mountains in the Northwest have a marked effect on precipitation, so the mountains of Upper Burma and the eastern Himalayas cast their rain shadow causing the rainfall to vary enormously in different localities, so that not all plants from that great region require the same cultural conditions. Those which come from the wettest and warmest sections are usually unsuited to our conditions. Some of the shrubs from the warmer fringes have been grown very little in this region because it has been assumed that they would not be hardy. *Pittosporum tobira* from China and Japan is an example of this sort, having been commonly cultivated in California for many years but considered doubtfully hardy here; however it has been growing happily in the Washington Park Arboretum in Seattle since 1969. Other examples are the crape myrtle (*Lagerstroemia indica*), *Camellia reticulata* (the wild type) and various rhododendrons belonging to the *Maddenii* series. Many more kinds are now being tested in our local gardens and in southern British Columbia.

The islands of Japan are also affected by the monsoons of eastern Asia, but they differ from the vast expanse of western China in having wet winters as well as moist summers. Japan, in proportion to its size, is even richer in broad-leaved evergreen trees and shrubs than western China, and in addition has given us some of the most beautiful of all our deciduous flowering trees, the cherries, apricots and plums. The climate of southern Japan, except for its summer rainfall, is very similar to that of the milder coastal sections of the Pacific Northwest. Therefore, it is not surprising that so many Japanese trees and shrubs grow to perfection in our watered gardens; for examples, the camellias (forms of *C. japonica* and *C. sasanqua*), hollies (*Ilex crenata, I. pedunculosa,* and *I. latifolia*), *Osmanthus* species, *Fatsia japonica* and many more. A few from the warmest lowland coastal sections of Japan will not thrive in our colder inland valleys, but Japan is a land of mountains and over ninety percent of the plants coming from those mountainous islands are among the most reliable of our garden plants. If you glance through a list of material selected for this region you will notice how many good old standbys carry the specific name *japonica—Aucuba, Skimmia, Camellia, Pieris,* and so on.

For centuries the Japanese have been great horticulturists and have cultivated many plants of Chinese origin. Special favorites have been extensively hybridized, and it is a matter of opinion as to whether some of them have not been spoiled by it. At any rate, we have the Japanese to thank for providing many of the finest garden plants for the Pacific Northwest.

The southwestern tip of South America has a warm temperate climate not too dissimilar to ours and has made some notable contributions to our gardens, including the showy orange-flowered barberries *Berberis darwinii* and *B. linearifolia,* the brilliant scarlet Chilean Fire-bush *Embothrium coccineum,* several species of southern beeches (*Nothofagus*), and the shrubby escallonias, flowering in midsummer and sometimes used for hedges.

Another region upon which we have hardly as yet begun to draw is New Zealand and southeastern Australia. On the whole, plants from this area present a much more fertile field for California gardens than for our own; many of the best Australian shrubs are already in cultivation there and have gained a well-deserved popularity but not proved sufficiently hardy for us. A few New Zealand shrubs such as some of the hebes and *Olearias* have been grown intermittently in gardens here for many years. However, they are usually given the same cultural conditions as plants which come from the monsoon area—in other words, a great deal of summer watering—and to this they strongly object. This lack of understanding of their needs has kept them from becoming more popular.

The Mediterranean is another very important region that has supplied us with shrubs which do not like summer moisture. These include the various *Cistus,* Laurustinus (*Viburnum tinus*), the Bay Tree (*Laurus nobilis*), True Myrtle (*Myrtus communis*), rosemary, lavenders and others which are invaluable for planting in locations where they are watered very little during the summer. Interplanted with shrubs from the monsoon region and heavily watered, they soon become miserable and are easily killed off by the first hard winter that comes along. This is the reason that many of these valuable shrubs have been grown for a time and then discarded as unsuited to our climate when actually they are ideal, given the right site.

The shrubs from these two regions, the southern Pacific and the Mediterranean, combined with our native drought-tolerant shrubs such as Manzanita and *Ceanothus,* can solve the problem of the gardener who has a small water supply and a hot dry bank to plant.

The British Isles and the west coast of Europe have a similar climate to our own, having about the same summer and winter temperatures and a winter rainfall, and more summer rainfall than we have, although less than that of Japan. Under these conditions we might expect an abundance of native plant material to be forthcoming, but compared with the islands of Japan their contribution is negligible. However, the British are a nation of horticulturists and have assembled plant material not just from one region but from all over the world, selected the best, hybridized and improved, and sent out again to gardens everywhere the wealth of the continents. The British Isles have been the Pacific Northwest's greatest source not only of garden plant material, but also of garden and plant information. A few of their own outstanding natives include the Strawberry Tree, *Arbutus unedo*, and many kinds of heathers such as *Erica vagans, E. cinerea, Calluna vulgaris*, and *Daboecia cantabrica.*

There are temperate and cool temperate zones at high altitudes in the tropics, where many plants of value to us are found, e.g., the *Vireya* group of rhododendrons from Malaysia and Borneo, *Vaccinium floribundum* from Peru and Ecuador, species of pines from Mexico. From the Himalayas come the popular Deodar Cedar (*Cedrus deodara*) and Bhutan Pine (*Pinus wallichiana*) as well as many well-known species of *Rhododendron*, including *R. thomsonii, R. campanulatum* and *R. ciliatum*, plus species of *Rosa, Cotoneaster, Pyracantha, Spiraea* and many other shrubs and trees. The tremendous mountain regions where western China meets Burma, India and Tibet have already been mentioned. The Andes of South America have still to be fully explored for plants although more work has been done there in recent years, and some plants have been introduced temporarily into cultivation. Numerous plants as yet scarcely tried in our local gardens are to be found in the high mountains of Mexico, such as evergreen oaks. We have reason to believe that some of them will thrive here because they grow in association with some of our natives such as *Mahonia, Ceanothus* and *Arctostaphylos* species.

This brief outline of the principal countries of origin of our best-known garden plants should open up vistas for further study of the subject. You can judge a plant's cultural requirements with surprising accuracy if you know where it originates and what some of its associates are. There are many more plants from these same regions which have not yet been thoroughly tested, need reintroduction, or are not yet readily obtainable. Anyone interested in further research will find this subject of plant geography fascinating to pursue.

Having traveled all over the world let us come back home and take stock of the material growing right at our doorsteps. Staying at home may not seem quite so exciting as journeying to distant countries, but the adaptability of our native plants certainly recommends them for use in our gardens. The better-known ones include the two Oregon grapes, *Mahonia aquifolium* and *M. nervosa*; the Salal, *Gaultheria shallon*; Kinnikinnik, *Arctostaphylos uva-ursi*; and the Evergreen Huckleberry, *Vaccinium ovatum.* The Manzanita, *Arctostaphylos columbiana*, is not yet as popular as it deserves to be, although its natural hybrid with Kinnikinnik, *A.* × *media,* is used often as a groundcover. For seacoast areas there is the beautiful California Wild Lilac, *Ceanothus thyrsiflorus,* which grows on the Oregon coast in association with the Evergreen Huckleberry; Oregon Grape; the native azalea, *Rhododendron occidentale;* and the evergreen Wax-myrtle, *Myrica californica,* which is also found in Washington. This plant association is breathtakingly beautiful in late April and early May; the white and salmon pink flowers of the azalea and the light touches of soft fluffy blue panicles of the ceanothus are sprinkled through great sweeping drifts of low wind-clipped bushes of the huckleberry.

The polished surfaces of the foliage of native broad-leaved evergreens catch the light and sparkle. The effect is lovely when the sun is filtered down through tall trees, the lustrous leaves a foil to the dark height and depth of the forest. This particular characteristic of broad-leaved evergreens is well illustrated by *Umbellularia,* the Oregon Myrtle; *Ceanothus velutinus;* and the mahonias, which can certainly hold their own among the best plants from other parts of the world.

CHAPTER V

Garden Maintenance

"Now, when I look at the affair more closely, I find that a real gardener is not a man who cultivates flowers; he is a man who cultivates the soil . . . if he came into the Garden of Eden he would sniff excitedly and say: 'Good Lord, what humus!' " Karel Capek.

SOILS

Soils can be divided into three basic components: sand, clay and humus. Almost all soils contain at least two of these components. A soil is usually named for whichever of these elements predominates. A well-balanced combination of them is called a loam. Sandy soil has rapid drainage and is generally spoken of as being light. Clay soil is very dense and compact, and is spoken of as heavy. Humus is defined as decomposed organic matter forming soil. A soil without humus is said to be sterile. The most readily available sources of humus include sedge peat, peat muck, peat moss, leafmold, and animal or vegetable manures, including compost. The addition of humus in generous quantities greatly benefits both heavy clays and light sands. It renders clay looser and more friable (easily crumbled), in this way greatly improving its working qualities and physical condition throughout the year, preventing it from forming a cold, soggy mass when wet or caking into bricklike lumps when dry. It acts like a sponge in sand, retaining both moisture and plant nutrients which might otherwise leach away. Humus in the form of large deposits of sedge peat, or mixtures of rich alluvial silt and peat, is found in bottomland and on the margin of lakes. The addition of coarse sand, or perlite, or other inert materials will render such a soil more easily worked. Peat soils are acid and may require the additional of lime to make them more nearly neutral.

The majority of garden plants require a loose, friable soil: a soil in which these components are balanced and the mixture kept in good physical condition. This is the hardest to achieve and maintain in clay soils, which are so much inclined to be sticky. Consequently they require special attention and careful handling. Avoid working a clay soil either when wet and sticky, or when dry and baked. Keep adding sand and humus and lime until the surface remains friable at all times. Clay soils will benefit from regular liming. Light sand soils need not be handled as carefully and require less preparation. A peat soil is easily cultivated as long as friability and adequate drainage are insured. However, peat soils should not be worked when wet for the same reasons as with clay soils.

SOIL PREPARATION

The principal object in growing plants under garden conditions is to attain a beautiful effect. Success with this endeavor will be in direct proportion to the preparation of the soil for planting, so only the penurious or foolish will waste time and money in halfway measures. It is true that there are a few shrubs which will thrive in poor soil, and in certain extreme cases plants are improved by starvation, but among the plants most generally grown these are decidedly in the minority. Most gardeners will probably wish to grow such broad-leaved evergreen shrubs as rhododendrons (both hybrids and species), *Kalmia, Pieris,* azaleas, viburnums, camellias and magnolias, and will be amply repaid for generous expenditures in thorough preparation of the soil. Eighteen inches may be regarded as a good depth of cultivation for a first-class shrub planting. Some enthusiasts go to the extent of working beds even deeper.

There is some controversy as to whether deep preparation is necessary, but anyone who has seen its effects does not question its value. No gardener with any sort of an eye to quality in planting will be satisfied with inferior results. Deep digging provides the plants with a better supply of nutrients than is found in shallow beds, which must be replenished at least every third year; it also improves drainage. Adequate enrichment of the soil in the first place is a sound investment considered even from a purely economic standpoint. The saving in maintenance over a period of years will pay for the original cost many times over.

Soils vary and even within a very small garden one may find several different types requiring somewhat differing treatment. Loose, friable soils may be worked to the required depth with a mechanical tiller or even with hand spading. Adding organic material such as rotted animal manure, compost or peat is a good practice. Heavy clay soils will require much more effort, and in extreme cases it may be necessary to excavate the soil to a depth of 30 inches or more, refilling with topsoil. If such drastic action is not possible, then use of a heavy-duty tiller may be the next best approach. Again, be certain to incorporate large quantities of organic material to lighten the soil prior to planting.

In some areas, a thin layer of topsoil may overlie a bed of gravel or sand, resulting in an excessively droughty condition in the summer. Here one should screen out larger rocks and replace their bulk with organic material.

Drainage is often a problem in heavy soils and has no simple answer. All too often there is a subsurface layer of tightly compacted soil called hardpan that resists penetration by water. Surface water percolates down until it strikes the hardpan, then flows laterally over it. The soil above remains saturated. Digging a hole into the hardpan and filling with gravel, as is sometimes done, will accomplish nothing—the hole will simply fill with water. The excess water must either be carried away through a system of drains or the impervious layer must be shattered, allowing it to drain into more permeable layers below. Keep this in mind when replacing heavy, poorly drained soils with a better growing medium—you may be adding the improved soil to a "bathtub" which will never drain.

The basic preparation of soil may be modified according to varying groups of plant materials. Holes for trees should be dug as large as possible, up to 3 feet or more deep, and up to 6 feet in diameter. Recent experiments and local experience have shown that container-grown or balled-and-burlapped trees do best if the native soil is backfilled around the tree roots. There is no need to improve this with amendments of any sort. However, the roots of the tree must be spread out so that they come in contact with the native soil. Again, drainage is important, and a poorly drained tree hole will surely encourage root rot.

Beds for heathers—*Erica, Calluna,* and *Daboecia*— should have larger quantities of humus mixed with the native soil. Four to 6 inches of peat spread over the surface and worked into the soil is usually adequate.

FERTILIZERS

The discussion of soil so far has been concerned almost entirely with its physical properties. Its chemical composition is also a vital factor. About a dozen elements are required for the healthy growth of most garden plants, but only four of these need to be added in sufficient quantity to be considered here. These are nitrogen, phosphorus, potassium and calcium (lime). The analysis found on the outside of every sack of fertilizer lists the first three elements in the above-mentioned order. A fertilizer which is advertised as having a "5-7-8" analysis contains 5 parts of available nitrogen, 7 parts of phosphate and 8 parts of potassium (potash).

Soils differ in their requirements and different crops require these elements in varying proportions. A knowledge of the effect of their absence or presence is helpful in diagnosing the needs of plants. Broadly speaking, nitrogen aids the formation of healthy green foliage, but an excess of nitrogen with a deficiency of other elements tends to produce soft, flabby growth. Nitrogen is liberated in the soil by decaying vegetable matter and animal manure. It may be obtained also from dried blood, sewage by-products such as Milorganite, cottonseed meal, soybean meal or inorganic chemical compounds such as ammonium sulfate, ammonium phosphate, (which also supplies phosphates), sodium nitrate and potassium nitrate (which also provides potash). These chemicals act rapidly and must be applied sparingly and with great care.

Phosphates contribute most toward the reproductive organs of the plant, and therefore are essential in producing flowers and fruits of quality. They are procurable as superphosphate, acid superphosphate, acid triple superphosphate, bone meal, and to a limited extent, from animal manures. It is usually necessary to supplement animal manures with super-phosphate. Triple superphosphate (48% water-soluble P_2O_5) is pre-ferable to ordinary superphosphate (18% P_2O_5) for plants which require an acid soil.

Potassium is essential in building sound wood structure, necessary to tuberous or fleshy-rooted plants such as potatoes and dahlias. It strengthens the stems of plants and is particularly necessary for the proper development of fruits. It is obtainable in the form of ashes from green plants (not logs), potassium sulphate or potassium chloride. These last two are powerful chemicals and must be applied very sparingly: it is easy to burn plants by using them too freely. Potassium sulphate is preferred to potassium chloride owing to its texture.

Commercial fertilizers are available in many formulations, often for specific purposes. They range from rapid-acting, high-analysis formulas suitable for turf to so-called slow-release products which allow nutrients to be "metered" into the surrounding soil at a predetermined rate and may be safely used with most trees and shrubs. There are formulas for azaleas, rhododendrons and other acid-requiring plants, and others for roses, lilies and similar lime lovers. Soils in the Pacific Northwest tend to be low in available nitrogen and deficient in potassium and phosphates. It may pay to have soils tested to determine what they need and in what quantities before deciding on a particular course of fertilization. This can be done through the Cooperative Extension Service or by private soils laboratories. Generally, a commercial fertilizer with nitrogen, phosphorus and potassium in the ration of 1-3-2, 1-2-2- or 1-2-1 are suitable for general garden purposes. The exact formulas may vary, but they might read 5-15-10, 5-10-10, or 6-10-7 for all-purpose fertilizers, 8-12-4 or 10-8-6 for rhodo-dendrons, and 6-10-4 for roses.

Formulations which include weed killers are also available, but these are not intended for lawns with trees planted in them, and should be used with care and only according to the manufacturer's directions.

In addition to the above three elements there are a number of so-called micronutrients or trace elements which, if deficient, can limit plant growth. Many fertilizers now on the market contain these in proper quantities for our region. They are often labeled F.T.E., for fritted trace elements, a reference to the way they are formulated. It is well worth the slight extra cost of these fertilizers to insure the well-being of expensive trees and shrubs.

Calcium is the fourth major element and is vital to the cellular growth in plants and a factor in controlling the degree of acidity or alkalinity of the soil. As a general rule, the soils east of the Cascade mountains are alkaline; west of the Cascades, more or less acid in reaction. Lime (calcium carbonate) is commonly used to supply calcium and to change the soil reaction from acid toward alkaline. The majority of shrubs and trees we grow in this region do not require lime, although they may need some source of calcium. Even ericaceous plants may benefit from some additional calcium. Skilled rhododendron and azalea growers have found that small quantities of dolomite lime (magnesium carbonate) will improve the growth of these shrubs.

It may be taken as a general rule that soils for broad-leaved evergreen shrubs need little or no lime, and that plantings of lilacs, herbaceous perennials, hybrid roses and vegetable gardens should be given regular applications. Lime accomplishes a number of valuable purposes for such plantings in addition to sweetening an acid soil: it increases the amount of available nutrients by stimulating the growth of soil bacteria; it also releases other soil elements by reacting chemically upon the compounds in which they are "locked"; and it greatly improves the physical condition of a heavy soil, making it more friable. Iron in several forms is sometimes added to soils which are too alkaline in reaction for ericaceous shrubs. It is often a component of the special-mix fertilizers mentioned previously.

Annual fertilizing is used as a growth stimulant to improve the quality of plants and to some extent to improve their flowering. There may be no "best" time to fertilize since this may depend on the soil and the type of fertilizer used. Traditionally it has been done in spring and early summer, usually not in late summer or fall. An excellent time to fertilize rhododendrons is just as the bloom buds begin to swell, and then again a month later. The fertilizer should be watered in if the weather is dry.

In addition to commercial fertilizers, animal manures are used to improve fertility of garden soils, and it is necessary to understand the relative value of each. Animal manures are superior over the long run. Commercial fertilizers alone do little permanent good to garden soils; they produce a temporary effect. Animal manures, rich in humus, build up the soil from year to year and improve its physical condition. Poultry manure is extremely rich and concentrated and should be used with the greatest care. It may be spread thinly on the surface of the ground in the fall, and allowed to wash in all winter, the remainder thoroughly mixed with the soil the following spring. This concentrated manure will burn the roots of plants if it comes in direct contact with them and is most beneficial administered in the form of weak liquid manure. Sheep and rabbit manure are also rich but much milder. Dried sheep manure is often lightly applied as a topdressing. Horse manure is especially valuable in heavy soils. It is rich in nutrients, but should not be applied when fresh. A ton of the best cow manure contains less than 35 pounds of actual chemicals available to plants, but it provides a slow and lasting supply, and in addition, a wealth of potential humus. Composted animal manures are commercially available and supply many of the same benefits. However since fresh farmyard manures are not readily available to the city gardener, the compost pile is perhaps the best substitute.

Since building up a garden soil consists mainly in maintaining and increasing the humus content, a compost pile is a necessary adjunct to every well-cared-for garden. It is even feasible to have one in a tiny city garden. Grass clippings, weeds, fallen leaves and the tops of herbaceous plants, when placed in a compost pile and allowed to decompose, have almost as much value as well-rotted cow manure. If these materials are constantly removed from the garden, the addition of chemical fertilizers alone does not prevent depletion of the soil. Humus returned to the ground continuously can improve even very poor garden soil.

A compost pile is very simply made by the following method: all waste vegetable material is piled in bins especially built for the purpose, and each foot or so of vegetable matter is covered with a thin layer of soil and a sprinkling of general-purpose fertilizer added to prevent the escape of valuable elements and to speed up decomposition. The heap should be kept constantly damp, though not soaking wet, and should be turned at regular intervals if possible to mix and aerate the contents.

There are many ways of composting and indeed a mystique surrounds this relatively simple and basic process. The components are vegetable matter, moisture, air and heat. The gardener supplies the plant material, the moisture if necessary and air by turning the pile; the decomposition process supplies the heat. An active pile can generate temperatures high enough to kill weed seeds and some soil pathogens. Literature on various composting techniques is widely available, and the gardener may wish to try several methods before deciding which is the most suitable for his/her conditions. Compost is excellent for mulching plants to keep their roots cool in the summer. Surface-rooting plants such as rhododendrons and azaleas especially appreciate this protection. As mentioned above, it may be used as a replacement for other manures when preparing new beds and serves the same purpose. Plantings of rye or vetch grown in the off-season and dug into the soil are referred to as green manures.

PLANTING

The best methods and seasons for transplanting plant material are important considerations. Deciduous materials can be moved at any time during their dormant period—between the beginning of November and the end of February. However, any deciduous material which is at all difficult to establish should be planted just before it starts into growth in the spring—that is, sometime during February or March. The actual date of planting will vary with the season, the site and whether the plant is bare-rooted, container-grown, or balled and burlapped (B & B). As a general rule small container-grown broad-leaved evergreens may be planted any time, provided they receive adequate water and the soil is warm enough to initiate new root growth. Larger broad-leaved evergreens in containers, B & B., or those being transplanted—any situation where the root system may be injured—should be planted just before new growth starts in the spring, late February to mid-April. Alternatively, planting in the autumn when the soil is still warm is equally successful. Waiting until after the fall rains start—late September through October and into November—saves on water bills and energy. Coniferous evergreens may be safely planted nearly any time during the late winter or until their buds begin to break in the spring. All evergreen material that must be ordered from distant nurseries, especially from those in warmer sections, should be obtained in the spring, never in the fall. Plants of borderline hardiness, which might succumb during a hard winter, should be set out in the spring rather than in the fall.

Great care should be taken in planting trees and shrubs to see that their roots can take hold of the soil at once. Every shrub or tree should be puddled in with water at the time of planting. This should be done even if the ground seems wet and it is actually raining at the time. Puddling in is more effective in eliminating air spaces around the roots than trampling soil around the root ball. The roots of plants should not be exposed to the air and sunlight a moment longer than is absolutely necessary. Cover them with wet burlap if you cannot plant them immediately.

Selection of sound nursery stock in the first place and its proper handling at the time of planting will go a long way toward eliminating trouble later. Whenever possible, obtain plants that have been grown in a good loam. Beware of nursery stock which comes out of a heavy black peat soil. When transplanted to a poorer soil, particularly clay soil, the roots of the plants may never take hold, and they then gradually fail as the supply of nutrients in the original rootball is exhausted. This applies especially to ericaceous plants with a mass of fine fibrous roots. Special precautions are necessary in planting them. A large hole should be dug, in well-prepared ground, and generous quantities of dampened peat or compost incorporated with the soil. Much the same thing applies in the case of shrubs taken from heavy clay and set in a porous, sandy soil. The shrub should be placed in the hole, the hole filled with water, the fine fibrous root system gently washed by swishing the shrub around in the water, then the amended soil filled in around it.

Nurseries vary in their methods of offering plant material for sale. Most firms now grow shrubs and trees in containers, and plants are usually graded by the size of the container in which they are grown. Local nurseries sell plants balled and burlapped as well as in containers. This method is excellent if the soil is moist at the time of digging and of a sufficiently heavy nature so that the rootball will hold together.

Container-grown stock moves readily unless the roots have escaped through the bottom of the pot. Avoid plants which are severely pot-bound, with roots curling up the sides of the container or projecting from the drain holes. If you must plant pot-bound material, wash out the roots in water, loosen and straighten them. This should enable them to resume normal growth. If the roots remain in a knot the plants may be stunted all their lives. Pines in particular grow poorly from pot-bound stock.

Many deciduous trees and shrubs are handled with bare roots during the dormant season. This is perfectly satisfactory as long as they are never allowed to dry out. They should be kept wrapped in wet burlap or covered with damp soil. The more difficult ones, such as magnolias with soft fleshy roots or deciduous azaleas with fine fibrous roots, are better moved only in early spring.

Beware of the danger of labels! The apparently innocent thin wire with which labels are tied on have been known to cause the loss of the entire top of a shrub or tree. If you want to leave labels on the plant, tie them loosely so that there is ample room for development for several years, and attach them to a side branch, not the main stem.

It is important not to plant any tree or shrub too deeply. Roots must be left close enough to the surface so that air can reach them. In general, the top of the root ball should be only 1–2 inches beneath the surface of the soil. Excessively deep planting severely retards of the growth of a shrub and may even cause it to die. Beware of mulching too heavily after planting, especially in sandy soils. There are a few exceptions, such as the deep planting of grafted lilacs. Plant surface-rooting shrubs such as rhododendrons in a slight hollow. This facilitates watering and topdressing, especially in sandy soils.

It is frequently necessary to protect a well-prepared flower or shrub bed from the encroachment of greedy neighboring plants. Trees such as poplars, willows, cherries and western red cedar will send out roots for a radius of 100 feet or more. You must defend your enriched soil from their ravages. This is done either with sheets of galvanized iron or fiber glass, or a thin concrete wall set in the ground to a depth of at least 30 inches. The voracious roots of certain hedge plants, e.g., laurel and privet, can be kept under control by this method; it can also be used to prevent the spread of plants like bamboos.

Turf or lawn can be equally competitive, especially with shallow-rooted trees on poor soils. It is not unusual to see a pair of magnolias, one planted in turf, the other in a well-prepared bed, in which the latter has outgrown its neighbor in the lawn and is much more vigorous. The culprit here is the mat of grass roots which remove both water and nutrients before they can reach the tree roots. A grass-free area, well mulched and at least 6 feet in diameter avoids this difficulty.

WATERING

Watering of trees and shrubs resolves itself into two very simple "do's" and "dont's":

Do water trees and shrubs from April or May onward; don't water after the middle of August, except in the irrigated areas east of the Cascades.

Do give a thorough soaking every time you water, allowing the hose to trickle for several hours; don't sprinkle lightly and often.

Most trees and shrubs in this region suffer from too frequent and too much watering at the wrong time of year. It is almost impossible to give trees and shrubs too much water in spring and early summer, except in poorly drained soils. Too-frequent light watering tends to check growth rather than stimulate it. This is especially so if the water which comes out of the tap or well is much colder than the temperature of the soil. Soaker hoses are a convenient method for slow, continuous watering. Both coniferous and broad-leaved evergreens, especially the latter, respond to overhead sprinkling. The ideal treatment is to leave a sprinkler running on them for several hours in the evening. Midday sprinkling in very hot weather can burn new foliage.

In established shrub areas the need for watering from midsummer on is less and the need for watering in the spring much more than is commonly supposed. Spring rains, while frequent, are seldom sufficient to soak the soil thoroughly and may be followed by drying winds. It is impossible to give hard and fast rules as to just when to water, but the following broad general outline will give a good indication of what is needed. Dig down and note the depth to which the soil is still moist. In spring and early summer soil moisture must be maintained to within at least one inch of the surface in light, sandy soil, and to within one-half inch in a stiff clay. Late in the summer a sandy soil should be moderately moist to within four inches of the surface, and a clay to within two inches.

During the first year when a planting is becoming established a thorough soaking every 10 days from May to mid or late August will generally be advisable. This will produce lush growth and less bloom, but for the first year strong root growth is of paramount importance. The second and third seasons watering can be cut down to once in two weeks from May until the middle of August. Thereafter the shrubs should receive approximately two thorough soakings each month during May, June, and July, and fewer in August and September unless there is an unusually hot and protracted dry spell. The really drought-resistant shrubs, such as brooms, *Cistus*, rosemary and lavender, need no watering at any time once they are established. It is essential to keep the ground free of weeds which otherwise rob it of a great deal of moisture. Until the ground is protected by the foliage of the shrubs, it is necessary to maintain a mulch on the bed. This may be ground bark, chips, leafmold, compost or even fresh grass clippings, which help keep the ground cool and conserve moisture. The grass clippings must be spread thinly enough so that they do not ferment, and a light layer added occasionally will greatly check the germination of weeds.

Lawns and flower areas require much more watering than shrubs, but here again, a thorough soaking once a week or in the hottest weather, at most twice a week, is all that is necessary. Sprinkler systems installed to water the entire garden may provide too much water for shrubs while keeping the lawn green. A partially portable system is a better answer to this problem. For this reason bulbs, which do not require late summer watering, make better companion plants for shrubs than do herbaceous perennials which are better in beds by themselves.

PEST MANAGEMENT
Sharon Collman

Over the years we have become conditioned to attacking pest problems with pesticides—often without considering which pesticide should be used, let alone *if* or when. In past generations we were scattered on farms with miles between cities. But now we live packed together in urban communities with one city blending into another. We live only a few feet from our neighbors, and we are all connected by a road system that channels rainwater and all it carries with it directly into our rivers, streams and lakes. These in turn must double as recreation areas and sources of food or irrigation water. Too often they serve also as dumping grounds for our wastes.

Even in gardening we must begin to consider the consequences of our actions, their impact on ourselves, our neighbors and on the community. It is easy to be outraged by the infractions of "industry" or "agriculture," but we must also consider the impact of our own fertilizers, pesticides and trash burning along with the problems of garbage and air pollution.

We can no longer say, My plant is sick, what do I spray it with? We must begin to ask *Why* is it sick? What can I do about it? What choices do I have? If pesticides are needed, which one is appropriate? How can I hit the target pest without hitting non-target creatures?

In developing our gardens we have created an unnatural and disturbed environment. We have rearranged the soil to suit our purposes, often upsetting the natural drainage pattern in the process. If we fail to select plants suited to the new conditions, or to the vagaries of our climate, we then blame our problems on disease or insects. Plants which have been selected to suit their site and grown under optimum cultural conditions are better able to withstand the attacks of insects or diseases should they strike, and are better able to activate their own defenses.

Landscape plants have significant aesthetic, emotional and dollar value. They must be protected if pests get the upper hand. But also the beneficial insects, people and pets must be protected. With care and some knowledge of pests or the help of people with that knowledge, we can have both healthy plants and a healthy environment—this is the challenge for today's gardener.

Sixty to seventy percent of the plant problems submitted to Washington State University Cooperative Extension have cultural or environmental origins. This indicates that the most important fundamental factor in the control of disease and insect pest in the garden is proper cultivation. There is little point in spraying a sickly plant for a condition which has been caused by or is aggravated by wrong cultural methods.

Some plant injuries are mechanical. Plant tissues can be killed by a sudden freeze or prolonged drought, but it may take a long time for the plant to actually turn brown. (Consider the Christmas tree: it still looks green months after it was cut.) Trees with tender bark may freeze on cold, sunny winter days. The bark warms up and thaws, but is suddenly frozen again when the sun goes down, killing the tissue beneath the bark. Later the bark splits open and falls away. No amount of spraying will cure plants of this kind of problem.

Insect populations are regulated by many forces. Often insects are present in low numbers and require no action. Only if they increase is action needed to reduce their numbers. Occasionally the insects seen in large numbers are beneficial ones. It is the gardener's responsibility to know which are which.

Sometimes insect damage will be apparent only after the insects are gone. They may have crawled away to pupate (transform to adults) or moved to an alternate host, or to an overwintering site. Before spraying, be sure the target insect is actually present and at a vulnerable stage.

Not all insecticides kill all insects. The insect must be at a vulnerable stage in its life cycle (usually not the pupal stage), and the pesticide used must be active against that particular insect.

Before automatically spraying, consider using nonchemical methods to control insects such as handpicking, trapping, placing barriers, pruning (to remove infested buds or caterpillars in tents), hosing off with water or replacing susceptible plants with resistant species or varieties.

Remember that general purpose insecticides will also kill beneficial insects such as ground beetles, lacewings, ladybugs, honeybees and tiny parasitic wasps and flies. Some insecticides are especially hazardous to certain groups of insects or animals. For example, when insecticidal dusts are used on blooms, bees take the dust with the pollen back to the hive where it will kill the entire colony; Diazanon is especially toxic to ducks; Rotenone is toxic to fish. Read the caution part of the label *carefully*. Be sure to select the right type of pesticide for the particular problem.

Root-applied systemics are taken up by the roots and moved upward through the plant system eventually concentrating in the leaves where they will kill some leaf-feeding insects, especially sap-sucking ones such as aphids, scales or whitefly. They are not generally effective against insects sucking on the bark of twigs, branches or trunks.

Foliage-applied systemics (excluding herbicides) may act as a contact pesticide or be absorbed into the leafy tissues. Generally they do not move within the plant. Acephate (Orthene) can be picked up in lower leaves and translocated upward but not downward. Thus it is more important to spray the lower leaves (where root weevil adults most often feed) rather than the top layers. Since the systemic is not moved into the roots it will not control the grub stage.

Bacillus thurengiensis is a bacterium which is primarily active against caterpillars (although some strains are being developed for mosquitoes and other pests), check the label! To be effective, it must be applied to the foliage and eaten by the pest. Thus timing of application must coincide with the stage of most active feeding. Large caterpillars often have stopped feeding and/or are moving away from the host.

Insects will always be with us. Frequent application of pesticides will never eliminate them entirely. Pesticides should, therefore, be viewed not as an end-all, but as just one of many tools for managing pests.

Fungi, bacteria and viruses usually enter the plant through wounds or natural pore openings. Some germinate and penetrate the plant cells. Once they are inside the tissues, it is difficult to cure the plant.

Some disease problems can be avoided or minimized by applying a protective fungicide that kills spores as they land on the plant, or before they can grow and enter into the plant. Additional applications later in the season may be necessary to protect new growth, or during wet summers, or when overhead watering is frequent, e.g., for dogwood anthrocnose.

The length of time leaves or flowers stay wet (several hours of wetness may be needed before spores can germinate) can be reduced by pruning to improve air circulation through the plant. Watering the plants at their base rather than overhead will minimize wetness on the leaves. Watering in the morning allows foliage to dry off during the day.

Sanitation is especially important in preventing many diseases. Remove fallen diseased leaves, flowers and fruits; prune to remove cankers and dead wood harboring disease. Discard with the trash—do not compost!

Choosing resistant varieties may be the best answer to persistent problems which require frequent fungicide applications. There are now scab-resistant apples including 'Akane', 'Jonagold', 'Spartan' and 'Tydeman's Early' and crab apples. Some varieties of cherries, such as the weeping *Prunus subhirtella,* are especially susceptible to brown rot and/or virus problems, and it may be best to avoid them altogether in our wetter areas.

Select the pesticide to match the host plant and the pest. Fungicides are for diseases caused by fungi (such as mildew); insecticides are for insects. When using these products mix only as much as you will need to treat target plants. Excess pesticide and rinse water from cleanup should be used up as per label instructions rather than poured down drains.

Don't spray on windy days, or allow the spray to drift on to blooming plants or weeds where bees might encounter it.

Don't aim the spray where it will shoot into the neighbors' yards unless you have consulted with them in advance, and children, play toys, pets, barbecues, picnic tables, etc., have been moved indoors or covered. In some states homeowners can be fined for pesticide misuse.

Be sure the pesticide label specifies the target plant (apple, rhododendron, shade tree) and the site (soil, garbage cans, etc.). Be careful not to let spray drift onto fruit, berry or vegetable crops unless it is labeled for those crops.

Do not hesitate to seek expert help when you need it. If your car has problems, your auto mechanic needs to know what kind of car it is and what is wrong with it before it can be fixed. The same is true with sickly plants. An accurate diagnosis is the key to solving the problem, and there is plenty of help available.

The Cooperative Extension of the USDA and the land grant university in each state (Washington State University, Oregon State University, University of Idaho) provides research-based information on growing plants and on their problems; there are Cooperative Extension offices in most counties. Their educational programs include training workshops, public lectures, public field days, etc., as well as publications and pamphlets. The Ministry of Agriculture in Canada provides similar assistance and information. Master Gardeners (volunteers who are trained to help diagnose problems for the public) are another source of help. Some community colleges and universities have programs on horticulture, landscaping, entomology and plant pathology. Quarter-long classes or one-day workshops provide excellent learning opportunities for the home gardener. Arboreta and botanical gardens also offer classes, publish newsletters, and some have public information services. Specialty plant societies and active garden clubs offer lectures and discussions on proper culture and garden problems.

There is no need to be intimidated by garden pests. They are simply a part of gardening. One need not rush into frantic overkill. Today's gardener can be equal to the challenge of keeping both the garden and the environment healthy.

PRUNING

The first rule of pruning is: *Preserve and accentuate a plant's natural habit of growth.* The prime contribution of a deciduous tree to the garden is the line pattern of its branches; each individual tree has its own distinctive pattern. The pruning of a deciduous tree, then, must preserve or accentuate its branching pattern. Lopping a tree back to an ugly mophead is not pruning; it is mutilation. The contribution of evergreens, both conifers and broad-leaved trees or shrubs, to the garden picture is the textured pattern of their foliage mass; pruning must therefore preserve this pattern as well as the graceful irregularities of the plant which bring out this texture. The contribution of deciduous shrubs is their flowers. Consequently, they need to be pruned in such a way as to produce the maximum number of blooms.

Pruning can be divided into the following three types. First, the removal of dead or weak and useless wood. Secondly, the cutting back of live growth with the specific purpose of invigorating or improving the shape of the plant. Thirdly, the pinching back of the current season's unripened new shoots, or summer pruning.

The removal of dead wood is a simple operation that requires no particular explanation except that a clean cut must be made back to live wood, leaving no stub to cause disease problems later. At the same time thin, weak shoots should be removed entirely to the base, to give more space and light to those remaining.

Pruning of ripened live wood makes a plant grow more vigorously. From this fact follows the second fundamental rule of pruning. *The required amount of pruning of ripened growth is always in reverse ratio to the vigor of the plant.* In other words, a robust grower should be pruned as little as possible, but a weak plant cut back relatively severely. But pruning should not be a means of keeping a large shrub or tree within the bounds of a small garden. Better to remove it and plant one more suitable to the space.

The purpose of summer pruning is to control and direct the energy of the plant in such a way as to continue growth only where it is wanted, and encourage the production of flowers and fruits. It is only directed to new, unripened growth so July is usually the month when summer pruning done.

Trees

Remove crossing branches which rub against one another, and ingrowing ones filling up the center of the tree, which should be kept open. If a tree has definite leader preserve it, shortening back any branches which show signs of competing with it. Most tree pruning is done in fall or winter when the trees are bare of leaves and it is easier to see the branch pattern. Trees which start growth early in the spring, such as the birches, walnuts, maples, and cherries, are best pruned in mid-summer to fall, and certainly before the end of the year. Conifers should also be pruned during the fall or early winter months, before sap starts to rise with warmer weather. When a tree such as *Prunus cerasifera* 'Pissardii', one of the flowering plums, has several branches arising from one point, or close together, treat each major branch separately, keeping the center as open as possible. Do not top the branches of any tree, as such treatment destroys their future shape and merely proliferates the branching habit. Cut out V-crotches, which can split in wind or snow storms and avoid such trees in nurseries, or eliminate the crotch if possible when the tree is still young. Side shoots on a main stem should be retained for a number of years, since they strengthen the trunk; just shorten them back annually to a few inches in length. However, strong suckergrowths (water sprouts) from the stem or main branches, especially in apples, crab apples, pears or plums, should be removed entirely. Shoots coming from the base of the stem or from below ground, which arise from the stock on which the tree was grafted, should be dug out rather than cut back.

Thin the branches of a weeping willow by following the main stems and cutting out the weakest branches hanging beneath them each winter. The tree's branching pattern can be improved steadily by removing all branches that are overlapped by heavier and more vigorous ones. The same method can be applied to other weeping forms of trees, such as the Camperdown elm and *Prunus subhirtella* 'Pendula'. Flowering peaches and almonds, if not grown for their fruits, should be pruned immediately after flowering to get the best results.

Shrubs

There are some genera, especially among the evergreen shrubs, which require little regular annual pruning save for removal of the old spent flower heads as soon after blooming as possible. These include *Kalmia latifolia, Pieris* species, most camellias and rhododendrons. If they are becoming too large for their allotted space and need branches pruned back, this should be done immediately after flowering. The evergreen species of *Viburnum* generally fall into the same category, unless they are fruiting plants of *V.davidii* or *V.tinus* and others, to be left for winter decoration. The deciduous species of *Rhododendron*, which include the native azaleas as well as some from China such as *R. davidsonianum* and *R.yunnanense*, seldom need regular pruning except to keep the bushes within their space limits.

Shrubs which flower on new growths of the current year must be pruned back in early spring (March) before they make much growth. Amongst these are species or hybrids of *Buddleia, Hydrangea paniculata*, the summer-flowering types of *Tamarix, Ceanothus* 'Gloire de Versailles', *Spiraea japonica* forms and its relatives, and most kinds of hypericums. All of these can be cut back to a strong shoot near the base of last year's

growth. With *Hydrangea macrophylla (H. hortensis)* the best flowers are produced on the strong shoots made last year; these should be retained their
full length and only the weakest shoots removed. Heathers which bloom
in August and September, including forms of *Erica tetralix, E.cinerea,* and
E.ciliaris, as well as the polymorphous *Calluna vulgaris,* should be clipped
back at this time, but not into old bare branches. The various kinds of roses
have to be pruned at this time, before they start growth. As a general rule
strong shoots should be left to nearly their full length, weak ones cut back
to near their bases. If doubtful as to how to treat a plant, visit a public rose
garden at this season and observe their methods with various types of
roses, or attend a pruning class if one is offered locally. The pruning of
Clematis is dealt with in the chapter on *Vines and Climbers.*

A greater number of deciduous shrubs flower along the branches
formed the previous year, beginning with the forsythias in March and continuing with several spiraeas in April and May, *Cytisus scoparius* hybrids in
late May, and the weigelas, then the *Philadelphus* and *Deutzia* species and
hybrids in June, with our native Ocean Spray, *Holodiscus discolor,* and
several species of *Spiraea* from eastern Asia, *S.canescens, S.nipponica,* and
S.veitchii. All these, and others with similar growth and flowering habits,
should be pruned as soon as the flowers have died, by removing the old
flowering branches completely, or down to a new young shoot if one arises
on a recently flowered branch, as is sometimes the case. This will allow the
maximum amount of time for the new shoots to extend and mature before
winter.

Summer Pruning

Summer pruning is especially needed by flowering and/or fruiting
trees belonging to the apples and crab apples (*Malus*), the pears (*Pyrus*),
mountain ashes (*Sorbus*), and plums and cherries (*Prunus*), but can also be
used to good effect on young maple (*Acer*), oak (*Quercus*), magnolia and
Sycamore (*Platanus*) trees, where crossing branches or duplicate leaders
can be removed when they are still young. In the case of the apples, pears
and plums, and especially those trained against walls for fruits, the principal shoots should be tied in to extend the branches as required, but the
short lateral shoots pinched back to three or four leaves, so as to encourage
the formation of flowering buds. For standard trees in the open remove
any crossing branches, especially in the center of the tree, or branches
overhanging another; longer branches extending out in one direction at
the expense of others should also be shortened. Espaliered shrubs against
walls or fences, such as *Camellia sasanqua* forms, should be treated like
espaliered fruit trees, to keep them within their space.

CHAPTER VI

Propagation

The methods of propagation discussed here could be enlarged upon considerably in their technical aspects. However, this information is not intended for professionals but for gardeners who may wish to grow small stocks of plants for their own use or their friends.

There are two principal ways of producing new plants, either by vegetative means or by seeds. Plants grown from seeds are likely to have greater vigor and may be longer lived. Seedlings, however, may not come into bloom as quickly, and the resulting plants may vary in essential characters. It is sometimes possible to obtain seeds, for example, of many herbaceous perennials, that will germinate freely, producing plants true to type that reach flowering stage in a reasonably short period of time. This is a satisfactory method when such seeds are available. However, the majority of garden plants must be propagated vegetatively because so many of them are either hybrids or special forms which do not come true from seeds. There is always the possibility of raising a superior seedling, but hybridization and selection are not within the scope of this discussion.

SEEDS

Some seeds can be raised out-of-doors, but the majority are better if given the protection of a cold frame or cool greenhouse: many seeds germinate more quickly with bottom heat below them. A temperature of 55°–60°F. is sufficient. Modern electrical heating with thermostatic control makes the raising of seeds in a heated frame a very simple affair. Many seeds are best sown in January or February when the days begin to lengthen, using bottom heat, but some need to be sown as soon as ripe. Among such genera are members of the buttercup family (*Anemone, Ranunculus, Thalictrum*) and those with very small seeds in the Ericaceae (*Cassiope, Erica,* and *Rhododendron*). If not sown when collected they should be kept in a refrigerator until the following February and sown then. Some seeds, if not sown promptly, will remain dormant for one or more seasons and then germinate; others rapidly lose their fertility. The chief reason for not sowing seeds as soon as ripe is the problem of caring for them during the winter months.

There are several ways of hastening germination. Exposure to severe frost or alternate freezing and thawing is one of the best of these, or to one or two sequences of 3–4 weeks in the refrigerator, alternating with a similar time at room temperature. A few kinds of seeds (members of the pea family) may benefit from soaking overnight in water before sowing, others by dropping into water heated to just below boiling point (*Arctostaphylos* and *Ceanothus*). It is therefore useful to know the requirements of individual species prior to sowing. Some seed catalogues supply this information; another useful source is the USDA publication *Seeds of Woody Plants in the United States.*

Opinions vary as to the best medium in which to sow seeds. One good mixture consists of one-third sandy garden soil (not if clay), one-third peat, one-third a coarse sharp sand (not builder's sand, which is too fine). Or Perlite may be used to replace the last ingredient. Mix them thoroughly. No fertilizer is necessary at this stage. Seeds are often sown in wooden boxes ("flats"), but except for large quantities of plants, pots or pans are preferable, made of polyethylene, not clay, which dries out too quickly. One quarter of the bottom of the pot should be filled with a coarse drainage material such as broken clay pots or pebbles; the former may harbor slugs or wood lice, so the latter are preferable. Some seeds may remain dormant for two or three years after sowing, in which case the tougher polyethylene pots are preferable.

Depth of sowing depends upon the size of the seeds, the standard rule being to cover the seed with its own depth of soil, the finest being sown on the surface. The soil should be pressed down firmly in the pots before sowing but the surface left loose. The upper soil surface can be sterilized by pouring boiling water on it 15 minutes prior to sowing the seeds. Care should be taken to have the soil just damp, neither too wet nor too dry. Chopped sphagnum moss is a good surfacing material for small seeds, especially those of ericaceous plants such as rhododendrons, heathers and their relatives.

Seeds are usually watered immediately after sowing but this must be done carefully so as not to wash them out of the soil. One good method is to stand the pot in a shallow container of water until the soil is completely soaked, but not so much that the seeds are floating. For seeds which germinate quickly this original soaking will last from one to two weeks until they appear. Each pot should be covered with a sheet of brown paper and a piece of glass to keep the soil surface moist without frequent watering. Or small pots may be enclosed in plastic bags and kept in a light place until germination is observed. This eliminates the need for watering until the seeds germinate. Tiny seedlings require special care, so control of moisture is vital. They may be watered with a fine hand spray, but soaking the pots from beneath is safest. If any sign of damping-off is seen, water with a solution of Benlate or other effective fungicide.

As soon as the seedlings form their first true leaf, prick them off carefully, using tweezers if necessary, into small boxes, 1 to 2 inches apart according to their size and probable rate of growth; then place the boxes in a shaded frame if possible. Transplant again as soon as they fill the allotted spaces, this time into individual pots of a suitable size, usually about 4 inches in diameter. At this stage, some fertilizer may be added to the soil mixture which should contain less sand or Perlite and more compost and garden soil. When they fill the pots with roots they are ready to be transplanted into nursery rows, or planted out into their permanent places. Seedlings of trees and shrubs, and of conifers in particular, should not be kept long in pots or their roots will become knotted and the plants restricted in their growth. If they form taproots at an early stage, e.g., oaks, walnuts, native western dogwoods, madronas, they should be planted straight into a nursery bed, or even into their places in the case of walnuts and hickories. A copper mesh screen in the bottom of the pots will prevent the growth of taproots.

The principal factor in raising seedlings successfully is to keep them growing steadily without a check of any sort until their normal dormant period. Some, if severely checked, will lose at least a season's growth. The essential considerations to avoid this are (1) good drainage in the pots, (2) evenly controlled moisture and temperature, (3) pricking them off at the right time, then potting them on when required. A compost heap to supply soil for this need is most valuable.

VEGETATIVE PROPAGATION

This is accomplished by cuttings of various types, layers, division, budding and grafting. Cuttings offer the best method for most shrubs. The amateur is particularly likely to want to propagate various broad-leaved evergreens to use in his or her garden. Some who might feel they could not afford to plant long drifts of heathers if they had to buy the plants, could propagate these for themselves by merely buying a few stock plants and then layering them.

Summer Cuttings

Propagation by cuttings has increased both in scope and number in recent years. There is virtually no closed season, but the busiest period in taking cuttings of half-ripened wood is from June to September. There are several distinct techniques and each propagator must develop and practice his or her own. The use of misting nozzles and automatic timing devices in recent years has facilitated successful new methods with summer cuttings. One, the Paris frame system, calls for using a cold frame which can be kept hermetically sealed or nearly so, situated in full sun and facing due south. Fill the bottom of the frame with sand and cover the glass sashes with two thicknesses of cheesecloth to prevent scorching. After first treating (the cuttings) with a powdered or liquid root-inducing hormone at the proper strength for the type of cutting, insert them in pots in a suitable porous rooting medium. Then water thoroughly and place them in the frame. Open it once a day in the early morning, sprinkle the cuttings lightly with a fine spray and also keep the sand wet. Otherwise keep the frame tightly closed. Cuttings of some shrubs will root in 10–14 days in warm weather under these conditions; the majority take two to four weeks.

Propagators vary in their choice of a rooting medium. Some prefer clean coarse sand, others a sand-peat mixture, some use Perlite, others a mixture of those three ingredients. Peat is more valuable for rooting acid-loving shrubs, particularly members of the Ericaceae, whose very fine roots benefit from its inclusion. This helps to conserve and control the moisture supply, but be sure that it is thoroughly wet when used.

A cold frame is not necessary when propagating in small quantities. Cuttings may be inserted in a pot filled with the sand-peat mixture, watered, then covered with a larger plastic sack. This should be shaded from direct sun, and the pot plunged in the ground to conserve moisture. Treat the pot the same as a small-scale frame. Or a wooden flat can be used instead of a pot and the plastic cover supported on a wire frame. It is important with soft summer cuttings that the humidity be kept high so that they do not dehydrate and die. A common mistake of the beginner is to attempt to root woody plants in water; most will rot rather than root, though willows are a well-known exception.

The most important factor for success is the proper choice of cutting wood. The growth should be half-ripened. If the cuttings are too soft they will quickly wilt. If the wood is too hard they will take a long time to root or may not root at all. To test a cutting, flex it between thumb and fingers. It should be springy, neither too soft nor too stiff. The required degree of stiffness varies with the individual plant. At the proper stage the wood will usually finally snap when tested but will bend somewhat first. If it is so soft that it doesn't break but only bends, it is too young. Choose normal growths, rejecting weak, thin shoots or abnormally thick ones. Where part of a plant is in the shade and part in the sun, take cuttings from the sunny side. Both deciduous and evergreen plants can be propagated from half-ripened wood, the former being taken in late June, the latter in July.

If a plant makes lush growth and does not ripen its wood early enough, those shoots intended for cuttings can be hastened by nipping out their tips; this may be done for some roses, for example. The earlier in the season that cuttings can be struck and rooted, the more growth they will make before the season is over, and the better they will be able to pull through the winter.

The beginner is usually tempted to make too large a cutting. Cuttings of small plants like heathers should be ½ to 1 inch long, 2 to 3 inches for larger shrubs. In handling material known to be difficult to strike, small lateral half-ripe shoots are pulled off ripened wood, leaving a "heel" at the base of the cutting (part of the bark and wood). Some propagators take all cuttings with such a "heel" and do not recut the joint. However, it is simpler in most cases to cut the selected shoots just below a leaf joint with either a pair of sharp shears or a razor blade or knife, if the operator is used to handling these implements. Leaves near the base of the cutting should be removed with care. Some plants such as *Clematis* root better when the cut is made halfway between two leaf joints; these are termed internodal cuttings.

In healing, the base of the cutting usually forms a callus. In some shrubs and trees, including camellias and certain conifers, this callus may develop at the expense of or in place of roots; in such cases cut it away on one side to encourage the formation of roots. Sometimes these emerge from the callus, sometimes from the stem of the cutting.

To insert the cuttings in the rooting medium, stand the pot in a bowl of water with the top of the sand less than an inch above the water level; then even the softest cuttings will slip down into the wet sand with no effort. Lift the pot out of the water when all the cuttings are placed and let it stand in a sink and drain. If a soil mixture of sand, peat and Perlite is preferred, cuttings may be dibbled into the evenly moist mixture, using a blunt, pointed short stick of a size appropriate to the cuttings. Then thoroughly water the pot overhead with a can and allow it to drain in a shady place. Cuttings may be placed as close together as the foliage will allow; those around the edge of a pot will root quicker than those in the center. With a number of one kind of plant it is simplest to keep them in one container, so that all can be handled together; do not mix different kinds in one pot, since they may root at different times. Label and date each pot. Since the sand is merely a rooting medium and provides no sustenance to young plants, as soon as cuttings have developed several short new roots transfer them to a sandy soil mixture or one containing either peat or compost with some Perlite to lighten it, from which they can obtain some nourishment. Good drainage in the containers and regular watering and shading is important at this stage of their new lives. Do not allow them to stand in a sunny situation until they show signs of new growth, and even then partial shade is desirable, especially in the afternoons. Then gradually give more light until they are thoroughly hardened. Cuttings which have not rooted or only feebly so by the end of September should be left in sand frames all winter, covered by glass or plastic but not allowed to dry out. Conifer cuttings, especially of true firs (*Abies*) and spruces (*Picea*) frequently require two years to make a good root system.

At the close of the summer cutting season frames equipped with electrical heating units may be used to propagate many broad-leaved evergreen shrubs, particularly those growing in shady sites where the young shoots are not so hard as those in sunny positions. In September and October especially, and from then on until early December, evergreens strike readily in a temperature of 55°–60°F. Some genera which may then be propagated include *Buxus, Berberis, Abelia, Escallonia, Osmanthus* and *Pieris*. Another possible season is in February, following any cold spell but before growth starts. Brooms (*Cytisus*) can be propagated at this time.

Hardwood Cuttings

Although many of the easily grown deciduous shrubs such as *Forsythia* and *Spiraea* root readily from summer cuttings, they may also be increased with a minimum of trouble from hardwood cuttings, taken in fall as soon as the leaves have fallen. Cut new shoots 8 to 12 inches long, and provided you have a sandy soil, insert them upright in the ground to about half their depth, opening a narrow trench with a spade for the purpose. Besides the two genera mentioned, deutzias and *Philadelphus*, privets (*Ligustrum*) and a number of kinds of roses can be propagated in this way. Make sure that the cuttings are firm in the ground so that frosts do not heave them out: a shady site is to be preferred, since they should remain there until the following fall.

Root Cuttings

A few trees and shrubs can be propagated from root cuttings. Small sections of roots 3 to 4 inches long can be dug out in October-November and planted in flats or pots, keeping the upper end towards the surface and covered with about an inch of sandy soil or a peat-Perlite-soil mixture. Keep them in a frame or under the bench in a cool greenhouse during the winter. When they show signs of growth in the spring, pot them individually in a richer mixture. Among trees which may be propagated thus are the Tree-of-Heaven (*Ailanthus*), *Aralia* species, the Empress Tree (*Paulownia*), the sumacs (*Rhus*), and Black Locust (*Robinia*) which often produces suckers, as does the White Poplar (*Populus alba*) and its relative the aspen (*P. tremuloides*). Root cuttings should not be taken from grafted trees, since in that case it would be the understock that would be propagated.

Layers and Divisions

Plants which spread by underground shoots, suckers or layers may be readily propagated by those means. They include *Daphne blagayana*, most gaultherias and pernettyas, and the hybrid *Gaulnettya*, our native *Mahonia nervosa* and *M. repens*, some species of *Rosa* including *R. nitida, R.*

virginiana and the native *R. nutkana* and its varieties on both sides of the Cascade Mountains: also *Sarcococca hookeriana* and its varieties, and the Yellowroot (*Xanthorhiza*) from the eastern United states. Such divisions are best made as soon as the plants show signs of new growth in early spring.

Layering is resorted to for shrubs that do not root easily from cuttings. The process is not complicated but takes longer than for cuttings. It is an adaptation of one of Nature's ways of propagation, when low branches become covered by drifting leaves and fallen twigs or branches, then form roots and develop a new plant. To accomplish this in the garden, a low branch of a tree or more often a shrub, is partly cut or broken through, covered with sandy soil or a mixture of soil, peat and sand and topped by a heavy rock to hold the layer in place; it may also be necessary to support an upright branch with a stake. In nurseries where this method is used, whole plants are dug up, laid on their sides, and then each branch layered. It was formerly much used in European nurseries for rhododendrons and azaleas. Two years will be needed to produce a sizable plant fit to be transplanted.

Budding and Grafting

These are essentially the same method of propagation, except that in budding the scion consists of a single bud but in grafting the scion holds several. Budding is usually done in July, grafting indoors in January and February, although it may be continued well on into the spring. Grafting should not be done during a severe cold spell. The scions should be cut from the parent trees in the previous October or November, then buried in the ground up to their tops in a cool place until required.

In many instances grafting or budding is the simplest method of propagating an individual tree of particular merit, and must be used where named clones are concerned, unless they can be propagated by cuttings, as can be done with many Japanese Maples. The named *Hamamelis* hybrids, for example, such as 'Arnold Promise', 'Diane' and 'Ruby Glow' are grafted on to seedlings of our native *H. virginiana*. With such plants, careful watch must be kept for suckers of the stock growing up from beneath the graft (or bud) union, and they must be removed promptly before they become large. A keen gardener will notice the difference in the foliage of the two plants. Modern hybrid roses are all budded onto vigorous stocks; fruit trees can be either budded or grafted. The stock used in the case of the latter group greatly influences the eventual size of the tree, particularly with apples and pears. Plants propagated by budding are obviously cheaper to produce than those which have to be grafted, since only one bud can form a new plant. To learn the techniques of budding and grafting, consult appropriate nurserymen's manuals.

CHAPTER VII

Broad-leaved Deciduous Trees

Deciduous trees are an essential part of gardens in this region. As used in this book, a tree usually will be a woody plant with a clearly defined trunk or trunks, as opposed to a shrub which branches from the base. We say "usually" because there are some woody plants that may be either large shrubs or small trees. Most of these can be grown single trunked and treelike, some are often allowed to have several trunks or stems (our Bigleaf Maple, dogwood, and many willows, for example) but definitely appear treelike in the landscape, and a few are distinctly shrubby and low branched but attain heights of 25–40 ft. in the landscape and so may fulfill a role of shrub/tree according to the observer.

Every tree placed in the garden constitutes an accent point in the design, and consequently the number of trees which can be used in a given area is definitely limited. This is a matter of garden design and cannot be fully discussed here, but we wish to emphasize the fact that, out of the hundreds of beautiful, desirable trees, the gardener will be able to use only a half dozen kinds in a garden of moderate size. This makes careful selection all the more important. The information that follows is intended as an aid to this process.

In the descriptions of individual genera and species the ultimate size of the tree in perhaps 50 years is indicated. This is a factor that is frequently ignored in planting gardens. It is possible to obtain trees which range in size from 10–150 ft. at maturity, so there is no excuse for the unsightly prospect of a butchered tree that is lopped back repeatedly to keep it from exceeding its position. However, a small tree is not automatically the answer, for sometimes a very large specimen is not only desirable but essential to the scale of a given design. Beware of planting a small flowering tree simply for its beautiful bloom where a larger though less spectacular shade tree is really what is needed. Most small trees flower no more than 10–15 days of the year, but some species offer a period of fall color as well as pleasing leaf patterns and attractive winter bark. The large trees recommended for garden use are mostly those which cast at least moderately light shade and do not have unduly voracious root systems. Also included in this revision are large trees suitable for street or park planting. A more complete discussion of many factors involved in their choice will be found in Chapter XV, *Trees for Street and Park Plantings*.

Finally, the most important qualification of a deciduous tree is the line pattern of its branches. This is its chief function in the garden design—to provide definition with the reach of its trunk and the swing of its branches. Whether one is conscious of it or not, this branch pattern will have a marked effect on the whole garden picture, especially in the winter when the rhythmic lines of the bare branches are revealed. Each tree has its own particular branching pattern. The drooping twigs of the Weeping Willow contrast with the upright stance of the Lombardy Poplar, the delicate tracery of a birch's slender twigs or the stout, gnarled, curling limbs of an oak; each will lend a different atmosphere to the garden. Trees of weeping and fastigiate lines—the two extremes—are often difficult to place, whereas those with an intermediate branching pattern, horizontal, gracefully arching, or gently upward curving, fit more easily into the composition. Selection of the proper tree for a given situation deserves the most careful thought.

Although a well-designed garden contains only a limited number of trees, this limitation can be partially obviated by training some of them as shrubs. A tree that is to be grown as a shrub should, if possible, be obtained when very young, preferably not more than three years old, and cut back almost to ground level at the appropriate season. This is usually during the dormant season for a deciduous tree, but it should be done at the time indicated as best for pruning that particular individual or group. The training of trees for hedges is closely allied to this, as they must be topped and encouraged to branch repeatedly while young if they are to make a successful hedge.

The propagation of deciduous trees is usually left to the nurseryman. However, a number of important points should be considered. Any large tree that is to be grown as a specimen should be on its own roots whenever possible. Large trees are best propagated from seed, except for selected cultivars which are usually grafted onto seedlings of the species. When buying a grafted tree, make sure that it is on the most desirable stock, for this may have considerable effect on the ultimate growth of the specimen. Nurserymen these days are propagating increasing numbers of deciduous trees (including cultivars) from cuttings, reducing the later-life problems sometimes encountered with grafted trees. It is vital to obtain a tree which will make a fine specimen in years to come, and neither care nor expense (negligible in the total equation) should be spared to obtain a sound tree in the first place.

Exercise great care in planting trees. The ground should be well loosened to a depth of 3 ft. in favorable soils, even deeper where subsoil is impervious. Perfect drainage is the goal; do your best to insure it. Except in naturally fertile soils, much fertilizing or amending with composts and peat moss tends to be counterproductive. A tree thus "assisted" will make quick growth for a few years in the small, improved area. If the surrounding soil is poor, however—gravel, sand, or clay—the tree roots will resist growing out into it as they ultimately must if the tree is to succeed. The result is a tree that becomes "pot-bound," its roots trapped in the small area of improved soil, sometimes actually circling around in it. Such a tree will be failing in 10–20 years, or it may blow down in a windstorm because it has an inadequate spread of roots to hold the apparently healthy top. The best commercial trees will have been grown in the nursery at exactly the right ground level, and should be planted in the garden at the same level. A large shade tree standing in a lawn is most attractive when the buttresses or thicker parts leading to the main roots are left exposed above the ground. This is governed almost entirely by the original planting. Trees planted 2–3 in. too deep in heavy or wet soils have no chance to grow properly and will die eventually. Young trees planted in lawns should have the turf kept back at least two feet from their trunks, both to minimize mower damage and because a lawn close around a young tree can reduce its growth rate by as much as half.

Deciduous trees, particularly in smaller sizes, are often transplanted with bare roots, and bare-root trees of any given size will normally have a better spread of roots than trees dug with a ball. Further, if the site soil is poor, a bare-root tree will adjust to it better than a tree with its nursery ball of improved soil which discourages the roots from leaving it. Most nurseries, however, dig trees of larger sizes (3 in. trunk diameter and up) with a ball of earth attached. Many genera—*Quercus, Fagus, Cornus, Betula, Carpinus, Ginkgo, Liquidambar, Liriodendron, Magnolia, Nothofagus, Stewartia, Styxax* and many ericaceous genera—are best dug with a root ball, since they resent root disturbance.

Many newly transplanted trees, particularly the larger balled-and-burlapped deciduous ones with multi-ton rootballs, need no staking except in locations exposed to very strong winds. The primary purpose of staking is to prevent wind-rock of the lower trunk at the ground level, which loosens new roots trying to get established in surrounding soil. Low staking or guying no more than 24 in. above the ground is adequate. Traditional tall, rigid, paired stakes, used with crossbars or crossties, are poorer, giving less support near the ground than the shorter stakes. Further, if the trunk is too rigidly staked it may fail to develop internal mechanical strength, actually making weaker growth than if left free to flex in the wind. The popular wrought-iron tree-guard cages share this problem. If the trunk is tied to them for several seasons it produces a weaker tree; if it is released the wind will bang the trunk against the wrought iron, injuring the bark. Such "tree guards" should be padded so the trunk is free to move with the wind, without ties. There is much evidence that they do more harm than good, being primarily a design element of minimal help to the tree. One successful newer staking method is that of using a steel reinforcing bar (⅝ in. "rebar," used in concrete construction) driven several feet into the ground alongside the tree. This flexes with the wind, but gives surprisingly strong ground-level support. The steel rebar should extend at least 5 ft. above the ground, with both a high and a low tie, the extra height not for support, but to foil vandals who can easily snap off trees staked with the traditional paired, rigid stakes. Cushion the stakes and wires so they don't injure the bark. Use old garden hose over the wires, fastened in a figure-eight configuration with loops around the tree and stake. Remove the wire after a year; otherwise, adjust it yearly. Wire carelessly left twisted around the trunk can become embedded in it, girdling the tree and causing the loss of the entire top if not detected in time.

The branches of deciduous trees should be thinned to a clean structure at the time of transplanting. Also, one should each year thin the branches of all trees growing under garden conditions, to preserve and accentuate a normal uncrowded branching pattern. This applies even more to flowering trees than to large shade trees. The misconception that a "solid mass of bloom" is the acme of perfection keeps many gardeners from having really beautiful flowering trees. The spare but rugged lines of old trees on windswept ridges or coastlines provide a more appropriate prototype for achieving an artistic composition in line and form to support the exquisite flower display. The chief difficulty is that under garden conditions a tree often makes an abnormally heavy growth with interlacing twigs and branches. It is better to maintain a more natural sort of beauty by judicious pruning, encouraging good line rather than merely mass. You can't just buy a flowering tree for your garden, forget about it and expect an artistic result. Pruning shears in hand, you create the structure of your tree as surely as a painter creates one on canvas with his brush, only your picture is in three dimensions and is never static.

ÁCER. The maples offer a notably wider choice of useful trees for Pacific Northwest gardens than any other genus. While the finest larger maples are mostly American species, there are many excellent mid-sized and smaller maples from Asia and Europe. The gardener who scorns maples as "common" will be wise to seek out some of these lesser-known species from among the over 100 possibilities. Many of them still require a search to find. Nurserymen, while stocking more maple species and cultivars than they did 25 years ago, still grow only a small number of the rarer and finer ones.

A. buergérianum (VI), the Trident Maple from China, is a favorite with bonsai growers. This species has small leaves, tri-lobed like an ivy, on a 25–30 ft. tree. The distinctive strong green summer color holds till autumn, then becomes orange or red.

The European Hedge Maple, *A. campéstre* (V), is of similar stature, though it can reach 40–50 ft. Hedge Maple makes a good, roundheaded tree adaptable as a street tree, and exhibits considerable drought and alkalinity tolerance. The small five-lobed leaves turn yellow in autumn.

A. circinátum (V), is the Vine Maple, probably our region's most useful native tree for the landscape. This small, often shrubby maple is among the loveliest in the genus, somewhat recalling the Japanese Maple, _A. palmatum_, but having a sturdier, more upright character than that species in sunny locations, and in shade developing an ethereal horizontal grace that few maples achieve. This maple tolerates the shade of conifers or woodland planting, and is often multitrunked. In woodland habitat it becomes open and angular with age, reaching 20 ft., and in such habitat its many-lobed leaves turn soft gold or chartreuse in fall. Trees grown or collected from shade will often perform poorly if suddenly moved to sunny sites. Those grown in sun will be dense and bushy, up to 15 ft., with smaller leaves that turn brilliant reds and oranges in autumn.

A. davídii (VI), is one of the species with white-striped bark. This is a 40–45 ft. Chinese tree of particular winter interest. Good seedling forms offer red-purple to orange autumn color. The upswept and vase-shaped young trees mature to a dense round-oval crown.

A. gínnala (II), Amur Maple, with small three-lobed leaves, has few rivals for warm scarlet autumn color. These leaves are borne on a normally low-branched bushy tree which requires careful pruning while young, especially if it is to be used as a street tree or park tree. Native of Manchuria and eastern Asia, it is very hardy.

A. glábrum var. _douglásii_ (IV), Douglas or Rocky Mountain Maple, is another native species similar to Vine Maple. Its leaves have fewer lobes and develop soft gold autumn color. Twigs of new growth are bright red. Having better tolerance of dry soils and low humidity than _A. circinatum_, it is worthy of wider use.

Paperbark Maple, _A. gríseum_ (V), is particularly showy in winter. In this Chinese species the cinnamon brown bark peels off like that of the best birches. The three-parted compound leaves give the plant a fine texture and turn a vivid red in late fall. Though rare, because it is difficult to propagate and slow-growing, this is a superior low-branched maple to ultimately 30 ft. in perhaps 50 years.

Fullmoon Maple, _A. japónicum_ (V), is a small, usually bushy, erect tree to 30 ft., stiff in its youth and taking 15 years to make any size at all, but gaining much more character with age. It is a superior small garden tree in either the type or in its 'Aconitifolium' form, which has leaves deeply divided into fingerlike formation, and which develops superb red autumn color. _A. shirasawánum_ 'Aureum' is the new name for the Golden Fullmoon Maple (V), beloved in its native Japan but less known here due to the popularity of Japanese Maple, _A. palmatum_.

A.lobélii (VII) is from Italy, a superior, but hard-to-find striped-bark maple for the coast and western valleys, growing to 50 ft. Its fine dark leaves are five-lobed on a tree like a compact-upright Norway Maple.

A. monspessulánum (V), Montpelier Maple, from Mediterranean Europe and Africa, is uncommon in nurseries. This 50-ft. roundheaded tree, similar to *A. campestre* but with three-lobed leaves, has been a successful street tree in Seattle.

Our native Bigleaf or Oregon Maple, *A. macrophýllum* (VI), is underrated in the Northwest because it is so common in the woods as to appear to be a weed. Too large a tree (100 ft.) for a small lot, with a hungry and shallow root system capable of breaking walks, drives or patios if placed too close to them, it must be carefully sited, and is best suited for parks. However, this is among the handsomest of maples with the boldest leaves and finest flowers of all the genus, and has good autumn gold color, excellent vigor and quick growth. Bigleaf Maple should be more often retained than it is at present when developing an existing wooded site, and is superior for moist hillsides with poor soils where only a few tree species succeed. One can cultivate under this tree by planting shade-tolerant plants and fertilizing and watering them liberally. Usually thought of as a coastal species, it occurs in central Washington and the Columbia River Gorge, which indicates that it can succeed east of the Cascades, if stock is taken from eastside sources.

A. negúndo (II), Box Elder, native over much of the United States, is a rapid-growing, mid-sized maple with large ashlike compound leaves. It is often seen as the cultivar 'Variegatum', with white-edged leaves and white seed clusters, giving an ivory-white garden effect. Box Elder is useful mostly in the cold-climate portions of the Pacific Northwest, being tough and drought tolerant. West of the Cascades it will be passed by for other superior species.

A well-grown specimen of the variegated form of the Box-Elder, *Acer negundo* 'Variegatum'. Photo by Don Normark.

A. palmátum (V), from Japan and Korea, comprises the dozens of Japanese Maples, growable over much of the U.S.A. in various forms. These include numerous leaf forms and both red and green summer foliages, all of which color well in autumn. Here belong most of the cut-leaf and lace-leaf maples, as well as a number of cultivars with brilliant red or bright green winter twigs. A. palmatum prefers a moist and rich soil, though it has somewhat greater tolerance to drier soils and lower humidity than does A. circinatum. Its delicate leaves do well in shade and usually in sun, but can be injured by hot, drying summer winds or late spring frosts. Pacific Northwest nurseries list as many as 100 cultivars of Japanese Maples. The enthusiast should consult the excellent descriptions in the book Japanese Maples by J. D. Vertrees (Timber Press, 2nd ed. 1988) to sort them out. These cultivars range from dwarf weeping shrubs 3–4 ft. in height to forms nearer the species which may grow up to 30 ft. or more.

A. platanoídes (III), Norway Maple, shares with Red Maple the honor of being the large maple which has most captured the attention of nurserymen, judging by the number of cultivars available on the market. Norway Maple grows tall, to 100 ft., like a slightly smaller-leaved version of the Bigleaf Maple (A. macrophyllum). Attractive blossom clusters of chartreuse green (or red, in the case of the red-leaved varieties) appear before the leaves. In our region, Norway Maple is tough, relatively trouble-free, quick-growing and a fairly heavy feeder from its shallow root system. While there are many maples that are more hospitable for other plants than Norway Maple, one can grow rhododendrons and actually quite a large number of shrubs beneath them. Old specimens (too large for a small garden) have a magnificent vigor of curved, arching branches forming roundheaded trees. Autumn color is generally soft gold with occasional sunset tints. Superior cultivars include:

'Cavalier', more compact than most, egg-shaped outline, to 40–50 ft. This often develops orange fall color.

'Cleveland', upright oval, fairly trim, narrow shape, to 60 ft.

'Columnare' ('Pyramidal'), narrow branching to 50 ft., twice as tall as wide. One Oregon nursery has its own strain, narrower than the type.

'Crimson King', ('Faasen's Black', 'Faasen's Red', 'Royal Crimson' are similar) 70 ft. rounded-upright, reddish black leaves throughout the season.

'Drummondii', 50 ft., leaves with bold white edge.

'Emerald Queen', quick-growing, upright oval shape that is fairly narrow, to 60 ft.

'Globosum' tends to ball shape, less vigorous, to 40 ft.

'Olmsted', to 50 ft., narrowly conical.

'Schwedler', superseded by 'Crimson King'. Red spring foliage, slate green by midsummer, to 65 ft.

'Summershade', to 75 ft., upright form, deep green foliage, developed specifically for hot-summer areas.

A. pseudoplátanus (V), the Sycamore-maple. In Britain this is the tree known as "Sycamore." This European species looks similar to our native *A. macrophyllum*. (When Menzies, the British botanist with the Vancouver expedition first saw and described this native species he called it sycamore.) It reaches a stature comparable to *A. macrophyllum*, to 100 ft. or more. It lacks good autumn color, but is tolerant of salt-laden winds near the ocean, and is thus much recommended for that purpose. Commonly seen on the market is the cultivar 'Atropurpureum' (also sold as 'Spaethii'). This sturdy form is like the species, but with red undersides to the leaves; the summer effect is slatey green rather than bright green. Sycamore-maple is an acceptable substitute for the ubiquitous London Plane (*Platanus*) in Pacific Northwest cities where soils are poor; it grows to the same size and dimensions but is much less damaging to sidewalks and paving.

A. rúbrum (III), Red Maple, is from eastern and central North America. It is one of the finest maples where its ultimately large size, 100–120 ft., can be accommodated. Because it is native from Quebec south to Florida, gardeners east of the Cascades will need to seek forms from strains grown in colder climates. This sort of data about the origin of seed stocks (the "provenance" of the parent stock) was once rarely available but is increasingly provided by better nurseries. Red Maple leaves are smallish (4–5 in.) for such a large maple, elongated, with three to five lobes. They cast a lighter shade than other large maples. Autumn color tends toward tomato red and orange shades, and the early spring haze of copper-red flowers on bare branches is briefly beautiful, as are the fruits on female trees. The smooth, silver-gray young trunks are attractive. Red Maple often inhabits swamp margins in native populations, so it will succeed better than most maples in areas with poorer drainage, but it may fail in soggy soil. Although not as brittle as Silver Maple (*A. saccharinum*), Red Maple is moderately brittle, so it is not recommended for planting in areas where ice storms are common. Some superior cultivars of *A. rubrum* are:

'Armstrong', narrow-columnar, upswept branching, to 60–70 ft.

'October Glory', roundheaded to 60 ft., bright to deep red autumn foliage, held late in the season; less hardy than the type (IV).

'Red Sunset', 60 ft., orange-red color early in fall; round head.

'Scanlon', 40 ft., conical shape and bright red fall color.

'Scarlet Sentinel', 50 ft., very uniform red; round shape.

'Schlesinger', 60 ft., orange-red fall color, one of the brightest; round-oval shaped tree; suffers from name confusion with Schwedler Norway Maple.

'Shade King', 60 ft., upright oval, quick-growing, red fall color.

A. saccharínum (III), is the Silver Maple from eastern North America. Its brittleness makes it highly vulnerable to windstorms once it reaches 20–30 years, yet it is a useful tree when properly placed. This quick-growing tree is capable of reaching over 100 ft. tall and as wide, tolerant of dry soils and poor conditions. The five-lobed, deeply cut leaves are silver beneath and are hung on thin, often pendulous branches so they ripple in a breeze. Nurserymen are selecting forms to expand the autumn color beyond the normal gold to pastel orange range. Carefully placed away from windy sites, and when not overhanging buildings and streets, this is a lovely landscape tree. Cultivars include 'Pyramidale' ('Columnare'), columnar in form to 50 ft. or more, and 'Wieri' with lacy, cut-leaved foliage.

A. *sáccharum* (III), Sugar Maple, in the Pacific Northwest may achieve perhaps 100 ft., but it grows more slowly than other maples and most of the specimens seen here are only half that height. Few trees can upstage its autumn color—gold-orange-flame—and it has the interesting habit of dropping all its foliage in about 48 hours, a leaf-raker's delight. The medium-sized leaves, five-lobed though occasionally three-lobed, are thinner than most maple leaves and may well sunburn in hotter and drier areas, or if placed where there is too much heat reflection from buildings or pavements. A. *saccharum* also has notably lower auto exhaust pollution tolerance than most maples. It is a better country tree than a city tree even in its native New England. Yet few maples are showier in a bright autumn than this famed species that lights up New England hillsides. If the gardener has room for a large maple and the site is not heavily sun-trapped, Sugar Maple is a good candidate. Some superior cultivars include:

'Globosum', round ball form, very slow growth to 20 ft.

'Green Mountain', a form developed for leaves with much thicker than normal protective coating, making it more tolerant of summer scorch and dry winds.

'Newton Sentry' ('Columnare'), columnar to 50 ft. with a central leader.

'Sentry' ('Monumentale', 'Temple's Upright'), another columnar form to 50 ft., this one without a leader.

'Sweet Shadow', 60–75 ft. with distinctive lacy cut leaves, very attractive.

AÉSCULUS califórnica (VII), California Buckeye, has proven an excellent ornamental tree in the Puget Sound area, surprisingly tolerant of poorly drained sites. In its California home it prefers extremely dry soils (though, to be fair, it does tend to seek out streamside locations that dry up very early in the season), and it is useful for such Northwest sites where temperatures do not drop below 0°F. Its showy gray-white trunks normally branch low, almost shrublike, and will grow wider than its 25 ft. height. The fragrant flowers in late summer are white to palest pink, freely produced and showy. California Buckeye's deep green foliage is unusually refined for this genus, the five or seven leaflets of the palmately compound leaves being about finger length and an inch wide. The entire tree is of most distinctive form. When it is better known it will be frequently

Trunk and branches of one of the striped-bark maples, *Acer tegmentosum,* in March. Photo by Brian Mulligan.

A mature tree of the Californian chestnut, *Aesculus californica,* flowering in Seattle, Photo by Jean Witt.

planted. This is not the easiest tree for the nurseryman; uncommon here, it is stocked in specialty California nurseries. With roots both large and coarse, it may be a tree that will need to be planted in a permanent garden location at a quite small size. Good examples can be seen on the grounds of the Chittenden Locks in Seattle.

A. × *cárnea* (III), the Red Horsechestnut, is a hybrid between *A. hippocastanum* and the shrubby Red Buckeye, *A. pavia*, with much of the size of the former, to 65 ft., and the showy inflorescences of the latter. It blooms in May with spectacular panicles of rose to red flowers. The cultivar 'Briotii' has even larger panicles—up to 10 in.—of slightly deeper color.

A. *hippocastánum* (III), the Horsechestnut itself, is a bold southern European tree of quick growth with large foliage (5 to 7 leaflets palmately compound), and imposing stature and size, up to 120 ft. in a dense, upright rounded head. It tolerates a wide range of well-drained soils. Too large for the small garden, Horsechestnut brings other problems; it casts a dense shade and has a vigorous, shallow root system that is difficult to garden beneath. As a park tree or a grand boulevard tree, for which purpose it is used in London and in Paris, in an autumn gold coat, it has few peers. The nuts, inedible and somewhat messy when they drop, are beloved of squirrels and children. A showy fruitless form is available, the cultivar 'Baumannii', with double white flowers. Otherwise like the species, it may be used where the fruit would be a problem.

Another superior Horsechestnut is *A. índica* (VII), the Indian Horsechestnut from the Himalayas, generally unavailable in American nurseries, but worth seeking out from collectors or specialty plant sales. The English authority W. J. Bean writes, "One of the most magnificent of all temperate trees, and equalling the common Horsechestnut in beauty, it is remarkable that this species is so little known in English gardens and parks." It can be grown from seed, which must either be sown while very fresh or overwintered in moist soil or peat. Here is a tree that is handsome over a long season, beginning with the delicately beautiful, copper-pink leaves unfolding in May, with palmately compound and narrowly fingerlike leaflets. By June these expand to tropical-looking foliage, shining green and as bold as the common Horsechestnut but with narrower leaflets. The Indian Horsechestnut blooms in July at a time when spring-flowering trees are past, including common Horsechestnut a month earlier. Its flowers are in upright panicles 1 ft. or more tall, similar to common Horsechestnut but showier. Individually the flowers are white blotched with yellow and red so that the whole tree looks palest pink in bloom. In autumn the leaf color is yellowish, and in the winter the rugged strength of the heavy-branched crown is dramatic. *Aesculus indica* grows to at least 75 ft. tall and perhaps 50 ft. in width with age. It will attract a lot of favorable comment, if one can get the plant!

AILÁNTHUS *altíssima* (IV), the Tree of Heaven from north China, is a tree whose time has come, the world's toughest urban tree. Rich green, quick-growing to 75 ft. and able to live more than a century, this tree gives a tropical landscape appearance with large compound leaves up to 2 ft. long. Young trees have a vigorous upswept look; with maturity they become more rounded in outline above tall, bare trunks. The male and female flowers are on separate trees, and the grower will probably wish to secure the female form, which in favorable seasons develops hanging clusters of ashlike fruit, yellow-green to striking copper-red. The male form lacks the summer fruit and offers only ill-smelling insignificant flowers. *Ailanthus* tolerates poor dry soils, but does much better on rich soil. It is tolerant of pollution and a wide range of acid to alkaline soil reactions. Better than any other tree this one can grow to maturity through cracks in concrete sidewalks, parking lots and buildings. *Ailanthus* is easily propagated from shoots that sprout when its roots are cut, a feature that does not endear it to those digging trenches for utility lines. Books report the tree is brittle and vulnerable to ice storms, but the city forester of Milwaukee, Wisconsin, says that this is not borne out by tests. While brittle, the tree's light, open branch structure tends to escape such damage. It is self-pruning, rarely needing assistance in this respect.

ALBÍZIA (ALBÍZZIA) *julibríssin* (VII), the Silk Tree, is a Chinese tree noted for its feathery, dainty, fernlike compound foliage. Its shape is flat topped, to 35 ft. and it grows wider than tall, often multitrunked. The exotic rose pink blossom effect is from the brushlike pompoms of stamens produced in August. Silk Tree must have a warm summer (place it in the warmest spot in Puget Sound gardens) and good drainage to succeed. It will grow in poor, gravelly soils. In many areas this tree is subject to a soil fungus that causes a fatal wilt, and it also develops a serious canker disease if it is stressed. Both can suddenly cripple a healthy tree, particularly on marginal sites.

ÁLNUS is Alder, a well-known native tree. *A. córdata* (V), Italian Alder, is a superior species because of its dark, lustrous, pearlike foliage. It forms a pyramidal oval tree to 70 ft. tall and tolerates poor dry soil, although it prefers moisture. The tree is newly available in Northwest nurseries.

A. rhombifólia (V), the White Alder, is native in our mountains where it prefers moist soils. Yet this 75 ft. species tolerates drought well enough to have become a recommended street tree in southern and interior California. It might be used more widely in the Northwest, though it is rarely seen in nurseries.

A. rúbra (V), is our native Red Alder, fast-growing to 75 ft. on poor or moist soils. Alders tolerate raw infertile soils, and their roots can help put nitrogen into such soils, making them valuable pioneer trees. Particularly along the coast, it can develop birchlike, gray-white bark, and the reddish dangling spring catkins and spring twigs have a subtle charm. In time the gardener may wish to replace existing native *A. rubra* groves with more interesting tree species, as the trees often blow over beginning at age 50–

60, posing real problems. Further, this tree is a favored host for tent caterpillars.

AMELÁNCHIER arbórea (IV), Shadbush from the eastern United States, is a small round-topped tree, often multitrunked like a large shrub, but it can be pruned easily to tree form. Showy white flower clusters appear in April with the unfolding leaves. The foliage turns to sunset colors in fall. Shadbush likes ample moisture, rich soil, and is intolerant of stressful sites. Its height is 15–25 ft. Birds are fond of the purplish black berries. This is a good specimen tree for the small garden.

A. láevis (IV), the Allegheny Serviceberry, is rather similar to *A. arborea* but has notable smooth bronzy new growth and a flesh pink tint in the flowers clusters. The ultimate size is perhaps 15 ft. This species has a particularly tasty fruit that makes good pies. The young trees of the *Amelanchier* are reminiscent of a small-flowered cherry in the garden. These amelanchiers are not readily found in western nurseries, but midwest nurseries stock them.

ARÁLIA eláta (III), Japanese Angelica Tree or Devil's Walking-stick, is a bold tropical-looking tree with large, coarse, dark green, doubly compound leaves, somewhat like *Ailanthus*. When these large leaves drop, the tree looks in winter like a stark and awkward hatrack, its top branches covered with small spines. In midsummer the tree is showy with large frothy umbels of small, cream-colored flowers which mature to small, black-purple berries, not poisonous. Autumn leaf color on this 30 ft. tree is in warm rose, gold and orange shades. This sometimes multitrunked tree suckers freely and can be a pest in a well-kept garden, but there are spots where it may be the right choice.

BÉTULA is Latin for birch. Birches cast only light shade, so they can be cultivated beneath. In the Pacific Northwest they may have aphid or borer problems which will be discussed below. Large birches can be difficult to transplant; for best results transplant with a root ball in spring just before growth begins. Relatively shallow rooters, birches like well-drained soil which need not be too fertile, but *B. nigra* and *B. papyrifera* tolerate moist soils. Most birches are short lived, with 50 years being a satisfactory garden life. The very light twigs which lend birches their beauty will break readily if loaded with ice in areas subject to silver thaws or ice storms, and the same problem can develop on windswept sites. Birches are sometimes classified as white, red, or black and yellow, referring to their notably colored bark. Almost all have a delicate pattern of fine twiggy branchlets. The main branches rapidly diminish in size as they divide into minor branches and twigs. The clean-cut lines of the trunk surrounded by this lacy network makes an attractive winter picture. They are more interesting in groups than as individuals, frequently growing this way in the wild.

B. albo-sinénsis and its variety *septentrionális* (V), the Chinese Paper Birch to 80 ft., is a singularly lovely tree, rare in gardens, but well worth a search. Its glory is its winter bark, luminous, rich rose-apricot or sometimes orange or gold. The bark peels freely exposing slightly paler layers beneath.

B. jacquemóntii (VII) is the Jacquemont Birch, a 40–50 ft. species from the Himalayas. This birch because of its showy bark will replace much of the European White Birch in our gardens. Bark color of seedlings can vary from the usual cream all the way to orange and brown. The Dutch nursery form of *B. jacquemontii* regularly seen in Northwest nurseries has startling milk white bark on trees as small as 1 in. in diameter. The leaves are quite large, not lobed, but entire, turning a typical birch gold in autumn. Recently imported from Europe, and unheralded in print, *B. jacquemontii* has been little tested in the eastern U.S., but it appears destined to be very popular. Early tests indicate it is less subject to aphid attacks than other birch species, and it may have some resistance to bronze birch borer.

The bark of *B. lénta* (III), Sweet Birch, Cherry Birch, or Black Birch, is cherrylike, chocolate brown to black, and its leaves and stems are pleasantly aromatic. This eastern American native tree grows to a shapely 75 ft., has leaves of a more luminous summer green than most birches, and boasts the finest fall gold. Uncommon in nurseries, this is a tree that is recommended by those who have grown it. It is not overly choosy about soils and is resistant to bronze birch borer.

B. maximowicziana (VI), Monarch Birch, is a Japanese tree with heart-shaped leaves larger than those of any other birch, changing from summer dark green to autumn yellow. This tree is open in habit, upright-angular in branch pattern, and quick-growing to as much as 80 ft. It appears completely resistant to borers, shows admirable tolerance of urban sites, and so would appear to have a good garden and park future.

B. nígra (IV), River Birch or Red Birch, native to eastern United States, is valuable for its tolerance of sites that are subject to winter or spring flooding. This ruggedly handsome 90 ft. tree has attractive bark that peels off in shaggy plates. The tree is upright-oval in form, becoming rounded with maturity, and rich green foliage color contributes to its being one of the best birches as a landscape specimen. *B. nigra* shows good borer resistance. There is a very large specimen in Marymoor Park, Redmond, Washington.

Paper Birch or Canoe Birch from North America is *B. papyrífera;* our native form is var. *commutáta* (II). This is another white-barked species with fewer insect problems than the common *B. péndula.* This tree often grows in colonies in the wild and looks attractive in clumps or groves in the garden. Its white trunks retain that color to an older age than those of many white-barked species. Leaves are large and medium coarse, autumn color is bright butter yellow. This 100-ft. tree performs best in average garden soil; it grows well in moist soils but is intolerant of soggy ones.

B. péndula (B. verrucósa, B. álba) (II), the 60-foot European White Birch, also called Silver Birch, is the species most often planted in Northwest

The European Silver Birch (*Betula pendula*) growing in a city garden. Photo by Don Normark.

gardens and includes most of the weeping types. This is the commonly seen birch in much of the United States, and hence the standard by which most people describe birches, but there are many more garden-worthy species. The good points of this species include a light and graceful form and good white bark on relatively young trees, though with age the bark becomes partially black and furrowed. It produces a light shade that is not difficult to garden beneath and has fine autumn color. It is unsatisfactory to dine beneath, constantly dropping small twigs, catkins, and some summer leaves. It is infuriating to park beneath for in our climate this tree is chronically infested by aphids which drip syrupy honeydew on vehicles below. East of the Cascades, *B. pendula* is often killed by attacks of bronze birch borer. It is best used west of the Cascades, in landscapes with shrubs or groundcover beneath the trees. There are numerous cultivars of *B. pendula,* including:

'Dalecarlica', 75 ft., much grown, very pendulous cut-leaved form.

'Fastigiata', narrowly erect, like a Lombardy Poplar.

'Purpurea', with purple leaves, which are interesting with the white bark.

'Tristis', weeping form with an erect leader.

'Youngii', Young's Weeping Birch, no tendency to grow erect unless forced to, rarely over 20 ft. tall.

B. *platyphýlla* and its variety *szechúanica (B. mandschúrica)* (V), Manchurian Birch, is as yet rather rare in cultivation. Reaching 50 ft. or more, this species is white-barked, growing into a rather open tree. The leaves are thick, dull blue-green, rather large and tough, and held until late in the fall. This species has performed well in Seattle at the Washington Park Arboretum. It appears to have some resistance to bronze birch borer.

CARPÍNUS bétulus (V), European Hornbeam, has only recently become a popular tree in the Pacific Northwest. Closely related to beech (*Fagus*), hornbeam is a superior small to medium-sized landscape tree and a good street tree, highly tolerant of heavy clay soils, but not of poor drainage nor of very light gravelly soil. Foliage is neat and trim on fine twigs that form a densely compact upswept tree that normally needs no pruning, though it will shear well into a hedge. Autumn color is soft golden tan, insignificant in some years. This is one of the toughest, most pest-and disease-free trees in existence. The cultivar 'Fastigiata', Pyramidal Hornbeam—which always looks as if it *had* been pruned—is the form most commonly seen in nurseries here. 'Quercifolia' and 'Asplenifolia' are named forms with lobed leaves.

C. *japónica* (IV), Japanese Hornbeam, makes a vase or fan shape at maturity as a 40-ft. tree. Though rare, it is an impressive species with larger, sharply veined leaves that sometimes color red in the autumn.

CÁRYA ováta (IV), is the Shagbark Hickory from eastern United States. This tree matures to a handsome 100 ft. specimen with fine, gold autumn foliage. It is one of the few trees to make a true taproot while young so is difficult to handle in nurseries, and the gardener will consequently probably have to raise it from seed or use newly germinated pot-grown seedlings planted directly into their permanent site. This same caution applies to the Pecan, C. *illinoiénsis* (V) and the Shellbark Hickory, C. *laciniósa* (V).

CASTÁNEA crenáta (VI) and C. *mollíssima* (IV), are the Japanese and Chinese Chestnuts, respectively. Both of these edible species are better choices here than C. *dentáta*, American Chestnut, or C. *satíva*, Spanish or European Chestnut, both of which are subject to a fatal blight. C. *crenáta* is a small tree, round topped and reaching only 30 ft., while C. *mollíssima*, which many observers claim has sweeter nuts, makes a tree twice as tall. The leaves of chestnuts are very distinct—long, pointed, and with regular, hooked, sawtoothed margins—and they usually turn rich gold in the fall.

Inflorescences of the European Sweet Chestnut (*Castanea sativa*) in early July. Photo by Don Normark, Campus Studios, University of Washington.

Chestnuts prefer good soil and can tolerate hot climates quite well. The branch pattern of *Castanea* is bold, upswept and strong. It is best used as a specimen though it can make a useful tree in large boulevard plantings where there is room for its growth.

CATÁLPA bignonioídes (IV), Indian Bean or Southern Catalpa, is one of America's most distinct native trees, which Bean has called "undoubtedly among the most beautiful of all flowering trees." Beautiful snow white flower panicles appear in early July, followed later by dangling beanlike fruits which persist into winter. There is a gold-leaved cultivar, 'Aurea', which holds its bright, golden, spring leaves well into summer, finally fading to a sharp yellow-green.

Twice as tall as *C. bignonioides* and upright-oval in form is *C. speciósa* (IV), the Western Catalpa, blooming earlier, in June, with similar very large, 10–12 in., heart-shaped leaves, and similar but fewer and larger flowers.

The flowers of both catalpas are exotic with yellow and purple markings on their white petals, and the bold leaves appear tropical. Yet these trees have a certain ponderous aspect that suits them better to the larger or more formal setting of a park lawn than a small garden. They succeed best in good soils, but tolerate difficult ones—wet, dry, alkaline—and are rather short lived, 50 years being old age for a catalpa.

The Katsura Tree from Japan, *CERCIDIPHYLLUM japónicum* (IV), is sheer elegance in a tree. It was relatively unknown in the Pacific Northwest until about 1950. This is one of the most pest-free and disease-resistant of trees and does not require extensive pruning past its youth. Katsura Tree is often multitrunked, almost shrubby at the base when young, and has been used thus as an informal screening hedge with branches retained low to the ground. One must prune out competing leaders if a single-trunked tree is desired, as for a street tree. Growth habit is medium fast, the columnar young tree shape finally giving way to a wide-spreading broad crown—old specimens can achieve trunks with greater than 6 ft. diameters and crowns 75 ft. or more wide, though such dimensions require well over a century! The foliage is small and airy, casting a shade comparable to that of birches. The heart-shaped leaves have a very clean outline; unfolding young leaves in spring can appear like amber glass when backlighted, and autumn color varies from yellow through orange-red or even maroon. It is quite common for several colors to appear on the tree at once. Katsura trees prefer deep soils and adequate summer moisture. *C. magníficum (C. japonicum* var. *magnificum)* (IV) is rare in nurseries, but it has performed exceptionally well in the Washington Park Arboretum in Seattle.

CÉRCIS canadénsis (IV), the Eastern Redbud from the United States, is a tree that appears to dislike the cooler maritime regions of the Pacific Northwest, performing better in the interior valleys and east of the Cascades. On the west side it must have a location with as much summer heat as possible and well-drained soils, since it hates wet feet or too much summer moisture. Because the native range extends from Florida north and west to much colder climates, gardeners east of the Cascades should seek stock grown from cool-climate seed sources. The leaves of *C. canadensis* are small and heart shaped, sometimes yellow in fall. Flowers of bright magenta pink are strung tightly along the branches at leaf-out time in April. The tree tends to be multistemmed with trunks gracefully upswept to 25 ft., and the plant is often grown as a large shrub. 'Alba' is a white-flowered cultivar and 'Forest Pansy' a selection with bright red-purple leaves.

C. chinénsis (VI), Chinese Redbud, becomes a 60-ft. tree in China, but is normally a multistemmed shrub less than half that height in the United States. Its very showy flowers are brighter color than those of *C. canadensis* and borne in short racemes.

C. siliquástrum (VI), the Judas Tree from southern Europe and the Middle East, is the third redbud often seen, more treelike than the others and like them preferring a hot climate. Mature *Cercis,* like most leguminous trees, are more permanent in the Northwest landscape if kept quite dry in summer, and this can become critical where they are being grown west of the Cascades. Redbuds should be transplanted when quite young because of their root systems.

CHIONÁNTHUS retúsus (V), Chinese Fringetree, is a small tree to 30 ft. Unless pruned to a single leader it has a tendency to develop several stems, forming a large shrub. The lovely June-July show of small, starry, white blooms in fleecy terminal panicles gives the tree its name. Sexes are on separate plants; on the female plants black fruit follows, which the birds like. The leaves are oval, and mid-sized, turning yellow in the fall on good forms. This rarely seen tree grows best in damp, rich acid soil.

Slightly better known but still rare is the White Fringetree from south-eastern United States, *C. virgínicus* (III), of similar size and attributes, but with larger and coarser leaves. Male plants are said to have longer flower petals for a finer bloom effect. Both species develop attractive gray bark, are most effective used in groups, and have been found to have good tolerance to air pollution. Locating sources of plants will be the greatest problem for the gardener who wishes to try fringetrees. They should be raised from seed and set out when small.

CLADÁSTRIS lútea (III), American Yellowwood, from the mid-South has been praised for years—a fine specimen stands on the University of Oregon campus in Eugene, and another on the west side of Anderson Hall on the University of Washington campus in Seattle—yet this 50 ft. tree is rarely seen in gardens or nurseries. Probably it shares the problem of most legumes in being difficult to transplant except as a small tree. The foliage is compound, of medium size and texture, a lively summer green, turning yellow in fall. Roundheaded, the tree tends to branch low, and is often broader than tall. The fragrant, white, wisteria-like bloom panicles are showy in June. Tolerant of well-drained soils ranging from acid to alkaline, Yellowwood has few pests.

C. sinénsis (V), Chinese Yellowwood, is similar and still rarer. It will skip flowering some seasons but is extremely handsome in July bloom. This tree leafs out very late in spring.

CÓRNUS alternifólia (III), Pagoda Dogwood, from eastern North America, is a small tree to 20 ft., often multistemmed, which is grown chiefly for the redpurple fall color of its alternate leaves. Its 2 in. clusters of small creamy white flowers are typical of the bractless dogwoods—not at all spectacular. It prefers soil kept reasonably moist but not wet.

C. controvérsa (V), Giant Dogwood from Japan and China, carries the clan's habit of flat-tiered branching to an elegant pagoda-like extreme, with spaced decks of horizontal foliage, forming a 60 ft. tree as distinctive as it is rare. This rarity is too bad; it is easily grown, hardy and immune to the twig blight affecting many dogwoods. Bractless flowers are small and white in cymes in early summer, followed by black fruits. Autumn color is good, red to purple. The variegated green and white foliaged form of *C. controversa*, 'Variegata', called by Roy Lancaster "perhaps the most beautiful and effective of all hardy variegated trees," originated nearly a century ago in England, yet is still a rarity there and is unavailable in U.S. nurseries. It is to be hoped that this can be rectified. In its new foliage in May it is the pride of many of the finest English gardens.

C. flórida (IV to V), is the popular Flowering Dogwood native to eastern United States from Massachusetts to Florida, capable of reaching 40 ft. The pink dogwoods also belong here, as variety *rubra*, with the redder cultivars 'Cherokee Chief' and 'Sweetwater Red' being color selections. 'Cherokee Princess', 'Cloud Nine' and 'Green Glow' are typical better white selections. Whether in white, pink or red, the flat-branching pattern of *C. florida* makes a spreading tree, round in outline, often wider than high, commonly reaching 25 ft. or less. The flat planes of flowers before the leaves appear make this dogwood one of our showiest April and May flowering trees. Summer foliage is a good lustrous green turning to an excellent red or plum fall color. Of the forms with variegated leaves, two good ones are 'Welchii' ('Tricolor') with leaves marked pink and ivory, and 'Rainbow', with green and gold leaves. The gray winter-twig beauty of *C. florida* has few equals among trees. This species does best in acid soils, but grows well east of the Cascades on neutral or even alkaline soils. In recent years it has been afflicted with several fungal leaf diseases, as has *C. nuttallii.* These diseases are serious but treatable.

C. kóusa and its variety *chinénsis* (V), are respectively Japanese and Chinese Dogwood and grow to 25–30 ft. They resemble *C. florida* in many ways, but are more airy and delicate in landscape effect, and the horizontal flower tiers are slightly up-tilted from the planes of the branches. Another important difference: bloom time of *C kousa* is about a month after *C. florida* and *C. nuttallii,* coming in early June when fewer garden trees are flowering. The floral bracts of *C. kousa* often turn from white to rosy pink upon aging. Variety *chinensis* is claimed to be preferable to the species, with larger and showier bracts, but this has not necessarily been shown in side-by-side growing comparisons with the type; possibly the two are mixed in nurseries.

C. más (IV), the Cornelian Cherry Dogwood from central Europe to western Asia, has no showy bracts, but the plant is cheerful and bright in March with its froth of little yellow flowers. Site the tree against a dark background, such as evergreens or a dark wall, to intensify this early-spring-blossom effect, which can make a pretty picture with bulbs beneath it. The large cherry red fruits, with their high pectin content, make good preserves. While the summer foliage is attractive, its autumn color is the poorest among the dogwoods. *C. mas* tends to be a broad-spreading shrub branching near the ground; it is one of the few dogwoods that will tolerate being pruned to open its trunk to the sun, which with most species would expose the very thin bark to serious sunburn. With lower branches pruned away, *C. mas* makes a small round-headed tree to 25 ft. tall. While it does best in good soil it is more tolerant than most dogwoods of poor, alkaline, and wet or dry conditions. This tree succeeds east of the Cascades in hotter, harsher climates than most dogwoods like, a reflection of its native home.

Flowers of a fine specimen of the Western Dogwood (*Cornus nuttallii*) in late April in Seattle. Photo by William Eng, University of Washington.

C. *nuttállii* (VII), the native Pacific Dogwood, is among the world's premier flowering trees, capable of reaching 80 ft. However, it is apt to dislike garden conditions, and can be extremely unhappy when its exacting needs are not met. Half-century-old specimens are dying as urban life overwhelms them, the decline accelerated in recent years by anthracnose leaf blights and certain cankers. Pacific Dogwood has very thin bark, in common with most dogwoods, but this species is more sensi-

tive than most to injury if hot sunshine hits the tree trunk. It is harmful to
remove the shading lower limbs from dogwoods growing in full sun for
this reason, which makes them poor choices for street trees. *C. nuttallii* wel-
comes ample spring moisture, but in nature is used to summr drought.
Old pre-existing trees incorporated into a garden will do best if kept relatively dry in mid and late summer; overwatering in summer appears to
hasten fungus diseases of this tree. Pacific Dogwood is very sensitive to a
wide variety of stresses, including root pruning or the addition of new soil
on top of existing root systems or against the trunk. Having listed the cau-
tions, we turn to the many fine qualities that make this our showiest native
tree. The white flower bracts are the largest of all dogwoods, blooming in
April and in some individuals a second time in August or September. The
red fruit can be showy in autumn, but is soon taken by birds. The tracery of
bare dogwood twigs against a winter sky is memorable; the buttons of next
spring's flowers are silhouetted at the twig ends. Two notable *C. nuttallii*
selections are 'Colrigo Giant', with extra-large bracts, and 'Eddiei' ('Gold
Spot') which has very bright green and gold variegated foliage. Also on the
market from British Columbia is a fine hybrid of *C. nuttallii* × *C. florida*
called 'White Wonder' ('Eddie's White Wonder'). Hardy to zone IV, it has
very showy flowers of intermediate size on slightly drooping branches. A
medium-sized tree, it has good autumn color.

The hybrid *Cornus*
'Eddie's White Wonder'
in bloom in May. Photo
by Brian Mulligan.

CÓRYLUS is the genus of nut trees commonly called filberts or hazelnuts. One often sees in gardens the Contorted Filbert, *C. avellána* 'Contorta' (IV–V), a twisted, densely branched tree slowly achieving a height of 10 ft. in 50 years. Its garden effect is that of a rounded shrub though it is usually single trunked, and its most interesting period comes when it is leafless in March, decorated with showy dangling gold catkins.

Turkish Filbert, *C. colúrna* (IV), has received attention in recent years as a rather formally upright tree to 80 ft. Its single central leader gives it a bold outline and it has been used as a street tree. Once established, it is able to resist summer drought well, staying a lively green. The leaves are large, lush, and appear pest-free. The male catkins in March are moderately showy, and the clustered nuts in autumn have strange bristly husks somewhat reminiscent of chestnuts.

Our native Western Hazelnut, *C. cornúta* var. *califórnica* (V), is a multi-stemmed shrub or small tree, reaching 12–20 ft., quite charming when hung with yellow catkins in March. It has no particular beauty the rest of the year, but is worth retaining in woodland or as screening planting. *C. máxima* 'Purpurea' (IV), Purple Filbert from the American Midwest is a shrubby often multitrunked tree to 15–20 ft. Its large red-purple leaves later fading to green, make a strong landscape accent. Even its catkins are purple. This is not a plant for the small garden, since it is capable of growing nearly as wide as high, developing a great many stems.

The hawthorns form the genus *CRATÁEGUS*, related to apples and other rose-family fruits. Some longtime stalwart garden trees are found here, many of them also being among the most problem-ridden trees in cultivation. The genus is regularly thorny, sometimes formidably so—the Cockspur Thorn's spurs can reach three inches long!—and thus it must be positioned with care in the landscape. This species, *C. crusgálli* (III), is a fine 30 ft. tree, one of the more attractive hawthorns in foliage, dark green in summer, coloring red-bronze to purplish in autumn, and in its large, red fruits like clustered crab apples. Like most hawthorns, the tree is densely rounded in form, with horizontal branching. Its white blooms in May smell unpleasant to most people, like pear blossoms.

C. laciniáta (C. orientális) (VI), Silver Hawthorn, 15–20 ft., is a rarely seen species from western Asia; it has done well in southern England and in the Washington Park Arboretum in Seattle. Nearly thornless, it has small triangular lobed leaves, dark green above and gray beneath. Silver Hawthorn makes a good June show of white flower clusters followed by large red-orange fruits.

Streets in Portland, Seattle and Victoria are colorful each May with the bright blossoms of *C. laevigáta (C. oxyacántha)* (IV), the English Hawthorn or May Tree. This native of Europe and North Africa grows to 25–30 ft., in an upright, oval shape, the branches being very twiggy and furnished with inch-long thorns. Trunks of English Hawthorn trees are distinctive, sinewy and corded like pulled taffy. These handsome trunks help redeem this tree which is often sheared hideously into ball shapes, a process which compounds the already serious problems that hawthorns have with fungus diseases. They may require yearly spraying to hold these plagues in check. Annual shearing promotes a dense central mass of branches which inhibits air movement through the foliage, and the result is often a nearly defoliated tree in August. In summer aphids feast on this tree, dripping their sticky honeydew wastes on parked cars. Of the many cultivars of this tree, 'Paul's Scarlet' is the best known. It originated in England before 1860, and with its double bright red flowers is one of the showiest trees in spring. Unfortunately the tree (along with other color forms of this species) is highly susceptible to leaf spot in the maritime parts of the Northwest. A seedling from 'Paul's Scarlet' named 'Crimson Cloud' ('Superba') overcomes this disease susceptibility. It has red single blossoms with white star centers, a very bright bloom effect, and it gives a good berry show in the fall, something the parent lacks. To grow these showy flowering hawthorns best, withhold extra fertilizing and watering, since this develops lush growth at the expense of flowers. Pruning should not be tip shearing, which thickens the tree's growth, but should consist of thinning the interior, to allow the branch pattern to show and let air move through the crown, thus discouraging leaf spot.

Closely akin to *C. oxyacantha* is *C. monogýna* (IV), Singleseed or Common Hawthorn. Similar to the previous species, it grows somewhat taller with longer thorns. This is the most common species seen in English hedgerows, though the former may also be present. It has a slightly larger leaf, similarly cut into several lobes, and makes a graceful tree. The flowers have the same scent, nicely sweet from a distance, but apt to be overpowering and unpleasant when too close to the nose. Two of Common Hawthorn's cultivars are worth noting. First is 'Biflora', the Glastonbury Thorn, which gives winter bloom any time from November to March (though not consistently in Seattle), as well as blooming in May. The fragrant white flowers are doubly welcome in winter; the cultivar is rarely found in American nurseries and will take a search. The second notable cultivar is the stiffly erect 'Stricta', sometimes as narrow as a Lombardy poplar, but other times twice that wide. Growing to 20–25 ft., it has good crops of white flowers, red berries and aphids. It has some potential use in formal designs.

Carrière Thorn, *C.* × *lavállei* ('Carriérei') (IV), is one of the best hawthorns, resistant to most hawthorn pests and diseases. This tree from France is believed to be a hybrid of the American *C. crusgálli* and *C. stipulácea*, a Mexican species. From the former it gets its bold foliage, large almost leathery leaves that are glossy and handsome in summer. From the Mexican parent comes the habit of holding the leaves until late in the winter and the large fruits like ¾-in. red crab apples, very noticeable for a long period in autumn. *C.* × *lavállei* is rounded and formal in appearance, with upswept branches to 25–30 ft. high and about as wide. It can be lightly sheared to achieve a very symmetrical effect without serious harm, and tends to look sheared even when unpruned. Its large white spring flowers are attractive. Carriere Thorn does best in well-drained soils.

C. móllis (III) is the Downy Hawthorn, a 40 ft. native of the eastern part of the United States and Canada, rare in nurseries. This has medium-sized lobed leaves with very downy undersides, and the branches are white-downy when young. Inch-wide white flowers make this a striking tree in blossom; the red fruits which follow are large and showy, but drop early in the autumn.

C. × *mordenénsis* 'Toba' (III) is a hardy hybrid from Canada between 'Paul's Scarlet' and *C. succulénta* from eastern North America. This 20 ft. tree has double white flowers fading to pink, which sometimes develop into red fruits, and is said to be resistant to leaf spot defoliation and to rust.

C. phaenopýrum (IV), Washington Thorn, is a 30 ft. species from eastern United States, one of the finest hawthorns for gardens. This wide-spreading species with arching-horizontal branches is one of the best trees available to offer four seasons of beauty. First is a moderate display of white flowers in June. Next comes excellent summer foliage, small dark green leaves from reddish new growth, relatively free of hawthorn ailments. Autumn color on this tree can vary from red branch tips to strong red-purple color over the entire tree. In winter, the tracery of delicate twigs against the sky is accentuated by ample clusters of beadlike, glossy red fruits that hang on well into the New Year. Washington Thorn has a moderate root system easy to garden under, but this means that the tree should not be planted in windy locations where it may blow over. An excellent patio tree, fine for closeup viewing, it should be planted more than it is.

C. pinnatífida var. *major (C. korolkówii)* (V), the Large Chinese Hawthorn, is a white-flowering species to 20 ft. tall with inch-wide red fruits in the fall, and thorns lacking or very small. The leaves are large and almost leathery, rich green. In fruit it is a singularly beautiful tree. It is rarely grown in the United States. Krussmann reports that in China the tree is used in reforestation on sandy soils, and this suggests another use in our region, as a seaside tree.

C. punctáta (IV), Dotted Hawthorn or Thicket Hawthorn, is another good choice from the bewildering array of American species. Growing to 30 ft. tall, it has strongly horizontal branching to as much as 40 ft. It has only small thorns and is grown for its large red fruits following masses of white blossoms. There is a superior thornless selection, var. *inérmis* or 'Ohio Pioneer'. *C. punctata* has performed well in Washington Park Arboretun in Seattle.

C.stipulácea (C. pubéscens, C. mexicána) (VIII–IX), the Mexican Hawthorn, can be grown successfully only in the most sheltered warm gardens of our region, but is so distinct as to be worth a trial. It performs satisfactorily in the south of England and the trees at Strybing Arboretum in San Francisco are lovely, holding their leaves until Christmas and studded with large yellow fruit like tiny oranges. This is a parent of C. × *lavallei*, which grows well here. The Mexican Hawthorn has diamond-shaped leaves, and white flowers in clusters in June. It can be grown from seed, and enterprising specialist growers may want to try raising seeds from trees grown in California or—better yet—seeds from Mexican trees in the colder part of the native habitat—and letting two or three winters help to sort out the seedlings to select a form hardy in the Northwest.

DAVÍDIA *involucráta* (VI), the Dove Tree or Handkerchief Tree from western China, is a startling sight to see in flower in May, with its large drooping white bracts looking like handkerchiefs hung to dry on the branches. First-time viewers form very strong impressions of the Dove Tree,—they either love it or hate it. Even when out of flower, this is a first-rate tree, its bold and upswept branches clothed with linden-like leaves of a particularly vibrant light green. *Davidia* is a very clean-appearing tree in the landscape, perhaps best used as a specimen. The tree may not bloom until it is 10 years old or more; it sometimes skips a year between flowerings, and in borderline climates it may grow but not bloom. Not a small tree, it can reach 60 ft. tall in a broad-based cone shape, and will perform best in a soil both fertile and well drained. The fruits resemble dangling brown walnuts.

ELAEÁGNUS *angustifólia* (II), the Russian Olive, is a most distinctive gray-silver tree with willowlike leaves, thriving better in the harsh dry areas east of the Cascades than in the mild western lowlands. Forming a round tree or sometimes a large shrub, this plant will grow to 20–30 ft. Russian Olive succeeds best on sandy well-drained soils, either seacoast or inland, and it is tolerant of alkaline soils, road salts and drought. It can make a very useful screening hedge; it is amenable to shearing. Here is a very light-textured tree which, coupled with its silver color about the same as desert sagebrush, makes it useful in the landscape, a fine foil for bright flower colors and dark conifers. Its hosts of tiny bell-shaped yellow flowers in June are fragrant.

EUCÓMMIA *ulmoídes* (IV). Hardy Rubber Tree, is a wide-spreading 60 ft. tree from China notable for attractive, cherrylike, deep green leaves. It also contains a low grade of rubber latex and is noted for this unique feature. Easily grown in a wide range of soils, this tree has been tried as a street tree with mixed ratings. Some sources report brittleness in the branches. As a specimen on a lawn a mature tree is quite handsome, and it is almost pest-free. The inconspicuous flowers are dioecious and the fruits negligible.

EUÓNYMUS *bungeánus* (IV), a Chinese and Manchurian species, is a large shrub or small tree to 20–25 ft. tall, of open habit, and taller than wide though the branches may weep somewhat. The tree's light green leaves are ovate, tapering to a point. When summers are hot and bright this small tree produces good crops of soft yellow-green fruit, often overlaid pink.

E. europáeus (IV), European Spindle Tree, is similar to the above, but generally smaller with a greater tendency to strong upright growth. This species has rose pink fruits which open to show bright orange-red seeds poking out, an uninhibited autumn show. *E. europaeus* fruits more dependably than *E. bungeanus* in cool summer areas. Several good selections, made for their fruit color, inclued 'Albus', a rare form with ivory-white fruits with the emerging red seeds, a striking combination much sought by flower arrangers; 'Aldenhamensis', with very large pink fruits; and 'Red Cascade' with red fruits.

A third worthy euonymus species is *E. sieboldiánus (E. yedoénsis)* (IV) Yeddo Euonymus from Japan, another tree or shrub according to pruning, 10–18 ft. tall, with pink fruits and red-purple fall leaf color, a showy combination. A sometimes serious pest on euonymus is scale, and the last-named is probably the most vulnerable of the species listed. All three species are tough and durable plants in sun or part shade, preferring good drainage, but not particular as to soil pH or fertility.

FÁGUS grandifólia (III), American Beech, is an imposing upright-oval-shaped tree to 100 ft. or taller. Almost never found in nurseries, it is so similar to the next species that the latter will suffice.

F. sylvática (IV) is the European Beech, a stately tree to 100 ft. tall, with notably beautiful smooth gray bark like elephant hide, casting a dense shade very difficult to garden under or keep a lawn beneath. The tree normally is low branched, handsome on a lawn where the scale is grand enough to accommodate its size. The new leaves are tender pale green, quickly turning deep green and shiny in summer, then bronzy like old leather in fall, with the dried leaves holding on quite a while before dropping. Beeches attain the size and outline shape of oaks, although their low-sweeping branches and dense foliage gives them different character. They are sensitive to badly compacted or poorly drained soil and are notably shallow rooting. Among the more distinct and worthy from the many cultivars that have been selected are the following:

'Atropunicea' ('Purpurea'), the Purple-leaved Beech, widely planted.

'Cuprea', the Copper Beech, with dark coppery purple leaves, very popular.

'Dawyck', narrowly upright to 80 ft. tall and less than 10 ft. wide; 'Fastigiata' is similar.

'Laciniata', with strongly serrated leaves.

'Riversii', a very dark black-purple selection.

'Rohanii', similar to 'Laciniata' but with purple leaves.

'Roseo-marginata' ('Purpurea Tricolor'). Tricolor Beech, purple leaves bordered rose and pale pink; a much slower growing sort because of the variegation; probably matures to 40 ft; leaves will scorch in too hot a situation.

FÍCUS cárica (VII–VIII) is the Common Fig, a fruiting tree that can be a handsome garden tree, often multistemmed, 20–25 ft. tall and wider than high in some cultivars. The coarse, bold leaves are lobed and dramatic. The tree has fair hardiness and will resprout from the ground after a hard winter, but will not fruit well in the open in the cooler parts of the Northwest. It needs the warmest site possible, usually near or against a south or west wall. In the warmer interior western Oregon valleys the tree fruits quite well in the open. 'Lattarula' is one of the varieties most dependable in fruit. The large leaves arranged closely on the branches cast heavy shade, and consequently the fig is to be recommended as a shade tree on a hot sunny terrace. It should be given ample moisture while the fruit is forming and will also respond to applications of superphosphate throughout the growing season. Figs grow easily in most soils but may not bear freely if given too much water and nitrogenous fertilizer. Figs that make rank growth and produce no fruit may benefit from a severe root pruning.

The Franklin Tree, *FRANKLÍNIA alátamaha (Gordónia a.)* (IV), comes from Georgia and is related to *Camellia* and *Stewartia*. The relationship is evident late in the summer when it blooms, with single 3 in. creamy white flower cups centered with gold stamens. Slow growing to 30 ft., it is as often shrubby as treelike, with large obovate leaves of shiny dark green that turn a blazing orange-red in autumn. Grow this as a specimen in a warm open location in well-drained soil with plenty of organic matter.

FRÁXINUS americána (III), the White Ash, is a fast-growing tree from the eastern United States and Canada, reaching 120 ft. It is much planted in colder climates, but is of no great garden merit. Its cultivars 'Autumn Purple' and 'Rosehill' are superior seedless forms with good red-bronze to red-purple fall color. Like the species they tolerate poor soils that can be anywhere from quite moist to quite dry. The leaves are compound and of fairly coarse texture. Like all ashes, White Ash trees are subject to a fairly long list of insect and disease problems.

Our native Oregon Ash, *F. latifólia (F. oregóna)* (VI), is somewhat valued as an ornamental in Europe, but less so here. Existing specimens may be worth keeping while other trees are being grown to replace them, and the 80 ft. tree is tolerant of near-swamp conditions and might be useful in badly drained sites. Oregon Ash is a coarsely bold tree with stiff branches and medium-coarse compound leaves that turn yellow in the fall.

Flowering Ash or Manna Ash, *F. órnus* (V), from southeast Europe and Asia Minor, makes a rounded tree to 50 ft. Its compound leaves are smaller and finer textured than most ashes. This is one of the few ash species with showy flowers, having panicles of small, fragrant, ivory-white blooms in May. Flowering ash is more trim appearing than most species and warrants more extensive planting than it has had.

F. oxycárpa (F. angustifólia var. *oxycarpa)* (V), is another very tidy-looking species from the same areas as *F. ornus,* with narrowly compound leaves which give a ferny look to the tree. This has not received much favorable comment from testing in the eastern U.S.A., but has a superior performance record in the West—a good example of regional trials not being accurate for all areas. Three cultivars merit attention:

'Flame', to 40–50 ft., rich green summer color, red-purple in autumn, this has created more favorable comment than any other Seattle street tree, as used on 35th Avenue Northeast.

'Golden Desert', 30–35 ft., golden twigs and bark on younger branches, a most attractive tree in winter; older bark becomes brown.

'Raywood', closely similar to 'Flame'; narrowly upright during its first 10 years, then wider and rounder.

F. pennsylvánica (F. lanceoláta) (II), Green Ash from eastern North America, grows quickly to 60 ft. at maturity. This is rather coarse in foliage and quite awkward in winter branching; it has been planted a great deal because it is tolerant of poor soil, drought or quite wet soils, high pH and winter road salt. It tends to produce unwelcome seedlings, but two of its selections avoid this: 'Marshall's Seedless', a vigorous sort with less disease problems than the species, and good yellow fall color; and 'Summit', a stiffer more upright selection with quite shapely form for an ash.

The Maidenhair Tree, GÍNKGO bilóba (IV) from eastern China is a tree with a glamorous history. Forests of it covered parts of the Northwest in prehistoric times. Long cultivated in China and still wild there in a limited area, it is now a sentimental favorite with tree lovers. Its small fan-shaped, fine-textured leaves are most handsome and resist virtually all pests and diseases. The butter-gold fall color equals that of the best birches. Young trees are irregular and open in shape, gaunt and unlovely for their first 10 years, after which they settle into a century or two of shapely maturity. This tree succeeds admirably in cities, being durable and resistant to air pollution and tolerant of a wide variety of soils, though it is happiest in good well-drained soil. Ginkgos are large trees, over 100 feet high, too large for small homes and small gardens, but they are majestic where they have room to develop. Male and female sexes are on separate trees. Propagated male forms are best, but seedlings may not fruit for 20 years, so these are a gamble. The female fruits, a food delicacy in Asia, are usually vile smelling, but a female tree at Filoli Garden in California produces nearly scentless fruits. Mature female ginkgos as street trees in Washington D.C. are sprayed in early summer with a solution that aborts the fruits before they develop, another answer to the problem. Good narrow ginkgos have been selected, sold as 'Fastigiata'; one of the best is 'Princeton Sentry', or just 'Sentry'. Another superior male selection is called 'Autumn Gold'.

Common Honeylocust is the name applied to GLEDÍTSIA triacánthos (IV), an American leguminous tree with doubly compound leaves bearing dozens of tiny leaflets, giving a lacy, fernlike effect. The greenish flowers are not conspicuous, but flat, foot-long dark brown pods may develop on female trees. The tree is large, to 75–100 ft. Unfortunately the species has clusters of large vicious thorns that make it an unwelcome guest in a garden—and these thorny forms can sucker freely—so the tree most often planted is *G. triacanthos* var. *inérmis*, Thornless Honeylocust. This form was planted very extensively in the Northwest, indeed all over America, during the 1960s and 1970s when the tree was discovered by designers and horticulturists. It has at best turned in a mixed performance in these shotgun-approach plantings, and a high percentage of 20-year-old honeylocusts in cities are showing dieback and decline caused by stress, insects and disease, so that the tree is now recommended only for moderate use in cities. When healthy it is a fine tree that succeeds best in well-drained soils. With poor drainage it often fares badly. Common Honeylocust is not a satisfactory garden tree in soils with insufficient moisture because then its root system will prove too voracious for the surrounding plantings. Once established, it will tolerate drier soils, high pH and winter road salts. Many cultivars, all thornless, have been introduced. Among the best are:

'Imperial', broadly spreading to 35 ft.; avoid in the coldest climates.

'Moraine', broadly rounded in outline to 50 ft., this selection has a good performance record.

'Shademaster' tends to grow taller and straighter than most, a superior choice for a street tree. Many Thornless Honeylocusts grow in nearly umbrella shape, with extended drooping branches requiring regular and extensive pruning to give street clearance.

'Skyline', branches angle upward rather than drooping downward; grows taller than most, making it a good street-tree selection.

'Sunburst', a well-known selection with yellow foliage in spring, turning green later; low-growing, umbrellalike drooping form; grows slowly to perhaps 30 ft.—too low to use as a street tree. Requires considerable pruning as a lawn tree; probably best as a specimen with shrubs or groundcover below.

Kentucky Coffeetree, *GYMNOCLÁDUS dioícus* (III), native to the northeastern U.S. is a rarely seen, slow-growing but desirable tree. It is tricky for nurserymen to propagate, for the seed must be soaked overnight in concentrated sulfuric acid! The tree is picturesque at maturity and its large doubly compound leaves are striking. As a big tree in a park or on a large lawn it has few equals, coarse-growing to 75 ft. with a bold and heavy rugged winter branch pattern. The bark, notably ridged and channeled, adds to the strong effect of this tree. Michael Dirr, an expert on American trees, cites this tree's great adaptability to drought and city conditions. It prefers rich, moist soil for best performance.

HÁLESIA carolína (H. tetráptera) (IV), the Silverbell Tree or Snowdrop Tree (not to be confused with *Styrax*, the Snowbell) comes from the southeastern United States. It is a charming flowering tree up to 50 ft. tall, slow-growing in gardens here and often multitrunked and shrubby. In early May the branches are freely hung with 1-in.-long white bells, harmonizing well with rhododendrons or evergreens.

The Mountain Silverbell, *H. carolina* var. *monticóla (H. monticola)* (V), is a taller version of the above, larger in all its parts and reaching 75 ft. Young trees are pyramidal, mature ones are broadly round topped. This woodland genus grows as an understory plant below other trees, but it can tolerate some sun. Grow it in well-drained soil rich in organic matter, with adequate moisture in summer.

HIPPOPHÁE rhamnoídes (III) is Sea-Buckthorn, native of Europe and Asia Minor, a small tree or large shrub to 25 ft. tall, often multistemmed and sprawling in growth. The leaves are narrow, willowlike, of a soft silvery gray-green, luminous in the landscape. The value of this plant lies in the heavy set of orange fruits clustered tightly along the spiny twigs, held through several months in winter. (Birds do not like them.) To have this display, both male and female plants must be present, a recommended ratio being six females per male plant. Sea-Buckthorn does best in sandy, poor soils, can tolerate salt spray, alkalinity and surface drought, but has a preference for moisture deeper in the soil. The plants establish slowly, then can make a thicket by suckering.

H. salicifólia (VI), Willowleaf Sea-Buckthorn is from the Himalayas, a spiny 30–40 ft. tree with broader dull green leaves that have silvery undersides. Its fruits are light yellow, not as spectacular as those of *H. rhamnoides,* but it is an equally worthy tree in a taller edition.

Black Walnut is *JÚGLANS nigra* (III–IV), a large rounded tree native to the central and eastern portions of the United States, reaching 120 ft. tall here in the Northwest. The tree is coarse branched, with bold, pungent, pinnately compound foliage which turns a clear light yellow in fall. It is grown for its large edible nuts, which can be a problem when they drop. The tree is often seen in older gardens in western Oregon where the early settlers planted nuts brought in wagon trains from the midwest. Old Black Walnuts can be quite stately; unfortunately, many such trees are being cut down for their very valuable wood. The tree grows best in rich, deep soils but will tolerate poorer and even dry soils. *J. nigra* grows quickly and is hard to transplant, so should be grown from seed sown in place, or seedlings transplanted young.

J. régia (V–VI), is English or Persian Walnut, native from southeastern Europe through the Himalayas to southwestern China. There are large commercial plantings of this roundheaded 100 ft. tree in western Oregon and in California. Its nut is the edible walnut of commerce. The tree is noble in aspect, with ascending heavy branches and smooth gray-white bark. The large leaves are high in tannic acid and potent-smelling when crushed. They must be raked off flower beds quickly when they fall or susceptible plants will be damaged. The leaves and nuts are messy on walking surfaces. English Walnuts need deep soils to do well, and are much less successful on thin glacial Puget Sound soils than in river valleys further south. The tree prefers warm summers. Newer cultivars such as 'Carpathian' have more winter hardiness than the commercial orchard variety 'Franquette'.

Less commonly found is the Japanese Walnut, *J. ailantifólia (J. sieboldiána)* (IV), a 60 ft. tree with a similar rounded head. This species, also with edible nuts, will tolerate much heavier soils than *J. regia*.

KALOPÁNAX píctus (IV), Castor-Aralia from Japan, Korea, China, and the Russian Far East has leaves that look superficially like those of maples or sweet gums, but lush enough to seem tropical (like *Fatsia* leaves but smaller). A closer look will reveal two distinctly unique characters— little, white, ball-like clustered flowers in midsummer, followed by small, blackish berries loved by birds. Prickly young twigs show its close relationship to *Aralia*. The tree grows quickly from awkward adolescence to elegant maturity, up to 80 ft., with a rounded crown. Donald Wyman of the Arnold Arboretum said "this tree should be grown much more than it is." Trouble-free, it prefers good soil but is said to be alkaline tolerant. Rare in nurseries, Castor-Aralia is easy from seeds which take two years to germinate.

KOELREUTÉRIA paniculáta (V), the Goldenrain Tree from the Orient, is not a common tree in the Northwest, and could well be planted more extensively. It might be confused with *Laburnum*, the Goldenchain, but apart from having yellow flowers the two are not similar. *Koelreuteria* has erect panicles in July and August, while *Laburnum* blooms in late May with pendulous flower clusters. *Koelreuteria* is a far superior tree, though *Laburnum* is flashier in bloom Goldenrain Tree grows slowly to 30 ft.; most specimens in this region have characteristically slow growth in their early years, making contorted, almost spiraling branch patterns. The tree appears to grow faster in the midwest where it is more popular. The unfolding compound leaves in spring are beautiful, emerging in shrimp to bronze colors before assuming their summer green. Flowers are bright yellow, individually small, but forming a 1 ft., upright, loose panicle in midsummer; when in full bloom the tree is lovely in the landscape. The blossoms are followed by paper-husked fruits, like Japanese lanterns, in late summer, at first pale apple green, then yellowish and finally copper or even rose colored, highly attractive and much sought after by flower arrangers. This is a thoroughly well-behaved tree, choice for the small lawn or patio, adaptable to air pollution and a wide range of soils, with drought and wind tolerance.

LABÚRNUM alpínum (IV), Scotch Laburnum, is one of the Goldenchain Trees so often confused with the Goldenrain tree above. From central Europe, this member of the pea family growing to 20 ft. tall is striking with its 12-in. long pendent flower racemes in May, like bright yellow wisteria flowers. Indeed, wisteria and laburnum are sometimes interwoven into plantings to drape over arbors in English gardens. The dazzled viewer walks below, impressed by this marriage of lavender and yellow tassels. *L. alpinum* is less common in gardens than the next species but has finer flowers; the foliage of the two is similar—trifoliate leaves of darkish green. Both trees are vase shaped, and after flowering bear dry gray-black seedpods. The seeds inside are poisonous, though the pods are not tempting to put in the mouth except when still green. Families with young children would do well to avoid Laburnums.

L. anagyroídes (V), is Common Goldenchain. This 30 ft. species, though the one most commonly seen, is inferior to *L. alpinum.* All laburnums are short lived, usually less than 50 years, but the species are quickly grown from seed, blooming by their third year. Goldenchain is not fussy about conditions, but is intolerant of soggy soil.

L. × *wátereri* 'Vossii' (V) is a superior selection from a cross involving the two species above. It makes a more dense tree intermediate between the parents, to 30 ft in height, with long racemes of fragrant golden yellow flowers.

LAGERSTRÓEMIA índica (VII), is the famed Crape-Myrtle, almost a trademark of the American South, although native to China and Korea. This showy 25 ft. tree (sometimes a large shrub) with flowers which can vary from rosy pink to white, red and purple, will grow in the Pacific Northwest but is often difficult to flower because of our cooler summers. Crape-Myrtle is often multistemmed, growing into a vase shape with little branching or foliage on the lower half of the tree, and so some sort of underplanting may be advisable. The peeling bark, pale brown to gray, is an attractive feature, especially in the winter. The plant likes good drainage, summer irrigation, and a warmer than average site to perform well in our climate. The upright panicles of small bright flowers are pyramidal in shape, up to 8 in. long, blooming in September. They do best when a warm fall follows a hot summer, and may fail to open properly in a cold, damp year.

LIQUIDÁMBAR formosána (VI–VII), Formosan Sweetgum from China and Taiwan, has distinctively three-lobed leaves, and its branches lack the corky wings of *L. styraciflua.* This tree is capable of reaching 125 ft. in height. Its fall color is usually a good, strong yellow, though leaves may occasionally be red as well. The long-stalked seed heads are bristly in appearance. This species also needs good soil and plenty of moisture.

In var. *monticola* the new foliage is plum purple, later turning dark green, then crimson again in the autumn.

The American Sweetgum from the eastern U.S., *Liquidámbar styráciflua* (V), has proven a very popular tree for Pacific Northwest streets and gardens. Sweetgum grows to 120 ft. tall, pyramidal in shape with a strong central leader. Its leaves are maplelike, strong green in most forms with autumn color varying widely, generally some shade of red, but it can be maroon, orange, yellow or a mixture of all these. Seedling color cannot be predicted, so if autumn color is of major importance try to choose your tree from a nursery field at that season. Sometime after age 15 the tree begins fruiting, with unique brown fruits the size of large marbles but with many pointed studs protruding. Some find these attractive as winter decorations, others find them mostly a nuisance. Of the many cultivars, these are four of the best:

'Burgundy', selected in California for wine-red autumn color.

'Festival', orange-gold autumn color, compact upright growth.

'Gold Dust', a very bright selection from Handy Nursery in Portland that lights up in the sunshine, one of the brightest of variegated trees, making a dramatically beautiful street tree on Portland's 12th Avenue. The leaves here are sprinkled with uneven gold patches; the effect looks better than it sounds. Pink fall color.

'Palo Alto', orange-red autumn color, dense and uniform habit.

American Sweetgum seedlings vary in the amount of corkiness along their branches and trunks, sometimes strongly winged or rough ridged or furrowed, again absolutely smooth. This is not an ailment, but merely genetic variation of the bark. While the tree does best in moist soils, it has shown surprising ability to survive poor soils and urban conditions in this region (tests in other regions have shown it not particularly tolerant of urban problems, but here it has done well). Sweetgum should always be moved balled and burlapped, and tends to take two to five years to get established and begin growing after transplanting. In mild winters some Sweetgum leaves hang on until Christmas or even until new spring growth pushes them off, and this feature may be accentuated if the trees are shaded by tall buildings.

LIRIODÉNDRON tulipífera (IV), the Tuliptree, Tulip Poplar, or Yellow Poplar, is native to eastern United States. It grows quickly to 150 ft., as large as our native cottonwoods, and has somewhat the same overall mature shape, but is a much more attractive tree. The foliage is superior, clean green leaves that look as if someone had clipped half the center lobe off a maple leaf. Tuliptree turns a dazzling gold in autumn, sometimes yellow-gold and occasionally tawny gold. The trees tend to have few low branches, showing magnificent straight trunks for a great distance above the ground. Flowers of the Tuliptree are beautiful but not showy, cup-shaped creations of greenish yellow with six petals stained bright orange inside. They are born singly near the branch tips, often so high in the tree as to be overlooked. Not a tree for small gardens, *L. tulipifera* is superior for parks and boulevards and other large-scale plantings. It looks ridiculous crowded to 30 ft. spacing in street planting strips. This tree grows best in deep, rich soils with ample moisture, but somehow succeeds in poor, gravelly glacial soils where it would not be expected to do well, as in the Washington Park Arboretum in Seattle. It should never be transplanted in autumn or early winter; much loss can result from the large fleshy roots remaining dormant all winter. Dig the tree with a good root ball and, as with magnolias, transplant it in spring just before growth starts so that roots can establish quickly. 'Fastigiatum' is a cultivar of very slender columnar habit. Variegated foliage is found in two forms: 'Aureomarginata' has leaves edged in pale chartreuse-yellow, with green centers; in 'Aureopictum' the pattern is reversed—the leaf margins are green and the centers yellow.

MAGNÓLIA campbéllii (VIII–IX), the Campbell Magnolia from the Himalayas, is the prima donna that leads off this listing of these aristocratic trees—and it is a fitting star, with huge 10 in. clean, deep pink blooms on bare early-spring branches. The star in this instance can keep its audience waiting a long time—up to 20 years until it is ready to appear with its first blossom. For this reason its variety *mollicomáta,* collected by Forrest in Yunnan, is preferred, since it blooms in about a third of the time. The variety, however, is more of a mauve pink color, less the clear rose pink that can be achieved in the species. Both are woodland trees that will someday reach 60 ft. or more under favorable conditions, and both have large, bold leaves and a regal bearing. Since spring frosts can damage the buds or blooms, choose the planting site carefully. Magnolias are intolerant of heavy wet soils and poor drainage, and do best in sandy soils. They are heavy feeders and respond to a rich diet of composts, fertilizers and manures. For the greatest transplanting success, move all magnolias in spring just as growth starts.

M. cordáta (M. acumináta var. subcordáta) (V), the Yellow Cucumber Tree, is a small species from the Carolinas and Georgia, growing to 30 ft., with cup-shaped pale yellow 2 in. flowers in May, set against a terminal ruff of the small, ovate leaves. The pods are somewhat cucumberlike in appearance, splitting open to reveal bright red seeds late in the season. The tree has strongly upswept branches.

M. fráseri (V), the Fraser Magnolia, is rare in nurseries, as is the preceding species, and this American tree from the Appalachian Mountains also has cucumberlike pods. Fraser Magnolia is showier, both for its fragrant, creamy white flowers 8–10 in. across in late spring, and for its coarse 12-in.-long leaves. It is distinctive enough in appearance to need careful use in design, perhaps as a featured tree, since it is capable of reaching 50 ft. in height.

Magnolia denudáta (V) has been reinstated as the correct name for Yulan Magnolia, and M. heptapéta rejected as being based on an inaccurate, non-botanical drawing according to a paper by Frederick G. Meyer and Elizabeth McClintock in *Taxon* 36, #3, August 1987. One of the most noble magnolias, the Yulan has been revered in the art and history of China and planted there around old temples. Except that it is one of the most difficult magnolias to propagate, this species would be seen in many more of our gardens; it is not new to the Northwest and does very well here. The goblet-shaped, fragrant, ivory-white blooms are out in late April or early May in great candelabra masses, before the leaves appear. This species tends to form a single trunk and looks more treelike than most magnolias, reaching to 45 ft. with horizontal branches that sweep upward at the tips. There is an elegance about this tree that is spoiled by much competing planting beneath it—Wyman recommends giving it 30 ft. of uncluttered space. A choice terrace tree, or one to plant near an entry where the early blooms can be appreciated, it is also lovely as a street tree; however, because of very limited availability we have rarely seen more than two Yulans together on the street. The blossoms can be hurt by late freezes, so site it carefully.

M. *kóbus* (IV), the Kobus Magnolia from Japan, is less choice than some magnolias, but it is another that makes a dependable flowering street tree; and the 40 ft. specimen against woodland at the Berry Botanic Garden in Portland shows that it rivals dogwoods in such a setting. Botanists now believe that M. *stellata* may be merely a compact bushy form of M. *kobus*, possessing double the number of tepals, 12–18 in each flower. M. *kobus* has similar white flowers but with fewer tepals, in April, before the leaves. It has a distinctly erect habit, though it can occasionally be multitrunked. The variety *boreális* (III), a selection, is said to reach 75 ft; this tree may not bloom for up to 10 years. One superior cultivar with better flowers, 'Wada's Memory', which was imported from Japan in 1940, has performed very well at the Washington Park Arboretum in Seattle, flowering at an earlier age. (Now referred to M. *salicifolia*).

M. × *lóebneri* 'Merrill' (IV) is a most satisfactory hybrid of M. *stellata* and M. *kobus* from the Arnold Arboretum in Boston. This cross bloomed 5 years after the seed was planted, and the form named Merrill Magnolia has performed well everywhere. The plant grows quickly in a strongly erect form when young, to an eventual height of about 50 ft. becoming rounded in outline. It blooms early, is free flowering, and shares the surprising resistance to air pollution that magnolias have. Further, it is not difficult from cuttings, so this will be a major magnolia for our gardens, and perhaps also as a street tree.

M. *macrophýlla* (V), Bigleaf Magnolia, is another American species from the southeastern states, with papery-textured leaves, the largest for any temperate North American tree—up to 32 in. long and 12 in. wide in some instances. Needless to say, a tree this coarse textured must be carefully used in the landscape, though when it attains its ultimate 50 ft. height the big leaves are in better scale. Michael Dirr calls the tree a "cumbersome giant ... for ... the insatiable magnolia collector". Fragrant, six-petaled white flowers are borne above the leaves in June, solitary, cupshaped, and up to 12 in. across.

M. *hypoléuca (M. obováta)* (V), the Whiteleaf Japanese Magnolia, is a big tree to 90 ft., with heavily fragrant, 6 in. creamy white flowers in early June, borne above the coarse 1-ft.-long leaves which are green above, blue-white below and of heavier texture than those of M. *macrophylla*. It also has conelike red fruits 5–8 in. long, with red seeds.

M. *salicifólia* (IV–V), is the Anise Magnolia from Japan. Sargent suggests that the bruised leaves smell gently of aniseed; the bark has a sharply fragrant odor of lemon-verbena. The tree is notable for its form, superior to that of most magnolias, often being narrowly compact and upright into quite old age, though some seedling forms grow broader. It can reach 40 ft. in height. Also notable are the leaves, dull green above, glaucous beneath, smaller and narrower than those of most magnolias, giving a fine texture unusual in this genus. Flowers are white and fragrant with 6 petals, 3–4 in. across, in April on naked shoots. The small green fruits are cucumberlike with the typical red seeds emerging, and are apt to be strongly pink cheeked. In 1961 the Washington Park Arboretum in Seattle introduced a superior selection of *M. salicifolia* named 'Else Frye', with flowers half again as large as the species, a fine, densely compact form. It has performed well in various tests across the U.S. and is worth seeking in nurseries.

A mature tree of *Magnolia salicifolia* 'Wada's Memory' in full bloom in early April in Seattle. Photo by Brian Mulligan.

M. sargentiána var. *robústa* (VII), Sargent's Magnolia from western China, has been called a pink-flowered *M. heptapeta,* and there is a good deal of flower similarity in the early-April blooms which appear before the leaves. The form of *M. sargentiana* known as var. *robusta,* however, tends to branch low and spread wide. It has very large flowers with up to 16 tepals (a magnolia's "petals") forming an 8–12 in. mauve-to-rose bloom. The leaves are medium-large, 6–8 in. and the tree needs a good deal of room to develop, since it can be 35 ft. each way. Wyman, who likes it, says "It is not a tree for the small garden." There is an excellent example on Arboretum

Drive in the Washington Park Arboretum in Seattle.

The magnolia most often seen in spring gardens in our region is the Saucer Magnolia, the hybrid *M.* × *soulangeána* (V), with *M. heptapeta* and *M. liliiflora* as parents. This vigorous, shrubby plant to about 25 ft. has strongly upswept branches and goblet-shaped blooms appearing just before the leaves in May. One can prune it readily to a single trunk if that is desired. This magnolia shows good air-pollution tolerance. A fine specimen, well over a century old, stands in the courtyard of a Christopher Wren church in the old city of London, having endured smoke, soot and wartime bombing. This hybrid has been around more than a century and a half and has spawned many cultivars. Below are some of the best.

'Alba' ('Superba'), very compact, white, outside of petals lightest purple.

'Alexandrina', large and early, white inside, rose-purple outside.

'Lennei', very dark purplish magenta, flowers quite large, goblet shaped; often lengthens the season with sporadic bloom in summer.

'Lombardy Rose', a 'Lennei' seedling, shares the reblooming habit; dark rose outside, white inside.

'Rustica Rubra', early flowering, large goblet-shaped blossoms, rosy red outside, white inside.

'Speciosa', large-flowered white, close to 'Alba'; late-blooming, rather dense, vigorous, upright tree.

'San Jose', very large, fragrant, rose-purple blossoms; vigorous grower.

Except for 'San Jose' and 'Lombardy Rose', these varieties are all a century old or nearly so.

M. spréngeri (VII), Sprenger Magnolia, is a 60 ft. tree of pyramidal shape from Central China which produces 8 in. rosy pink flowers before the leaves. It has a good deal of resemblance to *M. campbellii* and is known in gardens mostly in its cultivar 'Diva', which was raised from seeds sent by E. H. Wilson to England in 1900. This is a fine, rosy pink magnolia, described by Bean as being as good in color as some of the best forms of *M. campbellii*. It blooms a week or so later than that species, so is less often harmed by frost.

M. × *véitchii* (VII), the Veitch Magnolia, is similar in many respects to the above, being a hybrid of *M. campbellii* and *M. heptapeta* with 6 in. pink flowers before the leaves in April. Leaves are large and the growth rate is very fast. A tree planted in 1920 had by 1971 reached 85 ft. tall! Wyman suggests that it has brittle branches, but this has not been borne out on trees in Seattle.

M. wilsónii (VI), another Chinese species, is the 25 ft. Wilson Magnolia. This is one of the more satisfactory of the red-centered, white-flowered species. The 4–5 in. fragrant flowers show a bright ring of red stamens when the white blossoms open in May. Since the flowers hang from the leafy branches, it is helpful that this easily grown Magnolia assumes more of a tree form than do some of the related species of this group. They will show off to best advantage if the tree is planted some- where well above eye level, for the blooms are the main thing that it has to offer, and they are striking. Wilson's Magnolia is lime tolerant, not a problem in most Northwest gardens, and it is one of the hardier species in this group. It is one of the rarest in commerce, but a few Northwest nurseries list it.

MÁLUS. The apples and crab apples are a daunting lot to evaluate. Nurseries grow about as many varieties of this genus as of any flowering tree. In recent years many nurseries and hybridizers have come forward annually with new introductions. The connoisseur will undoubtedly wish to review the current listings before choosing. We will include only about 30 of the better species and cultivars, many of them older ones that have held their own against the novelties. Some *Malus* species and hybrids are valuable fruit trees, and others include some of the most important orna- mental trees, beautiful in flower and fruit. Many are useful for planting in heavy soils and some seem able to survive where drainage is by no means perfect. Consequently, the crabs entirely replace the cherries in gardens that are handicapped by poor drainage, or where the soil is a stiff clay. Their exquisite beauty is often fleeting, but most of them also make a fine showing of ornamental fruit which hangs on for a long time. They have another large problem west of the Cascades, and that is leaf and fruit diseases from apple scab and other fungi. In some *Malus* this is so serious as to remove the tree from consideration, since without a program of several spring sprays annually these susceptible sorts are brown-tattered in leaf or even defoliated from summer onward, an ugly garden picture. While this is less of the problem in the drier interior counties of the North- west, we have attempted to list only those species and cultivars with better-than-average resistance to apple scab and other leaf diseases.

Careful attention should be paid to the pruning of the flowering crab apples, and it is rare to see anyone pruning them correctly. They cannot attain their full beauty of form in the garden without judicious annual pruning which gradually eliminates any unwanted branches. Left to their own devices under garden conditions, the essential outline structure of the tree is soon lost in a mass of superfluous twigs. This can be prevented by systematic summer pruning of new growth. The restoration of a long- neglected specimen to an uncluttered branching pattern may take several years. It is unwise to try to reshape the structure of an old apple or crab apple in one or two large operations; it is better to spread it over several years. Cutting off huge portions of the tree—which still has its full vigorous root system—will result in its pushing out suckerlike sprouts in all directions. Sorting these out and working with them will take longer than keeping the operation slower but less frantic. It should be mentioned that fruiting orchard-type apples often make handsome garden trees, and usually if they have decent shapes, old existing apple trees can well be incorporated into a new or renovated garden design. Fruiting apples are derived from *Málus doméstica* (III), a European species in cultivation since ancient times. Many of its cultivars make excellent ornamental trees of fine garden behavior, and they should be grown far more often than they presently are. However, gardeners in areas where orchard pests are a problem will need to spray their garden apples diligently.

Here is an alphabetical listing of crab apple cultivars and species that we recommend for Pacific Northwest gardens: (all zone IV except where noted)

'Adams', red buds open to pink flowers in mid-May; ¾ in. red fruits in autumn; 24 ft.; originated in Massachusetts in 1947.

M × *arnoldiána*, a 20-ft. hybrid of *M. floribunda* × *M. baccata*, large fragrant pink flowers from red buds, early May; some susceptibility to scab—spray west of the Cascades.

M. × *atrosangúinea*, Carmine Crabapple, to 20 ft., hybrid of *M. halliana* × *M. sieboldii*; mounded, almost shrublike, rosy red blooms and red fruits.

M. baccáta 'Gracilis' (II), Siberian Crabapple, pink buds open white, very small red to gold fruits, to 40 ft.; branch tips tend to be pendulous; some fire-blight susceptibility, a problem east of the Cascades.

M. baccata 'Jackii' (II), of Korean origin; large blooms of pure white, purplish fruits, very deep green leaves, light fire-blight susceptibility.

'Baskatong', carmine buds open pink in mid-May, red fruits, red-bronze foliage; from the Central Experimental Farm, Ottawa, before 1950.

'Centurion;, red buds open to rose flowers in May, bright red fruit, bronzy foliage; notably columnar, vase shaped in age.

'Dolgo' (II), large white blooms in early May, larger, more conical fruit than most, red and good for pickling or jelly, 30–40 ft. tree, attractive glossy green foliage; from seed of Russian origin.

'Donald Wyman', white flowers from pink buds, small bright red fruits, rounded tree to 20 ft.; from the Arnold Arboretum, Boston, Massachusetts.

'Dorothea', semidouble rose pink flowers, small yellow fruits, on a rounded 25-ft. tree with dense branching; some scab susceptibility.

M. floribúnda, Japanese Flowering Crabapple. Carmine buds open pink, fade to white; 30-ft. tree, an old favorite that hangs on against the competition; yellow fruit; slightly susceptible to scab, moderately so to fire blight.

M. hupehénsis (M. theífera), Tea Crabapple, another old-timer from China that has held on in popularity despite susceptibility to fire blight in areas where that is a problem (mostly east of the Cascades). E. H. Wilson called this the "quintessence of crab apple loveliness." It looks more like a flowering cherry than a flowering crab apple, with its distinct pattern of stiffly spreading branches massed with clusters of large white or pink flowers on slender stems. Strong-growing tree, 25 ft., wide spreading; tiny red and yellow fruit is not significant; comes true to type when raised from seed.

M. ioénsis pléna (II), ('Bechtel's'), Bechtel Crabapple, fragrant double pink flowers; old-time variety, highly popular but about the most susceptible to every disease that comes by—choose an alternate!

'John Downie', pink-budded white flowers in late May, 20 ft., wide-spreading tree, large conical scarlet fruits make good pickles or jelly.

'Katherine', double light pink flowers, fading white, mid-May; small yellow fruit with red cheek, 20-ft. tree, open habit; origin, Rochester, NY.

'Liset', luminous large red flowers, purplish green leaves, red-purple fruit, dense 15–20 ft. shape, a tidy tree; originated in Holland.

'Marshall Oyama', narrowly upright habit, single pink buds open to white in mid-May; yellow and red fall fruit.

'Pink Spires', narrow upright tree with bronzy green leaves, copper in fall, 20 ft.; rose pink blooms, purplish fruit; some scab susceptibility.

'Professor Sprenger', densely upright-spreading tree to 20 ft.; white flowers, green leaves, long-lasting small orange-red fruits; highly disease resistant.

'Robinson', crimson buds open to deep pink flowers, 25 ft. dense tree, upright spreading, dark red fruits.

'Snowcloud', double white flowers from pink buds, very little fruit produced; upright grower to 20 ft., dark green foliage.

'Snowdrift', white flowers from pink buds, small glossy orange-red fruit; 20 ft., rounded form, good residential street tree in Seattle; origin in Ohio, 1965.

'Strawberry Parfait', red buds open to deep pink flowers; open, vase-shaped tree to 25 ft.; small yellow fruit with a red blush; may have some susceptibility to fire blight.

M. tschonóskii, (V) from Japan, white flowers not showy, 1-in. fruits yellow-green flushed purple; the beauty of this species is in its silvery gray leaves, green in summer, apricot-red fall foliage, one of the best for fall color; big tree up to 40 ft. high; a good performer as a Seattle street tree; some susceptibility to scab, prone to fire blight east of the mountains.

'White Cascade', a new variety, weeping, white flowers from pink buds; good foliage, fruits small and greenish in fall; 15 ft. tall; slight to moderate susceptibility to scab.

'Winter Gold', named for the persistent yellow winter fruit; late season white flowers from red buds; roundheaded tree to 25 ft.; slight scab susceptibility, moderate fire blight susceptibility; a good performer as a Seattle street tree; of Dutch origin.

M. × *zúmi* 'Calocárpa' (V), white flowers from pink buds in early May, fragrant; persistent bright red fruit make a long-time winter show, when birds don't eat them; 20 ft.

Having offered this list, we quote Michael Dirr: "I doubt if any treatment of flowering crab apples will ever be complete for as I write this someone is ready to introduce a new clone into the trade." About 500 cultivars are available in the U.S.

MÉSPILUS germánica (V), the Medlar from southeastern Europe or Asia Minor, is a sentimental favorite with students of gardening history and those interested in old-time fruits. Claimed by some authors to have been grown more than any other tree fruit in the Middle Ages, it has become a rarity everywhere now and is grown mostly by connoisseurs. The fruit, looking like a small russet crab apple with a prominent calyx persisting at the end, must fall to the ground, rot slightly, and then ideally be subjected to light frost (preferably on a lawn) before it is edible; the flavor is definitely an acquired taste. Americans have never clutched medlars to their bosoms, since they don't make good pies. The tree, apart from its fruits, is a very nice garden subject, preferably to view close up. It is small, no more than 15 feet tall in most cases, with an open structure of fairly heavy branches, like an orchard apple, but the branches have nice curves and arches. At the end of each branch in May is a single showy white flower, set in a collar of leaves larger than those of apples. This is followed by the solitary fruits, beautifully presented. The Medlar is tolerant of a wide variety of soils as long as they aren't too wet.

MÓRUS álba (IV), the White Mulberry, a native of China, is planted occasionally, particularly in the hotter interior parts of the Northwest. It is not highly ornamental, making dense growth in an uninspired form, without particularly good foliage, fall color or flower value. The fruit is edible; many people find it insipid, other people and most birds relish it. The fruit can be messy around paved areas; there is a fruitless cultivar, 'Kingan', which has quite large leathery leaves that have an attraction in themselves; and this one may have more future in some situations. The tree grows quickly, to 40–60 ft. survives virtually any soil and drought, and creates fast shade in hot climates. There are cut-leaved and pendulous forms. *M. nígra* and *M. rúbra,* both with edible red fruits, are more desirable trees, but difficult to obtain.

NOTHOFAGUS. The Southern Beeches, from South America, New Zealand and Australia, arrived—as did the eucalyptus—directly in western America without the usual nicety of a courtesy appearance in eastern arboreta. Indeed, they do not thrive except on the West Coast. Even here, they are only slowly making their way into nurseries because of difficulties in propagation.

N. antárctica (VII), Antarctic Beech from Argentina and Chile, is fast growing, a tree that can reach 50 ft. tall if single trunked. It often divides into several trunks close to the ground and in such cases would probably be half as tall. Antarctic Beech is one of the most distinctive of trees, making shoots up to 3 feet long in a season, with a strongly fishbone pattern of side branching, like elms, and set with very small closely placed, toothed ovate leaves, usually about an inch long and sometimes lobed.

The leaves are deep green and can be fragrant in some forms, and can color coppery in the autumn. The tree, best produced by seeds, needs an open, sunny position and is succeeding well in a variety of Seattle sites.

A quite different tree is *N. oblíqua* (VII), the Roblé Beech, native to the same areas as *N. antarctica,* but tending more toward the equator. Bean calls it the most warmth loving of the South American Beeches, and it likes almost Mediterranean warmth. This has much larger leaves that look like small chestnut (*Castanea*) leaves, grows to 100 ft. and more; it is a fast-growing species, and trees less than 100 years old in Britain are approaching that height. It is easy in a wide variety of soils, and can color nicely in the autumn—red, orange and yellow.

Larger still in leaf, with foliage like hornbeam (*Carpinus*), is *N. prócera* (VII) the Rauli Beech. It shares the quick growth and autumn color potential of Roblé Beech, growing to perhaps 80 ft. It has been little tried here, but has performed well in the Washington Park Arboretum in Seattle as an attractive landscape tree that would make a fine specimen. This tree succeeds best where rainfall is above 30 in. annually and should not be planted in frost pockets as it has some sensitivity to frost. In Britain, along with *N. obliqua,* it is being used in forestry as a plantation tree because of its quick growth. It is rare in Northwest nurseries, but can be raised from seed when available.

A comparatively young tree of one of the Southern Beeches (*Nothofagus antarctica*) showing its elegant habit. Photo by Brian Mulligan.

N. pumílio (VII), the Lenga Beech, is the most common species in Argentina. It has been introduced in Britain and the Northwest only during the past quarter century, so it very rare as yet, but has performed well. Leaves are like those of *N. antarctica,* but somewhat larger; they have two large blunt teeth along the leaf edge between each pair of veins, a key identification feature. In South American timber stands the tree reaches 70 ft. or more, but in open garden sites will probably be half to three quarters that size. Bean says "It is too early to judge whether this species will prove superior to *N. antarctica* as an ornamental tree, but it is certainly handsomer in foliage and grows faster."

NÝSSA sylvática (III), the Sour Gum or Black Tupelo, is an American species from the Atlantic Coast, Great Lakes and Gulf Coast, famed for its consistently beautiful fall color. In gardens, it is a medium-large tree of moderate growth to an ultimate 50 ft.; it grows larger in the wild. This is a swamp tree in nature, and quite tolerant of wet soils in the garden, though it is also quite satisfactory in well-drained soil. It is very difficult to transplant because seedlings have a taproot; move it only in spring and then balled and burlapped; trees moved in winter are apt not to survive. This tree is rare in nurseries, but has good-looking leaves not unlike dogwoods', with dark green color which often turns red-orange in fall but can range anywhere from bright yellow to purple. It is never a muted autumn color, always brilliant. It is dioecious, with small purple fruits on female trees.

Foliage and young fruits of the American Hop-Hornbeam (*Ostrya virginiana*). Photo by Brian Mulligan.

ÓSTRYA carpínifolia (III), American Hophornbeam, is a tree from eastern North America that is unusual in nurseries or in literature about trees, yet is considered to be "pretty" by Bean, "handsome" by Dirr, and "nice" by Wyman. All agree it grows well in gardens. It appears a bit touchy at transplanting (which would explain the nurserymen's aversion), must be transplanted with a root ball, and establishes slowly after transplanting. On the plus side, this rarely seen tree begins with a pyramidal outline in youth, becoming rounded with age as the branching becomes more horizontal. The medium-sized leaves look like large unlobed birch leaves. The male flowers are catkins, decorative in winter and early spring; insignificant female flowers become dangling clusters of bracts that look like hops in autumn, an interesting feature. The tree is pest-free.

OXYDÉNDRUM arbóreum (IV–V), the Sourwood or Sorrel Tree from southeastern United States, is one of the showiest small American trees, though as usually seen, it is more apt to be shrublike under 15 ft. rather than treelike. In the wild the tree reaches from 50–75 ft., but under garden conditions it takes quite a few years to break this 15-ft. barrier, then has a potential of growing to 40–50 ft. in Northwest gardens. There are some good treelike specimens in the Washington Park Arboretum in Seattle aged somewhat over 40 years. In the wild this ericaceous tree often grows in well-drained gravelly soils and has some tolerance for dry situations. Its resistance to pollution is low, and it is a better suburban tree than a city tree. The rather large leaves resemble those of a peach and are a good glossy green through the summer, then usually brilliant red in fall. In August one-sided panicles of small white flowers arch outward in pagodalike fashion, giving a strong, bold display. The individual bells look like lily-of-the-valley florets. The flowers are said to be attractive to bees. Select *Oxydendrum* in fall color in the nursery to be sure of the best leaf color.

PARRÓTIA pérsica (V), Persian Parrotia, in flower and leaf resembles its close relatives the witch hazels (*Hamamelis*). The flower effect on naked stems in March is dull red. *Parrotia* commonly has multiple trunks, like hazelnuts, and is often broader than its 20–30 ft. height. With old age, these trunks become very beautiful, with mottled and lacy patterns of brown, gray and green that are fine indeed. The deep green foliage trades its summer luster for bright sunset hues, one of the more reliable fall-coloring trees. This species should be better known and more used. It is attractive at all seasons and is spectacular in fall, it has no real pest or disease problems, and it is quite tolerant as to soils. From northwestern Iran, it likes a sunny location. Usually grown from seed, it can also be propagated from cuttings or layers of the lower branches.

The Empress Tree, *PAULÓWNIA tomentósa (P. imperiális)* (V), is well named when in May bloom, for then the 40-ft. tree is topped by big pyramidal panicles of fragrant lavender to purple flowers like large stubby foxgloves. The leaves are less empresslike but still regal, great green shields usually 6–10 in. across, generally heart shaped with five shallow lobes. Some gardeners, to achieve the maximum tropical jack-in-the-beanstalk look, annually slash Empress Tree to the ground during its younger years. The resultant stalk rises, phoenixlike to perhaps 15 ft. in a single season with leaves 30 in. across! The leaves resemble *Catalpa* leaves, the general form of the tree is much like *Catalpa,* and it has the same coarse weightiness in the landscape, casting dense shade. The tree is tough, withstands air pollution and a variety of soils and has become a significant roadside weed in the American South, though it is native to China. It grows readily from its multitudes of tiny seeds (protect the seedlings in a greenhouse their first winter). To understand how well it grows, consider that two years after the original plant in Europe flowered, there were believed to be between 20,000 and 30,000 of its progeny growing! The tree prefers warm sites and high summer temperatures; it sets fewer flower buds after cloudy summers, and in spring its developing flower buds may be nipped in some areas by late frosts, but seldom in and around Seattle.

PHELLODÉNDRON amurénse (III), Amur Corktree from the north of China, makes a 40-ft.-high rounded or wide-spreading tree with pinnately compound foliage rather like a Black Walnut's. Fall color is light yellow, but not dependable. There is no floral effect; little panicles of round black fruits are borne in late autumn on female trees. This tree tolerates a fairly wide range of soils, but has not shown much liking for urban conditions; it was a failure in its one trial as a Seattle street tree, and Dirr reports "from my observations not as urban tolerant as the literature would have us believe." It transplants easily and is pest-free. The best feature of the tree, when it is thriving, is the heavy horizontal branches, that like the trunk, are ridged and corky.

PLÁTANUS × *acerifólia* (IV–V), This is the London Planetree, a tough tree that withstands virtually any abuse heaped on it, and thus is a favorite with people planting trees in difficult places. It is known that this tree is a hybrid between the Oriental Planetree, *P. orientalis,* from Europe and western Asia, and the American Planetree or Sycamore, *P. occidentalis,* from North America. It is further known that the cross has occurred repeatedly, that the tree was known in England in 1663, and that it made its reputation in London where it was freely planted and where fine specimens are still to be seen. The last 20 years have seen the unravelling of much of the mystery of the origin of the London Plane, but the search is continuing. When one asks Frank S. Santamour, Jr. of the National Arboretum in Washington, D.C. about this tree (he has done many years of research on it), his response begins, "Which *Platanus* × *acerifolia* are you talking about? There are several." The tree has probably been more planted, and misplanted, in American cities in the past 40 years than any other tree, because it is tough and versatile, a classic survivor tree. Beyond that, it grows quickly on almost all soils except poorly drained ones, it has attractive maplelike leaves, and it forms an open rounded structure that looks like an old tree at about age 20, a highly desirable feature in today's cities where so much looks new. The tree has particularly handsome bark that flakes off in green and ivory patches. It is highly resistant to most city problems, but with some susceptibility to automobile exhaust, evident only where very high pollution levels are present. It is easily produced from cuttings with no problems in the nursery, and not difficult from seed. West of the Cascade Mountains, or anywhere where springs are apt to be cool and wet, anthracnose disease can be a serious problem, curling and blighting the leaves. It is controllable by spring spray with fungicides. The tree is susceptible any April that daytime temperatures don't rise above 65 degrees Fahrenheit, a not uncommon occurrence. In warmer climates, such as San Francisco's, the tree usually escapes anthracnose but may be damaged in late summer by attacks of mildew on the leaves. Neither disease is fatal unless repeated several years in a row, but both are disfiguring. The tree does cause allergies in some people in spring and summer when the leaves release hairs from their undersides. Some nurseries and tree companies issue face masks to employees who must work in the trees at this season. This point could be important for asthmatics or others with respiratory problems. Because these trees grow so well they can pry up sidewalks and paved areas more than most species, unless the soils in the area are deep and well drained; it is best to plant London Planes no closer than 6 ft. to paved surfaces. The trees used to be much pollarded (pruned hard, back to branch stubs) in Europe; this is done less now with labor costs higher, but the tree can tolerate this severe treatment better than most. London Plane is large, to 100 ft. or more, and the plants are best spaced 50 ft. or more apart in order that their potential majesty can develop.

P. orientális (VI), Oriental Planetree, from southeast Europe and western Asia, one parent of London Planetree, is similar, though much less planted than the hybrid. It has similar leaves, but these are deeply five-lobed, the lobes toothed, with the same hanging ball-like fruit clusters as London Planetree (though *P.* × *acerifolia* has usually two or sometimes three balls in the cluster, while *P. orientalis* has three to many more). The tree grows rapidly in a high, open pattern to 90 ft. tall, and the bark peels off as it does in London Planetree, though in this case it is less mottled, just revealing very pale greenish white bark beneath.

P. racemósa (VII), the California Planetree, was for many years suggested for Pacific Northwest gardens, once even making a "Six Most Recommended Trees" list. Nurseries seldom list it today, and we know of only a handful of specimens in the entire region, which have not shown any outstanding performance. In California where it is native, this 100-ft. tree with whitish peeling bark is a striking tree; in the Northwest it seems susceptible to several diseases and does not thrive.

PÓPULUS álba 'Pyramidalis' (III), Bolle's Poplar, is a form of the White Poplar, introduced as a cultivated tree from Central Asia and not known in the wild. Upright in habit like a Lombardy Poplar, but wider, up to 80 ft. tall, it has a smooth pale trunk, attractive in winter, and deeply lobed leaves, glossy deep green above, and white wooly beneath, turning yellow in autumn. It is easily propagated, and given to suckering freely, with all the problems that this entails, but is a stately and useful tree where quick results are needed.

P. nígra 'Italica' (III), Lombardy Poplar, is one of the most picturesque trees in existence, a favorite with landscape painters and creators of romantic natural landscapes. It has fine gold autumn color and a thoroughly distinct narrow upright form to 90 ft. Lombardy Poplar is extensively used east of the Cascades as a windbreak, and is often used west of the mountains as a quick-growing screen. Once the tree has grown to its quick maturity, problems begin. It is a voracious feeder, impossible to garden close to, which outlaws it for gardeners with limited space. Its roots seek out sewer lines and plug them; they run under and pry up sidewalks, streets and patios, which makes it a menace with those who must deal with the consequences. And it commonly throws up suckers in the neighbors' lawns, causing more problems. Every gardener should remember that the roots spread along the surface for hundreds of feet, robbing the soil of every scrap of moisture and nutriment that the rest of the garden should have. These poplars may be considered among the finest landscape trees for large areas of low-lying or swampy ground; they are useful for quickly screening, but for long-term effect—except on the grand scale of park planting—other trees will be far superior.

P. simónii (II) is the Simon's Poplar from northern and west central China, a graceful tree with ascending trunks and slender, almost weeping branches, to 75 ft. Spring is its best season, for the fragrant, bright chartreuse foliage appears very early; there is no fall color. Unfortunately, its twigs are brittle in windstorms, and the trunks suffer from disease, rotting and becoming dangerous as they age; but this is an attractive tree in its prime.

P. tremuloídes (I), Quaking Aspen, is the most widely distributed North American tree, from Alaska to Mexico. This poplar is fast growing, to 50 ft., with an irregular or roundheaded crown, living for 50 years or less. The effect is that of a white-barked birch, and the autumn gold color again echoes birch's. In our region, in some places, they intermingle in the wild with Paper Birches, in poor gravelly soils with the water table not far below; the trees will tolerate damp sites, but not soggy ones. In cultivation, this species has a series of diseases and insect problems, but still is often successfully used in landscaping, mostly in groups or groves.

In addition to the above, there are some good lesser-known poplars such as P. maximowíczii (II) from Japan, a fast-growing tree to 100 ft; and a host of hybrid poplars involving such species as P. deltoídes (II), the Black Cottonwood from eastern United States, and P. nigra (II) from Europe. Many are useful for parks, for screening or quick growth, but few are highly ornamental.

PRÚNUS. This large and diverse genus in the Rose family includes many of our fruit trees, and thus the flowering forms of them. We will consider the genus in this discussion under two main groupings: (1) The cherries and chokecherries (2) Other deciduous *Prunus*, including the plums, apricots, peaches and almonds.

A grove of aspens (*Populus tremuloides*) in the Cascade mountains, Washington. Photo by Brian Mulligan.

THE CHERRIES AND CHOKECHERRIES

This is a very important group of flowering trees for Northwest gardens, among which are many of the showiest trees that we grow. Diseases, particularly presently incurable virus diseases, have made major inroads in this group in the last decade or two, and some of the species and hybrids below will be noted as susceptible to such diseases. The wise designer will use such cherries sparingly so that should they be afflicted the entire garden design will not collapse. At the same time, many trees of even the susceptible types continue to perform satisfactorily here and nurseries continue to produce them. The wise gardener will not stay completely away from this group, either, unless she or he simply does not like cherries.

PRÚNUS *ávium* 'Plena' (III), Double-flowered Mazzard Cherry. The basic species here is a European native cherry, commonly used as an understock for many of the ornamental and fruiting (sweet) cherries. This is a white-flowered double form with substantial flowers, on a pyramidal 60-ft. tree, blooming in May. Foliage is that of the fruiting cherries, rather large. This is a little-seen cultivar, hard to find in nurseries, but it is much more cold hardy than most of the double-flowering cherries, so is important east of the Cascades. Like all cherries, it wants very good drainage—cherries die in soggy soils, or even with summer overwatering on clay soils in gardens. Sandy soils, or even gravelly ones, are ideal, with some annual addition of fertilizer. If the soil is clay, plant the tree on a hill.

P. campanuláta (VII), Taiwan Cherry from Japan and Taiwan. This cherry is not well tested in the Northwest; it succeeds well in California and is said to have survived 0°F. in the southeastern U.S. (Dirr); we suspect it is borderline hardy to about 10°F. Wilson considered this tree one of his finest introductions, a cherry with bell-shaped rosy red flowers, excitingly beautiful in bloom. The height of this tree is ultimately 25–30 ft., and it is densely branched. There is a hybrid of *P. campanulata* × *P. incisa* called 'Okame', carmine pink, available in a few Northwest nurseries; it is said to be hardier and has performed well in the middle Atlantic states, and is worthy of further trial here. It is very susceptible to bacterial blight.

P. × *híllieri* 'Spire' (V), is capable of growing rather quickly to its full size, 25 ft. high by 8 ft. wide. In April this gives single, light pink blossoms, and the foliage turns a good reddish bronze in fall. The parentage is *P. incisa* × *P. sargentii*, and this newer cultivar from England (1935) is making a good mark.

P. máackii (II), the Goldbark or Amur Chokecherry from Manchuria, is a very pleasant cherry, with 3-in. racemes of small, lightly fragrant white flowers in mid-May. It is extremely hardy, and can reach 45 ft. tall, but its prime feature beyond its great hardiness is its brown-gold bark, flaking off once the tree or branch reaches 4 in. in diameter.

P. pádus (III), is the European Bird Cherry or Hägg Tree, to 45 ft. with small, fragrant, white blossoms in drooping racemes 3–6 in. long in May. Of the named cultivars, var. *commutáta,* a wild selection from Manchuria, blooms about three weeks earlier than the type, usually by mid-April, with larger than normal blooms, and is very good except in regions with late frosts.

P. sargéntii (IV), the Sargent Cherry from Japan, to 75 ft., is one of the finest species, and seems to be much more trouble-free than most cherries. Wilson calls it "probably the finest of all the cherry trees, both as an ornamental and as a timber tree." It has single, pink blossoms in late spring, followed by bronzy new growth that then turns green as the season progressses, and finally ends up a good red color in early fall regardless of the weather. Two of its cultivars are outstanding: 'Columnaris', a notably upright form that is common as a street tree in newer U.S. city plantings, and can be spaced as close as 20–25 ft. on the street; and 'Accolade', with semidouble blush pink blooms up to 1½in. wide from deeper pink buds,

Trunks and branches of
Prunus maackii, valued
for its winter color.
Photo by Brian Mulligan.

A tree of Sargent's
cherry in full bloom at
the end of April in
Seattle. Photo by E. F.
Marten, University of
Washington, Campus
Studios.

the calyx bronze colored. This is a very beautiful cherry raised by Knap Hill Nursery, from Arnold Arboretum seeds. It is a hybrid of uncertain parentage, probably *P. sargentii* × *P. subhirtélla*. Wide spreading with perhaps a 40–50 foot span, this newer cherry is performing well in the Northwest.

P. serótina (III), the Black Cherry or Rum cherry from the eastern half of North America is one of the best cherries, its 80–100 ft. height also making it the largest. The oval-lanceolate dark green leaves look surprisingly like those of the Portugal Laurel (*P. lusitánica*), but this deciduous tree finally turns a pleasing yellow. When the flowers bear fruits, the pits can make a high-quality flavoring for rum and brandy. Its timber is valued for cabinetry. It will grow in any soils and frequently reseeds.

P. sérrula (V), Birchbark Cherry from western China, to 30–50 feet, is a bushy tree with small white flowers, known for its beautiful polished red-mahogany bark that finally peels off in older trees, a most unique and beautiful feature. The blooms are disappointingly small, borne with the narrow leaves in late April, but the fall color is rather good, and the winter effect is very good, the showy bark being most attractive at that time of year.

The large-flowered Japanese cherries are either selections from *P. serruláta* (V–VI) itself or hybrids between *P. serruláta* and other species. They are susceptible to serious virus diseases that can kill the trees; treatments keep coming but as this is written there are no dependable cures. Thus we suggest that these trees be used sparingly until a cure becomes available. We quote John Grant from the first edition of this volume.

Descriptions and pictures of individual flowers of these hybrids fail to convey the effect of their flowers massed on mature specimens. We are concerned here only with the effect of the whole tree, and not with the details of the individual blooms. Descriptions of individual blooms or even examining them at first hand may prove deceiving. Almost all are exquisite form and colour, but in many hybrids they are so massed on the branch as to lose all grace and charm.

The hybrid cherries carry the flowers on stalks of varying length. Those with short flower stalks, and blooms clustered around the stem, appear badly crowded. Those with flowers that hang on long stems in loose clusters below the branches are far more beautiful. The same criticism may be leveled at many of these cherries as at the 'vulgar mops' of coarse chrysanthemums. The Japanese, with all their feeling for attenuated refinement seen in exquisite economy of line, and delicacy of form, go to the opposite extreme when they hybridize. They produce enormous chrysanthemums, and tree peonies, huge iris, and clumsy, massive cherries. Their hybrids, in the words of Reginald Arkell "just keeps on getting bigger and bigger and takes no sort of account of their figure".... Although rated by many enthusiasts as of outstanding garden value, they will be shunned by the gardener to whom good proportion and refinement of form are a vital consideration.

These "shunned hybrids" include many varieties which can be found in good nurseries, and some enthusiasts will disagree with this dismissal of them. Our *P. serrulata* list of recommended sorts includes the nine that follow:

'Amanogawa', a columnar-formed tree like a miniature Lombardy Poplar done in soft pink, semidouble flowers in early to mid-May; distinctive accent form.

'Fugenzo' ('James Veitch', 'Kofugen'), rather wide-spreading, very double, pale pink fading to light pink, blooms with 'Sekiyama', which it resembles.

'Ojochin', a vigorous tree with stiff habit, young leaves bronzy green, leathery when mature; single or slightly double flowers, 1¼ in. wide, pink in bud, white flushed with pink when expanded; April and early May. 'Ojochin' has its flowers on 4–5 in. stems all around the branches, and they "develop a spreading deep pink eye as they fade so that they are especially attractive just before they drop.... It forms a broad 35–40 ft. specimen with irregularly upward-sweeping boughs. Here is a large fast growing showy tree which yet has no suggestions of coarseness or vulgarity" (John Grant).

'Sekiyama' ('Kwanzan') is the hardiest and most popular of the double Oriental cherries, a vase-shaped tree, with 2½-in. deep pink flowers over an early showing of coppery new foliage. Because they are on long dangling stems and are carried together with the bronzy new foliage, this mid-April bloomer appears deeper pink than it is. This is the cherry that covers the streets and lawns with "pink snow" when its petals fall.

'Shirofugen' ('White Goddess'), has double pale pink flowers up to 2½ in. in diameter which quickly fade white as they mature. The young flowers are elegant against the already developed deep bronze foliage, which appeals to those who object to the heaviness in flowering of the other double cherries; it also has a much longer season than most and is one of the latest to bloom. The initially bronzy foliage quickly turns to green for summer. 'Shirofugen' is somewhat taller than 'Shirotae' and less spreading.

'Shirotae' ('Mt. Fuji', 'Kojima') is considered by many the finest of the semidouble white Oriental cherries—the name means "snow white." The fragrant flowers are 2½ in. in diameter, and ruffled. This cultivar is very popular and tends to be quite horizontal in habit, often staying under 15 ft. tall with a 40-ft. spread. It can be in bloom as early as mid-March, and the flowers hang gracefully on long stems in loose clusters. Because of its low branching it is not a good street tree unless the tree lawns are 15–20 feet wide. This variety grows quickly and the snowy flowers are held nicely against the just-opening green leaves. When possible, this is a fine cultivar to set atop a bank with a path below.

'Shogetsu' ('Shimidsu Sakura') is another double cherry to 2 in. across. This has a horizontal form similar to that of 'Shirotae', but here the flowers are pale pink in bud, white when open. The tree grows 15 ft. tall and half again as wide. Grant's description says "daintiest of the doubles, with beautifully arching branches weighed down by loose long-stemmed clusters of delicate pale pink flowers, which are almost over before the green leaves develop." It has a weaker constitution than the others. It blooms late, in mid-May, with 'Shirofugen' and 'Fugenzo'.

'Tai-haku' ('Great White Cherry') is an old Japanese variety from near Kyoto; for some reason it became extinct there, and all trees in gardens are thought to have come from Collingwood Ingram's plant which he found half-dead in a Sussex garden in 1923; the owner had received it in 1900 in a shipment of cherries from Japan. This is a very vigorous tree to 20–25 ft. tall, more in width. The blossoms are pure white, 2½ in. wide, saucer shaped, in mid or late April, contrasting well with the richly colored young leaves; the leaves turn yellow or orange in fall.

Trees of the Japanese cherry, 'Tai-haku', flowering in mid-April in Seattle. Photo by Brian Mulligan.

'Ukon' has pendulous creamy chartreuse blooms in mid-April, giving a soft yellow blossom effect, opening out with the tree's warm bronze new leaves for a very rich combination that is somewhat more restrained than the color combinations of most other Japanese cherries. The medium-sized blooms are semidouble, hanging in loose profusion from the somewhat stiff branches which build up into a broad inverted cone shape.

A small tree of Von Siebold's cherry, *Prunus sieboldii,* in full bloom in Seattle in mid-April. Flowers pink, semi-double. Photo by E. F. Marten, Campus Studios, University of Washington.

P. subhirtélla (V), the Higan or Spring Cherry from Japan, can reach 40 ft. but usually grows to only 25–30 ft. We suggest four cultivars and one hybrid from this species as of especial merit:

'Autumnalis' is a particularly lovely cultivar in the Pacific Northwest, where winters are customarily mild enough for good autumn or winter bloom effect from November onward. John Grant tells it best:

"The autumn flowering cherry has become well known. The Japanese name, 'Jugatzu-sakura', means October flowering cherry. The blooming period depends on the season; the tree may come out with a mass of bloom in late fall and then almost stop and commence blooming again in March and April. In other seasons it sometimes makes less of a show in the early fall, and blooms steadily through a mild winter. Any fully opened flowers are damaged by sharp frosts, but the buds remain unharmed and continue to open whenever a warm spell comes along to lure them. The individual flowers are very daintily formed. They open a soft clear pink flushed deeper on the outside and at the tips of the petals, and lose very little of this colour as they age . . . one of the loveliest and most indispensable of flowering trees for warm sheltered gardens. Its loose branching pattern builds a rather bushy spready tree. It is slow growing but ultimately reaches a height of 20–25 ft. All the subhirtellas, but especially this variety, should be transplanted in late fall."

Many people position this cherry poorly as a street tree or somewhere it cannot be admired close up. This tends to waste the bloom in winter, as the effect is too thin; the tree should be sited near an entryway, outside a window, or where the blooms can be seen at close range, or against a dark-painted wall or evergreen trees.

'Hally Jolivette' is a small tree to an ultimate 15 ft. derived from *P. subhirtella*, developed at Arnold Arboretum near Boston by Professor Karl Sax in 1940. It is fast growing, and very popular as a bonsai subject. The pink-budded 1½ in. flowers open almost white, and not all at once, so it has a longer-than-average period of bloom in March and April. It strikes easily from cuttings.

'Pendula' is the best known of the spring weeping cherries. Its flowers are very early, small and pale pink, appearing before the leaves. Its branches are completely pendulous from the graft union, though unfortunately they are usually grafted on coarse understock, so that the trunks

Prunus subhirtella 'Pendula', showing typical growth habit. Flowering late March to early April. Photo by Brian Mulligan.

ultimately become disproportionally heavy for their crowns; more care in choosing grafting stock would give more pleasing results. As it is this otherwise desirable tree is usually passed by for more graceful weepers. Two clones of 'Pendula' exist—one a mushroom-shaped form, 'Eureka Weeping', and the other, the normal pendulous type. Of the latter there is also a double-flowered form, 'Yae-shidare-higan'.

'Whitcombei' was thought for years to be a hybrid cherry, but now is considered to be a clone of *P. subhirtella*, 'Rosea'. It was found in the Richmond Beach Nursery in Seattle not too many years ago and has quickly made its way into the nursery trade. Flowering at an early age, it comes from deep pink buds to pale pink blooms on a wide-spreading and quick-growing tree that is one of the earliest of all cherries to bloom. It can get tall, but is wide spreading and basically horizontal in form, so would have to be very carefully placed in a wide planting strip if used as a street tree. Unfortunately it is very susceptible to bacterial blight, difficult to control.

P. virginiána 'Shubert' (II) is the sole American chokecherry we list. It was introduced about 1950 by Oscar H. Will Nurseries of Bismarck, ND. Its leaves unfold green, then turn a dark reddish purple in June and remain this color the rest of the season, on a pyramidal 30-ft. tree. Easily grown, the tree is hardy anywhere in the United States and southern Canada. The small white flowers, borne in mid-May, make no great show.

P. × yedoénsis (V) brings this large group of good cherries and chokecherries to a close. The Yoshino Cherry, makes a bushy tree up to 50 ft. or more with single 1-inch blossoms of pale pink, slightly fragrant, in March-early April. This is a large and long-lived cherry. It is the main cherry around the Tidal Basin in Washington D.C. It tends to have the horizontal branching habit common in the genus, and so it is counterproductive to plant the trees too thickly to form "orchards," unless there is truly room to accomplish the desired effect. It is one of the showiest cherries in the world, one which benefits from a dark background since the blooms appear before the leaves. In 1920 the W. B. Clarke & Co. nursery in San Jose, California, introduced a new seedling called 'Akebono', which has had wide distribution and is very popular—the name sometimes translated as 'Daybreak'. It is somewhat deeper in color than the parent, and equally good. Both the Yoshino Cherry and its cultivar 'Akebono' are excedingly free flowering.

THE PLUMS, APRICOTS, ALMONDS, AND PEACHES

This smaller but still very important selection completes this horticulturally important genus. Our street-tree scene would be the poorer with the flowering plums gone—which might have some merit—but there are many useful species included in those which follow.

PRUNUS armeniaca (V), the Apricot, to 30 ft., is well known as a tree fruit and grown commercially in several parts of the Northwest, particularly east of the Cascades. While it can be grown west of the mountains, it is beset here by many problems, so one must consider how badly he wants the fruits. Most people decide they would rather just buy a box of fruit and skip the spraying. For those in warm west-side gardens, particularly in Oregon, apricots may be grown against a wall or barrier facing west or south, with good air circulation. In March they will produce off-white or pinkish blossoms an inch in diameter; and if things go well, a harvest of apricots in July. The variety 'Charles Abraham' has red buds and double deep pink petals, and is grown strictly for its flowers.

The purpleleaf plums form a group variously valued for their foliage color, floral beauty and even fruit, usually in that order. They have been much confused with one another. To help gardeners sort them out, we here account for every kind known in the Northwest.

The original is 'Pissardii' or 'Atropurpurea' (IV) which arose in Persia over 100 years ago. It has white flowers in earliest spring, the whole tree suffused with faintest pink from its buds. Its leaves emerge reddish but darken in the summer. Dark red, roundish plums are 1¼ in. long. The oldest Northwest specimens are nearing 50 ft. tall and are wider, but with regular summer pruning it is easily kept as small as 20 ft.

'Thundercloud' grows just as big and differs in its rich pink flowers, opening about a week later in spring, and has darker leaves. Virtually indistinguishable is 'Krauter's Vesuvius' which is better for drier, hotter sites and is therefore widely used in the Southwest. A third pink flowered dark-leaved one is 'Nigra' which is almost never sold in the U.S. but is common in B.C. nurseries.

Of the hybrids, most common is 'Blireiana' (V) with intense pink, double, fragrant flowers. It is very small, densely congested, with a burly little trunk. Mature height is usually 8–15 ft. Its summer foliage is a spotty mixture of red, bronze and green. Less dense, and larger growing (to 20 ft. tall and wide), with pale pink double flowers, is 'Moseri' which has been sold as "Prunus Pissardii Veitchii" and "Light Pink Blireiana." Both these hybrids almost never set fruit.

Three hybrids are useful as fruitful ornamental plums. 'Hollywood' has large white flowers, fragrant, giving a very full effect because on many blossoms extra petals are present. Its plums are roundish, red-skinned and fleshed and ripen late June to mid July. It can grow 40 ft. tall. 'Spencer Hollywood' makes a more useful garden tree because it is a natural dwarf with a compact head of dark, glossy foliage, the leaves both smaller and deper colored than those of 'Hollywood'. Its fragrant pinkish flowers give a good display. Very large red plums ripen from late July into August. 'Trailblazer' (often sold as 'Hollywood') has much smaller, pink-tinged flowers and egg-shaped plums, red-skinned with flesh the color of pink lemonade, ripening in August. It is usually less than 20 ft. tall. Both have relatively large, glossy leaves with much green in them, yet still a purplish dominance.

The only other cultivar much touted for its valuable fruit is 'Allred'—a 'Pissardii' seedling chiefly grown in California. A stiff, vigorous grower, its white flowers are followed by weakly purplish foliage and an abundance of red plums.

'Newport' is the hardiest purpleleaf plum tree. It is a hybrid from Minnesota and is the last to bloom in spring. Flowers on unpruned specimens make a poor display because of their paltry size and dull color. But the leaf color and branching habit are very good. It grows wider than tall and is almost never seen over 20 ft. in height. Winter pruning ruins its form (this is true of all *Prunus*) but makes it produce better flower shows, yet even then it is not as attractive as the preceding kinds.

Even less valuable as a flowering tree is the original 1907 'Vesuvius' of Luther Burbank. Unfortunately, this extremely distinctive tree has mostly been mixed up with the 1957 'Krauter's Vesuvius' which has now become so familiar that nurserymen are dropping Carl Krauter's name from it. Anyway, the Burbank tree is scarcely worth growing, at least as a flowering tree, because its pure white flowers are borne in miserly scantiness. The leaves are long, narrow and give a peachtree-like aspect. It is a natural dwarf and has a crown shape matched by none of its peers, a flaring, broad, inverted cone. It has been sold as 'Stribling Thundercloud'.

All the foregoing have been tried in Northwest gardens. A newcomer here, known in California for over 20 years, is a seedling of 'Krauter's Vesuvius' named 'Purple Pony' which is said to be a natural dwarf, absolutely fruitless, with pale pink flowers. From Oregon are two other new selections: 'Mt. St. Helens' (an improved sport of 'Newport') and 'Big Cis' (a tree version of the bush 'Cistena').

The edible plums can also be considered as garden subjects, provided one is aware that an extensive pruning and spraying program may be necessary to make them bear well. Two types are commonly grown, the Japanese plums, derived from *P. salicína,* and European plums, derived from *P. doméstica.* Both have white blossoms, not at all spectacular, and reach a height of 20–25 ft. Plums are not particular about conditions, but naturally performance is best in good, well-drained soil. Many varieties of both types are available in nurseries; consult your Cooperative Extension to find out which ones are recommended for your area. *P.d.* ssp. *insitítia,* the Damson, is occasionally grown for its small, tart, blue-black fruits which make good jam and jelly. Unlike the peaches and apricots, plums appear to have produced no ornamental flowering forms.

P. dúlcis (P. amýgdalus) (VI), is the Almond from western Asia and northern Africa. It is a fine tree for its flowers and its nutlike fruits, but production of the latter is not dependable except in the warmest spots in western Oregon because of its vulnerability to spring frosts. For this reason it needs deep, well-drained light soil in as sheltered a location as can be given. It flowers on the new wood of the previous year's growth and should be heavily pruned each year so as to produce a maximum of new growth (many newer selections will not carry on from year to year without this pruning). This 25-ft. tree flowers very early, with pale pink to white blossoms. Two varieties are needed for cross-pollination.

P. múme (VI), is the Japanese Apricot from China and Japan, an exquisitely fragrant early-flowering tree that has yet to become popular here. To quote from John Grant:

> The Japanese hold a festival to honour it in February, and poetry of both Japan and China abounds in descriptions of its beauty. It is the "plum blossom" of Oriental art, featured flowering among snow-clad landscapes—which it occasionally does even in our climate. The modern Chinese author, Lin Yu Tang, writes "The plum tree is enjoyed partly for its romantic manner in its branches, and partly for the fragrance in its flowers . . . like the orchid flower, it typifies the idea of charm in seclusion." The 'plum' with its delicate blossoms braving the winter snows, is taken to be a symbol of purity. Perhaps one reason *P. mume* has been so little known in gardens is the fact that it does not thrive either in England or in the eastern United States and, consequently, has never been praised in any of the widely read horticultural literature of those regions. Added to this is the fact that, in this climate at least, it requires so much care in the way of summer pruning to attain its full beauty both of form and of blossom. If its pruning requirements are not understood, it quickly degenerates into a meaningless twiggy bush and its potential tree character is completely lost.

It needs light, well-drained soil in a warm, sheltered position, and it should be given little or no water after mid-July. One of the most desirable of all trees in coastal areas or favorable locations inland, it should not be planted where spring frosts are severe. *P. mume* blooms from January to April, depending on the individual variety and the season. The flowers, both single and double, range in color from white through pink to crimson. The best forms last in bloom for fully a month, sometimes longer, and they are not difficult to force a few weeks early indoors. The San Jose Nursery of W. B. Clarke raised and introduced a number of new clones before World War II, including the following: 'Dawn', double pink; 'Peggy Clarke', deep rose petals and red calyx; and 'Rosemary Clarke', double white with red calyx. John Grant's advice not to buy a new cultivar until you had a chance to see the parent plant in bloom is still good, even if frustrating. This group of plants is a useful one that has yet to catch on in the Northwest.

P. pérsica (V) is the Peach from China, either the fruiting or the flowering type, though the newer flowering sorts have originated in several places. The fruiting peaches we shall pass by but will make mention of the flowering sorts, which can come in white, pink, or red, single or double, and in upright or weeping habit. The trees are generally only marginally showy unless one works hard at keeping pests and diseases away from them; they do make showy bonsai. Secondly, to assure really nice flowering branches for the following season (flowers and fruit are on new wood only), it is necessary to prune the tree drastically after flowering. This produces fine bloom but a less-attractive landscape specimen. Thus flowering peaches might well be grown somewhere in the border as shrubs or espaliered on a wall or fence.

PTEROCÁRYA fraxinifólia (V), the Caucasian Wingnut, native from the Caucasus to northern Iran, is capable of reaching 90 ft. but usually grows no more than 60. It is similar in overall appearance to black walnut, but without the big nuts; instead it has pendulous wingnuts ¾ in. across on a 12–20 in. spike. This is a big, bold-looking tree, almost subtropical in its aspect; certainly it could be used more as a park tree but it may also have some street-tree future. Seattle has a planting of it on 24th Avenue Northwest in Ballard.

PTEROSTÝRAX híspida (IV), the Fragrant Epaulette Tree from Japan, can achieve 45 ft. in height with an open head of small, slender branches. It blooms with fragrant white flowers in June, after the leaves develop, in pendent panicles up to 9 in. long, showy and distinct, the extra long stamens giving a fringed effect. It needs a warm site to flower well. The foliage is simple and alternate, medium-coarse texture, and pest free. It appears to be quite resistant to city stresses, but is rare in nurseries. It prefers loam, but is tolerant of clay or sandy soil, and is showiest if kept as a specimen with branches low to the ground. This plant is also decorative in the fruiting stage, in October.

PÝRUS. These are the pears, and in recent years cultivars of *P. calleryána* (IV), have been increasingly planted, though the species itself, from China, is rarely seen. They are excellent landscape trees where fire blight is not a problem; in areas where it is serious they must be sprayed. 'Bradford', the Bradford Callery Pear, grows to about 30 ft. or more, very compact in habit, looking as if someone had sheared it. It is narrowly upright when young, then expands to a fat teardrop shape, stopping just below most utility lines. Spring blossoms are off-white, with a fairly strong visual effect, but with less than ideal scent. Summer foliage is bright green and waxy-appearing, handsome, turning orange or red in fall. Most people like the tree's appearance, which is more formal than most; it is also pest free. Similar to the above cultivar but generally superior in the Northwest is 'Chanticleer', which has more frost resistance in its flowers and better autumn color, sometimes as bright as Vine Maple, *Acer circinatum.* 'Autumn Blaze' is a good-looking new selection from Oregon State

Inflorescences and foliage of the Japanese Epaulette tree, *Pterostyrax hispida*. Photo by William Eng, Campus Studios, University of Washington.

University by Dr. Mel Westwood, notable for its red-purple fall color.

P. salicifólia (IV), is the Willowleaf Pear, native from the Caucasus to Turkey and Iran. 'Pendula' is the form usually seen in cultivation. It is notably silvery gray in its narrow foliage, on a small tree to ultimately 20–25 ft. Where fire blight is a problem this tree should be avoided because it is quite susceptible. As an ornamental tree it is showy, with slender branches which appear to cascade down out of the crown, with a show of mid-May white flowers; the fruit which follows is small, as in the previous species, and of no value, but the habit of the tree is attractive. It is difficult to find anywhere in North American and will have to be sought out from specialty growers, plant sales, etc. There is a tree of the type in Washington Park Arboretun in Seattle. *(12 LISTED)*

QUÉRCUS. The oaks are one of the two most valuable genera of large deciduous shade trees, maple (*ACER*) being the other. Most oaks cast light or only moderately dense shade, and their root systems are less harmful than those of most trees of their size. They should be planted in their permanent positions as soon as possible since they form taproots early in life. The objection often made that oaks are too slow growing is largely untrue—many oaks grow more rapidly than most other large trees of garden value. In Arnold Arboretum trials, where oaks, hickories, walnuts, elms and maples were planted at about the same time, the largest of the oaks were taller and had thicker trunks than the other supposedly fast-growing trees, with the Pin Oak, *Q. palustris,* being the fastest. It is true that some species, such as our native *Q. garryana,* and those from south-western U.S. are very slow. Gardeners in this region should seriously consider the need to plant trees appropriate for a permanent effect, rather than quick-growing types such as poplars, willows and elms which have voracious root systems and are short-lived. Most of the over 200 *Quercus* species in the world are unavailable in our nurseries, but the following is a selection of the good ones which are in commerce.

Q. acutíssima (V–VI), the Sawtooth Oak from eastern Asia, is not well known here, but it is an adaptable species on many soils and can take the summer heat. Growing to 50 ft. when mature, it is dense and broadly pyramidal when young, with low branches causing it to flatten out more at maturity. Glossy, bristle-toothed, dark green leaves turn a clear yellow to golden brown in autumn. Like several of the less-common oaks mentioned, this tree may be hard to find in nurseries, but it is showy and easy, so is worth seeking.

Q. cérris (VI), the Turkey Oak from southern Europe and southeast Asia, grows to 120 ft. with a broadly pyramidal outline. One of the faster-growing oaks, its smaller than usual leaves are only 2–4 in. long, variably lobed, sometimes deeply so. This is one of the noblest of oaks, so might be seen more often as a park or boulevard tree. It has no notable autumn color, and is another tree not often seen on the Pacific Coast.

A cut branch of the Turkey oak, *Quercus cerris,* with partially developed acorns in early July. Photo by Campus Studios, University of Washington.

Q. coccínea (IV), the Scarlet Oak from the eastern and central U.S., is a deservedly popular oak to 75 ft. that is quite regularly grown in nurseries though it is a difficult tree to transplant. This illustrates a dilemma that the nursery industry faces: whether to grow the more difficult trees unless there is notable demand, and the answer is usually, "No." But this is a tree for which there is a considerable demand, and quite a few nurseries grow it. The fall color is an excellent red—often bright scarlet—and the crown of the tree is open, unlike the denser crown of the Pin Oak, *Q. palustris.* The lower limbs do not sweep downward so strongly as those of Pin Oak, meaning notably less pruning maintenance over streets and roadways. However, it does not fill in quickly as a young tree, and may look awkward and angular for its first 8–10 years, which does not endear it to those landscape designers who lose interest in a job after 3 or 4 years. It must be carefully transplanted, preferably early in spring, and given more attentive aftercare the first year than most oaks.

Q. garryána (IV) to 90 ft., is a slow-growing western American species with heavy ascending branches and a rounded outline. It usually takes some 25 years to break away from a shrubby growth style, and can easily live to 500 years. A beautiful tree in maturity, it is fussy about summer watering, and so should be underplanted only with some drought-tolerant groundcover—avoid rhododendrons because their summer need for water opposes its drought requirement. Also, this oak, like many in the genus, dislikes any fill placed over its root system, so homeowners and developers need to be careful about adding even a few inches of soil above an existing root system. The round-lobed leaves are a very dark green; autumn color is usually saddle brown, occasionally tinted gold or dull red. Its winter silhouette is ruggedly handsome. David Douglas named the tree for his friend Nicholas Garry of the Hudson's Bay Company, who assisted him in his early journeys in the Northwest.

Q. imbricária (V), is the Shingle Oak from the central U.S. It has simple unlobed 3–6 in. leaves, sometimes with wavy edges, dark green above. This rarely seen tree can grow to 75 ft. in height, changing from a pyramidal shape in youth to a round-topped and open habit with maturity. The foliage turns rich yellow or russet in fall and may hold on through the winter, excellent for sheared hedges. Shingle Oak is more easily transplanted than most oaks, and while it prefers moist, deep, well-drained soils, it is tolerant of drier soils and of city conditions.

Q. kellóggii (VII), the California Black Oak, is one of the red oak group, native down the Pacific Coast from mid-Oregon to California. It makes an open, roundheaded tree to 90 ft., with stout, spreading branches. The lobed leaves give a dense cover, and the tree will succeed in dry, sandy or gravelly soils.

Q. macrocárpa (II), the Bur Oak or Mossycup Oak, can grow to over 100 ft., but usually stops at 70–80 ft. It is another difficult-to-transplant oak that will not be readily encountered in nurseries. Native across North

America from Manitoba to Texas, and east to Nova Scotia and Pennsylvania, it can thrive in sandy soils or rich moist bottomlands, and succeeds well even in dry clay soils. It appears more tolerant of city conditions than most oaks. The lobed leaves, up to 10 in. long and about half as wide, change from a summer dark green to yellow-green, to yellow-brown in autumn. The general texture of the tree is "coarse in all seasons, but majestically so." (Dirr)

Q. palústris (VI), the Pin Oak, grows to 75–100 ft., and this native of the central and mid-eastern United States is a very popular tree. Its lobed leaves are very deeply cut and highly attractive, turning to bright autumn colors, usually pastel pink to orange-gold blends, but ranging to yellow and red as well. The tree is fast growing, averaging 2 ft. yearly for its first 5–7 years; and because it is one of the swamp oaks it has a very shallow root system that is readily transplanted. It is tolerant of a wide variety of stresses, but can become chlorotic when the soil is overly alkaline even though the tree appears to be growing well. It is probably the most widely used American oak for landscaping. Its strong tendency to drooping branches causes it to be a high-maintenance tree, for as each lower branch ring is removed, the one above it droops downward and causes the same problem. The cultivar 'Sovereign' partially solves this dilemma, Its lower limbs do not droop, but it is often plagued with graft incompatibility problems after a few years. Seattle trees of this cultivar that were planted in 1975 are now very showy in the triangle landscape at the intersection of Delridge Way SW and SW Roxbury Street.

Q. phéllos (V), is the Willow Oak from the eastern and southeastern United States. This 60-ft. species is used either as a specimen or as a street tree, having narrow, willowlike, entire leaves 3–5 in. long. It does well in our climate, or at least in maritime parts of it, and is considered easy to transplant because of shallow roots. However, it must be dug and transplanted in spring, as rather high losses can occur if the tree is transplanted in autumn or early winter. The autumn color is yellowish to russet red.

Q. róbur (IV), the English Oak, grows 75–150 feet tall and is a noble tree that can achieve massive proportions. It is less grown here than its pyramidal cultivar 'Fastigiata'. This grows in the narrow form of a Lombardy poplar, and often holds it leaves into or through the winter, the new leaves pushing the old ones off in the spring.

Q. rúbra (Q. boreális) (III), the Red Oak, has large, dense foliage, most often lustrous, and this eastern American species which can reach 75 ft. or more in height is used a great deal in plantings. It transplants easily and grows vigorously—in fact, it is the most rapid growing of all oaks. Red Oak has bright autumn color, usually medium or fairly dark red. It withstands polluted city air and makes a good boulevard tree, as well as being useful for specimens or groves in parks and on large lawns.

Q. shumárdii (V), the Texas Red Oak, or Shumard Oak from the south central U.S., is a superior species growing to 120 ft. tall. It has leaves similar

A superior form of the fastigiate English oak, *Quercus robur* 'Fastigiata'. Photo by William Eng, University of Washington, in early March.

to Red Oak, up to 8 in. long and half as wide, and variable autumn color, mostly scarlet. This handsome tree shapes up to its mature form after about 5 years, more quickly than *Q. rubra*'s 10 years to near maturity. As a Seattle street tree it has done extremely well, a performance echoed in most of the cities across the country where it has been tried. We consider it notably superior to *Q. rubra*, though both are good.

RHÁMNUS *purshiána* (VI), Cascara, is a native tree from whose bark the drug cascara is extracted. The tree can reach 40–50 ft., has no showy bloom, but forms a broad head of shining, rather alderlike leaves which turn yellow in fall. It attracts birds, and is a tree worth preserving in native woodlands, though probably not one to be purposely planted; birds may bring it unbidden.

ROBÍNIA × 'Idaho' (III–IV), Idaho Locust, grows to 40 feet, with pea-like rose-purple blooms in pendulous clusters in early June. This has the darkest flowers of any of the *Robinia* group. It does well on poor, dry soils where better trees often have a tough time, and it has been somewhat used as a street tree in dry parts of the west where borers and leaf miners are not a problem.

R. *pseudoácacia* (III), the Black Locust from the eastern United States, is a 75-ft. tree with pendulous racemes of fragrant, white, pea-like blossoms in early June. Much maligned as a specimen tree, this is a tough survivor in the dry areas east of the Cascades, and worthy as a shade or windbreak tree. Old specimens develop heavy rugged winter silhouettes. This tree transplants easily, withstands poor, lean soils, will grow on dry sandy soils but not wet ones, and is tolerant of alkaline conditions. Bees produce an excellent honey from the abundant blooms. 'Frisia' is a fine golden-leaved cultivar found 50 years ago in an old Dutch nursery. The gold color holds very well through the season, and it is one of the best-colored trees, becoming popular here.

R × *ambígua* (III) 'Decaisneana', the Decaisne Locust, is now considered to be a hybrid between R. *pseudoacacia* and R. *viscósa,* the Clammy Locust from the mountains of North Carolina. This vigorous cultivar with light rose-colored flowers grows to a height of about 40–50 ft. It needs plenty of summer heat to flower well.

SÁLIX. The willows are an important group of ornamental trees, but their use is limited because of their weak and brittle wood. This need not preclude their planting in moist spots and in park settings where there will be little harm if they do break up after a few years. Certainly we have no other weeping trees that look quite like them. They must have been a startling introduction to European gardens 250 years ago. As Wyman has pointed out, we have managed to get our weeping willows thoroughly confused in American nurseries. He says there are actually six distinct willows in nurseries as Babylon Weeping willow, five of which are impostors, worthy though they may be in the right situation.

S. *álba* (II), White Willow, native to Europe and western Asia is not a weeping willow in its pure species form, but is one of the best of the upright willows for landscape use, even though brittle and easily damaged by storms, diseases and insects. It grows to 75 feet. This willow is one of the first trees to leaf out in spring, and after turning bright golden, among the last to lose its leaves in the fall. The silver-leaved form 'Argentea' has made a striking 60–70 ft. tree by the lagoon at the north end of Washington Park Arboretum in Seattle. The cultivar 'Britzensis' has red young stems. This plant needs to be cut back heavily every year to maintain its color. Unpruned it becomes a 40–50 ft. tree of narrow habit. The cultivar 'Tristis' or 'Vitellina Pendula' is a weeping form to 70 ft., but this is not the Weeping Willow most commonly encountered in the United States or Europe. It is a female clone of French origin, dating from 1815. Its branches are deep yellow—Dirr says "almost eggyolk", but shorter and less pendent than in S. × *chrysocóma.* Leaves are shed much earlier in the fall, and it is a smaller and less vigorous tree, to about 70 ft. Its branches fall prey to disease and rot as it ages, but it is nevertheless a good tree on a short-term basis.

S. babylónica (VI). Many catalogs list Babylon Weeping Willow, but the true plant is not often seen. This species has no wild counterpart in Europe or the Middle East and is suspected of having come from China along the ancient trade routes. In spite of this romantic connotation, it is much less hardy than other Weeping Willows. It grows slowly to a height of 30–40 ft., its pendent branchlets are green rather than yellow, and both young branchlets and leaves are pubescent. 'Sacramento' is a male clone; most European clones are female. The various hybrids of this species are now more important horticulturally than their parent. It does appear in its cultivar 'Crispa' ('Annularis'), a curious form from China, with the leaves curled into rings or spirals, more intriguing than beautiful.

S. × blánda (IV), is called Wisconsin Weeping Willow, though it is of German origin, in 1831. It is a female clone, to 40–50 ft., said to be a hybrid between *S. babylonica* and *S. frágilis*. Its branches are gray-green, shorter than those of the Thurlow Weeping Willow; its large branches are brittle. The rather thick leaves, variously described as glossy, dark green or bluish green, fall early.

S. × chrysocóma (III), Golden Weeping Willow, is the name that applies to most of the weeping willows now grown in the United States, in spite of their being regularly advertised as *S. babylonica*. This plant is thought to be a hybrid between *S. alba* 'Tristis' and *S. babylonica,* but its origin is unknown. It is a male clone with yellow catkins, which occasionally produces female flowers. Its thin yellow branches arch over at the top of the tree, the branchlets hanging nearly vertical; the leaves, shiny on the upper surface and whitish below, remain late in the year. It is undoubtedly the most popular of the weepers in spite of its eventual large size—100 ft. high with an equal spread—but it is much better suited to park or lakeside plantings than for the home garden.

S. × elegantíssima (IV) is regarded by European authorities as possibly a synonym of *S. × blanda,* but in the United States this name is applied to the cold-hardy Thurlow Weeping Willow, which is considered to be the best weeping variety for our northern states. It is a 40–50 ft. tree, also with dull green branchlets, longer than those of the Wisconsin Willow.

S. × sepúlcralis (S. × salamónii) (IV), is of somewhat different aspect from any of the preceding—it has erect main branches to 60 ft. and only the branchlets are pendent, giving a silhouette more like that of a weeping birch. It is a female clone, from France before 1864, and is thought to be a hybrid between *S. alba* and *S. babylonica.*

Weeping willows are more useful trees than we make them out to be, but they must be carefully placed in the landscape so they will not fall on buildings or cars or invade sewer drain lines.

Many Northwesterners grow *S. matsúdana* 'Tortuósa' (V), the Dragon's Claw or Corkscrew Willow from north China, an erect, twisted variety to 30 ft. or more, without much interest except when the branches are bare in winter, exposing the wavy, contorted pattern of each branch and twig. Flower arrangers find this tree useful as line material in arrangements, but it is unsuitable as a specimen plant, better relegated to the rear of a shrub border because it suffers from severe fungus dieback and rarely looks completely healthy.

S. matsudána 'Navajo' (IV), 'Globe Navajo Willow' is a wide-spreading roundheaded tree to 60–70 ft., needing less water than many willows. It is grown primarily in the Southwest, and may be useful in eastern Washington and Oregon.

S. pentándra (IV), the Bay Willow, and our related native *S. lasiándra* (IV) are both of value for their large shining leaves.

SÁSSAFRAS álbidum (IV), the Sassafras, is a handsome small tree that can be very difficult to transplant successfully in the Northwest. Because we have been involved in some failures, we offer Michael Dirr's transplanting instructions: "Move balled and burlapped in early spring into moist, loamy, acid, well-drained soil; full sun or light shade; in the wild often found in acid, rocky soil . . . is difficult to transplant from the wild because of the deep tap root and the few spreading, lateral roots; could possibly be container grown and thus many of the transplanting problems would be avoided; if a single trunked tree is desired be sure to remove the suckers (shoots) that develop." Spectacularly bright fall color, yellow, orange, red or purple, varying with the plant, makes this one of the showiest of eastern natives. The tree usually grows to 30–40 ft. in this area, and there are a few trees around; the male and female blossoms are usually, but not always borne on separate trees in April before the leaves. The leaves come in a mixture of shapes on the same tree—simple lanceolate leaves "mitten" leaves with a thumb projection on one side, and tripartite leaves lobed on both sides. Root extracts of this tree yield the sassafras oil used in many flavorings—it is a key ingredient in root beer.

SÓPHORA japónica (IV), 75 ft., is the Japanese Pagoda Tree or Scholar Tree. Native to China and Korea, this tree was often used around Buddhist temples, thus the common names. Touted as a good city tree (which it is), it has not been used extensively in the Northwest, perhaps because, at least in the wetter areas here, this leguminous tree is sensitive to excess winter wet and often fails if sited on other than well-drained spots such as hills or slopes. When it is thriving it is indeed beautiful in July/August because its large clusters of small, fragrant, ivory-white blooms are most decorative. The tree's compound leaves are a fine background for the flowers. Natural dyers will be interested in the properties of the tree's flowers, which yield a good yellow dye. *Sophora* should be tried more often on the drier east side of the Cascades where it is more likely to succeed. Growth rate is up to 2 ft. yearly when young, into a roundheaded tree shaped rather like an ash. The tree may need special care up to the time the trunk reaches 1½–2 in. in diameter. It should be transplanted balled and burlapped and may need special attention to develop a leader on a young tree. The cultivar 'Regent' from Princeton Nurseries is one of the best for shapely, fast growth, and it blooms earlier than most; other clones may not flower until 10–14 years of age.

SÓRBUS. The Mountain Ashes include many very pretty flowering trees, shorter lived as a rule than most landscape trees, but often including kinds with showy autumn fruit clusters at the branch tips in a wider range of color than the common red. In some areas, and this may well be true in our drier east-side areas; they are quite subject to bark borers. There is an impressive collection of Mountain Ashes in the Washington Park Arboretum in Seattle, and in autumn these offer both outstanding fruit and leaf color.

One of the finest species is *S. alnifólia* (IV), Korean Mountain Ash, a tree from Japan, Korea and China, capable of reaching 60 ft., and one of the least subject to borers. It has simple leaves, not compound as in many *Sorbus* species. The tree has three very good features: silvery gray bark that is handsome at all seasons, a spring show of white blooms in May that lasts longer than in most *Sorbus,* and excellent fall color when the deep green leaves turn to yellow, orange or golden brown. These leaves, incidentally, look more like those of a Beech or a Hornbeam than a *Sorbus.* Growing rather quickly as a pyramidal tree, it becomes rounded with age. Few nurseries carry this superior species.

Fruiting branch of *Sorbus koehneana,* one of the white-fruited Chinese mountain ashes. Photo by Brian Mulligan, in late September.

S. ária (V), the Whitebeam, is another species with simple leaves; it is much planted in Europe where it is native, particularly in Britain where it is found on limestone soils. This tree is not much planted in the Pacific Northwest, but its performance in the Washington Park Arboretum in Seattle indicates it might well be used more. Showier of the two forms commonly planted is 'Majestica' which has reached 70 ft. in England; it has larger leaves than the type and large, red fruits which the birds quickly consume. The name Whitebeam refers to the pale whitish green reverse on the leaves, very obvious in spring when the wind blows. Of the often-grown Whitebeam cultivars, perhaps 'Lutescens' is the best known as it is occasionally used on our streets. It is similar to 'Majestica', but with smaller leaves, achieves about 50 ft. as a street tree, and has a paler-than-usual spring color on the leaf reverse, though nowhere approaching yellow, and soon changing to the normal light green. Both *S. aria* cultivars described have showy red fruits in fall.

S. aúcuparia (III), European Mountain Ash or Rowan Tree, which can reach 30–40 ft. in height, has become naturalized through much of the Northwest, even in Alaska. Of many selections available, we list three plus the species itself. To begin with the species, it has compound foliage which colors well in our region, with good yellows, oranges and reds. The flat clusters of small flowers are ivory-white in spring, followed by quantities of showy red fruits that are usually eaten by birds, creating problems on sidewalks or paved areas. It is surprisingly unpopular in the Northwest, perhaps because of its dispersal by birds, yet it is a good tree for the right place, and grows quickly. East of the Cascades, if its borer problems, low on the trunk, can be controlled, it could well be used more. We suggest the following three cultivars:

'Cardinal Royal' (II), a Michigan State University cultivar, vigorous, upright, and symmetrical, good green leaf color, good red fruits, evidently hardier than the species.

'Fastigiata', strongly ascending, upright branches, good red fruits.

'Fructu-luteo' ('Xanthocarpa'), orange-yellow fruits.

S. cashmiriána (IV), Kashmir Mountain Ash is a 20-ft. small tree from the western Himalayas. This species has showy white fruits in loose clusters. Its unusually large, pink-tinted white flowers from pink buds appear in May. Leaves drop early with little coloring, but the fruits remain.

S. forréstii (V), formerly grown as *S. prattii* in the Washington Park Arboretum in Seattle, is a 20-ft. tree from southwest China with white fruits holding late in the fall.

S. hupehénsis (V) from China is a tree to 50 ft. high of upright habit with compound pale green leaves and white or pink fruits which hang on until November/December. Both color forms are worthy trees, easily raised from seed.

S. 'Joseph Rock' is a tree to 40 ft. or more high in cultivation; its parentage is not known for sure and it may actually be a chance seedling from wild-collected seed. It has small, white flowers in late May/early June, followed by showy, amber-yellow fruits, paler on the shaded side, in autumn. Only vegetatively propagated stock can be considered true. Seedlings vary in fruit color. Fall leaf color may be crimson, purple or scarlet, a unique combination with the yellow fruits.

S. vilmorínii (V), the Vilmorin Mountain Ash from western China, is an excellent small tree to 25 ft., with rosy to pink fruits and bronze fall foliage, not generally available, but worth seeking out. It is easily raised from seeds and grows very rapidly.

STEWARTIA monadelpha (VI–VII) from southern Japan and southern Korea is a 30–40 ft. tree with 1–1½ in., cup-shaped white blossoms, smaller than those of the other species of this genus, and flowering later, in late July. Its leaves have mahogany red fall color, and its cinnamon brown bark is an attraction in winter.

S. pseudocaméllia (V), the Japanese Stewartia, can grow to 60 ft., but is more apt to be found at 25–30 ft., or less in our gardens. It prefers conditions with adequate moisture and humus. In late June/early July it produces 3-in. white flowers like white, single camellias. It has handsome leaves that turn orange or red in October. For the woodland garden it has few peers. Var. *koreána* has larger and more open flowers than the type. Both have good gray-to-brown flaking bark.

A tree of *Stewartia pseudocamellia* with two trunks, showing the flaking bark. Photo by Brian Mulligan.

S. serráta (V–VI), from Japan is a 30-ft. tree with about the same size blossoms as the above species, in June. It flowers freely, but is not much known yet in nurseries here.

S. sinénsis (V) is a 20–50 ft. tree from central and eastern China, another good small tree with fragrant white blossoms 1½–2 in. across in June. The bark is very handsome, the flowers moderately so. The outer bark peels away in autumn, exposing fresh tan inner bark.

STÝRAX *japónica* (V), the Japanese Snowbell from Japan, China and Korea, is one of the loveliest small flowering trees for the garden, to about 25–30 ft. The branches are slender, more or less horizontal, bearing great quantities of pendulous, fragrant white flowers like snowdrops, in June. While it much prefers a good soil, this tree will succeed in very much less than ideal situations. The small leaves turn a fine lemon yellow in autumn.

S. obássia (VI), to 30 feet, is the Fragrant Snowbell from Japan, Korea and China, introduced in 1879. The blossoms are borne in terminal 4–6 in. racemes, in June. It has large, ovate leaves, turning yellow in autumn, and is a worthwhile garden subject, though the leaves may partly hide the flowers. Both species root easily from cuttings taken in mid-July.

Leaves and flowers on a young tree of *Styrax obassia* in early June. Photo by Brian Mulligan.

SYRÍNGA reticúlata (III) was formerly called *S. amurensis* var. *japonica*, and is known as the Japanese Tree Lilac, having been introduced from that country in 1876. This fragrant tree or large shrub, 20–30 ft. in height, has cream-colored, somewhat Privet-scented flowers in June, and can be a very striking plant in the landscape, looking notably lilac-like. Flower clusters, which may be as much as 12 in. high and 10 in. wide, are extremely showy. There is no display of fall color, as with other Lilacs, but the winter bark is reddish brown, with prominent horizontal streaks like those on cherry trunks. It is easily propagated from cuttings taken in June.

TÍLIA is the Linden and this genus includes a great many useful trees for Pacific Northwest gardens. *T. americána* 'Redmond' (III), at first considered a selection of *T.* × *euchlóra*, is now thought to be a *T. americana* selection. It was introduced in 1927 by Plumfield Nurseries of Fremont, NE. The tree is densely pyramidal with large leaves that are intermediate between those of *T. americana* and those of *T.* × *euchlora*, more nearly approximating the size of the former. They have the typical Linden heart shape. This is a handsome street tree.

The most commonly planted species is *T. cordáta* (III), the Littleleaf Linden. This durable tree is native to Europe ranging from the Caucasus Mountains and northern Sweden into Britain. It can grow to over 100 ft., but slowly, and it tends to have a compact habit. The greenish white flowers are not showy but are sweetly fragrant. Unfortunately, aphids are often a problem in summer. Good cultivars include the following:

'Glenleven' is a fast-growing Canadian introduction with a straight trunk.

'Greenspire', from Princeton Nurseries, has good dark green foliage and compact habit, is tolerant of difficult sites and is a useful street tree.

'Salem' has upsweeping branches forming a rounded head, 35–50 ft. in height.

T. × *euchlóra* (IV) is the Crimean Linden, growing to 60 ft. with large, bright green leaves and fragrant, whitish blossoms in late July. It is freer of aphids than other Lindens and does not drip honeydew; it does have a slightly drooping branch habit, but is still a useful street tree. It originated in Germany about 1860, possibly as a cross between *T. cordata* and *T. dasystýla*.

T. mongólica (III), Mongolian Linden, is a small, graceful, round-headed tree to 40–50 ft. The flowers, small but numerous, appear in mid-July. The small leaves, deeply cut like those of a birch, are very different from those of other Linden species. This plant has been used as a street tree in Seattle on 25th Northeast, near University Village.

T. platyphýllos (III), the Bigleaf Linden, is native to Europe, growing to 80 ft. or taller, flowering in June before the other species. The leaves are the largest of the European species, rather coarse in texture and up to 5 in. long, giving a bold foliage effect. The habit is rounded to pyramidal in outline. The cultivar 'Orebro' from Denmark is outstanding but still uncommon here; it is a superior street tree in Seattle.

T. tomentósa (IV) is the Silver Linden, native from southeast Europe to western Asia. It grows to an eventual 60–80 ft., with a very regular outline that looks as if it had been clipped. The flowers in midsummer are not showy but are very fragrant. The leaf undersides, which show plainly on windy days, are silvery white. Softly hairy stems distinguish this species from other Lindens. The leaves drop without coloring.

ÚLMUS americána (II), the American Elm, to 120 ft. or more, from central and eastern North America, was probably the most commonly planted tree in the Northeast. It has been decimated by Dutch elm disease—250,000 trees removed in Detroit in 10 years! It is not advisable to plant this species until a resistant variety is developed or until a cure is found. Having said that, let us agree that this is one of our most shapely trees; however, it does require annual maintenance. At this writing, Oregon and all of Washington except the Walla Walla area are still free of the disease, but it is likely to appear on the west side soon. To quote Wyman, "The elms in general, and *Ulmus americana* in particular, are susceptible to more disease and insect troubles than any other tree. Those whose responsibility is to care for ornamental trees have long realized this fact, yet because of its unique habit of growth it has been the most popular shade tree, particularly for street and avenue planting. Now that the Dutch elm disease and phloem necrosis disease seriously threaten most elms, it seems at last advisable to limit the planting of the American Elm." Even so, in some instances a homeowner may still wish to plant this species.

U. glábra 'Camperdownii' is a formal, weeping cultivar of the Scotch Elm or Wych Elm. It is very distinct in its habit, like a living umbrella. The trees come grafted at 8–10 ft. high; if one wants to build it up higher into a more graceful form, he can splint a branch or two upward, using a stout stick or pole and tying them with soft ties. A year or two is enough time for the splinted branch to thicken up so that the ties can be removed. Since elm leaf miner can skeletonize the leaves quickly, this tree must be sprayed regularly.

U. parvifólia (V) is the 50-ft. Chinese Elm from eastern Asia, a round-topped and often multitrunked tree. This is a superior Elm, and has good tolerance to Dutch elm disease, though it is not immune. It is autumn blooming, which quickly separates it from the spring-flowering Siberian Elm. It is much more permanent than the latter, which grows very rapidly and splits badly in storms. *U. parvifolia* has smallish, dark green leaves which remain on the tree late into the fall. Autumn leaf color is red in some forms. Many California selections are more or less evergreen; these survive well in the Northwest, but drop their leaves like other Elms. Most beautiful of all, however, is the handsome bark of this Elm, mottled and flaking away in patches; the trees are worth growing for their bark alone.

U. púmila (IV) is the Siberian Elm, a 50-ft. species from eastern

An old specimen of the Camperdown elm in winter, *Ulmus* 'Camperdownii'. Photo by Don Normark.

Siberian and northern China. It is a fast-growing tree and is frequently offered incorrectly in nurseries as "Chinese Elm," which is really very different. It is useful in our drier, colder interior climates where the selection of hardy trees is limited. It is hardier than *U. parvifolia,* but west of the Cascades it should generally be passed by because it does not age well. It is resistant to Dutch elm disease.

ZELKÓVA carpinifólia (VI) is a little-known species from southern Russia and Iran, forming a 75-ft., usually multitrunked tree. It grows slowly and is long lived. The foliage is medium to fine textured, the oval leaves sharply toothed, turning red in the autumn. It has smooth, gray bark like a Beech. It may be a reasonable substitute for Elms. It is called the Elm Zelkova because it is basically Elm shaped, in spite of its many trunks.

Z. serráta (V), the Japanese Zelkova, which grows to 90 ft. is more frequently used and is equally good. It has the classic Elm vase shape, which is accentuated in the cultivar 'Village Green', a fine selection from Princeton Nurseries in New Jersey. It is a very good street tree and should be used more than it is at present. Both species are resistant to Dutch elm disease and insect pests.

CHAPTER VIII

Broad-leaved Evergreen Trees

Although their number is limited, broad-leaved evergreen trees make a notable contribution to the gardens of this region. They increase in number and variety as one goes south, being a more important feature of California gardens than of ours. Some of the broad-leaved evergreens that we treat as shrubs are trees in their native state. These are discussed in the chapter on Broad-leaved Evergreen Shrubs.

Whether a plant is to be trained as a tree or a shrub must be decided early on. If it is to be a tree, everything should be done to encourage a strong leader and to suppress side branches. Further details on this point are discussed under Garden Maintenance. If a broad-leaved evergreen is to be trained as a shrub, it is necessary to curb its arborescent habit from the start, and prune it to encourage a multibranched, well-distributed mass of foliage. All pruning should be done during the season of active growth.

As with other evergreens, these trees are best planted just before they start into active growth in the spring, or while the ground is still warm in early fall. The natives often transplant best as early as the end of September, just after the first autumn rains.

The most familiar example of a broad-leaved evergreen tree is our native Madroña, *ARBÚTUS menzíesii* (VII). This magnificent 75-ft. tree, with its rich red-brown bark and shining green leaves, is not fully appreciated here in its native region. It is usually found growing near salt water on dry bluffs or ridges, almost invariably in poor soil. Only very young seedlings transplant successfully. Since at present there is insufficient demand to justify nurserymen's carrying stock, anyone wishing to grow this plant will need to obtain a collected seedling, not more than 12–15 in. tall. Planted as a young tree in any good, well-drained soil, and not over-watered, it will grow rapidly and develop into a handsome specimen.

The criticism often leveled at Madroñas, which in fact applies to all broad-leaved evergreen trees, is that they drop their leaves during the summer and consequently are untidy. If they are planted in or near a patio

128

or lawn area, this can be very annoying. However, if the tree is surrounded by a shrub planting the shedding of its leaves will scarcely be noticed. Like the dogwood, a mature wild Madroña is likely to suffer if it suddenly becomes part of a garden which is fertilized and watered throughout the summer. Plants which may be used to good advantage under a Madroña include such shrubs as Salal, Manzanita, *Cotoneaster dammeri,* and other low-growing, drought-resistant species. The Madroña, seen from a distance, is not spectacular in bloom, although its flower clusters when examined closely are of exquisite form, texture and color. The pale greenish ivory bells, often fragrant, resemble those of *Pieris japonica,* only of heavier, waxier substance. The fruit which follows turns red in early fall, and remains on the tree during much of the winter, making a colorful display. Although this is one of the world's most picturesquely beautiful trees, it must be admitted that gardeners who value neatness will always find it a trial and an aggravation. There is scarcely a month in the year when it is not dropping something—first flowers and then leaves in the summertime, then berries and bark in the fall, winter and spring.

Arbutus unedo. See Broad-leaved Evergreen Shrubs.

CHRYSOLÉPIS chrysophýlla (VII). The Golden Chinquapin is allied to both the oaks and chestnuts. Formerly placed in *Castanopsis,* it has now been removed to its own genus. Like the Madroña, this broad-leaved evergreen tree thrives in poor, dry soils. Specimen trees in southwest Oregon and northwest California form massive, pyramidal 75-ft. heads, and occasionally reach twice that height. At the northern end of its range near Hood Canal and along hillsides in the lower Columbia River valley the Chinquapin grows as a 20–25 ft. shrub, forming a dense mass of lustrous, deep yellow-green foliage. In either form, it is an excellent, slow-growing plant for a dry, sunny situation. The narrow leaves, 3–6 in. long, are easily identified by the dull yellow fuzz on their under sides. The Chinquapin is especially showy in bloom in the summer, with its soft, fluffy spikes of cream-white flowers. These are followed by prickly burrs half the size of a sweet chestnut, which are quickly harvested by birds or squirrels when ripe. The Chinquapin is all too seldom found in cultivation either as a tree or a shrub, and deserves to be far more widely grown. While still rare in the nursery trade, it is now carried by a few specialists and is best planted out from container stock at a young age. Once established in the garden, it should not be moved since it transplants with great difficulty.

CÓRNUS capitáta (VIII) (*Benthámia fragífera*) from the Himalayas and western China is a handsome evergreen or semi-evergreen dogwood, worthy of a protected spot in favored gardens. It forms a round-headed 30–40 ft. tree. Its habit is something like that of *C. florida,* but its slightly longer and narrower leaves are dull green and minutely hairy, turning bronzy in winter. A well-grown specimen is very beautiful in June/July with its pale sulfur yellow bracts surrounding the true flowers. The flowers

are succeeded by fleshy, red strawberrylike fruits that are equally decorative. It requires a deep, light, well-drained soil enriched with plenty of
leafmold or steer manure, and a protected, sunny site.

EMBÓTHRIUM *coccíneum* (VII–VIII), Fire Bush, is a Southern
Hemisphere evergreen or semideciduous species with slender, glossy
leaves, native to Chile and Argentina. A somewhat gaunt, erect, small tree
to 25–30 ft., often with several trunks, it pays its keep with masses of
brilliant, tubular red flowers in early summer. This display is so striking
that careful thought must be given to locating the plant. Perhaps it is best
seen against a background of dark conifers, which will also serve to protect
it from the chill north winds of winter. It is propagated by seeds or cuttings and also from root suckers.

ERIOBÓTRYA *japónica* (VIII–IX), the Loquat from China and Japan, is a
superb foliage plant with gray-furry stems and strongly veined evergreen
leaves up to 8–9 in. long. It is a small tree or a large shrub, potentially 25 ft.
tall. In our area it needs some protection and benefits from the warmth of a
south-or west-facing wall. The small, fragrant white flowers in panicles
appear in autumn. The ovoid yellow fruits, 1½ in. long, are delicious,
when produced. Grafted plants of known hardiness are preferable to
seedlings. Several named clones are offered in California, but their performance in our area is untested.

EUCALÝPTUS (VIII–IX). These challenging Australian natives can be
successfully grown in the Pacific Northwest if two critical factors are considered. First, choose only the hardiest of the 500 species, and forget about
those from California with the striking foliage and colored flowers.
Second, be prepared to provide some protection for the plant when
young, and choose a site with full exposure to the sun. Young trees, container grown and less than 3 ft. tall, will do best in well-drained, poor, dry
soil. Do not stake, rather allow the rapidly growing trunks to develop their
own support. Bad experience has shown that over the years a cold winter
may be expected to cut them to the ground; good experience has also
shown that most species will recover and send up new shoots, eventually
making strong trees again. The following species have been relatively
successful in the Pacific Northwest.

E. *coccífera,* Tasmanian Snow Gum, may be a 70-ft. tree, or if
repeatedly cut to the ground by cold, a multistemmed shrub. Adult leaves
are slender, gray-green, set on silvery twigs. The clusters of fluffy flowers
are white.

E. *gúnnii,* or Cider Gum, has had the reputation of being the hardiest
of the eucalypts. Perhaps this is so, but plants have been killed to the
ground at regular intervals in Seattle, only to crown-sprout again. Reaching to 60 feet or more, it has a pale cream, flaking bark. The juvenile leaves
are rounded in opposite pairs on the branches, while the adult leaves are
slender, up to 3 in. long.

E. *mitchélliana,* Weeping Sally, showed signs of becoming a suitable tree for us, having survived with minor winter injury for some 10 years, but was lost after two severe winters in a row. Its open habit and gray-brown bark are most attractive; it has the potential of reaching 50 ft.

E. niphóphila, the Snow Gum, related to E. pauciflora, may actually be the species best suited for the cooler areas west of the Cascades—it has appeared to be the hardiest species in tests at the Washington Park Arboretum in Seattle. It is potentially 60 ft. tall with flaking gray-brown bark, silvery twigs, and glossy green, sickle-shaped leaves. Flowers, as in all the above species, are white.

Flowers and foliage of the Australian Snow Gum, *Eucalyptus niphophila*. Photo by William Eng, Campus studios, University of Washington.

E. parvifólia, Small-leaved Gum, is a dwarf among giants, rarely reaching 30 ft. It has slender gray-green leaves and an irregular habit of growth.

E. pauciflóra, Cabbage Gum, is a 60-ft. tree in the wild, but usually smaller in cultivation, often producing several crooked white to gray stems. The leaves are up to 6 in. long, slender and curved, greener than in many eucalypts.

Other species of *Eucalyptus* will surely prove their worth and hardiness in the Northwest in years to come, but only after many trials and failures.

EUCRÝPHIA. While most eucryphias are discussed in the chapter on Broad-leaved Evergreen Shrubs, two hybrids are large enough to be considered trees. E. × intermedia (VIII), appeared in Ireland more than 50 years ago. It is a small evergreen tree with both simple and 3-parted leaves. Four-petaled white flowers about 1–1¼ in. across, their centers filled with a brushlike mass of bright yellow stamens, appear during July and August. A location with full sun, but cool, moist soil suits this species admirably.

E. × *nymansénsis* (VII–VIII), is an elegant plant of erect habit and may be 40 ft. or more in height. Its leaves are of two types, compound and simple, lustrous dark green in color. The 2–3 in. wide white flowers have a boss of yellow stamens in the center and open in August. This English hybrid grows well in moist, rich soils, and is a superb companion for rhododendrons. Somewhat tender, it should be given some protection while young.

ILEX. The hollies include about 400 species found in temperate and tropical regions over much of the world, though not in western North America. Many of the hardier species can be grown here and are worthy of a place in Northwest gardens for their varied foliage and especially their ornamental fruits during the winter months. Since male and female flowers are usually produced on different plants, it is necessary to grow trees of both sexes to assure a good crop of fruits.

I. aquifólium (VI) is the common English Holly, although it is native throughout much of Europe and western Asia. It can become a thick pyramidal tree up to 50 ft. in height, but also makes an excellent dense and prickly hedge if properly trimmed and shaped in its early years. Seedlings form taproots in their first years and should therefore be moved annually for two or three years to induce a good root system. Named cultivars must be propagated by means of cuttings taken in October, or if under mist, then in summer as soon as the new shoots are hard enough. Large numbers of these are available commercially, varying in size and form of plant, the sex, and especially shape and coloring of the foliage, occasionally in the fruits.

'Bacciflava' is a yellow-fruited form.

'Angustifolia' and the very similar 'Myrtifolia' have unusually narrow leaves and an erect habit; they are good for hedges.

'Argentea' forms ('Argentea Marginata' is the commonest) have leaves margined with white; they are usually female and particularly attractive in winter.

'Aurea Medio-picta' and 'Golden Queen' are both yellow variegated, the former with a central blotch, the latter edged with gold; it is also female.

'Ferox' is distinguished by having spines on the surface as well as the edges of the leaves; there are both green and variegated forms of this.

'J. C. van Thol', a Dutch variety, possesses less glossy leaves, less spiny than usual, but plentiful bright red fruits annually.

I. × *altaclerénsis* (VII), is an early 19th century hybrid between *I. aquifolium* and the Madeiran Holly, *I. perado*. Because of its parentage, this group is less hardy than the common holly, but nevertheless contains some very ornamental varieties which can be grown in our region.

'Camelliifolia' is one of the best known and most easily recognized because of its large, glossy green, almost spineless leaves; this is a female form and bears good-sized red fruits.

'Hendersonii' is another female form, but with duller green foliage and usually fewer fruits.

'Hodginsii', named for an Irish nurseryman who raised it, is a male plant with large leaves 3–4 in. long, and purplish young wood.

'Golden King' is a bud sport from 'Hendersonii', raised in Scotland in the 1870s; the leaves are margined with golden yellow.

'Wilsonii' is another female form with leaves even larger than the others, of a rather glossy green and sometimes spineless.

These all make large trees, up to 40 ft. in height or more.

I. intégra (VII) is a handsome small tree from Japan and Korea which grows slowly to 30 ft. Its leaves—entirely spineless and 1½–4 in. long—are glossy green. Its fruits, carried close to the stems, are red and nearly ½ in. in diameter. Both sexes should be planted to secure fruits. Though possibly tender when young, this species is entirely hardy later on.

I. latifólia (VII) from Japan is an unusual and striking holly, its foliage resembling that of English Laurel. It is slow growing, with a loose habit of growth, and is said to reach a height of 50–60 ft. Professor Sargent declared it to be the "handsomest broad-leaved evergreen of Japan." The dull, lacquer red berries clustered along the branches are attractive, coloring in autumn and remaining on the plant a long time. It should be given a sheltered situation with partial or even deep shade, rich light soil, and moderate moisture.

I. opáca (V), American Holly, is the North American counterpart of English Holly. Much hardier, it may be had in a wide variety of cultivars including yellow-berried forms. Trees may reach 50 ft. or more in time, but this species is rarely grown in gardens here, since most gardeners consider it inferior to *I. aquifolium.* Its foliage is not as glossy green, and its fruits are not borne in such large clusters as in English Holly. However, where that species is too tender, then one might try *I. opaca.*

LIGÚSTRUM lúcidum (VII), Glossy Privet from China, has become a favorite small, broad-leaved tree for use in street and container plantings, and is considered the best of the evergreen privets. Reaching 30 ft. tall, it forms an oval-headed specimen with glossy, dark green, ovate leaves. Its large clusters of tiny white flowers in August are very effective, and show off well against the green foliage. Small blue-black fruits are carried through the winter. Although it will grow well in partial shade, it does even better in the open.

LITHOCÁRPUS densiflórus (VII), Tanbark Oak. This evergreen native of Oregon and California is similar to *Chrysolepis chrysophylla* in many respects, and is an equally desirable small tree. It develops a rather broad crown to 25–30 ft. in the garden, though it may be 70 ft. or more in the wild.

A flowering branch of
the Sweet Bay tree,
Laurus nobilis. Photo by
Brian Mulligan in late
April.

Fruiting branches of the
Chinese *Lithocarpus
henryi,* with unripe fruits.
Photo by Brian Mulligan,
in early October.

It has pale, woolly young shoots and stiff, leathery, heavily veined leaves, which are downy early in the season, becoming glabrous later. Male catkins are erect and creamy white in bloom; acorns are about 1 in. long, with reflexed scales on the caps. Tanbark Oak is shade tolerant in the wild and can be planted in either sun or partial shade in the garden, where it gradually makes a handsome specimen tree. Some forms in the wild are never more than shrubby, to 10 ft. or less.

MAGNÓLIA grandiflóra (VII), Bull Bay or Evergreen Magnolia. While this magnolia is usually treelike it may also be seen in the Pacific Northwest as a large shrub. Capable of reaching over 100 ft. in its native southeastern United States, it is slow growing and does best against a warm wall in the Puget Sound area. Further south where the summers are warmer it may be used as a specimen tree in the open. Its very large, glossy green leaves, often with a rich brown indumentum, and its intensely fragrant, waxy white flowers, 8–10 in. across, blooming from late May through September, make this an outstanding tree for the large garden. It should be planted in rich, well-drained soil, in full sun with protection from cold north winds. A number of cultivars are available, 'Glen St. Mary' has the reputation of flowering at a small size; 'Goliath' has extra-large flowers; 'Victoria' is a local introduction from Vancouver Island, B. C., and is perhaps the hardiest selection.

Even hardier and very similar to *M. grandiflora* is × *M. freemánii* (VII), a hybrid between the Bull Bay and *M. virginiana*. It is somewhat less treelike, but has the same large, fragrant flowers and shining foliage. It is not readily available from nurseries, but is worth searching for if one has a cold garden.

M. virginiána (V–VI), the Swamp Bay, while normally semideciduous, also includes evergreen selections from southern sources. A much smaller tree in all its parts than the Bull Bay, 30 ft. or less in height, it has gray-green foliage and 2–3 in. white flowers which appear for a long period in late summer. As its common name suggests it will grow in moist sites where few other evergreen trees would be happy.

NOTHOFÁGUS dómbeyi (VII) is a newcomer to the Pacific Northwest, yet has proved to be highly successful in Washington Park Arboretum in Seattle. A Southern Beech from Chile and Argentina, it will become a large tree, over 60 ft. tall, wide spreading at the base. Its very small leaves are dark green above and paler beneath, giving the tree a lacy texture. The flowers and fruits are inconspicuous. Not especially particular about soil conditions, it will grow in partial to nearly full shade, but develops a denser habit in sunny locations. Its ultimate size precludes its use in any but very large gardens.

PHOTÍNIA serruláta. See Broad-leaved Evergreen Shrubs.

PRÚNUS lusitánica (VI–VII), Portuguese Laurel from Spain and Portugal, is hardier than the Cherry Laurel, *P. laurocerasus* (VII), which is dealt with in the chapter on Broad-leaved Evergreen Shrubs. It may be

Inflorescences of the
Portugal Laurel, *Prunus
lusitanica,* in early July.
Photo by Brian Mulligan.

either a 10-ft. shrub or a 40–50 ft. tree. Small white flowers in 6–10 in.
racemes are produced at the shoot ends and in the leaf axils in June, often
making a considerable display. However, this plant is grown primarily for
its luxuriant, glossy, very dark green leaves, 5 in. long and 2 in. wide. It
makes a handsome specimen plant on a lawn or in thin woodlands. It is
easily propagated from cuttings or seeds. The white-variegated form,
'Variegata', is less hardy than the green-leaved type.

QUÉRCUS. It is strange that the evergreen oaks are so seldom used as
garden trees in this region. Trials by more venturesome gardeners have
indicated that there are a number of species which will thrive here.
Finding them in nurseries may be harder than growing them, although a
few specialists now stock several types. All need a warm, sheltered spot
and most should have well-drained soil. Among those worth trying here
are the following species:

Q. acúta (VII–VIII) from Japan, which seldom grows more than 30 ft.
tall. Its foliage is dark green, with leathery texture, the leaves up to 5 in.
long.

Q. chrysolépis (VII). California Live Oak, is often shrubby here, but can
become 50–60 ft. tall, spreading and round topped, with glossy, dark green

leaves 3–4 in. long, closely massed on the sturdy, arching branches. They can be either spiny toothed or entire.

Q. hypoleucoídes (VII), from southwestern U.S.A. may be shrubby but can become a small tree to 30 ft. Its leaves are narrowly oblong, up to 4 in. long, dark green above and beautifully white beneath, a pleasing foliage contrast.

Q. ílex (VII), Holm Oak, is quite widely used in European gardens as a hedge plant and is similar to *Q. chrysolepis,* but tends to be more treelike, to a possible 90 ft., and has darker green leaves, seldom toothed. It appears to succeed well in Seattle, and has possibilities as a street tree.

Q. myrsinifólia (VII), Chinese Evergreen Oak, has been most successful in this area. A tree, sometimes with several trunks, to 40–50 ft. tall, its graceful, narrow leaves are dark purple when they first appear in the spring. As they mature they become bright green. Given the proper site, warm and somewhat protected, this oak grows relatively rapidly, forming a handsome, upright green column.

Foliage of the evergreen oak, *Quercus myrsinifolia.* Photo by Brian Mulligan.

Q. phillyreoídes (VII) could be included among the broad-leaved evergreen shrubs, except that it may become 30 ft. tall. Its bright green foliage often clothes the plant to the base, giving it a somewhat moundlike outline.

Q. súber (VII–VIII), the Cork Oak of southwestern Europe, is another of the holly-leaved oaks with spiny, dark green foliage. Often with an open, irregular habit, its trunk and larger branches develop the thick, heavy bark

Trunk and limbs of an
old specimen of the
Cork oak, *Quercus suber.*
Photo by Brian Mulligan.

from which commercial cork is harvested. Although it is slow growing, it
may reach 50 ft. in height.

Q. wislizénii (VII) from California has been highly successful in
Washington Park Arboretum in Seattle, where several 50-ft. specimens are
growing. It has an irregular, open, strongly branched habit, and 1–3 in.
dark green leaves which may be entire or toothed on young trees.

TROCHODÉNDRON aralioídes (VII), the Wheel Tree from Japan and
Korea, should be more widely planted in this region since it has proved to
be remarkably hardy. It may be a small 25–30 ft. tree with open whorls of
branches or a large, roundheaded shrub. Its leaves, lanceolate and
leathery, 3–5 in. long are carried in whorls at the ends of the branches.
Dark to yellow-green in spring and summer, they change to red-bronze
during the winter, at least on plants in an exposed situation. The flowers,
while not showy, are interesting. They consist of green rims surrounded
by bright green stamens, appearing like the hub and spokes of a wheel,
and are carried in erect terminal racemes in April/May. Wheel Tree seems

tolerant of a wide range of soils; however, it is happiest planted in a moist site with good drainage. It will grow either in full sun or in nearly full shade, but does best at the edge of a woodland where it receives some protection.

UMBELLULÁRIA califórnica (VII), the Oregon Myrtle or California Laurel may be grown either as a tree or as a very large shrub. It is native in southwestern Oregon and northwestern California, where it forms a massive, densely foliaged tree, often reaching a height of 60–100 ft. with a trunk or trunks 2–3 ft. through. It is slow growing and a specimen 60 ft. in height is likely to be 150–250 years old. Its wood is very hard and close grained and is highly valued for making bowls and other ornamental objects. It is grown principally for its decorative, aromatic foliage and for the pretty clusters of small, creamy white flowers in early spring. The Oregon Myrtle in its native state is often found growing among other large trees. It has looser foliage in the shade, but in full sun it becomes a dense mass with rounded, humped-up form. It is a difficult tree to establish unless transplanted as a tiny seedling. However, it is easily raised from seed, and nursery-grown plants that have been transplanted a time or two are readily moved. When once established, it is easily grown in any rich, moist, well-drained soil in either sun or shade. This species deserves to be better known and far more widely used in garden planting, since it is perfectly hardy in the Puget Sound area.

CHAPTER IX

Broad-leaved Evergreen Shrubs

The broad-leaved evergreen shrubs as a group are more valuable to gardeners in this region than any other single group of plant material. They have not only the fleeting beauty of flower and fruit possessed by most other trees and shrubs, but also the varying patterns, colors and textures of their evergreen foliage are a constant delight throughout the year. This is their valuable contribution to our gardens and in describing them special attention has been paid to these attributes so that any gardener trying to select may have a picture of the size, pattern and color of their foliage, as well as discovering the essentials of their cultural requirements and the mature sizes of individual plants. The ultimate size given in each description should be carefully noted. There are plenty of shrubs of any given size for any given situation so that there is no need to put a shrub that ultimately will reach a height of 20 ft. where one of 4 ft. is required.

Correct pruning is important in the successful cultivation of broad-leaved, evergreen shrubs. In gardens many shrubs suffer from an excess of moisture during the summer which results in rank, straggly growth. Summer pruning is frequently necessary to correct this tendency. Long extension shoots should be pinched back to induce a more bushy type of growth. Shrubs which need this kind of attention include camellias, osmanthus, photinias, stranvaesias and many others. But note the difference between shortening individual shoots and going over the whole plant with a pair of shears and clipping it to a formal outline. Such clipping destroys the natural individuality of the plant, obliterating the irregularities which produce a textured pattern of light and shade, one of the chief beauties of a free-growing shrub. It is sometimes necessary to severely cut back certain shrubs such as camellias and rhododendrons when they have become leggy and straggly through age or overcrowding. Any such drastic pruning should be done in spring as soon as they have started active growth, or immediately following flowering.

With excessive late summer watering many shrubs form fewer bloom buds, so that a naturally floriferous plant may seem to be a shy bloomer. However, the majority of broad-leaved evergreens do demand considerable moisture during April, May and June when they may be flowering and then making new growth. They will ripen their wood and form bloom buds far more satisfactorily if watering is gradually diminished towards the end of summer, in August, and they are then allowed to become as dry as the season permits during September and early October. This the conscientious gardener is loath to do. He restricts the growth of shrubs by not watering them in late spring if the weather is dry, and then weakens them by keeping them growing into early fall, instead of permitting them to ripen the new wood gradually. In the case of shrubs of questionable hardiness such ripening is vital if they are to live through a severe winter.

Broad-leaved, evergreen shrubs should be planted in this region either early in the fall when the soil is still warm, from the last week in September to the first week in November, or just as they start into growth in early spring, from the end of February to early April. Fall planting, if not too late in the season, permits the plants to form new roots before winter sets in and gives them a flying start the following spring.

The best results are obtained by planting young nursery stock, about 3–4 years old from seeds, cuttings, or grafted or budded stock. Since so many plants are now grown continuously in containers it is possible to obtain them in various sizes and of different ages, as required for the site. Larger field-grown specimens should have been regularly root-pruned by some means to ensure the formation of an adequate ball of fibrous roots. However, it has often been observed that young vigorous stock will frequently overtake larger and older specimens set out at the same time and make more shapely plants.

Various methods are used in propagating these shrubs, but chiefly soft or hardwood cuttings for large quantities, and particularly for named individual cultivars. Layering is a useful method for the amateur grower. Consult the chapter on Propagation for details.

SELECTED GENERA AND SPECIES, AND HYBRIDS

ABÉLIA. Most kinds of abelias can be grown in the Pacific Northwest except the tender Mexican *A. floribúnda*. The most common is the hybrid *A. × grandiflóra,* (VI) (*A. chinénsis × A. uniflóra*) raised in an Italian nursery in 1886 and one of the best evergreen shrubs for a sunny location. The rich, coppery red coloring of the young shoots and leaves adds much to the clusters of pale pink flowers which are borne from July to October. The sepals are also colored and remain after the flowers have fallen, thus extending its season of value. It is an excellent shrub to form an evergreen hedge about 5 ft. in height, and once established needs only an annual pruning to keep it to the required height and in shape. This should be done in spring. Any long shoots formed should be pinched at the top to make them branch.

A. *schumánnii,* (VII) native of central China, is less common, at least in our area, and probably not quite as hardy as the former. The young shoots are also tinged purple, the leaves somewhat smaller and less reliably ever-green in colder winters; the flowers are rose pink, distinctly darker than those of *A.* × *grandiflora,* each about 1 in. long, swollen at the base of the tube. In height this species is unlikely to exceed 3 ft.

A. 'Edward Goucher' (VII) is a hybrid between this last and *A.* × *grandiflora.* It was raised at the USDA Station at Glenn Dale, MD, in 1911. In size the plant is about as large as *A.* × *grandiflora,* as are the leaves; the flowers, however, are definitely pink, although lighter in tone than those of *A. schumannii,* and have only two sepals as it does. For its richer color of the flowers it may be preferred to *A.* × *grandiflora.*

ANDROMEDA. For *A. polifolia* see Ground Covers. For *A. japonica* and *A. floribunda* see *PIERIS.*

ARALIA. For *Aralia japonica* see *FATSIA.*

ARBÚTUS unédo, (VII), the Strawberry tree, is indeed a tree in the wild state in its native homes in Ireland and southern Europe, but here is normally seen as a large shrub 12–15 ft. in height. It has a handsome pattern of medium-sized, pointed, dark green serrated leaves, 2–4 in. long and half as wide. The delicate, greenish-ivory, urn-shaped blossoms are carried in pendent clusters not unlike those of some *Pieris* species; they appear in October, at the same time that the fruits of the previous year are ripening into bright red, strawberrylike "berries," each about 1 in. in diameter. While these are edible they are insipid and not of any particular value. The production of these fruits depends at least in part on pollination of the flowers by both bees and moths.

A. *unédo,* like its relatives both in this genus and in *Arctostaphylos,* requires an acid or at least neutral soil to thrive, and a well-drained site in full sun. No summer watering is needed, which makes them ideal for dry banks. Once planted, they should not be disturbed, since they make taproots at an early age; for the same reason they should be planted out of a large container. Several varieties are in cultivation, including 'Compacta', which is well described by its name and will attain 5–6 ft. in height. 'Rubra', introduced by the University of Washington from England in 1964, possesses flowers of a rosy pink hue which are very distinct from the normal type. Its habit and eventual size are likely to be those of the type, but fruits have not yet been observed on it. Forms with red or pink flowers have been known in Europe since the late 18th century.

ARCTOSTÁPHYLOS. In this ericaceous genus, Manzanita, meaning "Little Apples," is a common name for most of the larger species of *Arctostaphylos* such as *A. columbiána* and *A. pátula,* although it has also been given as a specific name to a large Californian shrub or small tree, *A. manzanita*. All of them which can be grown in this region are excellent shrubs for dry, sandy or gravelly banks facing south or west, as is the smaller Kinnikinnick, *A. uva-ursi*, and the hybrid *A.* × *media* in its various forms.

A. columbiána (VII) is a native shrub found wild from southern British Columbia to northern California, and is particularly noticeable on the northern side of the Olympic Peninsula in Washington, forming densely rounded bushes 5–6 ft. high and wide on roadside banks. The shoots are bristly, the leaves oblong-ovate, gray-green and pubescent on both sides; the pale pink to nearly white flowers are produced in tight bunches in April–May and are followed later in the year by brown, mealy "berries." They are not easily transplanted from the wild, even though small plants, because of the long taproot produced at an early stage, and should therefore be propagated by cuttings taken in late summer, and planted in permanent sites when still small.

A. pátula (V–VI) can be seen wild from mid-Oregon southwards, a shrub usually of somewhat smaller size than *A. columbiana*, having tough, elliptical, green leaves and bunches of usually bright pink flowers. As it ascends to a great height into the Siskiyou Mountains it should be one of the hardiest species. *A. canéscens*, (VII) the Hoary Manzanita, is also found in southwest Oregon, and is notable for its very gray, pubescent foliage; the flowers are pale pink. *A. cinérea* (VII) is similar and closely related.

The tall *A. manzaníta* (VII) from northern California develops most attractive brown trunks with age, but needs space to expand, and full sunshine, such as on a bank facing south or west. The flowers appear in early spring, normally in March and April; they may be either pale or deep pink in color.

A. densiflóra (VII–VIII) and *A. stanfordiána*, (VII–VIII) with their various forms and hybrids are medium-sized shrubs growing 3–6 ft. in height and having the typical smooth, brown stems of the race but smaller elliptical leaves and clusters of pale to deep pink flowers. Both these species are native in the northern half of California and have been successfully grown in Seattle for the past 20–25 years. Some of the named cultivars are 'Harmony' and 'H. E. McMinn' (from *A. densiflora*), and 'Fred Oehler', 'Louis Edmunds' and 'Trinity', from *A. stanfordiana*.

For *A. nevadensis, A. nummularia* and *A. uva-ursi* see Groundcovers.

ARDISIA japonica. See Groundcovers.

ARTEMÍSIA. The artemisias, with their strongly fragrant or pungently aromatic foliage are plants for dry and open situations, in sandy, well-drained soils. Most are herbaceous plants, only a few are woody.

A. tridentáta, (V) the well-known native sagebrush of our western states, is seldom seen in local gardens, and certainly prefers the drier side of the Cascade range. However, the felted, gray leaves with their three terminal teeth, are very distinctive, as is the strong scent from the plants following rain. They could well be associated with lavender, rosemary and other shrubby aromatic plants, particularly in or around a garden of herbs. Anticipated height is 4–9 ft., but they can be clipped into shape as desired, like the others mentioned.

AUCÚBA japónica, (VII) the Japanese Laurel, is very well known both in its golden-mottled and plain green forms. It is a valuable, large-leaved shrub for planting in deep shade. In sun the foliage will scorch and lose its attractiveness, but in shade even the golden-mottled form, to which some people object, achieves richness and depth of hue. Aucuba is grown principally for its handsome, glossy foliage, but also for the brilliant red berries that are carried through the winter into the following spring, unless taken by birds. Like some other berry-bearing plants such as hollies and Skimmia, it is dioecious, requiring the presence of both male and female plants to ensure a crop of fruits. This is an important point to remember when buying plants from a nursery. One male plant is sufficient for pollinating several females, if planted in the center of them. This is a vigorous, hardy shrub of easy culture, apparently more or less indifferent to soil conditions so long as it has the necessary shade. It will even grow well under large trees such as horse-chestnuts or lindens, though even then it will appreciate an annual mulch of compost and some fertilizer. The golden-spotted form, 'Variegata', was introduced from Japan to Europe in 1783.

AZÁRA microphýlla, (VII–VIII) native of Chile and adjacent Argentina, is one of the most graceful of the smaller-leaved, evergreen shrubs. The neat, glossy, dark green foliage is carried in loose arching sprays. In addition to this handsome effect, it fills the air with a sweet vanilla fragrance in February from multitudes of tiny yellow flowers, of which the stamens are the most conspicuous part. It is a shrub for partial shade and may be trained to a north wall or fence; in a sheltered location it is quite capable of becoming a small tree 15–20 ft. in height. There is a rare variegated form, not known to be in cultivation in this area, but in California. Any necessary pruning should be done after flowering, in March.

Two other even more ornamental but unfortunately less hardy species are A. lanceolata, (VIII) from the rain-forest area of southern Chile, and A. petioláris, (VIII) also a Chilean native. Both are being grown in California but should be tried here only in gardens near salt water.

BÉRBERIS. This genus includes a large number of both evergreen and deciduous shrubs, often very similar to one another and not easily distinguished. Relatively few, however, are in common cultivation; many of them come from central or western China and were introduced late in the 19th or early in the 20th century by various French missionaries, E. H. Wilson, Forrest, Ward and other later plant explorers of that region. The only species which can be grown here are those immune to wheat rust disease.

B. calliántha (VII) is a comparatively recent introduction, by Kingdon-Ward from southeast Tibet in 1924, which forms a compact bush about 3 ft.

tall with glossy, spiny-margined leaves waxy white beneath. The solitary flowers are the largest of any *Berberis,* being up to 1 in. in diameter, produced at each leaf joint along the branches; the egg-shaped fruits are blue-black and covered with a waxy bloom. Taller, more erect species are *B. juliánae* (V–VI) and *B. sargentiána,* (VI–VII) both excellent for hedges. The former has angled, yellowish young shoots; in the latter they are distinctly reddish and not angled. Two more which can be recommended for forming very dense, compact shrubs 4–6 ft. tall are *B. triacanthophora* (meaning "bearing spines in groups of three"),—also a fine plant for hedges,—and *B. verrúculosa,* (V–VI) forming a shrub 4–5 ft tall, very dense in habit, and with small, dark green, shining leaves spiny on each side; the yellow flowers are often borne singly at each joint, the fruits blue-black.

Besides these Chinese and Tibetan species there are several from South America which have long been grown here, for various purposes. *B. darwínii,* (VII) from Chile, is probably the best known, with its small, hollylike leaves, clusters of bright orange flowers in April, to be followed later by bunches of dark purple fruits, often enjoyed by robins and other birds. It grows into a 6–8 ft. tall shrub, is of easy culture and sound constitution, hardy in all but the most exposed situations, and making a most attractive and useful hedge if so desired. It was discovered by Charles Darwin in 1835, during the voyage of the famous ship *Beagle,* but not introduced until 1849, by William Lobb.

In locations where *B. darwinii* can be injured by colder winters its hybrid *B.* × *stenóphylla* (V–VI) (*B. empetrifólia,* (VI–VII) a small Chilean shrub with very narrow leaves being the other parent) is an admirable though larger and less showy substitute for it. Its slender, whippy branches carry loose sprays of paler yellow flowers, in great quantities. Because of its eventual size and shape, (as much as 8–10 ft. high and wide), it is not as suitable for forming a hedge as *B. darwinii.* A number of different seedlings have been raised from it, of which perhaps 'Gracilis' and 'Corallina Compacta' are the best known. The former is a compact 3–4 ft. shrub with small clusters of orange flowers; the latter is never more than 1 ft. high, with tiny, dark green leaves, bright orange-red flowers and a densely twiggy habit of growth.

Another Chilean species similar to *B. darwinii* in habit and size is *B. linearifólia,* (VI) but very distinct from it in its narrow, entire leaves, up to 1½ in. long, very dark green above and tough in texture. The long-stalked flowers appear in April and are orange to apricot in color; the fruits in September black with a blue bloom. It is distinctly hardier than the former species, coming from a higher elevation in Chile. The hybrid between these two is *B.* × *lologénsis,* (VII) from Lake Lolog in Argentina where it was first discovered by Harold Comber in 1927. It is equally as useful and attractive as the parent species, and intermediate between them in its characters of foliage and flowers.

Any pruning required, mainly to keep them in shape and prevent overcrowding other adjacent plants, should be done immediately after flowering, generally in April or May. Old, neglected shrubs should have the oldest branches removed completely, in order to encourage younger growth from the base.

Since the serious black stem rust disease (*Puccinia graminis*) of wheat and other grains spends part of its life cycle on certain susceptible species of *Berberis* these cannot be grown in such wheat-growing areas as eastern Washington and Oregon and any existing plants must be eradicated. Amongst those already mentioned only *B. empetrifolia* is a susceptible species; others which fall into this category but are not in cultivation here as far as known include *B. glaucocarpa, B. hookeri, B. pruinosa* and *B. veitchii.*

BRUCKENTHALIA. See Heathers.

BÚXUS. Two species of Box are commonly cultivated here, namely *B. sempervírens* from southern Europe, north Africa and western Asia, and *B. microphýlla* from the eastern Asian Countries of Japan, Korea and China. Both are variable in habit and foliage, especially *B. sempervirens* (V–VI) which has about 50 different forms to its name, including the treelike 'Arborescens' which may grow 15–20 ft. in height, narrow leaved and broad leaved, variegated, and the dwarf 'Suffruticosa' frequently used in the past for making low hedges. The best local collection is probably that in the Washington Park Arboretum in Seattle, where more than 40 kinds are being grown.

B. microphýlla, is a compact shrub of some 3 ft. in height with smooth, square stems, (in *B. sempervirens* they are minutely downy) and oblong-elliptic leaves about ¾ in. long; the variety *japónica* (V) is taller, to 6 ft., with roundish-obovate leaves and winged stems. Both are used for various garden purposes in Japan, including hedges and clipped into desired forms. 'Morris Dwarf' and 'Morris Midget' are two dwarf forms from the Morris Arboretum in Philadelphia, growing wider than high and unlikely to exceed 12–15 in. in height in 25 years. Variety *koreána* (IV) will attain about 2–2½ ft., is compact in habit and has downy stems and leaf stalks; it makes a good low hedge but the leaves are apt to turn brown in winter, in colder areas. Variety *sínica* (VI–VII) is a native of central and western China, a shrub up to 10 ft. in height, with downy stems and shining, green obovate or elliptic leaves; it is also used as a garden shrub by the Chinese people. The plant grown as *Buxus harlándii* is a dwarf form of this variety.

All varieties or forms of both species are hardy shrubs of easy culture. They will grow either in sun or shade, but prefer the former to attain their proper habit; they do not like wet situations but have no objections to a calcareous soil, and in the case of *B. sempervirens* certainly prefer it; they will also tolerate regular clipping better than most evergreen shrubs, which is one reason why they have been so much used for hedges. However, they are most handsome when grown as free specimens in an open situation. The inconspicuous yellowish flowers in spring give off a distinct fragrance.

The Anderson collection of *Buxus sempervirens.*

In August and September, 1934, Dr. Edgar S. Anderson, then arborist at the Arnold Arboretum near Boston, MA, visited Jugoslavia with the aim of collecting hardier forms of ivy, yew and box for trial in the eastern U.S.A. He returned with both seeds and cuttings, and in the case of the *Buxus* especially, material collected from the Treska gorge near Skoplje.

Out of these came 'Vardar Valley', a wide-spreading, flat-topped plant which has proved to be hardy in Wisconsin; 'Edgar Anderson', an upright loosely pyramidal form reaching about 6 ft. after 25 years in Seattle; 'Agram', a compact pyramidal type; and 'Nish', of wider form and looser branching habit. These are growing successfully in the Missouri Botanical Garden at St. Louis, MO.

CALLUNA. See Heathers.

CAMÉLLIA. These popular and valuable shrubs of Japanese and Chinese origin include the commercial tea plant, *C. sinénsis,* which can be grown in Seattle and around Puget Sound; *C. japónica* in its now most numerous variations; the fall and early winter blooming *C. sasánqua, C. hiemális* and *C. vernális;* the Chinese *C. reticuláta,* less hardy but most beautiful whether in its wild single form or the semidouble garden selections and hybrids; *C. saluenénsis* from southwest China, the rather tender parent (with *C. japonica*) of the group of hybrids classified under *C. × williamsii,* most valuable new additions to our spring-flowering shrubs. One other species of fairly recent introduction from western China is *C. cuspidáta,* (VII) a shrub reaching some 10 ft. in height, with narrow, long-pointed glossy leaves, and small single white flowers borne in the leaf axils along the shoots. 'Cornish Snow' is an improved hybrid of this with larger flowers; another is 'Spring Festival'.

Camellias as a whole enjoy and appreciate a well-drained soil to which plenty of humus has been added, in the form of compost, leaf-mold or peat, plus an annual mulch of the same kind of material and an application of a well-balanced fertilizer immediately after flowering, when they are making their new growth. If the summer months are dry, they should be watered regularly up to the end of July or early August, then allowed to ripen the new wood and buds for the next spring. As to situation, they prefer some afternoon shade, and do not like to be placed against a west- or south-facing wall or fence; north or east is much better, especially for the *C. sasanqua* kinds, which lend themselves to training more readily. The high shade of native conifers, especially Douglas firs and hemlocks, or of deciduous trees such as oaks, western dogwoods and cherries, seems to suit them. Any necessary pruning to keep the plants in shape or in bounds can be done either immediately after flowering, or else deferred until midsummer when the new growth has been made.

The following is a selection of recommended cultivars of *Camellia japonica* (VII) for our region, arranged by flower color; however, personal preferences may dictate others than those listed and a comprehensive collection such as that at the Washington Park Arboretum in Seattle should be seen at flowering time in order to compare individual plants and their characteristics.

(a) *White.* 'Amabilis' (single); 'Auburn White'; 'Ecclefield'; 'Elegans Champagne'; 'Finlandia'; 'Lily Pons'; 'Nobilissima'; 'Purity'; 'Swan Lake'; *Miniature types.* 'Ginger'; 'Man Size'.

(b) *Pink.* 'Berenice Boddy'; 'Debutante'; 'Drama Girl'; 'Easter Morn'; 'Elegans'; 'Evelyn Poe Pink'; 'Grandiflora Rosea'; 'Giulio Nuccio'; 'Kumasaka'; 'Magnoliaeflora'; 'Marie Bracey'; 'R. L. Wheeler'; *Miniature types.* 'Hopkins Pink'.

(c) *Red.* 'Bob Hope'; 'Clark Hubbs'; 'Daikagura Red'; 'Flame'; 'Glen 40'; 'Grand Prix'; 'Grand Slam'; 'Maroon and Gold'; 'Mathotiana'; 'Monjisu Red'; 'Tom Knudsen'.

(d) *Variegated.* 'Amabel Lansdell'; 'Kickoff'; 'Margaret Davis'; 'Mrs. Lyman Clarke'; 'Nagasaki'; 'Sunset Oaks'; 'Ville de Nantes'; *Miniature types.* 'Fircone Variegated'; 'Tinsie'.

Camellia sasanqua (VII) blooms in fall and early winter, being at its peak in November and early December when such flowers are greatly appreciated. Although a less spectacular shrub than the spring-flowering *C. japonica,* the smaller foliage and more open habit of growth give it an undeniable charm and daintiness. The long shoots are well adapted to training on a wall or fence, where the added protection from the weather is an asset, especially if they can be seen from a window. The varieties of this species range in color from pure white through shades of pink to a bright red, and in form from single to fully double; many of them have a delicate fragrance, lacking in *C. japonica,* with rare exceptions. They need a reasonable amount of light to flower freely, and thus should not be placed in a position heavily overshadowed by dense evergreen trees. If planted against a house wall be sure that they do not suffer from dry roots during the summer months, especially if the wall faces south or west, or if the plant is beneath overhanging eaves. They will flower well even against a north or east wall. Popular and varied forms are:—'Apple Blossom'; 'Briar Rose'; 'Hana jiman'; 'Narumi gata'; 'Tago no tsuki'; 'Yae arare', and 'Yuletide', the brightest red, single. Double or semi-double are 'Bonanza', 'Jean May' and 'Setsugekkwa'.

Other similar camellia plants flowering at this season, being probable old hybrids between *C. japonica* and *C. sasanqua,* and often listed in catalogues under the names *C. hiemalis* (VII) or *C. vernalis,* (VII) are:— 'Chansonette'; 'Dawn'; 'Hiryu', double red; 'Shishigashira', double rose-red; 'Showa no sake', semidouble pink.

Following the introduction of *C. saluenensis* (VIII) from the mountains of southwest China to England about 1920 an entirely new race of hybrids between this species and *C. japonica* was created there, first by Mr. J. C. Williams in Cornwall, after whom they were named *C.* × *williamsii*

(VII–VIII) later by other growers such as Col. Stephenson Clarke. Although *C. saluenensis* is not reliably hardy in our region, unless grown against a wall or otherwise sheltered, the hybrids generally are and can be safely grown in the open, although they prefer to have some shade during summer afternoons. They vary considerably in habit, but are usually quite compact and upright. They begin flowering in February, although 'November Pink' may be earlier, before Christmas, and continue until April. The flowers are single or semidouble, some shade of pink, and are shed as they mature, which is an advantage over some forms of *C. japonica*. Single-flowered kinds are 'St. Ewe', 'J. C. Williams' and 'Mary Christian'; semidouble are 'Brigadoon', 'Donation', 'E. G. Waterhouse', 'Garden Glory' and 'Rose Parade'. The last is a backcross from 'Donation'.

One other handsome species which can be grown here in sheltered situations is *C. reticulata*, (VII–VIII) also a native of Yunnan, southwest China. This had been cultivated and improved over many centuries by the Chinese; it was first introduced to Europe in 1820 and 1824, in forms with large, semidouble, bright rose-red flowers about 6 in. across. The wild form with single flowers about 4 in. across, was not introduced until George Forrest collected it for his English sponsors about the same time as *C. saluenensis*, (1917–1924). The leaves are larger and more deeply veined than those of *C. japonica*, not glossy. The habit of the plant is upright, since in the wild or in warmer climates than ours it can form a small tree up to 30 ft. or more in height. In the Washington Park Arboretum in Seattle it flowers regularly in February, growing there in one of the open beds in the camellia collection. It can be propagated from seeds, sown as soon as ripe, or less easily from cuttings taken when the young wood is becoming firm in early summer. Two named English clones of this are 'Mary Williams' and 'Trewithen Pink'. Among the Chinese varieties introduced here in 1948 to 1950 are 'Buddha', 'Crimson Robe', 'Moutancha', 'Purple Gown' and 'Tali Queen'. Later hybrids derived from this species are 'Dr. Clifford Parks', 'Francie L.', 'Howard Asper', 'Lila Naff' and 'Leonard Messel'.

Also to be noted is the tea plant, *C. sinensis*, (VII) a smaller, more compact plant than the others, capable of forming a low hedge, as has been done in the Drug Plant Garden on the University of Washington campus, Seattle. The small white flowers are borne in the leaf axils in October.

CARPENTÉRIA califórnica (VII) is a beautiful shrub insufficiently grown here. Closely related to the mock oranges (*Philadelphus*), it grows wild only in Fresno County, CA, and consequently should be given the warmest available situation in local gardens, preferably facing south or west, in well-drained soil. Plants, however, have lived for more than 30 years in the open amongst the *Cistus* collection in the Washington Park Arboretum, Seattle, although somewhat burned in colder winters than normal. Their height range here is 6–8 ft. The leaves are narrow, paler beneath, 3–4 in. long; the fragrant, Anemone-like pure white flowers are borne on new growth about midsummer and continue for several

Carpenteria californica
flowering in Seattle, mid
to late June. Photo by
Brian Mulligan.

weeks—one of its good points. Be careful not to overwater it at any time. Since there is some variation when raised from seeds the best forms should be propagated by cuttings taken as soon as the new shoots are firm enough. Pruning should be limited to shortening some of the oldest branches annually.

CASSÍNIA. A small genus of shrubs from the Southern Hemisphere, chiefly found in Australia and New Zealand, belonging to the daisy family, Compositae. The species most frequently seen in cultivation is *C. fulvida*, (VII) growing 3–4 ft. high and very much like one of the larger heathers in appearance. The foliage, however, as well as the twigs, is golden in color; the leaves very small, about ⅓ in. long, but numerous. Flowers are produced at the ends of the branches in July, in heads, inconspicuous. This is hardy in our region, except in unusually severe weather. *C. leptophýlla*, (VII–VIII) also from New Zealand, is much grayer in appearance but otherwise similar.

CEANÓTHUS. Among the evergreen species and hybrids of this showy and useful race of shrubs few are reliably hardy in the Puget Sound area, suffering crippling damage from occasional cold winters. They require both a well-drained soil and full sunshine to thrive with us; a warm bank on sandy soil is desirable, facing south or west, but even there they can suffer in cold periods. Alternatively, against a wall or fence gives considerable protection, but they will then need annual pruning to keep them in order. Probably the hardiest is our native Greasewood, Soapwood or Tobacco Brush, C. *velútinus*, (VI) commonly seen on roadside banks in many parts of the Cascade Mountains in Washington and Oregon and northern California, where it forms rounded masses of glossy foliage sprinkled in summer with sprays of white flowers. However, it is difficult to transplant unless very small seedlings are taken, and not easy to root from cuttings, so is seldom seen in gardens, which is regrettable, considering its value for covering banks. C. *incánus*, (VII) from California, appears to be hardy here also, and likewise produces white flowers, in great quantities on old plants. The stems and foliage are distinctly gray-white, the leaves much smaller than those of C. *velutinus*, and not glossy. C. *gloriósus* (VII) is a valuable groundcover, forming mats only 12–18 in. high; the leaves are small and hollylike, the flowers dark blue. The plant named 'Emily Brown' is a taller selection of this species, not quite so hardy. C. *impréssus* (VII–VIII) is distinguished by its unusually small leaves, markedly veined; 'Puget Blue' is either a seedling of this, or more probably a hybrid with C. *papillósus*, raised at the Washington Park Arboretum in 1945, from California seeds. Other species worth trying here are C. *thyrsiflórus*, (VII–VIII) native in southern Oregon and southwards, and especially its variety *répens*, (VII) an excellent rock garden shrub in a sunny situation since it only grows 2–3 ft. tall, in contrast to the species, which can attain 15–20 ft. The flowers of both are rather a light blue shade. C. *gríseus* (VII–VIII) is closely allied, as is the old hybrid C. × *lobbiánus*. C. *dentátus* (VII–VIII) is another from northern California worth giving a trial. Among more recent hybrids raised in California are 'Julia Phelps', 'Mountain Haze', and 'Sierra Blue'; all must be regarded as speculative in this area, except close to the coast or in protected sites. Pruning should be done immediately after flowering, in all cases, so far as it is necessary.

CERCOCÁRPUS *ledifólius*, (V) the Mountain Mahogany, is a very tough, long-lived shrub from the Rocky Mountains, but also occurring in eastern Washington and Oregon. Growing 8–10 ft. tall, it is chiefly noticeable for its narrow lanceolate leaves, dark green on the upper side, paler and grayish beneath, but particularly for the long-tailed seeds formed in late summer, resembling those of a *Pulsatilla* or some species of *Geum*. The flowers themselves are quite inconspicuous. This shrub is well adapted to cold, dry climates, as is its relative C. *montánus*, (V) with broader, toothed leaves and less showy fruits.

CHAMAEDÁPHNE. A genus possessing only one species, in the family of Ericaceae, namely C. *calyculáta*, (II) circumpolar in its distribution throughout the world but not growing farther south than northern British Columbia on this side of the North American continent. The common name is Leather Leaf. It has a particular preference for bogs, so is a good plant for wet sites, where it may grow up to 3 ft. or so in height and produce racemes of tubular white flowers in April. The variety *nána* is more compact and better suited to garden use as a rule, especially for damp rock gardens.

CHÓISYA ternáta, (VII) the Mexican Orange, is certainly not a true orange, although belonging to the same family, the Rutaceae, as those fruits. However, the vivid yellow-green, aromatic foliage and the fragrant white flowers in April and May do have considerable resemblance to its namesake. The pattern of glossy compound leaves 3–4 in. across, with shadows and highlights, gives a broken texture. Here is another shrub that will grow in any well-drained soil but which frequently suffers from too much water in gardens which often results in large portions of the plant, or even the entire shrub, gradually turning yellow and dying back. The damage most often occurs in spring after a mild winter, so the hardiness of the shrub is not in question. Once a young plant has become established it will need no water at all during the summer and will give no further trouble in any sunny, well-drained location.

CÍSTUS (VII–VIII). The Rock Roses hail from around the Mediterranean, from the Canary Islands, North Africa and Portugal in the west, to Turkey in the east. Some 20 species are known, but few of these are really hardy here. They should be grown in sunny, well-drained locations in sandy soils. Many of them are excellent seaside shrubs and will stand exposure to salt spray, as well as having aromatic foliage, but they must be protected from low temperatures and cold winds in winter. They are best planted out as young plants from pots into permanent sites, and not disturbed thereafter. Almost all species can be grown easily from seeds, but the many hybrids must be propagated from summer cuttings.

C. laurifólius (VI–VII) is by far the hardiest species, growing at quite high elevations both in the Atlas Mountains of Morocco and in Turkey, but it is not the most ornamental, growing into a somewhat leggy shrub about 6 ft. tall with leathery, dark green leaves, 2–3 in. long and producing in June a succession of papery white flowers 2½–3 in. across at the ends of short lateral branches. It has been used successfully for planting along highways in Washington. Regular pruning after flowering will help materially to keep the bushes in shape.

The Gum Cistus, C. ladanífer, (VII–VIII) has longer and narrower leaves sticky to the touch, and with its usually crimson-blotched white flowers is a more attractive though less hardy shrub than C. laurifolius. In this the flowers are produced singly on the branches, but in the hybrid between these two species, C. × cýprius, several are carried on each branch and have the red blotch of C. ladanifer. It is also intermediate in hardiness between the two parents.

Another 6 ft. species is C. populifólius, with long-stalked, heart-shaped leaves up to 3 in. long and producing in June clusters of white flowers about 2 in. across. Smaller white-flowered species are C. monspeliénsis, with narrow, stalkless leaves and sprays of white flowers, and C. salviifólius, attaining about 2 ft. in height, the leaves smaller and more ovate in shape than the last, the flowers again white, often solitary on their stalks. This is a good species for the front of a border or planting. There are also several species with rose-pink to magenta-colored flowers, possessing soft gray-green foliage which acts as a foil to the somewhat harsh color. The best of these are *C. álbidus, C. críspus,* and the commonest in cultivation, *C. créticus (C. villósus).* These are all of approximately the same degree of hardiness (VII), but can be injured or even killed by prolonged cold weather.

Two hybrids of merit with paler pink flowers are 'Silver Pink' (*C. laurifolius × C. creticus*), raised in England about 1916, and 'Doris Hibberson', from a garden in Victoria, British Columbia, in the 1940s, or perhaps earlier. Both attain about 3 ft. in height, and must be propagated by cuttings. A larger hybrid with much brighter rose-purple 3 in. flowers with a dark red blotch at the base of the petals is *C. × purpúreus* (VII–VIII) (*C. ladanifer × C. creticus*); regrettably its parentage renders it less tolerant of cold winters and it is more successful in California than around Puget Sound. Height about 4 ft.

CLÉYERA. (VII–VIII) *C. japónica* is a shrub reaching 5–6 ft. in the Seattle area, having broadly ovate-oblong leathery leaves arranged alternately on the stems, and small, yellowish white, fragrant flowers produced in summer in the leaf axils of the previous year's growths. Native to Japan, but with other forms found in China and along the Himalaya range to Nepal. The fruits are first red, then finally black, quite small.

CORÓKIA (VII–VIII). *C. cotoneáster* is the hardiest member of a small genus of shrubs native to New Zealand, but even so is liable to having branches killed in severe winters, so a sheltered situation is advisable. The branches are extraordinarily thin and wiry, often twisted together; the leaves small, about ½ in. long, and spoon-shaped. The flowers are bright yellow, also small, five-petaled; the fruits, if produced, like little red peas. Altogether a botanical curiosity, belonging to the Dogwood family (Cornaceae). Height usually 5–6 ft.

COTONEÁSTER (V–VII). A large and important genus of shrubs centered, like *Rhododendron,* in western China and the eastern Himalaya, but with outliers in Europe and North Africa. Including varieties and hybrids some 50 different kinds are in cultivation; their hardiness varies according to their place and climate of origin, but most are normally hardy in the Pacific Northwest. In one section of the genus the petals are white and spreading (*Chaenopétalum*); among these are *C. microphýllus, C. salicifólius* and *C. lácteus;* in the other (*Cotoneáster,* or *Orthopétalum*) they are upright and often pink or even reddish. Here are *C. dielsiánus,* and *C. franchétii,* which are only semi-evergreen in mild winters around Puget Sound. Bees are much attracted to them when flowering.

Amongst the taller species are *C. henryánus* (VII) and its near relative, *C. salicifólius,* (VII) both natives of China and introduced by E. H. Wilson early in this century. Their leaves are leathery, dark green, lanceolate, wrinkled; the flowers are borne in close clusters in June, to be succeeded in autumn by bunches of bright red fruits packed along the branches. Both species can be expected to reach 12–15 ft. in height and 10–12 ft. in width, so they need room to develop. C. lácteus (C. párneyi) (VII–VIII) is not quite as tall or wide as a rule; the leaves are shorter and broader, persistently downy beneath. The fruits which are late in coloring and not at their peak until December, are valuable at that season.

Of medium size are C. dielsiánus (V–VI) and C. franchétii, (VI–VII) both Chinese natives, though the latter extends into Burma and eastern Tibet. They commonly grow 6–8 ft. tall, have small, ovate gray-green leaves borne on branches arranged in fishbone pattern, inconspicuus white or pale pink flowers in summer, and quantities of usually orange-red fruits in September–October. C. franchetii var. sterniánus (VII) is superior to the type and holds its fruits later. Another medium-sized species is C. conspícuous, (VI–VII) discovered by Kingdon-Ward along the Tsangpo river in south-eastern Tibet in 1925. This is closely related to C. microphyllus, having like it white flowers with spreading petals; both flowers and scarlet fruits are produced in great profusion if the plants are grown in full sun. Both dwarf and tall forms of this species are known. The leaves are small and glabrous.

Among low-growing or nearly prostrate species are C. microphýllus, (VII) native from the Himalaya into western China, well known for its small, very dark green, shining leaves, woolly beneath, and solitary white flowers and masses of bright red fruits. It is excellent for covering rocks or low walls. Variety thymifólius (V) has narrower leaves rolled under along their edges. C. congéstus (VI) is a closely related high alpine species from the Himalaya, of very compact habit with leaves not hairy beneath. C. dámmeri (V–VI), from central China, makes an attractive mat of small, dark green leaves, dotted in May and June with quite conspicuous white flowers, to be followed through the fall and into the winter months with bright red berries. It is an excellent groundcover, very similar in appearance to Kinnikinnick (Arctostaphylos uva-ursi) but not as well adapted to dry banks as that plant. Other low-growing or carpeting hybrids which have been raised in recent years include 'Saldam', 'Lowfast', and C. salicifólius 'Repens' (VI). They are all useful as bank covers in sunny sites. C. × 'Hybridus Pendulus', a remarkable weeping type of Cotoneaster of unknown origin, can also be used in this way if raised from cuttings, or trained against a wall. It is not, however, fully evergreen in cold winters.

CÝTISUS, GENÍSTA, SPÁRTIUM, ÚLEX (VI–VII). Although these shrubs are not evergreen in the strict sense they will all be dealt with here, since the stems are green all the year and largely take the place of leaves for photosynthesis, although some species of Cytisus and Genista do produce true leaves,—e.g., C. decumbens and C. demissus, G. pilosa and G. tinctoria. The common name Broom refers chiefly to species or hybrids of the genus CYTISUS, less so to species of GENISTA.

CÝTISUS. Natives mostly of central and southern Europe, with some extensions into North Africa and Turkey, much like the *Cistus,* they all prefer sunny, well-drained situations and show their capacity for free flowering in late spring or early summer. Like other deep-rooted, drought-resistant shrubs they resent root disturbance and should be planted out from pots when young. If the roots have wound themselves around in the container they should be straightened out and a deep hole dug to contain them. Many of them are rather short lived and are likely to need replacing after 10 years or so. The hybrids and selected forms are best propagated from summer cuttings in July, or alternatively in February when still dormant; the species by seeds, which are usually produced in quantity, but need watching and collecting before the pods split and scatter their contents far and wide.

C. scopárius (V), the common or Scotch broom, is too well known in the Pacific Northwest as a weed shrub to need any description or comment. The form 'Andreanus' has reddish wing petals and was the progenitor of many of the vari-colored hybrids or forms which now exist. Although they differ somewhat in size and habit, they are generally shrubs of 4–8 ft. in size. Growing rapidly in a few years to their full size, they should be kept in bounds by regular pruning following flowering. Older British hybrids include 'Cornish Cream', 'Lord Lambourne' and 'Lady Moore'; later Californian introductions are 'Pomona', 'St Mary's' and 'Stanford'. The hybrid *C. × dallimórei,* raised at Kew Gardens, London, in 1900, introduced a new species as one parent, the tall white-flowered *C. multiflórus (C. álbus)* (V–VI) from Spain and Portugal. The hybrid has small, rose-pink flowers and was used to produce others with the same characteristics, or better in some respects, such as 'Burkwoodii', 'Geoffrey Skipwith' and 'Johnson's Crimson'.

C. battandiéri (VI) is a very different plant from all the others, and in fact much more like a *Laburnum* in foliage and flowers, although a shrub having usually several branches from the base. Growing 10–12 ft. in height, it has trifoliate leaves about 2 in. long, silky-hairy on both sides which gives them a silvery appearance; they are only partially evergreen and likely to be shed in most winters. The flowers, produced in June in short dense racemes at the ends of lateral branches, are golden yellow in color and distinctly fragrant with a fruity odor. It is a difficult plant to propagate, unless seeds are produced, which does not happen regularly in this area. Native to the Middle Atlas Mountains of Morocco, at 5,000–6,000 ft. elevation, it is entirely hardy here.

Of medium-sized brooms, about 3 ft. or so, *C. púrgans* (V–VI) with golden yellow flowers, from France and Spain, and its much better-known hybrid, *C. × práecox,* (VI–VII) with creamy yellow, unpleasantly scented flowers, have their uses on roadside banks. For gardens the Dutch hybrid 'Allgold' is to be preferred, having deep yellow flowers.

DÁPHNE. The daphnes form a most useful and attractive group of small shrubs for the rock garden, although as a rule they are not very long lived and have an unfortunate tendency to lose entire branches or even the whole plant in a short time thereafter for no obvious reason. Consequently they should be regularly propagated either by seeds, if produced, or else by summer cuttings, to maintain stocks. They prefer a sunny site and a sandy, well-drained soil. Many of them grow naturally in limestone soils or rocks in Europe or Asia, so have no objection to alkaline soils, if not excessively so. Little or no pruning is necessary, but topdressing with a mulch of compost is usually advisable and beneficial.

Probably the best known is *D. cnéorum,* (V) the Garland Flower, native to Europe from Spain to the U.S.S.R. Growing only about 12–15 in. tall, it can spread to 3–4 ft. in diameter in old plants, and when covered with its rich pink, strongly fragrant heads of flowers in late April or early May, forms one of the most pleasing sights in any garden. If it can be set up on a rock ledge so much the better. Some larger species are *D. collína,* (VII) (or *D. serícea,* which is perhaps the same plant), native principally in Turkey and Crete in open situations on calcareous soils. Here it grows into a bushy shrub about 2–2½ ft. tall, flowering first in early May and often again in late summer. The rose-pink flowers are borne in tight clusters at the ends of the shoots and are sweetly scented. The leaves are about 1½ in. long and silky-hairy on both sides,—hence the name *sericea.* Fruits are never produced. Another, which does produce fruits annually and also flowers twice in the year, is *D. retúsa,* (VI–VII) from western China and southeastern Tibet. This becomes a dense, compact bush 2–2½ ft. tall, with tough, thick branches, the leaves a little larger than those of *D. collina,* blunt and often notched at the apex, not hairy. Flowers are borne in the upper leaf axils in April and again in August; the tubes are pink and the open, four-sepaled fragrant blossoms are white. Daphnes have no separate sepals and petals. The fruits are red with a fleshy coating, quite attractive to some birds. A near relative of *D. retusa* is *D. tangútica,* (VI–VII) also hailing from China but with a more northerly distribution in that country. The shrub is more upright in habit and taller, than *D. retusa* to 4 ft.; the leaves are lanceolate in shape and distinctly pointed, the tube of the flowers and the unopened buds purple rather than pink; it also comes into bloom in late rather than mid-April and is similarly scented. Fruits are also red. A hybrid of *D. retusa* is *D.* × *mantensiána,* (VI–VII) raised at White Rock, British Columbia, by nurseryman Jack Manten in 1941. The seed parent was *D.* × *burkwóodii* 'Somerset', *D. retusa* being the male parent. The offspring forms a low, compact shrub similar in habit to *D. collina* and producing clusters of flowers at the ends of the shoots from April onwards, and again in fall. This is a useful plant for its long flowering season but must be propagated by cuttings in summer to maintain it. The hybrid *D.* × *burkwoodii* is not normally evergreen, since one of its parents, *D. caucásica,* is deciduous.

Two other very different species which should be mentioned are (1) the Spurge Laurel, *D. laureóla,* (VI–VII) native over much of Europe

A bush of *Daphne collina* in bloom in mid-April. Flowers purple, fragrant. Photo by Brian Mulligan.

Foliage and flowers (male) of *Daphniphyllum macropodum* in late April. Photo by Brian Mulligan.

including Great Britain, as well as the Azores Islands and North Africa. This is a shrub of 3–5 ft. in height, wider at the top than the base, the foliage tending to be bunched at the top of the shoots, dark green, leathery, oblanceolate and tapering down to the base; when crushed the leaves have a pungent odor. The flowers appear very early in the year, usually in February, clustered together among the upper leaves; they are green in bud, becoming yellowish when open, and fragrant especially in the evening. The black fruits, set freely and dispersed far and wide by birds are poisonous. (2) *D. odóra,* (VII–VIII) the Winter Daphne, is a native of China but long cultivated in Japan like many other ornamental shrubs, and introduced from there to Europe in 1771. In the Puget Sound area it needs the protection of a wall facing south or west, where it will form a bushy plant some 3–4 ft. tall and as much in width, producing its highly fragrant pink flowers in tight clusters at the ends of short branches in April, or earlier in some favorable seasons. The form with variegated margins of the leaves is reported to be hardier than the green-leaved type. There is also a very charming white-flowered form, 'Alba'. This is a plant for zone 8.

ELAEÁGNUS púngens (VII), from Japan, is a handsome, spiny shrub with dark green, leathery leaves 3–4 in. long and about half as wide, the underside dull white and dotted with brownish scales. As it can grow to 10–12 ft. tall and as much in width it needs space and is therefore not a shrub for the average garden, but rather for a park or boulevard. The highly fragrant, silver-white flowers appear in October, borne in small clusters in the leaf axils; they are some of the latest flowers of the year on any shrub. There are several forms with variegated foliage; 'Aurea' and 'Variegata' have the leaves margined with yellow of different shades; in 'Frederici' and 'Maculata' the center of the leaf is colored yellow. All these should be propagated by cuttings taken in late summer. Another species from Japan and Korea which also flowers in October and November is *E. macrophýlla* (VII). This also forms a large rounded bush of similar size to *E. pungens,* but the leaves are much more ovate in shape, covered beneath with silver scales, as are the young shoots. Because of this silver foliage effect it is more ornamental than *E. pungens.* A hybrid between these two species is *E.* × *ebbíngei,* raised at The Hague, Holland, in 1929. *E. macrophylla* was the seed parent.

ÉRICA. Only the larger species, the so-called Tree-heaths, will be dealt with here. The others will be found among the Groundcovers, together with *Calluna* and *Daboecia.*

E. arbórea var. *alpína* (VI), a native of the mountains of Spain, is by far the hardiest of those we can grow in this region, tolerating temperatures down to or even below 0°F. Growing in a few years into a large bush about 10 ft. tall and as much in width, with vivid green foliage all the year, then bearing plumes of small white flowers in great quantities in May, it is always an attractive plant. Bees are very fond of it, as they are of almost all heathers, producing a delicious though strong-flavored honey. The type species, *E. arbórea,* (VIII–IX) growing around all of the Mediterranean region, is very much less hardy, as well as having duller, gray-green leaves. The Spanish Heath, *E. austrális,* (VIII), is a smaller plant, reaching only about 4 ft. as a rule, the narrow leaves dark green, flowers also in May, in terminal clusters of 4–8, rose-purple, the corolla cylindrical, ⅓ in. long, the largest of any of these heaths we can grow outdoors. In the form 'Mr Robert', named for Robert Williams who found it in southern Spain in 1912, the flowers are white. This form may be slightly hardier than the type, but cold winds and low temperatures are devastating to both, so they should be given protected sites against south or west walls or fences in gardens.

Another tall and not completely hardy heath is *E. lusitánica,* (VIII) the Portuguese Heath, but worth trying in sheltered or warmer gardens. This can grow 6–8 ft. tall but is usually smaller with us. The habit is quite stiff and upright, the foliage a light green; the flowers may open as early as February in a mild winter but more normally in March and on into April, white, but pink-tinged in the bud which is a distinctive feature of this species as well as the simple hairs on the stems in contrast to the branched hairs in *E. arborea.* The style is colored pink. The hybrid between these two, *E. × véitchii,* (VIII) is probably rarely grown here but certainly worth a trial if it can be obtained true to name. One other tall heath is *E. erígena,* (VII) better known for many years as *E. mediterránea,* a name which is really a synonym for *E. herbácea (E. carnea)* (V), the Winter Heath, and does not belong with the Mediterranean Heath. This species is found wild along the Atlantic coastal regions of Europe—Spain, Portugal, France and western Ireland—where it may attain 8–10 ft. in height with age. In cultivation 4 ft. is usually about its limit, and less with some clones such as 'W. T. Rackliff'. Plants are upright in habit, densely bushy in form, and very free-flowering. They are hardier than either *E. australis* or *E. lusitanica,* less so than *E. arborea* var. *alpina,* but because of their generally smaller size and free-flowering propensities more useful in gardens here. The flower color of the type is a rosy purple but in the clones 'Brightness' and 'Superba' the flowers are more pink than purple or reddish. 'W. T. Rackliff' is white. All are scented of honey, no doubt an attractant to the bees. The blooming season is from late March to early May, a useful one here for heathers.

ERIOBÓTRYA japónica (VIII). The Loquat Tree, native of China and Japan, is a handsome foliage plant for training or growing against a sunny wall facing south or west, in situations with a warmer than normal microclimate for this area. The wrinkled and toothed leaves may be 8–10 in. long, about 4 in. wide; the young branches and leaf stalks are thickly woolly. The flowers, which have a fragrance like hawthorn, are borne in terminal panicles like those of buckeyes (*Aesculus* spp), in September and October. Fruits are seldom if ever produced here because of this late flowering. Several named selections are grown in California where the climate is more to its taste.

ESCALLÓNIA (VII–VIII). The escallonias are some 40 species of almost entirely evergreen shrubs native to South America, chiefly in Chile and Argentina. Only a few are reliably hardy in this region but they include some of our best summer-flowering shrubs. *E. rúbra* and its variety *macrántha* are especially valuable in coastal gardens. (*E. punctáta* is a synonym of *E. rubra,* being a later introduction of the same species.) They make large shrubs 10–12 ft. high and with regular care form excellent hedges resistant to winds off the ocean. The young shoots are sticky glandular, the leaves glossy dark green on the upper side, glandular beneath, about 2 in. long and half as wide, serrated; the flowers appear in summer on the new growths and continue intermittently for some weeks. They are borne in short panicles and are rose-red, varying from pink to crimson with different forms, also very glandular on the pedicels and calyx. Two hybrids derived from this species are 'C. F. Ball', with very large, rich red flowers and 'Ingramii', smaller in its foliage but the flowers similar to *E. rubra.* There is also a dwarf form derived by cuttings from a witches'-broom, commonly called 'Pygmaea'; the proper name of this cultivar is 'Woodside'.

Hybrids derived from crossing *E. rubra* and the deciduous, very hardy species *E. virgáta,* with white flowers, include *E.* × langleyensis, the original hybrid of this group; 'Edinensis', raised at the Royal Botanic Garden, Edinburgh, before 1914; 'William Watson'; and a whole series raised by the Donard Nursery, Newcastle, Co. Down, N. Ireland, starting with 'Donard Seedling' prior to 1916. This is still frequently seen masquerading as 'Apple Blossom', a totally different hybrid also raised much later by the same firm. All those with the name 'Donard' in their title make excellent summer-flowering shrubs, with pink, rose or red flowers on bushes 4–6 ft. tall. They are hardy in most of our winters, except the coldest, and if cut back will usually recover during the following season of growth. A taller plant with white flowers borne in July and August is 'Iveyi' (VIII), a natural hybrid found in a garden in Cornwall, England, derived from the less-hardy species *E. bífida (E. montevidénsis)* (VIII) from southern Brazil and Uruguay. Its oval leaves are particularly dark green and glossy on the upper side, about 2 in. long and 1 in. wide; the flowers are produced in terminal panicles, like those of the parent species, so are more conspicuous than the hybrids of *E. rubra,* with which they can well be associated, as it forms a shrub of 6–8 ft. in height. All these escallonias can be readily propagated by cuttings taken in late summer. They flower best in sunny situations and appreciate an annual mulch of compost around and over their roots.

EUÓNYMUS. The evergreen *Euonymus* are valuable garden plants, generally hardy and tolerant of almost all conditions of shade and moisture, although preferring a light, well-drained soil in full sun. They are easily propagated from cuttings or layered branches. *E. japónicus* (VII) is a variable shrub, the type having obovate or oval leaves up to nearly 3 in.

long, 2 in. wide, blunt or rounded at the apex. The plant forms a large shrub or occasionally a small tree to 15 ft. or even more in height. Near the sea it can be used as a hedge with success, if regularly clipped, or trained against a wall or fence. Flowers are greenish white, if produced, the fruits pink. Variegated forms are 'Latifolius Albomarginatus', in which the leaves have a broad white margin; 'Aureus', with the center of the leaf bright yellow and the edge dark green; 'Ovatus Aureus', with the margin rich yellow, the center green. Entirely different in appearance is 'Microphyllus', a shrub of 3–4 ft., compact and upright in habit, having small ovate-lanceolate leaves about 1 in. long; this is very suitable for a low hedge. There is also a silver-variegated form of it.

E. *kiautschóvicus (E. pátens),* from eastern and central China, (VI) is somewhat hardier than E. *japonicus,* more open and spreading in its growth habit, the inflorescence a little larger, in August and September, the pink fruits with their orange-red seeds not ripening until November.

Most frequently cultivated is *Euonymus fórtunei* var. *rádicans,* (V) native to Japan, a creeping shrub that roots as it trails on the ground or may climb up a tree or other support like ivy. It has dark green, ovate leaves, shallowly toothed, about 1 in. long. It also resembles ivy in developing an adult bushy form which produces flowers and fruits like those of E. *japonicus;* the leaves likewise become larger. *Carrierei* is one of these, as is 'Silver Queen' with variegated foliage. 'Variegatus' may be either trailing or shrubby; the leaves are broadly margined with white. As might be expected, the variegated forms are somewhat less hardy than those with green leaves.

EUPHÓRBIA (VII). The only species which concerns us here is the subshrubby E. *wulfénii,* native to Yugoslavia and Greece, and therefore requiring a sunny, well-drained site in local gardens, where it is normally hardy except in the coldest winters. The rather fleshy stems with their numerous narrow leaves grow up to about 4 ft. in height and in April produce terminal panicles of many greenish yellow flowers which last for several weeks in good condition. It is best propagated from seeds and when well established is capable of producing its own seedlings around the plants. Like other euphorbias the stems contain a milky sap with which it is well to avoid contact; usually not long lived and should be repropagated regularly.

EURYA japónica (VII), a member of the Theaceae (Tea) family and therefore somewhat distantly related to the camellias, forms a somewhat upright to spreading, stiff-branched bush, with the leaves borne very regularly but alternately along the short branches. They are lanceolate-oblong, about 2 in. long, serrated, a glossy green. The flowers are white, produced beneath the branches early in spring (March), and although small are strongly scented. They are dioecious, so no fruits appear unless both sexes are present; these are small and black. This species ranges from the Himalayas through China and Japan to Taiwan and even Malaya.

Flowering stems of the Spurge, *Euphorbia wulfenii,* in early May. Photo by Brian Mulligan.

FÁTSIA japónica (VII) is a dramatic large shrub or small tree closely related to ivy (*Hedera*). The stems are often bare below and most of the large palmately lobed leaves borne near the top, so that it is better placed behind some other broad-leaved evergreen shrubs and not in the front of a border. The leaves may reach 1 ft. across and are shiny on the upper side. The heads of flowers in September–October are quite conspicuous and ornamental, and are normally followed by a crop of black fruits the next spring.

× *FATSHÉDERA lízei* (VII) is a bigeneric hybrid between *Fatsia* and *Hedera,* bred at a nursery in Nantes, France, in 1910, the *Fatsia* being the seed parent. Intermediate in both habit and foliage between the parents, it is probably best placed on a shady bank where it can trail down, or against an old stump which it can cover with its handsome glossy foliage. The compound inflorescence appears in October. It is easily propagated by cuttings, or branches can be layered.

GÁRRYA *ellíptica*, (VII) the Tassel Bush or Silk-tassel, is found wild ○ from Lincoln County in western Oregon down the coast as far as southern California. It is a choice shrub for a sheltered, sunny position, and should then be damaged only by exceptionally cold winters. A normal height here is 8–10 ft. but more if planted against a south or west wall or fence. The gray-green, leathery, undulated leaves form a perfect foil for the tassels of greenish male flowers in February; 'James Roof' is an especially fine selection with extra-long inflorescences. The female flowers produced by separate plants are inconspicuous, so that plants known as male should be grown. Any necessary pruning should be done in spring after flowering; flowering branches may be cut for decoration if desired.

G. *fremóntii* (VI) ranges from southern Washington in the Columbia Gorge through the Sierra Nevada to southern California. It is definitely hardier than G. *elliptica* though less ornamental in its shorter inflorescences; the leaves are a glossier green, lacking the thick coating of hairs on the underside found in the latter species, and are not undulated along the margin. It is also a smaller shrub, attaining only about half the size of G. *elliptica*.

G. × *issaquahénsis* is the name for the hybrids which have arisen in cultivation between these two species, firstly by Mr. Carl S. English of Seattle in 1956, using G. *elliptica* as the female parent; secondly in the garden of Mr. and Mrs. Page Ballard at Issaquah, Washington, where a female plant of G. *fremontii* was growing next to a male of G. *elliptica*. The hybrid plants vary in their characters of foliage and flowers, but all are hardier than G. *elliptica* and form a useful new group of early spring (or late winter) blooming shrubs, reaching about 8 ft. in height.

× GAULNÉTTYA (VII). The two genera *Gaultheria* and *Pernettya* are so closely allied that natural hybrids have been found between them in Mexico and New Zealand. × G. *wisleyénsis*, however, arose as a natural hybrid in the garden of the Royal Horticultural Society in southern England prior to 1929, where G. *shallón* and P. *mucronáta* were growing in close proximity. This hybrid reaches 3–4 ft. as a dense bush and has foliage and inflorescences resembling a small type of our native Salal, the *Gaultheria*. The flowers open in June, being produced at the ends of the branches in the form of a group of short racemes of small, urn-shaped, white flowers, of considerable decorative value. They are followed in September by purplish black fruits similar to those of the Salal, but smaller. This is a fertile hybrid and seedlings can be raised from it which vary considerably in form and characteristics.

GAULTHÉRIA (VII–VIII). A genus of more than 200 species in the family Ericaceae widely distributed in North and South America, eastern Asia, and Australasia, of varying hardiness in this region depending upon their origin. The native Salal, G. *shallón*, is well-known and commonly grown, being most useful in dry places under trees. The only possible difficulty that the gardener may have with it is in getting it established. The pattern of its handsome, dark green, leathery leaves is pleasing in combination with a great many other broad-leaved evergreen shrubs. Plants with red stems and pedicels are especially attractive. The pretty, pale pink, urn-shaped flowers, freely produced in May, are followed by edible purple fruits. Like the Evergreen Huckleberry (*Vaccinium ovatum*), another first-class native shrub, it may be grown either in full sun or in deep shade and takes on distinctive characteristics in either case. Usually it requires no pruning, but if necessary cut any damaged branches almost to the ground in March or early April and topdress the plants with compost, peat or leafmold.

Most of the Asiatic species are tender in this area so need to be grown in sheltered sites, excepting *G. hóokeri (G. veitchiána)* from the Himalayas and western China, which appears to be the hardiest and is well worth attempting, at least in warmer and somewhat protected gardens. This is a shrub about 2 ft. in height, with bristly stems, oblong, dark green, glossy, serrated leaves and small white flowers borne in short but dense terminal racemes in May. Its most conspicuous feature, however, is the bright blue fruits which follow in September, not an uncommon character in the gaultherias from this region. Several other American and Asiatic species will be found among the groundcovers. All appreciate an annual top-dressing in the spring. Some can be propagated by division of rooted underground stems, all by cuttings.

GENÍSTA. These differ botanically from species of *Cytisus* in several characters, especially in the absence of a wartlike swelling at the base of the seed (a strophiole), in the upper lip of the calyx being deeply cut into lobes instead of merely toothed, and in having spiny or thorny branches in some of the species which is never the case in *Cytisus* species. Some of them are tall shrubs, up to 15 ft. or even more, like *G. aetnénsis* (VII) from Sardinia and Sicily, bearing quantities of small, sweet-scented flowers in July, and *G. ténera (G. virgáta)* (VII) from the island of Madeira but normally quite hardy with us. These are easily raised from seeds, as are any other species which produce them. *G. cinérea,* (VII) from the mountains of Spain, is smaller in stature, definitely hardier, growing 6–8 ft., with bright yellow flowers in clusters in June and early July. *G. hispánica* (VI) is a prickly shrub up to 3 ft. tall, producing quantities of bright yellow flowers in May,—an excellent plant for dry banks.

× HALIMIOCÍSTUS (VII–VIII). These are natural hybrids between species of CISTUS and the closely related genus HALIMIUM, from European sources. The only one commonly cultivated is *H.* × *sahúcii, (H. umbellatum* × *C. salviifolius),* which originated in France. It is a long-lived, hardy, spreading shrub about 12 in. high, having narrow, dark green leaves about 1 in. long and in June a succession of small, white flowers held up above the foliage. An excellent plant for a dry bank, easily propagated by cuttings in late summer.

HALÍMIUM (VII–VIII). A genus of a few species found around the Mediterranean from Portugal in the west to Syria in the east. They are most closely related to the rock roses, *HELIANTHEMUM*, but the flowers possess only three sepals and the styles are straight rather than curved. The flowers are always yellow except in *H. umbellátum*, where they are white. The hardiest are *H. lasiánthum* from southern Portugal, having gray-green oblong foliage, and in June a succession of bright yellow flowers with a purple blotch near the base of the petals; *H. ocymoídes* also produces yellow flowers with a purple blotch but is a smaller shrub than the last, to about 2½ ft. tall. They can be raised from seeds, when available, or propagated by summer cuttings. A site in full sun on a southern or western slope is much to their liking.

HÉBE (VII–VIII). About 100 species of this genus are known, along with many natural hybrids from New Zealand, which is their principal home, although two are also found in southern South America. Propagation may be either by seeds or cuttings, taking the latter in late summer or early fall. The species mentioned below are normally hardy here except in more severe winters than the normal, with temperatures to 15°F or below. *H. amplexicaúlis* grows into a 4-ft.-tall shrub, branching from near the base; the foliage is distinctly glaucous about ¾ in. long, set in four rows, stalkless, as are the white flowers, produced in June, although not usually very freely until the plants are mature. *H. álbicans* is very similar and closely related. *H. brachysíphon,* formerly known as *H. travérsii,* grows into a bushy shrub up to 5 ft. in height, the leaves green, densely packed in four rows, the white flowers at the ends of the shoots in July; this is one of the hardiest species of the genus. *H. buxifólia* attains 3–4 ft. with erect shoots, small, to ½-in.-long dark green leaves, and white flowers in clusters in June and July. It is native to both the main islands of New Zealand. *H. odóra* is very closely related and similar to it: the flowers are scented. *H. cupressoídes* has, as its name implies, foliage like that of a cypress; it becomes a shrub of 5–6 ft. in height, the branches much forked and subdivided, the leaves scalelike, dusty green; flowers pale blue, in June and July. *H. salicifólia,* from the South Island of New Zealand, can grow into a tall, loose shrub to 8 ft. with lanceolate leaves 4–6 in. long and long racemes of pale blue or white flowers in summer. Although less hardy than the smaller species it is worth a trial, at least in more protected locations, for its showier flowers and greater effect in the garden.

HÉDERA hélix 'Arborescens'. The common English Ivy is well known as a rampant climber, but the flowering and fruiting branches are stiff and clothed with foliage of a different shape from that on the trailing branches. Cuttings rooted from these branches form shrubs up to 6 ft. or more in height. Their rounded clusters of greenish flowers are doubly welcome, appearing as they do in October, usually remaining uninjured by frosts and being followed by shiny black berries. They root freely from cuttings and should be used more often in dry shady corners where the choice of broad-leaved evergreen shrubs is strictly limited; they are, however, equally happy in a sunny situation.

HELLEBÓRUS angulifolius (H. córsicus) (VII). Although scarcely a woody-stemmed shrub this 2–3 ft. tall, stoutly upright plant from Corsica and Sardinia with its handsome trifoliate, serrated evergreen leaves certainly deserves a place in many gardens, both for the foliage effect as well as the loose heads of nodding chartreuse green flowers in March and April. The old stems die away in summer and are replaced by new ones for the following year. Plant in a sunny place and propagate by raising seedlings, sowing the seeds soon after ripening.

ILEX. The hollies include about 400 species found in temperate and tropical regions over much of the world except western North America and Australasia. Many of the former species can be grown here and more should be for their varied foliage and especially their ornamental fruits during the winter months. Since male and female flowers usually are produced on different plants, it is necessary to have both sexes in close proximity if fruits are to be produced.

For *Ilex aquifolium* and *I. × altaclerensis* see Broadleaved Evergreen Trees.

Ilex × aquipérnyi (VII) is a reputed hybrid between *I. aquifólium* and the Chinese species *I. pérnyi;* it is, however, very similar to *I. pérnyi* var. *véitchii,* which has longer, less-spiny leaves than the typical species. They form fairly compact upright bushes up to 12 ft. in height, and fruit freely and regularly; the fruits are bright red and remain on the plants until New Year or later. There is another selection of this hybrid, raised in California, named 'Brilliant'.

I. cornúta, (VII–VIII) from eastern China and Korea, grows into a compact bush 7–8 ft. high and wide; the shining green leaves have two prominent spines at their apex, which give the clue to its naming. It is not as hardy as some other species in this area and can be severely damaged in colder winters than normal. Female clones are 'Hume', 'National' and 'Shangri-la'. 'Burfordii' is a female form with almost spineless leaves, somewhat convex and blistered in appearance. 'Rotunda' is dwarf and very compact; 'D'Or' has yellow berries.

I. crenáta, (VI), the Japanese black-berried holly, is a very variable species, and many forms have been either introduced from Japan or raised in cultivation in nurseries in this country. The best known is probably 'Convexa', which forms a close bush some 6 ft. in height with very glossy, convex, bright green little leaves; it is an admirable plant for hedges, requiring little clipping once established. The normal type is a loose shrub with spreading branches, reaching perhaps 10–12 ft. in height eventually; the leaves are 1 in. or so long, lanceolate, inconspicuously toothed, tough in texture. The female flowers are borne singly in the leaf axils; fruits are small and black, so that they do not make any display in winter like the red-fruited species. 'Latifolia' has larger leaves than the type; 'Microphylla' smaller. Dwarf forms are 'Hetzii', 'Helleri' and 'Morris Dwarf'. 'Mariesii' has very small round leaves, a fastigiate habit of growth, and is female; it can reach up to 10 ft. in height or more. *I. glábra,* (IV), the Inkberry, native in the eastern U.S.A. and Canada, is a slow-growing shrub 3–4 ft. high, partial to swampy places in the wild but quite tolerant of drier positions in the garden. The leaves are glossy and dark green, also spineless; the fruits black, solitary, about ¼ in. wide; there is a form 'Ivory Queen' with greenish white berries. 'Compacta' is dwarf and compact as the name suggests.

I. × mesérveae (I. rugósa × I. aquifólium) (IV–V). A valuable race of hybrids raised by Mrs. F. L. Meserve of Long Island, NY, in the 1950s, between a very hardy, low-growing species from northern Japan (the mother parent) and the common European holly. Two, named 'Blue Boy' and 'Blue Girl', were patented in 1964; others are 'Blue Angel', 'Blue Maid', 'Blue Prince', and 'Blue Princess'. They have blue-green spiny leaves, red berries, and a dense habit of growth, up to 5–6 ft. in height. Very promising for colder climates. *I. pedunculósa,* (V–VI) a native of both Japan and China and becoming almost a small tree in time, is hardly to be recognized as a holly since the leaves lack any spines and are quite smooth; they are 2–3 in. long and 1–2 in. wide. The male flowers are produced on the new shoots in clusters; the female, however, are solitary on separate plants and borne on long pedicels, hence are of less value for ornament in winter than most other species. The habit of growth is upright and more or less pyramidal. *I. pérnyi* (VI–VII) is a very distinct species from western China, with small, wedge-shaped, spiny leaves about 1 in. long closely set along the slender branches. The fruits are bright red, ¼-in. in diameter, persistent into winter. The variety *véitchii* is to be preferred, having larger, less coriaceous leaves, bright green on the upper side, and more showy fruits. Both can attain 10–12 ft. in height or more under good conditions. The latter makes an excellent hedging or screening scrub.

ILLÍCIUM (VII–VIII) is a genus of some 40 evergreen trees and shrubs distributed widely in eastern Asia but also having some members in North America as far as south as Mexico. Few are reliably hardy in this region but at least two have been grown successfully in the Washington Park Arboretum, Seattle, for a number of years, namely *I. anisátum* and *I. floridánum,* so are worth trying in sheltered situations. The former, native in both China and Japan, is an erect large shrub with a central stem, attaining 12 ft. or so if placed against a wall facing west or south. The leaves are clustered towards the ends of the growths, glossy green on the upper side, about 2 in. long, smooth and smelling of aniseed when broken. Creamy white flowers are produced in the leaf axils in April and May; these are composed of many narrow petals but are not fragrant. The latter species is native from Florida to Louisiana, and is a shrub some 6 ft. in height with larger leaves than the former and similarly aromatic. The flowers, however, are dark red in color. Overhead shelter from large evergreen trees seems helpful to growing the latter species successfully. Both can be propagated by cuttings or seeds.

ITÉA (VII–VIII). *Itéa ilicifólia* belongs to a small genus of shrubs, all evergreen except *I. virgínica* from the eastern U.S.A. and the related *I. japónica* from Japan. They are botanically related to the escallonias from South America, but are all of Asiatic origin except the one from this country. *Itea ilicifolia* is perhaps not quite as hardy here as *Illicium floridanum*, and like it benefits from some overhead shelter. It forms in time a large, rounded bush about 8 ft. in height and perhaps more in width. The leaves are hollylike, with spines on each side, but thinner in texture than those of common holly; they are also borne alternately, as those are. The flowers, however, are very different in all respects, being long pendulous racemes of very small, greenish blossoms, appearing in August when few other shrubs are in bloom. It therefore has considerable value for this character alone. It must be propagated by cuttings, since it produces no fertile seeds.

KÁLMIA *latifólia* (IV), the Mountain Laurel from the eastern U.S.A. and Canada, is by far the most valuable species for the garden, and one of the loveliest of all native American, broad-leaved evergreen shrubs. Being an ericaceous plant it requires an acid, preferably sandy soil with a high humus content. In gardens in this region it seems to thrive best in partial shade, or on the east side of a house where it gets only the morning sun. With a moderate amount of shade and ample moisture during spring and early summer it makes vigorous growth and flowers freely. If given too much shade and water it may produce lush foliage but no bloom buds. If, on the other hand, it is grown in hot sun without adequate moisture the growth will be stunted and the foliage scorched. It is a relatively slow-growing shrub in gardens, taking many years to reach a height of 7–8 ft. It blooms in early to mid-June, with abundant clusters of puckered pink flowers above the bright green, 3–4 in. long leaves. In all the kalmias the 10 stamens in the individual flowers are held in pockets in the corollas until released by the touch of an insect, an unusual feature, but a means to ensure pollination. In recent years many selections of various color forms have been made and propagated by cuttings. Colors range from clear pink to very deep rose-pink, with buds which are bright red, especially effective and striking at that stage. 'Ostbo Red' was one of the first of these, named for Endre Ostbo, nurseryman of Bellevue, WA. Others are 'Dexter Pink', 'J-1', 'Nipmuck', and 'Sharon Rose'. 'Silver Dollar' has unusually large, almost white flowers. In 'Fresca' and 'Goodrich' they are banded with purple inside the corolla.

LÁURUS *nóbilis* (VII–VIII), the Bay Laurel or Sweet Bay from the Mediterranean region, is the famous laurel of the ancient Greeks and Romans, the laurel of history and poetry from which wreaths were made to crown the winners in the Olympic games. This large shrub or small tree has not been grown a great deal in our area, although it is hardier than generally supposed, if grown in full sun in a well-drained soil, although liable to be burned by cold winds or even cut back by unusually cold winters. However, established specimens will recover from these set-backs the following season, if not hit two years in succession by similar conditions. They form 25–30 ft. tall shrubs or small trees with a slender conical outline and quite compact growth habit. Being able to withstand frequent trimming it has been used a great deal in topiary work, especially in Europe, (Belgium and France), or even as a hedge. The pointed leaves, 3–4 in. long and 1 in. wide, are aromatic and used for flavoring in cooking. Flowers are small, yellowish, and produced in clusters in the leaf axils in spring. Male and female are borne on different plants, so that fruits are seldom seen in cultivation.

LAVÁNDULA (V–VI). The common lavender is L. angustifólia, often formerly called L. officinális. It is a most useful and attractive small shrub, especially for dry banks and sunny corners, being native to the western Mediterranean region and in the mountains up to 5,000–6,000 ft. It has been cultivated in Europe for many centuries and is the source of oil of lavender. Flowering time of the typical plant is mid- to late June, but there are many forms which may bloom at slightly differing dates. The white form is 'Alba', the pink 'Rosea'. Taller (to 3 ft. or so) varieties with violet or purple flowers are 'Bowles' Early', 'Folgate' and 'Twickel Purple', raised in Holland before 1922. Dwarfer kinds, to about 20 in., are 'Compacta', 'Hidcote', and 'Munstead'. They make excellent low hedges in suitable situations and can be used as such around herb gardens. Any pruning required to keep them in shape should be done immediately after flowering. If done in spring much of that season's flowering will be lost. Propagation is easy by means of cuttings taken after the new growth has hardened sufficiently.

Spike Lavender, L. latifólia, also from the same region as L. angusti-folia, but from lower altitudes and is therefore somewhat less hardy. It is a larger shrub, has broader leaves and the flowering stems are often branched; it also flowers about two weeks later than the common lavender. The oil produced is inferior to that of the latter species.

Hybrids between these two are quite common, and bear the name of Lavandin in commerce; the Latin one is L. × intermédia. There is also a white-flowered form, 'Alba'. Some cultivars of the hybrids are 'Dutch', 'Grappenhall', 'Hidcote Giant', and 'Old English'. They average 3–4 ft. in height when flowering, so should be planted behind the smaller forms of L. angustifolia.

LÉDUM. The ledums are small, hardy shrubs particularly adapted to living in bogs in cold regions. They are characterized by their low stature, usually 2–3 ft. tall, narrow often rolled leaves, aromatic when rubbed, and terminal clusters of small, white flowers in May or June. L. glandulósum (IV) is native from British Columbia east and south to the Rocky Mountains (Wyoming), Oregon and California. The leaves are nearly smooth and pale beneath, in contrast to the two other species in which they are rusty-hairy. Flowers are lemon scented. *L. groenlándicum,* the Labrador tea, (I–II) has a much wider distribution, being found right across northern North America from Alaska to Labrador and also in Greenland. The oblong leaves are somewhat rolled at the margins and covered beneath with brownish wool. The common name derives from the use made of these leaves for tea by early travelers in the regions. The third species, *L. palústre,* (I–II) is chiefly of European origin, but very widely distributed there, and into northern Asia and even Japan. The leaves are narrower than either of the other two, being much more rolled at their edges, covered beneath with similar brown wool. All species have a reputation for being poisonous to animals, particularly to sheep. They can be propagated most readily by seeds, which are produced in quantity, but also by cuttings if needed, or by layering branches. An acid soil is essential for them.

× *LEDODENDRON.* See Small Shrubs.

LEPTOSPÉRMUM (VII–VIII). This is an attractive genus of shrubs native chiefly to Australia, and ranging in size from low groundcovers to small trees, but unfortunately lacking sufficient hardiness to be generally growable around Puget Sound, though some are worth a trial, if obtainable from Californian sources. From southern coastal Oregon and southwards they can certainly be grown with success.

The hardiest species are those from Tasmania and the mountains of southeastern Australia. They include *L. lanígerum,* with very hairy shoots and white flowers in summer; *L. flavéscens,* flowering in July with somewhat larger white flowers; *L. nítidum* and *L. rodwáyanum,* the last having flowers 1 in. in width. All form tall shrubs with heathlike narrow foliage on willowy shoots. They need a sandy soil and full exposure to sun. *L. scopárium,* the Manuka of New Zealand, having white, pink or even red flowers, is unfortunately the least hardy species. Propagation is by seeds or cuttings.

LEUCÓTHOE. There are three native North American species with evergreen foliage in this genus of about 45 species, most of which are found in Central or South America in mountainous regions. *L. axilláris (L. cátesbaei)* (VII) is a shrub of the coastal plain from southern Virginia to Florida and Louisiana, attaining 4–5 ft. with us, the leaves leathery, 3–4 in. long, serrated in the upper part only. The short racemes of white, bell-shaped flowers appear in April and May along the branches. Because of its origin it is less hardy in cool winters than *L. fontanésiana* (V), which is found in the mountains from Virginia to Tennessee and Georgia, a very handsome shrub with more acuminate leaves than the preceding species, but of similar habit. 'Girard's Rainbow' is a form with variegated foliage, originating from a nursery in Ohio. The third species we grow is *L. davisíae,* which will be found in the Small Shrubs section.

LIGÚSTRUM. Privets. These include a number of valuable garden shrubs. The old common European Privet, *L. vulgáre* (V), formerly much used for hedges especially in Europe, has been superseded by the so-called Californian Privet, *L. ovalifólium*, (VI), a native of Japan, with its golden-variegated form 'Aureum'. These usually retain their leaves until late in the fall, when the latter form is particularly noticeable. Another drawback to the Common Privet is the heavy scent of the flowers in midsummer, although the resulting black fruits are appreciated by birds.

Two ornamental and useful Asiatic privets are *L. japónicum* (VII) from Japan and Korea, and *L. lucídum* from China. The former has thick, glossy foliage resembling that of *Camellia japonica*; it is best planted in partial shade to retain the leaves in good color and condition. This species makes an excellent hedge plant, as can be seen on the University of Washington campus, to 5–6 ft. in height. The panicles of white flowers appear in July and August. There is a dwarfer form of slow, congested growth named 'Rotundifolium' ('Coriaceum'), suitable for rock gardens.

L. lucidum can become a small tree, up to 40 ft. or even more in height; it is used as a street tree in warm climates, e.g., in southern Italy. The leaves are larger and of a more olive green than those of *L. japonicum*. The flowers appear later, in August and September, and occur in larger panicles, so that it is a more handsome shrub in all respects. Another Chinese privet, *L. sinénse*, (VI–VII), is sometimes seen here and is certainly worth growing for its quantities of flowers in July, smothering bushes up to 9–10 ft. in height. The fruits are very small, black, and remain on the plants for many weeks or even months.

LONÍCERA. Honeysuckles. There are two shrubby evergreen species from China grown in our area, namely *L. nítida* and *L. pileáta*, both first introduced by E. H. Wilson. *L. nitida*, (VI–VII), the Box Honeysuckle, with small, shining leaves and a dense habit, is admirable for forming hedges up to 4–5 ft. in height. If allowed to grow freely it will form a looser shrub with more spreading branches. The flowers are produced in pairs in the leaf axils, and are small, yellowish white and fragrant; the fruits are amethyst purple, though not always formed or easily seen. Several clones have been named, including 'Ernest Wilson' and 'Yunnan'. The second species, *L. pileata*, (VI), is of low, spreading habit, the branches tending to overlap one another; the leaves slightly larger, also glossy on the upper surface; the flowers and fruits quite similar to those of *L. nitida*. It has considerable value as an evergreen cover for banks but not in too shady a site. Both species are resistant to salt spray. They can be propagated very easily by means of cuttings taken in fall or early in spring.

LYÓNIA. A genus of some 30 species, both evergreen and deciduous, spread over eastern Asia and North America, and related to *Pieris*, in Ericaceae. We are only concerned here with one evergreen species, *L. lúcida*, (VII–VIII), native from Virginia to Florida and Louisiana, and known as the Fetter-bush. The elliptic leaves are 2–3 in. long, more or less ovate with a rolled margin, bright green and glossy on the upper side. The white flowers appear in short racemes towards the end of the shoots, in April and May. A shady site in soil which does not readily dry out is to its liking. It is a good companion for the leucothoes.

MAHÓNIA *aquifólium* (V), the tall Oregon Grape has proved to be one of the most valuable shrubs for garden use in a variety of sites, and probably has received more recognition in other regions than any other of our native shrubs. A plant of easy culture, thriving under the most adverse circumstances, including near the seashore or on roadside banks in eastern Washington, its foliage is unsurpassed in the quality of blending with that of other species. The compound leaves have leaflets varying from 5–9; some have dull leaf surfaces with prominent veining while others are smooth and glossy as if coated with varnish. Some are as crinkled and spiny as common holly's, others are flat and almost spine-less. The best forms should be selected either in the wild or in a nursery and propagated vegetatively. In most forms the new growths are copper to bronze in coloring; during winter the old leaves may change to red or dark purple. Flowering, in April, is often profuse, with clusters of rich yellow, fragrant little blossoms. These will be followed in due course by bunches of blue-purple berries like miniature grapes, so this is indeed a shrub for all seasons and many climates and situations. Its average height, in the open, is 5–6 ft.; the dwarf form, 'Compacta' grows to about 2 ft. In shade, which is less desirable for good flowering and fruiting, they can reach 8 ft. Periodic pruning, either in early spring or preferably immediately after flowering, is needed to keep the plants from becoming too tall and leggy.

M. béalei (VI) is a native of China, from which country it was intro-duced by Robert Fortune in 1848 to England. This, and its near relative *M. japónica* (VII), are two of the most striking members of the genus which we can cultivate, because of their large, leathery pinnate leaves 1 ft. or more in length under favorable conditions, in good soil and partial shade. They do not enjoy being exposed to hot and sunny conditions in the summer after-noons. The fragrant flowers are borne at the ends of the shoots early in the year, usually in February, in clusters of several racemes in each inflores-cence. Those of *M. bealei* are comparatively short (4–6 in.), and held upright; in the case of *M. japonica* they are longer and held horizontally or are somewhat pendulous. The foliage of the two also differs: that of *M. bealei* has shorter and broader leaflets usually touching or even over-lapping each other; in *M. japonica* they are more ovate-lanceolate in shape, acuminate at the tip, and may be separated from each other; all have several spines on each side. Eventual height of both species, 8–10 ft. Propa-gated by either seeds or cuttings.

M. lomariifólia (VIII) is a fairly recent (1931) introduction from south-west China, where it can become a small tree 30 ft. in height. It is not suffi-ciently hardy to be grown in the Northwest, unless in a very protected situation, such as under the eaves of a house and facing south or west. The leaves are 15–20 in. in length, with 10–18 pairs of leaflets, so it is a striking

Mahonia lomariifolia in full bloom at the end of October, or later. Photo by Brian Mulligan.

plant for this feature alone. Add to this the fact that the flowers open in late October to December, borne in clusters of upright racemes at the ends of the branches as in *M. bealei* and *M. japonica,* and you have a very unusual and valuable shrub, in the appropriate climate such as southern Oregon near the coast, or in coastal California. However, a hybrid derived from it, by a fortuitous cross with *M. bealei* in San Francisco, and named 'Arthur Menzies' after its raiser, has proved to be very much hardier and an excellent new plant for winter flowering. The leaves are about as long as those of *M. lomariifolia,* up to about 25 in., with 8–10 pairs of leaflets each 3–4 in. long, dull green on the upper side, paler beneath. The inflorescences open in December or January and last well, even during cold weather. A site where it will not receive the morning sun is advisable. The habit of the shrub is tall, usually with several main stems from the base. It can be pruned back to a lower whorl of branches after flowering if it is desired to keep it at a lower height. Otherwise they should be planted at the back of a border behind other more bushy shrubs. Other similar hybrids have been raised in Britain, but with *M. japonica* as the second parent. These have been described under the name *M. × média.* Some of them are 'Charity', 'Winter Sun' and 'Lionel Fortescue'.

One of the best groundcover plants for our Northwest gardens is the native *M. nervósa* (VI), found wild from British Columbia into Idaho and

The hybrid *Mahonia* ×
'Arthur Menzies'
flowering in early
February, or earlier.
Photo by Brian Mulligan.

Foliage and a few fruits
of *Mahonia repens*. Photo
by Brian Mulligan.

south to northern California. It grows well under native evergreen conifers but is better suited to a partially shaded situation and is often found in conjunction with Salal, *Gaultheria shallon,* a happy combination and a very permanent one once established. It does resent transplanting from the wild and will take 2–3 years to reestablish thereafter. Its average height is about 2–2½ ft., but it can be taller in dense shade, shorter in a sunny position. The flowers are borne in terminal clusters of upright racemes in April and are followed by bunches of juicy purple fruits in September which are edible but acid. *M. répens* (V), another native species with much less spiny, shorter and broader leaflets, is sometimes recommended as a groundcover, especially in eastern Washington, but is certainly inferior to the former for this purpose. Both spread by means of underground stems.

MÝRICA califórnica, the Californian Wax Myrtle or Bayberry, (VII), grows along the Pacific coast from southwestern Washington to southern California. In the wild it sometimes reaches a height of 30 ft., but in local gardens 10–12 ft. is about the average. The habit is upright, the branching pattern rather loose. The leaves are narrow, lanceolate, dark green, regularly toothed. Flowers are inconspicuous, but the small, dark purple, almost black fruits are evident in fall. This is a good screening shrub for the back of a border or along a fence, particularly for damp locations. It can be kept in shape by regular pruning as required.

NANDINA (VII). The Sacred Bamboo, *N. doméstica,* (VII), is a native of China but long cultivated in Japan. The graceful horizontal pattern of its compound leaves, 12–20 in. long, and its tall, slender, unbranched stems are somewhat suggestive of bamboos. The new leaves are tinged with pink and bronze as they unfold, mature to a soft, light green, then are again rose-tinged in fall, or sometimes have bright red foliage into winter. The loose clusters of small white flowers in summer may be followed by bright red fruits, but another pollinating plant may be necessary to achieve this. Individual plants may not bear fruit. It should be grown in a sheltered position, such as beside a house door, as is frequently the case in Japan. 6 to 8 feet is its usual height with us. Several clones have been introduced, including 'Moyer's Red' & 'Royal Princess'.

OLEÁRIA (VII–VIII). The Daisy Bushes, as the species and numerous hybrids of this genus are commonly known, are regrettably not generally hardy enough to withstand our sometimes colder than average spells of winter weather, with the exception of *O.* × *haastii,* a natural hybrid originating in New Zealand between *O. aviceniifólia* and *O. moscháta.* This forms a dense, bushy shrub 6 ft. in height, having ovate leaves 1 in. or less in length, thick in texture and covered with a white felt beneath. In July and August it covers itself with flattish clusters of small white flowers of the typical daisy form, with yellow disc florets in the center. These have an aromatic or musky fragrance, derived from *O. moschata.* Some other species which might be tried in sheltered gardens, especially those near salt water, are *O. phlogopáppa, (O. stelluláta)*, from southeastern Australia, a shrub of 5–6 ft. with narrow leaves 1–2 in. long, the young shoots covered with a white felt of hairs, and small clusters of white, pink or pale blue flowers in early May. *O. ilicifólia* and *O. nummuláriifolia* are two others from New Zealand worth seeking out and trying in warmer gardens. If fresh seeds can be obtained from their native countries this is the best means of propagation, except for cuttings from established plants.

OSMÁNTHUS is a small genus of evergreen shrubs or trees, native mostly in eastern Asia, but with two representatives in the U.S.A., one in western Asia. Some flower in the spring, others in the fall; most have fragrant, white flowers. *O. armátus*, (VII), introduced from western China by E. H. Wilson in 1902, has some of the largest leaves in the group, up to 5 in. long and 1½ in. wide, sharply toothed on each side like some holly; they are glossy green on the upper side and taper to each end. The small white flowers are produced in axillary clusters in October, and are faintly fragrant. As it can easily attain 12 ft. in height, it should be placed towards the back of a border with some lower, more bushy shrubs in front of it. *O. × burkwóodii*, (VI), a hybrid between *O. delaváyi* and *O. decórus* produced in England before 1928, becomes a large bushy shrub attaining about 8 ft., freely producing masses of small, white fragrant flowers in April, like the parent *O. delavayi*. It is an excellent hedge plant, if regularly trimmed to shape, and is easily propagated from cuttings, like other species of this genus. *O. decórus (Phillyráea decóra)*, (VII), is a native of the region around the southeastern corner of the Black Sea, and a handsome foliage shrub growing 8–10 ft. in height and as much or more in width. The leaves are not normally toothed. This is a spring-flowering species, in April. Fruits, if produced in September, are oval and dark purple, as are those of *O. delaváyi*, (VII), a native of western and southwestern China, from whence it was introduced into France in 1890 by the Abbe Delavay. This is probably the gem of the genus so far as our local gardens are concerned. The twiggy growths, well clothed with small oval, toothed, dark green leaves gradually builds itself up into a very neat and graceful shrub, perhaps 8 ft. high and more in width. The showers of fragrant, waxy, white flowers that appear in March and April in clusters from both the leaf axils and the ends of the shoots, produce an enchanting effect. It appears to be perfectly hardy in any well-drained soil in a sunny position. Some regular annual pruning in summer will probably be necessary to keep it in bounds. *O. × fórtunei*, (VII–VIII), is the hybrid, of Japanese origin, between *O. frágrans* from western China and *O. heteróphyllus (O. aquifólium)* from Japan. The leaves are large and toothed, like those of *O. armatus;* the flowers appear in late summer or early fall and are white and fragrant, as one would expect. 'San Jose' is a selection of this hybrid, raised in California in 1934. *O. heteró- phyllus*, (VI) is the hardiest and best known of these shrubs. The leaves of an adult specimen are very much like those of the common holly in size, shape and spiny margins, but can easily be distinguished from hollies by the fact that they are set opposite one another on the branches, while in hollies, genus *Ilex*, they are alternate. However, when mature, the leaves at the top of the plant will often lose their spines and look quite different; this can also happen in old hollies. *O. heterophyllus* bears its axillary clusters of highly fragrant, small white flowers in October, when there are few other shrubs blooming, so it is worth its space for that reason alone. In habit it is more or less upright, very bushy and well branched, so it does need plenty of space to fully develop, to a height very often of 15 ft. It is a good screening plant along a fence line. The form 'Myrtifolius' has spineless leaves only 1½–2 in. long, blunt and notched at the tip. For small gardens it is to be preferred. There are also forms with leaves variegated with creamy yellow along their margins ('Aureomarginatus') and white margined ('Variegatus') which are attractive in the winter for their coloration.

PAXÍSTIMA (or *PACHÍSTIMA*). Both spellings are in use by different authorities, but the former is preferred. *P. myrsinites,* the Mountain Box, (V) is a low shrub 2–3 ft. high found in the Cascade Mountains from British Columbia to California as an undergrowth beneath thin coniferous forest. It may be used in the same way in any partly shaded area in the garden, preferably in light, well-drained, slightly acid soil. Small plants, or portions of them, carefully collected from wild stands, can readily be reestablished in the garden. Although not showy, there is a certain charm in the pattern of its upright slender branches and small dark green leaves resembling those of *Buxus.* The very small reddish flowers are quite inconspicuous unless sought for in spring.

PERNÉTTYA mucronáta (VI–VII), native to southern Chile and Argentina, is an invaluable, small-leaved, ericaceous shrub grown principally for variously colored fruits, but also for its masses of flowers in May, small individually though they may be. The plants are commonly unisexual, so that to obtain a good crop of the fruits it is essential to have plants of both sexes growing near each other; one male in the midst of 5–6 female plants should be adequate for successful pollination. The fruits are berries, up to ½ in. in diameter; they range in color from pure white through rose and pink to maroon red; they should be seen in fruit in the nursery before selecting particular plants. They prefer a light sandy soil in which they can run easily, and will then soon cover a considerable area. The leaves are small, about ½ in. long, hard, spiny toothed, glossy green. Variety *angustifólia* has narrower leaves with a very short spine, or none at all. Some clones of this variety are male and bear no fruits. *P. mucronata* grows to about 4 ft. in height, likes a sunny situation in the company of other ericaceous shrubs, and can be easily propagated either by running shoots (stolons) or by cuttings in the case of extra good forms.

PHILLYRÉA (VII). This is a small genus with probably only two species, native around the Mediterranean Sea, in North Africa, and as far east as the shores of the Black Sea in Turkey and south to Israel. It is a common constituent of the maquis in those countries, together with the

Kermes Oak, *Quercus coccifera,* and other tough, woody shrubs. This species is *P. latifólia (P. média),* a large shrub or even a small tree, up to 15–20 ft. in height in time, with a dense habit of growth, making it an excellent subject for hedges. The leaves are quite variable in shape, from ovate to lanceolate, serrate or entire, sharply pointed, about 1–2 in. long. The flowers are small, greenish white, not showy, borne in May or June, in axillary clusters like those of *Osmanthus heterophyllus,* and slightly fragrant. A form with strongly toothed leaves is *spinósa.* The other species sometimes grown is *P. angustifólia,* native of much the same area, but in the western half of the Mediterranean more than in the east. In this species the leaves are very narrow, up to 2 in. long and about ½ in. wide, not toothed. It forms a dense shrub up to 10 ft. in height, and can be used in the same way as *P. latifolia.*

PHOTÍNIA. A genus containing both evergreen and deciduous shrubs and small trees, nearly all native to eastern Asia, except for one in California (*P. arbutifólia,* the Toyon), which unfortunately is not hardy in the Northwest. Of those evergreen species which we grow, *P. glábra* (VI–VII) from Japan, forms a compact shrub up to 10 ft. in height, 6–8 ft. in width, valued chiefly for the vivid coppery red coloring of its young foliage, maturing to a shining, deep green. The flowers, which appear in June, are borne in branching panicles 4–5 in. wide, are pinkish in bud becoming white when fully open and hawthorn scented. They make quite an attractive display at that season. If grown as a hedge and regularly clipped, more young foliage is produced and the coloring thereby prolonged. *P. serruláta* (VII–VIII), a small tree from China, is most commonly seen in our area, often planted against walls of houses and facing west or south, since it appreciates such a site, although in time usually growing too large for it. This is certainly one of the handsomest of the larger-leaved evergreen shrubs or small trees which we can grow, except for some of the rhododendrons of the *Falconera* subsection. As generally seen it grows to 25 ft. in height, though it can be larger under favorable conditions. As a young plant the red coloring of the young leaves is very noticeable; if the plant is regularly pruned by pinching back the young shoots this feature can be extended for some weeks, as well as encouraging it to become bushy in habit, which is desirable. The leaves are oblong, serrate and pointed, 5–7 in. in length; flowers are not produced until the plant is of some size and age—then in May, in large terminal panicles, the petals white. Fruits, if produced in the fall (October), are red, like small hawthorns. Since they start into growth earlier than most broad-leaved evergreen shrubs they should be planted early in the year, preferably in March.

P. × *fráseri* (VII) is the name given to the hybrid between the two preceding species, raised from seeds of *P. serrulata* at the Fraser Nurseries, Birmingham, AL, in 1940. In appearance and habit it more resembles the seed parent than the pollen parent, *P. glabra.* The leaves are approximately intermediate in size between the two parents, but notable for the brilliance of their red coloring, especially in spring. The inflorescences are also intermediate in size and are freely formed on established plants. Because of the ease of propagation by cuttings it has been planted on some highways, especially east of Seattle, almost to excess. Shrubs with such brilliant foliage coloring over an extended period should be used with discretion, and balanced by some less vivid foreground plantings. The original clone has been named 'Birmingham'. Others are 'Robusta' and 'Red Robin', of Australian origin.

PIÉRIS. Like the photinias, this genus contains both evergreen and deciduous species, most of them hailing from the Himalayas, China and Japan, with one native American plant, *P. floribúnda*. They are all valuable shrubs for our gardens, generally flowering profusely in the spring, from February to May according to the location and species, and free from pests or fungus diseases. Because of its greater hardiness *P. floribunda* (V) is more useful in colder climates than our own, where we can grow the other, more ornamental species. In it, the flower racemes are short and held up in clusters of several at the ends of the branches in late March and early April, surrounded by the dark green, 2–3 in. long leaves. The bushes are rounded in form, compact, and attain 5–6 ft. in time. *P. formósa* (VII–VIII) has the widest range of any member of the genus, being found from Nepal in the west to central China in the east, along the Himalayan chain, from whence came the earliest introductions to England in the 19th century. Later ones from China have proved to be hardier. The plants may grow up to 10–12 or even more ft. height in favorable situations where they are sheltered from cold winds and have some overhead protection from higher evergreens such as Douglas firs. The leaves are generally larger and glossier than those of the commonly grown *P. japonica*, although both can vary considerably in size and coloration; in *P. formosa* they are sharply serrated to the base, but much less so in *P. japonica*, being hardly more than crenate on their margins. The drooping panicles of pure white, pitcher-shaped flowers appear in May, much later than those of the Japanese species and as the new foliage is being produced, in clusters at the ends of the branches up to 6 in. long and wide. The spring coloring of the new growths, which may be bronze, copper or almost red in the best forms, adds greatly to the garden value of this splendid shrub. An annual mulch of compost or woodland humus, as for rhododendrons, is most beneficial. The variety *forréstii*, originally from Yunnan, southwest China, is said to have a more pendent habit, and a rounder and longer corolla, among other slight differences from the type. A clone of this variety is 'Wakehurst', named for the garden in Sussex, England, where it originated, now a branch garden for the Royal Botanic Garden at Kew in Surrey, near London. 'Wakehurst' is noted for the brilliant red coloring of the young foliage, which eventually turns to the normal green in summer. The flowers are large and urn shaped. 'Forest Flame' (VII) is a natural hybrid between *P. japonica* and one of the forms of *P. formosa* which arose in a nursery in the south of England. It is likely to attain 10 ft. or so in height with us, has an upright habit, and best of all is hardier than *P. formosa* and carries the rich red coloring of the young growths in spring which is so valuable a feature of the best clones of that species. 'Valley Fire' is an Oregon-bred hybrid with similar characteristics. *P. japonica* is certainly one of our most useful and valuable spring-flowering shrubs. When well cared for, the spreading or drooping glossy green leaves, and the masses of pendent trusses of pearly white flowers are conspicuous in many gardens and in many situations. Flower buds are formed during the previous season and are quite evident all winter, especially in the pink-flowered forms, of which there are now many named clones. Two of Japanese origin are 'Christmas Cheer' and 'Daisen'; others are 'Coleman', 'Mountain Fire', and two from the Willamette Experiment Station of Oregon State University, namely 'Valley Rose' and 'Valley Valentine'. It would be well to see them flowering before purchasing plants. 'White Cascade' is a selected white-flowered plant, also from Oregon. 'Crispa', of Japanese origin, has especially bright green, glossy leaves with an undulate margin; it makes an excellent informal hedge 5–6 ft. high. *P. taiwanénsis,* found in the mountains of Taiwan and formerly considered to be a distinct species, is now included by recent authority in *P. japonica,* so that name can be dropped from our gardens. Plants originating from that source are generally shorter and more compact than typical *P. japonica,* and the racemes are sometimes held upright or are spreading; they are considered to be somewhat hardier.

PITTÓSPORUM. This genus of both shrubs and trees is centered in Australasia, with outliers in eastern Asia, Africa, the Canary Islands and Madeira. At least two of the shrubby types can be grown here, and more might be possible in warmer areas near the coast, certainly from southwestern Oregon southwards. *P. glabrátum* (VII–VIII) is native to eastern China but has proved hardy in Seattle in all but the very coldest winters. Here it grows into a rounded bush some 7–8 ft. in height, well clothed with shining lanceolate leaves 4–5 in. long, and about 1 in. wide, undulate along their margins. The small tubular-campanulate yellow flowers are produced singly in the leaf axils in May, but are not conspicuous. This shrub can be propagated by cuttings taken as soon as firm in summer. It should be given a sunny position in well-drained soil to succeed here. The second is the Tobira of Japan, *P. tobíra,* (VII–VIII) native also to Korea, China and Taiwan as well as central and southern Japan. It is a more compact shrub than the former species and recommended for resistance to seaside conditions for its tough foliage, widest at the apex and tapering down to the base, each leaf about 3 in. long and 1 in. or so in width. Clusters of fragrant, creamy white flowers are produced in May at the ends of the branches, turning yellowish with age. In warmer climates it can reach 12–15 ft. in height, but with us 5–6 ft. is more normal. A sunny location in well-drained

Part of a flowering bush of *Pittosporum tobira* in Seattle in late May. Photo by Brian Mulligan.

soil is essential; some protection in exceptionally cold winters may be necessary. Propagation by either seeds or cuttings is possible. There is also a variegated form in cultivation, 'Variegatum'.

PRUNUS laurocerásus (VI–VII), the Common Laurel or Cherry Laurel, is found wild in southeastern Europe (Yugoslavia and Bulgaria) to western Asia (Turkey and the Caucasus region), where it is often associated with *Rhododendron ponticum,* the native beech tree (*Fagus orientalis*), as well as ivy (*Hedera*) and hollies. It may occur as high as 6,000–7,000 ft. in elevation in those areas, so should be thoroughly hardy here if obtainable from there, which may not be easy. It also extends into northwestern Iran. Under cultivation it has produced about 30 cultivars of great variety. Around Puget Sound this ubiquitous shrub is most often seen grown as a hedge, for which purpose it is least suited. Its coarse texture and greedy root system make it a poor background for other plantings. It cannot be clipped without damaging the handsome leaves, so each shoot must be pruned individually, which makes the cost of maintenance exorbitantly high. When allowed to grow freely it becomes a superb shrub or even a small tree, but here we are concerned with the former types, which can be used as hedges or large groundcovers or on highway banks or dividers. For such purposes the best are probably 'Schipkaensis' and 'Zabeliana', both growing to about 6 ft. in height and spreading as widely or more if not restricted; their leaves are narrow, entire, 3–4 in. long; they produce short racemes of white flowers in May, even on clipped plants. A third clone of more recent German origin is 'Otto Luyken', very compact in habit, up to about 4 ft. in height, the leaves dark green, also narrow; it is very free-

The popular form of the common laurel, *Prunus laurocerasus* 'Otto Luyken', in flower in early summer. Photo by Don Normark.

flowering and a useful shrub for covering banks. The dwarfest form is 'Mount Vernon', reaching only 1 ft. or little more in height. This originated at Everett, WA, and has been propagated and named by Wells Nursery of Mount Vernon, WA. Generally, no form of laurel likes a hot dry situation, so they should have some shade in the afternoon if possible and not have to compete with tree roots. They are propagated by cuttings taken in late summer, or earlier if under mist.

PYRACÁNTHA. The firethorns are perhaps the most widely used wall shrubs in this region, with their masses of yellow, orange or red fruits in October–November, until the birds strip them off. They should be grown more often as freestanding specimens, smothered with tiny white flowers in June, then becoming 10–12 ft. high, dense, leafy shrubs, usually thorny, and consequently making good barrier plants if required. If possible, they should have the benefit of a warm southern or western exposure, since most of them hail from warmer climates than ours. To train them as wall shrubs, distribute the growths over a sufficiently large area so that the plant does not have to be mercilessly butchered after it has reached certain limits. Encourage the plant to make plenty of basal growth before allowing it to stretch upwards. Pruning is best done in spring before new growth commences. They are susceptible to the bacterial disease fire blight, as are the evergreen cotoneasters; any affected flowers or shoots should be immediately cut out and burned. *P. angustifólia,* (VII–VIII) from southwestern China, is distinct in its downy gray shoots, narrow oblong notched leaves up to 2 in. long and ½ in. wide. Bunches of orange fruits ripen in November but remain on the plants until the following spring. In habit it is a very dense thorny shrub up to 9–10 ft. in height, and about as wide. *P. coccínea* (VII), the best-known and commonest of the firethorns, is native to southern Europe and western Asia. Of dense irregular habit of growth, it is also thorny and should be treated with respect when handling branches. The leaves are more or less evergreen, except in unusually severe weather; the white flowers are borne in clusters (corymbs) along the previous year's branches in early June, and are followed in October– November by masses of the brilliant orange-red fruits, each about ¼ in. across. Several such plants together create an almost overpowering splash of color, at least for a short time until the birds remove them. 'Lalandei' is an improved form originating in France about 1874, having a more upright habit of growth, larger leaves and fruits, the latter more orange in coloring. More recent hybrids or selections of Dutch origin are 'Keessen', 'Orange Giant' and 'Orange King'. Unfortunately this species is quite susceptible to apple scab disease, and in areas where this is prevalent it would be better to plant one of the following Chinese species, or their hybrids, which are much less affected by this problem. *P. crenáto-serráta (P. fortuneána)* (VI–VII) is native to west and northwest China, growing to about 15 ft. in height, with obovate leaves about 2 in. long and half as wide, rounded at the apex and coarsely toothed; the fruits are coral-red and can remain until spring if they are not eaten by birds. 'Orange Glow', from Holland, is probably a hybrid between this species and *P. coccinea.* The fruits begin to color in late September and are orange-red. The plant is reputed to be resistant to scab disease. *P. koidzúmii* (VII) comes from Taiwan, has oblanceolate, entire leaves tapering to the base, and a downy inflorescence. According to Dr. Donald Wyman it is frequently grown in the southeastern States. Many selections of it have been made by Californian nurserymen; some of them are 'Rosedale', 'Santa Cruz', 'San Jose' and 'Walderi Prostrata'. Whether these are fully hardy in the Puget Sound region has yet to be proved. 'Mohave' is a hybrid between *P. koidzumii* and *P. coccinea* bred at the U.S. National Arboretum, having large orange-red fruits in September; it is also resistant to disease. 'Shawnee' is a hybrid between *P. crenato-serrata* and *P. koidzumii,* also from the same source, so we have many more forms of pyracanthas now than we did in 1940. One other species from southwest China is *P. rogersiána,* introduced to England by George Forrest in 1911. Becoming a spiny shrub 8 ft. or so in height, it has the smallest leaves in the genus, oblanceolate, 1 in. or little more in length, rounded at the tip, gland-toothed, shining on the upper side. The flowers are small but very numerous, again opening in June like the flowers of most of these shrubs, the inflorescence glabrous. Fruits can be either orange, red or yellow, which adds to the attraction of this species. Selected color forms can be raised from cuttings taken in late summer or early fall. Because of its smaller size this is an admirable plant for city gardens. Two Dutch hybrids between *P. coccinea* and *P. rogersiana* are 'Golden Charmer' with orange-yellow, and 'Orange Charmer' with deep orange fruits.

QUÉRCUS. Most of the species in this very large genus are definitely trees, and usually of considerable size when mature. There are, however, two shrubby species found in southwestern Oregon and northern California which can be grown in our area with confidence and pleasure. These are *Q. sadleriána* (VI), the Deer Oak, which forms a bush usually 4–5 ft. high and as much or more in width in the course of time, with tough, smooth, gray-green branches and oblong-obovate leaves 3–4 in. long and about half as wide, toothed on both sides to near the base. The upper side is dark green, the lower much paler, making a nice contrast between them. The 10–12 pairs of parallel veins are conspicuously raised beneath, making in all a very distinctive leaf for an oak. This plant prefers an open site but will also tolerate some shade and remain fairly compact; soil drainage should be good. It is best propagated by seeds, but layering the lower branches would be a possible method of increase. The second species to be included is *Q. vacciniifolia,* (VI) the Huckleberry Oak, a bushy shrub attaining about 6 ft. in cultivation, but often less in the wild state on southwestern Oregon or northern California hillsides. The leaves are very much smaller than those of *Q. sadleriana,* only 1 in. or so in length, light green on the upper side, white-hairy beneath, not toothed. It definitely appreciates the sunniest spot in the garden that can be found for it, such as on a bank facing south or west; there it will live long and give much pleasure to its owner.

RHÁMNUS. Of the Buckthorns, only two need concern us, one from southern Europe and around the Mediterranean, the other from southern Oregon and California. The former is *R. alatérnus* (VI–VII), a shrub much resembling *Phillyrea latifolia,* but having alternate instead of opposite leaves, 1–2 in. long, about half as wide, usually toothed when young but often entire later. Flowers, in April, are inconspicuous, yellowish, in the leaf axils in short racemes; the fruits small and black, as is usual in this genus. The plant will grow up to 10 ft. in height and can be used for a hedge or screen like the *Phillyrea.* Propagation by cuttings is relatively easy. Plants are dioecious, the two sexes on different individuals. They enjoy calcareous soils. The second species we can grow here is *R. califórnica,* the Coffeeberry, (VII–VIII), a more open bush in its habit than the last, reaching 8–10 ft. in height, with oblong, yellowish green leaves some 2 in. in length and 1 in. wide, with markedly parallel veining. The fruits are somewhat larger than those of *R. alaternus,* at first red then turning black when mature. Seeds provide the easiest means of propagation. Californian selections are 'Compacta' and 'Sea View'.

RHAPHIOLÉPIS umbelláta, (R. ováta, R. japónica), (VII), the Yeddo Hawthorn from Japan and Korea, is a sturdy shrub with leathery, dark green, rounded leaves 2–3 in. long on a stout stalk, toothed towards their apices, very downy when young but glabrous later. The white flowers are held up on terminal panicles, in June, and are fragrant. The fruits are black when ripe. It is a slow-growing shrub eventually reaching 3–4 ft. in height and as much or more in width. It is well suited to a sunny situation on the south or west sides of a house, where it will never become a nuisance. A much less hardy species is *R. índica*, (VIII), a native of China despite its specific name, having thinner, narrower, serrated leaves, and racemes of pink flowers, especially in the numerous selected California-raised forms such as 'Rosea', 'Flamingo', 'Pink Cloud', 'Coates Crimson' and others. These can be grown around the Northwest only in the warmest and most sheltered gardens, but even in such cases it would probably be safest if grown in containers which can be moved under cover in severe weather. A hybrid between these two species is *R. × delacóurii*, (VII–VIII), bred in France at the end of the 19th century. Its leaves more resemble those of *R. umbellata*, being obovate, leathery and toothed at the apex; the flowers, however, are pink. This cultivar can be expected to reach 5–6 ft. in eventual height. Propagation can be by cuttings taken as soon as firm in summer, or later in the fall.

RHODODENDRON. The rhododendrons constitute without question the most important genus of broad-leaved evergreen shrubs for this region. Such great advances have been made in breeding new hybrids during the past 50 years or so that the kinds now being grown in our local gardens have completely changed from those seen prior to the Second World War. This breeding first took place in the British Isles and Holland, then in the Pacific Coast states with their similar climate, if west of the Cascade Range; the eastern and to a lesser extent the middle western states, for greater hardiness, and more recently in Australia and New Zealand. With so many new introductions appearing in these and other countries such as Germany and Sweden, it becomes increasingly difficult for the average gardener to make a choice, unless he or she can see fair-sized plants growing in a test garden, arboretum or large nursery. Container-grown plants give little or no idea of how the plants will eventually develop in size, form and flowering qualities.

Distribution. In the wild state rhododendrons are found principally in the temperate and warm-temperate regions of the world, chiefly in eastern Asia, with a center of distinction located between Sikkim and Nepal in the Himalaya Mountains, eastwards to western China. This is where the bulk of the finest and most attractive species now known have originated and then been introduced, thanks to the work of such collectors as Dr. J. D. Hooker in the mid-19th century and E. H. Wilson, F. Kingdon-

Ward, George Forrest and Dr. J. F. Rock in the present century. In the matter of numbers and kinds introduced Forrest was certainly the acknowledged leader. Japan is also the home of a number of species of the Subsection (formerly Series) *Póntica,* including the now famous *R. yakushimanum,* but of many more azaleas, with which we shall deal later. In North America we have three relatives in the same group, *R. maximum* and *R. catawbiense* in the east, and *R. macrophyllum* along the Pacific Coast, with one deciduous species here (*R. occidentale*) and some 16 in the eastern states and southeastern Canada. The huge Section *Viréya,* from New Guinea, Borneo and adjacent countries in the tropics, is outside our consideration here.

Cultivation. It is essential that rhododendrons have a lime-free soil, although they will tolerate one containing magnesian limestone. They definitely prefer a sandy, gravelly or peaty soil which drains readily to one which remains wet in winter, or a clay type with very poor drainage and a tendency to drying out in the summer. Clayey soils can all be improved by the addition of humus in some form,—leafmold, peat, old stable manure, old sawdust in limited quantities, or whatever other vegetable matter may be locally available. Heavy soils can be improved by the addition of coarse sand or small grit, but the question of good drainage is all-important. As a general rule it can be safely stated that all rhododendrons of any size benefit from an annual mulch of some vegetable material such as peat or leafmold or compost. It is more important than any commercial fertilizer, although these may be necessary additives in some cases.

It may be taken as a general rule that most rhododendrons except the smallest alpine types prefer partial shade, especially during the afternoons in summer, and also that the larger the leaves the more shade they will need. The large-leaved species of the *Falconéra* Subsection (or Series *Falconeri*), such as *R. falconeri, R. rex,* or *R. hodgsonii,* accustomed to heavy monsoon rains in the summer, particularly need shade and regular moisture when in growth. Planting each individual in a shallow basin makes watering very much easier during the first two or three years; the depression will be gradually filled by annual mulching. If it is important to provide sufficient water during the growing period it is equally important to slow it down and then cut it off once new growth has been completed and flower buds formed for the following year, unless the summer is exceptionally dry. Many of the older, hardy hybrids grow surprisingly well under rather adverse conditions, even when lacking regular watering and facing west against walls or fences; the newer, less-vigorous or less-hardy cultivars need more care in their siting and subsequent treatment, but will amply repay this in the quantity and color of their blooms, as well as in extending the flowering season both early and late. Pruning, except for the annual removal of the old flower heads as soon as possible after flowering, does not have to be done regularly but chiefly when individual branches tend to grow out in one direction and then need shortening, or when an old neglected plant has to be severely pruned back to rejuvenate it. In this case care should be taken to cut back to visible dormant buds at the base of an annual growth, and not beyond that point. It will probably require two years after such treatment for new flower buds to be formed. This should be done in early spring before growth commences. Watch should be kept for suckers arising from the base of any hybrid which has been propagated by grafting. Promptly remove them before they become large, tearing or pulling them away from the graft above. However, fewer plants are now being propagated by this means; more either by cuttings or micropropagation under sterile conditions. Disbudding vigorously growing hybrids in their early years is good practice, if they produce two or three flower buds together. Extra-long shoots can be made to branch by removing the terminal growth bud early in the year.

Propagation. Rhododendrons can be propagated by seeds, cuttings, layers, grafting or budding. For the amateur grower, cuttings or layers are the simplest methods. Cuttings should be taken of the smaller-leaved species and hybrids as soon as the new growths are firm enough, usually in June or early July, inserted in a mixture of peat and coarse sand in flats or pots (not clay pots, which dry out too quickly), watered thoroughly, then covered by a plastic sack kept off the cuttings by means of a wire support and placed in a shady site until rooting occurs. A cool greenhouse or cold frame are useful for this purpose. During the first winter they should not be allowed to freeze as the cuttings will be killed. Artificial light in a basement can be beneficial in hastening their development. In the spring they should be individually potted in a richer soil mixture to grow on, later transplanting them into a frame or nursery row.

Larger-leaved hybrids can be attempted by similar methods, but the cuttings should be inserted around the perimeter of plastic or neoprene pots after first being wounded on one or both sides and dipped in a hormone rooting liquid or powder to increase their rooting chances. Again, cuttings should be taken as soon as the new growths are firm enough, probably in July or August, but the time varying considerably with the individual variety. Layering of lower branches of particularly desirable plants can be done either in fall or early spring. The selected branch should be bent upwards until it cracks but does not break, then fastened down and covered with a quantity of mixed sandy soil and compost into which the plant can root. On top of this place one or two rocks to hold the branch in place during the two years necessary to form a good root system, after which it can be separated from the mother plant and transplanted elsewhere. More details on methods of propagation can be found in various books dealing with the culture of rhododendrons. The chapter in W. J. Bean's *Trees and Shrubs Hardy in the British Isles,* 8th edition, vol. III, (1976), is recommended; also many articles in the pages of the *Quarterly Bulletin of the American Rhododendron Society* (see the two Indices).

Species classification. For about 50 years the only available system of classification of the species of *Rhododendron* was that published in the book *The Species of Rhododendron* (London, 1930), edited by J. B. Stevenson but having three principal authors, namely Dr. A. Rehder from the Arnold Arboretum, Boston, MA.; Dr. John Hutchinson from Kew, London; and H. F. Tagg, at the Royal Botanic Garden, Edinburgh. The species described in this classification system were arranged into Series, based on a tentative classification proposed by Sir I. Bayley Balfour at Edinburgh, who died in 1922. Keys were provided for distinguishing the different species within each Series, and short descriptions of each were given, making it a very useful handbook for growers of these plants. The next botanical classification was that by Dr. H. Sleumer, of Leiden, Holland, in 1949, published in a German botanical journal and therefore not easily accessible to the amateur grower. Sleumer divided the genus into subgenera, sections and subsections; by far the largest being those having scales beneath the leaves, the Lepidote group, with about 500 species. The others, the Elepidote, have no scales and constitute the subgenus *Hymenánthes*. Most recently (1978–1979) Drs. Cullen and Chamberlain, working at Edinburgh, have published a third arrangement of the species, dividing them into two subgenera following Dr. Sleumer, then into smaller sections and subsections. The two arrangements (of 1930 and 1978–1979) are published side-by-side, together with a parallel horticultural revision by the Royal Horticultural Society (author C. D. Brickell) in *The Rhododendron Handbook* (R.H.S., London, 1980). In the present work we shall adhere to the Cullen and Chamberlain arrangement, since this has been adopted by the American Rhododendron Society.

Descriptions. The length of the rhododendron blooming season is not approached by any other genus of shrubs, which is one reason why they are so valuable in our gardens. Starting with the deciduous species *R. mucronulatum* in January, succeeded by the dwarf *R. moupinense* a month or so later, others take up flowering in quick succession until a peak is reached in May; then a decline in numbers sets in until the final display is made by the huge *R. auriculatum* with its papery white trusses of blooms in August,—a time when all thoughts of rhododendrons flowering have long passed.

The following list, it is believed, will include most, or at any rate a fair selection of the best species now available commercially from specialist growers. It is of course realized that everyone will have his own ideas and reasons for selecting certain species for his own garden, especially habit, time of flowering and color of the blooms, and the quality of the foliage, which is important when the plants are not in bloom. We shall start with the smaller-growing, smaller-leaved types, and work up towards the larger in both respects, since fewer people have room for planting the latter and some of them are scarce in nurseries. We shall also indicate the earlier- and later-flowering kinds, by giving the former priority over the latter. The dwarf species, less than 18 in. in height, will be found in the chapter on Small Shrubs. Primary hybrids between species are included here.

Smaller species. *R. moupinénse* (VII), already mentioned, is the first of the fully evergreen species to flower, in February and early March, weather permitting. Growing 2–3 ft. high and somewhat wider, it is usually well decked with 2-in.-wide, white to pale pink flowers; however, it is very susceptible to frosts, so it should be given a place where the morning sun will not strike it. The small, oval, convex leaves are reddish when young and quite attractive. This character is frequently passed on to its hybrids, e.g., 'Cilpinense', 'Bo-Peep', and 'Bric-a-Brac', all of which are valuable early-flowering shrubs; 'Bo-Peep' has pale yellow flowers, the other two pale pink to white. *R. fletcheriánum,* (VI–VII) discovered by Dr. Joseph Rock on the borders of China and Tibet in 1932, is a shrub of 3–4 ft., with rather bristly green leaves and wide, funnel-shaped, pale yellow flowers opening in late March or early April. It is related to *R. ciliátum* (VII) and *R. valentiniánum* (VIII) of the *Maddénia* Subsection. The first of these two was found in Sikkim by Dr. J. D. Hooker in 1850 and introduced by him to England; it is also found in other countries along the Himalayan chain. A shrub 3–4 ft. high, the bristly stems and leaves are very conspicuous; flowers are open, funnel shaped, appearing in late March and early April, pale pink at first then almost white.

Two closely related species in the subsection *Triflóra* are *R. lutéscens* (VII) from western China and *R. kéiskei* (VI–VII) from Japan. Since the former flowers earlier than the latter, sometimes even in late February and always by March, and *R. keiskei,* named for a Japanese botanist who discovered it, in April, they could well be planted together to provide a succession of pale yellow blossoms in early spring. *R. lutéscens* is taller, to 7 ft. or so, so should be in the rear; its leaves are narrow-lanceolate, reddish when young, but those of *R. keiskei* pale green and shorter.

Two other related species in Subsection *Lappónica* blooming in March and April are *R. hippophaeoídes* (VI–VII),—the long name means resembling a *Hippophae,* the Sea Buckthorn shrub,—and *R. russátum.* Both come from the same region of western China and were introduced by George Forrest to English gardens in 1913 and 1917 respectively. Both form shrubs about 4 ft. tall, have scaly, gray-green leaves in the former, but greener above in the latter, and tight clusters of small lavender flowers in *R. hippophaeoides,* purple in the other species. They are admirable shrubs for the front of a border, and can easily be propagated by cuttings.

Subsection *Triflora* contains a number of most useful, garden-worthy species, including *R. augustínii* (VII) with flowers in various shades of blue in late April and early May, borne on shrubs 9–10 ft. high. There is a fine group of them near the north entrance to the Washington Park Arboretum in Seattle, planted about 1944 or perhaps earlier. The bronze coloring of the young foliage is an additional attractive feature. Selections chosen for their improved color are 'Barto Blue' and 'Marine'. 'Electra' is a hybrid between the type species and subsp. *chasmánthum* which has larger flowers in clusters of up to seven, violet-blue in color with a green patch in the throat. The subspecies *rúbrum* has red flowers.

Two other nearly related species here are *R. davidsoniánum* (VII) and *R. yunnanénse* (VII), both coming from southwest China but introduced at different times, the latter to France in 1889, the former by E. H. Wilson in 1904. *R. davidsonianum* is evergreen, growing up to 10 ft. in height and having clusters of pale pink flowers spotted with red dots in mid-April. *R. yunnanense* flowers three or four weeks later, is only partially evergreen, and can vary in color from white to pale pink or pale lavender, spotted brown or red. Because of their different flowering times these two can well be planted together, using several plants of each if space permits. Although placed in the same subsection, *R. oreotréphes* (VII) is very distinct with its elliptic leaves about 2 in. long and 1 in. wide, gray-green on the upper side but scaly and glaucous beneath. The flowers, produced in clusters at the ends of the shoots in early May, are funnel shaped, about 2 in. across, pale lilac-pink as a rule although they can vary somewhat in color when raised from seeds. Another related species but with flowers of a very different color is *R. concínnum* (VII), native to Mt. Omei in western Sichuan, China, and another of Wilson's introductions. This makes a shrub 9–10 ft. high; the leaves are dark green, scaly on both sides, especially beneath, elliptic, 2–3 in. long; the widely funnel shaped flowers are purple, held in terminal clusters usually of five or six flowers. This color creates a strong contrast to the other paler-flowered species at this season and should be used more often.

An early-blooming, red-flowered species is *R. neriiflórum, (R. euchaítes),* (VII), found in the wild in southwest China (Yunnan) to the eastern Himalayan region. Introduced by George Forrest in 1910 to Great Britain, it is a shrub of rather open habit growing usually 5–7 ft. in height, with oblong leaves 2–3 in. long and about 1 in. wide, noticeably glaucous white beneath; the tubular-bell-shaped, blood red flowers appear in late March or April, each about 1½ in. long, borne in groups of five or seven at the ends of the branches. In the wild this species has been known to reach 15 ft. or more. A related species is *R. floccígerum,* with flowers varying from red to yellow. Another lower-growing species with rich red flowers is *R. haematódes* (VI–VII), also from Yunnan Province, China, at elevations of 12–13,000 ft. This is a much more compact, slower-growing shrub than the last two and well suited to a larger rock garden. The leathery, obovate leaves are dark glossy green on the upper side, but covered beneath with a dense brown wool, a character which no doubt makes it hardier than the almost glabrous *R. neriiflorum.* The funnel-shaped flowers are carried on long pedicels, in trusses of six or more, and are nearly 2 in. long and wide. It has been used as a parent for many well-known hybrids including 'Grosclaude', 'Humming Bird', and 'May Day'.

From Nepal and the eastern Himalaya comes *R. glaucophýllum,* (VII), introduced originally by Sir Joseph Hooker in 1850. This species forms a rather loose-habited bush about 4–5 ft. high, the oblong leaves quite glaucous beneath and with a strong aromatic smell when rubbed or broken. The calyx is large for the flower, green and scaly; the flowers rose pink, campanulate, produced in clusters of five or six in May. More than 100 years later, in 1953, a yellow-flowered plant was discovered by Frank Kingdon-Ward in Upper Burma which proved to be the same species; this is var. *luteiflórum* and even more attractive than the original pink form. They are most effective if planted in groups at the front of a border of larger plants. Propagation can be done by either seeds, cuttings or layers. *R. charitópes* is a closely related species well worth acquiring, with appleblossom pink flowers, as is *R. tephropéplum (R. deleiénse)* (VII–VIII), found by several collectors at the eastern end of the Himalayas and in Assam and Upper Burma, but somewhat less hardy than the preceding species. This is a small bush, up to 4 ft. tall, the leaves oblong, 3–4 in. long, glaucous and scaly beneath, the flowers appearing in loose trusses of four to seven in April and May, funnel shaped, of some shade of pink or rose. A very different species both in habit and flower characters is *R. abercónwayi,* discovered in eastern Yunnan Province, China, and introduced in 1937 as a new species, later named for the second Lord Aberconway, financial supporter of the expedition which discovered it. It forms rather a stiff shrub, more upright in habit than most, the leaves tough, oblong-ovate, somewhat convex above, about 2 in. long and 1 in. wide; the flowers are borne in May or June, on a short raceme of six to ten, each 2 or more inches wide, saucer shaped, white with crimson spots. A selected form has been named 'His Lordship'.

R. *williamsiánum* (VII), is a near relative of other species in the Thomsónia Subsection, native to only a few localities in western China but a most valuable addition to our gardens, and introduced by E. H. Wilson in 1908. In an open situation it will form a rounded, dense bush some 4–5 ft. high, 5–6 ft. in width; the leaves are small, ovate with heart-shaped bases, copper colored when young, opening with the pale pink, bell-shaped flowers in late April, usually borne in pairs on slender stalks. If shaded by surrounding trees it will not flower freely, so be careful of the site when placing it. Like many of its kin with leaves lacking any protecting indumentum or scales, the leaves will curl up in cold weather but unfold again when this is past. It will certainly tolerate temperatures below 10°F., if not accompanied by much wind. As a parent it has been widely used and often successfully. The taller 'Bow Bells' is one of its best-known offspring; others are 'Moonstone', (pale yellow or pink); 'Humming Bird' (low growing, red); 'Brocade', (blush pink), and 'Jock', a hybrid with *R. griersonianum* and consequently late flowering with rose-red, more tubular flowers.

One other species, borderline in hardiness, which should be

included here, is *R. edgewórthii (R. bullátum)*, (VIII), first found in Sikkim by
Dr. J. D. Hooker in 1850, later by other collectors farther east into western
China (Yunnan and Sichuan provinces). It frequently grows as an
epiphyte in moss and humus on tree trunks, but can attain 5–6 ft. in height.
The young shoots are covered with a thick brown felt of hairs, as is the
underside of the leathery, ovate, deeply veined leaves. Usually two or
three flowers are produced in May at the ends of the branches; they are
trumpet-shaped, often tinged pink in the bud stage but white with a yellow
blotch inside, 1 in. long and nearly as wide, highly fragrant. A most lovely
plant and worthy of receiving tender, loving care, in the form of protection in the winter, if grown outdoors, though better if in a container which
can be brought into a cool greenhouse or basement if necessary. Attractive hybrids derived from it include 'Princess Alice' and 'Fragrantis-
simum', which are also tender.

Species of larger size. Here we have a very wide choice and again
personal tastes must dictate individual choices. Beginning in March there
are two very similar species with pink flowers borne in profusion on established shrubs; these are *R. oreodóxa* and *R. fárgesii*, (VII) both hailing from
western China, growing into large shrubs about 10 ft. tall, with oblong,
smooth leaves about 3 in. long and half as wide, noticeably paler on the
underside than above, the flowers borne in trusses of six to eight, having
seven-lobed corollas 2–2½ in. long and nearly as wide. In early spring
large plants of these species can be a most cheering sight when in full
bloom. For a brilliant red at about the same time *R. strigillósum* (VII–VIII)
can be recommended, though of quite different habit than the two
preceding, being denser and more compact in its branching, with very
narrow, lanceolate leaves, 5–6 in. long and bristly beneath. The flowers are
held in a tight terminal truss and are tubular-campanulate in shape with
nectar pouches at the base. These flower characters often reappear in its
hybrids. It is also native to western China.

One of the finest for its blood red, bell-shaped flowers borne in loose
trusses in late March or early April is the Himalayan *R. thómsonii*, (VII)
another of Dr. Hooker's introductions from Sikkim in 1850, becoming
here an open-habited shrub some 10 ft. in height, the foliage very attractive with oblong, smooth leaves, dark green on the upper side but waxy
white beneath. The large fleshy calyx is a feature of the flowers, sometimes tinged red. It has been much used as a parent of many hybrids; some
of them are 'Luscombei', 'Cornish Cross', 'Barclayi' and 'Shilsonii'. They
are not always as hardy here as *R. thomsonii*, so care needs to be taken in
selecting any of them.

Two other very similar Himalayan species flowering in April are *R.
campanulátum* and *R. wallíchii*, (VII). Both form large shrubs 10–12 ft. tall,
often with a central leader. The leaves are oblong-oval, 3–4 in. long, about
2 in. wide, pubescent on the underside and sometimes completely coated
there with a felt of brown hairs, sometimes with only a few tufts of hairs.

The nature of these hairs is the only distinguishing character between the two species, since the flowers are similar, being usually some shade of lilac or purple, occasionally white, the five-petalled corolla about 2 in. wide, bell shaped. The selection 'Knap Hill' has flowers more blue than purple and is desirable. A Chinese (n.w. Yunnan Province) species chiefly grown for its remarkable foliage is R. buréavii, (VI), a dense bush generally 8–10 ft. high but perhaps wider in the course of time. Its leaves are ovate-elliptic, 3–4 in. long, dark green and veined above but covered beneath with a thick coating of rust red hairs, as are the young branches, which no doubt protect the plant from low temperatures in its mountain home. It may take some years to produce blooms; these appear in April or May, in trusses of 10 or 12, the corollas funnel- to bell-shaped, nearly 2 in. long, white spotted crimson. It is perhaps best used as a background or filler specimen, because of its dense habit and sparse flowering until older. Another useful background shrub is R. rubiginósum (VII), likewise of Chinese and Tibetan origin, but with much smaller leaves only 2–3 in. in length and covered beneath with reddish scales; flowers also in April and May, in groups of four to six, the corollas rose-lilac in color, spotted on the upper petal, funnel shaped, about 2 in. across. This species has potential as a hedge plant, as does its later-flowering relative, R. heliolépis.

For those who like yellow-flowered plants there is the Himalayan R. campylocárpum (VII), discovered and introduced by Dr. Hooker from eastern Nepal in 1848 and named by him for the curved seed pods. Forming a rather open shrub with slender branches, it is not one of the more robust species and appreciates shelter from cold winds or hot sun. The leaves are elliptic, blunt, dark and shining above but paler or even glaucous beneath, 2–3 in. long; flowers borne in a loose cluster of four to eight, on glandular pedicels; the calyx also is glandular. The corolla is bell shaped, five-lobed, about 2 in. across, pale or deeper yellow, sometimes with a crimson blotch. When flowering well this is a very beautiful plant and worth extra care and attention. Some of its numerous offspring are 'Exminster', 'Damaris', 'Gladys', and 'Goldsworth Yellow'. R. caloxánthum, from Upper Burma, is a smaller shrub now considered to be a subspecies of R. campylocarpum. Its flowers are orange-red in bud opening to yellow or apricot; height to 5 ft. R. wárdii (R. cróceum; R. litiénse) (VII) is closely related to R. campylocarpum but has a more easterly range, from southeastern Tibet where it was collected by Ludlow, Sherriff and Taylor in the 1930s, but much earlier, in 1913, by both George Forrest and Kingdon-Ward in northwest Yunnan Province, China. This is a much more robust shrub than R. campylocarpum, growing up to 10 or more ft. in height and having larger leaves of varying shapes from nearly round to oblong, up to 4 in. long and 2 in. wide, always paler beneath than above. The flowers open in mid-May, borne in loose trusses at the ends of the branches, on long pedicels; the corolla is saucer shaped, yellow, 2 in. or more across, sometimes with a crimson blotch inside. This is a very handsome and valuable plant for our Northwest gardens but should be placed so that it receives only morning sun, with shade in the afternoon in the summer. Named English clones are 'Ellestee' and 'Meadow Pond'. Some of its hybrids are 'Idealist', 'Cowslip', 'Prelude', 'Hawk' and 'Crest'. For a species with rose to pink flowers to match these two well in foliage *R. orbiculáre* (VII) is available. This species forms a rounded bush up to 8 ft. in height eventually and about as wide. The leaves are almost round, as the name indicates, about 3 in. long, glaucous beneath. The flowers are widely bell shaped, almost bowl shaped, about 2 in. across, seven-lobed, usually rose-pink but varying somewhat in shade of color depending upon the sources of the stock. Flowering time April–May. 'Fortorb' is a handsome, vigorous hybrid with *R. fortunei*, while 'Temple Belle' resulted from crossing *R. orbiculare* with *R. williamsianum.*

R. fórtunei (VII), named for Robert Fortune who introduced it from seeds collected in eastern China (Zhejiang Province) in 1855, is undoubtedly one of the fines! of its race, both for the quality of the large, oblong leaves supported on stout, purplish stalks, but especially for the loose trusses of fragrant, blush pink flowers produced in May. Each may be 3 in. across and has seven lobes to the corolla. It has proved to be quite hardy in Seattle despite its origin, but needs space to reach its attainable size of 10 ft. or more in height and width. Many hybrids have been derived from it, including the most famous of them all, *R. × lóderi*, of which the Himalayan *R. griffithianum* was the male parent; *R. × lúscombei*, when crossed with *R. thomsonii*, and 'Gladys' and 'Letty Edwards' when *R. campylocarpum* was the other parent. The 'Naomi' series is derived from *R. fortunei* crossed with 'Aurora', a hybrid which included *R. thomsonii* in its pedigree. If *R. fortunei* is a prince amongst *Rhododendron* species then *R. decórum* (VII) might be considered his princess, being in the same subsection of the genus (Fortúnea) and very similar in appearance and habit, except that the latter tends to be a taller plant as it ages. The leaves are usually somewhat smaller, more wedge shaped than rounded at the base, the stalk not purplish. The flowers are more often white than pink, also very fragrant, borne in 8–10 flowered trusses in June; the corolla has six to eight lobes and the style is covered with white or yellow glands, a distinguishing character. Native to western China, where it is widespread. Because of its probable eventual height of 10–12 ft., it should be planted in the rear of the border.

An April-flowering species from Japan is *R. degroniánum,* (VI–VII) a member of the important Subsection Póntica, which has contributed several valuable species from various parts of the world to North American gardens, including *R. pónticum,* so much used as a stock in past years but less so nowadays; *R. máximum* and *R. catawbiénse* from the eastern U.S.A., our own western *R. macrophýllum; R. caucásicum* from southern U.S.S.R. and others. *R. degronianum* is a variable plant in nature but generally has long usually elliptical leaves, shiny on the upper side,

The handsome, fragrant pale pink flowers of *Rhododendron fortunei*. Photo by Brian Mulligan, in late May.

Rhododendron × loderi and seedlings flowering in mid-May in Seattle. Photo by Brian Mulligan.

A thirty-year old tree of *Rhododendron sinogrande* in midsummer.
Photo by Brian Mulligan.

covered beneath with a thick layer of brownish hairs. The flowers are
borne in loose trusses of 10–15, and are some shade of pink, some deeper
than others and therefore preferable. The plants form bushes 5–6 ft. in
height and rather more in width. The corollas of the type plant have five
lobes, but seven in the variety *heptámerum (R. metterníchii)*.

The best-known species in this group is undoubtedly *R.
yakushimánum,* (VI) found only on Yakushima Island south of Japan proper
and introduced into England in 1934 from the nursery of K. Wada.
Botanically it is very closely related to the preceding species but has somewhat shorter, more convex, very glossy leaves densely covered with fawn-
colored felt beneath. On the island it grows at about 5,000–6,000 ft. elevation, being of course smaller in size at the higher elevation. In the garden
plants should be placed where they will receive sufficient sun to mature
the growths and buds, but at the same time not be too dry in the summer
months. Facing west is desirable if possible, and without too much overhead shade. Flowers are borne in a dense, compact truss in late May and
number up to 12 in each; the bell-shaped corollas are pale pink in the bud,
opening to pure white. The finest form is named 'Koichiro Wada', after the
Japanese nurseryman who introduced it. Innumerable hybrids have been
raised from this superb plant or others similar to it, and more are introduced each year, both in the U.S.A. and Great Britain. They should be seen
in flower before purchase, since the color of the flowers may not

A group of *Rhododendron yakushimanum* flowering in late May. Photo by Brian Mulligan.

harmonize with other plants in the garden. The habit of hybrids may also be influenced considerably by the second parent. The type species is certainly one of the finest rhododendrons ever introduced and worthy of a prominent place in any garden. Mature height about 5 ft., but wider in diameter.

Very different in habit and flowers is *R. cinnabarinum* (VII) and its near relatives and variations. They generally grow into rather leggy bushes 6–8 ft. in height, the leaves tending to cluster towards the ends of the branches or be thinly scattered along them, ovate or elliptic, 2–3 in. long, often with reddish stalks; the flowers appear in May and June, borne in loose trusses at the ends of the shoots; they are tubular-funnel-shaped, variable in color in different forms, waxy and solid in texture, dark red in the type but sometimes with an orange throat (var. *blandfordiiflórum*) or paler or darker red (var. *róylei*). They need a fair amount of sun to bloom regularly and freely so should not be placed in a shady location. A west-facing site will light up the red flowers in the late afternoons. The species is found wild along the Himalayas from Nepal eastwards to southwest Tibet. It was both discovered and introduced by Dr. J. D. Hooker in Sikkim in 1850. Many hybrids have been raised from it in Great Britain; one of the best known is 'Royal Flush', of which the other parent was the tender species *R. maddénii* (VIII) so that this requires a more sheltered site in our gardens to be successful; the flowers are orange-rose outside the tube, buff or yellow within. By crossing 'Royal Flush' back to var. *roylei* the hybrids 'Lady Chamberlain' (orange-red and rose-pink) and 'Lady Rosebery' (deep red and pink) were produced in the Rothschild garden at Exbury, near Southampton, prior to 1930. All are very beautiful and handsome plants when flowering well. Related species are *R. concátenans,* (VII) found by Kingdon-Ward in southeast Tibet in 1924; in this the foliage is distinctly glaucous, especially when young, and the flowers shorter in length, apricot-yellow in color. Another is *R. xanthocódon,* (VII) also from the same region but having creamy yellow flowers and leaves scaly on the upper side. Both are well worth growing for their different coloring of both flowers and foliage, especially alongside any forms of *R. cinnabarinum* or its hybrids. In the Cullen and Chamberlain revision the two Kingdon-Ward plants are considered to be only subspecies of *R. cinnabarinum,* but these opinions will not reduce our regard for them. Both have been used in hybridizing and have produced some useful offspring.

We must not overlook our native *R. macrophýllum,* (VII) especially for planting in partially shaded often dry situations under native conifers, which it seems able to tolerate and still flower, although not as well as in an open site. The flowers appear in May and are rose-pink in color; there is also a white form. Height is usually 7–8 ft. but larger in old plants. A tough species, flowering in late May and early June, is *R. smirnówii* (VI) from northeastern Turkey, in the mountains. In cultivation it forms a dense sturdy shrub 5–6 ft. in height; the young shoots are covered with a thick white wool, as are the undersides of the oblong, leathery leaves which later become pale brown. It is a useful plant for sunny, wind-swept places which more tender species resent. The flowers are purple, very similar in color to those of its relative *R. ponticum,* but bluer in shade. Avoid planting it next to a red-flowered rhododendron of the same season!

One of the latest of the species to flower, in June, is the remarkable and beautiful *R. griersoniánum,* (VII–VIII), native only on the borders of southwest China and Burma, where it was first discovered by George Forrest in 1917 and introduced to British gardens. It is remarkable because of its botanical characters which make it quite distinct from all other species of rhododendrons—the hairy and glandular young shoots, the large and prominent winter buds, the lanceolate leaves covered with a tawny felt beneath, as is the ovary, and the loose trusses of glowing red flowers with their trumpet-shaped corollas, besides the late season of flowering. Becoming a rather loose, open-habited shrub of 6–7 ft. in height and about as much across, it does need some protection to grow success-fully until it becomes large enough to withstand our average winters, with low temperatures around 20°F. However, too much overhead shade will inhibit flowering, so a happy median has to be sought, especially where it will receive some late afternoon sun in the summer.

Literally hundreds of hybrids have been raised from *R. grier-sonianum* since the first, 'Vanessa', at Bodnant garden in North Wales in

1924. Some of these, now well known and often grown locally, are 'Aladdin' and 'Azor', both flowering late in June and July and having masses of salmon-pink flowers on large plants; 'Fabia', in several different color forms; 'Daydream', with the flowers red in the throat, early May; 'Jock', mentioned earlier under *R. williamsianum;* 'Ibex', 'John Coutts', 'May Day' and 'Matador' all flowering in late April or early May. The former of these two is one of the brightest reds among the dwarfer hybrids, and of compact habit. It is as well to see them in flower before placing them in a garden, although most of the red colors will agree and blend with one another, if their flowering times overlap.

Some larger growing species. Commencing with the earlier-flowering species there is none better than *R. sutchuenénse* (VII) from western China, introduced in 1900 by E. H. Wilson. The species in time make massive bushes 10–12 ft. in height; the leaves are oblanceolate, 8–10 in. in length and 2 in. wide. Flowers are not produced until the plants are of some age and size, but thereafter fairly regularly and often profusely. It is a plant for an open space at the edge of woodlands or the side of a lawn, at some distance from any building to allow space for future development. Eight to ten flowers are produced in each of the heavy trusses in March, varying with the season; they are normally rose-pink in color and may or may not have a crimson blotch within the corolla, which is solid in texture and about 3 in. long. Because of the risk of frosts damaging the flowers at that season they should not have an eastern exposure; facing north or west is better. An annual mulch of compost or decaying leaves from deciduous trees is advisable for these handsome plants, whose own leaves decay very slowly.

The oldest-known of the tree types of rhododendrons is the Himalayan *R. arbóreum* (VII–VIII), which may reach 60 or more ft. in height in the wild state and is well known to travellers and explorers from Kashmir to Nepal and Sikkim, with its rich red flowers in spring, starting in late February or early March. In our gardens they will be a few weeks later, depending upon the temperature. The leaves of the typical form are densely covered with silver indumentum beneath, especially noticeable on the young new growths after flowering. More common however, since it is hardier, from higher elevations above 8,000 ft., is the subspecies *campbélliae,* in which the leaves have a brown indumentum and the flowers are often pink or even white. The plants make a strong central leader and are indeed treelike in habit, so should be placed at the back of a border where they can overtop others of smaller size in front of them. Because of their early flowering season some high overhead shelter will be desirable, as for *R. sutchuenense.* More desirable than either of these two is subspecies *cinnamómeum* (VII), primarily a native of Nepal and from higher altitudes than the others already mentioned. In this the leaf underside is coated with a dense covering of rust-brown wool and is most attractive when turned over; the flowers are normally white, though often spotted in the corolla.

The hybrid 'Sir Charles Lemon' probably derives from this form of R. arboreum, and is a very lovely plant when in bloom, although it may take some years to do so. The flowers are bell-shaped, 2 in. or more across, white with some spotting, about 10 in each truss. In typical R. arboreum the trusses are conical in form, densely packed with up to 20 flowers in each, on very short stalks (pedicels). The species was first introduced to British gardens about 1815, so there has been plenty of time for plants there to grow to their maximum site, especially in gardens on the wetter west coast of Scotland and in southern Ireland, and for many hybrids to have been produced. One of the earliest of these, in 1829, was R. × nobleánum, of which the seed parent was R. caucasicum from Turkey.

A little later in the spring we can have R. fúlvum, (VII) a larger shrub or small tree up to about 15 ft. in height, native from southwest China to southeast Tibet at elevations of 10,000–12,000 ft., so it is hardier than some others with large leaves coming from lower elevations. In this species the leaves are oblong or oval, 6–8 in. long, dark green above but covered beneath with a handsome cinnamon or fawn-colored felt. The flowers appear in March and April, in close trusses of up to 20 on short stalks; they may be white, pale pink or even have a crimson blotch in the throat. The corolla has five or six lobes. As a specimen plant in thin woodland they are admirable. They prefer the kind of situation which suits most of these large-leaved species and hybrids; they do not like a windy or unduly sunny site, nor, of course, a frost pocket, in view of their early flowering.

Three closely related species of similar habits and requirements are R. arizélum (VII) from the eastern end of the Himalaya to Upper Burma and the borders of China; R. ficto-lácteum from southwest China at elevations of 12,000–13,000 ft., whence it was introduced by both George Forrest and Dr. J. F. Rock; and R. réx, from the same region as the last named. However, Cullen and Chamberlain now regard R. arizelum and R. fictolacteum as subspecies of R. rex, the earliest of the trio to be named. All are capable of becoming small trees under favorable conditions and have large oblong or oblanceolate leaves tapering to their bases, covered beneath with a dense brown felt, except in R. rex in which it is gray or buff. The flowers are borne in compact trusses of 12 to 15 or even more, in April. The bell-shaped corollas may be 2 in. long, usually have eight lobes, and can vary in color from white (the most common) to cream, pink-tinged, or even to bright crimson (var. rubicósum, introduced by Dr. Rock in 1923). Botanically they belong to the Subsection Falconéra, where also we find R. falcóneri, R. hódgsonii, and R. basílicum, all currently available from specialist nurseries.

Taking R. falcóneri (VII) as representative of its subsection, it can become a very large shrub, branching from the base, or grow as a small tree if pruned to a single leader. In either case it can be expected in time to reach 30 ft. in height and in old plants as much in width, especially in climates with a heavy rainfall, as along the Pacific coast. However, it has to be remembered that in their native homes in the Himalaya, Upper Burma and western China, they are accustomed to heavy summer rainfalls which we do not receive here, so should be regularly watered to remain healthy and happy.

R. *falconeri* was introduced to British gardens in 1830 and 1850 by Dr. J. D. Hooker from Sikkim, but probably nearly a century later to gardens in this region, especially to California, where the climate of the north coast suits this species extremely well. It is especially notable for the size and quality of the leaves, which may be 1 ft. or more in length and 5–6 in. wide, dark green and deeply wrinkled on the upper surface, covered beneath with a brownish felt of hairs similar in color to those on the R. *rex* group, though quite different when examined under a microscope, the upper layer being funnel or cup shaped; the veins on the underside are very prominent and the petiole stouter and longer than usual to support these heavy leaves. Even as a foliage plant it is well worth growing, since it will be many years as a rule before flowers are produced. These are formed in dense, compact trusses of about 20 creamy white, bell-shaped flowers, each with a deep purple blotch in the base; corolla lobes 8–10. Subspecies *eximium* (VII–VIII) (R. *eximium*) differs in the leaves, having their upper surfaces covered with a brown, mealy tomentum while they are young; the flowers are pink or rose. It is native to the Assam Himalaya and less commonly cultivated here.

R. *basilicum* (VII) comes from western China and Upper Burma and was found and introduced by George Forrest in 1912. The leaves are covered beneath with a dense, reddish brown felt of hairs, the petiole is thick and flattened; the flowers, in April, are pale yellow flushed pink and blotched crimson within.

Another species of the same type and requiring similar conditions to thrive is R. *macabeánum* (VII–VIII), from the mountains of Assam at 8,000–9,000 ft. elevation, but not quite as hardy in the Seattle area as R. *falconeri*. Nevertheless it is an attractive plant recognizable for its large oblong leaves covered beneath with a gray felt of hairs, as are the young shoots. The flowers open in March and April, borne in dense, tight umbels of 20–30, tubular-bell-shaped corollas of some shade of yellow, each with a purple spot in the pouched base; they are about 3 in. long and 2 in. wide, with eight lobes, so are worth some care and protection to bring them to the flowering stage. Shelter in their early years is especially necessary, until they become sufficiently woody to withstand colder conditions than the normal experienced.

A selection of species for a small garden (arranged in approximate order of flowering, from early to later). R. *moupinense*; R. *lutescens*; R. *keiskei*; R. *augustinii*; R. *fletcherianum*; R. *russatum*; R. *degronianum*; R. *williamsianum*; R. *ciliatum*; R. *davidsonianum*, or R. *yunnanense*; R. *yakushimanum*; R. *concatenans* or R. *xanthocodon*; R. *aberconwayi*.

The hybrids. Our remarks made earlier on the matter of personal choices in selecting species of rhododendrons for any garden apply even more forcefully to the hybrids, where there are now so many hundreds available to choose from, varying in every conceivable character, including size and form, foliage, and especially the flowers, being that part of the plant which probably most influences a buyer. Nevertheless, since the foliage is there to be seen all the year and the flowers for only a short period, it is important to choose plants with good foliage characteristics to blend with other broad-leaved, evergreen shrubs near them in a garden, particularly in size.

The following is a selection of hybrids, both older and of more recent origin, chosen in consultation with some of the leading growers in the Northwest. It would be well, if possible, to see established plants in bloom either in public or private collections or in nurseries before purchasing. A flower truss on a show bench may look most attractive but the living plant may not be desirable in some ways to add to a particular collection. After flowers and foliage the habit and growth form of the plant are the most important features in judging its value amongst other plants.

Arrangement of these hybrids is by size of plant, starting first with the largest, and by flower color, basically in five categories:—(a) red; (b) rose to pink; (c) white; (d) yellow to orange; (e) blue.

A. Large plants, attaining 12–15 feet or more in time.
   (b) 'Alice'; *Loderi* 'Pink Diamond' and 'Venus'; 'Luscombei'; 'Pink Pearl'.
   (c) 'Beauty of Littleworth'; 'Lodauric'; *Loderi* 'King George' and 'White Diamond'; 'Loder's White'; 'Sir Charles Lemon'; 'White Pearl'.

B. Medium-sized; 6–12 feet.
   (a) 'Britannia'; 'Grace Seabrook'; 'Halfdan Lem'; 'Markeeta's Prize'; 'Taurus'.
   (b) 'Anna Rose Whitney'; 'Azor'; 'Betty Wormald'; 'Faggetter's Favourite'; 'Furnivall's Daughter'; 'Lem's Monarch'; 'Naomi' forms; 'Trude Webster'.
   (c) 'Gomer Waterer'; 'Mrs A. T. de la Mare'; 'White Swan'.
   (d) 'Carita'; 'Crest'; 'China'; 'Mrs Lamott Copeland'.
   (e) 'Blue Ensign'; 'Blue Pacific'; 'Blue Peter'; 'Purple Lace'.

C. Smaller; 4–6 feet.
   (a) 'Elizabeth'; 'Jean Marie de Montague'; 'Thor'; 'Unknown Warrior'; 'Vulcan'.
   (b) 'Bow Bells'; 'Christmas Cheer'; 'Cary Ann'; 'Jock'; 'P. J. M.'; 'Tessa'; 'Pioneer'.
   (c) 'Belle Heller'; 'Chionoides'; 'Helene Schiffner'.
   (d) 'Fabia' forms; 'Full Moon'; 'Harvest Moon'; 'Hotei'; 'Virginia Richards'; 'Unique'.
   (e) 'Blue Tit'; 'Blue Diamond'; 'Blaney's Blue'.

D. Dwarf. 1–3 feet.
   (a) 'Carmen'; 'Ethel'; 'Little Gem'; 'Scarlet Wonder'.
   (b) 'Cilpinense'; 'Molly Ann'; 'Rose Elf'; 'Winsome'.

(c) 'Bric-a-Brac'; 'Cream Crest'; 'Dora Amateis'; 'Ptarmigan'; 'Snow Lady'; 'Tessa Bianca'.

(d) 'Chikor'; 'Curlew'; 'Golden Witt'; 'Jingle Bells'; 'Shamrock'.

(e) 'Blue Bird'; 'Oceanlake'; 'Ramapo'; 'Sapphire'.

For descriptions of these consult the catalogues of specialist retail nurserymen or books on rhododendrons. See Bibliography.

A selection of hybrids for a small garden (in approximate order of flowering). 'Christmas Cheer'; 'P. J. M.'; 'Cilpinense'; 'Blue Diamond'; 'Carmen'; 'Bow Bells'; 'Elizabeth'; 'Ramapo'; 'Dora Amateis'; 'Unique'; 'Scarlet Wonder'; 'Jean Marie de Montague'; 'Helene Schiffner'; 'Full Moon'.

Evergreen Azaleas

These form a large, ever-increasing group of complex origin, derived primarily from several evergreen or nearly evergreen species of *Rhododendron* native to Japan, especially *R. káempferi, R. kiusiánum, R. sataénse, R. ripénse, R. macrosépalum* and *R. índicum*. The last-named is indeed native to Japan and not to India as Linnaeus believed when naming it. One other species occurs in eastern China, *R. símsii,* which was a progenitor of the less-hardy Belgian azaleas, much propagated in Europe for forcing purposes in spring. Plants formerly grown under the names of *R.* 'Obtusum', 'Amoenum', 'Mucronatum', 'Sekidera', 'Phoeniceum', 'Omurasaki' and 'Linearifolium' are all old garden clones or hybrids and not wild species.

Among the principal groups of hybrids are the Kurume azaleas, derived from *R. kaempferi, R. sataense* and *R. kiusianum.* They were first seen in this country at the Panama-Pacific Exposition in San Francisco in 1915, then introduced into commerce by the Domoto Brothers of Hayward, California, between 1917 and 1920. In 1918 E. H. Wilson introduced 50 clones to the Arnold Arboretum, Boston, Massachusetts, of which 'Hinodegiri', 'Kirin' and 'Otome' are examples. Few of these seem to still be in cultivation, perhaps having been superseded by other later, superior kinds, or proved insufficiently hardy in the eastern United States. In 1983, however, the U.S. National Arboretum distributed 33 clones of what are said to be the finest Kurume hybrids in Japan; these should become available from nurseries during the next few years. They were collected at Kurume, in southern Japan, by staff members of the Arboretum. Hybrids raised by A. Pericat, of Collingdale, Pennsylvania, in the 1930s, between some Belgian hybrids and Kurume forms produced some plants such as 'Sweetheart Supreme' which are still being grown.

The Beltsville hybrids were raised at the U.S.D.A. Research Division at Beltsville, Maryland, by G. E. Yerkes and R. L. Pryor between 1950 and 1959. Forty-seven plants were named at that time, one of which is the white-flowered 'Casablanca'. Mr. Pryor selected a dwarf race from these and named 19 of them; they grow less than 30 in. high, so are useful for placing in front of taller kinds.

The well-known Glenn Dale race was produced by B. Y. Morrison, then Chief of the U.S.D.A. Plant Introduction Section at Glenn Dale, Maryland, from 1935 onwards. It was by far the most ambitious and successful program of its kind undertaken, at least up to that time, with over 70,000 plants being raised and 440 named and introduced, mostly between 1947 and 1949. In October 1953, an illustrated booklet was published by the U.S.D.A., (*Agricultural Monograph*, No. 20) describing these hybrids in detail, with some illustrations. Many have proved to be excellent garden plants useful over a wider area from zones 6 to 9. Some of the most popular are 'Buccaneer', 'Dayspring', 'Gaiety', 'Geisha', 'Glamour', 'Helen Close' and 'Martha Hitchcock'. Some of these hybrids were further used as parents of another race by Bill Gutormsen of Canby, Oregon, by crossing them with some of Joseph Gable's hybrids. These are the Greenwood hybrids, and 'Can-Can', 'Greenwood Orange' and 'Royal Robe' are now available. The last has deep purple, hose-in-hose flowers.

The Kaempferi hybrids are of course chiefly derived from the Japanese species *R. kaempferi*, introduced into the U.S.A. by Professor Charles Sargent to the Arnold Arboretum in 1892 and soon found to be hardy there as well as in northern Europe. This species, however, is to all intents and purposes deciduous in winter, even in the Pacific Northwest, only retaining small leaves at the tips of the shoots. Some hybrids were raised from it at the Arnold Arboretum about 1910; more in Holland following World War I by P. M. Koster, A. Vuyk and others. The Vuyk hybrids were given names of music composers such as 'Bach', 'Beethoven', 'Mozart' and 'Strauss'.

An important group raised in this country by Joseph Gable, of Stewartstown, Pennsylvania, from 1927 onwards, was named for him. To obtain necessary hardiness, he frequently used the Korean *R. poukhanense* as well as *R. kaempferi* and others; e.g., in 'Caroline Gable', 'Purple Splendor' and 'Springtime'. 'Caroline Gable' and 'Stewartsonian' have vivid red flowers, 'Louise Gable' is deep pink with a darker blotch, and 'Rosebud' a charming, double-flowered rose-pink. The Gable hybrids are certainly reliable and attractive plants.

Other races using *R. kaempferi* as one of the parents have been raised in the U.S.A. by such growers as Peter Girard of Geneva, Ohio; Dr. C. Fisher, Jr. and G. A. Reid of Linwood, New Jersey; A. M. Shamarello of South Euclid, Ohio, and more. For detailed information see the records in *Azaleas,* by F. C. Galle, (Timber Press, Portland, Oregon, 1985).

Three other important groups of evergreen azaleas must be mentioned. One is the Japanese Satsuki race, bred and cultivated for hundreds of years in Japan but originally derived from *R. tamúrae (R. eriocárpum)* and *R. índicum.* The former is more southern in its range and therefore somewhat less hardy than *R. indicum.* They are commonly grown as Bonsai subjects in Japan where annual shows are held to display them. The race is a very large one, with great variation in size of plant, form, though often compact and even cushionlike, and especially flowers—their size, shape and especially coloration, which can vary from pure white to pink, red, orange or near purple, sometimes flaked, striped or even edged with another color. Frilled petals can add to their charm. They generally flower late in the azalea season, from late May on into June, which is a useful characteristic for the gardener wanting some to carry on the season after earlier kinds have finished; it is well to place them in a shaded site in the afternoon or they may suffer from too much sunshine. A group of several of the same kind is more effective than planting one each of five or six, but they can easily be moved in fall or early spring should this be necessary. To increase the stock, lower branches can be layered, or cuttings taken as soon as the new growths are firm enough.

In 1938–1939 the U.S.D.A. introduced 53 clones of this type from the Chugai Nursery Company of Kobe, Japan. Some of these are still in cultivation at the Washington Park Arboretum in Seattle. Available commercially are 'Bunkwa' (salmon-pink); 'Chichibu', 'Eikwan' and 'Kagetsu', all white with some flaking or variegation; 'Gumpo White' and 'Gumpo Pink'; 'Gunrei' (rose-pink with red variegation), and 'Shinnyo-no-tsuki' (white-flaked red). Their habit of growth is spreading and cushion forming, so they should be kept in the front of a border. Pruning is seldom necessary.

The second group of importance is the Robin Hill hybrids, raised between 1937 and the mid-1960s by Robert Gartrell of Wyckoff, New Jersey. The parents of these included Belgian, Gable, Glenn Dale and Satsuki hybrids so that great variation in all principal characters could be expected from the progeny, of which about 70 have been named. Most, however, are low growing in habit and flower late in the season like the Satsukis, although they are generally hardier than those plants. The flowers are large and of stout texture. Available clones include 'Betty Ann Voss' (pink), 'Conversation Piece' (pale pink, variegated), 'Lady Louise' (rose-pink), 'Robin Dale' (semi-double, white striped pink), and 'Watchet' (pink with ruffled petals). After Mr Gartrell's retirement to North Carolina with his stock plants in the late 1970s, a nursery in Hawkinsville, Georgia, took over propagation of his named plants and introduced 22 more, under the title of Cripple Creek Gartrell azaleas. Several of these begin with the name 'Cherokee'.

The third and most recent of these later races are the forms and hybrids of *R. nakahárae** introduced by Mrs. Julian Hill of Martha's Vineyard, Massachusetts, in 1975, from seeds or cuttings sent her by Dr. T. Rokujo of Tokyo, Japan. This species is native to northern Taiwan, in the mountains, where seeds were also collected in 1969 at 2,600 ft. elevation. One plant was raised from these which flowered three years later and had vivid red flowers; it has been named 'Mount Seven Star', from its source.

---

*Specific names ending in "a" take the Latin terminal "e", not "i" as is usually the case.

R. nakaharae is naturally prostrate in habit and because of its late-flowering characteristic (June to early July) is a valuable introduction, especially for rock gardens, since it will tolerate a good deal of sun and then flower better than if shaded. Propagation again can be by either layers or cuttings. The plants grow wider each year, but not higher. Clones now in commerce from specialist nurseries include 'Alexander' (salmon-red), 'Jeff Hill' (deep salmon-pink), 'Marilee' (salmon-pink with a deeper blotch), and 'Pink Pancake' (pale pink), the plant quite flat. They are known collectively as the North Tisbury hybrids.

Clones Recommended by the Seattle or Portland Chapters of the American Rhododendron Society and Available Locally.

Flowers pink
'Coral Bells' (K)
'Gumpo Pink' (S)
'Gaiety' (GD)
'Pearl Bradford' (GD)
'Lorna' (G)
'Louise Gable (G)
'Rosebud' (G)
'Bunkwa' (S)
'Nancy of Robinhill' (RH)
'Sir Robert' (RH)
'Watchet' (RH)

White
'Snow' (K)
'Everest' (GD)
'Gumpo White' (S)
'Gunrei' (S)
'Helen Close' (GD)
'Martha Hitchcock' (GD)
'Matsuyo' (S)
'Midori' (S)
'Robin Dale' (RH)
'Shinnyo-no-tsuki' (S)
'Treasure' (GD)

Red to Purple
'Hinodegiri' (K)
'Hino-Crimson' (K)
'Sherwood Red' (K)
'Hexe' (K)
'Sherwood Orchid' (K)
'Buccaneer' (GD)
'Alexander' (NT)
'Caroline Gable' (G)
'Glamour' (GD)
'Greta' (RH)
'Joseph Hill' (NT)
'Lady Louise' (RH)
'Purple Splendor' (G)
'Red Fountain' (NT)
'Stewartsonian' (G)
'Susannah Hill' (NT)
'Twenty Grand' (P/Leach)

Key to Abbreviations
K = Kurume
G = Gable
GD = Glenn Dale
NT = North Tisbury
RH = Robin Hill
P = Pericat

ROSMARÍNUS officinális, (VII–VIII) the well-known and loved rosemary from the Mediterranean region and North Africa (Morocco) is an aromatic shrub for dry banks in full sun, or against west or south walls, where it will produce pale blue flowers freely in early spring, growing up to 4 ft. or so in height. It is not, however, as hardy as the common lavender, which enjoys similar conditions in our gardens, and can suffer in colder winters than normal. Several different clones are in cultivation, especially in California, including 'Lockwood de Forest', 'Tuscan Blue', 'Collingwood Ingram', which is probably the same plant as 'Benenden Blue', a narrow-leaved form introduced from Corsica by Mr. Ingram before 1930, and 'Prostratus' (IX), the least hardy of them all. Any pruning necessary to keep the plants in shape or bounds should be done immediately after flowering. Selected forms can be propagated by cuttings in summer.

RÚSCUS aculeátus (VI), the Butcher's Broom, is scarcely shrubby, although it appears to be so with its green stems and stiff branches bearing spine-tipped false leaves, termed cladodes, on which the small white flowers are borne. The plants are dioecious, so that unless plants of both sexes are grown no red, berrylike fruits will appear. Height about 2 ft. An excellent plant for dry, shady places, where it will slowly spread by means of basal suckers.

RÚTA gravéolens (VII), the rue of Shakespeare and other authors and an herb of various uses in former times—though much less so in these days of modern medicines and drugs—is a native of southeastern Europe and like lavender and rosemary most suited to sunny places in our gardens. It is about as hardy as rosemary in such situations, and with its glaucous gray foliage can be an attractive addition to a border in summer. The dull yellow flowers are borne in corymbs in May at the ends of the branches and are usually followed by a plentiful crop of seeds by which the plants can be easily propagated. 'Jackman's Blue' is a selected clone which must be increased by cuttings. It is dwarfer in habit and has distinctly bluer foliage than the type.

SARCOCÓCCA. Sweet Box. Of these useful small shrubs three species are commonly cultivated here, namely S. confúsa, S. hookeriána, and S. ruscifólia. A fourth, S. salígna, is on the borderline of hardiness and not as ornamental as the others, so is seldom seen or grown except perhaps in California or southwestern Oregon. All are Asiatic in origin. They are particularly valuable for planting in shady places, which they tolerate well, if not too dry in summer.

S. confúsa (VII) is probably of Chinese origin, although this has never been confirmed by wild material. Attaining 3–4 ft. in height, it forms large clumps but does not spread by underground shoots like the next species. The leaves are lanceolate, shining green on the upper side, about 2 in. long and half as wide, with a long-drawn tip. The flowers appear in January or February, carried in the axils of each leaf, and although small are fragrant and quite noticeable at that dull season of the year. The fruits, which take a year to ripen, are black, shining, oval, about ⅓ in. long.

S. hookeriána is represented by its Chinese variety digýna, (VII), which has two styles to each flower instead of three as in the Himalayan type. The young shoots are distinctly rosy red in color, the leaves longer and narrower than in S. confusa, to 3–4 in. in length, with, as for that species, an attenuated tip. It flowers at the same time as *S. confusa* and is even more noticeably fragrant. The fruits are round, black and glossy. This plant is stoloniferous, spreading easily by underground stems so that it can soon cover a large area, as can be seen in the Washington Park Arboretum in Seattle on a bank beside Arboretum Drive East.

The third species is *S. ruscifólia* (VII–VIII), definitely known from central and western China from whence it was introduced by E. H. Wilson in 1901. It is not as hardy here as the other two species, which is regrettable, since it possesses equally attractive though shorter and broader foliage, similarly scented flowers very early in the year, followed by red fruits. Those who can safely grow this plant should certainly do so. Like all the others it can be propagated either by cuttings or seeds. Pruning is seldom necessary except in old plants which may have outgrown their allotted space; if so, this should be done in early spring (March).

SKÍMMIA. There are about six species of *Skimmia* native to Asia from the western Himalayas east to Japan and Taiwan, but only two of them, namely *S. japónica* (VII) from Japan and *S. reevesiána* (VII–VIII) from China, are commonly cultivated, along with the hybrid between them, *S.* × *foremánii* or *S.* × *rogérsii.* Both names have been applied to it, since it was raised first by a Mr. Foreman in Scotland sometime in the 1870s, then in 1877 by W. H. Rogers of Southampton, England. All bear red fruits, except that *S. japonica* has a white-fruited form, 'Fructu-albo', which was mentioned in the first edition of this work in 1943 as a rare plant. It is now much more common in West Coast gardens. This species is dioecious, so that both male and female plants are required to produce a crop of fruits; even then some hand-pollination at flowering time may be helpful to ensure a good crop. Plants normally grow to about 4–5 ft. in height, but different clones vary in this respect—some are quite dwarf and make useful groundcover plants. The leaves are more or less obovate, aromatic when broken, often yellowish green. If the plants seem chlorotic they may be given dilute liquid magnesium sulphate, one tablespoon to a gallon of water. Flowers appear in April at the ends of the branches; those of the male plants are in larger panicles and more highly fragrant than the female. Fruits normally remain through the winter and are especially valued for this habit. 'Rubella' is a male clone having reddish buds through the winter months, carried on the flower stalks in spring, and larger flower panicles than usual. 'Veitchii' is a female form with leathery blunt leaves and tight bunches of fruits.

S. reevesiána was introduced to Great Britain by Robert Fortune from China in 1849. It is apparently less common in cultivation here than *S. japonica,* growing to only about 2 ft. in height, of much less vigorous growth, the leaves more elliptical than obovate in shape, and smaller with a sharper apex. The flowers, however, are hermaphrodite, with five petals instead of the four usually found in *S. japonica,* so that each plant is capable of producing fruits by itself. These are deep red, oval instead of round, or even pear shaped, and also carried through the winter to the following spring. Most plants of the hybrid, *S.* × *foremanii* or *S.* × *rogersii,* are male and have large, pure white flowers; the leaves are oblong, dark green, thick and stiff with recurved margins; fruits depressed globose. Since skimmias prefer some shade during summer afternoons and an acid soil, they associate well with rhododendrons, or can be planted under high shade trees, so long as they do not get too dry.

SPÁRTIUM *júnceum* (VII–VIII). Spanish Broom. Native to southern Europe, North Africa, east to Turkey and Syria. Forming a tall, rather leggy shrub up to 10 ft. in height it should be planted behind other smaller shrubs or at the back of a border. Regular pruning after flowering in July and August is advisable to keep the plants bushy. Flowers large for the broom family, about 1 in. long, fragrant, bright golden yellow. It is propagated by seeds and should be planted out permanently when still young.

STRANVÁESIA. A small genus of shrubs, or occasionally small trees, native in Asia from the Himalayas east and south to China and the Philippine Islands and Borneo. It is so closely related to *PHOTINIA* as to be hardly separated botanically from that genus, and in fact has been combined with it by at least one botanist, in 1973.

S. davidiána (VI–VII) is the species commonly cultivated here, becoming a large shrub with usually several branches from the base, 10–12 ft. in height, but sometimes larger and more treelike, up to 25 ft. or so. The leaves are 3–4 in. long, lanceolate, and undulate along the margin, more than 1 in. wide; old leaves turn red before falling. Bunches of white flowers, rather strongly scented, are produced in June–July, much enjoyed by bees and flies, to be followed in fall by clusters of bright red fruits which persist through the winter until the following spring. This is the chief value of these shrubs, but as plants of the typical species frequently become bare at the base with all branches in the upper part, it is necessary to cover this with some other evergreen shrub of lower stature. For this purpose the variety *unduláta* succeeds admirably, since it is in effect a smaller edition of the larger plant but does not grow more than 20–24 in. high at its maximum, although spreading widely, a feature which makes it an excellent cover for sloping banks. It will stand a good deal of sunshine, so long as the soil does not dry out too much in summer, due, for example, to adjacent tree roots. Self-sown seedlings may be found around established plants, no doubt distributed by birds eating the fruits. *S. davidiana* is a native of wide regions in China and is another of Wilson's introductions, in 1903.

SYCÓPSIS *sinénsis* (VI) is the only member of a small genus of evergreen shrubs or small trees belonging to the witch-hazel family (*Hamamelidaceae*) and native to eastern Asia. *S. sinensis* comes from central China, again thanks to the indefatigable Mr. Wilson, and has been cultivated in Seattle since around 1940, brought in by the U.S. Department of

Agriculture. It becomes a bushy large shrub about 15–20 ft. in height; the leaves are tough and leathery, 2½–3 in. long, ovate in shape, dark green on the upper side, strongly veined. The flowers, which appear in February or March depending upon the weather, consist of clusters of stamens, orange-yellow in color; they have no petals. Cuttings are the best means of propagation, since seeds are not regularly produced. As a tall, evergreen background shrub this has merit, at least for larger gardens. Pruning is rarely necessary.

TERNSTRÓEMIA *gymnánthera (T. japónica)* (VII), found wild in India as well as China, Japan and southern Korea, is a distinctive shrub reaching 8–10 ft. in height, closely related to *CLEYERA* from the same parts of the world, but distinguished by its tough, obovate, smooth leaves carried on red petioles. It also produces rather small, creamy white flowers hanging at the leaf axils in July and August. A sunny location against a west or south wall is indicated for both these shrubs, which can be expected to attain 8–10 ft. with us. Some pruning in spring may be necessary to keep them in shape.

ÚLEX (VII–VIII). Gorse, Furze, Whin (in Ireland). *U. európaeus* is a European shrub which has become naturalized in some places along the Pacific Coast, as has the common or Scotch Broom (*Cytisus scoparius*), but because of its habit of continually shedding the old dry twigs and branches, the gorse constitutes a serious fire hazard and should not be planted except perhaps as a single specimen and then kept regularly pruned and the old branches raked up. Since it will withstand wind and flowers for some weeks in spring it does have particular values, especially as the flowers are a rich gold in color and are scented. Even more showy is the double-flowered form, 'Flore Pleno', if it can be obtained. Since this cultivar forms no seeds it must be propagated by cuttings in late summer.

VACCÍNIUM. Unfortunately only one of the evergreen Asiatic species appears to be reliably hardy with us, and that is *V. moupinénse* (VII), native to western China and introduced to British gardens by Wilson in 1909. In the wild state it often grows as an epiphyte on tree trunks, but in gardens locally seems quite happy in a light soil with adequate humus, as for rhododendrons, with which it can well be associated, since its maximum height is about 30 in., its habit dense and bushy, though tending to throw out lateral extension branches. The Boxlike leaves are about ⅝ in. long, shining green on the upper side, blunt at the tip, quite densely arranged along the branches. The flowers are carried on short racemes at the ends of the branches in May and are dark red in color, no more than ¼ in. long so quite inconspicuous, but unusual in their coloring. The edible fruits are likewise very small and purple-black.

A near relative is *V. delaváyi,* (VIII) from southwestern China and Upper Burma, but this has white flowers and leaves notched at the tip. It is definitely less hardy than *V. moupinense.*

V. ovátum (VII), the native Evergreen Huckleberry, found along the Pacific coast from British Columbia to California, is an invaluable shrub for our gardens, with its neat, upright habit of growth, dark green glossy Boxlike leaves set closely along the reddish stems, and mahogany to bronze or coppery young shoots in spring just after flowering. The urn-shaped flowers are borne in short racemes and are pale pink in color; the fruits in late summer are purple-black or glaucous blue and edible, though somewhat acid. The flowers are most popular with bees, no doubt for their nectar, resulting in good crops of fruits annually. This shrub will form an excellent hedge, if trimmed to the size and shape required. Normal height 6–8 ft. Selected forms can be propagated by cuttings in late summer.

VIBÚRNUM. The evergreen viburnums include several valuable and excellent garden shrubs, many of them having a bold, distinctive foliage pattern desirable in the garden. In addition, many bear beautiful flowers and fruits, but as some of them are dioecious, both sexes are necessary to produce the latter; all probably fruit more freely if two or more forms of one species are grown together, or two closely related species, such as *V. davidii* and *V. cinnamomifolium.*

V. × *burkwóodii* (VI–VII) is an artificial hybrid between the evergreen *V. utile* from China and *V. carlesii* from Korea, which is deciduous. The hybrid retains some of its *utile*-like leaves each year, but sheds most of its foliage during summer. In form it is a more or less upright shrub with arching branches, reaching about 9 ft. in height, so should be given a place behind other more compact, shorter shrubs in a border. The flowers are produced in April, formed in globose, loose trusses at the ends of the shoots; individually they are pink in the bud, opening white, to about ½ in. across, extremely fragrant like the *V. carlesii* parent. Branches should be cut at this stage to enjoy them indoors. Prune immediately after flowering if needed.

V. cinnamomifólium (VII), native to western China, is a larger-scale edition of *V. davidii,* to about 8 ft. high and wide, the leaves twice the size of that species but of the same shape and texture. The flowers are carried in larger trusses, so somewhat more conspicuous; the fruiting characteristics are similar. It is at least as hardy as *V. davidii* in Seattle, where it can be seen on the University of Washington campus and in Washington Park Arboretum.

V. davídii is now so well known and so frequently grown, even along city streets and in planted city parks, that it needs little description. The shining green, deeply veined, ovate leaves 3–4 in. long and half as wide, the petioles reddened on the upper side, are familiar and easily recognized wherever seen. The plants form compact rounded bushes about 3 ft. high but often more in width, if in an open situation; in shady sites they will be less compact and probably flower less freely. However, avoid placing them in a full south-facing site, or the foliage will suffer from sunburn, especially when young, in June. The bright blue fruits, held up on red pedicels, are only ¼ in. or less in length. Both sexes must be planted to obtain fruit.

Another Chinese species in the same group as the two preceding is *V. propínquum* (VII–VIII), established for many years on the University of Washington campus where plants have formed large, dome-shaped bushes along Rainier Vista on the north side of Johnson Hall. The young shoots are tinged red; the leaves only 2–2½ in. long, lanceolate, shining on the upper side but not prominently veined like the other two species. The flowers are extremely small and insignificant, and fruits have not been seen. Nonetheless, this is an excellent medium-sized evergreen shrub for grouping or filling in borders, hardy enough for normal winters around Puget Sound.

V. rhytidophýllum (V–VI), the Leather-leaf Viburnum, native to central and western China and another of Wilson's introductions, in 1900, is well known and easily recognized by its large, coarse, deeply veined leaves, glossy on the upper side but covered with a gray felt of hairs beneath. Becoming a shrub often 12–15 ft. in height, it is not one to be planted casually in the average small garden but rather at the back of a fairly wide border or at the edge of woodland amongst rhododendrons, where it fits very well. The flowers are dull white, in May/June; the fruits, when formed, which is not always on solitary plants, are bright red turning to black when ripe. Birds appreciate them.

Hybrids between *V. rhytidophyllum* and several other species are known. The best is probably the recently bred *V.* × *pragénse* (VI), of which the evergreen Chinese *V. útile* was the male parent. This was produced in the Municipal Nurseries at Prague, Czechoslovakia, hence its name. The leaves resemble those of *V. rhytidophyllum* but are much smaller, averaging about 3 in. in length, 1 in. in width; the twigs are much more slender and the plant more graceful in appearance, less strictly upright in habit. It is one which needs to be propagated and distributed more widely, for the value of its foliage. Neither flowers nor fruits are particularly significant.

V. tínus (VII), the Laurustinus from the Mediterranean and North Africa, is an almost indispensable shrub which can be used in many ways, including forming a hedge which when in flower can be a most pleasing sight and far superior to common laurel or privet in its decorative qualities, as well as annual maintenance. Typically it becomes a large, densely branched shrub, 10–12 ft. high and nearly as wide. The leaves are oblong, or ovate-oblong, very variable in most characters, especially size, form, and hairiness or otherwise; the best in this respect is 'Lucidum' (VIII), which has large, 3–4 in. long and 2 in. wide leaves, very shiny on the upper side; the flowers appear late in the season for this species, in April, and are larger than normal. Against these good points, however, must be set the fact that it is less hardy than the usual type so needs a more sheltered location to thrive. *V. tinus* in some forms can begin flowering before Christmas and continue for several weeks if the weather is not severe. Others will bloom in early spring, (February to March), so it pays to observe and propagate these different clones. This can be done by cuttings in late summer, or sometimes by obtaining rooted pieces from the base of the plants. Other clones are 'Hirtum', having stems and leaf stalks clothed with short hairs, and 'Variegatum', with yellow-variegated foliage, not very attractive. 'Compactum' and 'Nanum' are dwarf forms sometimes listed.

A hedge of *Viburnum tinus* in an Irish garden. Photo by Brian Mulligan.

CHAPTER X

Deciduous Shrubs

Deciduous shrubs are grown principally for their spring or summer displays of flowers, and are very commonly spoken of as flowering shrubs. Some of them are also valuable for their fall foliage color, and a few are grown primarily for the bright color of their winter twigs or fruits. While their leafless winter state puts them at some disadvantage compared with the year-around effect of broad-leaved evergreen shrubs, they have nevertheless a well-deserved place in the garden scene. As a class they are hardier than their broad-leaved evergreen counterparts, and therefore play a larger role in gardens east of the Cascades than in those of western Washington and Oregon. A few of the shrubs included in this chapter can be grown equally well as trees, and this is indicated in such cases in the individual descriptions. Some which are commonly regarded as shrubs, such as *Styrax japonica* and *Cornus kousa,* are better grown as trees and are described only in that chapter. The training of a shrub into tree forms, and vice versa, is fully discussed in the introduction to Deciduous Trees.

In general, deciduous shrubs are much less demanding of good cultural practices than are most evergreen shrubs, even those within the same genus. They are thus a good choice when it is impossible to give plants more than minimal care. While they can withstand considerable abuse, they also repay good care with greatly improved performance and increased beauty and profusion of bloom.

A valuable attribute of many deciduous shrubs is that great branches of bloom may be cut for decoration without in the least injuring the plant or reducing the bloom in succeeding years. This is particularly true of those that are pruned immediately after flowering, such as *Forsythia, Spiraea, Philadelphus, Weigela,* and *Deutzia.* Even gardeners devoted to broad-leaved shrubs may want to plant a few deciduous species simply for cut flowers.

Most deciduous shrubs are propagated readily from hardwood cuttings. This is an inexpensive process for the nurseryman, so the shrubs can be sold fairly cheaply. By the same token, it is easy for the amateur to strike

214

cuttings. Specific instructions for procedures will be found in the chapter on Propagation. It may be assumed that all deciduous shrubs included here are propagated by this simple method unless otherwise indicated in the individual descriptions. A few such as *Magnolia* and *Hamamelis* do not strike readily, so are grafted or layered. Others are best raised from seed, but such exceptions are not common.

All deciduous materials should be transplanted during the dormant period, that is, when they are leafless. Container-grown plants have largely superseded bare-rooted stock, so with care these may be planted at any time of the year. A few species which are more difficult are usually dug with a root ball and are best moved immediately before they start into growth in the spring. This is especially true of plants with soft fleshy roots such as magnolias.

ABELIOPHÝLLUM dístichum (V), the White Forsythia from Korea, is a multistemmed shrub to about 5 ft. high, with oval leaves. Small, four-petaled fragrant white flowers are borne profusely on the naked stems in early spring. Adapted to hot summers and cold winters, this species is more useful on the east side of the Cascades than on the west.

ÁCER negúndo 'Flamingo' (II) can be grown as a small tree, but is more effective if it is kept as a shrub and cut back to the ground repeatedly to encourage new shoots. New growth is variegated with bright shrimp pink as well as white, the tricolored leaves making the plant as colorful as any flowering shrub. This variety will do best in a fully sunny location.

AÉSCULUS parviflóra (IV), Bottlebrush Buckeye, is a native of south-eastern United States. Usually several-stemmed and suckering, but occasionally becoming a single-stemmed small tree, it varies in height from about 8–15 ft., and is usually broader than high. Leaves have the typical five-fingered, palmately compound leaflets of the Horsechestnuts, and turn a good, bright yellow in the fall, depending somewhat on growing conditions. The flowers, white with conspicuous red stamens, are borne in July in panicles up to 1 ft. long. This is an outstanding, summer-flowering shrub, suitable for a specimen plant in a lawn, or equally good massed in a shrub border. It prefers acid soil and can take full sun, but blooms well even in the shade. Var. *serótina* and its selection 'Rogers' bloom 2–3 weeks later than the species.

AMELÁNCHIER, the Serviceberry, includes some 12 species distributed throughout the temperate regions of the Northern Hemisphere, most of them in North America. The species native to our regions, *A. alnifólia* (IV), is a conspicuous feature of the early spring flora on both sides of the Cascades. An erect shrub to 20 ft. its clusters of pristine white flowers are followed by ½-in. edible purple berries, more useful to birds than man. The neat foliage takes on attractive autumn tints. Serviceberry thrives in any good garden soil, in sun or light shade. Selections 'Regent', a compact shrub, and 'Success', with an abundance of fruit, may or may not be available in our area.

ARÓNIA arbútifolia (IV), Red Chokeberry, native to eastern North America, is a vigorous, bushy shrub to about 10 ft., with oval, tapered leaves and white or rose-tinted flowers. The small, red fruits live up to their name, and are avoided even by birds. Fall color is excellent, crimson or purplish red. Though a rather leggy shrub, it is very effective in mass plantings, and the colorful fruits hold well; Dirr suggests that it would be useful in highway plantings. 'Brilliantíssima' is a selection with especially good berries and scarlet fall color.

A. melanocárpa (IV), Black Chokeberry, is somewhat similar, but with darker fruits, and tends to sucker profusely, forming large colonies to a height of 5 ft. Adaptable to either dry or wet situations, its fall color is also good. Var. *eláta,* larger than the type and twice its height, to 10 ft., is preferred for landscape use. These two species hybridize rather easily, even in the wild.

AZALEA. See *RHODODENDRON.*

BÉRBERIS, the Barberries, are grown for their bright fruits and their hedging properties. *B. koreána* (III), a hedgerow plant from Korea, is a 6-ft. shrub with grooved, red-tinted young shoots, curiously branched spines, and dark green foliage, turning deep red-purple in fall. Drooping racemes of yellow flowers, 3–4 in. long, bloom in May and are followed by small, egg-shaped red fruits, which hold well into winter. This species is extremely cold hardy, suited to any soil except soggy, and is especially useful as a barrier plant.

The Japanese Barberry, *B. thunbérgii* (V), and its dark purple-leaved form, var. *atropurpúrea,* is the best-known deciduous species. The type has small, bright green leaves, which change in autumn to yellow, red, and orange. When they drop they reveal the arching, spiny branches festooned with small, slender, beadlike scarlet fruits. A rounded shrub to 5–6 ft., the Japanese Barberry is useful principally for summer and autumn foliage color. It thrives in dry, sunny locations, in any well-drained soil. Many cultivars have been selected from this species over the years, including erect forms, dwarf forms, and forms with many types of leaf coloration.

'Aurea' has vivid yellow foliage which maintains its color well and does not sunburn.

'Crimson Pigmy' is a compact-mounded miniature form.

'Erecta' is a fastigiate form useful for hedging.

'Kobold' has green foliage and dwarf habit.

'Rose Glow' has rose-pink new foliage, mottled deeper purple.

'Silver Beauty', also listed as 'Argenteo-marginata', has green and white variegated leaves.

'Sparkle' is mounded, with green foliage, turning red, orange, and yellow in fall.

There is even a thornless variant of this species, which would seem to defeat part of the landscape use of barberries.

BÉTULA glandulósa (2) Bog Birch, or Scrub Birch, occurs in Greenland and at high latitudes and elevations across North America including the mountains of the Northwest. It is a graceful, small shrub, rarely more than 5–6 ft. tall, with conspicuously glandular young shoots; small, green catkins, and small, rounded leaves, which take on orange and coppery tones in the fall. Plants are best raised from seeds, and those of lowland provenance will probably give better results in coastal gardens than the alpine forms. This attractive little birch is a promising answer to that ever-soggy spot in the garden.

BUDDLEIA, Butterfly Bush. There are many species of *Buddleia* in subtropical and temperate regions, but comparatively few of them are in common cultivation.

B. alternifólia (V), the Alternate-Leafed Butterfly Bush, from northwestern China, flowers in May and June all along the previous year's growth, with compact little clusters of clear lavender or lilac-purple flowers that show to good advantage against the soft gray-green foliage. It thrives in any poor soil in a hot, dry situation. The arching branches soon build a spreading shrub 10–12 ft. high. Prune severely immediately after flowering if it becomes straggly; otherwise, removal of weak, twiggy growth in March is sufficient.

B. davídii (V–VI). The Summer Lilac or Common Butterfly Bush from China, is also known as *B. variábilis,* and variable indeed it is. This vigorous shrub in most of its forms is too coarse for the small garden, especially the 15–20 ft. var. *magnífica.* The finest selected forms earn their place at the back of the herbaceous border, and are valued for their summer flowering. The better named varieties include:

'Black Knight', dark violet, considered the best named clone by Arnold Arboretum.

'Charming', pink flowers in 1–2 ft. panicles.

'Dubonnet', with dark reddish purple flowers.

'Empire Blue', rich blue-violet with an orange eye.

'Petite Indigo', much branched dwarf with lilac-blue flowers.

'Petite Plum', red-purple flowers with an orange eye.

'White Bouquet' and 'White Profusion' are white-flowered forms.

Var. *nanhoénsis* from North China is smaller in all its parts and more compact in habit, usually not more than 3–5 ft. tall, quite suitable for the small garden. It is probably hardier than the type. 'Nanho Purple' has clear purple flowers.

B. fallowiána (VII), from southwestern China is a vigorous 8-ft. shrub with white, felty leaves and very fragrant, lavender flowers in clusters along the current year's shoots. Somewhat less hardy than the preceding species, it is not permanently damaged even if cut down by a severe winter, since it blooms on new wood. Var. *álba* has white flowers.

B. globósa (VII–VIII), from Chile and Peru, differs from the foregoing species in having bright yellow flowers gathered into ¾-in. balls, in a panicle 6–8 in. long. It has long, slender leaves, wrinkled and dark green above and felted beneath. It develops into a 15-ft. shrub if not cut back by hard winters, as it can be here. It needs a sheltered location.

CALLICÁRPA, the Beauty Berry, is grown principally for its handsome magenta-purple fruits; the minute lavender flowers are rather inconspicuous. The two species most common in cultivation here, C. americána (VII) and C. japónica (VI) are 4–5 ft. shrubs not unlike our native Snowberry in general appearance. C. japónica is the more worthwhile of the two. C. bodiniéri (VI), from southwestern China, is more spectacular. It is a vigorous 10-ft. shrub similar to the preceding, except that the clustered berries are a metallic violet; fall leaf color in muted violet and pale yellow complements the fruits. 'Profusion' is a more free-fruiting selection. White-berried forms of all three species have been described. C. j. 'Leucocarpa' is attractive for both the plant and its white fruits. Callicarpas prefer light woodland conditions. They flower and fruit at the tips of the new wood and should be cut back severely in late winter or early spring to get the best flowers and fruit. An annual mulch of compost is beneficial.

CALYCÁNTHUS flóridus (IV), the Carolina Allspice, is a quiet, almost uninteresting 8–10 ft. shrub, principally grown for the rich fragrance of its small, chocolate brown flowers produced in May and June. It prefers light, well-drained soil in full sun. C. occidentális (VI), California Allspice, is a somewhat larger shrub than its eastern counterpart, the crushed leaves and twigs having a stronger spicy odor, with paler and redder flowers. Though it grows by streams and ponds in the wild, it takes well to ordinary garden conditions, in either sun or shade. Fruits are flask shaped, green, becoming brown, nearly 2 in. long. It flowers in June/July, sometimes into August. Both require a good deal of space to fully develop.

CARAGÁNA arboréscens (II), Siberian Pea Tree, native to Siberia and Mongolia, is an upright shrub to 15–20 ft., with pinnately compound leaves and a profusion of bright yellow flowers in early May. Though of limited ornamental value for the average garden, it is extremely hardy and tolerant of the harshest conditions including drought and alkaline soils, making it useful for screens and windbreaks in the semi-arid parts of our region. Dwarf, weeping, and fastigiate forms, suited to various uses, are commercially available. The most distinctive cultivar is 'Lorbérgii', which has linear, threadlike leaflets, giving it a ferny appearance.

CARYÓPTERIS incána (C. tangútica) (VII), Blue Beard or Blue Spiraea, from northwestern China, is a gray-foliaged shrub with upright, twiggy branches attaining a height of 4–5 ft. The tips of all the branches produce slender spikes of violet-blue flowers from the axils of the leaves in September/October. A sunny location and well-drained soil are its chief requirements, and it is a valuable addition to the late summer and early fall garden. 'Blue Billows' is a low, trailing form; 'Candicans' is white flowered.

C. × clandonénsis (V), an English hybrid between C. incána and C.

mongólica, is a low-mounded and barely woody shrub to about 2 ft. It has given rise to a number of named varieties ranging in color from powder blue through deeper blue to blue-purple. 'Heavenly Blue', 18–24 in. tall, is typical.

CEANÓTHUS × *delílianus* (VI) covers a group of hybrids made in France in the early 19th century between the tender blue-flowered Mexican *C. coerúleus* and the hardy white-flowered *C. americánus* from eastern United States. 'Gloire de Versailles' is the most common of these in cultivation. Its large panicles of powder blue flowers are borne in summer on the new wood; old wood should be pruned out in early spring before growth starts.

C. integérrimus (VII), Deer Brush, is a freely branched shrub to 10 ft., sometimes partially evergreen, which ranges from California through western Oregon to south central Washington. The 6–10 in. panicles of small flowers, airier and daintier than true lilacs, appear in late spring, varying in color from nearly white to lilac-blue, occasionally with deeper color. This is one of our more attractive native shrubs, at its best massed in thickets in the wild garden; it should not be overwatered.

C. sanguíneus (V), Buckbrush, is a 3–10 ft. shrub native from British Columbia and Idaho to California, which takes its name from the reddish bark of its twigs. Its panicles of creamy white flowers, 2–4 in. long, have a sweet but cloying fragrance. While not a species that one would seek out for planting, except possibly in the dry wild garden, it is well worth saving from the bulldozer. It would be no great trick to select plants for larger flower clusters, since both this species and the preceding one come readily from cuttings.

CERATOSTÍGMA wilmottiánum (VII–VIII), from China, is a delightful 3–4 ft. upright, late summer-blooming shrub. The brilliant, sky blue flowers are freely produced from July until frost. They are of a color that is always welcome in the garden, and doubly so at this time of year. This shrub should be grown in the warmest possible location, in deep, light, perfectly drained soil. In severe winters it may be cut to the ground, but in a favorable location will always spring up again from the base.

CHAENÓMELES is now the accepted botanical name for the Japanese Quince, colloquially called 'Japonica', and still occasionally listed in catalogs as *Cydónia or Pýrus.* True *C. japónica* (IV) is a small, twiggy, low-spreading shrub, less than 3 ft. high. Apricot, scarlet, or blood red flowers arise in clusters from year-old wood, in April, followed by richly fragrant, round yellow fruits. It is an excellent shrub for the large rock garden if the soil is lean and the location hot and sunny.

The 'Japonica' of popular parlance is actually *C. speciósa (C. lagenária)* (IV), native to China, but long cultivated in Japan. Introduced in England before 1800, it is one of the most colorful and best-beloved deciduous, spring-flowering shrubs in our area. A large shrub, forming a tangle of rather spiny branches, it can reach to 10 ft. in height with a spread of more than 20 ft. This species, as well as the others, often suffers from over-watering during the summer and fall months, which results in rank vegetative growth. The appleblossom-like coral to red flowers are then formed only in the heart of the bush on the older wood, all but hidden by the mass of flowerless branches on the outside. This shortcoming can be partially corrected by reducing water in summer. Persistent pruning throughout the growing season—the same method as that used for the summer pruning of flowering trees—will bring them into bloom right to the tips of their branches. Quinces flower well when trained against a warm south or west wall. They make no special demands as to soil except that it be well drained, but they must be given full sun. Variants include white-flowered forms, vivid reds, and also double flowers. 'Rubra Grandiflora' has very large crimson flowers and a low, spreading habit of growth.

Both of the above species have participated extensively in hybrids, collectively known as *C.* × *supérba* (V), and many of the named varieties now offered in the nursery trade fall into this category. Spreading shrubs 4–5 ft. in height, with habit and foliage intermediate for the two parents, their color range runs the gamut from white through pink and crimson to orange, orange-scarlet and brick reds. 'Crimson and Gold' is deep red with golden anthers.

C. × *califórnica* (V). This group of hybrids originated in California from the work of W. B. Clark, who crossed *C.* × *supérba* with the large-fruited, white-flowered *C. cathayénsis* from China. These stiffly erect, spiny shrubs have slender leaves and pink or rosy red flowers up to 2 in. across. 'Cardinal' is considered especially good.

Cultivars listed in catalogs as *C. japónica* may well include some plants of hybrid origin. The following selections illustrate the available color range:

'Cameo', soft apricot pink double, low growing.
'Hollandia', red, 1½ ft., flowering later.
'Low and White', white flowers; low, spreading habit.
'Minerva', cherry red; low, spreading habit.
'Orange Delight', orange to red; low and spreading.
'Pink Beauty', tall, upright rose pink.
'Super Red', large bright red flowers, upright habit.
'Texas Scarlet', scarlet flowers, low and spreading.

C. cathayénsis (VI), long cultivated in China, is an open, rather crookedly branched, spiny 8–10 ft. shrub, with shining, finely toothed leaves up to 5 in. long, reddish-downy beneath. It appleblossom-like flowers are white, tinged pink in bud. Very large, green fruits, 4–6 in. long and almost sessile on the branches, are quite freely produced and make good jelly. It is grown primarily for these curious fruits, and is a plant for a sunny location, away from traffic patterns. Seeds are the usual method of increase.

CHIMONÁNTHUS praécox (VII), Wintersweet, from China, is a bushy 9–10 ft. shrub. Its small, richly fragrant flowers, pale yellow outside, shading to chocolate in the center, are clustered along the stem throughout January and February in mild winters. Plant on the south or west side of some larger evergreen shrub; in such a situation it gets all the sun and warmth in winter. It can also be grown against a wall, where it will flower more freely but require more pruning. It needs little moisture during the latter part of the summer, and will thrive in any good garden soil. The variety 'Grandiflórus' has larger and more brightly colored flowers than the type, but is less fragrant. In 'Lúteus' they are distinctly more yellow. Wintersweet needs no pruning other than the thinning out of weak twigs in the center of the shrub or the occasional removal of heavy old branches.

CLERODÉNDRUM búngei (C. fóetidum) (VI–VII), from China, has heart-shaped, toothed leaves and large clusters of purple-red flowers in August/September from vigorous, woody shoots of the current year's growth. Flowers are fragrant, but the crushed leaves are ill-smelling. It spreads rapidly by suckers, forming dense thickets which may need to be restrained.

C. trichótomum (VI), Harlequin Glorybower, can be treated either as a shrub or as a tree. It forms a somewhat coarse shrub to 15–20 ft. in height, with leaves 4–8 in. long, resembling those of a *Catalpa*. Native to China and Japan, it is grown principally for its rather spectacular bloom in late summer and early fall. The clusters of fragrant, tubular, white flowers are quickly followed by bright blue berries surrounded by the persistent crimson calyces. Var. *fargésii* is said to be hardier than the type, but somewhat less colorful. *Clerodendrum* prefers a deep, light, well-drained soil in a warm, sunny location.

A plant of the Glorybower (*Clerodendrum trichotomum*) flowering in late August. Photo by Brian Mulligan.

CLÉTHRA acumináta (V), Cinnamon Clethra, is a shrub under garden conditions, but can be a 20-ft. tree in the wild. It is a native of southeastern United States, and is less hardy than the next two species. Its fragrant white flowers borne in solitary racemes up to 6 in. long, in August and large leaves clustered at the end of the shoots, have much to recommend them.

C. alnifólia (III), Summersweet Clethra, or Sweet Pepper Bush, a native of the Atlantic Coastal States, is an attractive 8–10 ft. shrub with erect stems ending in 4–6 in. racemes of fragrant white flowers in August. It likes a rich, moist soil, and a position in full sun. In the cultivar 'Paniculata' the flowers are borne in terminal panicles rather than racemes, for a somewhat showier effect than the type. 'Rosea' is an outstanding form with deep pink buds and soft pink flowers. 'Pink Spire' is another colored selection. Foliage turns a bright yellow or orange in the fall.

C. barbinérvis (V), from Japan, is a beautiful large shrub or small tree to about 10 ft., distinctive for its polished gray-brown bark. Large, toothed leaves, obviously hairy on the midribs and veins, cluster at the ends of the branches, giving a somewhat whorled appearance. Fragrant white flowers in large, compact clusters, bloom from July/September. Clethras are best pruned in early spring; part of the old wood should be removed each year. Propagate by seeds or cuttings.

COLÚTEA arboréscens (V), Common Bladder Senna, native to the Mediterranean region and southeastern Europe, is vigorous and fast-growing to about 12 ft. It has pinnately compound leaves, and small, yellow, pealike flowers followed by 3 in. long inflated pods. Easy and adaptable in all but the wettest conditions, this shrub is especially useful in poor, dry locations where choicer shrubs would fail. Pruning back to old wood in winter will keep it tidy. 'Bullata' is a dense, dwarf form with leaves smaller than those of the type. 'Crispa' is low-growing, with wavy margins to the leaves.

COMPTÓNIA peregrína (II), Sweet Fern, from eastern North America, is an attractive small plant, with an interesting, "woodsy" texture, suckering to form wide, flat-topped mounds to about 3–4 ft. Its long, slender, deeply cut leaves resemble fern fronds, and are pleasantly aromatic—hence the common name. A nitrogen fixer, it is adaptable to infertile, peaty, or sandy acid soils, in sun or shade, moist or dry. Separate male and female catkins flower in April or early May, but are not especially showy. Propagate by root cuttings; it is not easily transplanted from the wild.

CÓRNUS. The shrubby dogwoods put forth no display of large and decorative bracts—they depend for their garden value on brightly colored barks or good fall foliage. The clusters of small creamy white flowers are followed by small, white, bluish or black berries which appeal to birds.

C. álba (II), Tatarian Dogwood, from Asia, is a rampant shrub to 10 ft. high and as many wide, forming a great mass of arching stems, quite capable of engulfing choicer plants, and thus suitable only for the largest areas. Its variety 'Sibirica' is a less rampant grower with bright coral-red stems; it needs good, damp soil to be successful. 'Elegantissima', also known as 'Sibirica variegata', has white-variegated foliage, giving a good garden effect in summer as well as winter. 'Spaethii', with yellow-margined leaves, is considered one of the best deciduous shrubs of this type. The yellow color does not scorch. It makes an attractive specimen plant for the large lawn, and could be useful to brighten a dark corner.

C. *sangúinea* (IV), Common or Red Dogwood, is a European native up to 12 ft. in height, having fine red fall color and shiny purple-black berries, but not particularly good color to the winter twigs. Since this shrub can be rather untidy unless pruned regularly, it is best used for screening, and possibly for highway plantings. Redder-stemmed, green-stemmed, and variegated-leaved forms—not as good as those of C. *álba*—have been offered from time to time.

C. *stolonifera* (II) Red Osier Dogwood, native across North America, has rich red winter branches and twigs. Like some of the yellow-barked willows with which it may be grouped, it is excellent for winter effect when planted near water or in low-lying swampy places. Cut to the ground yearly, in early spring, it produces luxuriant, brightly colored new growth. It will throw up a mass of 5–8 ft. shoots in a single season when once established, and is easily increased by taking off the rooted stolons. Of value chiefly in large-scale plantings, its stoloniferous habit makes it difficult to contain in the average garden. Its clusters of white berries are ripe as early as August, and its crimson to red-violet fall color is often good. The form 'Flaviramea' with a yellow stem makes an interesting foil for the red stems of the type, as does the pea green 'Nitida'. 'Cheyenne' is a selection with particularly good red color. 'Kelseyi', low-growing and compact, could be used in the small garden, since it reaches to only about 30 in. 'Sunshine', with golden variegated foliage is a recent introduction from the Washington Park Arboretum in Seattle.

CORONÍLLA *émerus* (V), Scorpion Senna, from central and southern Europe has been in cultivation for several centuries. Described by Bean as having an "elegant habit," this shrub grows up to 8–9 ft. tall, with an equal spread. It has pinnately compound leaves, with clusters of small, yellow, pea-shaped flowers in the leaf axils, followed by slender, jointed seed-pods. It is well suited to warm, dry situations in Northwest coast areas.

CORYLÓPSIS *pauciflóra* (VI), Winter Hazel, from Japan, is one of the choicest and most delightful of early spring-flowering shrubs. In March, its fine network of slender branches is bejeweled with fragrant, pale yellow bells. The delicate little hazel-like leaves are beautiful when they first unfold, changing from varying tints of soft rosy pink through pinky copper to pale, lucid green. C. *pauciflora* ultimately makes a spreading shrub as much as 5 ft. high, but is slow growing. It should be given protection from full sun and drying winds, such as a sheltered corner in a woodland setting. It prefers light, well-drained soil enriched with leafmold or manure, and is not suited to alkaline soils.

C. sinénsis (V–VI) from China, is a much larger shrub than the preceding, reaching a height of 15 ft. Its primrose yellow flowers in short, drooping racemes appear in early to mid-spring, undeterred by chill weather. Var. *calvéscens* now includes plants formerly known as *C. platypétala* and *C. veitchiána*.

C. spícata (V–VI), is another Japanese native, blooming in March and early April. Up to 6 ft. high and as much wide, with a hairy inflorescence of small, soft yellow, fragrant flowers, it is larger and less graceful than *C. pauciflora*, and not as well suited to the small garden.

The fall leaf color is yellow in most *Corylopsis*.

CÓRYLUS, Hazel. Most of the many species of Hazel are grown for their edible nuts, but some have ornamental qualities as well. All are large, multistemmed shrubs or small trees, 15–20 ft. in height. The drooping male catkins turn yellow with pollen as early as January/February in mild climates; the less conspicuous female flowers display small, red style tips.

C. avellána (III), the Hazelnut from Europe, is better suited to woodland plantings than to small gardens. 'Contorta', Harry Lauder's Walking Stick, has curled and twisted twigs and branches and does not achieve the full size of the type; contorted leaves in this form may be evidence of disease, 'Fusco-rubra' is a handsome purple-leaved cultivar.

C. cornúta var. *califórnica* (V), our native Hazel, is decidedly worth including in large woodland areas, and when fine specimens are found growing on any proposed garden site, they should, whenever possible, be incorporated into the garden planting. Found in both eastern and western parts of our area, it is the first native shrub to come into bloom in the spring; its leaves turn a pleasing yellow in the fall. It is a considerably less dense plant than its European relatives, the branching pattern stiffly erect rather than arching, to 20–30 ft.

C. máxima (IV), Filbert, from southern Europe, is similar in habit to *C. avellana*, but somewhat larger, to 20 ft. or more. Most named varieties are nut selections. 'Purpurea', which has purple catkins as well as purple foliage, is one of the more effective shrubs of its type, though definitely too large for the small garden. Its dark purple leaves fade to green in late summer and do not color in the fall. All three species are of the easiest possible culture in any garden soil, sun or shade. Defending the nuts from squirrels or jays may pose problems.

COTÍNUS coggýgria (V), Smoke Tree or Smoke Bush from southern Europe and western Asia, forms a broad, bushy shrub or small tree 10–15 ft. tall, and as much or more across. The small, rounded, slightly glaucous leaves turn golden to red-purple in the fall. Smoke Bush is an apt description of the clouds of smoky pinkish purple fluff—the long, sterile hairs of the inflorescence—which enshroud the shrub in midsummer. In the form

The Smoke Tree, (*Cotinus coggygria*) in midsummer. Photo by Brian Mulligan.

'Purpureus' the leaves are green, but the "smoke" is purple. Other interesting cultivars, selected for variations in "smoke" color, leaf color, and fall color are available. 'Velvet Cloak', with richly colored foliage and spectacular reddish purple fall color is perhaps the best of a number of purple-leaved forms. In 'Flame' the smoke is pinkish, and fall leaf color is orange-red. 'Royal Purple' has very dark purple foliage, narrowly edged with crimson. To be assured of the most colorful display, select this shrub in the fall of the year. Smoke Bush is easily grown in full sun and any well-drained garden soil. Fall color is best when watering and fertilizer have been minimal; a hot summer helps. Its branches may be thinned lightly from time to time during the dormant season; avoid excessive pruning.

C. *obovátus* (III), Chittamwood or American Smoke Tree from southeastern United States, has less conspicuous inflorescences than the preceding species, but much larger leaves and even more spectacular fall color. It can be a tree up to 30 ft. tall, but is usually smaller, a roundheaded plant with scaly gray or gray-brown bark. Again, select this one in fall leaf, and give it lean conditions to assure the best coloring.

COTONEÁSTER. Most species of *Cotoneaster* are evergreen or semi-evergreen and are discussed under Broad-leaved Evergreen Shrubs. However, a number of the deciduous species are well worthy of a place in Northwest gardens.

C. *adpréssus* (IV), from western China, is one of the choicest of the small cotoneasters for the rock garden. Very dwarf, stiff branching, and seldom over a foot in height, with oval leaves scarcely ½ in. long, it can spread over several square yards of ground, rooting as it goes. The small, rose-tipped white flowers produce quantities of ¼-in. red berries which show to advantage on the bare winter twigs.

C. *bullátus* (V), is a 10–12 ft. shrub from western China and Tibet, with arching branches and blistered leaves, downy on the underside. Its small flowers pass too quickly to be important—as with most cotoneasters—but they leave a legacy of handsome 2-in. clusters of brilliant red, pear-shaped fruits.

C. *dístichus* (V), is a stiffly branched 4–8 ft. shrub from the Himalayas. Its dark, glossy, ½-in. long leaves may be deciduous or semi-evergreen. Bean considers this the best of the smaller cotoneasters by virtue of its brightly colored and very abundant fruits, which persist until early spring, making a splash of scarlet in the winter garden.

C. *divaricátus* (V), from western China is another good red-fruited species. This spreading 6-ft. shrub with glossy dark green leaves ½ to 1 in. long, rose-colored flowers and tiny egg-shaped fruits makes an attractive informal hedge plant.

C. *horizontális* (IV), Rock Spray or Rock Cotoneaster, from western China, is a spreading 3–4 ft. shrub with a flat, dense branching structure, giving it a layered effect. Its tiny, pink-tinted flowers are very attractive to bees, which can be something of a hazard; avoid placing plants near entrances or principal traffic patterns in the home garden. The fine, glossy, dark green leaves turn red-orange before dropping, and the many small, red berries provide good winter color. 'Saxatilis' is dwarfer and more prostrate than the type, with a distinctive "fishbone" branching pattern, and is useful for the rock garden. 'Variegatus', with leaves edged in white is a very dainty plant for the small rock garden, the leaves turning pink in autumn. It is sometimes attacked by red spider mites or web worms.

C. *simónsii* (V), from Assam can be semi-evergreen or deciduous. It is a handsome vigorous shrub to about 10–12 feet, with glossy, dark green leaves 1 in. long or a little less, and scarlet fruits. It can be used to advantage in mixed shrub plantings, and is suitable for hedges.

C. *spléndens* (V–VI), from western China, is allied to the evergreen C. *dielsiánus,* but is shorter in growth habit and has larger red-orange fruits. A recent introduction.

C. *zabélii* (IV), is a 6–9 ft. shrub from China, having small, dull green leaves, with felty, pale beige undersides. The small, rose-colored flowers are borne in clusters, and the small red fruits are downy and pearshaped.

Var. *miniátus* is a more compact plant having red-orange fruits and leaves with yellow autumn color.

Cotoneasters thrive in most well-drained garden soils, in full sun, and fruit freely, since bees are much attracted to the flowers. Fire blight can be a hazard with some species of this genus, which will make them unwelcome in commercial fruit-growing areas. Prune out and burn affected branches as soon as noticed.

DÁPHNE × *burkwóodii* (IV), Burkwood Daphne, is a hybrid between *D. caucásica* and *D. cneórum*. The flowers, pale pink and fragrant, are borne in dense 2-in.-wide clusters in late spring. Foliage is semi-evergreen. The several clones in commerce are vigorous, rounded shrubs 3–4 ft. each way. 'Arthur Burkwood' is somewhat taller than 'Somerset'. 'Carol Mackie' has delicate cream-edged leaf margins to go with its pink flowers. This attractive, fragrant plant is useful in shrub borders or foundation plantings, in sunny or lightly shaded sites.

D. *mezéreum* (IV), from Europe, is an upright, slow-growing, 5–6 ft. shrub with a well-deserved place in the winter garden. In February the stiff little twigs are tightly packed with sweetly scented, rose-magenta flowers. These are followed in summer by handsome but poisonous scarlet berries. Gardeners with preschool children will do well to postpone their acquisition of this plant! 'Autumnalis' flowers in the fall, with blooms larger than the type. The dull-white-flowered form, D. *m. álba*, has been supplanted by the pure white selections 'Paul's White' and 'Bowles' White'; fruits of this form are yellow. This *Daphne* is easily grown in any good garden soil with moderate moisture, but prefers a deep, light, sandy medium with plenty of humus. It is propagated most readily from seed.

DEÚTZIA. The Deutzias are a group of May- and June-blooming shrubs from Asia, related to *Philadelphus*, and are represented in gardens by both species and hybrids. Their leaves have a characteristic scratchy feel, from the stellate hairs on their surface. In general, they are a winter-hardy group, but bloom may not be satisfactory in areas subject to late spring freezes.

D. × *elegantíssima* (IV) is a French hybrid of D. *purpuráscens*. The clone 'Rosalind' grows 4–5 ft. tall and has deep carmine flowers in June.

D. *grácilis* (IV), Slender Deutzia, native to Japan, produces many arching stems to 3–4 ft. high, with a 5-ft. spread. It has soft, dull green foliage, and pure white flowers in late May, and is one parent of many of the best hybrids.

D. × *lemóinei* (IV), Lémoine Deutzia, is a hybrid between D. *grácilis* and D. *parviflóra*, from north China, considered more beautiful than the parental species. It grows to a height of about 7 ft., has white flowers in late May, and is one of the hardiest, able to survive in Minnesota. 'Compacta' is a dwarf selection.

D. × *rósea* (IV). This name applies to a group of hybrids between D. *grácilis* and D. *purpuráscens*, also raised by Lémoine in France. They make rather dense shrubs, to about 3 ft. Their flowers, white inside, pink outside, are borne in small clusters. 'Carminea', a dwarf selection, has pale pink flowers, darker in the bud, blooming in May/June.

D. scábra (V), Fuzzy Deutzia, from Japan and China, is a leggy shrub 6–10 ft. tall, rather straggly in appearance, and flowering in June. Its white flowers, sometimes tinged pink on the outside, are borne in upright panicles 3–6 in. long. Color and flower variants include pure white 'Candidissima', double white 'Florepleno', with flowers pink tinted on the outside, 'Goodsall Pink', with double pink flowers, and 'Pride of Rochester', with double flowers, rosy purple on the outside.

Deutzias are of easiest culture in any garden soil in sun or shade, and are best pruned immediately after flowering, to stimulate clean, new growth. The taller varieties, like so many of the June-flowering deciduous shrubs, are very good as a background for herbaceous material. Treated in this way in full sun in rich soil with ample moisture, they are more showy than when grown in drier conditions on the edge of woodland. In the many forms available it is possible to obtain either tall, intermediate, or dwarf shrubs ranging in height from 3–10 ft. They are probably less important in our region than in colder climates where a narrower range of shrubs can be grown.

DISÁNTHUS cercidifólius (VI), A Witch-hazel relative from Japan, is a broadly spreading 8–10 ft. shrub, rather rare in nurseries here, but worth seeking out for its orange, claret red, or purple fall color. Its dark red flowers, about ½ in. in diameter, appear in October. Not always an easy plant to grow, but well worth the effort, it requires a deep, rich, moist soil, in light shade, and needs protection from strong, drying winds.

ELAEÁGNUS multiflóra (IV), the Cherry Elaeagnus of China and Japan, is a deciduous or semi-evergreen shrub forming a dense mound 10 ft. high and as much across. Brownish or reddish brown scales cover the twigs and branches. Its leaves, silvery green above and silvery brown below, are also scaly, as are the small, fragrant flowers which appear in April or May. This shrub is especially handsome in midsummer when its abundance of ½-in. oblong orange-red fruits are ripe; it is a very useful plant for attracting birds.

E. umbelláta (III), Autumn Eleagnus, from the Himalayas, China, and Japan, is a spreading 10–12 ft. shrub with graceful arching branches and leaves bright green above but silver below. It is quite a variable plant in vigor and habit of growth; some forms are slightly broader than high, while others are said to gain a spread of as much as 30 ft. The small, fragrant, silvery cream flowers in May and June are followed by very beautiful globose fruits—at first a silvery brown, gradually changing in a delightful sequence from palest chartreuse green through soft yellow and orange to a clear red, all dusted with silvery scales.

ENKIÁNTHUS is a genus of attractive ericaceous shrubs closely related to *Andromeda* and *Zenobia*. The species most often grown are

Japanese natives and are highly valued as garden plants in their own country. They require the same acid soil conditions as the deciduous azaleas and need no pruning other than prompt removal of dead flower heads before seed pods form. Best propagated from seed, they can also be struck from summer cuttings.

E. campanulátus (IV), a relatively showy species, is an erect shrub that ultimately reaches 10–15 ft. The small, bell-shaped flowers, hanging in loose, long-stemmed clusters under the foliage in May, are a pale, luminous apricot, delicately veined or striped with candy pink. This species is not only lovely in bloom when properly placed, but both it and the following species are grown almost as much for the vivid red fall coloring of their neat, pointed leaves. 'Albiflorus' has greenish white flowers. 'Hollandia Red' has flowers with much darker color than the type. In var. *palibínii* the flowers are red and smaller than the type.

E. cérnuus (V) is slightly smaller than the preceding species, seldom reaching more than 10 ft. in height. Its flowers are likewise small and bell shaped, but with the petal edge fringed or toothed, and they are short stalked, 10–12 to a cluster. Var. *rúbens* with rounder leaves than the type, and deep red flowers, is an especially handsome plant.

E. perulátus (V) has small, urn-shaped, white flowers that appear in early April before the leaves. It is smaller in all its parts than the two preceding species, a slender shrub seldom exceeding 5–6 ft. Its leaves have an even more brilliant scarlet coloring in autumn.

All three species are highly desirable for the small garden.

EUÓNYMUS. The many species of Spindle Berry are grown principally for the fall coloring of their foliage and their very unusual seed pods, which are usually rose, crimson, or magenta, splitting open to show vivid orange seeds. The larger species may be grown almost equally well as either trees or shrubs. To get the maximum effect of autumn coloring and heavy crops of fruit, the Spindle Berries must not be overfertilized. They need full sun and will thrive in almost any soil. Little pruning is required other than occasional thinning of the branches.

E. alátus (III), Winged Spindle Berry from Japan and China, so called because the horizontally spreading branches have 2–4 corky wings all along their length, forms a broad 6–8 ft. shrub. The fruit pods, purplish magenta with orange seeds, are small, but are freely produced when the plant is grown in lean soil. The small, dark green, pointed leaves turn in the fall to a brilliant scarlet. 'Compactus' is a tighter-growing form, but not smaller, with wings less pronounced or absent.

E. európaeus (III), European Spindletree, is a narrowly upright shrub or small tree, to about 30 ft. Its fruits, which vary considerably in color, are its chief ornamental feature. Cultivars with white, pink, and bright red capsules are in the nursery trade, all with the same bright orange seeds. Scale can be a problem with this species, so one should be prepared to spray to keep it under control. *E. europaeus* is, nevertheless, one of the most consistent performers in the cooler sections. 'Red Cascade' and 'Aldenhamen-sis' are named selections.

E. *hamiltónianus* (V), native to the Himalayas and the Far East, and closely related to the preceding, is a deciduous or semi-evergreen shrub or small tree of similar height and habit. Var. *sieboldiánus*, the Yeddo Euonymus, which comes from Japan and Korea, has leaves up to 5 in. long, pink capsules, orange-coated seeds, and good rose to red autumn color.

E. *latifólius* (V), from southern Europe and eastward, is a splendid 10–15 ft., broadly spreading shrub or small tree with broad leaves coloring well in the fall. Its long-stalked, magenta-crimson seedpods, nearly ¾ in. across, are more effective than those of E. *europaeus* even though borne in less profusion. This is perhaps the best of all the species in Northwest gardens.

E. *plánipes* (V), from northeastern Asia, is allied to the preceding species and is of similar size and habit. It has the merit of both good fruits and good fall color.

EXOCHÓRDA *racemósa (E. grandiflóra)* (IV), Pearl Bush, from Northern China, is a close relative of the Spiraeas, which will thrive in any good garden soil in a sunny location. A bushy 10–12 ft. shrub with soft green foliage, it bears a profusion of pearly white flowers 1–1½ in. across in erect racemes in late April or May. Spent flowering branches should be removed immediately after blooming.

E. *giráldii* (IV) from northwestern China is perhaps an even better garden shrub than the preceding. It has pinkish young shoots, and in its variety *wilsónii*, flowers up to 2 in. across; but it is, unfortunately, less commonly available in nurseries.

E. × *macrántha* (IV–V), a hybrid between E. *korolkówii* and E. *racemósa*, is a beautiful shrub with 3–4 in. long racemes of large, pure white flowers, of which the cultivar 'The Bride' is a compact, free-flowering version.

FORSÝTHIA species from China and Japan are the indispensable 'Golden Bells' so welcome in early spring. They are happy in any garden soil in sun or light shade. They require severe pruning immediately after flowering, or can be cut when in bloom. Unless the old bloomed-out growth is removed, the shrub quickly becomes untidy with the old weak wood forming a tangled mass. There are about six species, but most of the plants readily available in commerce today belong to F. × *intermédia*, a hybrid between F. *suspénsa* and F. *viridíssima*, which arose in Germany toward the end of the last century.

F. × *intermédia* (IV), is a vigorous 8–10 ft. shrub with many erect or arching branches thickly set with 4-petaled, yellow flowers, appearing before the leaves from February to early April. Cut stems force well from late winter on. Useful as a specimen plant or in the shrub border, the leaves of this hybrid hold a good green color all summer, turning yellow, sometimes tinged with purple, in the fall. Some of the better named clones are:

'Karl Sax', deep gold, with flowers up to 1¾ in. across.

'Lynwood' ('Lynwood Gold'), with flowers slightly lighter yellow than those of 'Spectabilis', bright yellow garden favorite of long standing.

'Spring Glory', which has primrose yellow flowers and is very floriferous.

F. ováta (V), Early Forsythia, from Korea, is a smaller shrub than the preceding, seldom over 5 ft. in height, neat and compact in habit. Its short twiggy branches are laden with small, bright yellow flowers in February/March, well ahead of those of the other species and hybrids.

F. suspénsa var. *siebóldii* (V), Weeping Forsythia, a native of China, is an 8–10 ft. shrub with upright stems and gracefully drooping or weeping branches which root where they touch the ground, enabling it to ramble about the garden at an alarming rate. However, this characteristic makes it a useful plant for covering steep slopes; it can even be used as a climber, against buildings or tree. Golden yellow flowers bloom later than those of *F. × intermedia,* the three types together making possible a greatly extended *Forsythia* season.

FOTHERGÍLLA gardénii (V), Dwarf Fothergilla, is a 4 ft. tall Witch-hazel relative native to southeastern United States. One-inch-wide clusters of fragrant, bottlebrush-like flowers, consisting of great tufts of white stamens, appear before the foliage in April or early May. The broadly ovate, somewhat leathery leaves take on gorgeous yellow and orange tones in autumn, most intense in full sun. This species likes acid soil with good drainage, and does well planted with rhododendrons and azaleas.

F. májor (F. montícola) (IV), Large Fothergilla, also native to the south-eastern states, is a beautiful and unusual 8–10 ft. shrub, often multi-stemmed. In May, its pleasing and distinctive pattern of broadly spreading branches (up to 10 ft. across) is clothed in a cloud of fluffy, fragrant, white flowers. In fall the foliage develops spectacular autumn color, turning to fiery orange-red or red before it drops. This species grows well in any good garden soil, but prefers one on the acid side, and needs only moder-ate moisture. Prune sparingly, just enough to keep the branches open. This is an excellent plant for the shrub border and makes outstanding groupings since no two individuals color quite the same.

FÚCHSIA. There are about 100 species of *Fuchsia* in tropical and sub-tropical America and New Zealand, but only one which is reliably hardy in our area, and then only west of the Cascades. This is *F. magellánica* (VII–VIII), from Chile and Argentina. Although it can grow upwards of 15 ft. in the wild, the forms in cultivation are seldom more than about 5 ft. high and as much across, with many gracefully arching, red-tinted stems. The 1½ in. long, pendent flowers—crimson with rich purple petticoats—are carried in profusion from July till frost. This is a choice late-summer-flowering plant for a favored position in the garden; even so, it will be periodically cut to the ground by severe winters. If it does not form permanent shrubby growth, it will still come back freely from the ground each spring and can be considered thoroughly satisfactory as an herbaceous plant if not as a shrub. Grow it in the warmest possible situation, in rather rich, well-drained soil. Fuchsias are best propagated by late summer cuttings kept in the frame all winter. Hummingbirds are fond of their flowers. In addition to the usual crimson-and-purple-flowered form, a pink and white variety, 'Molinae', is available.

GAYLUSSÁCIA baccáta (II), from northeastern North America, called Black Huckleberry there, is a small, much-branched shrub 3–5 ft. high, with oval, resin-dotted leaves and drooping racemes of tiny, bell-shaped pink flowers resembling those of *Vaccinium*. Edible but variably tasty, shining black berries follow. It will grow in full sun, in sandy or rocky soil to which peat has been added, and is propagated by cuttings.

HAMAMÉLIS móllis (V), from China, the handsomest of the Witch Hazels, is one of the most uniquely beautiful of winter-flowering shrubs when its vigorous upright branches are set with its spidery, bright yellow, richly fragrant flowers. These may last a month or more, beginning around New Year. The heavy, hazel-like foliage takes on rich yellow tints in autumn. Ultimately a large shrub, 25–30 ft. high, it is slow-growing, and unfortunately, both difficult and slow to propagate. For this reason it has remained an expensive shrub all too seldom seen in gardens. Lower branches can be layered.

H. japónica (V), Japanese Witch Hazel, is almost as showy, a variable, widespreading shrub to about 10–15 ft. tall. The slightly scented flowers are paler and more greenish yellow than those of *H. móllis,* the leaves smaller and less hairy.

H. vernális (IV), Vernal Witch Hazel, comes from southeastern United States, but grows well in Northwest gardens. A multistemmed, densely branched shrub to 10 ft. or more, its blooms can last 3–4 weeks in January/February, the flowers rolling up on very cold days. The ½-in.-long petals are yellow, and pungently fragrant, based in a red calyx. This species also has good yellow to orange fall color, and as a stream-bank native is well suited to damp locations. 'Sandra' blooms in the fall with very small flowers, but has plum purple new growth and rivals *Acer gríseum* in scarlet red fall color.

H. virginiána (III), Common Witch Hazel, found over much of eastern United States and into Canada, is a large, multistemmed shrub or small tree to 25 or more ft., and is thus probably too big for the small garden, but well suited to a woodland or park setting. It can flower as early as October, and the small, fragrant, yellow flowers are sometimes lost in the bright gold fall foliage. This species is the source of the witch-hazel extract used in astringents. It is frequently used as understock for grafting other species.

The name *H.* × *intermédia* (V) covers a group of hybrids between *H. japónica* and *H. móllis,* a combination that has been made repeatedly and is now represented in nurseries by a considerable number of named cultivars. Large shrubs, to 15 ft. or more, multistemmed and of spreading habit, they vary considerably both in flower and fall leaf color, those with the redder flowers also having red fall color.

'Arnold Promise' has fragrant, clear yellow flowers, and yellow-orange fall color.

'Diane' has flowers of bright bronzy red, with orange-red fall color.

'Jelena' (also known as 'Copper Beauty'), has yellow petals flushed coppery red; autumn color also is fiery red.

'Fire Charm' ('Feuerzauber') has orange-red flowers.

'Moonlight', with pale sulfur yellow flowers, has yellow fall color as well.

Witch Hazels thrive in deep, well-drained soil, preferably sandy loam enriched with plenty of leafmold or compost. They prefer light woodland conditions, but do well in full sun, especially if given ample moisture during the growing season. The pattern and tracery of branches so essential to the beauty of the plant in bloom can be kept open by light winter pruning. Branches cut in December open quickly in the house.

HIBÍSCUS is a large genus of some 200 species almost all of which are tropical. The only woody species reliably hardy in our region is H. syríacus (V), Shrub Althaea or Rose of Sharon. It is actually a cultivated plant in Syria, and native only farther east in India and China. Its flowers, similar in shape to those of hollyhocks, are freely produced in August/September on a shrub of rather stiff habit, to 10 or more feet, and sometimes an equal spread, branching upward and outward in the shape of an inverted cone. Plants that become too leggy may be cut back severely in early spring. They are easily propagated by cuttings or layering; named varieties are grafted. A surprisingly large number of cultivars, both single and double flowered, can be found in nursery lists, in a color range from white and pink through lavender to magenta or purplish red:

'Diana' is a white single with very large flowers, bred at the U. S. National Arboretum, Washington, D.C., in 1963.

'Red Heart' is a white single with a red center.

'Jeanne d'Arc' is a late-flowering double white.

'Morning Star', a double white, has a red throat.

'Blue Bird' is a large blue-mauve with a deeper center, of French origin.

'Coelestis' has slightly smaller flowers with a reddish purple throat.

'Woodbridge' is a single rose pink with a red eye, of English origin.

'Collie Mullens' is a lavender-purple double with a crimson eye.

'Anemonaeflorus' and 'Paeoniflorus' are double pinks.

'Lucy' is a double magenta red.

'Boule de Feu' is a double violet-pink.

HIPPÓPHAË rhamnoídes (III), the Sea Buckthorn, native to both Europe and Asia, is a somewhat spiny shrub or small tree to 20–30 feet, related to *Elaeagnus* and *Shepherdia*. Its flowers are inconspicuous, but the narrow, silvery gray foliage is most attractive, particularly when the small orange fruits are clustered thickly along the stem from September onwards. The fruits are not eaten by birds and last well into February making it one of the more colorful shrubs for the winter garden. Only female plants bear fruits, so that at least one male plant will be necessary as a pollenizer. Layering is the most satisfactory means of propagation, since the sex of the new plants will be known at the outset. Sea Buckthorn is a useful shrub for a dry, sunny location, especially for seaside plantings or hedges.

HOLODÍSCUS díscolor (V), our well-known native Ocean Spray, is under-appreciated as a garden shrub, even though its soft, airy panicles of creamy white lace are highly visible in many parts of the Northwest in June. In the wild it is a rangy shrub up to 20 ft. tall. Grown in the garden in any good soil, in either sun or partial shade, and pruned severely each year after flowering, it forms a loose, graceful 10-ft. shrub well deserving a place among the most distinguished exotics. It is particularly beautiful at the back of the herbaceous border, where its creamy trusses can contrast with the spikes of pale blue delphiniums.

HYDRÁNGEA, most familiar to gardeners in the heavy-headed, sterile-flowered 'Hortensia' type, is simultaneously both a very popular and a much reviled shrub. With its bold leaves, and round, mounded outline, it is probably the most conspicuous summer-flowering shrub west of the Cascades. Those who find these stiff, pudgy "mop-heads'" of bloom objectionable can forego them in favor of the daintier, but not so well-known 'Lace Cap' forms, in which a few sterile flowers decorate a flat-topped inflorescense of many small, fertile flowers.

H. macrophýlla (VI), the Bigleaf Hydrangea from Japan, has a rather odd history, having been described originally from its sterile horticultural form, rather than its fertile-flowered wild type (now called var. *normális*), which was not discovered by Western botanists until more than 100 years later! Also, peculiar to this species, the flower color is affected by the pH of the soil: the best blues are produced in very acid soils; the same variety in only slightly acid or neutral soils will give pink or bluish pink flowers. A little aluminum sulfate sprinkled on the soil around the plant can be used to maintain the blue color; lime or superphosphate can be used to induce pink. Color is more reliably fixed in some varieties than others; a few seem immune to the effects of pH. All require rich, well-drained soil with ample moisture. If given sufficient water they will thrive in full sun in the coastal areas, but in interior valleys require partial shade, even with ample moisture at the roots.

In choosing varieties of Hydrangeas, see them in bloom if possible, either in public plantings or in nurseries. Hortensias will be found in violet and crimson as well as blue, pink, or white. Plants with fairly modest heads blend in better in the general garden scheme than those of the very largest size.

'All Summer Beauty' blooms prolifically, and may be blue or pink depending on the soil.

'Forever Pink' has clear pink flowers.

'Mme. Moullière' is the best white 'Hortensia', perpetual flowering.

'Pink and Pretty' is pink flowered, with compact habit.

'Otaksa' is deep blue.

LaceCaps come in blue, pink or white, with most of the color contributed by the small fertile flowers.

'Blue Wave' is rich blue in acid soils.

'Lanarth White' has white ray flowers, the fertile flowers colored pink or blue.

'Mariesii' has pink or mauve-pink flowers. A blue-flowered form with white-variegated leaves is also available.

H. arboréscens (III–IV), the Smooth Hydrangea, is a native of eastern United States. A vigorous, hardy species, with roundish, toothed leaves up to 8 in. across, it flowers on new wood, from June through September. 'Grandiflora', referred to as 'Snowhill Hydrangea' or 'Hills of Snow Hydrangea', is the clone most commonly available in nurseries. It has large, round heads of greenish ivory sterile flowers, similar to those of the Hortensias, and will stand considerable shade. 'Annabelle' is a newer selection from Illinois.

H. áspera (H. villósa) (V) comes to us from China, though its range extends from Nepal to the East Indies. It can be a shrub or a small tree to as much as 12 ft. tall. Both the stems and the large, pointed leaves are densely hairy. Flat-topped clusters of flowers up to 10 in. across consist primarily of tiny, colored, fertile flowers with the larger, sterile florets grouped around the outside—white, pale pink or purple—the veins with increased intensity of color. This species is said to do best in somewhat dry soil, where water never stands; it is lime tolerant, and hardy enough when established, but may need some protection through its first winters.

H. paniculáta (IV) is a Japanese species most usually seen in the cultivar 'Grandiflora', the "PeeGee" Hydrangea. An irregular but graceful shrub to 20 ft., it can be trained as a single-trunked small tree, and is especially useful in areas where *H. macrophylla* is too tender. It has foot-long panicles of creamy white sterile flowers in late summer or early fall, which turn a beautiful pinky-bronze as they age. Its cultural requirements are the same as for *H. macrophylla*. It should be hard-pruned in the spring before growth starts.

H. quercifólia (V), the Oak-Leaved Hydrangea, native to the southeastern states, in a handsome 6-ft. shrub all too little known in gardens here. As its name suggests, its leaves resemble large oak leaves. They are

The oak-leaved
Hydrangea quercifolia in
bloom in July. Photo by
E. F. Marten, Campus
Studios, University of
Washington.

leathery and deeply veined, a rich, dark green with a gray-green felt on the underside, turning to scarlet-crimson or purple in the fall. In addition to the striking character of its foliage, large, loose trusses of creamy white flowers are freely produced in June, lasting until September, turning pinkish as they age. Several named cultivars are showier than the type, to the point of weighing down the branches. This species requires rich soil in a not too shady location, with adequate moisture, and a mulch of humus to do its best.

HYPÉRICUM, St. Johnswort, is perhaps most familiar to gardeners in its herbaceous species, but several shrubby or subshrubby species are also useful garden plants. They are valued for their extended summer flowering and for their handsome, long-lasting foliage, useful for hiding the legginess of taller shrubs. All come easily from cuttings, the species from seed.

H. *androsaémum* (VI), 'Tutsan', found from western Europe and north Africa to the Caspian and Black Sea regions, is a 2–3 ft. woody-stemmed plant with large, handsome leaves and clusters of small yellow flowers. Pea-sized berries (actually capsules) progress from red to almost black by September. This is a shade-tolerant species, more desirable for its leaves than for its flowers.

H. *forréstii* (VII). Native to southern China, Assam, and Upper Burma, this species is an almost deciduous shrub with small stiff-pointed leaves and golden yellow flowers 1½–2 in. or more across. Red color in the young fruits and orange-red fall foliage extend its season of brightness in the garden. Now somewhat eclipsed by H. × 'Hidcote', it is nevertheless still worth planting.

H. frondósum (IV), from southeastern United States, grows to a height of 3–4 ft. and about the same width. It has handsome blue-green foliage and bright yellow 1–2 in. flowers all summer. Later, cone-shaped red fruits rise from a collar of sepals. The named clone 'Sunburst', slightly lower growing than the species proper, is particularly good, and will thrive in either sun or shade.

H. × 'Hidcote' (VI) is an English hybrid which originated in the garden at Hidcote Manor. It is an almost evergreen shrub up to 5 ft. high and more across, with slender leaves, dark green above and pale below. Three-in. wide golden yellow flowers cover the plant continuously from midsummer to September; fruit is rarely set.

H. pátulum (VII), Goldencup St. Johnswort, is a spreading, almost evergreen shrub from southwestern China, but cultivated in Japan, rarely more than 3 ft. high with oval dark green leaves and golden yellow flowers 2 in. across, from July to fall.

ÍLEX. Hollies are widely distributed around the world, except in western North America. Though the name conjures up a mental image of the spiny evergreen types, there are also a few garden-worthy deciduous species grown chiefly for their berries which are especially good against a background of conifers.

I. decídua (IV), "Possumhaw", from southeastern United States can be a 30-ft. tree in the wild, but is usually an 8–10 ft. shrub under garden conditions. Glossy dark green summer foliage—not spiny—turns yellow in the fall. Orange-red to scarlet berries, borne singly or 3 together, remain on the tree until the following spring. 'Byer's Golden' is a yellow-fruited form; 'Reed' is a selection that fruits more heavily than the species; 'Warren's Red' has especially good foliage and superior bright red fruits.

I. laevigáta (IV), Winterberry, is also a native of eastern United States, where it grows in low, wet situations and may be expected to put up with a similar situation in the garden. A deciduous shrub 6–8 ft. high, with glossy, pale green leaves, it produces quantities of orange-red fruits, borne singly, but giving a vivid winter effect. There is also a yellow-fruited form.

I. verticilláta (III). Common Winterberry, Coralberry, Michigan Holly, or Christmas Berry, from eastern North America is considered the most ornamental of the American deciduous hollies. It is a 6–10 ft. shrub, dense and multistemmed, with leaves dark green in summer. Bright red fruits, which ripen in September and persist well into winter, are attractive to birds. Male as well as female plants are necessary for good fruit set, in this species as well as others. A native of swampy areas, this plant prefers rich, moist, acid soil, in full sun or semishade. It provides a bright bit of color for the shrub border in winter and makes a good massed effect. 'Winter Red' is a new selection.

ÍTEA virgínica (V), Virginia Sweetspire, is an upright 3–5 ft. shrub, much branched at the top, well suited to naturalizing in moist locations in the garden, in good, damp soil. Native to southeastern United States, and blooming after most other shrubs are past, it produces a host of long, narrow racemes of fragrant, white flowers in June and July. In the fall, its scarlet to red foliage color can be spectacular. Propagated simply by division, it also comes easily from cuttings.

KÉRRIA japónica (IV). This deciduous shrub from central and western China—though originally described from Japan—is perhaps most familiar in its showy double form, 'Pleniflora'. The slender branches of bright green foliage are weighed to the ground in April with soft orange-yellow flowers like small, double roses clustered along the stem. The less popular single *Kerria* with flat 5-petaled flowers is more airy and graceful, but less colorful in total garden effect than the double form. *Kerria* prefers light shade with a moderate amount of moisture, and thrives in any good garden soil. It will run around by underground shoots and rapidly form a loose graceful shrub up to 8 ft. tall. It should not be planted where there is danger of crowding less energetic neighbors. All flowering branches should be removed immediately after blooming. Forms with white-variegated foliage, 'Picta', and yellow-variegated foliage, 'Aurea-variegata', are also available, but are said to be somewhat less vigorous than the type.

The flowers of the normal single form of *Kerria japonica*. Photo by Brian Mulligan, in late April.

KOLKWÍTZIA amábilis (IV), Beautybush, from central China, is an 8–10 ft. shrub with many heavy, arching branches, perhaps most attractive where their outer ends can cascade down a bank or over a wall. It needs full sun, and fairly dry soil to bloom well, and is then covered with hordes of small, flaring, bell-shaped pink to lavender-pink flowers in June. These are followed by fluffy pinkish-brown seedpods which continue the color display (often with a few flowers) throughout the summer. Spent flowering branches should be removed to encourage new growth. Newly established plants are best pruned after flowering, to conserve the energy of the shrub. 'Pink Cloud' and 'Rosea' are selections with improved pink color and give much better garden effect than run-of-the-mill seedlings.

LEYCESTÉRIA formósa (VII) from the Himalayas is an attractive, tall, slender shrub with bright green, hollow-jointed stems growing stiffly upright, but with gracefully arching laterals. These carry drooping clusters of dark purple bracts up to 4 in. long with small, pinkish white flowers set in their axils, blooming from July to September, and followed by small red-purple fruits. This shrub is easily grown in any good garden soil in full sun but prefers a rich, moist loam. It may achieve a height of as much as 15 ft. in a sheltered position. The rootstock is perfectly hardy, but the top is occasionally cut to the ground in exceptionally severe winters. If pruned almost to the ground every year, which is one method of treatment, it will send up lusty 6-ft. shoots and flower freely during the latter part of the summer. Birds are partial to the fleshy black fruits.

LÍNDERA benzóin (IV), Spice Bush, a native of eastern North America, can grow to a height of 12 ft. or more, and is rather loose and open as an understory plant, but rounded and dense in full sun. It takes its common name from the pungent spicy odor of the crushed leaves. Its small, yellow-green dioecious flowers are not showy, but the leaves provide good yellow fall color, and the small red fruits of female plants can be quite effective after the leaves are gone. A useful plant for the shrub border, it does best in moist but well-drained soils. 'Rubra' has brick red male flowers. In 'Xanthocarpa' the fruits are orange-yellow.

L. obtusilóba (VI), the Japanese Spice Bush, is a somewhat larger multistemmed shrub or small tree from China, Japan, and Korea. The large, leathery leaves turn a truly magnificent golden yellow in the fall, unrivalled by those of any other deciduous shrub.

LONÍCERA. The deciduous shrubby Honeysuckles are legion, but only a few of these are sufficiently striking to be worthwhile garden plants. As a group they are adapted to many types of soil, except extremely wet, and will take full sun or partial shade. They are easily renewed by cutting them back to the ground when they become overgrown.

L. fragrantíssima (V) from China is not a showy plant but is valued for its extremely fragrant flowers. Deciduous or partially evergreen to 6–8 ft., it blooms from December to March depending on the weather, with pairs of small, creamy white flowers at the stem joints. Its small, red berries tend to be hidden by the paired leaves. *L. standíshii* (V) is similar, but more freely flowering, with lemon-scented, white blossoms. It also is winter blooming.

L. involucráta (III), Black Twin Berry, is a Northwest species, native to moist thickets from Alaska to California and eastward, and therefore especially useful for the wild garden in open, poorly drained locations. A large-leaved shrub to 10 ft., it has conspicuous red or red-tinged bracts cupped below paired yellow flowers. The shining, black fruits, also paired, are said to be distastefully bitter and somewhat poisonous.

L. korolkówii (IV), Blue Leaf Honeysuckle, from the mountains of Soviet Central Asia, Afghanistan, and Pakistan, is a graceful 6–10 ft. shrub with downy shoots and pale pubescent foliage, giving the entire plant a gray-blue aspect. Pairs of pale rose-colored flowers appear in the leaf axils of the lateral branches in late May or early June. Red berries follow in July and August. Var. *zabélii* has deeper rose pink flowers and should not be confused with the cultivar 'Zabelii' of *L. tatarica*.

L. syringántha (IV) from northwestern China is an erect, twiggy shrub 6–8 ft. tall, with small, slightly glaucous leaves, and clusters of small, lilac-pink and lilac-scented flowers in great profusion in late spring. It is very pretty in a quiet way and worth growing for its fragrance alone.

L. tatárica (III), the Tartarian Bush Honeysuckle, native to southern Russia and central Asia, is the commonest of the bush honeysuckles in cultivation. Many cultivars are available, varying in color from white through pink and rose to deep, dark red. The type is a vigorous, upright 8–10 ft. shrub, forming a dense mass of thin, twiggy branches with bluish green foliage. It is of the easiest possible culture in sun or shade, but has a looser and more attractive growth habit in partial shade. 'Arnold Red' is a superior selection for flower color; 'Hack's Red' is of Canadian origin, with deep purplish red flowers; 'Alba' and 'Grandiflora' are white flowered, the latter sometimes listed as 'Bride'; 'Virginalis' has the largest flowers, in rose pink; 'Lutea' has pink flowers and yellow fruits; 'Morden Orange' has pale pink flowers and orange fruits; fruits in most varieties are red.

L. xylósteum (IV), Fly Honeysuckle, native from Europe through Asia Minor to western Siberia, is a very bushy shrub to 10 ft. with slender branches arching to an equal spread. The ovate leaves, 1½–2 in. long are pale green and slightly downy above, grayish and more densely pubescent below, arranged in pairs up the stems. Yellowish white flowers, sometimes tinted pink, not scented, are produced in pairs in the leaf axils in May. The translucent, dark red fruits, nearly ½ in. across can be quite showy in July/August. 'Clavey' is a dwarfer selection, from 3–6 ft. in height; 'Hedge King' is a narrow, upright form; 'Emerald Mound' or 'Nana' is said by Dirr to be one of the best of the low, mounded honeysuckles. It has handsome, bluish green foliage and grows to about 3 ft. in height, with a possible spread of 6 ft. This species roots easily from cuttings.

LYÓNIA mariána (V), Staggerbush, native to coastal plains of eastern and southern United States, is a 6-ft. shrub with small, glaucous leaves, coloring red in autumn, and clusters of pendulous, cylindrical, white or pink-tinted flowers. It thrives in acid, sandy, and somewhat dry soils and is a suitable companion plant for rhododendrons.

MAGNÓLIAS. The deciduous magnolias, with their spectacular, fragrant blossoms, are such choice and valuable plants that special care should be taken in preparing their soil. They must have perfect drainage, and prefer a soil that is basically light—ideally, a rich, sandy loam. In heavy soils, ample sand must be incorporated to insure friability, and drainage must be provided. Magnolias respond to generous quantities of partially rotted manure used as a mulch. They resent root disturbance, and should whenever possible be planted in their final location and left undisturbed. They must not be transplanted with bare roots as are most other deciduous materials. When first becoming established they require plenty of summer moisture. Propagation is usually by grafting or layering, or by seed which should be sown when fresh, after removing the outer skins. Magnolias require little pruning other than the occasional thinning of branches to improve shape. The smaller shrubby ones prefer to grow in very light shade.

M. liliiflóra (V), (*M. quinquepéta*), the Lily Flowered Magnolia, native to China, but much cultivated in Japan, is a rather awkward, multitrunked shrub to 10–12 ft. tall, with obovate, dark green leaves about 4 in. long, downy on the underside. The flowers, which stand upright on the branches, are purple and white outside and white inside. Those of the variety 'Nigra', up to 4–5 in. long and somewhat pointed, are a very dark purple. 'Gracilis' is smaller and more upright in habit than the type, with both petals and leaves narrower. 'Betty' is a hybrid with *M. stellata* 'Rosea', raised at the National Arboretum, having more open flowers, rose-pink outside, white within. 'Ann', 'Jane' and 'Susan' are sister seedlings.

The ever-popular *M. × soulangeána* (V), or Saucer Magnolia, is a hybrid between the preceding species and *M. denudáta (M. heptapéta)*, which was raised in the garden of Soulange-Bodin, in France about 150 years ago. The pink to white, cup-shaped flowers put on their most spectacular display in March and April, before the leaves appear, but blooms may still be opening into June, with a few final ones in late summer or early fall. It is as tolerant as it is beautiful, withstanding city conditions, mediocre soils, or cold temperatures. The Saucer Magnolia has numerous variations, all of them desirable garden shrubs from 10–30 ft. in height. Though young specimens may be somewhat gawky initially, like the ugly duckling, they become handsome in maturity. These are a few of the many cultivars offered:

'Alba Superba' is perhaps the loveliest of the whites.

'Amabilis' has ivory white flowers, tinted purple.

'Grace McDade' has rosy flowers.

'Lennei' is outstanding in bloom, late in the season, with full, rounded chalices, purple on the outside and creamy white on the inside. The petals are very waxy. Most other forms have slender, pointed flowers of less massive proportions. All last well in bloom and make a display for a month or more.

'Lilliputian', a slow grower with smaller flowers and habit, is tempting for those who are short of space.

'Picture', has very large flowers, flushed pink up the midribs, white inside.

'Rustica Rubra', with goblet-shaped blooms 5½ in. in diameter, is more rose colored than 'Lennei' and earlier flowering.

M. siebóldii (VI), native to Korea and southern Japan, is one of a trio of closely related Asiatic magnolias, with small, fragrant white flowers filled with great masses of red or rosy crimson stamens, and bearing flesh pink fruits with scarlet seeds. It is a small tree or a large, multistemmed shrub to 12–15 ft., of rather loose, spreading habit, with obovate leaves about 4 in. long, abruptly pointed at the tip. The cup-shaped flowers, 3–4 in. across, on long pedicels, face outward "looking one in the eye", so to speak. They appear intermittently from May onwards throughout the summer. This species layers more easily than other magnolias, and the fact that it flowers quite young has contributed to its popularity.

M. wilsónii (VI), from western China, is more treelike in habit than the preceding species and can be up to 25 ft. tall. Its pendent white cups, 3–4 in. across, are strongly scented. They appear in June, with the 4–6 in. elliptical leaves. This species comes easily from seed and is said to be the hardiest of the three.

Magnolia wilsonii, flowering in early May in Seattle. Photo by Brian Mulligan.

M. sinénsis (VII) from the mountains of western Sichuan, usually takes the form of a very large bush, up to 20 ft. tall, and half again as wide; though it can be pruned, it does not form a tree shape well. It blooms in May and June, after the leathery, broadly obovate leaves are out. Erect flower buds descend to become pendent white flowers, cup-shaped at first, then opening flatter, so their crimson stamens are more visible. A well-developed specimen will be heavily laden with fragrant blooms. This species also comes easily from seed, and flowers when quite young.

M. stelláta (V), the Star Magnolia, is deservedly the most popular of the smaller species, intricately branched, and wide spreading, forming a broad shrub 8–12 ft. tall, or occasionally much larger. Its bare branches make a striking pattern, especially if thinned to reduce conflicting twig growth. Furry bud scales drop away as a lavish profusion of fragrant, slender, many-petalled white flowers emerge in late March and early April, before the leaves. Flowering continues as the plant leafs out. Although this Japanese species is perfectly hardy, it should be grown in a sheltered location to protect the frail flowers from damage by inclement spring weather. 'Royal Star' has large, fragrant, double flowers opening from pink buds, blooming later than the type. In addition to the white-flowered forms, a number of pink-tinted to rose-colored varieties have become available in recent years. These include:

'Sundew', with white flowers striped pinkish purple.

'Centennial', flowers 5½ in. across, tinged pink on the outside.

'Kikuzaki', with 2-in. flowers of light pink.

'Rosea', dark pink, fading lighter.

'Jane Platt', with more petals than 'Rosea'.

'Waterlily', light pink, opening white, with many petals.

M. × *thompsoniána* (VI), a hybrid between *M. tripetala* and *M. virginiana,* which appeared in an English nursery about 1808, has large leaves, up to 10 in. long Fragrant, creamy white flowers, 3–5 in. across—much larger than those of *M. virginiana*—open from pointed buds in May and June. In spite of its desirable flowers, this is a large shrub of rather awkward habit, given to throwing up great long shoots in a single season, and thus more manageable in the wild garden than as a specimen plant. 'Urbana', a modern hybrid, has flowers with less yellow color than the original, and a delightful scent.

M. × *wiesenéri (M. watsónii)* (V–VI), a hybrid of Japanese origin between *M. hypoleuca* and *M. sieboldii,* is a small, stiff tree or bushy shrub with obovate leaves 6–8 in. long. Golf-ball-sized buds open to upward-facing flowers—the legacy of *M. hypoleuca*—twice the size of those of *M. sieboldii.* Their ivory-white petals, tinted rose, are filled with crimson stamens and scented with pineapple fragrance.

MÁLUS. Most species of Malus are trees, but *M. sargéntii,* the Sargent Crab Apple, is a bushy shrub, 5–8 ft. tall, spreading twice that wide. Fragrant white flowers, about 1 in. across, open from red buds in mid-May, and are followed in turn by small red fruits ⅓ in. in diameter, which birds enjoy. The deep green foliage takes an orange and yellow fall tints. Dirr includes this species as one of his favorite crab apples, and adds that it is only slightly susceptible to scab and fire blight. This species was collected near a marsh in Japan, so it could be expected to succeed in poorly drained soils. It is also most attractive when grown as a miniature tree. 'Rosea' and 'Roseglow' are named cultivars.

MENZÍESIA ciliicályx (V–VI), is one of the most attractive of the smaller ericaceous shrubs, but the type with its plump, nodding, bell-shaped flowers of yellowish green, tipped purple, has been all but eclipsed in commerce by its variety, *purpurea*, in which the flowers are entirely pinkish purple. Buds, glaucous blue before opening, provide an added touch of color. This species takes its name from the long, bristly hairs edging the sepals; the leaves also are similarly hairy. In a good, sunny location it will make a bushy plant about 3 ft. tall and about as broad. A native of Japan, it is quite hardy and will thrive in conditions suitable for rhododendrons.

OEMLÉRIA cerasifórmis (V–VI), more recognizable as *Osmarónia cerasiformis,* Indian Plum or Oso Berry, the shrubby harbinger of spring in lowland westside forests from British Columbia to California, can grow to 15–20 ft. tall, with many long, slender stems. It often appears spontaneously in gardens, brought by birds who relish its small, oval, red-purple fruits. The pendent, greenish white clusters of flowers—male and female on separate plants—appear in early March, and the thin, pale green leaves quickly follow, long before most other deciduous shrubs in our area leaf out. This modest, under-appreciated native is a most useful shrub for wild plantings where its size and suckering habits are not a disadvantage.

PAEÓNIA suffruticósa (V), Moutan or Chinese Tree Peony, the best known of the few woody species in this primarily herbaceous genus, has been in cultivation in China since the 7th century, and long celebrated in Oriental art for the beauty of its large flowers. It is a rather open shrub 6–8 ft. tall, frequently with gnarled or twisted branches of great character, gaunt in aspect out of leaf. The foliage as it first comes out is bluish green, with glaucous bloom, its pink and bronzy pink shadings a telling foil for the flowers in May. The flowers, varying from 4 in. to as much as 12 in. across, were originally single, and either a clear magenta-crimson or white with a purple-maroon blotch at the base of each petal, with many golden stamens. In China and Japan in the course of the centuries, hundreds if not thousands of garden varieties and hybrids of this species have been developed. While many of the single and semidouble ones are very beautiful, others have lost much of their original charm, becoming over-large and overfull, like colored cabbages. Moreover, they tend to be less well suited to the average garden scene than their simpler predecessors. Tree Peonies in general do well in this region. They are propagated in one of two ways: either by grafting on *P. suffruticosa* or on herbaceous peony roots. Hybrids are likely to be much more robust on the former, but the gardener must keep a constant vigil for suckers springing up from below the graft. Many growers prefer grafting them on the herbaceous peony even though this results in a short-lived specimen with a weak constitution. However, Bean advises that tree peonies grafted on herbaceous peony roots—the usual commercial method—need not be short lived, if the graft union is placed about 3–4 in. below the soil surface to encourage the tree peony to develop its own roots.

P. suffruticosa itself is not a difficult species, for it thrives in any well-drained soil in sun or partial shade. It should not be given too much summer moisture. Its hybrids, on the other hand, are best grown in rich, moderately heavy loam, preferably in light shade, and good drainage is essential. Tree Peonies are heavy feeders and will profit from a yearly topdressing with well-rotted—not fresh—manure or compost. Peony blight (*Botrytis*) can be a problem if springs are wet, but can be controlled with fungicide. Planting in open areas with good drainage and good air circulation reduces the problem.

Subshrubby *P. lútea* (VI), also from China, is a much dwarfer plant, seldom more than 3–4 ft. tall, with a short woody, stem and large deciduous leaves, 12–15 in. long, glaucous beneath and deeply cut. Its small yellow flowers in May tend to be somewhat hidden by the foliage. In var. *ludlówii* from eastern Tibet the flowers are larger, up to 4–5 in. across, and the plant itself is taller, up to 7–8 ft. This species is easily increased by seeds.

Hybrids between *P. suffruticosa* and *P. lutea* are known as *P.* × *lemoínei*, and modern varieties came first from France, although many have since been raised in the United States, particularly by the late Prof. A. P. Saunders. They are prized for their exquisite and very large flowers varying in color from soft yellow to apricot, flushed wine at the base. Some are fragrant. However, the heaviest headed ones droop under their own weight, particularly in the rain. Single-flowered or semidouble ones show off their blooms to better advantage. The legginess which adds character to plants of *P. suffruticosa* itself may be undesirable in the hybrids which are much less vigorous. Therefore, they should be pruned immediately after flowering to encourage strong new growth for the following season's bloom.

P. delaváyi (V), a third Chinese species, is a handsome shrub to 6 ft., with elaborately dissected leaves as much as 18 in. in length, which persist after frost, hanging wraithlike on the stems in winter. Nodding, blood-red flowers filled with golden anthers appear in June and are 3–4 in. across. This species is closely related to *P. lutea*, and will hybridize with it where they are grown together. Named varieties have also been developed from planned crosses. These are propagated by grafting, but the species itself is raised from seed.

A bush of the double-flowered *Philadelphus* 'Bouquet Blanc' in full bloom in mid-June. Photo by E. F. Marten, Campus Studios, University of Washington.

PHILADÉLPHUS, the Mock Orange, is also commonly called 'Syringa' (correctly the generic name for lilacs) perhaps because of its strong, sweet fragrance. Though the species are widely distributed over North America, southern Europe, and eastern Asia, they cross readily when grown together in gardens, and European hybridizers, especially Lémoine in France, named and introduced countless hybrids. The species themselves are much less common in cultivation. All are white-flowered shrubs, usually four-petaled, with varying numbers of flowers per cluster, and with opposite leaves. They bloom from May until July, and are deservedly popular for their showiness in bloom as well as for their spicy fragrance. If they have a fault, it is that many of the most beautiful varieties are really too large for the average modern garden—those under 6 ft. in height are much more satisfactory.

P. coronárius (IV), a native of southeastern Europe and Asia Minor, has a long history of cultivation, but except for its golden-leaved form, 'Aureus', it is now largely supplanted by its hybrids. Its flowers are over-poweringly fragrant if brought indoors. Among the hybrid Phildelphus offered are:

'Avalanche', single 1-in.-wide flowers, height 4 ft; one of the most fragrant.

'Enchantment', large semidouble flowers, height 6–7 ft.

'Belle Etoile', single flowers, 2½ in. wide, with purple blotch at the base; height 5–6 ft.; late June.

'Marjorie', double flowered, fragrant, on a compact 3-ft. shrub.

'Minnesota Snowflake', 2 in. double flowers, height 8 ft.; there is also a 'Dwarf Snowflake' or 'Miniature Snowflake', which reaches only 3 ft.

'Mont Blanc', single 1¼-in.-wide flowers; height, 4–5 ft.

'Norma', single flowers 1-¾ in. wide, to 6–8 ft.

'Silver Showers', single flowered, to 3–5 ft.

'Virginal', semidouble, 2 in. flowers in June with orange blossoms fragrance, to 10 ft. This has long been the most popular of the taller *Philadelphus,* but the gardener may want to consider some of the smaller ones where space is limited.

Northwest native *P. lewísii* (IV), the state flower of Idaho, is a common shrub both east and west of the Cascades, well suited to gardens, either in the shrub border or as a specimen. Plants vary in height from 4–10 ft, many stemmed and much branched, blooming in late June with elongate, full-flowered clusters, deliciously fragrant. Surfaces of the coarsely toothed, paired leaves are characteristically scratchy to the touch. Selections of this species from the wild to give us plants of dwarfer habit and wider-petaled flowers would be welcome additions to our gardens.

Philadelphus will thrive in almost any garden soil in either full sun or partial shade, and are of the easiest possible culture. The hybrids respond noticeably to generous cultivation, fertilizer, and water. They belong to the group of summer-flowering shrubs that are best pruned immediately after flowering. Branches cut for decoration will last longer if most of the foliage is stripped off and the stems pounded before they are put in water.

PHYSOCÁRPUS. Our two Northwestern species of Ninebark are worth saving for the wild garden if either comes with new property. Their small, lobed leaves resemble those of a currant, and their small, creamy white flowers, in 1½–2 in. clusters in late May or early June are pleasant and sometimes quite numerous, but hardly exciting. The common name refers to the peeling, shredding bark of the stems. *P. capitátus* (V) occurs in open woodland and thickets along stream banks, west of the Cascades (and also in northern Idaho), reaching a height of 10 ft., occasionally 20. *P. malváceus* (V) is a somewhat shorter plant, 3–6 ft. high, with smaller leaves and flower clusters, and thus in better scale for the average garden. It is hardier also, since it is found chiefly east of the Cascades, and into the Rocky Mountains. Both species come easily from cuttings.

P. opulifólius (II) from eastern North America is more common in cultivation than either of the preceding species. It grows 8–10 ft. high, occasionally much wider. Its small, white flowers, in 2-in.-wide clusters, are tinted rose with contrasting purple stamens, and the plant is quite decorative in June. It cannot, however, compete with viburnums for show, and is probably most useful in the wild garden. Several horticultural selections are available:

var. *intermédius* is a more refined plant, reaching only 4 ft., with reddish brown fall color.

var. *nánus* is a dwarf selection, to 2 ft.

In 'Luteus' the new foliage is golden yellow, turning green by midsummer.

'Darts' Golden' holds its yellow spring color better than 'Luteus', and is also a more compact grower.

Eastern Ninebark is a good plant for difficult dry situations, in sun or shade. All three species are easy from seed.

PHOTÍNIA. The photinias, relatives of the Hawthorns, have clusters of white flowers followed by small, red berries, which hang on the branches well into winter.

P. villósa (IV) from Japan, Korea, and China, is noted for the brilliant orange color of its autumn foliage. The flowers appear in May on lateral branches from the previous year's growth. These 10–15 ft. shrubs or small trees are easily grown in full sun or light shade, in any well-drained soil, preferring a light, sandy medium with plenty of humus incorporated. They color best in the fall if the soil is not too poor but kept on the dry side toward the end of the season. Fruits are like small red hawthorns. Propagation is easy from seed.

PONCÍRUS *trifoliáta* (VI), the Hardy Orange from Korea and northern China, is a small tree or shrub 8–20 ft. tall, with small, trifoliate leaves and crooked green branches armed with vicious 2-in. spines. Fragrant white flowers in the spine axils come out before the leaves. Fruits like small, downy oranges in September and October, are too sour to eat fresh, but suitable for candying or for marmalade; they rarely ripen here. Possibly useful for hedges, in our area this plant serves chiefly as an interesting conversation piece for a warm, protected location in well-drained, acid soil. It is not a plant for gardens with small children!

POTENTÍLLA *fruticósa* (2), Shrubby Cinquefoil, distributed throughout the colder parts of the Northern Hemisphere, is a variable shrub with flowers like small roses. The prostrate or low mounded forms are eminently suitable for the rock garden, while the upright types, 3–4 ft. tall, have been extensively planted on highway embankments and other public areas. It is also one of the most attractive small shrubs for the home garden. The color range continues to expand and now includes besides the typical golden yellow seen in 'Goldfinger', and 'Goldstar', plants with white flowers, such as 'Abbotswood', canary yellow 'Katherine Dykes', pale yellow 'Moonlight', and orange-colored 'Tangerine'. Pink-flowered plants such as 'Princess' are the latest additions to the color range. 'Sundance' is a double-flowered light yellow. 'Red Ace' has vermilion red petals with a yellow reverse. Cinquefoils flower intermittently all summer and all are readily grown in any light, rather poor, dry soil in full sun. They are quite drought resistant and well suited to calcareous soils.

The shrubby species of *PRÚNUS* are less important as garden plants than those of tree habit. Nevertheless several are worth mentioning:

P. bésseyi (III), Western Sand Cherry, from the central Great Plains, is a small shrub only 3–6 ft. tall, with oval gray-green leaves and ½-in. white flowers borne in such quantities as to turn its branches into white wands in April or May. Its ¾-in., glaucous black fruits are attractive to birds and can be used to make jellies and jams. Extremely hardy and drought resistant, it will probably be more useful in gardens east of the Cascades than on the west side.

P. × cisténa (II), Purple-leaf Sand Cherry, a hybrid between Eurasian *P. cerasifera* 'Atropurpurea' and the dwarf American *P. púmila,* is one of the hardiest of purple-leaved shrubs. It reaches a height of 7–10 ft. with about an equal spread, has intense reddish purple foliage, and fragrant white flowers, and black-purple fruits in July. It is not particular about soil.

P. glandulósa (IV), Dwarf Flowering Almond, from northern China and Korea, and long cultivated in Japan, is a bushy 4–5 ft. shrub, usually seen only in its double-flowered forms. 'Alba Plena' is white flowered, while 'Rosea Plena' ('Sinensis') is pink flowered. The slender, upright branches become arching sprays of bloom in May. Like the arborescent species of almond, these need cutting back severely immediately after flowering or while in bloom. This is necessary to maintain vigor, and remove the unsightly dieback to which this plant is subject later in the season. Flowering Almond prefers a deep, light, well-drained soil in full sun, with a moderate amount of moisture.

One of the double-flowered forms of the dwarf almond in bloom in spring (*Prunus glandulosa*). Photo by Don Normark.

P. tenélla (II), Dwarf Russian Almond, is a very hardy small shrub from southeastern Europe and the USSR. Growing to no more than 5 ft. tall, it has small, rosy red flowers in April. In 'Alba' the flowers are white; 'Fire Hill' is redder than the type. Layered plants are said to be better than those grafted on plum stock.

P. tomentósa (II), Nanking Cherry, Manchu Cherry, from China and Japan, is another very hardy species, valuable for its early flowers. It is a large, downy-twigged shrub 6–8 ft. high and spreading to as much as 15 ft. wide. Small pink-tinted white flowers appear in March or April. The dark green leaves are densely furred on the underside. The red fruits are edible, ripening in July.

P. trilóba 'Multiplex' (III), Double Flowering Almond from China, with flowers like double pink roses in May, is a 15-ft. shrub which is satisfactory here only in the warmest locations in light, not-too-rich soil. Like *P. glandulosa,* it should be pruned back heavily immediately after flowering. It is sometimes recommended as a tree, but because of its need for drastic pruning, it is better grown as a shrub in this region.

PÚNICA *granátum* (VII), the Pomegranate, in cultivation from southern Europe to the Himalayas since ancient times, can be grown with fair success in western Washington and western Oregon, in any warm, sheltered garden. The type is a 15–20 ft. shrub, with shining, dark green leaves. Small scarlet red flowers with crumpled petals bloom from June to September, followed by yellow to reddish fruit. Varieties with double flowers, white flowers, and flowers of other colors can be found in nursery lists, but may not be as hardy as the type. There is a hardier dwarf form, var. *nana,* smaller in all its parts, with orange-red flowers, and less than 3 ft. tall. 'Plena' is a showy shrub with double red flowers. 'Wonderful' has orange-red flowers. The pomegranate must be given the warmest possible situation, a south or west wall, to flower freely. Fruits will probably not ripen in the Northwest. Keeping the plant on the dry side toward the end of summer so that growth will ripen, will encourage hardiness. Culture, including pruning, is the same as for Flowering Quince.

RHODODÉNDRON. The deciduous species of *Rhododéndron* were originally placed in the separate genus, *Azálea,* and though they have long since been united with their evergreen relatives, from a horticultural standpoint they tend to remain azaleas. The deciduous azaleas prefer a basically light soil, in which ample fibrous material such as peat or leafmold has been incorporated. However, they are not at all exacting and make themselves thoroughly at home in any well-prepared, lime-free garden soil. In common with most ericaceous plants they are usually happiest growing in association with other shrubs of a similar kind. Heathers will help to keep their roots cool, or they can be interplanted with such shrubs as *Pernettya mucronata* or our native Evergreen Huckleberry, *Vaccinium ovatum.* Most of them need full sun to produce maximum bloom, although many flower freely in partial shade, if they receive a little moisture during the summer. Many provide beautiful autumn foliage color. Remove the old flower heads as soon as possible after blooming. Other than this deciduous azaleas rarely require pruning, except for some thinning out as they grow older. They are readily propagated from seeds, grown from summer cuttings, or layered.

R. *lúteum* (V), the Pontic Azalea from western Asia and the southern USSR, is a thoroughly hardy and very popular species, making a densely branched shrub ultimately 10–12 ft. high and wide. It has long been valued not only for its very fragrant yellow flowers with a darker blotch, freely produced in May, but also for its glowing orange to red autumn foliage. It has bequeathed its yellow color to many hybrid strains; beekeepers should avoid this species since it produces poisonous honey. It has often been used as a stock for grafting named azalea clones.

R. *mucronulátum* (IV), Korean Rhododendron, from Korea, Japan and northern China, is a slender 6-ft. shrub which puts forth a cloud of inch-wide, orchid pink flowers from late January to March, depending upon the season and weather, but always long before the leaves appear. It is a most welcome addition to any garden in winter, although its delicate blossoms can be spoiled by frosts. 'Cornell Pink', is a pure pink-flowered form, raised at Cornell University in 1952. Dwarf forms are now also in cultivation.

R. *occidentále* (VI–VII), the fragrant Western Azalea of the Pacific coast, from southern Oregon to California, needs no introduction to gardeners in our area. Its large, honeysuckle-like blooms carried in heads of 6–10, show a wide variation in color shades from those which are dark crimson in bud, opening to salmon-pink, with or without a yellow blotch, to those which are pure white. 'Yaquina' is a pink selection, and 'Coquille' a white with a yellow blotch. Double-flowered forms also occasionally appear. The majority are in bloom in the wild by the middle of May in most localities, but some may flower as late as the middle of July, so careful selection of these clones will provide a long period of bloom. Old plants in the State Park at Brookings, in southwest Oregon, are 12–15 ft. high and as much through. They are estimated to be hundreds of years old, but in the garden 8–10 ft. is a reasonably mature size. This species has contributed extensively to the modern hybrid races, adding fragrance to many of the older hybrids. Fall coloring is lemon yellow to orange.

R. *quinquefólium* (IV), from Japan, is a slow-growing bushy shrub generally only 4–5 ft. tall, but capable of becoming larger in time; it is noted for its distinctive foliage. The small, diamond-shaped leaves, 1½–2 in. long, are borne in whorls of five at the ends of the branches and are especially attractive in spring when their pale green coloring is bordered with reddish purple. They also color well in autumn. The flaring, funnel-shaped flowers, 2–3 together, each about 1½ in. wide, appear with the leaves in April, and are white with some green dots in the throat. Altogether a very beautiful shrub, requiring light shade in a garden, but with some summer moisture, since Japanese plants receive summer rainfall.

R. *schlippenbáchii* (IV), the Royal azalea, from Korea and Manchuria, is a very beautiful and distinctive species. Its leaves, in groups of 5, appearing as if whorled, unfold a pinkish bronze just as the first flowers appear in late March or early April; in autumn they turn orange. Saucer-shaped flowers 2½ in. across are some shade of pink, spotted reddish brown on the upper petal. This species is happier in open woodland than in full sun, and does not seem to need as acid a soil as most other azaleas. It is slow-growing when raised from seeds.

The numerous Azalea species native to the eastern and southeastern United States have become increasingly popular in Northwest gardens in recent years. All have narrowly tubular flowers, but often flaring out into a funnel shape, with styles and stamens much extended beyond the corolla. Most of the pink to white-flowered species are intensely fragrant, the flamboyant red to yellow-flowered species less so, or not at all. These are good understory shrubs for woodland gardens, but coming as they do from habitats with summer moisture, they will require watering during our drier summers. Deep fertile soils suit them best. Several of them hybridize extensively in the wild and in gardens, and have been used in the development of some of the popular hybrid strains.

Plants of *Rhododendron schlippenbachii* flowering in late April. Photo by Don Normark, Campus Studios, University of Washington.

R. *alabaménse* (VII). The Alabama Azalea is a stoloniferous but compact shrub 3–6 ft. in height, from dry open woods and rocky slopes in northern Alabama and western Georgia. Clusters of lemon-scented white flowers with a yellow blotch, with greatly extended stamens, appear in April, together with the new leaves, making a pretty show in the spring woodlands.

R. arboréscens (IV), the Sweet Azalea, native along streamsides and in rich, damp woods from New York to Georgia and Alabama, is a most useful hardy species blooming as late as July or August. In habit, it is low and spreading in the open, tall and lanky in shade, but not stoloniferous. The heliotrope-scented flowers are white, tinged pink or blotched yellow, with conspicuous styles and stamens.

R. atlánticum (V), the Coast or Atlantic Azalea, occurs on wet or sandy soils along the Atlantic coastal plain from Pennsylvania and Delaware to South Carolina. It is one of the dwarfer species and is definitely stoloniferous. From knee-high to 3 ft. tall, it blooms in April and May with arching sprays of very fragrant white or pink-tinged blossoms, the tube being more deeply colored.

R. calenduláceum (V), the Flame Azalea, is perhaps the best known of the eastern American azaleas, and certainly possesses the showiest flowers. Native in the mountains from Pennsylvania and Ohio to Georgia, it is a hardy upright shrub 8–12 ft. tall, blooming in May and June. The flowers, about 2 in. across, are borne in umbels of 5 to 7, opening just as the leaves are expanding; the stamens can be two or three times as long as the glandular tube. The flowers are not fragrant but make up for that by their vivid coloration; they range from scarlet to pink, through salmon and orange to yellow, with an orange blotch on the upper lobe. It hybridizes easily with related species, both in the wild and in gardens, and is one parent of the Ghent hybrids.

R. canéscens, (V), the Piedmont Azalea or Florida Pinxter, may be a 15-ft. shrub of streamsides and low-lying woodlands from North Carolina and Tennessee to Florida and Texas. The flowers, normally white-petaled with a pink tube, the stamens long exserted, appear in April or May at the same time as the young leaves, and are slightly fragrant. In the wild it grows in damp woodlands, often in sandy soils.

R. flámmeum (V), (*R. speciósum*) the Oconee Azalea from Georgia and South Carolina, is the earliest to flower of the red species, blooming in April or May as the leaves appear. It forms a 3–6 ft. shrub, with leaves smaller and thinner than those of *R. calendulaceum.* The flowers, borne in umbels of 6–15, are each about 1¾ in. long, not fragrant; the color can vary from bright red and scarlet through orange, coral-pink and salmon, often with an orange blotch on the upper lobe. However, red is the normal color in wild plants. Other color forms may be hybrids.

R. oblongifólium (VII), the Texas Azalea, is a shrub of 6 ft. or less found in moist valleys and along streams in Arkansas, eastern Oklahoma and southeastern Texas. The small pink or white, funnel-shaped flowers appear in May after the leaves have developed; they have stamens about twice as long as the tube. It is related to *R. viscosum,* but both flowers and leaves are larger in this species.

R. prinophýllum (R. róseum) (III). This is one of the hardiest species, growing wild from Quebec Province in Canada west to Illinois, south to

Virginia and Missouri; it does not object to limestone. It makes a much-branched shrub, usually 6–8 ft. in height but occasionally to 15 ft. The branches, buds and underside of the leaves are noticeably hairy, in varying degrees. It flowers in May, either before or with the leaves; the blossoms are bright pink, clove scented, funnelform with a cylindric tube. It is an attractive woodland shrub.

R. prunifólium (V), the Plumleaf Azalea from the borders of Georgia and Alabama, is one of the finest American species. Growing 8–10 ft. tall, it inhabits moist ravines or stream banks and prefers a shaded location in gardens; it is not stoloniferous. The lateness of its flowering season—July and August—makes it valuable. The flowers, borne in umbels 4–5, are typically crimson in color, but variations can produce others ranging through scarlet to orange; these are likely to be hybrids with other species. They are not fragrant.

R. periclymenoídes (R. nudiflórum) (III). The Pinxterbloom or Honey-suckle Azalea. This is a much-branched, stoloniferous shrub growing 9–10 ft. tall, native chiefly in the mountains on open slopes from Massachusetts to the Carolinas, and west to Ohio. It is as hardy as *R. prinophyllum,* flowering in late April or early May just before the leaves expand, with rather dense racemes of 6–12 flowers which are not scented. They are white or pale pink with deeper pink or almost red tubes; the stamens may be almost three times as long as the tube.

R. serrulátum (VII), the Hammock-Sweet Azalea, is native from Georgia to Louisiana where it grows in wooded swamps and forms a large shrub 10–20 ft. in height. Blooming from mid-June even to August or per-haps later, the flowers are the smallest of any of this group, white in color, clove scented. It is closely related to *R. viscosum.* The reddish-brown branches are densely hairy.

R. váseyi (III). Pink-Shell Azalea, from the Blue Ridge Mountains of North Carolina, is another hardy one, since it grows there at elevations from 3,000 to 5,000 ft., and may be 10–12 ft. in height. The flowers, borne in umbels of 5–8, open in May before the leaves; they are saucer to bowl shaped, quite different from those of most other native species with their tubular flowers, excepting for *R. calendulaceum,* and some shade of pink in color; there is also a white form of great beauty, named 'White Find'. Fall color is usually orange-yellow in this species.

R. viscósum (III), the White Swamp azalea, or Honeysuckle Azalea, is a plant of swamps, damp woods and moist pine barrens from southern Maine to South Carolina and Tennessee. It may be low and stoloniferous, or up to 10–12 ft. tall, blooming from late May or early June into July, a very variable species. The flowers, carried in heads of 4–9, are white to pink, tubular, opening after the leaves have developed, glandular and sticky, spicily fragrant.

All of these species from eastern United States will require watering during our dry Northwest summers, as will those from eastern Asia. In

A mature plant of *Rhododendron vaseyi* in full bloom in early May. Photo by Campus studios, University of Washington.

spite of their unquestioned merit as garden plants, the deciduous species of *Rhododendron* are today greatly outnumbered by hybrids of many types, and often complex parentage.

Ghent Hybrids (V), the oldest in point of time, were developed in Belgium early in the 19th century, from crosses of *R. luteum* with some of the red-flowered eastern American species. This group is noted for its extreme hardiness, upright habit from 6–10 ft., and brilliant fall foliage color. Its flowers, which are not as large as those of more recent strains, include whites, pinks, pure yellows, orange and scarlet, both single and double. They are trouble-free and valuable plants for the woodland garden. ;'Gloria Mundi' and 'Coccinea Speciosa' are two still in cultivation. Some have double flowers, e.g. 'Narcissiflora'.

Knap Hill-Exbury Hybrids (V) originated in the Knap Hill Nursery of Anthony Waterer in England in the 19th century with the addition of *R. mólle (Azálea sinénsis)* to the *Ghent Hybrids*. The resulting large flowers come in all colors from white and pink to yellow, orange and red, sometimes with contrasting blotches, ruffled petals and often fragrant. Plants vary from spreading to upright in the 4–6 ft. height range. This line was further developed in the 1920s and 1930s by Lionel de Rothschild at Exbury near Southampton, England. Hybrids of this type originally

Azaleas of the Knap Hill
or Exbury types in full
bloom in May. Photo by
Don Normark.

reached the United States as seedlings identified by color only, but large numbers of named varieties are now available as well, and development of new ones is continuing.

Mollis Hybrids (V–VI), are derived mainly from *R. japónicum* (*Azalea móllis* of 19th-century gardens) and its Chinese relative *Azalea sinensis*, now *Rhododendron molle*. They were developed in Belgium and Holland during the second half of the 19th century. They are May blooming, in the yellow, orange and red range, and have good fall color as well. Variations in salmon-pink and apricot-orange are especially good.

Occidentale Hybrids (VI). Our western *R. occidentale* has made its contribution to garden azaleas by crossing with the *Mollis Hybrids,* first in England at the Knap Hill Nursery before 1890; later in the Netherlands by Koster. In this group plants are taller, up to 8 ft., and tend to bloom later, in late May or early June. Flowers are similar to those of the *Mollis Hybrids,* but are more delicately colored and usually fragrant. 'Graciosa' and 'Exquisita' are examples of this type of hybrid.

RHODOTÝPOS scándens (IV), the Jet Bead from China and Japan, resembles the better-known, closely related *Kerria japonica* in having toothed, heavily ribbed leaves and green arching stems to about 6 ft. The flowers, which are pearly white instead of yellow, appear in May or early June. They are borne singly, looking like four-petaled white roses 1½–2 in.

across. The shining pea-sized black seeds which give the plant its name, may still be present from the previous season. Like *Kerria* this is an adaptable shrub for sun or shade, tolerant of harsh conditions including air pollution.

RHÚS. The sumacs are ornamental shrubs grown chiefly for their brilliant autumn coloring. Their flowers are of negligible importance.

R. aromática. (III), Fragrant Sumac, from eastern United States, has three-parted leaves, glossy blue-green in summer, turning orange-red to purple-red in autumn. Female plants produce a host of small, hairy, red fruits. Given to rooting where stems touch the ground, this 2–6 ft. species is well suited for holding banks, both in the home garden and in roadside plantings.

R. copallína (IV), Shining Sumac, a widespread species in eastern United States, can be either a small, dense shrub or a picturesque small tree to 20–30 ft. tall and as much wide. Its many untoothed leaflets, on winged central stalks, turn scarlet or crimson in the fall. While Dirr considers this "the most ornamental of the sumacs," and Wyman "the best of the sumacs," it is not the one most commonly planted in the Northwest, which is regrettable.

R. glábra (II), the Smooth Sumac, is widely distributed over North Ameica, and is one of our best native shrubs for fall color east of the Cascades. It is an erect 8–10 ft. shrub with smooth branches, and clusters of sticky, dark red fruits. It has a cut-leafed form, 'Laciniata', and is of easy culture in any sunny location, doing best in rather poor, dry soil. It is propagated readily by root cuttings. R. glabra, in fact, forms its wild colonies by suckering which makes it more useful for parks and roadside plantings than for the small garden.

R. trilobáta (IV), is the western counterpart of R. aromatica, and is known as Skunkbush because of the unpleasant odor of its foliage when bruised. The twiggy bushes, with ½–1 in. fan-shaped leaflets, form dense thickets 3–5 ft. tall, useful for dry, sunny places or highway plantings. The three-parted leaves color rich orange-red in the fall. The small red berries are attractive to birds, and can be used to make a lemon-flavored drink.

R. typhína (III), Staghorn Sumac, a handsome 25–30 ft. shrub or small tree native to eastern North America, has vigorous upward-swooping branches clothed in brown velvet, and dramatic dark red velvet fruit clusters. Fall coloration is orange to red in the type, but only yellow to orange in the lower, irregularly shrubby form with deeply cut foliage, 'Dissecta'.

RÍBES. Of our several native species of currants and gooseberries, at least three have showy enough flowers to be desirable garden plants.

R. aúreum (II), Golden Currant, a streamside plant from the eastern part of our area, is happier in eastside gardens than it is west of the Cascades. A large, multistemmed shrub to 10 ft., it comes into bloom in April or early May, well covered with small clusters of fragrant, bright yellow flowers, which are sometimes speckled with red. A heavy crop of edible berries follows in July—yellow, red or black, with the black ones having the best flavor.

In *R. menziesii* (VII), the Canyon Gooseberry, or Menzies' Gooseberry, from coastal northwestern California and southern Oregon, the shoots are covered with bristles and armed with spines at the leaf axils. Small flowers like tiny white and rose-purple fuchsias occur singly or in pairs, and are followed by bristly, unpalatable fruits. This species likes moist, shady situations and is well suited to the damp wild garden. *R. lóbbii* (VII), is a closely related species from the Cascades and Olympics, with white petals and a reflexed red calyx, the stems with bristles but no spines.

R. sanguíneum (V), Red Flowering Currant, is the most commonly cultivated of our native species, a handsome, many-stemmed shrub to about 8–10 ft. tall. Pendent 1–3 in. flower clusters cover the branches in early spring, those with the longer clusters providing the most color. The best forms are a rich carmine red, but the color varies to include pale pinks and an occasional white. This species thrives almost anywhere west of the Cascades, but will also succeed in sheltered locations east of them. If it shows a tendency to become leggy, it may be pruned severely immediately after flowering. In England where this species has been highly prized since the early 19th century, several named color variants are available. In the Northwest, more plants are probably distributed by birds than by nurseries. 'King Edward VII' is a good, long-clustered red clone. 'Pulborough Scarlet' has deep red flowers on a 12-ft. plant.

ROBÍNIA híspida (V), Rose Acacia from southeastern United States, has the largest and showiest flowers of any of the Robinias, but they come on a rather leggy 6–10 ft. shrub, which suckers freely to form great thickets. Its rose-pink, pea-shaped flowers, good blue-green foliage and twiglets covered with red-brown bristles are all attractive, but it remains a shrub of limited value to the home gardener. It does find a place in highway plantings and on dry soils in need of stabilization, where the suckering propensities are an asset and not a liability.

RÓSA. There are two distinct groups of bush roses, the species roses and the modern hybrids. Each has a separate place in the garden. The species are very valuable for shrubbery groups on sunny slopes or as a background for herbaceous plantings. Some of them make a telling background for bearded iris, which flower at approximately the same time in May and June.

R. foétida (IV), Austrian Brier, a 6–8 ft. shrub from western Asia, has been in cultivation for hundreds of years. It has sulfur yellow flowers and a heavy fragrance, hence its Latin name. In var. *bícolor,* the smaller Austrian Copper Brier, the flowers are a brilliant coppery orange on the inside of the petals and a soft yellow buff on the reverse; occasional branches revert to the yellow of the type. Though fleeting, it is one of the loveliest roses in

The Sweet-brier rose (*Rosa eglanteria*) flowering in late June. Photo by E. F. Marten, Campus Studios, University of Washington.

bloom. Unfortunately, it does not have a strong garden constitution, although it does much better in Spokane and Idaho than on the coast. This species is the source of the copper and orange hues in the modern Hybrid Tea roses. Another variety, *persiána*, the beloved old-fashioned 'Persian Yellow', which wreathes its arching branches in clusters of small, soft yellow, double roses, was introduced in the early 1800s and still holds its own. A hybrid of the same period, *R. foetida* × *R. pimpinellifolia* known as *R.* × *harisónii* (V), 'Harison's Yellow', raised in New York state, has paler and less double flowers than 'Persian Yellow'; this is the yellow rose of old farmsteads east of the Cascades and in the Willamette Valley. It is more satisfactory in our area than 'Persian Yellow'.

R. *gláuca* (*R. rubrifólia*) (II), a 6–8 ft. shrub from the mountains of central and southern Europe, is unique for its glaucous coloring of stems and leaves, which has almost a violet hue on young shoots. Leaves are a mauve-tinted blue-green in shade, turning to coppery mauve in full sun. Clear pink flowers are followed by glossy red hips; the nearly thornless winter twigs are a warm red-brown.

R. *hugónis* (V), Father Hugo's Rose, from western China, is one of the loveliest of the single yellow roses. It forms a very bushy 6–8 ft. shrub of erect young branches covered with reddish brown bristles and some thorns that bend over in graceful sprays under the profusion of bloom. Small red fruits are occasionally formed. It flowers early, in May.

R. *moyésii* (V–VI), also from western China, is a beautiful species much more upright in habit than *R. hugónis*, but forming a less dense shrub. A well-established plant sends out great, arching 8–10 ft. sprays weighted down with clusters of large, single blood red flowers. G. S. Thomas considers this one of E. H. Wilson's greatest treasures from the

China. Intensely red, flask-shaped hips extend its decorative season well into winter. This species is quite variable from seed. The pink-flowered form is known as 'Fargesii'. 'Geranium', of more compact growth than the type, has brilliant red flowers and especially good hips. In 'Sealing Wax' the hips are scarlet while the flowers are pink. 'Nevada', a R. *moyesii* hybrid of Spanish origin, is a 7–8 ft. arching bush with great semidouble creamy white flowers with a center of golden stamens, not fragrant. It blooms in June and again in August, with a scattering of flowers till October.

R. *multiflóra* (V) from Japan and Korea, is a particularly vigorous climbing rose with single white flowers; Chinese forms have single pink flowers. This is the species which gave rise to such early climbers as 'Crimson Rambler'. It is also a parent of the dwarf *Polyanthas,* and thus a forebear of the *Floribundas.* This species makes a dense thicket of long, arching shoots, interlaced like blackberry tangles, and because it can take care of itself, it is much used as windbreaks and snow fences, and in roadside plantings. The large trusses of tiny blooms are followed by equally large numbers of dainty, bright red fruits, attractive to birds. Var. *cathayénsis* from China has single pink flowers; var. *platyphýlla,* the 'Seven Sisters Rose' is a double-flowered pink from Japan.

R. *nutkána* (V) from western North America, is an upright-growing, stoloniferous, 5–6 ft. shrub with slightly fragrant 2-in. pink flowers and good orange-red hips, suitable for the wild garden or seaside plantings. The eastern form, var. *híspida,* is more fragrant than var. *nutkana.*

R. *pimpinellifólia (R. spinosíssima)* (IV), Scotch Rose or Burnet Rose, is the most widely distributed of all rose species, occurring from Iceland to eastern Siberia, and south to Armenia. It is a 4–5 ft. suckering shrub with extremely bristly stems, and a multitude of small flowers, borne singly. Its leaves may color a plum-maroon in the fall, and the large hips are black. Described as forming "wide, hummocky bushes," it thrives under the most adverse conditions. Easily raised from seed, with single, semidouble or double flowers, it varies in color from white through pink to dark red, and pale to dark yellow—the latter probably hybrids with R. *foetida.* This species can be found in a number of named forms and has given rise to many hybrids. It is useful in difficult situations, enjoys sandy soils, and has value as a cover for birds in the wild garden.

R. *rugósa* (II), from northern China, Korea, and Japan, is one of the hardiest species, capable of withstanding subzero temperatures. It is especially valuable in regions having severe winters, and is even grown in Alaska. In our region it has been used in parks and freeway plantings, but it is also attractive and very useful for home garden sites such as hot, dry banks, and for seaside plantings. The 5–6 ft. stems, prickly and suckering, support a dense, spreading mass of dark green, wrinkled foliage, which takes on golden autumn tints. Large, fragrant flowers, single in the type or double in garden forms, are sprinkled among the foliage continuously throughout the summer. They come in a variety of colors from white

('Alba' and 'Albo-plena') through pink ('Rosea') to the typical deep, purplish red. The bright orange-red hips, about 1 in. across, are large enough to be useful in jam as well as highly decorative on the plant. This species has been the parent of a number of especially hardy and useful garden hybrids, including 'Agnes', 'Hansa', 'Frau Dagmar Hastrup'.

R. serícea (VII), native to the Himalayas, northern Burma and parts of southwestern and central China, is a large, spreading shrub to about 12 ft., which can be very effective as a specimen plant. Its numerous small leaflets give the foliage a ferny effect. White or creamy yellow flowers 1½–2 in. across appear in May, and, curiously, have only 4 petals instead of the usual 5. In f. *pteracántha* the young stems are armed with large, winged and translucent red prickles. Hips, borne on thickened stalks, are variable in color, some red, some yellow or orange. Hybrids of this species are also available, 'Doubloons' being an example. 'Cantabrigiensis', has light yellow flowers, somewhat cupped, and grows to about 7 ft.

R. wóodsii (III), Woods' Rose, another Northwest native useful for the wild garden, is widespread from the east side of the Cascades into the Rockies, along stream banks and in other moist locations. Arching stems 3–10 ft. tall bear showy clusters of fragrant, rose-pink flowers in early June, and quantities of bright orange-red hips in autumn. This would make a good informal hedge plant.

Detailed discussion of the various types of hybrid Roses is beyond the scope of this book; but, in general, they require considerably more care than the species. Thorough soil preparation is essential for their success, with the addition of plenty of organic material and fertilizer. They require a sunny location, and adequate water throughout the growing season. Mulching around the base of the plants is helpful. They also attract more pests than species roses—be prepared to spray as necessary for mildew, rust, black spot, aphids, etc. Only a few of the more popular types of hybrids can be mentioned here.

The elegant *Hybrid Tea Roses,* hybrids of *R. foétida,* highly prized as cut flowers for the home and for exhibition, deserve a plot of their own, where their special needs can be met without competition from adjacent shrubs or trees. Though they grow adequately in a wide range of soils, they will do best in a well-drained, loamy one with a high organic content. To obtain the best flowers, repeated applications of rose fertilizer formulated for our region are necessary—once before the plants leaf out, again in early summer, and again in late autumn. Roses also require severe pruning in early spring, before the plant breaks dormancy; they will certainly require regular spraying as well. Hybrid Teas are available both as container-grown plants from local nurseries and bare root from mail order catalogs of rose specialists. Either source should be satisfactory, provided planting directions are followed carefully, and that the varieties selected are chosen for their suitability to the Northwest.

Polyánthas—hybrids of *Rosa multiflora*—produce large sprays of small flowers on low-growing, bushy shrubs, and are excellent for mass bedding. They are nearly evergreen, and fairly disease resistant. Their color range is not as great as in their descendants the Floribundas, nor are they usually fragrant.

Floribúndas, derived from *Hybrid Teas* and *Polyanthas,* live up to their name, producing large clusters of single, semidouble, or double flowers throughout the summer. Short or medium in height, 3–6 ft., with vigorous, bushy habit, they are the most useful of the modern hybrids for the average garden—especially valuable for their masses of color, for informal hedges, or for use in mixed shrub borders. They come in all the modern rose colors, including many bi-colors, but are not usually fragrant. They are customarily not pruned as heavily as Hybrid Tea Roses, some shortening back and removal of old and weak canes being sufficient. They are both hardy and disease resistant.

Grándiflora roses are a fairly recent group derived from *Floribundas* and *Hybrid Teas,* and are not always clearly distinguished from the latter. They bear their flowers either in clusters or singly, and are vigorous shrubs up to 6 ft. in height. They are hardy and considered more disease resistant than the Hybrid Teas.

Climbing roses and pillar roses. See Vines and Climbers.

"Tree Roses" are bush roses budded on 3–4 ft. standards instead of at the ground line. Substantial staking is usually necessary to prevent the top from breaking off under its own weight. Although both *Floribundas* and *Hybrid Teas* are available in this form, tree roses are of limited usefulness in the average garden. They find their place chiefly in formal rose gardens.

For further information on roses of all kinds, performance ratings, and lists of award-winning varieties, the *American Rose Annual* published by the American Rose Society should be consulted. Most of our larger cities have public rose gardens, and Portland, Oregon, has an International Rose Test Garden. Visits to any of these during the blooming season is by far the best way to choose colors for one's own garden.

RÚBUS. Species of the genus *Rubus,* the Blackberries and Raspberries, make a greater contribution to our table than to our gardens, but a few are worthy of mention as ornamentals. *R. parviflórus* (III), our native Thimbleberry, with its large, downy, maplelike leaves, forms dense thickets of upright 4–6 ft. stems and does well in the moister parts of the wild garden, though it will tolerate drier sites. Its white flowers, about 2 in. across, are larger than most in the genus; the pleasantly tart red fruits are attractive to children and birds. *R. × 'Tridel'* (VI–VII), a hybrid between *R. deliciósus* of the Rocky Mountains and *R. trilóbus* from southern Mexico, was bred in England in the 1950s. Its arching, thornless canes, reaching 8 ft. or more in height, produce a fountain of bloom in May or June, with numerous single, roselike white flowers 2–3 in. across.

R. spectábilis (V), our native Salmon Berry, with its rose-colored flowers in early spring, is not as spectacular as its name implies, but is nevertheless a better answer for naturalizing in low-lying, damp soils than most introduced species. Birds may bring it unbidden, and it is not always welcome, due to its suckering habit and prickly stems, but children enjoy its somewhat bland orange or red fruits.

SÁLIX, the Willows, bear their male and female flowers on separate plants, with the male plants furnishing the best "pussy willows." Commercial clones are therefore male, selected for the size or unusual color of the catkins. Most species root easily from cuttings, and if well watered during dry spells will thrive under average garden conditions, though they generally come from wet or damp sites in the wild. Care should be taken in siting willows, so that their water-greedy roots will not plug sewers and downspout drains.

S. cinérea (II), Gray Willow, also called French Pussy Willow, is a European native, a shrub to 15 ft., sometimes treelike, with densely gray-downy twigs, and long, narrow leaves, gray-felted on the underside. Its male catkins are very large, rose-tinted with yellow anthers.

S. gracilistýla (V), from Japan, Korea, and northern China is said by Bean to be "one of the most ornamental of willows." Slender, red-tinted gray male catkins line the shoots in March and April. This species grows to a height of 6–10 ft. In var. *melanostáchys* (IV), the Black Pussywillow, which is a male clone, the anthers show a bright brick red between the almost black scales of the catkins, finally opening yellow—a highly decorative and striking combination. Bark of the winter twigs also is a deep purplish black. The slender, many-ribbed leaves are attractive during the summer months. This species requires moist soil, in full sun, and needs to be cut back every spring, after the catkins have dropped.

S. irroráta (IV), a native of southwestern United States, is a 15-ft. shrub or small tree. The young stems are covered with a conspicuous white bloom, and the 1-inch-long catkins burst with reddish anthers as the flowers open. This species should be pruned back hard each spring after bloom, to get the best effect from the new shoots.

S. purpúrea (III), Purple Osier, is a large Eurasian shrub to 10 ft. or more, long valued for its wealth of slender, graceful shoots, used in basketry. It is grown in present-day gardens primarily for its shining purple bark and glaucous blue-green foliage. The catkins, which appear in April, are 1 in. long or less. 'Nana', Dwarf Blue-Leaf Arctic Willow, is a compact form only 3–5 ft. in height, with silvery blue foliage. It can be used as a small hedge if clipped annually, or grown as a specimen plant, for the blue-green color of its slender leaves. It is especially useful for heavy, wet soils. 'Streamco', developed by the USDA, is useful for protecting stream banks from erosion, making a medium-sized thicket, profusely layering and suckering.

Among our Northwest natives *S. scouleriána* (V), Scouler's Willow, is worthy of a place in the wild garden. A large shrub or small tree widespread in both streamside and upland habitats, it should probably be pruned regularly to maintain the large catkins, the older branches being removed.

S. hookeriána (V), Hooker's Willow, is a stout, stiffly branched shrub or small tree with a preference for growing within a few miles of salt water, and is thus useful for seaside plantings. In March, or earlier, its large catkins burst with a halo of yellow-dusted anthers borne on extra-long, shining filaments, far more spectacular than their tight gray-fur stage.

SAMBÚCUS. Our two native Elderberries are scarcely choice shrubs for the small garden, but they thrive in almost any soil, and in large areas they provide useful background material. Both have large compound leaves and large clusters of creamy white flowers.

S. canadénsis (III), American Elder of eastern North America, is a stout, multistemmed shrub to about 12 ft. Large umbels of white flowers, up to 8 in. across in June or July, produce clusters of purple-black fruits in August and September, better for wine and jelly than *S. cerulea.* Cultivated varieties include, among others, 'Aurea' with yellow foliage and red fruits; 'Acutiloba' with deeply cut leaflets; 'Maxima', with extra-large flower clusters and extra-long leaves; and 'Adams' and 'John', selected for their fruits.

S. cerúlea (S. gláuca) (IV), Blue Elderberry, can become a 30-ft. tree, but is better kept to a tall, shrubby habit by vigorous pruning in early spring. Its glaucous blue berries, in large flattened clusters, are edible, though not very tasty. It prefers a sunny, forest-edge location.

S. racemósa (IV), is lower and more widely branching, with bright red berries borne in a short conical head. It will tolerate deep shade, and is dispersed by birds. Var. *melanocárpa* is a later-flowering form from higher elevations with purple-black fruits, in denser heads.

SHEPHÉRDIA argéntea (II), Silver Buffalo Berry from the Rocky Mountains and northern Great Plains, is an ironclad 6–10 ft. shrub (sometimes to as much as 25 ft.), tolerant in cold, drought and alkaline soils. Both sides of the leaves, the spine-tipped branchlets, young stems, and even the small, edible red berries are covered with scurfy, silvery scales, so that the entire plant has a silvery sheen. It finds a place chiefly in gardens in the drier parts of our area. Male and female plants should be grown together to assure a crop of fruits.

SORBÁRIA, False Spiraea, is a genus of summer-flowering Asian shrubs closely related to *Spiraea* and *Hólodiscus* bearing their flowers on the current year's growth. *S. arbórea* (V) from western China, considered by Bean to be the finest of the genus, is a spreading shrub 10–20 ft. tall, with pinnately compound leaves and pyramidal clusters of tiny white flowers in July.

S. aitchisónii (V–VI), from Afghanistan, western Pakistan, and Kashmir, is a vigorous 9–10 ft. shrub with bright green, ferny foliage, and large, loose panicles of soft, fluffy, creamy white flowers in June and July.

S. sorbifólia (II), with a wide distribution from western Siberia to

Japan, is the commonest species in cultivation. It is a much smaller plant than the two preceding species, growing only 3–6 ft. tall, but is extremely invasive, traveling rapidly by underground shoots, and for that reason is less desirable than the others. All three are easily grown in sun or light shade, and while tolerant of poor soils, will do much better under moist, well-fertilized conditions. Sorbarias will flower more freely if old shoots are pruned out from time to time to make way for new growth. All spent flowering branches should be removed immediately after flowering.

SÓRBUS. Our two native species of Mountain Ash are of shrub stature and both have garden possibilities. *S. scopulína* (IV), and *S. sitchénsis* (IV), the Sitka Mountain Ash, both put up many stout 3–10 ft. stems, with compound leaves and clusters of small, white flowers. However, their chief merit is their display of bright fruits, beloved by birds—glossy orange-red in *S. scopulína,* and bloomy, carmine-red in *S. sitchénsis*—and their good fall color in the yellow to red-orange range. Though mountain species, they are not averse to lowland situations, and do well in the shrub border, with full sun and adequate summer moisture. They may not fruit quite as well in their native habitat, unless planted in groups.

The native *Sorbus sitchensis* in fruit in mid-September. Photo by Don Normark, Campus Studios, University of Washington.

SPIRÁEA, Bridal Wreath or Spiraea, is a north temperate genus of about 70 species, but only a few of the more commonly grown ones will be mentioned here; and only a few of the many hybrids. All are shrubs of the easiest culture in full sun or light shade, and while they will grow in almost any situation, a rich, light soil with plenty of moisture suits them best. More than most shrubs they respond to careful pruning. Removal of old wood after flowering is most necessary to stimulate the loose, graceful growth, which is the most pleasing characteristic of these shrubs.

S. × *'Argúta'* (IV), Garland Spiraea, a complex hybrid more than 100 years old, is a 6–8 ft. shrub of rounded habit, with slender, downy branches, one of the most beautiful and free-flowering of the spring-blooming types. Clusters of tiny white flowers wreath the plant in April or May. Variety 'Compacta' grows to only 4 ft. tall.

S. betulifólia (IV), a native of Japan and northeastern Asia, is a low, rounded shrub to about 2 ft. White or rose flowers are borne in dense, flat-topped clusters up to 3½ in. wide, during June. Our native var. *lúcida,* from open, coniferous woods, mainly east of the Cascades, is a good under-story plant for the unwatered woodland garden, seldom more than 3 ft. tall. It blooms in June. Where this variety comes in contact with *S. douglásii,* a hybrid, × *S. pyramidális,* often occurs, with a pale pink, broadly cone-shaped inflorescence. This too is an easy, attractive garden plant, preferring slightly more moisture.

S. cantoniénsis (VI), from China, is known in gardens chiefly in its double-flowered state, 'Flore Pleno' (var. *lanceáta*). It forms a graceful 6–8 ft. clump of erect or widely arching stems, heavily laden with rounded clusters of fragrant white flowers in April.

S. densiflóra (V), Subalpine Spiraea, is one of a number of native species suited to Northwest gardens. A low, freely branching shrub, with small, toothed leaves and rose-pink flowers in flat-topped clusters, it is found along stream banks in the mountains and requires similar damp, but sunny conditions in the garden.

S. douglásii (IV), Hard Hack, another Northwest native, is better known in English gardens than in our own. A many-stemmed shrub 4–8 ft. high, it colors lowland swamps in June and July with its plumes of rose flowers and is the perfect answer for naturalizing in soggy places or the wild garden. It is propagated easily from its creeping underground stems, and spreads slowly to cover large areas.

The Japanese Spiraea, *S. japónica* (V), has a long history of cultivation and has produced many cultivars and hybrids. It is a 4–5 ft. shrub, bearing large, flat-topped clusters of rose-colored flowers in late July and August, trouble-free, of great garden value. 'Albiflora' is a dwarfer form, with white flowers. In 'Goldflame' the expanding leaves are at first reddish, changing to bright gold in summer and finally putting on fall colors similar to its spring tints; rosy-red flowers last all summer. 'Shirobana' has red, pink and white flowers mixed on the same plant. 'Little Princess' is a desirable dwarf variety of mounded forms, with rosy crimson flowers. 'Bumalda', sometimes listed as a hybrid, but correctly considered a variant of *S. japonica* itself, has carmine-pink flowers, and variable foliage, often marked in yellow. The widely planted selection, 'Anthony Waterer', with deep carmine flowers, originated as a sport of 'Bumalda'; unstable coloration is characteristic of its foliage too. More than one variation of the original may now be in commerce. 'Lime Mound' has lemon yellow new growth, which changes to lime green in summer. It is a dwarf, mounded form with light pink flowers and orange-red fall color.

S. *nippónica* (III), also from Japan, is a desirable shrub 6–8 ft. tall with somewhat the aspect of a smaller, stiffer, more compact S. × *vanhoúttei*. Its leaves are a dark blue-green, its branches thickly set with clusters of white flowers in May/June. Its cultivar 'Snowmound' grows rapidly to a height of 4–5 ft., and as much or more wide. This species needs good, moist soil to do well, somewhat more so than most spiraeas. 'Rotundifolia' is the original introduction from Japan to the Netherlands, about 1845.

S. *prunifólia* (IV), Bridal Wreath Spiraea, is hardly known in cultivation except in the double-flowered form first introduced from Japan in 1845. The single-flowered type is native in China, Korea, and Taiwan. It is a slender 4–6 ft. shrub, its branches arching to an equal width, and thickly set in April/May with clusters of tiny rosettes, like miniature double roses. Its foliage turns red and orange in autumn. Careful pruning is required to keep this species from becoming leggy.

S. *thunbérgii* (IV), Thunberg Spiraea, from Japan and China, is the first of the early-flowering spiraeas to bloom. A low, graceful shrub 3–4 ft. high, with slender, arching branches, it has very fine, feathery, bright green foliage which turns orange and bronze in autumn. A great profusion of small, dainty, flowers covers the shrub in a billowy cloud of white in March, occasionally as early as February. It blooms on old wood, and pruning after flowering is necessary to keep it from becoming straggly.

S. × *vanhóuttei* (IV), VanHoutte Spiraea, Bridal Wreath, is a showy and widely grown hybrid between S. *trilobáta* and S. *cantoniénsis*. It grows to a height of about 8 ft, the stems arching to a slightly greater spread. With its dark green foliage and profusion of small flower clusters in June, it is probably the handsomest of the white-flowering species. Older wood should be thinned after flowering to make way for new growth. It makes an excellent hedge plant.

STACHYÚRUS *práecox* (V–VI) from Japan is an interesting, late-winter-blooming plant for the shrub border, growing to 10–15 ft. or more, coming into bloom as early as February. Small yellow-green, bell-shaped flowers in 4-in.-long racemes hang stiffly from the tall, arching, red-brown stems. The ovate, long-tipped leaves turn straw yellow and rosy purple in the fall. Flowers and leaves tend to be congregated at the top of the plant leaving long stems in need of foreground planting.

STAPHYLÉA pinnáta (V), Bladder Nut, is a Eurasian shrub up to 12–15 ft. high, with leaflets in 5s. Pendent clusters of white flowers in May/June develop into bladderlike fruits about 1½ in. long. It thrives in any good, moist soil, and is useful in the back of the shrub border.

STEPHANÁNDRA inćisa (V), Cutleaf Stephanandra, from Japan and Korea, is a mounded 4–7 ft. shrub grown for its ferny, fine-textured foliage, red tinged in spring and turning red-orange or red-purple in autumn. Its greenish white flowers are inconspicuous. The taller forms are suitable for hedges and screens. It prefers acid soil and can take either full sun or light shade. The brown branches are attractive in winter.

— *STEWÁRTIA ováta* (V), (also often spelled *Stuártia*), Mountain Stewartia, a 15-ft. shrub from the understory along stream banks in southeastern United States, has the reputation of being difficult to transplant except when young. It is worth the trouble, however, for as a specimen plant it will provide a host of 2–3 in. wide, 5-petaled white flowers in July/August, fine orange to scarlet color in the fall, and interestingly mottled bark in the winter months. Var. *grandiflóra,* which has flowers up to 4 in. in diameter, has conspicuous purple stamens rather than the usual yellow.

SYMPHORICÁRPOS álbus (III), Snowberry, is a well-known native shrub, widely distributed across North America, easily recognizable for its clusters of small, fat snowballs hanging on the thin winter stems. It is generally regarded as being too rampant a grower (spreading by underground roots) to be admitted to the garden, but in woodland areas or on roadside banks, it may be permitted to ramble at will. If pruned to the ground in early spring and given a topdressing of compost and fertilizer, it will more than repay this slight attention with luxurious growth and abundant masses of large berries. *S. móllis* (V), another Northwest native, found from B.C. to California and east into Idaho, has a trailing habit, rooting at the nodes, and accordingly can be used as a groundcover, particularly in woodland settings. Its berries are somewhat smaller than those of *S. albus.* Both species have small, bell-shaped pink flowers in summer.

S. × *chenáultii* (IV), the Chenault Coralberry, is a hybrid between the Mexican *S. microphýllus* and *S. orbiculátus,* the Coralberry of the Great Plains and eastward. It is an erect or spreading shrub, 3–6 ft. tall, with pink flowers and round white fruits, tinged pink on the sunny side. The Canadian selection 'Hancock' makes a good groundcover, no more than 2 ft. in height.

S. orbiculátus (II), Coralberry, or Indian Currant, found from the Great Plains to New Jersey, is a shade-tolerant, spreading shrub 3–5 ft. tall and nearly twice as wide. Its tiny whitish flowers and small, rounded leaves have limited garden merit, but the clusters of ¼ in. purplish red fruits, which last into late winter, bring a nice touch of color to shaded corners. It is also valuable for planting on banks.

SYMPLÓCOS paniculáta (IV), Sapphire Berry, is a shrub or small tree from 10–20 ft. high, of wide distribution in eastern Asia, but most prized in the blue-fruited form from Japan. Starry clusters of small, fragrant, white flowers accompany the dark, shining, leathery, green foliage in May and June, but the really unusual feature of this shrub is the color of its fruits, which are turquoise blue. Fruits will be more plentiful if several seedlings or clones are grown together, since this species is partially self-incompatible, and cross-pollination helps to achieve good fruit set. It prefers full sun and a well-drained soil, and is deserving of a conspicuous place in the shrub border.

⁓ *SYRÍNGA* × *chinénsis* (V), Rouen Lilac, an 18th-century French hybrid between *S. laciniáta* and *S. vulgáris*, is a graceful, arching shrub 8–15 ft. tall, and usually as broad, with large, loose panicles of fragrant, purple-lilac flowers in May. 'Alba' bears light pink, nearly white, flowers, while those of 'Saugeana' are lilac-red. Propagate by cuttings taken in summer when firm.

S. josikáea (IV), Hungarian Lilac, is an upright shrub to 12 ft., with elliptical leaves and a rather narrow panicle of deep lilac flowers. Blooming somewhat later than the common lilacs, it is a useful species for extending the season. Crossed with other species, it has given rise to a number of late-flowering hybrids.

⁓ *S. meyéri* (V), Meyer's Lilac, was introduced into the United States in 1908 from China, where it is known only in the cultivated state. It is a neat, densely mounded shrub about 5–6 ft. in height and as much or more wide, with oval leaves and downy shoots. It is covered with 4-in.-long panicles of fragrant, violet-purple blossoms in May and June. Since the flowers tend to appear before the leaves are out, this shrub looks best against an evergreen background.

⁓ *S. méyeri* 'Palibin', (*S. palibíniana*, of gardens). One of the smallest lilacs both in foliage and flowers, although eventually growing 5–6 feet tall. The leaves are oval to obovate, 1–1½ in. long, less in width, with two pairs of veins on each side. Flowering profusely in May, even when young, with many short dense panicles of small, fragrant, light purple blossoms. This could be an attractive hedge plant if properly cared for. Propagate by cuttings in summer.

⁓ *S. pátula (S. velútina)* (III), Korean Lilac, is usually a shrub to 10 ft., but is most commonly seen in its dwarf cultivar, 'Miss Kim', which is rarely over 5 ft. tall, but can be 5 ft. wide. Its fragrant, bluish flowers open from pinkish purple buds in June, thus extending the lilac season some weeks.

⁓ *S.* × *pérsica* (V), Persian Lilac, is a loose, graceful 5–7 ft. shrub with slender, privetlike leaves, which has been in cultivation in Europe since the 17th century, but is an ancient garden plant in India and Iran. It bears a profusion of small, soft panicles of lilac-colored and lilac-scented flowers in May. 'Alba' is a white-flowered form.

S. refléxa (V), Nodding Lilac, is a 12-ft. shrub which comes to us from central China and differs from the other lilac species in having nearly cylindrical inflorescences, with tier after tier of densely packed, small blossoms weighing down the branches. The individual flowers, like tiny trumpets with reflexed tips, are a rich pink or purplish pink outside and white inside. Leaves, 4–6 in. long, dark green above, paler beneath, are ovate lanceolate with long points. Hybrids of this species with *S. villósa, S.* × *prestóniae,* developed by Isabella Preston at Ottawa in the early 1900s, are extremely hardy and the color range includes violet and lavender as well as pinks. Cultivars of this type are still appearing. 'Isabella' and 'Ursula' are two of the originals.

S. vulgáris (III), the Common Lilac from the mountains of eastern Europe, is one of the most beloved and widely grown of all deciduous shrubs. Its rather leggy, upright manner of growth and heart-shaped plain green leaves are forgotten when the large trusses of fragrant flowers burst forth in May. They have given us the adjective that describes their light bluish lavender color: lilac. The tall, slender forms reach a height of 12–15 ft. or more, while the broadly spreading ones are usually not less than 8–10 ft. high. Flower color ranges from a light blue-mauve to rich wine purple, crimson and pink, as well as white. It is possible to extend the blooming period from the last week in April to the first week in June by growing a number of different hybrids. There are many hundreds of named varieties, but relatively small number of outstanding ones. Lists of "best" varieties appear from time to time in horticultural publications, not necessarily well suited to the Pacific Northwest. In any case, the gardener choosing lilacs is more likely to be guided by personal color preference and local availability. Lilacs bloom best in areas of winter chilling. The following list gives an idea of the range of colors and types.

Single, white: 'Angel White', 'Vestale' 'Jan van Tol'.

Double white: 'Ellen Willmott', 'Edith Cavell', 'Mme. Lémoine'.

Single violet: 'De Miribel', 'Cavour'.

Double violet: 'President Poincaré', 'Violette'.

Single, lilac to blue: 'President Lincoln', 'Firmament'.

Double, lilac to blue: 'Alphonse Lavallée', 'Belle de Nancy'.

Single pink: 'Lucie Baltet', 'Esther Staley' (hybrid with *S. oblata*).

Double pink: 'William Robinson', 'Katherine Havemeyer', 'Maréchal Foch'.

Single red-violet: 'Ludwig Spaeth', 'Congo', 'Reaumur'.

Double red-violet: 'Charles Joly', 'Paul Thirion'.

'Sensation', single red-violet with a white edge to its petals, is in a class by itself, as is 'Primrose', a pale yellow single, not a strong grower. Both are of Dutch origin.

Lilacs as a group require full sun and are favored by warm summers. The species are easily grown in any good garden soil, provided it is not more than slightly acid. Prior to planting, the site should be dug to a depth of at least 2 ft., generously limed and augmented with manure or compost. A yearly topdressing of bone meal and a mulch of compost will enable hybrids to produce their best blooms. The plants should have ample moisture during the blooming season and for a short period afterward. Watering should then be sharply reduced to allow growth to ripen off during July and August. Lilacs are drought resistant during August and September.

Lilac blossoms are much prized for cutting, but this should be done judiciously, with an eye to the shape of the shrub. Beyond removal of dead flower heads immediately after blooming, lilacs should require no regular pruning except cutting out weak twiggy growth in the center of the shrub. Drastic pruning may be necessary if a plant has been neglected or become misshapen through crowding by its neighbors. Old branches can be cut back in winter to within 3–4 ft. of the ground to force strong new growth from the base. Bloom will be sacrificed for a year or two, and it may take 2–3 years for the shrub to regain a shapely form. They are very long-lived shrubs if properly cared for.

Lilacs can be propagated by layering or by cutting off suckers. They may also be rooted from mature cuttings, with the encouragement of mist or bottom heat. Many modern cultivars are grafted.

TÁMARIX. Tamarisks are distinctive, fluffy-looking shrubs with hordes of minute, pink blossoms in tight panicles and fine, gray or green, scalelike foliage. Native in the Mediterranean region and eastward, they are found in coastal sites or on salt flats inland, and make good hedges for seaside gardens. Hardy and extremely drought resistant, they do well east of the Cascades. In west-side gardens they should have a sunny, well-drained position, with a minimum of watering. At least one species has gone wild in the semi-arid parts of the West. All can become rather leggy and untidy unless properly pruned, but no plant is easier to propagate—it is only necessary to set the cuttings in the open ground at the beginning of winter.

T. gállica (V), French Tamarisk, from western Europe and northern Africa, is a shrub or small tree to 25 ft. Slender 1–2 in. long racemes of tiny, pink-tinged white flowers cover the branches in June/July. The closely related *T. africána* (VII) with a similar distribution in southwestern Europe and northern Africa flowers either on the previous season's wood or that of the current season.

In *T. ramosíssima (T. pentándra)* (II), Five Petaled Tamarisk, widely distributed from Asia Minor through southern Russia and Central Asia to China, the racemes are longer than those of the other species, 2 in. or more, gathered into panicles, blooming in late summer on the current year's wood. In its best forms it is a very beautiful shrub up to 15–20 ft. tall. Like all tamarisks, it makes a far better garden plant if pruned severely every year. It should be cut back almost to the ground in early spring. When pruned in this way it will send out 5–10 foot plumes of misty sage green foliage tipped with loose, airy panicles of soft lavender-pink flowers. Forms with darker rose flowers are sometimes available, 'Rosea' or 'Rubra'.

In *T. parviflóra* (IV), Small Flowered Tamarisk, native to southeastern Europe, the tiny 4-petaled flowers are light pink and borne from April to June on the previous year's growth. Spent flowering branches should be pruned out immediately after bloom is over. This species can reach 15 ft., so is better planted behind other shrubs.

VACCINIUM. The Vacciniums, deciduous or evergreen, are commonly called Huckleberries in our area, though this name refers to *Gaylussacia* in other parts of the country.

V. parvifólium (V), Red Huckleberry, is a 3–12 ft. shrub, widely distributed in lowland forests west of the Cascades, and deserving wider use in our gardens. Its pale green, pink-tinted flowers are barely noticeable, but the small, pale green leaves give it a dainty aspect, useful for lightening a dark corner; they turn a clear, pale yellow in the shade, red or orange tinted in full sun. Angled green twigs, in erect sheafs in exposed locations, more spreading in shade, develop considerable red color in winter. Translucent red berries ¼–½ in. across, borne singly but often in great numbers, ripen in July. They are tart in flavor even when ripe, but children and birds love them—they also make good jelly and pies. This plant, often found growing on old stumps, is worth saving from the bulldozer on new lots, or bird-brought seedlings can be rescued and encouraged; it is rarely offered for sale. It will thrive in conditions suitable for rhododendrons.

V. corymbósum (III), the High Bush Blueberry of eastern United States, need not be relegated to the kitchen garden. The type is a 10–12 ft. shrub, but named cultivars vary in size and habit of growth. All are attractive garden plants valuable for their small white or pinkish white blooms in April and brilliant red autumn foliage, as well as for their tasty glaucous blue fruits. A sunny position and moist soil well enriched with organic matter will suit them—summer watering is essential. They require little if any pruning to keep the bushes shapely, and are easily propagated from summer cuttings of half-ripened wood stuck in peat and sand. More than one variety is necessary for cross-pollination to assure a good fruit set. Consult the Cooperative Extension Service for varieties suitable for your area.

VIBURNUM. More than 100 species of *Viburnum*, both deciduous and evergreen, occur in the Northern Hemisphere, and a large percentage of them are worthy garden subjects. The species which have become the most widespread in cultivation are grown for their flowers. Others are grown principally for their beautiful berries, and would be equally common except for their fruiting idiosyncracies. Many species tend to be self-sterile, so that—like cherries—several seedlings or propagations from different cultivars must be planted together in order for cross-pollination to assure a good set of fruits. Groups of plants originating from a single individual are self-sterile. Viburnums are easy, undemanding shrubs, preferring a deep, rich soil and plenty of moisture, but capable of good performance under less favorable circumstances. Some drying out toward the end of summer is desirable for the best display of autumn color. They require little pruning other than occasional thinning or removal of weak growth in early spring. Cuttings or layering are the usual methods of propagation. Seeds are slow to germinate and may not come true to type.

V. × *bodnanténse* (VI) covers hybrids between *V. fárreri (V. frágrans)* and *V. grandiflórum* dating from the 1930s, which are more or less intermediate between the two parents. One to 2-in.-wide heads of fragrant flowers, rose pink in bud but pale pink when open, are borne on short branches on a stiffly upright stem. Flowers may appear as early as November, persisting through to early spring, depending on the severity of the winter. 'Dawn' is the original cultivar; in 'Deben' the flowers are much paler, almost white.

V. carlésii (IV), Korean Spice Viburnum, from Korea, but cultivated in Japan, is a dense, rounded shrub, 4–8 ft. tall and about as wide, with oval, almost heart-shaped leaves, downy dull green above, and thickly grayish downy below. The extremely fragrant flowers are waxy in substance, rich bronzy pink in the bud, opening pure white in April/May, and carried in roundheaded clusters 3–3½ in. across. It is of comparatively easy culture under a fairly wide range of garden conditions, but will prove happiest in open woodland under deciduous trees where it will receive full sun in winter and light dappled shade in summer. This species is propagated by cuttings taken in July and is said to resent disturbance after planting out. Several named selections are an improvement over the type. 'Carlotta' has larger flowers. 'Compacta' is of more compact habit than the type. This species has also contributed to a number of hybrids.

V. × *carlcéphalum* (VI), raised in England about 1932 from a cross between *V. carlesii* and *V. macrocephalum,* is a somewhat larger, coarser plant with flowers of "semi-snowball" type, opening white from pink buds. It also is fragrant, but less graceful in the garden than some of the other hybrids, or *V. carlesii.*

V. cassinóides (III), Witherod Viburnum from eastern North America, is a handsome shrub from 5–10 ft. tall, with slightly arching branches. Purple-tinted new foliage becomes dull, dark green, then orange-red to crimson-purple in the fall. Creamy white flowers in flat-topped clusters are good, but the fruits are even better: turning from green to pink, then red, and finally dark blue-black by September. This is a valuable, easily propagated shrub, deserving of greater use in woodland plantings and in the shrub border.

V. dentátum (II), Arrowwood Viburnum, from eastern United States, is a hardy, multistemmed 8–15 ft. shrub with coarsely toothed leaves which turn yellow, brilliant red, or red-purple in autumn. Flat-topped clusters of creamy white flowers, 2–4 in. across bloom in May/June, followed by small blue or blue-black fruits in September/October. While not as choice as ornamental as other Viburnums, this species is a tough, tolerant plant able to survive in heavy or alkaline soils, useful for seaside plantings, and good for hedges or screening, or in the wild garden.

V. dilatátum (V), Linden Viburnum, from Japan and China, is an upright, bushy, 6–10 ft. shrub with large, hairy, ovate leaves, and attractive clusters of white flowers in May; its young branches also are hairy. Its beautiful, red fruits last well into winter, but are produced in decorative quantities only if more than one clone is present in a planting. This species does best in slightly acid soil and will need some summer watering. A number of variants are available:

In f. *xanthocárpum* the berries are yellow.

'Erie' forms a 6-ft. mound, covered with flat-topped white flower clusters in spring, yellow to orange-red fall color, and scarlet berries, fading to coral after frost, which literally weigh down the bushes.

'Catskill' is a dwarf selection, with small leaves and good fall color.

'Iroquois' has glossy dark scarlet fruits.

'Oneida', a cross between *V. dilatátum* and *V. lobophýllum,* raised by Dr. D. Egolf at the U.S. National Arboretum, produces an abundance of flowers in May, with some second bloom. Its glossy, dark red fruits are long lasting; leaves have good fall color in the pale yellow to orange-red range.

V. fárreri (V. frágrans) (V), Fragrant Viburnum, from Kansu in Northern China, is a rugged, early-spring-flowering shrub with the fragrance of heliotrope, made popular by the writings of Reginald Farrer whose name it bears. It can reach 12 ft. or more in height, but varies considerably in manner of growth, from erect to sprawling. Flowers, in clusters up to 1–2 in. across, are pale pink or pure white (f. *candidíssimum*). Reddish purple fall color and fruits turning from red to black complete the picture. Softwood cuttings root easily. This species needs a sunny location and prefers a light soil over a heavy one.

V. × *híllieri* (VI) arose as a chance hybrid between *V. hénryi* and *V. erubéscens,* in Hillier's Nursery in England. Flowers are intermediate between the species—leaves are broader than in *V. henryi,* and the plant is of a more graceful habit. The same hybrid has also occurred in the wild in China.

V. macrocéphalum (VI), Chinese Snowball, is a deciduous or partly evergreen shrub from China, possibly the showiest of all viburnums in bloom, with huge, spherical flower clusters as much as 6 in. in diameter, produced freely from May onward. The plant may ultimately reach a height of 15–20 ft. Its pointed, oval leaves are dull green above and downy beneath; young shoots are also downy. They are semi-evergreen in this area. Forma *keteléeri* is the wild type—in it the showy, sterile flowers are limited to the outer edge of the flat and otherwise fertile flower clusters.

V. ópulus (III), the Common Highbush Cranberry or Guelder Rose, native from Europe to Central Asia, is a rapidly growing, multistemmed 10–15 ft. shrub with broadly lobed leaves 3–5 in. across, turning deep wine red, crimson or scarlet in autumn. In the type, the flower clusters, 2–3 in. across, are flat-topped and edged with an outer ring of showy, sterile flowers. Clusters of translucent, bright red fruits follow, hanging on into winter, shrunken, but still colorful. To obtain maximum fall color this shrub should be kept dry toward the end of summer. It can be lightly pruned when in bloom or immediately after flowering, but remains tidy in its habit unless overwatered and overfertilized. This species is very easy to propagate from cuttings inserted in the fall. It is susceptible to attacks by leaf curling aphids.

'Roseum' ('Sterile') is the common Snowball in which all the flowers are sterile, gathered in 2–3 in. heads, pale green changing to white, sometimes pink-tinted with age. This form is one of our most widely planted May-blooming shrubs, particularly east of the Cascades, being of the easiest culture in any soil or situation. It produces no fruits, but fall color is excellent.

'Aureum' is a yellow-leaved form which needs the protection of a shady location to look its best.

'Compactum', about half the height of the species and dense in habit, is in much better scale for today's smaller gardens and fruits well.

'Notcutt' or 'Notcutt's Variety' has larger flowers and fruits than the type, and superior fall color.

'Xanthocarpum' has golden yellow fruits.

V. plicátum (V), Japanese Snowball, is a most pleasing 9–10 ft. shrub with spreading horizontal branches and pointed, oval leaves—again with both flat-topped and globose, sterile forms. Forma *tomentósum* is the wild form, native to Japan and China. Its dull green, toothed leaves are grayish-downy beneath, and reddish-purple in fall color. The flat umbels of bloom on short twigs with a pair of leaves below them, consist chiefly of small, fertile flowers with a few large, white, sterile ones around the edges. Clusters of small, egg-shaped fruits turning from coral-red to blue-black, ripen in August/September and are a favorite with birds. Several cultivars are available.

'Mariesii', with flower clusters larger than the type and sterile flowers up to 1¾ in. wide, is distinctly horizontal in habit of growth, and has dull crimson or purplish red fall color.

'Pink Beauty' is said by Dirr to have "outstanding deep pink" petals.

'Rowallane' is less vigorous than the type and has smaller leaves as well. Its sterile florets are still large, but the fertile ones are less numerous.

'Shasta' from the National Arboretum, 6 ft. tall and about twice as broad, has 4–6 in. wide inflorescenses with marginal sterile florets up to 2 in. across, and additional somewhat smaller sterile florets scattered among the central fertile ones.

V. plicátum f. *plicátum* is the name given to the handsome snowball variant of this species with its heads of ivory white, totally sterile flowers rounded up into 2–3 in. globes. They march in two ranks down the arching branches, hence the name 'Double-File Viburnum', and make a spectacular show in April/May.

'Grandiflorum' is a form with even larger flower heads.

'Rosace' has pink flowers and bronze-tinged foliage.

These sterile forms produce no fruit. This species is an elegant spring-flowering shrub in either form, useful as a screening plant or as a foil for the upright lines of adjacent shrubs. It is particularly good against red brick buildings. It prefers a moist, but well-drained site and does not thrive in heavy, poorly drained soils. It needs regular watering in summer if in sandy soils and an annual mulch to cover the root area.

V. prunifólium (III), Black Haw, is a multistemmed shrub but can be trained as a small tree, and may reach 20–30 ft. It is native to eastern North America, and is similar in habit to the hawthorns. Flat-topped flower clusters with numerous yellow stamens appear in May. Small fruits, pinkish at first, but finally a powdery blue-black are decorative and can also be used in preserves. Fall color varies from dark red to purple, and some selection from seedlings may be necessary to find individuals with good color. Easily transplanted and adaptable to many soil types, this is a useful plant for dry locations.

V. setígerum (V), Tea Viburnum, from central and western China, is an erect, rather leggy, gray-stemmed shrub 8–12 ft. tall, with long-tapered, narrowly ovate leaves that are a soft blue-green in summer and sometimes reddish purple in autumn. Small white flowers, all perfect, in clusters 1½–2 in. across, are of limited interest in May, but in October the egg-shaped, bright red fruits, nearly ½ in. long, are among the most handsome of any of the viburnums. In the cultivar 'Aurantiacum' the fruit is bright orange rather than red.

V. siebóldii (IV), Siebold Viburnum from Japan, is a handsome, vigorous shrub or small tree from 10–20 ft. in height, with gray-downy stems when young. Leaves, prominently veined and glossy dark green, are up to 5 in. long and about half as wide, shallowly toothed and pointed, with a disagreeable odor when crushed. In May the creamy white flowers, in long-stalked, flat-topped clusters 3–6 in. across, are borne in such great abundance as to mask the foliage. Small fruits, rose-pink changing to blue-black by October, are popular with birds—the rose-red stemlets of the inflorescence are decorative even after the fruits are gone! This is a plant that thrives in cold winters and warm summers, highly thought of in eastern United States. It will be useful east of the Cascades, but its leaves may scorch unless it has sufficient summer moisture.

VÍTEX ágnus-cástus (VII), Chaste Tree, native from the Mediterranean region into southwestern and central Asia, is a gray-downy, multi-trunked shrub to 10 ft., chiefly valuable because of the lateness of its bloom, in September and October. Its large, palmately compound, aromatic leaves are decidedly coarse-looking, but the whorls of small violet flowers, gathered into large panicles like those of a *Buddleia* at the ends of the current year's growth, are fragrant. This plant tolerates many soil types, but requires plenty of summer heat for best flowering. 'Alba' is a form with white flowers. 'Rosea' has pink flowers. 'Latifolia' has broader leaflets than the type.

WEIGÉLA flórida (V) from Korea and northern China is a sturdy 6–9 ft. shrub with spreading branches that arch gracefully under the weight of its tubular pink flowers in May/June. Leaves, 2–4 in. long, are oval and long-pointed, with felty midribs on the underside. Flowers vary in color from white through pale appleblossom pink to deep rose and red. Leaf color also varies. Weigelas need good, rich soil, adequate summer water, and considerable pruning—removal of bloomed-out stems after flowering—to keep them looking their best. They are one of the easiest shrubs to root from softwood cuttings. Hybrid forms have all but eclipsed the original species.

'Bristol Ruby' is one of several red-flowered varieties, which are very popular but not necessarily as attractive in the garden scene as the pink ones.

'Eva Supreme' is one of the best reds, with a height of about 5 ft.; others include 'Red Prince'; 'Newport Red', flowering in late May; and 'Evita', a red-flowered miniature, more or less everblooming.

'Bristol Snowflake', 'Candida' and 'Mont Blanc' are white flowered.

Pinks of varying intensity are also offered. 'Centennial' is said to be extra hardy. 'Pink Princess' has bright pink flowers. 'Seduction' is magenta-rose.

'Variegata' has white-variegated foliage; 'Variegata Nana', with compact rounded form to about 3 ft., has soft pink flowers and leaves edged creamy white.

'Java Red' has deep pink flowers and reddish foliage on a plant of compact habit.

'Minuet', with dark rosy purple flowers and purple-tinged foliage, is one of the smallest varieties.

W. middendorffiána (IV) from northeastern Asia, grows to only about 5 ft. and has bell-shaped sulfur yellow flowers about 1¼ in. long and 1 in. wide. It flowers in April/May, but is often damaged in areas where late frosts are the rule.

ZANTHOXÝLUM piperítum (VI), Japan Pepper, from China, Japan, and Korea, is a small, compact bush, with dainty, pinnately compound leaves and spiny stems. Its flowers are small and green, and not particularly conspicuous, but the small, red fruits, splitting to reveal black seeds, add a touch of color in September. This plant is grown primarily for its lacy foliage. It prefers good, fertile soil in full sun, and is easily propagated from seeds or from cuttings of young wood in July.

ZENÓBIA *pulverulénta* (V), Dusty Zenobia, from Virginia and South Carolina, is a beautiful 6-ft. shrub related to *Leucothoe* and *Pieris,* often deciduous, but semi-evergreen in the Seattle area. Its rounded leaves and shoots are covered with a bluish white, glaucous bloom. Small clusters of anise-scented white flowers like large lilies-of-the-valley bloom in June and July. It thrives in the same conditions as rhododendrons, and will require summer watering in our area, particularly if it has to compete with tree roots. It does best in full sun, since it has a tendency to become leggy in the shade. This plant can be raised easily from seeds or cuttings, but the latter method is best for perpetuating extra-good individuals. In f. *nítida* neither the leaves nor the stems are glaucous. In 'Quercifolia' the leaves are margined with shallow, wavy lobes.

CHAPTER XI

Groundcovers and Small Shrubs

These plants are valuable for covering areas of bare ground fairly easily and quickly, and thereby reducing annual maintenance. They can be either evergreen or deciduous; the former predominate in the following lists and descriptions, and are of course preferable to deciduous plants for their winter effect. Some are stoloniferous and spread by means of stems extending underground, e.g., *Cornus canadensis, Andromeda polifolia,* and *Vaccinium vitis-idaea,* Lingonberry; others by means of their long new shoots covering the ground around them, e.g., *Arctostaphylos uva-ursi,* the Kinnikinnick; *Juniperus horizontalis* and *Leptospermum humifusum;* heathers such as the smaller species of *Erica* (*E. herbacea (carnea), E. vagans* and *E. tetralix*), and the related species of *Cassiope* and *Daboecia* by annually enlarging their size until they grow into each other. Some prefer to be in the sun, others in full or partial shade. These characteristics will be mentioned in the individual descriptions.

AETHIONÉMA (VII). is a genus of small subshrubs 9–18 in. tall from the eastern Mediterranean region, definitely needing full sunshine and good drainage. Foliage is glaucous gray; flowers April to May, pale or deeper pink, in racemes at the ends of the branches. *A. arménum* and *A. pulchéllum* are most commonly grown; *A.* 'Warley Rose' is dwarfer and more compact, with deeper pink flowers.

ALYSSUM. See *AURINIA.*

ANDRÓMEDA. (II). *A. polifólia,* the Bog Rosemary, An ericaceous shrublet native to peat bogs in Alaska, Japan, northern Canada and the extreme northwestern U.S.A. Height 6–8 in. Flowers bell shaped, in terminal clusters in May, normally pale pink but there are also white-flowered forms introduced from Japan. Suitable only for damp places in the garden, and acid soils.

ARCTERICA. See *PIERIS.*

Andromeda polifolia 'Nana Compacta' flowering in late April. Photo by Brian Mulligan.

ARCTOSTÁPHYLOS (II–VII). *A. nevadénsis,* Pinemat Manzanita, native in the mountains of California, Oregon and Washington where it likes to scramble over rocks to a height of about 18 in., and expose its tan-brown, woody stems, generally thicker and tougher than those of Kinnikinnick. The leaves are similar to those of the latter species but more definitely pointed; the fruits are brown when ripe, not red. The small flowers are pale pink. Less vigorous and slower to establish than *A. uva-ursi,* but like it, enjoying a sunny, well-drained site. *A.* × *média* is the hybrid between *A. columbiana* and *A. uva-ursi,* liable to be found wherever the two parents occur together, notably in Kitsap County, Washington. Being hybrids between two very different species, the offspring can vary greatly in form and habit but are generally about 18–24 in. in height, the branches spreading out or trailing from a humped center. The leaves also vary in their form and color, some being grayer than others; the flowers may be white or pink. Fruits have not been observed. *A. uva-úrsi* (II), Kinnikinnick or Bearberry, is widely distributed throughout the Northern Hemisphere, from near mountain tops to the seacoast, even along river beds in the shingles, in Idaho for example. As an evergreen groundcover 4–6 in. high for sunny banks it is unexcelled, and when bedecked with its numerous, tiny, bell-shaped flowers or the glowing red, globular fruits it becomes an object of considerable attraction. Propagation is easy by cuttings taken in late summer, or by layering the long trailing shoots. Selected named forms are to be found in gardens and nurserymen's catalogs. 'Point Reyes', from California, is one of these. 'Wood's Red' may a be hybrid with *A. nevadensis.*

ARDÍSIA, (VII–VIII). *A. japónica* is a shade-loving plant with woody stems, growing about 12 in. tall, native of Japan and China. The leaves are clustered together near the tops of the stems, are evergreen, though quite often killed here in severe winters, about 2–3 in. long and 1 in. wide, sharply toothed. The white flowers are produced from the upper leaf axils in August and may be followed by red fruits. The plant is stoloniferous, spreading by underground stems; it prefers a sandy type of soil.

AURÍNIA *(ALYSSUM) saxátilis* (III). Basket-of-Gold. This early-spring-flowering rock garden and wall plant, well known under its former name of *Alyssum saxatile* is still useful and popular, whether in its normal, golden yellow type or the pale yellow form 'Citrina'. The compact clusters of flowers are well supported by the gray, evergreen foliage. The plants in height attain only about 8 in. in height, so need to be in the front of any other plants in a border. Propagate either by seeds or by cuttings taken in summer. These plants are long lived and need little care or attention, which is an asset.

BÉRBERIS. *B. thunbérgii*, (IV–V), the well-known deciduous barberry from Japan, has produced a number of dwarf or compact forms including 'Crimson Pygmy' ('Atropurpurea Nana'), 'Globe' ('Nana'), 'Kobold', and 'Minor'. These vary in height from 18–30 in. and are useful for filling spaces in front of larger shrubs, or as edging plants along a path. The reddish or purpleleaved forms, 'Crimson Pygmy' and 'Intermedia', supply more color in summer. 'Aurea' is vivid yellow even in summer, but taller.

BÉTULA (II). *B. nána*, the Dwarf Birch, native of the Northern Hemisphere, is a deciduous shrub growing to about 2–3 ft. tall, with a distinct preference for cool, moist, acid soils. The branches are slender, the leaves almost round, notably toothed, dark shining green on the upper side, only about ½ in. across, the smallest of all the shrubby birches.

BRUCKENTHALIA. See *ERICA*.

CALLUNA. See *ERICA*.

BÚXUS (VI). Box shrubs. *B. microphýlla* (V–VI), native to Japan and Korea, is the hardiest of the Box family and varies considerably in form and stature, depending upon its origin, but is usually 3–4 ft. tall. The leaves are obovate in shape, about ½ in. long, glossy on the upper side, which makes it an attractive small bush in a sunny situation. The angled stems are quite smooth, which distinguishes it from the Korean and Chinese varieties. Dwarf forms are 'Compacta', 'Morris Dwarf' and 'Morris Midget'; the last two were raised at the Morris Arboretum in Philadelphia. They grow so slowly that no pruning is required. Of the European Box species, *B. semper-vírens*, only the very dwarf form 'Suffruticosa' (VII) is appropriate to this list. It is the type used for Box edgings, growing to about 15–20 in. in height, but requiring an annual clipping to keep it in shape.

CASSÍOPE. A genus of "false heathers" distributed over the mountains of the Northern Hemisphere, not easily cultivated here with our dry summers., despite the fact that *C. mertensiána* (V) is so common in the Cascade Mountains of Oregon, Washington and British Columbia, growing 6–8 ins. in height and flowering profusely there in midsummer. The Japanese *C. lycopodioídes* (III) is perhaps somewhat more amenable to cultivation, but any of them need to be grown in shady, cool situations in this region, in a well-drained soil with plenty of humus added annually. They can be propagated by either seeds or cuttings. The Scottish hybrids 'Muirhead' and 'Badenoch' are probably more easily grown than the species.

CEANÓTHUS. *C. gloriósus* (VII), the Point Reyes Ceanothus, appears to be the hardiest and most useful of its race here as a groundcover 6–10 in. tall, having been grown successfully for a number of years on a steep bank facing east on the University of Washington campus in Seattle. The leaves are thick and leathery, dark green above but paler beneath, about 1 in. long and wide, conspicuously toothed; flowers purplish blue, in dense short-stalked umbels. Should be grown in full sun, like Kinnikinnick, with which it associates well. *C. prostrátus* (VI) is a smaller edition of *C. gloriosus*, native to dry hillsides from southern Washington into northern California where it forms flat mats on sandy soils but it is much less easy to establish and grow in western Washington or Oregon. Flowers ashy blue. *C. thyrsiflórus* var. *répens*, from the northern California coast, (VII) is taller and bushier, not mat forming like the two previous species, the leaves ovate, about 1 in. long, evergreen; flowers clear bright blue, in May. Height about 18–24 in., but more in width when happily sited on a sunny bank.

CERATOSTÍGMA *plumbaginoídes (Plumbágo larpéntae)* (VI). An herbaceous plant with deciduous leaves turning red in autumn; flowers bright blue, about 1 in. in diameter, in late summer. Height 9–12 in. Needs a sunny location to flower freely. Native of China.

CÓRNUS *canadénsis* (IV–V). A charming and useful little groundcover for shady, moist places, familiar to anyone who has hiked trails in the Cascade mountains from British Columbia to Oregon. Attaining only 6 in. or so in height, it runs through the humus and soon forms colonies bedecked in summer with its bright four-bracted white "flowers" (the true flowers are concealed in the center of the inflorescence). Later these turn to clusters of shining red fruits, attractive to rodents as well as humans. It may take time to establish this plant in local gardens, but is well worth the effort. An annual mulch of humus or compost is very beneficial. The correct name for the plant from the Cascade range is *C. unalaschkénsis*. True *C. canadensis* is found only to the east of the Continental Divide. The closely related *C. suécica*. is found in Alaska.

COPRÓSMA. A genus of trees and shrubs from the southwestern Pacific region and New Zealand, of which only two or three from the latter country are in cultivation here and concern us. These include *C. brúnnea* (VII), and *C. pétriei* (VII), both possessing a wiry habit of growth, forming mats or up to a foot in height, small lanceolate leaves, inconspicuous flowers but fleshy berries later on, pale blue in the case of the former, white or red in the latter. However, since these small shrubs are dioecious, having male and female flowers on different plants, one of each sex is necessary to obtain fruits. They are easily propagated by cuttings.

COTONEÁSTER dámmeri (VI), native in central China, quickly forms a mat of trailing shoots covered with obovate shining leaves about 1 in. long. The white flowers are borne singly, in May, each about ½ in. in diameter, followed by bright red fruits which remain long into the winter or early spring. The branches root as they elongate, especially if covered with a little soil. 'Lowfast' and 'Skogholm' are taller-growing hybrids of C. dammeri, up to 2 ft. 'Hybridus Pendulus' has a weeping or trailing habit of growth, but much larger leaves, up to 3 in. long and 1 in. wide. It fruits freely in any situation. Another species producing prostrate forms with smaller foliage is the Chinese C. salicifólius. Of this, 'Gnom', 'Herbstfeuer' and 'Repens' are in cultivation on the West Coast. All are excellent groundcovers, but will flower and fruit better when in a fairly open situation.

CYATHÓDES colensói (VII), native to the mountains of New Zealand, is a heathlike shrub 12–18 in. tall, though often smaller. The lanceolate leaves are shining above, glaucous gray beneath, with conspicuous veins. The flowers are very small, tubular, white; fruits, produced of course only by the female plants, may vary in color from white to red. It enjoys conditions similar to those for small ericaceous shrubs in our gardens, belonging to the related family Epacridaceae.

CÝTISUS. Several small species or hybrids of these brooms are admirable groundcovers. One of the most attractive and useful is C. decúmbens (V–VI), which forms a mat only 6 in. high but up to 3 ft. across. The leafy green twigs lie one over another and in May produce quantities of bright yellow little pea flowers for about two to three weeks. Native to southern Europe, from France to Jugoslavia. Propagate either by cuttings or seeds. C. × kewénsis is (V–VI) a hybrid between two very different species, (C. ardoinii, dwarf and yellow flowered, and the tall, white-flowered C. multiflórus), made at Kew in 1891. The attractive result is a plant growing only 1 ft. or so in height but spreading to 3–4 ft. across, producing creamy yellow flowers along the branches in May. Propagated only by cuttings. C. procúmbens (V). Native to the mountains of southeastern Europe, where so many of these plants grow, this one attains about 18 in. in height, but spreads wider by its arching branches. The leaves are small and simple, green. The golden yellow flowers are carried along the stems in mid-May to early June. Very tolerant of dry conditions. Propagate either by seeds or cuttings. C. purpúreus (V). An upright type, to no more than 18 in., with trifoliate leaves up to 1 inch long; in May the stems produce many purple flowers each ¾ in. long. This is valuable for its different color amongst these dwarf brooms. There is also a rare white form, álbus, from northern Italy. Propagate by either seeds or cuttings.

DABÓECIA cantábrica (D. polifólia), (VII). The Irish Bell Heath, found wild from western Ireland to northern Portugal, grows in acid soil conditions as a moorland plant about 18 in. tall in large colonies. The large, eggshaped flowers are borne in racemes from June to October and are purple in the type species but darker in 'Atropurpurea' and varying to white in forma *álba*, pink in 'Pragerae', found in Connemara, Ireland. The leaves are dark glossy green, white beneath with a thick coating of hairs. Useful for its long if somewhat intermittent flowering, this species is about of equal hardiness to *Erica erigena (E. mediterranea)* and like it liable to be cut back severely or even killed to the ground in colder than normal winters. So it is wise to propagate a few plants annually by cuttings and keep them in reserve and under cover through the winter.

There is one other species of *Daboecia*, namely *D. azórica* (VIII), found only in the Azores Islands, which is not hardy in the Puget Sound region as a general rule. However, hybrids occurred between this and *D. cantabrica* in a garden in Scotland which are intermediate in habit of growth and other characters, including hardiness. One of these has been named 'William Buchanan' for the breeder, another 'Jack Drake' for the nurseryman who propagated it. Both are low-growing, more compact plants than *D. cantabrica*, some 6–8 in. high, but becoming wider as they age. Flowers are carried on stems a few inches taller than the plant and are much more red in tone than purple. Altogether quite desirable little heath-like plants which will be more widely grown as they become available and better known. A well-drained site in a rock garden is indicated, as is temporary protection if the winter should be unusually cold without snow.

DÁPHNE cneórum (IV), the Garland Flower, native in the mountains of central Europe and apparently indifferent to the presence of calcium in the soil since it grows equally well in either calcareous or acid soils. Growing to about 1 ft. in height, it may in time reach 3–4 ft. in width, especially if annually topdressed with compost or a mixture of coarse sand or Perlite and peat. In late April and May the plant is covered with highly fragrant heads of pink flowers; some variation in color can be found in different clones. One of these is 'Eximia', which forms long trailing stems and has large, deep rose-pink flowers. White forms exist but are rare and more difficult to keep in good health.

DRÝAS octopétala (II), the Mountain Avens, is an Arctic-Alpine species of great value for rock gardens, where it will slowly creep over rocks, covering them with its mats of small evergreen, crenated, oblong leaves, and in spring producing the large white flowers on stems about 3 in. high. Later these become heads of silky-plumed seeds, like a *Pulsatilla* or some species of *Clematis*, thus giving a second season of ornament in the garden. It also makes a good cover for small bulbs such as the *Crocus* species and others. *D. drummóndii*, found chiefly in Canada and rarely in the U.S.A., has smaller yellow flowers not opening so widely but can be used in the same way. The hybrid between the two species is named *D.* ×

suendermánnii; its flowers are at first yellow turning or fading to white. Height in flower 6 in. or less.

EMPÉTRUM *nígrum* (II), the Crowberry, is a circumpolar, heathlike shrub 6–9 in. high with evergreen foliage and inconspicuous flowers, the two sexes usually borne on different plants; fruits a small black berry. Easily propagated by cuttings or layers, they can be used as groundcover plants in the same way as the heaths (*Erica* spp.).

EPIGÁEA *répens* (II), the Mayflower or Trailing Arbutus, is a well-known native of the eastern U.S.A., where it grows in acid soils often in pine woods, covering the ground with mats of its leathery, oblong ever-green leaves and producing the sweetly scented, tubular, pale pink or white flowers at the ends of the shoots in April. To be propagated by layers, or seeds if obtained fresh and sown as soon as ripe. Even Donald Wyman says "Very difficult to transplant, it needs specific growing condi-tions in which to thrive." Our dry summers add to the difficulties of growing it here. The only other species in the genus is *E. asiática* (V) from Japan, with deeper pink flowers; The hybrid between the two has been named *E.* × *intertéxta.*

ÉRICA and CALLÚNA. ERICA constitutes the largest single genus of heaths, but since they are so closely allied and require similar cultural conditions CALLÚNA and BRUCKENTHÁLIA are included here; DABOÉCIA has already been discussed. By making a heather garden it is possible to have color either of flowers or foliage throughout the year, with a minimum amount of maintenance, so if the soil and climatic conditions are favorable there is much to recommend such a planting. All need full sun, excellent drainage, and a light, slightly acid soil with peat, compost or leafmold incorporated in it. It cannot be too strongly stressed that they are community plants, happiest and looking best when planted in groups of one kind. Obtain young plants two years old, set them 1–2 ft. apart depending upon the habit of the particular variety, letting their inter-mingling foliage create a protective mat for the fine fibrous root systems. It is wise to leave ample space between groups of different kinds so that a strong-growing variety does not smother its neighbor. The first year that a planting is being established it will probably require generous watering throughout the summer, but heathers normally do not require heavy summer watering.

We will deal with the species alphabetically, starting with ERICA *cárnea.* See *E. herbácea. E. ciliáris* (VII), the Dorset Heath, from the county in England where it is common, or the Fringed Heath. Height about 12–15 in.; flowers in the type rose-pink, borne in upright racemes in summer, but varying from rose-red to white ('Stoborough'). 'Mrs. C. H. Gill' is almost crimson. Leaves are formed in whorls of three, thus distinguishing it from the rather similar but hardier *E. tétralix,* in which they are in fours. Flowering season, July to October. *E. cínerea* (V), the European Bell Heather, has probably produced more varieties (clones) than any other species of *Erica*. More than 100 are now known, differing in habit of growth (from 4–18 in.), foliage or flower color. They should be seen in bloom at some specialist nursery in July or August before making a selection. The color range is from white through bicolored ('Eden Valley') to rose-pink ('Cevennes' and 'Knap Hill Pink'), to purple ('Colligan Bridge' and 'P. S. Patrick') and bright ruby red ('Atrorubens' and 'Coccinea'). Those with colored foliage include 'Golden Drop' and 'Golden Hue'; these are more yellow in the summer but bronze or copper during the winter. Any necessary pruning should be done immediately after flowering, particularly of the taller-growing kinds such as 'Colligan Bridge'. Topdressing with a peat/sand mixture should be done in the spring when growth commences. *E.* × *darleyénsis* (VI) (*E. herbácea* × *E. erigéna*) although a natural hybrid, must be included in our list here. Becoming a larger plant than the former, up to about 20 in. in height and as much or even more in width, it may start to show its earliest flowers in November or December and continue until the following March or April, thus overlapping the flowering periods of both its parents. In the original hybrid these are lilac-pink in color, but later forms such as 'George Rendall' and 'Arthur Johnson' have deeper-toned flowers and a more compact habit, so are to be preferred.

 E. herbácea (E. cárnea) (V). Winter Heath. Native to the mountains of central and southeastern Europe, this is consequently the hardiest of the ericas and also tolerates or perhaps appreciates a calcareous soil. The plants form cushions or mats from which the flowers spikes arise or extend from November ('Eileen Porter') to April ('Loughrigg' and 'Vivellii'). They are invaluable plants for providing color in the garden at that dull season of the year, but need a fairly sunny site to flower well and

Erica herbacea (carnea) used as edging along a small stream. Photo by Don Normark.

keep their compact habit. Height in bloom, about 9 in. Other available clones are 'Springwood White', the best for white flowers, but with a more trailing habit then most; 'King George', deep rose, 'Praecox Rubra', 'Ruby Glow', and 'Sherwoodii', all varying shades of rosy red. They should be planted in groups of at least three plants of each kind to achieve the best effect. They can also be used as a edging along a border, preferably of one kind only.

E. *tetrálix* (III), the Cross-leaved Heath, also native to northern and western Europe like E. *ciliaris* but hardier than that species and distinguished from it by the leaves which are arranged four in a whorl instead of three, prefers damp places and acid soils, even growing under Scots Pines in the wild state. Height about 12–15 in. as a rule. The young shoots and leaves are distinctly downy and the latter edged with glandular hairs. Flowering time, from June to fall. The flowers are carried in a tight cluster at the ends of the shoots, pink in the typical form but white in 'Alba Mollis', much darker rose in 'Con Underwood'. 'George Fraser' and 'Hookstone Pink' and other clones which sometimes may be found in nurseries.

E. *vágans*, the Cornish Heath, (VI), native to western Europe as well as the county of Cornwall in England, is a reliable free-flowering species for late summer, from July to September, generally fairly compact in habit, especially if regularly lightly pruned in spring when growth is commencing. Some kinds such as 'St. Keverne' (deep pink) and 'Lyonesse' (white) form tighter and denser plants than others such as 'Birch Glow' which are taller (to 18 ins.) and more open with age. 'Mrs D. F. Maxwell' is a rich pink and one of the best both for color and habit of growth. E. × *watsónii* (VI), a natural hybrid between E. *ciliaris* and E. *tetralix*, is found wherever the two species grow together, usually possessing the rather elongated corolla of the former, but much shorter inflorescences and leaves in whorls of four as well as greater hardiness of the latter. 'Dawn' is probably the best known of these hybrids, with pink flowers over a long period in summer and early fall and a dense, bushy habit of growth. Others, equally valuable, are 'Gwen' and 'H. Maxwell'. Height, about 12 ins.

CALLÚNA *vulgáris* (IV), the Ling or Heather, of European and western Asian origin but also now naturalized in some New England states. In Scotland, northern England and Ireland thousands of acres of moorland may be covered by this one plant, turning them purple in August when they flower. *Calluna* is distinguished from *Erica* most obviously by possessing a colored calyx longer than the corolla which persists after flowering, making them of some value for dried material for winter decoration. Forms of this variable plant are indeed numerous. Bean's *Trees and Shrubs*, 8th ed. (1970) lists 25; a recent list from a specialist nursery has 34; Wyman's *Encyclopedia* (1971) lists 14 which he considers "among the best." Of single white forms there are 'Mair's Variety', 'Serlei' and 'Silver Spire'; double whites are rarer, but 'Kinlochruel' is listed; single purple to lilac are, 'David Eason', 'Silver Knight', 'Elegantissima'; double pink to lilac forms are more plentiful now, with the tall 'H. E. Beale' and 'Peter Sparkes', and dwarfer 'County Wicklow' and 'J. H. Hamilton'. Deepest red flowers are to be found in 'Alportii', 'Barnett Anley' and 'Darkness'. For colored foliage effects in winter we have 'Cuprea', 'Golden Feather', 'Robert Chapman' and 'Red Haze', many more than were available a few years ago. Very dwarf forms are 'Minima', 'Mullion' and 'Sister Anne'.

The callunas are quite drought resistant when once established and may be grown on any dry sunny bank of light, well-drained soil. To get the best results with both callunas and ericas they should be planted out from pots when small and not yet root-bound; they resent disturbance of their root systems and an old plant does not like to be moved. They need to be pruned annually each spring to prevent their becoming leggy, each flowering branch cut back to its base. There can be a high mortality rate among them if severely pruned late in the year.

BRUCKENTHÁLIA spiculifólia (V) is a dwarf shrub from southeastern Europe and western Asia, the sole representative of its genus, growing there in alpine pastures in the mountains. It is very closely related botanically to Erica and distinguished from it only by slight characters of the flowers. Growing 6–8 in. high, it can be used in the same manner as the smaller ericas, planted in groups of five or more plants. The flowers, which are pale pink, are borne in tight clusters at the top of the stems in May and June, a period when there are not many other heathers in bloom, so it can fill a gap in their flowering seasons.

ERINÁCEA ánthyllis (E. púngens) (VI). Hedgehog Broom. A spiny dwarf, compact shrub 18 in. high but more in width, from Spain and north Africa, leafless, since the stems take the place of the leaves in photosynthesis, as with some other spiny members of the Genista genus. The flowers, produced in May towards the end of the branchlets, are pale blue, a rare color in this family; each is surrounded by a large inflated calyx. Seeds seem to be rarely produced by our local plants but they can be propagated by cuttings taken in late summer. A site on top of a sunny wall or bank facing south is appropriate. Like the Bruckenthalia, this is the sole known representative of its genus.

ERIÓGONUM. A large genus of herbaceous or semiwoody plants, mostly native to the western states and growing in mountain habitats or under semidesert conditions. A few have been tried and sometimes successfully cultivated in gardens around Puget Sound, planted on sunny banks or among rocks facing west or south. E. umbellátum (V–VI) is one of the most widely distributed in nature, from British Columbia to California, then east to the Rocky Mountains. A mat-forming plant up to 18 or 24 in. in diameter, with oval spathulate leaves usually green above but woolly beneath, its flowers are carried in simple or compound umbels on stems from 6–15 ins. tall in May to June, depending upon their location and elevation. They may be either white to cream or yellow according to their particular variety; they are also quite ornamental in the fruiting stage later in the year. In the garden they may be planted on well-drained slopes in a sandy or gravelly soil, facing south or west. Propagation is relatively easy by means of collected seeds from wild plants.

EUÓNYMUS fórtunei var. *rádicans* (V). Trailing Euonymus; Winter Creeper. Native of Japan, this is a smaller creeping edition of the larger Chinese *E. fortunei,* most useful for covering the ground quickly, especially in shady places, where it is preferable to most types of ivies. It will also climb up a wall or tree trunk if given the opportunity. Propagation is easy by means of rooted layers. In the miniature form 'Kewensis' the leaves are only ⅜–½ in. long, of a light green color but with the veins much paler. This will also climb over a stump or other support if available; it can be formed into a border edging if desired, with little maintenance needed except pruning back about once a year. Also of Japanese origin.

EURYOPS. This is a genus of African shrubs belonging to the Compositae (Daisy) family, Only one is in cultivation here so far as known. This is *E. ácraeus* (VII–VIII), native to the Drakensberg mountains of Natal and Basutoland at nearly 10,000 ft. elevation, so it should be fairly hardy with us given a sunny situation and a well-drained soil, such as on top of a rock wall facing south or west. Height, 2–3 ft. The leaves are silver-gray, linear, about 1 in. long, condensed towards the ends of the branches. The flower heads, which open in May, are bright yellow and very conspicuous against the light gray foliage. Some protection during extended cold weather may be advisable, especially during the plant's early years.

FORSÝTHIA. Here we have two dwarf clones which can be used as groundcovers, namely *F. viridíssima* 'Bronxensis' and the hybrid 'Arnold Dwarf'. Both are hardy in Zone V. The former was raised from Japanese seeds at the Boyce Thompson Arboretum, Yonkers, NY, in 1928, attains only 12 in. in height but flowers quite freely in March and early April. The flowers are primrose yellow. Propagate by cuttings in summer when firm enough. The latter was raised at the Arnold Arboretum in the 1940s from a cross between *F. × intermédia* and *F. japónica,* grows 2–3 ft. tall and flowers only sparsely; with greenish yellow flowers. It is, however, more useful as a groundcover than the first, since the branches root wherever they touch the ground and a few plants will soon cover the space between them. Both of course are leafless in winter, so of less value to us in the Pacific Northwest where we can grow many evergreen ground covers.

A distinctive plant in this latter category is *GÁLAX urceoláta (G. aphýlla)* (III), native to shady woods in the southeastern U.S.A. and particularly valuable for its shining almost orbicular leaves, 2–3 ins. across and toothed all around the margin. The small white flowers are carried on slender stalks a foot or so high, appearing in June or July. These are not especially showy, so the chief value of the plant lies in its handsome foliage. Propagate by division in spring.

The genus *GAULTHÉRIA* includes several excellent groundcovers, in addition to the species mentioned elsewhere in this book. First among them would be Checkerberry or Wintergreen, *G. procúmbens* (III), native to a wide area of the eastern U.S.A. and Canada. This is a stoloniferous plant no more than 6 in. high, enjoying woodland conditions and an acid soil, where it will cover the ground with its shining ovate leaves held at the top of the stems and largely concealing the the small bell-shaped flowers produced from the upper leaf axils. These are followed in the fall by the bright red fruits with a flavor of wintergreen.

Several gaultherias in this category have white fruits; all are Asiatic in origin. One is *G. miqueliána* from Japan (V), which forms a 12 in. high shrublet with oval, leathery leaves about 1 in. long, globose white flowers in June, followed by the pearly white fruits in September–October. *G. cuneáta* (VI) is of about the same height and also spreads by means of underground stems (stolons) if in a suitable light soil. The leaves, however are quite different, being much narrower, wedge shaped at both ends and finely toothed. The flowers are carried in auxillary racemes at the ends of the old shoots and are white and urn shaped; the fruits ripen in September, are oblong, about ⅜ in. long, white flushed pink. Native to western China and introduced by E. H. Wilson in 1909. A third, less common species, from Taiwan, is *G. itoána (G. merrilliána)* (VI), also attaining about 8 in. in height but more in width as it ages. It is perhaps best described as a miniature edition of the last, with leaves of the same shape but only ⅜ in. long and half that in width; they are set much more closely together on the stems which gives the plant a different aspect, more like some heath. Fruits are also white, but smaller than the others described. All can be propagated most easily by means of cuttings taken in late summer or early fall and kept in a cold frame or cool greenhouse over winter. Seed propagation, if the seeds are fresh, will give more plants. *G. nummularioídes* (VII) is a mat-forming species from the Himalayas and western China. The trailing shoots are brown and covered with bristles; the leaves are heart shaped, the largest at the base of the stems about ¾ in. long, but tapering to about half that size towards the tip—an unusual feature. The flowers are produced in August on the underside of the shoots, so are not easily seen. Fruits, if produced, are blue-black. 'Minuta' (VI) is a form totally appressed to the ground, the leaves ovate-elliptic, ¼–⅜ in. long, tapering very slightly towards the tip. This is of Chinese origin and hardier than the Himalayan plant. Both should be grown in shady places in rock gardens.

GAYLUSSÁCIA brachycéra (V), the Box Huckleberry, is a rare plant both in the wild where it is found in a few locations from Pennsylvania to Kentucky, and in gardens, except those of a few collectors who have learned how to treat and cherish it. Growing up to 18 in. in height and spreading by means of underground stems, it can eventually cover a considerable area. The evergreen, ovate leaves are leathery, toothed, up to 1 in. long and about half as wide. The cylindrical white flowers are borne in

The Chinese *Gaultheria
cuneata* in fruit in late
September. Photo by
Brian Mulligan.

The Japanese *Gaultheria
miqueliana* in fruit in late
September. Photo by
Brian Mulligan.

The Checkerberry or
Partridgeberry
(*Gaultheria procumbens*)
in flower. Photo by Don
Normark.

short racemes near the ends of the shoots in May and June. The fruits, if produced, are blue, like those of some species of *Vaccinium,* to which genus *Gaylussacia* is closely allied. It can be propagated by cuttings, division or by seeds, if obtainable. In the garden it should be planted with other ericaceous plants of similar size and requirements, namely partial shade and an acid, sandy soil.

GENÍSTA. Several species of this European or Mediterranean genus are useful for sunny banks on well-drained sites. G. *lýdia* (V), from southeastern Europe and western Turkey, is one of the most adaptable, making a low tangled bush some 24 in. high, but wider in a few years, then producing quantities of bright yellow flowers on short spurs in late May and early June. Usually propagated by cuttings. G. *pilósa* (V) has been longer in cultivation, being native over a large part of Europe from southern Scandinavia to the Balkan Peninsula. It forms a mat of interlacing branches, which in May are covered with the numerous golden flowers. An excellent small shrub for the rock garden, very similar in habit to *Cytisus decumbens.* G. *sagittális* (V) is slightly taller than the last, rising to about 9 in. and different in appearance owing to its flattened stems which largely take the place of leaves in their functions. The yellow flowers are borne in upright terminal clusters in June, somewhat later than most of the others. G. *delphinénsis* (V) is a smaller edition of G. *sagittalis* from the Pyrenees mountains in southern France. It is best suited to a scree or trough.

HEBE. We have already dealt with a number of these New Zealand shrubs in the chapter on Broad-leaved Evergreen Shrubs, but there are some which can be included amongst the Groundcovers. H. *buchanánii* (VII) grows on rock outcrops of the drier mountains of the South Island, up to about 12 in. height. The stems are dark, the stalkless leaves thickish, concave and glaucous, about ¼ in. long. Clusters of white flowers appear at the ends of the shoots in midsummer. An even smaller form is 'Minor', appropriate for growing in a stone trough. H. *decúmbens* (VI) from the same region, may be prostrate or grow up to 2–3 ft. in height. The branches are almost black, the leaves rather obovate, green with a red margin, flat. Donald Wyman reports it as "the only one of this genus capable of withstanding the winters of the northern U.S.A." If not now in cultivation it should be reintroduced and given further trial in various regions. H. *héctoris* (VI) may be taken as a typical example of the so-called "whipcord" hebes, a term which clearly describes the effect of the yellow-green scalelike leaves closely set and tightly held against the stems. These plants range from about 12–20 in. in height. The white flowers may not appear for some years until the plants are fully mature; when they do they are in clusters at the ends of the branches. H. *lycopódioides* and H. *tetrágona* are other species in the same group. They are certainly the hardiest of the hebes but not the most ornamental. An attractive low-growing one is H. *pimeleoídes,* (VII) native to the South Island in dry places and only attaining some 9–12 in. in height, making it very suitable for a rock garden or as an edging to a border. The young branches are purplish, the leaves acutish, glaucous, closely set in four rows. The flowers appear in summer, borne in short spikes, and are violet-blue. 'Carl Teschner' is a hybrid of *H. pimeleoides* but less hardy. *H. pinguifólia* 'Pagei' (VII) is a selected clone of this species, larger in all respects than the last, the leaves wider and more glaucous, the flowers opening in May (and sometimes again in late summer), white, in compact clusters. So with these various kinds the dwarf hebes have a good deal to offer, although it would be wise to propagate them regularly by means of cuttings in case of severe cold weather cutting them down or killing them.

HÉDERA hélix forms (VII). Many ivies make first-class groundcovers but some are apt to grow too fast and cover the ground too densely to be safely introduced into a small garden, particularly the larger-leaved kinds. 'Deltoidea', the Shield or Sweetheart Ivy could be included in the first category and should be avoided, and the Irish Ivy, 'Hibernica', in the second along with the various forms of *H. cólchica*, the Persian Ivy, all of which have large leaves. Better selections are 'Buttercup' with its golden yellow young leaves; 'Green Feather', which will form a dense mass of interweaving shoots covered with tiny trilobed leaves no more than an inch long; 'Ivalace', somewhat taller, to 15 in., the leaves larger, glossy on the upperside, undulated along the margin as well as lobed. 'Baltica', about 6 in. high, with its lighter-colored leaf veins, is also to be recommended, and is hardier than most. Propagation of most ivies is extremely easy, either by means of rooted portions of the shoots (layers) or by cuttings in late summer or fall.

HELIÁNTHEMUM (VII) The sun roses are useful and attractive small evergreen shrubs for sunny places, hailing mostly from southern Europe but extending as far north as the British Isles and east into western Asia. *H. alpéstre* is probably the smallest of the genus, being only about 3 in. high even in flower, with leaves green on both sides; in *H. cánum* they are gray beneath. Flowers of both are yellow, about ½ in. across. The most widespread species is *H. nummulárium*, which may be 1 ft. in height but twice that in width; the leaves up to 1 in. in length, gray-hairy beneath, the flowers yellow, about 1 in. wide, each opening successively for a day or less, as with other members of this group, in May and June.

A large number of hybrids were bred in Scotland and England in the early part of this century, with flowers varying in color from bright red through flame to orange, yellow, pink and white. Some of these are named after Scottish mountains ('Ben More', 'Ben Nevis'), others after places where they were raised ('Wisley Primrose', 'St. John's College Yellow'). With double flowers are 'Cerise Queen' (rose pink), 'Jubilee' (yellow), and 'Mrs C. W. Earle', scarlet with the base of the petals yellow. If any of these are found in cultivation they should be propagated by means of cuttings in late summer when the new shoots are firm.

HELICHRÝSUM *bellidioídes* (VII), the Everlasting Daisy of New Zealand, is a mat-forming plant well suited to rock gardens and especially for covering small bulbs such as the *Crocus, Narcissus, Cyclamen* and others flowering in spring. The small leaves are white beneath; the flowering stems about 3 in. high, clothed with similar leaves; the flower heads white, about ¾ in. across, usually produced quite freely on established plants. It would be advisable to take a few cuttings annually each summer or fall to avoid losing the plant in cold winters. A covering of snow is more to its liking than cold winds combined with freezing conditions.

HYPÉRICUM. This is a large genus containing both herbaceous and shrubby species: however only a few can be utilized as groundcovers, but one is particularly important and frequently grown in our area. This is *H. calycínum* (VII), the Rose-of-Sharon or Aaron's Beard, native to southeastern Europe and western Asia, and soon forming a dense mat on any sunny bank or highway roadside. Often losing most of its leaves during winter, it soon replaces them in spring and in summer produces its bright golden flowers at the ends of foot-high stems over a long period. Individually these are about 3 in. across, so a large planting can be very showy and effective. Propagation by division in spring is easy.

H. cerástioides (VII) is a mat-forming species from the same regions possessing very hairy stems and leaves, which are borne in opposite pairs like all species of *Hypericum* but are only about ½ in. long, oval and stalkless. The bright yellow flowers appear at the ends of the shoots in May, each 1 in. or more in diameter. An excellent plant for a wall or bank in the sunshine, best propagated by seeds, although cuttings are possible. It has also been known, incorrectly, as *H. rhodópeum*. A third attractive small

Hypericum calycinum, the Rose of Sharon, used as a groundcover between sidewalk and street. Ivy on the wall in the rear. Photo by Don Normark.

species from the same parts of the world is *H. olýmpicum,* (VII) rather more woody at the base than the last, the stems rising 9–12 in. high, bearing also rich yellow flowers 1½–2 in. across. It is reported to be a variable plant both in its growth habit and the size of the flowers, so good forms should be sought out and propagated by cuttings. Seeds, however, are the usual method. The form 'Citrinum' has lemon yellow flowers.

One species native to North Carolina and Georgia must be mentioned, and that is *H. búckleyi* (VI), a very small shrub no more than 12 in. in height and sometimes less. Both leaves and flowers are reduced in size, the latter 1 in. or less in width, appearing in June. It is a plant for a cool site in a rock garden where it will not be overgrown by more vigorous competitors.

IBERIS. The candytufts contain several species suitable for rock gardens in warmer areas, but one is especially valuable and frequently used as a groundcover in drier places, including beneath trees so long as the shade is not too dense. This is *I. sempervírens* (VI), native also to southern Europe and western Asia like several of the hypericums just described. The plants attain a height of 12 in. or so but spread much wider, to 3–4 ft. in a few years. The leaves are narrow, linear-lanceolate, bunched towards the end of the shoots, evergreen as the specific name indicates. The pure white flowers appear in spring, from March onwards depending upon the season, in condensed racemes which lengthen later. A large plant or group of them can be very showy at that time. After flowering, the plants should be cut over to restrain their growth, unless this is desired to make an extensive cover. No seeds are produced, so propagation must be by means of cuttings.

JASMÍNUM. Most of the jasmines are climbing plants, or will become so if given some support. *J. párkeri* (VII), from the northwestern Himalayas, is an exception to that general rule, being only a dwarf shrub up to about 12 in. in height, spreading over the surrounding ground in all directions if permitted to do so. The stems are green, grooved or ridged, the leaves composed of either three or five leaflets, the whole no more than ¾ in. long, including the stalk. The ½ in. wide, yellow flowers appear in June, like miniatures of the winter jasmine, *J. nudiflórum.* A rock garden would be a suitable place for this little shrub, preferably where it will receive sufficient sunshine to flower well. Propagate by cuttings in late summer.

JUNÍPERUS. In this large and varied genus of both trees and shrubs there are several which are first-class groundcovers, notably some forms of *J. communis,* all of *J. horizontalis, J. procumbens, J. conferta,* and a few other particular cultivars or varieties.

Most forms of the Chinese Juniper are either trees or eventually large shrubs, but *J. chinénsis* 'San Jose' (IV) is low qrowing, up to about 30 in. but much wider, in color sage green, with a mixture of juvenile and adult (scalelike) foliage, as is common in most forms of *J. chinensis.* It was introduced by the W. B. Clarke Nursery of San Jose, California, in 1935, and is popular in that state as well as elsewhere.

J. cómmunis (II) is the common European Juniper, although the alpine form is found in mountains throughout the Northern Hemisphere, including the Cascades and Olympic ranges, where it forms slowly spreading cushions 12–15 in. high on or among rocks, including calcareous strata. This is var. *montána* (also known by the names of *nána* and *saxátilis*). The leaves are arranged in whorls of three, are boat shaped, thick, spiny pointed, with a broad, white band of stomata on each side of the main vein on the upper surface which is very conspicuous on wild plants. In the garden they should be placed on a bank or among rocks in full sun at an early age since they object to being moved later when established. Owing to their slow growth they seldom require any pruning and seem to be resistant to the leaf and stem disease which can fatally attack forms of the Savin Juniper (*J. sabina*) and some other species. The junipers are all dioecious, so that individual plants are either male or female. If the berries are desired then it will be advisable to plant individuals of both sexes to ensure them. They can be propagated by cuttings taken in late summer or early fall, or even later in winter, although they will probably be slow in rooting. 'Hornibrookii' is a desirable prostrate form of *J. communis*, found in Co. Galway in western Ireland. Var. *jáckii* is a very distinct trailing type from the Siskiyou Mtns. of S. Oregon and N. California.

J. conférta (*J. litorális*) (V), the prostrate Shore Juniper of Japan, is particularly well adapted for seaside planting in view of its native habitat, but can also be well used on banks or even roadsides well inland. The leaves are greener and less noticeably glaucous than those of *J. communis* var. *montana*, with only one broad line of stomata instead of two. The leaves are sharply pointed. 'Emerald Sea', introduced by the U.S.D.A. through Dr. John Creech's collection in Japan, and 'Blue Pacific' are two recent clones of this species.

The Creeping Juniper, *J. horizontális* (II), is found wild over a large part of the North American continent, from southeastern Alaska and Colorado in the west, to Maine in the east. It is completely prostrate in habit and therefore excellent for covering banks in dry situations, like the Kinnikinnick, *Arctostaphylos uva-ursi*, with which it will compete favorably, providing a gray covering as opposed to the green foliage of the latter. 'Bar Harbor', from the coast of Maine, is compact, gray-green in summer. 'Douglasii', the Waukegan Juniper, is a clone from sand dunes in Illinois, the young foliage gray-green, but turning purplish in fall and winter. 'Plumosa', the Andorra Juniper, behaves similarly as to coloring but is taller, to about 18 in. 'Emerson' ('Black Hills Creeper'), from South Dakota, is bluish in general effect, very slow growing, quite prostrate. 'Wiltonii', or 'Blue Rug', from the island of Vinal Haven off the coast of Maine, is one of the bluest forms in foliage color throughout the year.

J. procúmbens (V), native to Japan and introduced from there to Europe about 1844, is similar to *J. communis* var. *montana* in habit, making a

Juniperus horizontalis, an excellent groundcover for dry banks. Photo by Don Normark.

mound rather than a mat or carpet in time, and like it quite glaucous gray in its effect in the landscape. It is an admirable plant for a sunny rock garden, in well-drained soil. It can be expected in time to reach 7–8 ft. in diameter, 10–25 in. in height. The leaves have two glaucous bands on the upper surface with a green midrib and margins; on the underside there are two white streaks near the base which are a good distinguishing feature for this species. The ends of the branches all turn upwards. *J. procumbens* 'Nana' is a dwarf form of the same species, very compact.

J. sabína (IV), the Savin Juniper from Europe, has leaves of two kinds, awl shaped in the juvenile, scalelike in the adult state, as does *J. chinensis.* This plant has a strong, pungent odor when the foliage is crushed. Like *J. communis* there are both upright and bushy forms as well as prostrate kinds. The best known because it is so commonly planted in all kinds of situations, both in cities and the suburbs, is "Tamariscifolia', which grows into a dark green cushion several feet across, 15–20 in. high. Owing to its suceptibility to the juniper disease (*Phomopsis*), which begins by killing parts of branches, then finally the entire plant, it is advisable to avoid planting this species in the future. Clones raised from Russian seeds in 1934 and reputed to be resistant to the disease are 'Arcadia', grass green in color, growing to about 24 in. tall; 'Broadmoor', a male form, becoming larger than 'Arcadia' in time, bright green in coloring; 'Buffalo', a female plant, spreading in habit and not as tall as the others; 'Skandia', a low-growing form having somewhat glaucous foliage which gives a gray effect to the plant.

J. squamáta (IV), native to the Himalayas and western China, is a shrub which has produced several distinct forms such as 'Meyeri' and 'Loderi' with which we are not here concerned. However, an excellent dwarf type is now available named 'Blue Star', a mutation from 'Meyeri' which was observed in a Dutch nursery in about 1950. This is a slow-growing, dense little shrub with vivid blue-gray foliage very noticeable in the landscape. It associates comfortably with *J. communis* var. *montana* on a sunny bank or wall, but not perhaps with the greener clones of *J. sabina*. Height probably about 15 in.

KÁLMIA *polifólia* (II), the Swamp Laurel, is a rather straggling inhabitant of boggy areas throughout North America, on both the east and west sides of the continent and up into Alaska and the Yukon. The flowers are a bright rose, quite pretty when seen in the wild state, but fugitive and not making any great display in a garden. The variety *microphýlla*, however, is much more attractive and useful to us for its carpeting propensities, growing only 6–8 in. tall and forming quite a close mat of its upright stems with their small glossy leaves. In too much shade it will not flower well.

KALMIÓPSIS *leachiána* (VI), the sole representative of its genus anywhere in the world, is found only in the counties of Curry and Douglas in southwestern Oregon, where it is to be seen growing on rocky slopes or cliffs in the mountains, often in extremely hot and dry situations. Here it forms large clumps or mats from 9–15 in. in height, but a yard or more across in old plants. Flowers appear towards the end of April and in early May, of some shade of pink, either bright or pale; they are shallowly bowl shaped and do not possess the pouches seen in all species of *Kalmia*, which retain the stamens until ripe. The plants from Curry County, found originally by Mr. and Mrs. John Leach, are of more upright habit and have longer inflorescences generally of a brighter color than those from the Umpqua River valley, discovered later. In the garden this charming little shrub proves rather difficult to maintain and should be propagated regularly by seeds or cuttings. A site on the upper slopes of a rock garden facing south or west, in well-drained soil, is appropriate.

LEIOPHÝLLUM *buxifólium* (V), the Box Sandmyrtle, native in the eastern U.S.A. from New Jersey southwards, in various habitats from sand dunes to mountain tops and varying accordingly in its local form, is a very pleasing small shrub usually 18–30 in. in height, with reddish brown stems, opposite or alternate oblong or spoon-shaped leaves about ¼ in. long, glossy on the upper sides. Clusters of tiny white flowers almost hide a healthy plant in May. The buds are rose-pink, the petals pure white when open, so that it is really most attractive before the buds burst. Being a member of the Ericaceae it needs a light, sandy, acid soil and can be associated with some of the summer or winter-flowering heathers. The variety *prostrátum* is the mountain plant from the Appalachians, distinguished by its glandular flower stalks and opposite leaves; in the typical species they are alternate. To be propagated by seeds or cuttings, the latter taken in late summer.

The Sandmyrtle
(*Leiophyllum buxifolium*)
in bloom. Photo by Don
Normark.

LEPTOSPÉRMUM. A genus of shrubs or small trees, native chiefly to Australasia and few of which are hardy in the Puget Sound region, except for one or perhaps two prostrate kinds. The hardiest of these is *L. humifúsum* (VII), introduced from the mountains of Tasmania by H. F. Comber in 1930. This is capable of forming a mat or hummock no more than 6 in. high of radiating stems and branches overlapping on another, if given a site where it can creep over a bank or rock and obtain a fair amount of sunshine. The leaves are borne alternately on the stems, are elliptical to obovate, about ½ in. in length, dark green, with a blunt tip; The white flowers are produced singly, in May, each about ½ in. across. It can tolerate one cold winter, but two in succession are likely to cause its demise, unfortunately, so some cuttings should be taken annually as a precaution. The second prostrate species is *L. scopárium* 'Prostratum', (VIII), definitely less hardy than the preceding, originally from New Zealand, where it is known (the type species) as the Manuka, or New Zealand Tea Tree, since early settlers made tea from its leaves. The flowers of this may be pink or white, since different clones exist; the leaves have a sharp point which readily distinguishes them from *L. humifusum*.

LINNÁEA boreális var. *longiflóra* (II) is our native Twin-flower, a circumpolar species which extends as far south as Arizona and New Mexico in the Rocky Mountains and is frequently found creeping over the ground and forming a mat in wooded sites in the Cascades and Olympic mountains of Washington state. In the garden it is best to provide it with an open space where it can be allowed to wander freely, or have only other small shrubs to contend with, such as the *Cassiope* species or hybrids, the smallest rhododendrons, e.g., *R. keleticum, R. camtschaticum* or *R. forrestii.* The pale pink, fragrant, tubular, paired flowers appear in May; they are most effective when seen en masse as along the edge of a trail in the wild state.

LITHOSPÉRMUM diffúsum (Lithodóra diffúsa) (VII), is well known especially to rock gardeners in its clone 'Heavenly Blue', which can form dense hummocks or mats of semiprostrate, evergreen, narrow foliage on hairy shoots, illuminated in May and June and often again in late summer by the brilliant blue flowers. If given some natural support such as an adjacent shrub, the straggling shoots will often climb up on to it for 12–18 in. and decorate it unexpectedly. This plant is easily propagated by cuttings in late summer. A more recent clone is 'Grace Ward', said to have larger flowers than 'Heavenly Blue' and less trailng habit. The species is native to southwestern Europe, in France and Spain.

MITCHÉLLA répens (III). The Partridge-berry of the eastern U.S.A. and Canada. A more aggressive groundcover than *Linnaea,* forming a closely woven mat of slender trailing branches bearing pairs of heart-shaped leaves from ¾–1 in. apart. These are about ½ in. long with the main vein lighter in color than the blade of the leaf. The four-petalled, white, fragrant flowers open in June, borne in pairs at the ends of the shoots. In nature they will be followed by bright red fruits, but this is by no means the case in many local gardens, unfortunately. Perhaps it is a matter of pollination by another clone? Or perhaps we do not have the right insect to perform the act?

PACHYSÁNDRA terminális, the Japanese Spurge, (V), is one of the most useful, subshrubby evergreen groundcovers, especially for planting in the shade. The deep green, leathery, toothed leaves, from 2–4 in. long, are clustered on the stems to form a rosette pattern. The plant spreads rapidly by underground runners, to form a carpet of these rosettes. Even in the densest shade is never more than 12 in. high, and in partial shade half that height. The short spikes of whitish flowers are carried at the ends of the shoots in early May. The fruits, if produced, are white, but are not likely to appear unless two different clones are growing together. Propagation by division of the plants in spring is extremely easy.

P. procúmbens (IV), the Alleghany Spurge, is herbaceous in habit, about 12 in. tall, and consequently not so useful as a groundcover as the Japanese species. The flower spikes appear in spring before the new leaves develop.

PARAHÉBE. This is a small genus of dwarf subshrubs from New Zealand, several members of which are now in cultivation. Formerly they were included in the polymorphic genus *Veronica,* but have now been extracted from it by New Zealand botanists. *P. catarráctae* (VII) is the largest, growing to 12 in. or so in height, the ovate or lanceolate, toothed leaves about 1 in. long and half as wide. The flowers are borne in short racemes at the ends of the new shoots in summer; they are white, streaked with purple lines on the petals. *P. lyállii,* from the South Island of New Zealand, is a smaller edition of the former, prostrate in habit. Coming from mountainous habitats it can be expected to be somewhat hardier. *P. decóra,* a shingle or scree plant in the wild state, is prostrate and creeping in habit, possessing extremely small leaves no more than ⅛ in. long. The racemes of white or pale bluish flowers may be up to 8 in. in length, held up well above the foliage. *P.* × *bidwíllii* is a natural hybrid between *P. decora* and *P. lyallii,* most resembling the first of these two parents, but with flower stems only 3 in. or so above the mat of foliage. It is excellent for a partly shady spot in the rock garden. All need well-drained soil conditions to thrive.

PAXÍSTIMA (or *PACHÍSTIMA*); the former name is now preferred by most authorities. *P. cánbyi* (V), from the mountains of Virginia, is a neat and attractive little evergreen shrub, growing 10–12 in. in height, the dark green, lanceolate, toothed leaves set close together on brown stems. Minute flowers are borne in the upper leaf axils in May and June, but its chief value is in its use as a low groundcover. In winter months the foliage becomes more bronze in coloring, especially in colder climates. Propagation is quite easy by means of cuttings or layers.

PERNÉTTYA. Some dwarf species are now coming into cultivation, chiefly through the efforts of amateur growers, since they are easily propagated either by seeds or by cuttings. Two of these are *P. leucocárpa* (VII) from the Andes Mountains of Chile and adjacent Argentina, and *P. púmila,* found only in extreme South America (the Magellan region) and on the Falkland Islands. The former is a stoloniferous little shrub, attaining some 9 in. in height; the leaves are lanceolate, about ½ in. long, paler green on the underside than above, only bluntly pointed. The small, bell-shaped, white flowers are produced singly in the leaf axils in June. Since the plants are dioecious, the white or pale pink fruits will be produced only if both sexes are present, or if perhaps a plant of *P. mucronata* nearby might serve the same function.

P. púmila (VII), of which *P. empetrifólia* is a synonym, is lower growing and mat forming, the leaves a brighter green, very closely set along the slender branches, decreasing in size towards the tip of the shoot. Both flowers and fruits are similar to those of *P. leucocarpa* but smaller. As a groundcover for bulbs such as the smaller daffodils, *Crocus,* scillas or *Chionodoxa* species it is excellent. A slightly acid soil is preferred by both these plants, as well as partial shade, especially in the afternoons in summer.

PÉNSTEMON. Several of the native species from the western U.S.A. have considerable value as groundcovers for sunny situations, especially in rock gardens where the drainage is rapid; they will not tolerate wet sites. Taking them alphabetically, we first have *P. cardwéllii* (VI), to be found wild from southern Washington down to southern Oregon, west of the summits of the Cascade range. They form dense little shrubs about 9–10 in. in height; the leaves more or less spoon shaped, finely serrated, and about 1 in. long. The late spring or early summer flowers are carried several inches above the plant in the typical short racemes of this group of penstemons (Section Dasánthera), typically lavender-purple in color, but variations with rose or white ('John Bacher') flowers are to found in specialist nurseries.

P. davidsónii and its variety *menzíesii* (V–VI) are mat-forming plants, and therefore most suitable for the rock garden, or to be placed on the top of a sunny bank where they can trail down it in due time. *P. davidsonii* (V) is found wild from northern Washington down to California. The inch-long leaves are light green, more or less spoon shaped, not toothed. The flowers, in May, are held a few inches above the mat of foliage and are purplish lilac in color, each about 1½ in. long. The sunnier the situation the better they are likely to bloom, as with most penstemons. The variety *menziesii* is smaller in all its parts and the leaves are distinctly toothed. Its range is from southern British Columbia to northern Oregon.

Most frequently cultivated is *P. fruticósus,* widely distributed in the mountains from British Columbia south to central Oregon (east of the Cascade range summits), then east into Montana and Wyoming. It is an amenable and useful plant for local gardens, long lived, free from pests, and in appropriate situations flowering profusely in May each year. The lavender-purple flowers are likewise held up above the foliage, which usually attains 12–15 in. in height, carried on strong woody stems. The leaves are lanceolate, up to 2 in. in length, lightly toothed. 'Charming' has pleasing shell pink flowers. In the variety *scóuleri,* from northeastern Washington and adjacent Idaho and British Columbia, the leaves are linear-lanceolate, no more than ¼ in. wide. Propagation of all the above species is quite easy by means of cuttings in summer or early fall, then planting the resulting individuals the following spring before they become root-bound in their pots.

A very different-looking species is *P. pinifólius* (VI–VII) from Arizona, New Mexico and northern Mexico, but it seems able to cope with our wetter winters in the Puget Sound region if given a well-drained and sunny site, facing south or west. This grows into a small bush about 10–12 in. tall, woody at the base; the leaves are heathlike, ¼–½ in. long; the flowers are carried on stems 4–6 in. above the plant, are bright red, and open in July and August, late for any penstemon, but conspicuous.

PIÉRIS (or *ARCTÉRICA*) *nána.* (I). An extremely hardy, very small member of the Ericaceae family, hailing from northern Japan, and Kamchatka. It forms a compact cushion no more than 6 in. high, spreading slowly by means of underground stems. The leaves are leathery, oblong-ovate, about ½ in. in length, arranged in pairs or threes. The white, urn-shaped flowers appear in April, borne in tight clusters at the ends of the shoots; they are fragrant, no doubt to attract pollinating insects in their native habitat. This is a choice little plant for an acid soil suited to other members of the same family such as the cassiopes and phyllodoces; a shady site is indicated, plus an annual mulch of peat or compost. A second flowering in the fall sometimes occurs.

PIMÉLEA. This is a genus of shrubs from Australasia, some of them alpine plants from New Zealand; they belong to the *Daphne* family, Thymeleáceae, and usually have small, white, tubular flowers which may be followed by berries of various colors. The only one we are concerned with is *P. próstrata* (VII) from various parts of New Zealand, but not alpine in its habitat. Here it forms a tangled mat of interlacing branches, hairy and brown in color, carrying opposite pairs of glaucous-gray leaves, each about ¼ in. long. The white flowers are held in clusters at the ends of the branches, appearing in May. Fruits, if produced, are white also, but both sexes are needed to ensure their production. Both completely prostrate and semi-upright forms 6–8 in. high are in cultivation. Propagation is easy by means of cuttings taken in fall, or earlier if available. This is another good cover plant for small bulbs.

PHYLLÓDOCE. A genus of about 6 species of dwarf shrubs, found wild from Japan around the North Pacific south into California, with one (*P. caerúlea*) extending into northern Europe and Asia. Two species grown here are *P. bréweri* (VI) from California, in the Sierra Nevada, and our native *P. empetrifórmis* from the Cascade Mountains and widely distributed elsewhere in the western states as well as British Columbia. These mountain heathers are by no means so easy to grow at lower levels around

Phyllodoce aleutica in flower in mid-April. Photo by Brian Mulligan.

Puget Sound as the European species of *Erica,* for which they substitute in our mountains. Our dry summers make life difficult for them at that season, so they need shade in the afternoons and regular watering to keep them in good condition. On the other hand, too much shade will result in poor flowering, so that considerable thought should be given to placing them in local gardens. A rock garden facing between northwest and southeast, with a sandy soil to which humus in some form is added annually, might be suitable. *P. breweri* will grow to about 15 in. in height, has the typical heathlike green foliage of this genus, but the bright rose-pink flowers are saucer shaped, produced in May at the tops of the shoots of the previous year, more like those of *Kalmiopsis* than the other species of *Phyllodoce.*

In *P. empetriformis* (V) they are bell shaped, more purple in hue than rose, although variations can be found in the field, some brighter than others. This plant tends to grow wider than tall, up to about 12 in. in height but more in width in older specimens. Propagation can be done by means of cuttings, or from fresh seeds collected in the wild in October, kept in the refrigerator for three or four months then sown in February. Another native western U.S.A. and Canadian species is *P. glanduliflóra* (V), the Yellow Mountain Heath. In this the leaves and flower parts are all quite glandular and sticky to the touch; the flowers are chartreuse-yellow, urn shaped and thus very distinct from *P. empetriformis.* The plants also are usually shorter and more compact in habit. Hybrids between these two species are frequently found in the wild where they overlap in distribution. The flowers are often a washy pink in color and seldom as desirable as the parents. They have been named *P. × intermédia.*

POLÝGALA chamaebúxus (V), Milkwort, is a small evergreen shrublet about 6 in. high, with Boxlike leaves about ¾ in. long, and a creeping habit of growth by which it extends its area annually. The flowers, produced in April to June, are borne at the ends of the shoots singly or in pairs; in form they look like some member of the pea family, Leguminósae, having two sepals enlarged to resemble the "wings" of the latter flowers, the three petals united to form a "keel' and the stamens also united into a tube. The fruits, however, form a capsule, not a pod. It has a definite preference for calcareous soils in the wild state in the mountains of Central Europe, which indicates its gardening requirements here, where it does not always flower freely. A sunny situation is certainly preferred.

POLÝGONUM vacciniifólium (VII) is the only representative of its large and varied genus in the Dock family of use to us here. Native to the Himalayas, this is an almost prostrate little shrub rising only a few inches above the ground but capable of covering several square feet of soil from one rootstock. It is deciduous, unfortunately, so is bare in the winter months. The elliptic leaves average about ¾ in. in length and are glaucous beneath; many of them turn red before falling in October or November. Flowers are pink, carried in spikes on short stems above the foliage, in

September when few other plants of any kind are flowering. This is an excellent plant for a sunny spot in the rock garden or on a bank down which it can trail. Since the stems root as they extend it is easily propagated by this means, or by cuttings of the new shoots in summer.

ROSES—DWARF KINDS. "Fairy Roses". These had their origins in the dwarf form or sport of *Rósa chinénsis*, the China Rose, named 'Minima', introduced into France in 1810. The flowers of this were single and pink. In England it was called *Rósa lawranciána*, after Mary Lawrance, a well-known painter of roses at that period. By 1837 about 16 such dwarf forms had been raised there by nurserymen, so they have been in cultivation for more than a century and a half. Modern forms, however, are quite different from those old ones.

A much more recent introduction is *Rosa* 'Rouletii', found in cultivation in Switzerland early this century. This grows only 9–12 in. in height, the foliage is semi-evergreen, the flowers ¾–1 in. wide, pink and double. It is believed to be a mutation from *R. chinensis* 'Pumila', which possessed double pink flowers and was raised in an English nursery in 1806. Two modern sports or hybrids derived from 'Rouletii' are 'Oakington Ruby' and 'Tom Thumb'. These can be grown here successfully on rock gardens, given a sunny but not too dry location.

Modern breeders have introduced into this race genes of many kinds of larger types of roses, giving them a complex genetic history but at the same time much greater variety in size and coloring of the flowers. As a result the gardener can now obtain miniature roses in colors comparable to those of the hybrid teas and Floribundas, though not as large, but fully double. They should be seen in bloom before ordering, or at least judged from a colored catalogue from a specialist grower. Most attain 12–18 in. in height and should be treated like their larger brethren in matters of pruning in early spring, though less severely and with a small pair of garden scissors rather than pruning shears, as well as fertilizing then and later if necessary, and spraying for pests. Plant them in groups of three or more of one kind to avoid spottiness. Propagation is accomplished by cuttings taken in September–October.

RÚBUS. One member of this large and polymorphic genus is a most useful groundcover, *R. calycinoídes* (VI–VII), native to the mountains of Taiwan, creeping over the ground or over rocks in a manner similar to the smaller kinds of wild strawberries, *Fragaria* spp. It also has the same habit of rooting at the nodes as it progresses, making it easy to increase. The leaves are evergreen, trilobed, 1–2 in. across, dark glossy green and wrinkled on the upper side, silvery gray beneath with markedly netted veins. The white flowers are scarce as a rule, as are the red fruits, but even in their absence it is a valuable groundcover in partly shaded sites.

RÚSCUS *aculeátus* (VII) Butcher's Broom. This semishrub, since it is not truly woody at the base, grows wild over much of Europe, as far north as southern England, east to Turkey, south to North Africa, so it is widespread. This is a striking and unusual plant for a dry and/or shady place; it prefers to be in the sun but will tolerate shade very well, growing about 2 ft. in height, the dark green stems branching near the top and bearing the apparent leaves which are really modified stems and properly termed cladodes. These are ovate, spine tipped, up to 1½ in. long and half as wide. The inconspicuous whitish flowers are borne in the center of these cladodes in spring. Rarely they may be followed by red, cherrylike fruits, but plants of both sexes are necessary to achieve this desirable end. There is an uncommon hermaphrodite form in cultivation which will fruit on its own. Propagation is by division of the plants when growth commences in spring, or by seeds if obtainable.

SANTOLÍNA chamaecyparíssus, (VII) the Lavender Cotton, native to the western and central Mediterranean region of Europe, is a low shrub usually about 18 in. high, having strongly aromatic, finely cut, woolly-white leaves 1–1½ in. long which are covered with a white felt as are the young stems. The plants should be given the hottest and sunniest place in the garden. The bright yellow flower heads are held up on short stems during summer. Prune the plants immediately after flowering to ensure compact growth. Propagate by means of cuttings in spring or summer.

SÁLIX. Several more or less prostrate or low-growing willows are now in cultivation. One from the mountains of northern Japan is *S. nakamurána* var. *yezoalpína* (IV–V) which forms a prostrate, creeping shrub 3 ft. or more across but only 8–10 in. tall. The leaves are large, more or less orbicular or heart shaped, rounded at the apex, netted on the upper side; the flowers are borne on erect catkins in spring, either male or female on different plants as is usual in this genus. The stems are distinctly olive-brown in winter and the fat buds a tan-brown.

S. répens subsp. *argéntea* (IV), from northern Europe where it grows on sand dunes, is notable for silvery gray coloring of its foliage in summer. The leaves are oblong-elliptic, about 1½ in. long, covered with silky hairs which are responsible for the silky effect. This shrub grows 2–3 ft. tall; the stems are very slender, upright or somewhat spreading; the flowers, borne along the bare branches in April, are very pretty and useful for cutting. It is a most vigorous plant, needing plenty of room for expansion. A sandy soil in full sun seems to its liking.

Two very similar hybrids, with *S. herbácea* as one parent of both, are *S.* × *grahámii* (IV–V), first found in northern Scotland and *S.* 'Moorei' (IV–V) from County Donegal in northwest Ireland. Both are creeping shrublets rising to about 6 in. in height; the leaves elliptic in shape, 1 in. or little more in length, and pointed, distinctly green on both sides. The female catkins are small, tinged red. These are definitely plants for rock gardens.

SARCOCÓCCA hookeriána var. *húmilis (S. húmilis)* (VI), native to central and western China, is a low stoloniferous shrub of tufted growth habit with yellowish stems, spreading quite rapidly in a shady place if conditions are to its liking, such as a sandy soil with sufficient humus in it.

Growing to about 15 in. tall, the leaves are similar to those of its elder brother, *S. hookeriána* var. *digýna* (VI) in shape but somewhat shorter, to about 2 in. long. The inconspicuous flowers also open February, or sometimes even in late January, and are noticeably fragrant. Fruits are black.

SHÓRTIA *galacifólia* (IV), Oconee Bells, is a charming little evergreen groundcover, native to North and South Carolina in the mountains, first discovered by Michaux in 1787, identified from a herbarium specimen by Asa Gray in Paris in 1842, but not found again in the wild and introduced into cultivation until 1877. The oval, glossy, upturned leaves are 1–2 in. across, carried on petioles as long or longer; in the winter the leaves turn bronze and thus add to their decorative value. The solitary flowers are carried a few inches above the foliage in May or early June; each is about 1 in. in diameter, open bell shaped, at first white, then fading to flesh pink. This is a shade-loving woodland plant needing plenty of humus in its site to thrive. Propagation is by division in spring or by cuttings of the new shoots when firm enough. Or by seeds if sown as soon as ripe.

S. uniflóra, from Japan, has thinner, more distinctly toothed leaves, and larger, more open pale pink flowers but is otherwise very similar to the former species. Hybrids between the two species have been made and are very attractive, free-flowering plants.

SÓRBUS. A species of mountain ash seems unlikely to be used as a groundcover, but one at least has been, in England. This is *S. redúcta*, native to southwestern China, introduced to Europe in 1937. This shrub is stoloniferous, sending out underground stems to form new plants a few feet away. It also seeds freely when established, at least in sandy soil. Growing up to no more than 2 ft. in height and often less, it bears pinnate leaves typical of the Aucuparia Section of this genus, with four to seven pairs of small leaflets; the stalks are tinged red. White flowers are produced in May, in loose terminal heads, to be followed in September–October by rose-pink fruits each about ¼ in. across; these are its chief attraction, so it should be placed at the front of the border or on a rock garden where it can be easily seen.

SPIRÁEA *japónica* 'Nana', (VI) is a very compact dwarf form of this Japanese and Chinese species, reaching about 20–24 in. in height but much more in width. The leaves are no more than 1 in. long and often less; the young stems and inflorescences distinctly woolly-hairy; flowers lilac-pink, in flattish heads, in July. As a dense groundcover it has much to recommend it, though the flowers are not conspicuous. It is also sometimes called 'Alpina', but 'Nana' is the correct name. *S. japonica* var. *alpina* was described from a wild plant found in the mountains of Japan and is not known to be in cultivation here.

S. japonica 'Norman' (or 'Normanii') originated in the garden of Mr. T. R. Norman, of Painesville, Ohio. It grows only about 12 in. high, the stems are very slender, the leaves slightly larger than those of 'Nana', and remarkable for their brilliant red fall coloring, lasting for nearly a month in

October into November. Because of its dwarf habit it should be placed in the rock garden or at the front of a border.

STEPHANÁNDRA incísa 'Crispa' (V) is a compact form of this Japanese and Korean shrub, growing about 2 ft. tall but several times more in width. It is very similar in habit to *Spiraea japonica* 'Nana', and these two forms can be seen growing side by side in the Japanese garden in the Washington Park Arboretum in Seattle. The minute flowers are white and of little value for ornament. Fall leaf color is orange.

TEÚCRIUM chamaédrys (V), the Wall Germander, native to central and southern Europe and North Africa, is well known as an edging plant for herb gardens or borders. From a creeping rootstock it sends up stems 9–12 in. in height, bearing opposite, hairy, toothed leaves about 1 in. long. The flowers are carried in a terminal raceme in summer; the bracts and sepals are purplish, the two-lipped flowers typical of the Labiátae are rose colored. Easily propagated by division in spring.

THÝMUS. Thymes come in a variety of sizes and scents. The tallest is *Thýmus vulgáris* (V), the garden thyme, growing to about 12 in., quite woody stemmed, with aromatic leaves used for flavoring in cooking or in salads; there is also a variegated foliaged form, 'Argenteus'. The flowers of both are lilac in color. This species is native to the Mediterranean region, from Portugal to Greece, so should be given a sunny site in our local gardens, as indeed should all the thymes. They certainly prefer a sandy, well-drained soil, but most have no objection to a calcareous one. *T. × citriodórus* (VI) is an old hybrid between *T. vulgaris* and *T. pulegioídes*; the leaves of this are somewhat larger and noticeably lemon scented.

Of the prostrate, mat-forming thymes, the plant or plants known as *T. serpýllum* (III) is undoubtedly the most common in cultivation, although probably many grown under that name are *T. drúcei* or another near relative. These creeping thymes are very difficult to separate and identify, but nevertheless are valuable groundcovers on sunny rock gardens, producing sheets of lilac to purple flowers in summer and making excellent cover for small bulbs. The Caraway Thyme, *T. hérba-baróna* (IV), a native of Corsica, is one of them, though less conspicuous in flower than for its fragrance. *T. nummulárius* (V), from western Asia, possessing opposite pairs of spoonshaped stalked leaves ⅓–½ in. long on semiprostrate stems 6–8 in. long, with a scent similar to that of the common thyme, is also in cultivation.

VACCÍNIUM vítis-idáea (V), the Cowberry or, in Sweden, the Lingonberry, native to the mountains of Europe and northern Asia, is a neat, low-growing subshrub spreading by underground runners and thriving in a soil with plenty of humus such as peat or compost: it ordinarily reaches a height of about 9 in. The reddish stems carry Boxlike, evergreen leaves of varying sizes from ½–1 in. in length; the paler underside is sprinkled with black, glandular dots. The bell-shaped, pale pink flowers are borne in tight clusters at the tops of the stems in May and June. The fruits, if produced, are dark red, acid to taste but making good jelly. *V. vitis-idaea* subsp. *minus* (II), our native N. American plant, is much smaller in every respect, growing to only about 4 in. tall and the dark green leaves about ½ in. long. It is a charming little groundcover for shady places.

VIBÚRNUM *ópulus* 'Compactum' (III–IV), is a dwarf form of the European Guelder Rose shrub, originating in Holland. This grows 2–3 ft. tall, flowers like the type in May, but produces heavy clusters of bright red fruits in September–October. It is a much more useful garden plant than the old form 'Nanum', which never flowers.

VÍNCA, the periwinkles, are useful groundcovers particularly beneath trees, where they are a good alternative to ivy and more ornamental because of their flowers. *V. májor* (VII), the Greater Periwinkle, is native to the western and central Mediterranean region and less hardy than its smaller brother, *V. mínor*. The nonflowering stems carry ovate leaves 1–2 in. long in opposite pairs, dark green and shining on both sides. The flowering stems may be a foot or more above the others and produce pairs of bright blue flowers, each about 1½ in. across, during the summer. A form with variegated leaves also exists, 'Variegata'. *V. minor*, the Lesser Periwinkle, is found wild from southwestern into central Europe and as far east as western Asia. Both leaves and flowers are smaller than those of *V. major*, but the latter are usually borne more freely. Although the typical flower color is blue, there are also white ('Alba') and purple-flowered variants. Propagation is easy in both species by means of the rooting stems.

CHAPTER XII

Vines and Climbers

The word vine originally signified the wine grape, but has been extended to refer to any plant with limber, trailing stems that need support. This chapter deals with those which are of woody or partially woody habit. Some, like grapes, climb by means of tendrils, while others such as *Clematis* and *Akebia,* use leaf stems as tendrils. In still others, such as *Wisteria* and honeysuckle, the new shoots themselves wind in an ascending spiral around anything they contact. Ivies and the climbing hydrangeas cling tightly by means of aerial rootlets. Boston Ivy and Virginia creeper develop little sticky suction cups at the tips of their tendrils, giving them a powerful grip on their support. It is usually unwise to plant any of these scandent shrubs against wooden walls, especially shingles or shakes, since the shoots may work their way inside and cause damage. A few vines, such as *Jasminum nudiflorum,* prefer to remain prostrate and trail on the ground; these are best positioned where they can cascade over a wall or down a bank. Climbing roses are in a group entirely by themselves—in the strictest sense they do not climb, but send out long arching or trailing shoots which must be fastened to supports, though some are capable of ascending into trees on their own.

The majority of the clinging or twining vines grow under woodland conditions in the wild—that is, their roots are in the shade of trees and they scramble up toward the light so their tops are in full sun. They are happiest under similar conditions in the garden. Indeed, this is the simplest way to grow them, since no further training is required once two or three lead shoots have been directed up into the branches of a shrub or tree. There they can be allowed to ramble to their hearts' content without assistance or restraint; however, vines planted at the base of conifers may need extra water during dry periods. Shade at the roots is essential to the well-being of vines of this class and frequently makes the difference between success and failure.

In our gardens, however, vines are not usually given free rein, but fastened to artificial supports such as fences, trellises, or pergolas, or directed along wires and encouraged to cover walls or provide shade for porches and patios. Under these conditions, vines quickly form an untidy tangle if left to their own devices. They have a great tendency to run up to the highest point they can reach. There, especially if space at the top is limited, they send out an ever-increasing mass of shoots. The secret of managing vines lies in training the shoots when young, forming a framework for future growth. In the individual descriptions which follow the approximate height of each species or variety is given, or the area which it can be expected to cover. Be sure to choose a vine that is suited in size to the space allotted. Decide first whether you want simply a solid mass of foliage, or an open tracery of stems and leaves, which requires a larger space. Allot sufficient area so that new growth need not be cramped by excessive cutting back. Unfortunately for the gardener on a small lot, many of our very best vines are also very large, but fortunately, the roses and clematis come to his rescue.

Once their initial path of growth has been firmly established, the care of vines is comparatively simple, and they require only intermittent attention. However if a vine gets out of control to form a tangled mass of shoots at the top of a wall or trellis the gardener may have to start all over the following year. Nor are vines for those of a super-tidy mindset; part of their charm lies in the grace of their vigorous new growth.

The time for planting vines is the same as that for shrubs of similar type. All vigorous, deciduous vines can be moved at any time during their dormant period when they are leafless. Any that are at all difficult to transplant should be moved just before they start into growth in the spring. Broad-leaved evergreen vines are best planted just after they start into growth. Cultural differences have been somewhat blurred by the prevalence in today's market of container-grown nursery stock, which can be planted at almost any season.

Most deciduous vines are propagated readily either from hardwood cuttings or from layered shoots, which tend to form spontaneously. The broad-leaved evergreen kinds are propagated either from layers or from summer cuttings of half-ripened wood. Exceptions are the named selections of *Wisteria* and *Clematis,* which are grafted. Other exceptions will be noted in the individual descriptions.

ACTINÍDIA chinénsis (VII), the Chinese Gooseberry, or Kiwi Fruit of grocery stores, is a handsome, strong-growing, deciduous vine, needing an area of not less than 200 square feet. The broad, heart-shaped 3–5 in. long leaves are softly hairy when young, and the young twining shoots and veins on the underside of the leaves are covered with velvety dark red hairs. Creamy white flowers, an inch and a half across, occur in June, and fade to a soft yellow as they age. Brown-furry egg-shaped fruit, green on the inside, are produced in late summer. As with hollies, both male and female plants must be planted to achieve fruit production. Named selections—capable of ripening their fruit under Northwest conditions—

have recently become available in our area. A south-or west-facing location will provide added warmth to assure their ripening. If fruits would be a nuisance, a single plant is still worth growing for its attractive foliage. Well-drained loam suits it best, but *Actinidia* will grow exuberantly in any good fertile soil.

A. *argúta* (IV), a very hardy species ranging from China and Japan to the Amur River region of Asia, has recently become available in nurseries here. It, too, is a very vigorous grower, to 60 ft., with almost glabrous leaves and greenish white flowers containing clusters of purple anthers on male plants. Inch-long edible greenish yellow fruits are produced on female plants if male plants are also present.

A. *kolomíkta* (IV), from China and Japan, is a more slender climber than the preceding species, reaching about 20–30 ft. Its deciduous deep green leaves are strikingly variegated with rose and white splashes. The ½-in.-long, white flowers appear in May and June and are fragrant; edible inch-long berries ripen in September. Male plants, however, are said to have the best color. This plant thrives in any well-drained soil. Too much fertilizer and too shady a location are said to reduce the coloration on the leaves.

AKÉBIA *quináta* (VI), Five-leaf Akebia, is a lacy twining vine from Japan and China, deciduous or almost evergreen, depending on winter temperatures. Its dark green leaves are palmately compound with five blunt-tipped leaflets, and it clings by twining its leaf stems. Male and female flowers with a marked spicy fragrance are borne together in pendent clusters, the female at the base, as inch-wide triads of chocolate-purple cups, with the more numerous male flowers, smaller and paler rose-purple, toward the tip. Fruits 3–4 in. long, glaucous and pale purple, like fat sausages, are produced somewhat inconsistantly. This species ultimately makes growth 30–40 ft. long and must always be planted with its roots in the shade, even though the top likes to climb into full sun. It may be grown either against a partially shaded wall where it will require careful training on some kind of framework to maintain a pleasing tracery, or over an arch, trellis, pergola, or any structure where a light covering is wanted. The reflected heat of a south or west wall is rather too much for it; it is more useful for a north wall where comparatively few vines thrive.

A. *trifoliáta* (A. *lobáta*) (IV). the Three-leaf Akebia, also comes from China and Japan and differs from the preceding species in having three leaflets instead of five, and female flowers of somewhat darker color. Pale violet fruits split when ripe, showing rows of black seeds embedded in a white pulp. It is deciduous, perfectly hardy, and grows to about 50 ft.

A. × *pentaphýlla* is a hybrid between the two preceding species, and intermediate in appearance between them.

Both species and their hybrid prefer a rich, light soil in which plenty of leafmold has been incorporated, but will grow in any well-prepared garden soil, given ample moisture during the growing season. Once they

Ripe fruits of *Akebia quinata* in late September. Photo by Brian Mulligan.

have reached mature size, after midsummer, they will flower more freely if they do not receive too much moisture. They do require some annual pruning even with careful initial training.

AMPELÓPSIS *brévipedúnculáta* (VI). Porcelain Ampelopsis, once included in *Vitis* as *V. heterophylla*, from Northeast Asia, boasts the most brilliant and striking fruit of all our deciduous vines. The small greenish flowers are hardly discernable and the typically grape-shaped leaves do not change color particularly in the fall, but in September and October its abundant clusters of ⅛–¼ in. grapes put on a spectacular display, turning slowly from white or pale yellow through brilliant turquoise to clear violet-blue. A rampant vine that should be grown in rather poor dry soil, it can reach 15–20 ft. in a season. Since it clings by tendrils, it needs good support, such as a pergola, and is well suited to growing up a large tree through which it can ramble. The effect is especially fine if it is allowed to climb through richly colored autumn foliage, such as that of *Viburnum opulus*. A position in full sun is needed for the best crop of fruits. 'Elegans' has slightly smaller leaves then the type, variegated with greenish white and tinged with pink when young, and is said to be somewhat less vigorous. Plants with variegated foliage are also offered as 'Variegata'. In var. *maximowíczii* the lobing of the leaves is highly variable, from deeply cut to nearly heart shaped. It is definitely a vigorous grower!

ARISTOLÓCHIA *macrophýlla* (*A. dúrior*) (IV), called Dutchman's Pipe from the shape of the flowers, is a handsome, deciduous vine native to eastern North America. Robust and of twining habit, with dark green, heart-shaped leaves 6–12 in.long, its curious hook-shaped yellowish-green and purple-lipped flowers in June are intriguing rather than showy. This vine is very desirable for covering arbors, porches or similar structures with heavy foliage. It will quickly grow to 20–30 ft. in length, so should be allowed plenty of room to prevent crowding out less robust neighbors. Easily grown in any good garden soil with a moderate amount of moisture, it is a gross feeder and responds to generous fertilizing. Its roots do not need shade. Grown as a simple covering vine, it requires little care once the twining shoots have been evenly distributed; the surplus is simply cut back each spring. If the growth becomes too heavy, it should be removed during the dormant season, and the vigorous new shoots spread out in place.

BIGNÓNIA *capreoláta* (VII), Cross Vine, is a semi-deciduous or evergreen climber, from southeastern United States, clinging by tendrils, ascending in trees up to 50 ft. Its deep green oval leaflets, 2½–5 in. long, are paired at the nodes of the stems. Clusters of plump, tubular, orange-red flowers with reflexed petal tips, up to 2 in. long and 1¼ in. across, are borne in the leaf axils. This slender but vigorous vine will do best in a warm sunny location.

CÁMPSIS *grandiflóra* (VII), Chinese Trumpet Creeper, is unfortunately somewhat less hardy than the next species, *C. radicans.* Its wide-mouthed, trumpet-shaped flowers—deep orange and red—are borne in panicles at the end of the current season's growth during August and September. 'Thunbergii' is considered hardier than the type. Both need a warm wall for best performance in our area. They can reach a height of 20 ft.

C. rádicans (IV), Trumpet Vine, is another beautiful, hardy, deciduous climber from the southeastern United States. Quite capable of covering 300–400 sq. ft., it clings by aerial roots like ivy, and develops a heavy woody trunk. The pinnately compound leaves end in long waving tendrils. Fat trumpet-shaped flowers 1½ in. across are produced in late summer. This plant likes summer heat and blooms better in Portland and in eastern Washington than it does in Seattle and Vancouver. Annual pruning will be necessary to keep its vigorous growth from becoming a complete tangle. Deep, well-drained soil, and a south or west exposure will suit it best; do not overfertilize! 'Flava' has apricot-yellow flowers.

C. × tagliabúana (VI) is a hybrid which arose in Italy in the 19th century between *C. radicans* and its tender Chinese relative, *C. grandiflora.* 'Mme. Galen', considered the finest named clone, is intermediate between the two parents to 30 ft. or more and has salmon-orange flowers.

CELÁSTRUS *orbiculátus* (IV–V), Oriental Bittersweet, from northeastern Asia, is said by Bean to be the most striking of all hardy climbers during November and December when the gold and scarlet fruits are at their best. A deciduous plant of twining habit, it needs the support of a trellis or tree and can climb to 30–40 ft. Its minute flowers are scarcely noticeable and partly dioecious, so that two plants—male and female—

may be necessary for good fruit set. It prefers good loamy soil.

C. scándens (IV), American Bittersweet of the eastern United States, is somewhat smaller than the preceding species to about 20 ft. with glossy green, toothed leaves, and tiny flowers. It also is dioecious, so obtaining plants of both sexes from unspecified nursery material poses a problem. The orange-yellow and crimson-seeded fruits are desirable for dried arrangements, but the vine itself is probably most useful to hide unsightly areas, or relegated to the wild garden. It is not particular about soil or location and can withstand considerable drought when well established.

Clematis

CLÉMATIS. This large genus of more than 200 species has probably contributed a greater variety of climbing plants to our gardens than any other except Rosa. The hardy species come chiefly from the north temperate regions of the world, and range in size from delicate plants rambling over the ground or into low shrubs, to vigorous, rampant types fully capable of running to the tops of tall trees. A few are evergreen, but most are deciduous, woody-stemmed vines, twining their way upward by wrapping their leaf stalks around any handy support; their leaves are paired at the nodes of the stems and divided into varying numbers of leaflets. Some bloom in early spring; other wait until late summer or early fall; some of the hybrids bloom both early and late. A good many species are attractive in fruit as well as in flower; the seeds develop long plumose tails as they mature, extending the season of interest well into winter. C. alpina is a good example of this feature.

Clematis are not difficult garden plants, provided a few important points are kept in mind. Clambering over shrubs and trees as they do in the wild, they need a cool, shaded position for their roots in the garden—preferably a north or east exposure—and they must be well watered during our dry summers. As with other vines, their tops should be out in full sun. Clematis do better in water retentive soils than in sandy ones. Soil should be dug deeply before planting and well enriched with compost and fertilizer. The addition of lime is often recommended, but a fully alkaline soil is not necessary—a neutral or slightly acid one is quite satisfactory.

The large-flowered hybrids are often regarded as temperamental due to a fungus disease, know as Clematis Wilt, which causes the shoots to die suddenly during the growing season. Trimming away the diseased portions and treatment with a garden fungicide will usually restore the plant to health. Preventative applications during the season of active growth are a wise precautions, particularly for young plants.

Pruning strategies for clematis are geared to their season of bloom, and the size of the area that they are planned to occupy. With spring-flowering types, pruning should be done right after bloom season, and only just enough to remove spent flowers and keep the plant tidy. Those of the large-flowered hybrids that bloom in early summer on short shoots from last year's wood need very little pruning, but some attention should be paid to the training of new growth. Many of the species hybrids blooming in late summer on the current season's growth either die back in winter or tend to form top-heavy tangles if left to themselves; they are typically pruned back heavily in late winter or early spring.

Descriptions of the most attractive, commonly cultivated, and readily obtainable species follow. All are deciduous unless otherwise noted. More complete listings of the large-flowered hybrids will be found in specialty catalogs and nurseries.

C. alpína (V) from Europe and central Asia, is a dainty climber 10–15 ft. in height, producing solitary, nodding, lavender blue flowers in April and May. The sepals are the most prominent feature of the flower, but small white petaloids clustered around the stamens give it somewhat the appearance of a four-petaled, spurless columbine. Our native *C. columbiána* (VI), Rock Clematis, is similar in size, but with sepals only, in lavender-blue. It is a small-scale, trailing vine, 6–10 ft. long, suitable for naturalizing, or the sunny rock garden, blooming in late spring. *C. macropétala* (V). Downy Clematis, is a very desirable little Chinese species to about 8 ft., similar in habit to *C. alpina*. Its stems are downy when young; the nine leaflets, in three sets of three, are irregularly toothed. The 2–3 in. flowers, produced in May or June, consist of four outer sepals and a center filled with slender downy petaloids varying from violet-blue to almost white, giving the effect of a double flower. 'Markham's Pink' has rosy lilac flowers. 'Blue Bird' is a July-flowering blue selection. All of these small species are seen to best advantage climbing up through some deciduous shrub, such as our native Red Flowering Currant, *Ribes sanguineum,* or one of the deciduous azaleas; but it should be one with a root system that will not compete too strongly with that of the clematis. These spring-blooming species should be pruned immediately after flowering.

Evergreen *C. armándii* (VI) from central and western China, is a vigorous woody species with leathery, dark green, three-parted leaves. It is capable of climbing to 20–30 ft. With proper initial training it requires no pruning save for the removal of old flower clusters. The slender, pointed leaflets make a fine facade along a roof edge or a fence. Showy clusters of fragrant white flowers, 1–2 in. across, appear in April. Several selected forms are available: 'Appleblossom' has larger and more spectacular flowers than the type, very slightly tinted pink. 'Snowdrift' is a large-flowered white form. One word of caution in siting this species—if sun falls on frozen leaves, they may be damaged in a more severe than average winter, but the plant itself is able to recover the following spring, though it may not bloom.

C. campaniflóra (VII) from Portugal, is a vigorous climber up to 20 ft., with much-divided foliage. The small, nodding, bowl-shaped flowers—woolly surfaced and with pointed, recurving tips—are white tinged with violet and bloom in July and August.

Though *C. chrysocóma* from China is a semiwoody 6–8 ft. shrub, its variety *serícea (C. spóoneri)* (VII) is truly climbing, to as much as 10–15 ft. New shoots, leaves, and flower stalks are covered with a conspicuous yellow down. Pink-tinged white flowers 1¾ in. across, have broadly ovate sepals. Seed tails are plumed with golden hairs, so that this plant is particularly attractive in fruit. In the hybrid 'Rosea' the flowers are truly pink; there are also pure white forms. It blooms from June to October on old wood, and should be pruned or thinned in February.

C. cirrhósa var. *baléarica* (VIII), native to the islands of the western Mediterranean, is a 10–15 ft. evergreen vine with ferny, finely divided foliage, turning bronzy in winter. Flowers, 1½–2½ in., with oval cream-colored sepals, downy on the outside, bloom on and off from September to March. Plumose fruits form large silken tassels. Its bronzy foliage and winter-blooming habit make this a desirable vine for a sunny, protected location.

C. flámmula (VI), a southern European native, is one of the few fragrant species of *Clematis,* blooming in August and September. The individual white flowers are less than 1 in. across, but they come in enormous panicles up to a foot across, and their almond or vanilla fragrance carries some distance. Seed plumes are white. Lower stems tend to be bare, so this species is best grown with other plants in the foreground. Its stems reach to 10 ft. or more.

C. ligusticifólia (IV), western North American native, common in canyons east of the Cascades, is a 20 ft., late-summer-flowering vine, with male and female flowers on separate plants. The large clusters of small, white flowers are fragrant, and followed on the female plants by puffs of feathery-tailed seeds which persist into winter. The ready availability of many more handsome species relegates this plant to use in dry sites or roadside plantings where it can scramble around at will. It combines well with our native sumac, *Rhus glabra. C. vitálba* (IV), Traveller's Joy or Old Man's Beard, is a very similar European species which has escaped from cultivation in some places west of the Cascades. It can be distinguished from the native *C. ligusticifolia* by the flowers which are perfect rather than unisexual, and almond scented, in bloom much of the summer. While both the panicles of small, white blossoms and the silvery-silky fruits are attractive, *C. vitalba* is an aggressive and fast-growing 40 ft. vine quite capable of smothering more desirable plants, and useful only for large wild areas.

C. montána (V), perhaps the best known of the spring-flowering species, is a native of the Himalayas. It is a vigorous grower, to 20 ft. or more with fragrant white flowers 2–2½ in. across, and three-parted leaflets. Among the varieties available are the following selections: 'Elizabeth', with large light pink flowers; 'Grandiflora', with white flowers up to 3 in. across; and 'Tetrarose', a tetraploid variety from Holland with

Clematis montana var. *grandiflora* trained over a wall. Photo by Brian Mulligan, in early June.

large purplish pink flowers and bronzy foliage. Var. *rúbens,* from China—said by Bean to be "the most beautiful and useful climber distributed in the twentieth century"—flowers later and more freely than the type. It has rosy sepals and purple-tinged leaflets and young stems—a marvelous vine to run up tall trees! This species should be pruned after flowering, if necessary.

C. *maximowícziana,* better known as C. *paniculáta* (V), the Sweet Autumn Clematis from Japan, is a very vigorous climber, to 30 ft. or more, with heartshaped leaflets resembling lilac leaves. Clusters of fragrant, 1-in. white flowers wait until September and October, so that this is a very desirable companion plant for trees and shrubs with early fall color.

C. *viticélla* (IV), Italian Clematis, is a dainty, partially woody 8–12 ft. species from southern Europe, with lobed tripartite leaflets and stalked, bell-shaped flowers 1½ in. or so across. Sepals are blue or rosy purple in the type, borne in profusion from early to late summer. Old growth which has died off during the winter should be cut back to the main stems in February. Several color forms are in cultivation, as well as a number of hybrids with the general aspect of the species: 'Abundance', soft red-purple, overlaid with darker veins; 'Alba Luxurians', white flowers with green recurved tips; 'Etoile Violette', velvety rich purple; 'Minuet', white with mauve veins and margins; and 'Kermesina', deep red.

Large Flowered Hybrids

The large-flowered summer-blooming clematis are among the most colorful and decorative of all our deciduous vines. Their breeding began in the middle of the 19th century with the introduction of C. × *jackmánii*, which remains in commerce today, highly valued for its 4–5 in. flowers of rich violet-purple. The species involved were the Italian clematis, C. *viticella*, which blooms on the new season's growth, and three oriental species, C. *lanuginósa*, also blooming on new growth, and C. *flórida* and C. *pátens*, which bloom on the the previous season's wood. Flowers of the oriental species are pale in color, but very large, opening out flat, while in C. *viticella* the sepals flare out at an angle, so that the flowers are somewhat bell shaped and the crimson to violet colors are rich and deep. The resulting hybrids are frequently grouped according to the species which they most closely resemble, but the typical gardener is more interested in when a variety will bloom, and how to prune, than in its background.

In general, those which bloom early—in May or June—on short shoots from the previous season's wood, need very little pruning beyond the removal of spent flowers, and an occasional bit of shaping. These include 'Barbara Jackman', bluish purple with a carmine bar down the center of the sepals, and cream stamens; 'Dr. Ruppel', strawberry pink with carmine bar; the ever-popular 'Nellie Moser', mauve pink with deep carmine bar; and 'Vyvyan Pennell', reddish lilac with the center filled with staminodes.

Those hybrids which bloom from mid-June onwards on the new wood are generally more vigorous, so they are pruned back hard in early spring, as soon as it is possible to distinguish the live shoots from the dead ones. Many cultivars put out two flushes of bloom; others are in bloom more or less continuously from early to late summer. Colors range from light to dark; contrasting stamens add further interest. The pale-flowered kinds look best against dark walls or evergreens; while those with dark flowers are set off to especially good advantage when they are allowed to come up through white-variegated shrubs such as *Cornus alba* 'Argenteo-marginata'. The number of named varieties available has increased greatly in recent years.

Among those that begin early and flower into late summer, in light to dark blue are 'Lasurstern', deep lavender-blue with white stamens; 'Ramona', sky blue; 'Mrs. Cholmondeley' (pronounced 'Chumley'), lavender blue, veined darker and with a deep pink stripe down the center of each sepal; 'Lady Betty Balfour', violet blue, with prominent, yellow stamens. Whites include 'Henryi', with a circle of brown anthers; 'Huldine', in which the reverse of the petals is tinted mauve; 'Miss Bateman', white with a cushion of purple anthers; and the very large flowered 'Mme. Le Coultre'. Reds include 'Ernest Markham', petunia red; 'Niobe', ruby red with white stamens, and 'Ville de Lyon', a wide-petalled carmine red with creamy stamens. 'Comtesse de Bouchaud' in bright mauve pink and 'Hagley Hybrid', rose mauve with purple stamens, come closest to true pink. Double-flowered varieties include 'Belle of Woking', with blossoms of pale silvery mauve; fragrant, white 'Duchess of Edinburgh'; 'Sieboldii', which has an eye-catching ruff of purple petaloid stamens backed by six white sepals; and the very large and extremely double mauve pink 'Proteus'.

Best of the late-flowering types in deep purple are 'Gipsy Queen', in which the stamens are dark as well; and 'Jackmanii Superba', larger and fuller than 'Jackmanii' itself, which is also still widely grown. These are all pruned heavily in early spring.

In a complete departure from the flower colors found in the foregoing species and hybrids, there are a number of oriental species in which the sepals are pale to bright yellow.

C. orientális (IV), is native from eastern Europe across to western China. It is a climbing vine to about 15 ft. with glaucous, more or less lobed leaflets. Small yellow or greenish yellow flowers with reflexed sepals, furry both inside and out, are borne in large, compound clusters that bloom in August / September. The true species is not common in cultivation.

C. rehderiána (IV), Rehder's Clematis from western China, another of the yellow-flowered Asiatic species, is a 25 ft. climber with downy three-lobed leaflets. The clusters of little bell-shaped flowers are pale primrose yellow and fragrant; sepals are velvety on the outside, with recurved tips. Its late period of bloom—August to October—and the fragrance of its flowers makes this a highly desirable species for use in combination with trees and shrubs which develop their fall color early.

C. tangútica (V), Golden Clematis from northwest India and western China, is much more common in cultivation than the two preceding species. It is a vigorous climbing shrub, reaching 12–15 ft. The green lanceolate leaflets are toothed and more or less lobed at the base. The long, pointed lemon yellow sepals form pendent lanterns, short stalked and solitary or two or three together, and are silky outside, smooth and shiny inside. 'Bill McKenzie', one of several cultivars derived from this species, has open flowers showing off the cluster of black anthers in the center. 'Gravetye' is probably a selection of C. tangutica ssp. obtusiúscula, a form in which the flowers are wide open rather than lanternlike. Obtaining correctly named cultivars often poses a problem, in that many of the plants offered under their names appear to be seedlings of the original rather than clonal material. Plants should be chose in bloom if possible. Seed-heads in this species are especially attractive, with their golden plumes swirled into small shining turbans.

C. tibetána ssp. vernáyi (VII), from Nepal and Tibet, has leathery leaflets, narrowly lanceolate and lobed at the base on 20 ft. vines. The flowers, yellow flushed brownish purple on the outside, are long stemmed and solitary or two or three in a group. The sepals are unusually thick sub-

Clematis tibetana subsp. *vernayi* flowering and fruiting in early October. Photo by Brian Mulligan.

stanced, silky-hairy only on the inside. This species is much confused with *C. orientalis* in the nursery trade, so that the cultivar 'Orange Peel', which belongs here, is usually listed in catalogs as *C.o.* 'Orange Peel'. The original introduction of *C. tibetana* ssp. *vernayi* is known as 'Sherriff's Variety', and sometimes listed under number as L. & S. 13372. Both this species and *C. tangutica* are easily grown and will succeed under drier conditions than most, though they like plenty of moisture. All of these yellow-flowered species can be pruned back hard in early spring if necessary. New growth should be carefully trained to avoid a mere tangled mass at bloom time.

    C. texénsis (V), Scarlet Clematis from Texas as its name indicates, is the most vividly colored of all clematis, its small long-stalked scarlet urns, nearly closed at the mouth, contrasting nicely with its glaucous leaflets. In our area this species will need a favored location, such as a south-facing wall, and winter protection for its base, since it is not evergreen here and tends to die back in winter. The 6–9 ft. long shoots will need the support of an adjacent shrub, or some framework to cling to against a wall. It flowers in July, and is sure to be a conversation piece in any garden. Its hybrid, 'Duchess of Albany', has semi-open flowers of bright rose pink, and blooms in late summer.

    HÉDERA canariénsis (VIII–IX) 'Azorica' (*H. algeriénsis*), Algerian Ivy, is native from the Canary Islands to Portugal and Algeria, and has 4–6 in. shallowly lobed leaves. Young wood and leaves are felted with tawny hairs. Evergreen and vigorous, this 75–100 ft. vine is useful for covering large areas. There is also a white-variegated form 'Variegata', Variegated Algerian Ivy.

H. cólchica (VI–VII), Persian Ivy, native from the Caucasus to Asiatic Turkey, has very large leathery leaves with heart-shaped bases and also grows to 75–100 ft. It is useful for dry sites in full sun where a vine capable of covering a large area is needed. 'Dentata Variegata' is a white-variegated form, the leaves having patches of green, gray-green, and white.

H. hélix (V), English Ivy, is a European species which has made itself very much at home in the Pacific Northwest, even to the extent of going wild upon occasion. The typical 100 ft. ivy vine, with its glossy, lobed leaves and stems clinging by rootlike holdfasts, is actually an extended juvenile state; fruiting occurs only on short, bushy branches with smaller, entire leaves, produced high in the air. Umbels of greenish yellow flowers are followed by clusters of black, allegedly poisonous berries. All three species are evergreen.

The ivies are especially useful as groundcovers for steep and inhospitable banks of poor soil, or in the dense shade of large trees. The type is too rampant a grower to be trusted under more favorable circumstances in anything but very large areas such as highway banks. However, some of the innumerable forms which have been selected over the centuries it has been in cultivation are much less robust and can be used in more limited settings. The following are among those currently in commerce.

'Argenteo-variegata', Silverleaf Ivy, is a white-variegated form.

'Atropurpurea' ('Purpurea'), in which the central lobe of the leaves is long and the two laterals short, becomes purple in winter with the veins remaining bright green.

'Baltica', a form with smaller leaves, is said by Dirr to be less hardy than advertised.

'Glacier' is a variegated form, margined white with green and gray-green center.

'Goldheart' has golden-variegated leaves, very dark green with an irregular central blotch of yellow, and red stems when young.

'Hibernica', Irish Ivy, is descended from a plant found growing wild in Ireland; it has large leaves with five triangular lobes, the terminal one longest.

'Pedata', Bird's Foot Ivy, has dark green leaves veined with white, the central lobe much longer than the others, and the two basal ones pointing backwards.

'Pittsburgh' ('Hahn's Self-branching') is a small-leaved form, light green and densely branched; origin in Pennsylvania about 1920.

Ivies are not at all particular about soil, but they require pruning, about the middle of April just a they start into growth. As groundcovers they may need pruning more than once. Those growing into trees must not be allowed to smother them.

HYDRÁNGEA anómala ssp. *petioláris* (IV) or *H. petioláris*, Climbing Hydrangea, from Japan and Korea, is a very hardy, deciduous climber, clinging by aerial roots as in ivy. It may be slow to establish at first, but is capable of climbing 60–80 ft. up a tree. Its leaves are ovate, nearly as wide as long, pointed and finely toothed; winter bark is a rich cinnamon brown, peeling with age. Loose, flat-topped clusters of blossoms, 6–10 in. across, cover the plant in June—the large white sterile flowers around the edge, the smaller fragrant fertile flowers in the center. This vine will stand considerable sun, providing it has a cool, moist root run, and does well on a north- or east-facing wall. It can also be used as a freestanding shrub, if kept within bounds with pruning, or mounded over a large stump, and is very highly rated in spite of its large size.

JÁSMINUM. The Jasmines, well known for their fragrant flowers, are of easy culture in good garden soil, given a warm sunny position. *J. nudiflórum* (V), the Winter Flowering Jasmine from China, is really a deciduous trailing shrub with tiny leaves, rather than a vine. It is seen to greatest advantage draped down over a wall in a flowing 10–15 ft. curtain of growth. It can be grown as a shrub on an open slope, or fastened up to grow against a bank or fence. When properly grown in a dry, sunny location, the bright yellow flowers appear during the winter along the bare, bright green branches of the previous season's growth, creating a colorful and most welcome display in January and February. When the plant becomes untidy it can be lightly pruned immediately after flowering, or flowering branches can be cut for decoration—they force well as early as December. Stems root where they touch the ground.

J. officinále (VII), the common White Jasmine, is a well-known, semi-evergreen twinging climber to 40 ft. with a long history of cultivation, native from Iran to the Himalayas and China. The dainty, soft green, divided foliage is sprinkled with fragrant white flowers all summer. It is an indispensable vine for covering a trellis or pergola in sun or light shade, with a spread of 75–100 sq. ft. This jasmine prefers cool soil for its roots, well enriched with humus, but is easily grown in any good garden loam with moderate summer moisture. Pruning is not usually necessary unless the plant becomes top-heavy, in which case any trimming should be done after growth begins in early spring.

J. × stephanénse (VI), a hybrid between *J. officinále* and *J. beesiánum*, was bred in France about 1920, but is also known to occur in the wild. Its small, fragrant, pale pink flowers bloom in June and July; the deciduous foliage runs the gamut from simple to pinnately divided. It is a vigorous climber, with slender stems to about 15–20 ft.

LONÍCERA. The hardy climbing honeysuckles are legion. Only a few of the most outstanding will be mentioned here. They are all rambling twining vines which quickly become untidy without adequate training. They thrive in any good garden soil, providing their roots are cool and moist, and can be grown over fences and pergolas or allowed to run up into the branches of large trees. Two of our Pacific Coast species are useful in the wild garden.

L. × *brównii* (V), Brown's Honeysuckle, covers a number of deciduous hybrids between two species from eastern North America, *L. sempervírens* and *L. hirsúta,* growing to about 20 ft. 'Dropmore Scarlet', of Canadian origin, is essentially everblooming, with clusters of slender scarlet trumpets, and is the hardiest of the vine honeysuckles. It is not fragrant, however. Both parents seem to have been eclipsed in the nursery trade by the hybrids, perhaps because of their lack of fragrance; but also, in the case of *L. sempervirens,* because of a susceptibility to aphids. *L. sempervirens sulphurea,* a yellow-flowered form, is occasionally offered.

L. ciliósa (V), native to the Rocky Mountains and the Pacific Coast, takes its name from the hairy margins of its deciduous oval leaves. Unlike many of our commonly cultivated vines, this is a plant of relatively modest growth to about 15 ft., not apt to smother its neighbors. Its yellow-orange or orange-scarlet flowers will show to best advantage climbing up through shrubs or small trees as it would in the wild. Its flowers are not fragrant.

L. etrúsca (VII). This native of the Mediterranean region is a very vigorous climber, to at least 15 ft. with a tendency to be partially ever-green. The glaucous leaves are somewhat downy beneath; those toward the upper ends of the shoots are united at the base; young shoots are reddish. The flowers—yellow tinted with red—begin to bloom in July and are fragrant. 'Superba' has larger panicles than the type. This species has gone wild in some places on the southern Oregon coast.

L. × *heckróttii* 'Goldflame' (V), thought to be a hybrid between *L. sempervírens* and *L. americána,* is almost a shrub rather than a vine, wide spreading and loose in habit, 12–15 ft. in height, with deciduous foliage, the upper leaves connate (joined at the base). Carmine buds open yellow on the inside, giving the clusters of fragrant flowers a two-toned effect. Because of its long season of bloom—from June through the summer—this plant is known as the Everblooming Honeysuckle.

L. hénryi (V), from western China has purplish red flowers, clustered two to a stalk at the shoot tips, blooming in June. This evergreen or semi-deciduous climber can grow to 30 ft. or more. Its fruits are black.

L. hispídula (VI), Hairy Honeysuckle, a native of the Pacific Coast states west of the Cascades and Sierras, has small, pink or pink-tinged yellow blossoms, and variously hairy leaves, glaucous beneath. Its small flowers are not fragrant, but it can be useful for covering dry banks; rather dainty and delicate with stems 3–9 ft. long, it will not go out of bounds where space is limited. The fruits are red.

L. japónica (IV), Japanese Honeysuckle, is a vigorous twining vine to 15–30 ft. with dark foliage, evergreen or deciduous as winter allows. The fragrant flowers are white, tinged purple, turning yellow with age, and blooming continuously from June onward. Several forms of this species are available, and all are worth growing as vines or groundcovers. They thrive in either sun or partial shade and if properly trained require little pruning. One plant will quickly cover an area of 100–150 sq. ft. In the cultivar 'Aureo-reticulata' the veins of the leaves are yellow on a green background, best developed in full sun. 'Halliana', Hall's Honeysuckle, is said by Bean to be the most beautiful form, with pure white flowers, changing to yellow, very fragrant. The leaves of var. *purpurea* are purple tinted, and coral-red fruits follow the white and yellow flowers.

L. *periclýmenum* (IV), the English Woodbine, native throughout Europe, scrambles over thickets and hedgerows in the wild. With twining stems up to 20 ft. long, it is a strong and rather untidy grower, needing plenty of room in the garden. Its deciduous, pointed, oval leaves are mostly stalked, but never connate. In June large, pinkish purple buds open into sweetly scented, creamy white flowers, which fade to a deep creamy yellow, sometimes followed by clusters of bright red berries. 'Belgica', Dutch Honeysuckle, has a rather more bushy habit, with flowers purplish red outside and yellow inside. 'Serotina' blooms over a long period in July/August with flowers dark purple outside, fading paler.

L. × *tellmanniána* (V), bred in Hungary, is considered by Bean to be one of the best honeysuckles of hybrid origin. It combines the showy Chinese L. *tragóphylla* with the colorful American L. *sempervírens* 'Superba' in a hardy deciduous plant of luxurious growth with clusters of large yellow flowers, tinted bronzy red.

MUEHLENBÉCKIA *compléxa* (VII) comes from New Zealand, and is a deciduous climber to 20–30 ft. with wiry, much-interlaced stems, which have given it the common name of Mattress Vine or Wire Vine. Its glabrous dull green leaves vary in shape and size. Tiny greenish white flowers are produced in small spikes in autumn—their perianth lobes persist and expand to become showy waxy white coverings for a black nutlet. Its dense tangle of wiry stems makes a useful and interesting cover for stumps or rock piles, though it may be killed to the ground by an unusually cold winter.

PARTHENOCÍSSUS *quinquefólia* (III), the well-known Virginia Creeper, is a handsome deciduous native of eastern United States, a rampant, fast-growing vine to 30–50 ft. The five-parted compound leaves turn brilliant scarlet and crimson in autumn. The small, dark blue, grapelike fruits, in clusters, ripen at about the same time. This species is at its best rambling up large old trees—its draperies of brilliant color contrast pleasingly with the somber foliage and dark trunks of Douglas Fir. Clinging by means of tendrils, it actually adheres to buildings. It comes easily from cuttings and will thrive in any well-drained soil. It is also tough enough to survive in adverse situations, making it a good choice for dry places or harsh city conditions. The form *engelmánnii* differs from the type in having smaller individual leaflets.

P. *tricuspidáta* (IV), Boston Ivy, from China and Japan, is another popular deciduous vine of great climbing ability to 80–100 ft. It clings tightly to walls in a dense sheet of foliage, making it valuable for softening large stark areas of stone or brick. Its glossy green leaves, varying from broadly ovate to lobed and 3-parted on different parts of the same plant, take on bright reddish autumn hues. 'Beverly Brooks' has large leaves, coloring brilliantly. 'Lowii' has small 3–7 lobed leaves when young and colors as well as the type. In 'Purpurea' the foliage remains purple throughout the summer, changing to scarlet and orange in the fall. Boston Ivy, though not quite as hardy as Virginia Creeper, has a "cast iron" constitution, thrives in any well-prepared soil, and is especially useful in cities because it withstands pollution well.

PILEOSTÉGIA viburnoídes (VII), from northern India, China, and Taiwan, is a scandent, broad-leaved, evergreen shrub, closely related to *Schizophragma* (and sometimes included in that genus). The handsome, leathery, oblong leaves are similar to those of *Viburnum odoratissimum;* leaves and shoots are scurfy when young, but later glabrous. Showy 4–6 in. clusters of white hydrangea-like flowers are plentifully produced in September and October. This is the finest of evergreen climbers for a shady north or northwest wall, and will cover an area of 50–100 sq. ft. It is said to climb over cliffs and up into trees to a height of 20 ft. or more in its native state. In cultivation it seems to prefer a light, porous soil well enriched with peat or compost. The extent of its hardiness has not been entirely determined, but it can be expected to succeed throughout the coastal sections and in sheltered gardens inland if given a shady wall.

POLÝGONUM. The 300 or more species of Dock, are in general a weedy lot, mostly herbaceous. However, a few species are valuable vines for the garden. *P. baldschúanicum* (IV), the Fleece Flower from Bokhara, is an extremely fast-growing deciduous twining climber that will run to 50–60 ft. into a tree, forming a mass of woody growth well clothed with pale green, heart-shaped leaves. Like other vines of its type, it should be given plenty of room and carefully trained when young to prevent its becoming untidy. This is one of the prettiest of the vigorous climbers, especially useful where shade is needed quickly, and capable of succeeding under adverse conditions where other vines might fail. In late summer and early autumn, compound panicles of small white or pinkish white flowers are borne in great profusion, all but hiding the foliage.

In *P. aubértii* (IV), Silver Lace Vine, or Chinese Fleece Vine, from western China, the panicles are erect and spikelike, and the fragrant flowers somewhat smaller than in the preceeding species; but it is otherwise quite similar in size, manner of growth and in the purposes it serves in the garden. There seems to be considerable confusion from one source to the next as to which species is the more common in cultivation, and they also appear to be mixed up in the trade. There are not many characters to allow the layman to separate them.

Roses

RÓSA. Climbing roses might better be described as "leaning roses," since their long, limber branches must have support of some kind. In the wild they run up into trees and over shrubs. In the garden they can be fastened to trellises, or trained against walls and along fences. They are also very effective for hiding old sheds and other eyesores, and because of their graceful, arching habit are much more useful in the informal garden scene than either the Hybrid Teas or the shrub roses. Most of today's varieties are either hybrids of climbing species no longer important in themselves, or sports of Hybrid Teas or Floribundas. A very few species of particular merit have persisted in gardens in their original form; some have a long history of cultivation in the Orient before their introduction into western gardens. All appreciate good soil and proper care, but many of the older ones in particular, will thrive under quite adverse garden conditions.

R. bánksiae (VII), Lady Banks' Rose, from China, is a favorite in the southeastern United States. Its nearly thornless stems are capable of reaching up 30–40 feet. The clusters of white or yellow flowers, a little more than 1 in. across, appear in May. 'Alba Plena' is a white-flowered double, with the fragrance of violets. 'Lutea', with double yellow flowers, and only slightly fragrant, is said to be the hardiest form, and is the most common in cultivation here. All need the protection of a warm sunny wall and are deciduous. Occasional removal of a few of the oldest canes is the only pruning necessary. They are easily propagated by cuttings taken in the fall.

R. brunónii (VII), the Himalayan Musk Rose, is another 30–40 footer, growing into the tops of tall trees in the wild. The grayish-downy leaves are either deciduous or semi-evergreen, and the stems are armed with hooked prickles. Large clusters of fragrant white flowers 1½–1¾ in. across open from pale yellow buds in late June or early July.

R. fílipes (VI), is native to western China, its arching 30-ft. shoots armed with hooked spines. The leaflets are coppery when young, later light green and deciduous. Small, fragrant, white flowers in massive clusters 1 ft. or more across are centered with a tuft of conspicuous gold stamens. Peak bloom comes in late June or early July. 'Kiftsgate' is a named selection from the English estate of that name, the original plant of which is said to now be 100 ft. wide. This species takes time to become established, but can then shoot up 20 ft. in a season, and may overwhelm adjacent plants.

All three of the foregoing are suitable for large areas only. Most named varieties of climbing roses are of much more modest proportions. Except for those which are sports of Hybrid Tea roses, the climbers found in today's gardens are of rather diverse background and few of them are of really recent origin. They have, however, stood the test of time. Many are

Rosa brunonii 'La Mortola' trained against a fence. Photo by Brian Mulligan, in early July.

Rosa 'Polyantha Grandiflora' covering a chain link fence. Photo by Jean Witt, in June.

representative of types popular in the 19th century and must be sought from dealers in old roses.

'Crimson Rambler' is typical of climbers derived from *R. multiflóra* which created a sensation with their great clusters of small bright flowers when they first appeared toward the end of the 19th century. They had, however, the disadvantage of being scentless, and were very subject to mildew, especially in our area. They have long since been superseded by healthier, fragrant types. Hybrids of similar characteristics, derived from *R. wichuraiána* (V), were popular as "Pillar Roses" in the early years of this century. The best of these inherited glossy foliage from *R. wichuraiana,* but were still largely scentless. Pink 'Dorothy Perkins' (18 ft.) is an early example, common in old gardens. 'American Pillar', (20–25 ft.) with large clusters of single bright pink flowers with a white eye, is also scentless. Ramblers as a group require an annual summer pruning to remove the canes which have bloomed and allow new ones to replace them for the following year's bloom. However, 'Hiawatha', with single white-centered red flowers and golden stamens, needs little or no pruning; about 10 ft. long, it will grow horizontally without support, and is useful as a ground-cover. 'Climbing Cecile Brunner', a sport of a Polyantha variety, grows to 20 ft. It has pink blooms deeper in the center like miniature Hybrid Teas, and can be pruned like the ramblers.

Additional climbers of assorted types and ancestries include the following:

'Alberic Barbier', with clusters of soft yellow to creamy white flowers, very double and with the fragrance of green apples, is a graceful rambler to 20 ft. or so with luxurious shining dark green foliage, blooming in mid-summer and not dependent on an annual pruning. Graham Thomas considers this one of the very best climbing roses.

'Alister Stella Gray' is a 20-ft. plant, blooming from June to October with 3-in. double, yellow, fragrant flowers.

'Blaze' has been supplanted by 'Improved Blaze', which has greater disease resistance. Its clusters of semidouble scarlet red blossoms, 2–3 in. across, begin in June and continue all summer. Old shoots should be pruned out as new ones grow up. Height 8–10 ft.

'Félicité et Perpétue' has clusters of tiny, tightly double flowers, creamy white, tinted flesh, from crimson-flushed buds. It is semi-evergreen to 12–15 ft., needing only light pruning. It was raised in France in 1827.

'Gloire de Dijon' blooms continuously throughout the summer with fragrant, double, buff-yellow flowers tinted pink and apricot, on 15-ft. canes.

'Handel' is creamy white with a pink edge, deepening in color in warm weather, with canes to about 8 ft.

'Max Graf', a *R. rugosa-R. wichuraiana* hybrid, is a good groundcover rose, hardy and disease resistant, to about 7–8 ft., bearing a wealth of small bright pink flowers. 'Dortmund', its tetraploid descendant, is a recurrent bloomer, with clusters of very large single blossoms in crimson red with a white eye and shiny foliage. It also grows to about 7–8 ft.

'Mermaid', a *R. bracteáta* hybrid, to 20–30 ft., produces large, pale yellow flowers, flat and single, blooming continuously from summer into autumn. This is a great favorite with climbing rose buffs, but is not as hardy as might be desirable and can be killed by a cold winter, even in the Puget Sound area.

'Mme, Alfred Carrière', a climbing Tea-Noisette Hybrid, runs easily up to 20 ft., blooming over a long season with fragrant, very full, creamy-centered flowers, fading to white. It needs full sun in the Northwest.

'New Dawn', a perpetual flowering sport of pale pink, June-blooming 'Dr. Van Fleet', is at 12–15 ft., slightly less vigorous than its 20-ft. parent, but has the same merits of fragrance and disease-resistant foliage.

'Paul's Scarlet Climber', with clusters of medium-sized, semidouble flowers of intense scarlet red, requires very little pruning and is very free flowering, to 20 ft., but has been rather overplanted in the past.

'Réveil Dijonnais', a Floribunda climber, produces sweetly fragrant, semidouble flowers in midsummer, in a brilliant cerise-scarlet with yellow centers and a yellow reverse to the petals. Although it grows to 12 ft., it makes a better shrub than climber because of its rather bushy habit.

'Rhonda' has double flowers 3–4 in. across, in pink shaded with coral, blooming all summer on 7–8 ft. canes with good glossy foliage. It is suitable as a pillar rose.

'Ruth Alexander', raised in the Pacific Northwest, was highly acclaimed in its day for its rich, glowing orange semidouble flowers, flushed with red. However, styles in climbers have shifted toward varieties with a longer season of bloom, on shorter and less heavily armored plants. While the color remains unusual, and the buds are elegant, the 15–20 ft. canes with their horrendous thorns seem miserly with their blooms by today's standards.

'Sombreuil' is another great favorite, reaching 10–15 ft., with fragrant ivory cream flowers.

'White Dawn' has 2–3 in. slightly fragrant double flowers on canes up to 12 ft., blooming over the entire summer.

Many Hybrid Tea roses have produced climbing sports over the years, and while their plants are rather stiffer than those of the preceding varieties, they are useful against walls or pillars, and produce many more blooms than their shrub counterparts. Among the most attractive and durable varieties are:

'Climbing Dainty Bess', with exquisite single pink flowers with red-brown stamens, the plants reaching 8–12 ft.

'Climbing Ena Harkness' is a fine older variety with very fragrant crimson flowers, blooming over a long period and reaching about 15 ft.

'Climbing McGredy's Ivory' is one of the few Hybrid Tea sports with white flowers; its height is about 12 ft.

'Climbing Talisman', with flowers blended red, gold, copper and yellow, reaches about 8–9 ft.

SCHIZOPHRÁGMA hydrangeoídes (V) is a deciduous 40-ft. climber from Japan, which clings to tree trunks or walls with aerial roots. Its leaves, coarsely toothed and broadly ovate in outline, are 4–6 in. long, and turn a pale yellow in the fall. The small yellowish-white flowers appear in July, gathered into flat-topped inflorescences as much as 10–12 in. across. Pale yellow heart-shaped bracts, like little paddles, float peripherally around the clusters of fertile flowers, and are the most eye-catching feature of the plant. In 'Rosea' the bracts are tinged with rose. This vine is easily grown in any good garden soil, preferably with plenty of moisture.

SOLÁNUM críspum (VII) is a partially woody, semi-evergreen vine from Chile and Peru, up to 30 ft., suitable for the milder parts of our area. Dainty bluish-purple flowers are borne from June to September. Quick growing and tolerant of poor soil, it can be trimmed back each year in early spring.

S. jasminoídes (VII–VIII), from Brazil, is a beautiful vine popular in California gardens, but not nearly so well known as it should be in the coastal sections of this region. It should be grown in the warmest possible location in light sandy soil. If not cut to the ground by frosts during the winter, it is better pruned severely to produce the maximum amount of new growth (up to 15–20 ft.), and the best bloom. The type has pale blue flowers, but the 'Album' form is commoner in cultivation, blooming all summer long with a profusion of large white flowers against neat dark green foliage tinged with bronze-purple. Being evergreen, this species is more likely than *S. crispum* to be cut back in severe winters, but this is not a problem since it blooms on the current year's growth. Summer cuttings of half-ripened wood strike readily.

S. dulcamára (IV), European Bittersweet or Bitter Nightshade, a small purple flowered twiner spread by birds and sometimes naturalized in our area, hardly qualifies as an ornamental vine, and in any case is to be avoided since its poisonous red fruits are far too attractive to children.

STAUNTÓNIA hexaphýlla (VII–VIII), from Southern Korea and Japan, is an evergreen climber to 30–40 ft. developing stoutly woody primary stems. The handsome, leathery foliage is divided into several pointed, radiating leaflets. The small, violet-tinged white flowers are fragrant and unisexual. This is a plant for a warm south or west wall, deserving wider use in protected locations.

VÍTIS. There are about 50 species of wild grapes, all from the Northern Hemisphere; and grapes are, of course, among the most ancient of cultivated vines. A few of the former are outstanding garden plants, and the fruit-producing varieties can most certainly double as ornamental vines. Grapes grown for their fruit demand a deep, light, rich soil; a position in full sun with a free circulation of air; and support on wires or trellises. They require careful pruning in winter, before growth starts in the spring. Branches from the previous season are cut back to within 2–4 buds of older wood, so that the vine builds a permanent trunk very slowly. However, when a grape is grown primarily for ornament, it may be allowed to build a large skeleton structure, 200 sq. ft. or so, and can then be cut to this outline each spring. Grapes respond to generous applications of fertilizer, and a little pruning—pinching out of the tips of the shoots—is advised to check the growth in midsummer after 2–3 fruit clusters have formed. Plenty of water is necessary during the time the fruit is growing, but water should be withheld after fruit ripens, to allow the wood to harden off.

Both slip-skin grapes—fox grapes of the 'Concord' type derived from *V. labrúsca* (V) of eastern North American—and European wine grapes, derived from *V. vinifera* (V–VI), can be grown in the Pacific Northwest. Consult the Cooperative Extension Service for information on varieties suitable for your particular area. In addition to the fruiting forms, *V. vinifera* has a form with purple foliage, 'Purpúrea,' which brightens to crimson in the fall. All are deciduous, in the 12–15 ft. range.

V. coignétiae (V) from Japan is a very vigorous species to 60 ft. or more with large, only slightly lobed leaves, most effective when allowed to run up into the tops of tall trees as it does in the wild. Flowers, as in all grapes, are tiny and inconspicuous, but the leaves color wonderfully in autumn, with vivid scarlet and crimson tones. Carefully trained, this species can also be used as a bank cover and to cascade down walls.

V. davídii (V. armáta) (VI) from China is another large-leaved species which colors brilliant red in autumn. Its stems to 50 ft. or more are distinctively armored with glandular, hooked bristles. The toothed, heart-shaped leaves can be up to 10 in. long and 8 in. wide. Its rather large black fruits are edible.

V. califórnica (VII), which reaches into the Umpqua and Rogue River valleys of southern Oregon, does not color as well and has little to recommend it except rampant growth; but it could be used similarly, allowed to run up trees in the wild garden. It can reach a height of 60–70 ft.

WISTÉRIA. This genus has North American as well as Asian species, but only the latter are of horticultural importance. They are among the finest of our spring-flowering woody climbers, as well as some of the very largest.

W. floribúnda (IV), Japanese Wisteria, is a deciduous vine of very large proportions, 30 ft. or more high, ultimately developing a heavy twining trunk and needing a stout framework for a support—a pipe or a tall evergreen tree is recommended. The glossy, dark green leaves, pinnately compound, with a dozen or more small leaflets, are downy when young. The slender, pendent racemes of fragrant violet flowers bloom successively from base to tip. The horticultural forms, developed through centuries of selection in Japan, have been derived from the spectacular variety 'Macrobotrys' ('Multijuga') and may have racemes 3–4 ft. long. Among the varieties available from nurseries are 'Alba', with white flowers; 'Rosea', in which the flowers have pale rose standards and purple wings and keels; 'Royal Purple', with darker than usual color; and 'Violacea Plena', a double in which the flowers are little rosettes, rather than pea shaped, and somewhat less attractive.

W. sinénsis (V), Chinese Wisteria, carries shorter, broader racemes of fragrant flowers, individually larger than those of Japanese wisteria, but less graceful than the longer clusters. *W. sinensis* flowers in April, a week or two before *W. floribunda,* and does have the advantage of producing additional bloom off and on throughout the summer. 'Alba' is a white-flowered form. Gray-velvety, bean-shaped pods may hang on the vine all winter, exploding with an audible pop when warmed by the early spring sun. This species displays its blooms to good advantage when trained against a wall, and since it grows very rapidly, can cover a great deal of space in a short time, a 100 ft. or more in each direction! On the other hand, *W. floribunda* is more attractive running along a porch or over a pergola where its very long racemes can hang down to form a curtain. The white varieties show up best against a dark or shadowed background.

W. venústa (V), Silky Wisteria from Japan, is similar to the Chinese Wisteria and takes its name from the downy hairs on the shoots and leaves. Its pendulous flower clusters, blooming in May and June, are short and broad, with fragrant white flowers which individually are larger than those of the two preceding species. There is also a variety with soft, lavender-purple flowers, f. *violacea.* This species, though available in nurseries, is not

The Japanese *Wisteria venusta* flowering in a Seattle garden in early May. Photo by Brian Mulligan.

as common in Northwest gardens as the other two and deserves to be better known.

When buying wisterias, it is necessary to select them in bloom to be certain of obtaining plants of suitable form in the color and fragrance desired. Both grafted and vegetatively propagated plants are offered in the nursery trade. Grafted plants should be watched, so that suckers do not come up from below the graft. Wisterias respond favorably to a rich, heavy soil and ample moisture in the early part of the growing season. They can be planted with their roots in either sun or shade, but the top must be in full sun. They need very careful training to obtain maximum bloom. A plant producing masses of whiplike shoots but little bloom may be receiving too much moisture in late summer. If persistent shortening of the shoots fails to curb the masses of growth, it may be necessary to root prune the vine, or face the fact that it really should be covering a greatly increased area. A single vine can easily be trained to a distance of 350 to 500 feet, and can in fact be extended almost without limit. Wisterias can also be obtained in standard form to be trained as free-standing shrubs. This method displays the beautiful panicles of bloom to good advantage, but requires a great deal more pruning to maintain a proper shape.

CHAPTER XIII

Palms, Yuccas and Bamboos

PALMS

Palm trees are hardly more than a curiosity in Northwest gardens—only two species can be considered at all successful.

CHAMAEROPS húmilis (VIII), Dwarf Fan Palm, is of interest as the only palm native to Europe, around the western Mediterranean Sea. Never more than a few feet in height, and often more bushlike than treelike, it needs a good loamy soil, and a sunny sheltered location, such as a south-facing entry way, or perhaps an atrium. Its fibrous trunk gives rise to numerous short-stemmed, fan-shaped leaves, the segments varying from a few inches up to a foot or more in length.

TRACHYCÁRPUS fórtunei (VII), Chinese Windmill Palm, is hardier than the preceding species, and considerably larger as well—up to 20–30 ft. Its trunk is strongly patterned with the coarse, fibrous remains of leaf bases. The fan-shaped leaves up to 2 ft. long and 4 ft. wide, pleated toward the base and raggedly pointed at the tips, persist for several seasons. Specimens in the Carl English Gardens at the Hiram M. Chittenden Locks in Seattle have survived the worst winters of the last 30 years without injury, and have even bloomed upon occasion, producing great clusters of tiny, bright yellow flowers. The marble-sized blue-black fruits, falling to the ground beneath, germinate in great numbers, constituting a possible nuisance. However, as this palm is normally dioecious, the chances of a single plant fruiting excessively are remote. This species will do best if sheltered from cold north winds in the winter; it does not seem to be fussy about soil, but will need supplementary watering during our dry summer months.

YUCCAS

YÚCCA. These evergreen shrubs are members of the lily family usually associated with the southwestern United States, but actually ranging from Central America as far north as North Dakota and New

335

Mature trees of the Chusan palm, *Trachycarpus fortunei,* along a street in California. Photo by Don Normark.

The Chusan palm, *Trachycarpus fortunei,* growing in Seattle. Photo by Don Normark.

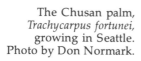

Jersey. Several species do quite well in the Northwest. With their rosettes of stiff, swordlike leaves and immense panicles of creamy white flowers, they are difficult to place in the average garden setting, but they can be very dramatic as accents for large dry-area plantings. Some of the stiffer types could be used as barriers.

Y. *baccáta* (VII), Datil Yucca or Blue Yucca, is native to desert areas from southern Colorado to eastern California. Its basal rosettes, with pale gray-green leaves, 2 in. wide and 2 ft. long, grow at ground level or up on short trunks. Two-foot-long clusters of white flowers, red-brown on the outside, come in May or June.

Y. *filamentósa* (IV), Adam's Needle, is a thoroughly hardy species of sandy habitats on the eastern and southeastern coastal plains, as far north as New Jersey. It takes its name from the threadlike filaments curling off the edges of the leaves. This is a stately plant in the garden. Its leaves, in basal tufts, may be up to 1½ ft. long, with flowering stalks from 3–6 ft. tall bearing great masses of large, creamy white flowers during July–August.

In Y. *fláccida* (IV), another southeastern species, the leaves are 1–1¾ ft. long, the outer ends hanging downward with long tapered points and marginal fibers. The flower panicles are shorter, with downy branchlets and stems. This is a vigorous, free-flowering species, fragrant in the evening. 'Golden Sword' and 'Bright Edge' are forms with striped foliage, the former with green margins and yellow centers, the latter with the color pattern reversed. These cultivars may also be found listed as Y. *filamentosa*.

Y. *gláuca* (IV), Small Soapweed, from the west-central United States, has slender, glaucous, white-margined leaves rising from a prostrate stem. The 3–4 ft. racemes of flowers are greenish white rather than creamy; they flower in July and August. 'Stricta' has a more branched inflorescence than the type. In 'Rosea' the flowers are tinted pink on the outside.

Y. *gloriósa* (VI–VII), Spanish Dagger, is a sand dune plant from the southeastern United States. It has short thick stems, sometimes branched, topped with rosettes of stiff, spiny-tipped leaves. It flowers from July/September with a narrowly conical panicle 3–8 ft. tall and up to a foot wide. The creamy white flowers are sometimes tinged with red on the outside. Forms with variegated foliage also are listed.

Y. *harrimániae* (V–VI) is another small, summer-flowering species from the southwestern United States which has been growing success-fully in the Carl English garden at the Hiram M. Chittenden Locks in Seattle and could be expected to succeed in other parts of our region. It has narrow leaves under 18 in. in length and relatively large, greenish white flowers in unbranched clusters 1–3 ft. tall.

Y. *recurvifólia* (VI), from coastal southeastern United States, has leaves, 2–3 ft. long, tapering to a thin point, and reflexed downward. Its flower clusters are raised up on short, more or less branched stems. The flowers are more loosely arranged and the inflorescence accordingly somewhat more graceful in the preceding species. It flowers in late summer and is said to resist snow and dampness well.

Yuccas can be propagated by taking cuttings of their underground stolons. The tips of these dormant underground shoots can be used without disturbing the main plant. Some of the smaller species can also be propagated by divisions of the crown, or from seeds.

A Yucca in bloom in the summer, probably *Y. flaccida.* Photo by Don Normark.

BAMBOOS

Bamboos are woody members of the grass family. Their beauty has long been proclaimed in Oriental art, and since World War II they have been making their way into Northwest gardens in increasing numbers. With their jointed "fishing pole" stems—known as culms—and their graceful, drooping foliage, they are distinct in habit from all other woody evergreens, suggesting the lushness of the tropics, while being normally quite hardy. To grow well they need a deep rich soil with plenty of moisture and a generous fall mulching of manure or compost, coupled with a well-balanced fertilizer. A site protected from north winds is desirable.

The main problem in the cultivation of bamboos, however, is not in getting them to grow, but rather in preventing them from spreading too vigorously. Except for those of tufted habit, which are mostly tropical and not hardy, they spread rapidly by means of underground rhizomes. When placing bamboos in the garden it is therefore necessary to plan as well for their control. This can be accomplished by surrounding the area they are to occupy with either a thin concrete wall or a galvanized sheet metal barrier 2 ft. deep. Another alternative is to dig a foot-deep perimeter trench around the plants, allowing it to fill with the leaves, which are shed in late summer. Wandering rhizomes can be located easily within the trench and chopped off before they invade the surrounding terrain.

Bamboos are propagated by division of clumps and can be grown from small portions of the creeping woody rootstock which contain one or more "eyes" or dormant buds. The first year after planting the divisions will throw up shoots varying from 6 in. to 3 ft. in height. Under favorable conditions new shoots twice as long will be thrown up the following year. Each succeeding year stronger and taller shoots will be produced until the maximum height is achieved. The larger bamboos seldom receive sufficient watering and fertilizing in gardens to enable them to reach their full size; moreover, restricting the roots tends to restrict the height also.

One of the most interesting features of bamboos, after they are well established, is the ability of their culms to reach their maximum height—be it 6 in. or 60 ft.—in a matter of a few weeks. The lateral branches do not develop until the second year in a few cases, but the main shoot does not increase in height or girth after the first season. This is why water and fertilizer are so important. Individual stems live from 5–10 or more years, becoming completely woody after about 3 years. They may be thinned from time to time so that the clump or group does not become too dense—meandering paths through a bamboo grove have a charm all their own. Thinned culms come in handy for stakes or trellises.

The flowering habits of bamboos are curious and catastrophic. Most of them flower only at long intervals—decades or up to 120 years apart—and bamboos of a given species will bloom simultaneously in widely separate parts of the world. The death of the plant follows, wiping out entire stands of some species. Others die back, then make a slow recovery. Bean suggests that plantings may possibly be saved by cutting off all stems close to the ground when they show the first signs of flowering; but recovery is slow at best, if it takes place at all. Fortunately, this phenomenon of flowering and dying occurs in only a single species at any one time, so alternative species are available if one loses an entire planting. Japanese Timber bamboo (*Phyllostachys bambusoides*) bloomed in Seattle in the 1970s with many losses; but Black Bamboo (*P. nigra*) has not bloomed since 1907.

This infrequent flowering habit has led to problems in nomenclature. Species which bloom only rarely may be reassigned to a different genus after botanists finally have a chance to observe their flowers. Some species have been in several genera since they were originally described.

ARUNDINÁRIA dísticha (V), Dwarf Fernleaf Bamboo from Japan, is a dainty plant only 1–3 ft. in height, well described by its common name. Small, bright green leaflets, distinctive for their two-ranked arrangement, are borne on culms only ⅛ in. in diameter.

A. japónica (VI), (*Sása japónica, Pséudosasa japónica*), Japanese Arrow

Bamboo, presents a somewhat tufted habit, spreading only slowly. Its culms average 10–12 ft. in height, though they can go higher under good conditions. Its leaves are large—up to 2 in. wide and 12 in. long, with a long tapered point, and are a glossy dark green.

A. simónii (VI), Simon Bamboo from China is a vigorous creeper with deep green culms 1 in. in diameter and up to 24 ft. tall. The leaves are broadly wedge shaped at the base, with long tapered points, and can be up to 1 ft. long. In the cultivar 'Variegata', some of the leaves are striped with white.

A. variegáta (VI–VII), the Dwarf White-striped Bamboo from Japan, has ¼ in. pale green stems growing 1–3 ft. tall, and is a fast spreader needing containment. Its leaves, up to 7 in. long and 1 in. wide, are striped lengthwise with creamy white—sometimes almost more white than green. This is the most attractive of the white-variegated bamboos. *A. argénteo-striáta* and *A. chíno* var. *váginata* 'Variegata' also have green and white striped leaves.

Three foot high *A. víridistriata* (VI), also from Japan, has slender purplish stems and striking golden-variegated leaves 8 in. long and 1¼ in. wide. The leaves are actually mostly golden, with narrow green stripes, making it distinct from all other bamboos. It needs full sun to develop the best color.

SINARUNDINÁRIA *nítida* (V), the Blue Bamboo from China, is leafless except at the tips during its first year. The deep purple stems can reach 10–12 ft. in height, though they are only ⅜ in. through. The mass of the second year's slender, pointed leaves—2–3 in. long and less than 1 in. wide—leads to graceful arching of the stems. Although this is a very vigorous species, it is adversely affected by drought and too much sun, and requires a semishaded location with plenty of moisture. This species forms crowded clumps of stems rather than running.

PHYLLOSTÁCHYS. This genus includes the best of the taller bamboos. Its distinguishing character is that the flattened side of the culm alternates between each pair of nodes up the stem. All species mentioned here are loosely and openly branched. They spread at a moderate rate, but still need to be kept under control.

P. áurea (VI), Golden Bamboo, comes from China, but has long been cultivated in Japan. It is a graceful 15–18 ft. species, and is one of the best known bamboos in gardens here. Its popular name refers to its bright golden stems.

P. bambusoídes (VI), Giant or Japanese Timber Bamboo, came originally from China, and grows to 15–25 ft. or more if not confined. Stem diameter can be as much as 6 in., but is not more than 2 in. under our conditions. Its leaves, up to 6 in. long and 1 in. or more across, are bright green. This is one of the finest of the hardy bamboos, but its availability has been sharply curtailed since its flowering in the 1970s. In the cultivar 'Castillonis' or 'Castillon', the culms are bright yellow with the alternating flat portions bright green. Leaves, too, are striped with yellow in varying amounts, making this the most colorful of the hardy bamboos.

P. flexuósa (VI), Zigzag Bamboo from China, is a graceful medium-sized plant with leaves ½ in. across and up to 4 in. long, dark green above, and glaucous beneath. Its slender stems—6–8 ft. tall (or more in warm climates)—turn from green to almost black as they age.

P. nígra (VI), the Black Bamboo of China, so called from the very dark color of its culms, is one of the most elegant and distinctive of bamboos. Slightly smaller than the Golden Bamboo or the Timber Bamboo, it has slender willowly canes to about 8–10 ft. if restricted, almost double that if allowed to spread. Arching branches bear drooping sprays of foliage, the leaves 2–3 in. long, and about ½ in. wide. In the cultivar 'Boryana', also listed as 'Bory Bamboo', the stems are yellow rather than black at maturity. 'Henon Bamboo' has green stems and is known for its luxuriant foliage.

SÁSA is a genus of dwarf bamboos, two of which can be highly recommended as garden subjects, while a third is a menace. *S. palmáta* (VI), from Japan, is an extremely handsome species up to 6 ft. tall, with broad, rich green leaves as much as 12–15 in. long and 3–4 in. wide, flaring out like the fingers of a hand. Although decidedly invasive, this bamboo gives such a dramatic effect that it is well worth the effort of keeping it under control.

S. tesselláta (VI) from China is somewhat shorter than the preceding species—4–5 ft., but has even larger leaves—up to 18 in. long. The stems supporting them are tiny—¼ inch through or less—but durable, and this species spreads slowly, forming a rounded clump.

S. véitchii (VI) from Japan is about half the height of the two preceding species and has much smaller leaves, which die off at the edges, appearing as interesting tan variegation or merely tatty, depending on one's point of view. The looks of the leaves is rather a moot point, however, since the plant is such a rampant spreader that it is best avoided altogether—except possibly in containers. Once established it is very hard to eradicate. With so many other highly desirable bamboos available any use of *S. veitchii* would seem ill advised.

SEMIARUNDINÁRIA fástuosa (V), Narihira Bamboo, from Japan, is a beautiful and stately species, less rampant than *Arundinaria simonii*. Its culms, up to 15–18 ft. tall, are olive green, with large red-purple tinted sheaths. Its leaves are 4–8 in. long and up to 1 in. wide. This is one of the hardiest of the bamboos.

THAMNOCÁLAMUS spatháceus (VI–VII). This Chinese species, long known as *Sinarundinária muriélae,* flowered recently and was found to belong neither to *Arundinaria* nor *Sinarundinaria*. It puts up leafless, bright green stems ½ in. thick one year, while its cloud of graceful foliage appears the following year. Its stems eventually turn bright yellow. Quite similar in its clumping habit to *S. nitida,* and equally graceful and attractive when mature, it will attain 10–12 ft. in height in a suitable, partially shaded site.

CHAPTER XIV

Conifers

Conifers have strong character, whether evergreen or deciduous. The aggragated mass of their needlelike leaves, in contrast to the glossy foliage of broad-leaved evergreens, reflects less light and produces a darker effect. In the Pacific Northwest where the majority of evergreen conifers grow readily, they have been rather overworked as garden plant materials. The use of trees as accent points is discussed in the introduction to the chapter on Deciduous Trees. These recommendations apply even more strongly in the placing of conifers.

The coniferous evergreen trees and shrubs do have an important part to play in large scale plantings, lending great strength and dignity to the landscape scene. They may be grown as freestanding specimens on expanses of lawn, with their foliage coming right down to the ground, but this treatment is feasible only in large areas. Big conifers occasionally may be used to advantage in comparatively small area if they are grown with trunks bare to a considerable height, furnishing a canopy of branches high overhead. A stand of native Douglas Fir is often incorporated in the garden in this way. Certain practical considerations must be taken into account when this is done. Any garden planting underneath conifers will need a great deal of watering, because not only do the trees draw heavily on the moisture in the soil, but also less rain reaches the ground where it is over-hung with their branches. Some particularly tough and sturdy ground-cover, such as ivy or *Pachysandra,* may be used if it is necessary to reduce maintenance to a minimum.

Our best native conifers, unfortunately, are the largest species in their respective genera, of stature more suitable for parks than for small home gardens. Homeowners frequently find, after only a few decades, that their prized Douglas Firs or White Pines have become a menace in windstorms or are shading half the lot. Topped conifers are a visual disaster in a landscape—the best answer for specimens grown too large is to remove them completely and replace them with smaller, slower-growing species.

Coniferous evergreen trees of medium size have an important part to play in the garden, but they should be used with restraint. They take their place both in foundation plantings and shrubbery groups as accent points, and combine well with broad-leaved evergreen shrubs. Golden-needled and blue-glaucous forms add brightness to the winter garden scene, much needed in our cloudy winters. It is essential when selecting conifers for any purpose to have accurate information as to their ultimate height and also their normal outline and approximate spread. With a wide range of sizes to choose from, there is no reason for selecting species or varieties which will exceed their position.

DWARF AND SLOW GROWING FORMS

Conifer species that have been in cultivation for many years have given rise to a variety of small forms, some of which are so diminutive as to fit into the smallest rock garden. These are not specimens which have been grown in pots or tubs and dwarfed as bonsai, but forms which retain their small habit under normal garden conditions. Dwarf varieties have originated in three ways:

(1) Some conifers vary tremendously when raised from seed, and in certain cases, exceptionally dwarf forms have been selected and propagated by nurserymen, given clonal names and distributed to the public. One of the best examples of this is *Picea abies*, the Norway Spruce. There are over 60 distinct dwarf forms of Norway Spruce in cultivation, a number of which originated as seedlings. Dwarf clones have also arisen from plants found in the wild and propagated vegetatively.

(2) Another source of dwarfs are the bud mutations known as "witches'-brooms". They may occur on Norway Spruce, or on *Cryptomeria japonica*, or on pines, and are common on Douglas Fir in our own mountains. High up in a large, well-developed tree of normal habit, a congested, twiggy mass of branchlets forms, with decreased growth rate and needle size; this is spontaneous, and not the result of fungus or other disease. Cuttings taken from this and rooted or grafted usually retain the dense, slow-growing habit of the broom, producing a dwarf plant of distinct and striking characteristics. Shoots which revert to normal habit should be pruned out immediately.

(3) The final group of valuable dwarfs are those known as juvenile forms. This term needs explanation. Anyone who has observed a typical seedling of the native Western Red Cedar, *Thuja plicata*, will recall that it has a fine, almost heatherlike foliage, which is quite different from the scale leaves produced later on. Normally, these needlelike seedling leaves, or juvenile foliage, soon disappear. However, some junipers always retain a mixture of distinct juvenile and mature foliage, while seedlings of certain *Chamaecyparis* fail to produce any adult foliage. The resulting variant

specimens are known as juvenile forms; they are also usually smaller in stature at maturity than their normal foliaged parents. The native Lawson Cypress or Port Orford Cedar, *Chamaecyparis lawsoniana,* has produced several good juvenile forms. One of these, 'Fletcheri', has fine, soft, gray-green foliage and grows no more than 25–30 ft. high, while the typical Lawson Cypress is a 150-ft. tree. The Japanese Hinoki Cypress, *C. obtusa,* and *C. pisifera,* the Sawara Cypress, and *Cryptomeria japonica* have also given rise to interesting juvenile forms. The fluffy foliage of all of these fits readily into the ordinary garden planting. With their softness of outline, they are less dominant than the average conifer with adult foliage and do not stand out in sharp contrast to their surroundings. Dwarfs which have crisp outlines and stiff foliage, such as the miniature pines and spruces, are best used in the rock garden where their positive character is set off to good advantage. Juvenile forms usually prefer some shade and tend to require much more moisture than their parents. Also, they frequently need judicious pruning during the growing season, especially when young, to make neat, shapely (though not too regular) specimens.

The majority of the dwarf conifers readily obtainable are discussed here. Anyone wishing to study them in greater detail should refer to the *Manual of Dwarf Conifers,* revised edition, by Humphrey J. Welch, published in 1979 by Theophrastus Publishers/Garland STPM Press, New York.

NOMENCLATURE

A great deal of confusion has arisen in the application of common names to some of the conifers. The terms "cedar" and "cypress" are especially ambiguous. Our native Western Red Cedar or Arbor-vitae belongs to the genus *Thuja, T. plicata.* The native Port Orford Cedar, or Lawson's Cypress, is correctly *Chamaecyparis lawsoniana*—literally, False Cypress. Incense Cedar from southern Oregon and northern California is *Calocedrus decurrens.* The Red Cedar of eastern United States, from which cedar chests are made, is a juniper, *Juniperus virginiana.* Then there are the true Cedars of the Old World—*Cedrus libani,* the Cedar of Lebanon of biblical fame; the Deodar Cedar from the Himalayas, *C. deodara;* and the North African Cedar, *C. atlantica.* Finally, there are the true cypresses, *Cupressus,* of which the Italian Cypress, *C. sempervirens,* and the Monterey Cypress, *C. macrocarpa,* are representative species. For added confusion, the Bald Cypress of southeastern United States is *Taxodium distichum.* Thus, there are in common usage seven distinct botanical genera included under the names cedar and cypress!

Botanical nomenclature has also undergone changes. The Big Tree, formerly *Sequoia gigantea,* is now *Sequoiadendron giganteum. Libocedrus decur-*

rens has become *Calocedrus decurrens*. There are sound botanical reasons for these changes.

Conifers may be transplanted at the same seasons as broad-leaved evergreens, either in the early fall, or in the spring, or during the winter months. Detailed soil preparation and planting instructions will be found in the chapters on Garden Maintenance and the introduction to Deciduous Trees.

All of the large arborescent conifers are best raised from seed or obtained as small plants grown in the open ground—not in containers—and planted out in their permanent position as soon as possible. This is particularly important in the case of any of the deep-rooting kinds that resent disturbance, such as pines, the Monterey Cypress, the Incense Cedar, and some of the junipers. Selected forms, such as those with unusually fine foliage color, or distinctive habit of growth, must be propagated vegetatively. The simplest method of vegetative propagation is by means of cuttings taken in fall or February. Most conifers except *Pinus*, *Cedrus* and *Abies*, strike readily. Those which do not are usually grafted on seedlings of the type. Cuttings should be planted in a shaded cold frame using a soil mix of perlite, peat and coarse sand.

The smaller or medium-sized conifers may require more or less moisture according to their position in the garden, whether they are high on a dry slope or down in a moist hollow. Since they are small, they can always be given enough water from the hose to meet their needs. The large conifers, as a rule, must fend for themselves, so they should be chosen according to the cultural conditions of the site. Spruce (*Picea*), fir (*Abies*), or hemlock (*Tsuga*) should not be planted unless there is ample available moisture in the soil. Pines and junipers are best in deep, light, well-drained soil even if it is rather poor. The native Douglas Fir is a cosmopolitan tree, thriving under a very wide range of conditions.

Any pruning necessary for the training of conifers should be done during the season of active growth. It is absolutely imperative to leave some foliage on any branch or portion of the tree that is being pruned. Most conifers will not re-sprout when cut back to old wood, and for this reason they must have careful training when young. Two notable exceptions to this are the yews, *Taxus*, and the China Fir, *Cunninghamia*. The best time for the removal of large limbs is during the months of July and August. Cutting at this period will reduce the bleeding of the wound to a minimum. It is necessary to decide early in the life of the tree whether it is to be grown with a clear, bare trunk, or with the branches spreading to the ground. If the branches are to be removed, this should be a gradual and progressive process that starts when the tree is small. Limbs on the smaller conifers are not usually trimmed up. Conifers which are still too large for their space after being limbed up should be removed. Trying to reduce their size by constant trimming is futile, and they should never be topped, which completely destroys their outline.

ÁBIES are the true firs. (Our native Douglas Fir is not a true fir, but a false hemlock—*Pseudotsuga!*) There are about 50 species distributed throughout the Northern Hemisphere. All are handsome, stately trees with crisp, symmetrical, conical outlines and horizontal branches thickly clothed with rich green needles. Most of them carry attractive cones which stand upright on the branches and disintegrate on ripening. This is one of the best characteristics for distinguishing the true firs from spruces, Douglas Fir, and other genera with which they might be confused. True firs thrive in gardens in our region in any good, friable soil. They are moisture-loving trees, and although fairly adaptable to a variety of conditions, are not drought resistant. They are, however, with a few exceptions, far too large for plantings of average size.

A. *álba* (IV), the Silver Fir from the mountains of Europe, has long been in cultivation there. The type is a slender, pyramidal tree up to 150 ft. tall, which forms a regular, dense mass of dark green foliage, silvery on the underside.

A. *amábilis* (V), the Pacific Silver Fir, which ranges from southeastern Alaska to southern Oregon, is quite similar to the European Silver Fir. In Washington it is usually found at elevations of 3000 ft. or above. It is slow-growing, ultimately reaching a height of 120–150 ft. or more, but is much too large for the average garden.

A. *balsámea* (III), a native of eastern North America, which takes its name from the fragrance of its needles, is a tree of more moderate size, to 75 ft. It is perhaps best known in its cultivar 'Hudsonia', a tight dwarf seldom more than 2 ft. tall, with needles arranged semi-radially around the stems. This is a useful conifer for the large rock garden. 'Nana' is a loose, 1-ft.-high shrub with very short needles densely packed around the twigs.

A. *bracteáta* (VII), Bristlecone or Santa Lucia Fir, from the mountains of central California is a moderately rapid-growing tree, with flat 2–2½ in.-long, very sharply pointed needles of dark, shining green. Handsome while young because of its shaggy texture and shining foliage, it may grow to over 100 ft. tall. Called Bristlecone Fir because of the long, stiff bracts which extend from the 4-in.-long, barrel-shaped cones, it may take 20 or more years to produce these decorative features. It is best used as a specimen tree and should be given a sunny location. Avoid planting it in frost pockets since its new growth is somewhat tender; a hillside location is preferable.

A. *cóncolor* (IV), the Colorado White Fir, is another western North American species of *Abies* quite common in cultivation. With its beautiful, soft, glaucous foliage it resembles the popular Blue Spruce. However, it is not so stiff or crisp in outline, and this softness renders it more easily accommodated in the garden setting. It forms a broadly based pyramidal tree attaining a height of 100–120 ft. with a spread of as much as 30–40 ft. at the base. It has produced several varietal forms, a number of which are dwarfs or foliage-color variants.

'Argentea' is a good, bright silver form.

'Candicans' is a vivid blue-gray.

'Compacta' is a slow-growing silver-blue dwarf, somewhat irregular in shape.

'Gable's Weeping' is prostrate with pendulous branches and needles shorter than normal.

'Green Globe' is a sage green dwarf, said to be drought resistant.

A. grándis (VI), the Grand Fir, is the only native fir commonly found at lowland levels throughout this region, almost always in moist situations. The glossy, bright green leaves form characteristic flat sprays on the olive-brown twigs. The large cones are brown when mature. Although not a tree of any great horticultural value, it may well be incorporated in the garden planting where it occurs on ground that is brought under cultivation. Unfortunately, it is the largest species of the genus, ultimately 200–250 ft. tall!

A. koreána (V), Korean Fir, is slower growing than most firs although it may eventually be 60 ft. tall with a columnar habit. Its blunt needles are dark green above, shining silver beneath, making a pleasing contrast. It is remarkable in coming at a very young age, unusual in *Abies*, and it may bear its 2–3 in. long purple cones at eye level. It makes a fine small specimen plant for use in lawn or other plantings.

A. lasiocárpa (IV), Subalpine Fir, is one of several conifers sold as "alpines." A slender spire of a tree to 80–100 ft. in its home above 3000 ft. in the mountains of western North America, it is often seen in our lowlands as an accent plant in rock gardens. Unfortunately, most of these trees soon lose their picturesque shape either outgrowing their site or succumbing to some pest such as the wooly balsam aphid. This species is more successful when planted in a cool, moist situation, perhaps as a companion for rhododendrons or camellias. 'Compacta' is a silvery blue dwarf form. 'Argentea' is a silver-needled form of var. *arizónica*.

A. nordmanniána (IV), Nordmann Fir from northeastern Turkey and the western Caucasus region has been grown a great deal in Europe and can also be found in nurseries in our area. It forms a slender, tapering cone up to 150–200 ft. The stiff, dark green needles, notched at the ends, shining on the upper side, and white banded beneath, point forward on the upper side of the branches, but spread comblike below. The handsome reddish brown cones are 4–6 in. long. Dwarf and weeping forms are in the trade.

A. pinsápo (VI), the Spanish Fir, is the stiffest of all the firs, with short, thick needles arranged radially around each branchlet. Large specimens attain a height of 75 ft. or more with a spread of 30 ft. They have a very distinctive appearance and are attractive from a distance, but out of place in a small garden. Forms with either yellow or glaucous foliage are available. This species enjoys a calcareous soil.

A. prócera (V) Noble Fir, is another of the "alpines" from our western mountains, and like the Subalpine Fir, is difficult under lowland condi-

Cultivated specimens of the subalpine fir, *Abies lasiocarpa*, in a garden near Seattle, Photo by Don Normark.

A handsome specimen of the Spanish fir, *Abies pinsapo*, in California. Photo by Brian Mulligan.

tions unless its cultural requirements can be met. These include cool, moist but well-drained soil, and full exposure to sunlight. Given these, Noble Fir can be noble indeed, forming a narrow spire of grayish green foliage that may be over 100 ft. tall. In time, its 8–10 in. cones, brown-purple with greenish bracts, will decorate the top of the tree. This species, along with its California counterpart, *A. magnifica,* is commonly used as a Christmas tree. 'Aurea' has golden needles in full sun. In 'Glauca' the needles have a bluish cast. 'Glauca Prostrata' is a bluish dwarf form.

ARAUCÁRIA araucána (VII), the Monkey Puzzle from Chile, is ultimately a 75–80 ft. tree. One plant explorer who visited Chile reported that he went there expecting at last to see Monkey Puzzle trees looking as though they "belonged" in their surroundings, but came back feeling that they were almost as much out of place in their homeland as they are in our gardens! Despite their bizarre silhouette, there is something intriguing about these strange trees, with their whorls of stiff, spreading branches and heavy, overlapping, spiny-pointed leaves. They found their niche as a lawn tree in front of large Victorian homes at the turn of the century and are still popular for this purpose today. Female trees may produce large globose cones which fall apart at maturity; the cylindrical male cones are 4–6 in. long. Female trees are said to grow larger than male trees.

Arbor-vitae. See *Thuja.*

An avenue of conifers in an estate in Ireland. A very large monkeypuzzle tree (*Araucaria araucana*) on the extreme right. Photo by Brian Mulligan.

CALOCÉDRUS decúrrens (VI), formerly known as Libocédrus decúrrens, is the native Incense Cedar from southern Oregon and throughout California, and is a beautiful, fast-growing ornamental tree with densely massed, vivid green, lustrous foliage. The small, oblong, pale brown cones are carried in clusters at the tips of the foliage sprays, and open from the top down when ripe. Both the flowers and the cones are very decorative, and branches of this tree make effective Christmas greens. A young tree has a narrow, columnar outline. Grown in the open in rich, moist soil, it retains its heavy foliage mass right to the ground and makes a handsome specimen tree for the park or large estate. It greatly resents root disturbance and should be planted in a permanent position when quite young. It deserves to be much more widely grown, but will reach 80 ft. or more in height, and this must be kept in mind when choosing its site in the garden.

An incense cedar tree (*Calocedrus decurrens*) in southern Oregon. Photo by Brian Mulligan.

CÉDRUS includes three closely related species which are the only true cedars. Probably the best known of these is the Deodar, Cedrus deodára (VII), from the Himalayas, with openly spaced branches, pendulous at the tips, clothed with clusters of soft green needles. It will attain a spread of at least 50 ft. at the base and a height of 100–150 ft. The Deodar is not suitable for foundation planting or the front yard of a small house! Because of the loose and irregular spacing of the ends of the branches, and their rapid increase in spread, this tree does not lend itself to background planting. It may be used to advantage in the open, with its branches sweeping the ground, and is also attractive with a bare trunk for the first 25–30 ft. The cones take 2–3 years to mature and then disintegrate on the branches. An effective avenue of these trees can be seen on Stevens Way at the University of Washington in Seattle. Several foliage-color variants can be found in nurseries. In 'Albospica' the tips of the shoots are a creamy white, later turning green. 'Aurea' has golden foliage. 'Glauca' has silvery blue foliage. 'Kashmir' is an extra hardy selection, said to take −20°F. 'Pendula' is weeping. 'Snowsprite' has whitish new growth.

C. *atlántica* (VI), the Atlas Cedar from the mountains of Algeria and Morocco, is most often grown in its glaucous-foliaged form, 'Glauca', the Blue Atlas Cedar, which rivals the popular Blue Spruce in color. This species has stout, upward-curving branches and rapidly assumes a regal silhouette. It is much stiffer than the Deodar in all its parts, but its clear, silvery blue foliage makes a strong appeal. It is ultimately a 100–120 ft. tree with a 60–80 ft. spread. Old specimens may be damaged by heavy, wet snowfalls. Besides the 'Glauca' form, there is a golden form, 'Aurea', with shorter needles. 'Glauca Pendula' is weeping and can be staked or trained into unusual forms. 'Fastigiata' is an attractive columnar selection.

C. *libáni* (V), the Cedar of Lebanon of biblical fame, is a stately tree which as a young specimen has better form than either of the others. It develops into a columnar or broadly pyramidal tree 100–120 ft. high with a 60–80 ft. spread at the base. Its branches are held horizontally. The foliage

A mature tree of the true Cedar of Lebanon (*Cedrus libani*). Photo by Brian Mulligan.

of the type is bright green, but there are also rare golden-leaved and glaucous forms which are seldom grown. 'Sargentii' ('Pendula') must be grafted on a high standard to obtain a truly weeping tree. 'Nana' is a dwarf form.

All three species thrive in this region. They need a deep, well-drained, fairly rich loam with a moderate amount of moisture. The Blue Atlas Mountain Cedar requires more moisture and heavier soil than the other two. All three species have unusually beautiful cones which take 2 or 3 years to mature, and then disintegrate on the branches. They bloom in the fall and winter, and the flowers may be damaged by frost, so it is only after a mild winter that the trees produce cones.

CEPHALOTÁXUS, the Plum-yews, are small shrubby, dioecious trees from Japan and China with foliage similar to but coarser than the true yews (*Taxus*), shining on the upper surface. Thin-fleshed, plum-shaped fruits a little more than 1 in. long are borne singly or in clusters on short stalks and take two years to ripen. Suitable for heavy to moderate shade, they thrive best in rich, moist soil.

C. *harringtónia* var. *drupácea* (V–VI), the Japanese Plum-yew, has handsome, coarse-textured, dark green foliage, and is usually grown as a shrub. In its native habitat it can be a tree with a height of 30 ft; however, in cultivation it grows as a broadly spreading, irregularly shaped shrub seldom more than half that height. The olive green fruits which give the plant its common name are about 1¼ in. long, with small prickly tips set in dimples. 'Nana' grows only 4–6 ft. high, but sends out suckering shoots from below ground and in time can become as much as 25 ft. across. The very narrowly upright cultivar 'Fastigiata' is a slow-growing plant useful wherever a moderate-sized, erect and formal shrub is wanted.

C. *fórtuni* (VI–VII), the Chinese Plum-yew, is very similar to its Japanese counterpart, though thinner and lighter in appearance, less hardy, and less common in cultivation. Its leaves are usually curved, much longer and more gradually tapering at the apex than in the preceding species. It can reach a height of 30 ft.

CHAMAECÝPARIS. The species of *Chamaecyparis* have provided us with some of the most useful of all garden conifers. They are easily identi-fied in fruit by their characteristic small, round cones not more than ¼ in. across, with a little horny knob at the apex of each scale. This distinguishes them from *Thuja*, which has small ovoid-oblong cones splitting open from the top downward. Minute, scalelike leaves closely follow the twiglets in the forms with adult foliage; in juvenile forms the foliage is needlelike. The *Chamaecyparis* need adequate moisture and an acid soil. Their juvenile forms are best with some shade, and should be protected from cold winds. The species may be raised from seed, but selected forms, especially juvenile forms, should be propagated from summer or fall cuttings.

C. *lawsoniána* (V), the Lawson Cypress or Port Orford Cedar from southwestern Oregon and northern California, usually forms a slender

100–150 ft. pyramidal tree, which varies in color from yellow-green to blue-green. The soft, loosely arranged foliage has no severity of outline such as is found in the Firs and Spruces. This is an extremely variable species, and since first introduced into cultivation in 1854 has produced over 200 named forms. It is represented in commerce by a great variety of color and habit cultivars, only a few of which will be mentioned here.

'Allumii' is a stiff column with bluish green foliage.

'Erecta Viridis' is a bright green, upright, fastigiate form. Both of these are commonly grown, but neither has the grace of the type.

'Fletcheri', with soft, feathery, glaucous foliage is the best known of several juvenile forms, taking on a faint purplish tinge in winter. It grows to a height of 30 ft. or more. 'Ellwoodii' is similar, but smaller in size and tightly columnar to about 25 ft.

'Golden Showers' has bright yellow-green foliage.

'Oregon Blué is fast-growing, its foliage a sea-blue green with nodding tips.

'Stewartii' is an erect tree to 45 ft. with rich yellow foliage, especially on the sunny side, changing to bright green as it ages.

'Wisselii' is striking and distinct, with narrow, spirally twisting branches of blue-green foliage loosely and irregularly arranged within a slender, columnar outline; Male flowers, often produced in great quantity, are distinctly red.

Several dwarf forms will be found listed under such names as 'Nana', 'Nana Glauca', 'Minima' and 'Minima Glauca'. The first two have a central leader and conical shape, while the latter two are without definite leaders and tend to be bun shaped. 'Tamariscifolia' ('Nestoides') is a handsome, broadly spreading plant to 8 ft. high and considerably wider.

Phytophthora root disease can be a serious problem in both wild and cultivated plants.

C. *nootkaténsis* (IV), the Alaska or Yellow Cedar, grows in the mountains of this region, just reaching northern California, and at sea level in Alaska. It thrives planted near water in rich, moist ground. Mature trees in the wild reach a height of 80–120 ft., with conspicuous white bark. The twigs and branchlets of dull green foliage, with a catty odor when crushed, often hang limply from the main branches, producing a weeping effect. The little round cones, about ½ in. across, are first green then brown, ripening in the second year. An even more weeping form, 'Pendula', is a slender, gray-green column, with branches hanging nearly parallel to the main stem. In 'Aurea' the young sprays of leaves are yellow, turning yellow-green with age.

C. *obtúsa* (III), the Japanese Hinoki Cypress, is an invaluable Oriental species, widely planted in our area. The type is a 100-ft. tree with a broadly pyramidal head of deep emerald green foliage, but in cultivation it has given rise to a host of variations in both the size of mature specimens and rapidity of growth, as well as variations in foliage form and color.

'Gracilis', 20–25 ft., with shell-shaped foliage sprays, and bright, dark green 'Nana Gracilis', 5–10 ft., are excellent, slow-growing trees for the small garden or large rock garden. They are among the most aristocratic of the medium-sized conifers. In 'Nana Lutea' the twigs give the appearance of rosettes.

'Ericoides' is a juvenile form with soft, fluffy foliage, forming a loose bush, pyramidal or slightly rounded, less than 4 ft. high, with an equal spread. The coloring of its foliage in summer is a lovely sea green with a glaucous tinge. At the approach of winter it gradually turns plum purple. This form seems particularly susceptible to cold winds. It is better grown in the sun, but then needs more moisture.

'Filicoides' slowly forms a 20–30 ft. specimen with slightly arching branches ending in stringlike branchlets.

'Lycopodioides', the Club-moss Cypress, is a striking small tree to 6 ft. in 30 years, but ultimately 40 ft. or more. The branches and branchlets are very irregular, densely crowded, curled and twisted. The foliage is a brilliant blue-green in color; there is also a golden form, 'Lycopodioides Aurea'.

'Crippsii', Golden Hinoki Cypress, is slow growing to 50–60 ft., broadly conical in form, with branchlets fan shaped, golden yellow in color.

'Kosteri' is dwarf, 3–4 ft. high and 2–3 ft. wide, with short, tight twiglets.

'Tetragona Aurea' is a bushy plant to 6 ft., with pale to golden yellow, mosslike foliage.

Probably the smallest of all the dwarf forms of this species are 'Caespitosa', the Golfball Cypress, and 'Minima', the Tennis Ball Cypress. Their names give an indication of the size of a mature specimen of each.

All forms of the Hinoki Cypress grow readily in any good garden soil if given ample moisture; the dwarf forms do not like to be in full sun in summer.

C. pisifera (III), the Sawara Cypress from Japan, is a 150-ft. tree of slender pyramidal outline. The type, an excellent tree for city gardens, is of rapid growth, with a rather loose, open branching habit and thin, yellow-green foliage. Many of its varieties rapidly lose their lower branches, revealing slender, reddish brown trunks. This species can be found in a number of foliage forms of varying size and color.

'Squarrosa' is a popular juvenile form, with fluffy gray-green foliage, which can be 50–60 ft. tall. There are also medium and dwarf varieties of this type, which make compact bushes of irregular shape, from 15 ft. to less than 3 ft. high.

'Boulevard' ('Cyanoviridis') is a 'Squarrosa' form with gray-green leaves that are a brilliant silver beneath. It is of conical growth to at least 15 ft.

'Squarrosa Minima' is smaller, a dense, seafoam green bun.

The gold and silver 'Squarrosa' variants are not at their best in full sun and dry soil, but in light shade with ample moisture they are lovely. Dead foliage should be removed once a year with a jet of water from the hose to keep them looking neat and attractive. They may be allowed to grow loosely, revealing their branching structure, or kept more compact by judicious pruning, preserving their natural irregularities of shape while discouraging any tendency to become leggy.

'Plumosa' has deep green foliage intermediate between that of the type and of the juvenile 'Squarrosa'. It makes a dense pyramidal mass that slowly reaches a height of 50–60 ft. The golden-variegated form, 'Plumosa Aurea', is golden in the spring, and green later. 'Plumosa Aurea Compacta' is very dwarf, with yellowish new growth. These do not need shade or as much moisture as 'Squarrosa'.

'Filifera' has drooping, stringlike twigs and foliage. Its branching pattern is loose and open, the whole plant forming a spreading, dwarf tree, 10–15 ft. high and almost as wide, though ultimately as much as 50 ft. high. 'Filifera Aurea' is slower growing, with light yellow-green new growth to 15–20 ft. 'Filifera Nana' forms a squat, humpy, little shrub 2–3 ft. through. 'Golden Mop' is similarly dwarf, but golden yellow. 'Filifera Aureovariegata' is yellow variegated and somewhat easily burned by sun or frost.

CRYPTOMÉRIA *japónica* (V), Japanese Cryptomeria, is a forest tree in Japan, to 180 ft, comparable in manner of growth to our native Western Red Cedar. Narrow and pyramidal in habit, with red-brown bark peeling off in long shreds, its bright green, cordlike foliage and twigs give it a distinctive appearance even when young. The cone-bearing branches are especially attractive for winter decoration, with their vigorous linear pattern, bunches of round, prickly cones, and clusters of next year's flower buds. It requires deep, well-drained, acid soil, with ample moisture and may be grown in either sun or partial shade. Although the type is too large for the average garden, it has produced many valuable dwarf and juvenile forms selected for a variety of unusual characteristics.

'Bandai-sugi', broadly conical in outline to 6 ft. and bluish green in color, has a peculiar mixture of long and short needles and branchlets.

'Cristata', narrowly conical in outline to 6–8 ft. or more with stiff, irregularly ascending branches, has heavy, fasciated, cockscomb-like growths on the tips of the branches, more novel than attractive.

'Elegans', a juvenile form with soft, fluffy green foliage, turning rich red-brown in winter, is a first-class garden tree to 10–15 or sometimes 30 ft., but subject to damage by wet snow. 'Elegans Viridis', similar in growth habit, but green in winter as well as summer, is a beautiful plant for a shady location.

'Jindai-sugi' is a taller, more conical bush than 'Bandai-sugi', up to 8 ft. in height, its foliage regular and dense, and light green in color.

'Nana' is a rather dense and compact form to 5–6 ft., light green in color, the branches with pendulous tips.

'Spiralis' is flat-globose and compact, with the leaves curiously twisted around the branches, most noticable in winter.

'Vilmoriniana', a very tight and compact small bush to 3 ft. in height, is suitable for rock gardens. 'Compressa' is very similar, but its foliage turns bronze in winter.

CUNNINGHÁMIA *lanceoláta (C. sinénsis)* (VII), the China Fir, is a striking evergreen suggestive of the Monkey Puzzle Tree. Irregularly or broadly pyramidal, it grows to 50–80 ft. in height. Its coarse, sharply pointed needles, about 2 in. long and flaring near the base, are glossy green above and paler beneath, often taking on a bronzy or reddish tint in the winter time. The cones are ovoid, up to 2 in. long, green at first, finally brown. It is easily grown in this region, preferring a light, well-drained, acid soil, with ample spring and summer moisture. A site protected from cold north winds is recommended, and it seems to do best in sheltered locations near buildings; however, it also pays to set it away from close human contact, since its stiff needles are painful to brush against. This conifer is noteworthy in that, like the redwoods, it sprouts from the stump if cut down or winterkilled. 'Glauca' is a blue-needled form, also turning bronzy in winter.

× CUPRESSOCÝPARIS *leylándii* (VI–VII), the Leyland Cypress, a hybrid between Monterey Cypress, *Cupressus macrocarpa,* and Alaska Cedar, *Chamaecyparis nootkatensis,* originated in England in 1888, and again at the same estate in 1911, and is considered one of the most important tree introductions of recent times. It is a vigorous, rapidly growing tree to over 100 ft., with a narrow crown, often quite dense. Somewhat similar to Lawson Cypress in habit, its somber green foliage resembles that of *C. nootkatensis,* while its cones are somewhat intermediate in size between those of the two parental species. Hardy, and seemingly resistant to root rot, it makes a quick screening plant, useful for windbreaks. In Seattle, at Washington Park Arboretum, it has suffered somewhat from tip moth.

Since neither the original set of seedlings, nor those from subsequent occurrences were entirely uniform, several have been given clonal names:

'Castlewellan' is a beautiful form with golden foliage, said to be the first golden-foliaged conifer to grow over 100 ft. in height.

'Green Spire' is a narrowly columnar form with rich green foliage.

'Haggerston Grey' has a branching system resembling *Cupressus macrocarpa,* and foliage with a grayish cast. It is tolerant of coastal conditions, as is 'Leighton Green'.

'Leighton Green', pyramidal in form, and the commonest of the clones around Seattle, has rich, green foliage which resembles that of *Chamaecyparis nootkatensis.*

'Naylor's Blue', the most glaucous of the available clones, is also the nearest to Monterey Cypress in appearance.

'Silver Dust' has white-variegated, silvery blue foliage, and is more widespreading in habit than some other selections.

CUPRÉSSUS. The true cypresses are trees for warm, sunny situations, perfect drainage, and poor, dry soils. The western American species, at least, should receive no summer irrigation. Cypresses grow quickly and often lack the root system needed to support their tops. Although useful as screens, they are perhaps at their best as specimen trees, especially the gray-foliaged forms and the slender, erect ones.

C. arizónica (VIII), the Arizona Cypress, native to central and southern Arizona, New Mexico and Mexico, has strongly glaucous foliage. The bushy growth varies in outline from broadly spreading to slender pyramidal, up to 35–40 ft. in height. It is hardy, tolerant of hot, dry situations, and thus particularly useful in the intermountain west. It is easily recognized by the fissured bark, while the related C. glábra has smooth bark and markedly glandular leaves. It does better in the Northwest than its origin might suggest. Its round, knobby cones are about an inch in diameter.

C. bákeri (V), the Modoc Cypress, from southwestern Oregon and northern California, has glaucous gray foliage, and although the hardiest of all the Cypress, it is still uncommon in gardens. It is similar to the Arizona Cypress in general characteristics, but preferable to that species in that it is an attractive, bushy tree even as a very young specimen. It is not such a fast grower, and in maturity is much smaller, 25–30 ft.

C. macnábiana (VII), Macnab Cypress, is a closely related species from northern California, found on serpentine soils. Branches and leaves are sage green in color; the brown cones are about 1 in. in diameter. This species should be valuable for planting on hot, dry slopes with sandy or gravelly soil.

C. macrocárpa (VII), the Monterey Cypress, famous for its picturesque growth on the California coast, was once commonly used for seaside shelterbelt plantings and hedges. It has been largely superseded for these purposes by × Cupressocyparis leylandii. Where not shaped by the wind it is often merely an awkward, gawky tree, particularly when young. It has dark green, densely branched twigs and foliage, and knobby, rounded cones 1–1½ in. across, much valued for decoration. Height may reach as much as 120 ft. 'Golden Pillar' is a slow-growing, columnar form with dense, golden yellow summer foliage. 'Lutea' and 'Donard Gold' are other golden cultivars.

C. sempervírens (VII), the Italian Cypress, is perhaps best known in its columnar form, var. strícta (var. fastigiáta). This is the dark green, columnar tree associated with Italian and Spanish architecture. It is admirable for California gardens, and although not entirely hardy throughout our region, it can survive for some years in sheltered gardens. The species itself will reach a height of 50–75 ft., forming broad heads in windswept locations. Cones are slightly smaller than those of Monterey Cypress.

A ginkgo tree (*Ginkgo biloba*) in a city park in autumn. Photo by Brian Mulligan.

JUNÍPERUS. More than 60 species of Juniper are widely distributed from the Arctic Circle to subtropical regions, including North Africa. They vary in habit from low-growing shrubs to large, pyramidal trees. Foliage may be needlelike or scalelike. The small, rounded or oval berries are technically cones. Junipers are rugged plants, generally capable of withstanding severe cold, drought and neglect. They thrive in full sun, doing less well in partial or full shade. Soil should be well drained, but they are tolerant of a wide range of conditions if not too wet. Propagation is by seeds or by cuttings in the case of special cultivars. Cones are clearly smaller than those of Monterey Cypress, gray or brown when mature.

J. chinénsis (IV), the Chinese Juniper, native to China, Japan and Korea, is a very variable species with many garden forms, the majority of which are shrubs. This species is dioecious like most junipers, and some selections have been made from female plants and others from male plants. Some forms have awl-like juvenile foliage, and others have scalelike adult foliage; still others may have both. The type is a 50–60 ft. tree, the form most common in cultivation being 'Pyramidalis', which grows as a tall, slender round-topped column to a height of 20–25 ft., and has ascending branches with fine, dense, prickly gray-green foliage. It is a male clone much superior to the better-known Irish Juniper, *J. communis* 'Hibernica', having neater foliage and holding its shape much better, especially in old age.

'Kaizuka', the Hollywood Juniper, is a picturesque large shrub of upright habit, up to 16 or more ft., with vivid green, scalelike foliage. The outward-slanting branches have a slight twist to them, adding to the exotic effect. The fruits have a waxy coating.

'Pfitzeriana', considered by some authors to be *J. × média,* a hybrid of *J. chinensis* with *J. sabina,* is probably the most widely planted of all junipers. A flat-topped shrub with branches angled out at about 45 degrees, it frequently exceeds the listed height of 5–6 ft., and may attain a spread of as much as 25 ft., becoming more open in old age. Drought resistant, it is well suited for planting at the base of madroña trees or on trunks. Selections with gold or blue-green foliage are available, as well as forms with less exuberant habits. 'Pfitzeriana Aurea' with gold-tinged young shoots is an example. 'Gold Coast', a male form, is a more compact version, with the golden yellow tips to the shoots. 'Old Gold', of Dutch origin in 1958, is bronzy gold in winter, and flatter in habit.

'Hetzii' is a large, upright-spreading form which can be as much as 15 × 15 ft. in size, with mostly scalelike leaves, blue-green in color, and many small, glaucous berries. It is sometimes listed as a form of *J. × media.*

'Plumosa Albovariegata' is the name given to the well-known shrub with splashes of white scattered here and there among the foliage. Unfortunately, this variation suggests disease rather than giving a sparkling ornamental effect. Other variegated forms, with either white or golden areas distributed over the plant are far more attractive and desirable.

J. cómmunis (II), the Common Juniper, is another extremely variable species found throughout the entire Northern Hemisphere. It has the widest distribution of any conifer. The type, from Europe, is an erect tree of pyramidal habit to about 15 ft. Native Northwest American forms are var. *depressa,* low-spreading or prostrate shrubs, only 3–5 ft. high. The many varieties of *J. communis* are desirable garden subjects, closely similar in their glaucous, awl-shaped foliage, but with a wide range of habit, growth rate and size of mature specimens. They are thoroughly drought resistant if planted in deep, light soil, and will grow well under normal garden conditions, but resent root disturbance once they have become established.

Var. *depréssa,* Canadian Juniper, native to Canada and northern United States, including Washington, is spreading in habit, seldom over 4–5 ft. tall, and usually wider than high. The cultivar 'Depressa Aurea' is low and spreading with arching branches. Its new growth in spring is a rich golden bronze becoming green later in the year. This is one of the most attractive of golden conifers, but decidedly lacking in vigor. It requires rich, light soil and ample moisture during the growing season.

The upright, arborescent forms of this species include the columnar Irish Juniper 'Hibernica', to 15 ft., with silvery gray foliage, and erect outer twigs, more tender and slower growing than some of the other upright types; and forma *súecica*, the Swedish Juniper, native to Northern Europe, a fastigiate tree with blue-green foliage to 30 ft; its branches are erect, but the branch tips are nodding.

'Compressa', the Noah's Ark Juniper, is a tight, very narrowly conical shrub with light green, awl-like leaves, one of the very slowest growers, achieving only 1½ ft. in 20 years, but 3–4 ft. eventually. It is definitely less hardy than the type and should not be planted in an exposed situation. It is also subject to attacks by red spider mite.

'Suecica Nana' is a dwarf, columnar variant of f. *suecica* with short, bluish green leaves, larger and faster growing than 'Compressa' and probably hardier.

J. occidentális (IV–V), Western Juniper, our beautiful glaucous native species from south central Washington and the high deserts of eastern Oregon, will be more useful in gardens east of the Cascades than in western Washington and Oregon. A large shrub or small tree to 40–50 ft., with erect, columnar habit when young and open, very irregular branching in older specimens, it has peeling reddish brown bark, gray-green, scalelike foliage, and small, glaucous blue berries. This species is very drought resistant, as befits a desert tree, and is said to be difficult to transplant except when young.

'Sierra Silver' is one of a number of named selections, mostly with extra pale coloration.

J. rígida (V), a native of Japan and Korea, can be either a shrub or a small spreading tree up to 40 ft. The foliage is needlelike and very prickly to handle. Fruits are dark brown. It is reported to be useful in seaside locations.

J. scopulórum (V), the Rocky Mountain Juniper, is also found in the San Juan Islands where rainfall is light. This is the western counterpart of *J. virginiana*, a large, broad-headed shrub or shaggy tree up to 35–40 ft., with shredding bark, scalelike leaves, and glaucous, light blue fruits which take two years to ripen. It has come into gardens only within the last 30–40 years with the introduction of a number of named cultivars, and is an excellent plant for dry, sunny sites, needing no summer water. The many named varieties now in the trade include globe-shaped as well as narrowly cylindrical and weeping forms, ranging in color from green or blue-green to silvery gray.

'Blue Haven', is a silvery blue-green, of upright habit, loose and stringy.

'Chandler's Blue' is hardy to southern Canada.

'Chandler's Silver', broadly pyramidal, with bluish green foliage, may require occasional pruning.

'Gray Gleam' is slow-growing and narrowly columnar, with silvery gray foliage, brighter in winter.

'Pathfinder' is pyramidal, with silvery blue foliage.

'Skyrocket', sometimes listed as belonging to *J. virginiana*, is one of the narrowest of the columnar junipers.

'Table Top' is more or less horizontal, 3–4 ft. high, but as much as 15 ft. across; it has very glaucous foliage and sets fruit.

'Welchii' has silvery foliage and a compact, narrowly conical habit.

J. squamáta var. *fargésii* (IV) from Sichuan, is a shrub or small tree to 40 ft., with branches more spreading than the dwarf forms from the Himalayas and central China, and with distinctly longer needles. The foliage effect is green, the habit compact, and the tips of the branches droop. This form is rare in cultivation, but attractive. It should probably be rated as a distinct species, *J. lemeeána*.

J. virginiána (II), the Red Cedar or Pencil Cedar of eastern and central United States and Canada, is a variable tree or shrub with peeling bark, ranging from a low, sprawling thicket to an occasional stately 100-ft. specimen. The foliage is dark green and scalelike; awl-like juvenile foliage is sometimes present as well. Cones ripen in one year rather than two as in *J. scopulorum*. Numerous varietal forms, dwarf, variegated, and pendulous, have been described, including the following:

'Canaertii', with erect, columnar habit to 35 ft. has rich, green foliage and is especially attractive when covered with its freely produced, bluish white, waxy fruits.

'Burkii', with compact, columnar habit to about 20–25 ft. and blue-green foliage, is exceptionally hardy and vigorous.

'Grey Owl' is spreading in habit to 4 ft. tall, with soft, silvery gray foliage. It is probably a hybrid with *J. chinensis* 'Pfitzeriana'.

The numerous shrubby forms do not for the most part seem as well adapted to Northwest garden conditions as those of the other species.

LÁRIX. The larches are the best-known of the deciduous conifers. Their principal attraction is the bright green of their new spring foliage, and the clear yellow of their autumn color. The several species are widespread in the cooler parts of the Northern Hemisphere, usually in the mountains. Larch trees have a tendency toward self-pruning, but can be trimmed in July or August if required, to keep bleeding to a minimum and allow rapid healing of wounds. They are usually propagated from seed.

L. decídua (II), the European Larch, native in the mountains of central Europe, has bright grass green foliage which is especially vivid when it first unfolds in the spring. It can be 100 ft. or more tall. The cones are usually longer than but similar to those of the Japanese Larch, except that the scales do not reflex when mature. It prefers deep, moist, neutral soils and is not suitable for exposed locations. 'Pendula', the weeping form, is very attractive. There is also a fastigiate form as well, as upright as a Lombardy Poplar.

L. kaémpferi (L. leptolépis) (IV), the Japanese Larch, is a handsome, fast-growing tree to 90–100 ft., and is the most satisfactory species in cultivation. Its foliage, thickly clothing the short, horizontally spreading, reddish branches, is a soft, bluish green. Dead twigs are brittle in the wind, providing an endless supply of arching sprays of small, decorative brown cones, each about 1 in. long and wide, with reflexing scale tips. This species is sometimes grown as an artificially dwarfed specimen in Japanese gardens, and does not seem to mind close clipping. New branches can arise directly from the trunk. *L. × eurolépis,* the Dunkeld Larch, a hybrid between this and the preceeding species, is a valuable tree for forestry purposes in the U. K., particularly in Scotland where it first arose.

L. laricína (I), the American Larch or Tamarack of the eastern United States, swings across the north of the continent to within the Arctic Circle and is found in Alaska and northeastern British Columbia. Rarely grown in our area, as other species are considered preferable, it has a horizontal branching pattern, reddish, scaling bark, very small cones, and the usual fresh green needles and golden fall color common to all the larches. It grows to a height of 65 ft.

L. lyállii (III), Lyall's Larch, is a small tree of picturesque form, to 15–25 ft., usually found at elevations over 5000 ft. in the Cascades and Rocky Mountains. Like many alpine plants, it does not take kindly to lowland gardens, and regrettably must be eliminated as a horticultural subject.

L. occidentális (V), Western Larch, is the largest of the larches, a long-lived tree attaining a height of as much as 150–200 ft., forming a slender, pyramidal head above a 4–6 ft. thick trunk covered with reddish, scaling bark. The small cones, 1–1½ in. long are conspicuously bracted. In its native state and in cultivation it prefers a rich, light, moist soil, and is a tree of rapid growth, ultimately too large for the average garden, but then making good firewood. It is native in the Cascades and northern Rockies from southern British Columbia to Oregon and Idaho.

The genus *METASEQUÓIA* has the rare distinction among cultivated plants of having been known as a fossil before living trees were discovered in the wild in China in 1941. The single species, *M. glýptostroboídes* (IV), the Water Fir, has become widespread in cultivation since its introduction in 1948. A rapid and remarkably easy grower in good, moist soils, it is a far less demanding tree than *Taxodium distichum.* Some specimens have already reached 100 ft. in height. The reddish brown trunk develops a distinctive furrowed and buttressed base after only a few years. As with *Taxodium, M. glyptostroboides* is deciduous. The soft green needles, borne opposite one another on small twiglets, turn rosy brown before they are shed in the fall. Many trees in the Northwest are now old enough to bear the small, long-stalked cones. It is not a tree for the small garden nor for dry situations. 'National' is a narrowly pyramidal selection

The Dawn Redwood (*Metasequoia glyptostroboides*) showing its branching habit and grooved trunk. Photo by Don Normark.

from the National Arboretum in Washington, D.C.

MICROBIOTA decussata. See Groundcovers.

PÍCEA, Spruce. The more than forty species of spruces throughout the temperate regions of the Northern Hemisphere are handsome, stately trees with sharp outlines. They thrive in deep, rich soil with plenty of moisture and are perhaps the least drought resistant of the conifers. As noted under *Abies,* the stiff needles of these two genera are not dissimilar seen from a distance, but in spruces they are set on small pegs. Another simple distinguishing characteristic is that in *Abies* the cones stand upright on the branches and disintegrate at maturity, while in *Picea* they hang downward and fall entire. In our area spruces are plagued by a number of insect problems, among them an early season February–March aphid, which causes defoliation; the Cooley spruce gall; as well as other aphid infestations later in the season. They are also attacked by the spruce-leaf sawfly, which consumes mature foliage. The best way of dealing with this pest is to spray with a good insecticide 2–3 times starting in February if the weather is warm, or again later. Acid rain and the air pollution of cities are also proving to be very hard on spruces.

P. ábies, (II), the Norway Spruce, has a conventional "Christmas Tree" form with dark green, somewhat somber foliage, and reddish brown bark, attaining a height of 150 ft. or more. The tapered, cylindrical cones, 4–6 in. long, have considerable decorative value. There are 200 or more named cultivars of *P. abies*, many of which are dwarf, slow-growing forms or abnormal shapes, while others have colored foliage. Mature specimens of the dwarfs vary in size from one to several feet high, and there is as much variation in habit of growth as in size. Some are slender and tapering; others are short, dumpy pyramids. Many take on an inverted bowl or bun-like shape, and there are several distinct weeping and prostrate ones. The dwarf spruces are most valuable in the rock garden. Their use in general landscape effect is limited because of their stiffness and hard outline. These are a few of the more distinct ones currently offered:

'Clanbrassiliana' is slow-growing with a tight, round habit of growth, often wider than high and still under 3 ft. after 30 years; branchlets thin, white, shining.

'Compacta' covers a number of round, bushy types with slender branches and short leaves.

'Gregoryana' is a tight, compact cushion to 2 ft. tall, but wider, with leaves arranged radially on the branches, gray-green, and pointing forward.

'Nidiformis', the Bird's Nest Spruce, is dense and spreading, to 6 ft. high usually with a dip in the center of the plant, giving rise to the common name.

'Procumbens' grows as a tight, twiggy pancake, with branches overlapping up to 8 ft. wide, but only 1 ft. high; its leaves are yellow-green.

'Pumila' is dwarf, 3–4 ft. tall, but wider, globular, flattened, and compact, the reddish brown lower branches spreading, the upper more erect; leaves thin, flexible, bright green.

'Repens', Prostrate Norway Spruce, is another flat one, arching in the center, the yellowish green shoots noticeably in layers; leaves thin, very crowded, becoming shorter toward the ends of the twigs.

'Argenteospica', which has creamy white new shoots, later turning dark green, and 'Cupressina' of columnar habit with ascending branches are among the more interesting nondwarf variants.

'Pendula', covers a variable group of weeping forms, much confused in commerce. They are useful to cascade down walls, and the leaders can be staked to give more swing to the trailing branches.

P. breweriána (V–VI), Brewer's Weeping Spruce, an endemic from the Siskiyou Mountains of southern Oregon and northern California, is one of the most beautiful of the large, weeping, evergreen conifers. Reaching 120 ft. in the wild, with its swooping main branches draped with 5–6 ft. long, nearly perpendicular branchlets, it has whitish, scaling bark, and purple-tinged cones 4–5 in. long. Uncommon and very slow-growing in cultivation, it needs cool temperatures and adequate moisture.

P. engelmánnii (II), Engelmann's Spruce, inhabits our mountains,

A fine example of the native Engelmann spruce (*Picea engelmannii*) in northeastern Washington. Photo by Brian Mulligan.

usually at elevations above 3000 ft. A slender, spire-shaped tree to 100 ft. or more, with a dense habit and sharp, stiff, often silvery foliage, it is relatively slow-growing in cultivation and is unfortunately susceptible to Cooley spruce gall and aphid attacks in early spring. Collected seedlings, however, have thrived in the Washington Park Arboretum in Seattle for 30 years, with regular spraying.

P. gláuca (III), the White Spruce of northern Canada and northeastern North America is a medium-sized tree to 60–70 ft. with habit similar to *P. abies*, but grayer, silvery green foliage.

'Conica', Dwarf Alberta Spruce, is a valuable dwarf form of the White Spruce. The parent plant was found in the Canadian Rockies and is now growing in the Arnold Arboretum in Boston, Massachusetts. This spruce has grassy green foliage much softer than any of the varieties of *P. abies*. It forms a very slender, conical tree, to 12–15 ft. in 25–30 years, which requires a great deal of moisture, some shade and protection from cold winds. It has become one of the most commonly planted dwarf conifers in spite of its susceptibility to red spider mite.

P. mariána (II), Black Spruce, comes from swamps in northern North America. The type is not a particularly attractive tree in the wild, having a long, short-branched leader, like the tail of an outraged cat. The small, ovoid, gray-green cones may remain for many years on the branches. It needs moist, well-drained soil and could be useful for planting in frost pockets.

'Doumetii' is a compact conical form to 15 ft. or more.

'Nana' is a very slow-growing dwarf, no more than 1½ ft. high, with blue-green foliage.

P. omórika (IV), the Serbian Spruce from southwestern Yugoslavia, is a narrow, short-branched, slender-trunked tree with a distinctive, almost columnar silhouette, eventually to 80–100 ft. Its needles are a glossy, dark green. The bark is coffee brown, scaling off in small pieces. The cones, about 3 in. long, are blue-black when young, turning a shining brown when mature. It is an excellent tree for smaller gardens on account of its narrow habit of growth. It, too, has a 'Nana' form, a dense, slow-growing dwarf shrub to about 10 ft.

P. orientális (IV), Caucasian Spruce, from the Caucasus Mountains and northern Asia Minor, is one of the most attractive spruces, pyramidal and densely branched when young, with shining, dark green, very short needles, almost as small as those of the pigmy forms of other species. The cones, which are purple when young, brown when mature, are 3–5 in. long and curved, produced even on young trees. This species can eventually reach 60 ft. There is also a rare golden form, 'Aurea'.

P. púngens (II), the Colorado Spruce from the central Rockies, is by far the most popular spruce in gardens today, though not necessarily the most suitable species for a number of reasons. This is a magnificent tree for planting where it can be viewed from a distance—at the end of a vista or as a specimen on a lawn,—but beautiful as it is, it is not a tree for the small garden, since it will reach 150 ft. in the wild and 70–80 ft. in cultivation. It grows well and very quickly in our area, forming broadly pyramidal specimens which are particularly attractive when the branches reach clear to the ground. It has grayish brown bark, and 2–3 in. long, light tan cones, often freely produced. Although this species is very adaptable and more drought resistant than other spruces, in our area it is subject to a number of disfiguring plagues, including spruce gall aphid, spruce budworm and spider mite, as well as defoliating aphids in spring. Regular spraying may be necessary to maintain its beauty. The green-foliage type of *P. pungens* is rarely seen, since all the cultivated selections are some variation of the blue-green f. *glaúca,* a name used collectively for glaucous selections in the nursery trade.

'Compacta' is a slow-growing, flat-topped miniature tree, broader than high, with stiff dark green needles. The original specimen in Massachusetts is now about 10 ft. high and 14 ft. in diameter.

'Globosa' is compact and rounded, to 3 ft. high, wider than high at maturity, of Dutch origin.

'Hoopsii' is perhaps the most glaucous cultivar, with lovely silver-blue foliage. Dirr says it is also the best grower.

'Koster', Koster's Blue Spruce, is a commonly offered pyramidal form, which seems immune to the spruce gall, but not to the defoliating aphid.

'Moerheim', also silvery blue, is a more compact shape than 'Koster', with a slender, conical habit to 30 ft. or more.

'Montgomery' raised in northeastern United States is dwarf, slow-growing and broadly conical in shape, with needles tightly packed.

Forms listed as 'Glauca Pendula', 'Glauca Procumbens' and 'Glauca Prostrata' are all more or less spreading, groundcover types suitable for large rock gardens. Some of the flatter sorts can present a rather "bony" appearance in time, when their leaves and twiglets no longer cover the central limbs.

P. sitchénsis (VI), Sitka Spruce or Tidewater Spruce, is the giant of the spruce family, a moisture-loving Northwest native, to 250 ft. or more in the wild and thus scarcely suitable for cultivation, especially since it resents city conditions. As a young tree it forms a rather irregular crown with widely spaced branches building to a broadly pyramidal outline. It has somewhat silvery foliage, small pale brown cones, and scaling gray bark. Cooley spruce gall is a major problem in our area. This tree is much happier near salt water on the coast.

Two dwarf forms are available, 'Papoose', which is of rounded habit with bluish foliage, to 3 × 3 ft., and 'Tenas', somewhat triangular in outline, with needles green above and silvery below.

P. smithiaña (VI–VII), Himalayan Spruce, from the western Himalayas, is another of weeping habit, to 120 ft., with horizontal branches and pendulous branchlets, distinctive for its needles which are longer than those of other spruces, and for its large, brown cones, to 7 in. In our area it is subject to frost injury in spring, especially when young, but forms a very beautiful tree. It prefers a moist, loamy soil.

PÍNUS. This genus contains some of the most distinct and striking of all the coniferous evergreens. Their one common characteristic is the needles arranged in bundles, varying from 2 to 5 in number and greatly in length, according to the species. One of the principal means of identification is the number of needles per bundle. Although pines in general are excellent garden subjects, they do have a number of problems. Pine shoot moth kills the tips of the new shoots of 2-needled species such as *P. contorta* and *P. mugo*. White Pine blister rust affects the 5-needled pines, especially our native *P. monticola*. Air pollution has become a very serious problem with this genus, as attested by freeway plantings in some of our major cities.

Many species grow to be enormous trees and have a regular columnar or pyramidal form when young. In the wild old pines are frequently irregular in outline, with rugged, sturdy branches that speak eloquently of battles with the elements down through the centuries. Many of them grow in exposed situations by the seashore, or on windswept mountain ridges.

All the pines mentioned here are drought resistant preferring rather dry, sandy, gravelly or rocky ground. They do not thrive in heavy wet soils. Their foliage color varies from the soft blue-gray of *P. monticola,* the Western White Pine, through the dark, almost black greens of *P. mugo,* the Mugho Pine, to the bright grass green of *P. radiata,* the Monterey Pine. The cones are an attractive feature of this genus. They are spectacularly large in some species. The heavy cone of the Digger Pine, *P. sabiniana,* and the Coulter Pine, *P. coulteri,* is nearly as large as a man's head, while those of the Sugar Pine, *P. lambertiana,* are lighter and more slender, but may be 18 in. long. A number of species have reddish or golden bark, (*P. densiflora, P. sylvestris*) which adds a welcome touch of color to the winter garden scene.

    P. albicáulis (III), the Whitebark Pine, native from the Cascades and Sierras into Wyoming, is a slow-growing tree of picturesque, irregular habit to 40 ft. or more. Its short, stiff needles, 2–3 in. long, arranged 5 to a bundle, are clustered densely at the tips of the spreading branchlets, so that the white bark which gives the plant its name is very obvious. Its red male cones are fleetingly colorful; the purple female cones dry slowly and disintegrate at maturity, and then they are frequently attacked by Clark's Nutcracker for their seeds. This is a fine subject for the large rock garden, but may be less than permanent as it often develops blister rust in cultivation. It is very difficult to establish near sea level, and is seldom seen in gardens.

    P. aristáta (III), the Bristlecone Pine, is a slow-growing species from the mountains of southwestern United States (Colorado, Arizona, and New Mexico) which does surprisingly well in lowland Oregon and Washington. Its short needles, also in fives, are coated with small, white dots of resin and are densely set on stout ascending branches. It is often multitrunked, and seldom more than 30 ft. in height. The small, dark brown oval cones are more noticeably spiny than in most species of pines, hence its name.

    P. bungeána (III), the Lacebark Pine from northern China, is usually a multistemmed tree from 30–50 ft. tall, with grayish-marbled bark which scales off like a Sycamore (*Platanus*). A 3-needled pine, its foliage is aromatic when crushed and rather sparse so that the attractive, patterned bark is well displayed. Cones are about 2½ in. long, light yellowish brown in color. Rare in cultivation.

    P. cémbra (IV), the Swiss Stone Pine or Arolla Pine, native from the Alps to the Carpathians, is a slow-growing, pyramidal tree to 60–100 ft, branched from the ground, and of especially good form when young. The needles, 5 to a bundle, are rich green and fragrant. The small, ovoid cones are purple, but young trees rarely fruit in cultivation. With sufficient moisture it will do well under rather severe conditions of cold and poor soil.

    P. cembroídes (IV–V), Piñon, is a 3-needled pine from the American Southwest and northern Mexico, usually no more than 15–25 ft. tall, but

Young trees of the bristlecone pine (*Pinus aristata*) planted against a public building. Photo by Don Normark.

occasionally up to 50 ft. Var. *édulis,* which is found further north in Utah and Wyoming, has 2 needles, and is a plant of neat, dense habit under garden conditions. Its small, lumpy, resinous cones are the source of piñon nuts. Var. *monophýlla,* which has only a single needle in each position, is a good small tree for dry conditions.

P. contórta (III–VII), the native Lodgepole Pine or Shore Pine, ranges in different varieties, from the coast of Alaska to the mountain regions of Arizona and New Mexico. This tree grows under a wide variety of cultural and climatic conditions, frequently in bogs or moist, sandy soil, and also on poor, dry soils; but not all strains are adapted to both wet and dry conditions. It is easily identified as our only native 2-needled pine. In windswept locations near the coast or on mountains, it is the most picturesque of our native pines; but growing in dense stands in more protected places, it is a slender straight tree 80–100 ft. tall. It is an excellent garden tree, and should be more widely grown. Its small cones are persistent, in the wild opening only after fire.

Var. *contórta* (VII), Shore Pine, from windswept coastal areas has an irregular, rounded crown, deep green needles, and dark grayish brown bark, growing to 50 ft.

The Shore Pine (*Pinus contorta*) in its native habitat. Photo by Brian Mulligan.

Var. *latifólia* (III), Lodgepole Pine, the interior form, is a columnar tree, especially in even-age stands, with yellow-green needles and reddish brown bark.

'Spaan's Dwarf' has ½-in.-long needles, on a very dwarf plant.

P. densiflóra (III), the Japanese Red Pine, is a favorite garden subject in Japan. The type is a tree up to 100 ft. tall, forming a broad head with irregularly spaced, horizontal branches. It is a 2-needled pine with rich green, rather soft foliage, and a reddish, scaling trunk. Its species name, referring to the dense clusters of flowers (and consequently dense clusters of cones), describes the most noticeable characteristic of the tree. It is often artificially dwarfed by the Japanese, but also has a number of naturally dwarf forms, which are known as Japanese Table Pines, Umbrella Pines, or Tanyosho Pines.

'Umbraculifera' makes a bushy, rounded, and broadly spreading tree, 10–12 ft. high, flat topped, and multitrunked, giving it a distinctly umbrella shape. Great clusters of small green cones about 1 in. long are borne near the tips of the branches, with older tan-brown ones of previous years still present in the interior of the bush.

In 'Oculis-draconis', Dragon Eye Pine, needles and branches are banded with yellow giving the shoots a ringed effect.

'Pendula' is a weeping form with trailing branches, but the framework of the young plant can be unattractive and sprawling, especially if the leaders have been pruned out to keep it low.

P. fléxilis (III), the Limber Pine, is a slow-growing 5-needled species, from the dry interior mountains of western North America. It has a dense, bushy habit, with rugged gray bark and dark yellow-green foliage, and 4-inch tapered cones. Though frequently dwarfed by the harsh conditions of its alpine habitat, it can be a 50–60 ft. tree in Utah and Wyoming. This species does much better under lowland conditions than *P. albicaulis*. Several cultivars have been described:

'Glauca Reflexa' has attractive blue foliage, upturned branches, and a pretty 4-in. green cone, studded with white gobs of pitch.

'Firmament' is another blue-needled form, said to be immune to blister rust.

'Nana' is a bushy dwarf form from the Sierra Nevada in California.

P. jéffreyi (IV), the Jeffrey Pine from southwestern Oregon and northern California, is slow growing to a height of 200 ft., and is ultimately too large for the average garden, but suitable for park plantings. It is a 3-needled pine, similar in appearance to *P. ponderosa*, but has longer needles and much larger cones, and also a different fruity scent to the crushed leaves, not of turpentine.

P. montícola (IV), the Western White Pine of northwestern North America, is a stately forest tree to 200 ft. or more, with whorls of branches regularly spaced up the checkered, gray trunk. It is pyramidal in form when young, becoming irregularly columnar in outline and often flat topped with age, a very fast-growing tree reaching 2 ft. through and 80 ft. tall in 50 years. Blue-green needles are borne in clusters of 5. Cylindrical, pitchy cones, either purple or bright green when young, are up to 8 in. long. This is not a tree for patio areas, since the cones drip pitch in warm weather. Dwarf and weeping forms have been described, but are less common in cultivation than the similar forms of the eastern White Pine, *P. strobus*.

P. múgo (II), the Mugho Pine from the mountains of Europe, is one of the best known of the dwarf or medium-sized pines commonly planted in rock gardens. A dark green 2-needled pine extremely variable in habit and size, it is drought resistant and easily grown in almost any soil. Several very dwarf forms have been described, but dwarfness in *P. mugo* as usually offered is relative. It is never really treelike, but the numerous spreading and ascending stems can reach 6–8 ft., and easily outgrow the position that was suitable when they were young and tightly clustered.

Var. *pumílio* has cones with off-center rather than central bosses, but otherwise does not differ in habit from the type.

'Wintergold' is a dwarf form with needles golden in the winter.

'Valley Cushion' is a dwarf from Oregon State University.

'Alpineglow' has green foliage, and 'Oregon Jade' is blue-green; both are improvements in color over the type.

P. nígra (IV), the Austrian Pine, is a variable 2-needled species from western and central Europe eastward into the Balkans, Crimea and Turkey,

A young tree of one of
the varieties of the
Austrian pine (*Pinus
nigra* var. *cebennensis*).
Photo by Brian Mulligan.

which in all its forms is desirable for planting in this region, given sufficient space for a large tree.

Ssp. *nígra,* the Austrian Pine itself, has rich, deep green foliage and
shiny brown cones 2–3½ in. long. The spreading branches of a young tree
form a pyramidal outline, but in old age it sometimes achieves a picturesque flat-topped head.

Ssp. *larício,* the Corsican Pine, and ssp. *pallásiana (caramánica),* the
Crimean Pine, are regional forms of *P. nigra* with crisper foliage, the former
with longer leaves and cones 6–7 in. in length; the latter is well suited to
sandy soils. All are vigorous 100–125 ft. trees, not especially particular
about conditions, tolerating calcareous soils in their native mountains.

P. parviflóra (IV), the Japanese White Pine, another of the 5-needled
pines, is a small dense tree, 50–70 ft. high, with gray-green foliage. It cones
freely and the 2–3 in. long cones can remain on the tree for 6–7 years. In
'Glauca' the needles are dense and twisted, glaucous on the under side.
Many dwarf forms exist, of both Japanese and European origin. It is the
principal pine used for bonsai in Japan, and is an attractive species for
gardens as well.

P. péuce (IV), Macedonian Pine from the Balkans, also a 5-needled
species, is a small, slow-growing tree with densely branched pyramidal
habit, suitable for small gardens, although it can ultimately reach 120 feet
in the wild. It has pitchy, light brown cones up to 6 in. long. It is regrettably
rare in cultivation.

P. pináster (VII), Maritime Pine, native to southwestern Europe and
North Africa, carries its large, stout, dark green needles in pairs, is of very

rapid growth and is well suited to poor, sandy soils. Old specimens develop a picturesque dark trunk, and can ultimately reach 100 ft. or more; young trees are often merely gangling. The tapering cones, 6 or more in. long, are often borne in large clusters, and can persist on the tree for many years.

P. *ponderósa* (IV), Western Yellow Pine or Ponderosa Pine, is the most frequently planted of the large, long-needled native pines. The deep green needles, 6–10 in. long, are arranged in bundles of 3. Although occasionally found in the interior valleys of western Washington and Oregon, its principal range is east of the Cascades. It thrives in cultivation here, planted in a deep, light, porous soil and given plenty of room. Native stands of young trees have been retained by developers in parts of Spokane, where they provide welcome shade in hot summers. However, homeowners will ultimately be faced with removal problems, since *P. ponderosa* is one of the largest of pines, to 200 ft. or more after 100 years or so, and eventually 6–7 ft. through. Unfortunately, the fine yellow trunks with their scaling, jigsaw-puzzle bark, develop only in older specimens; trunks of young trees are merely dark gray. The squat brown cones, 3–4 in. long, are prickly.

A fine specimen of the western yellow pine (*Pinus ponderosa*). Photo by Brian Mulligan.

P. púmila (III), Japanese Stone Pine or Dwarf Siberian Pine from northeastern Asia, is a slow-growing, sometimes prostrate shrub, suitable for rock gardens and useful in exposed locations. Its needles are blue-green, 5 to a bundle. Plants cone at a young age. Male cones are deep red and quite conspicuous; female cones, in clusters, are at first deep purple, finally yellowish brown. This species is usually under 4 ft. in height, but can be as much as 8 ft., or as small as 12 in. It is one of the few pines which will remain in proper scale in the rock garden.

P. radiáta (VII–VIII), the Monterey Pine, is a handsome 3-needled pine with bright green leaves, robust in growth. It is a native of the California coast in three separate stands, of which that on the Monterey Peninsula is the best known. It is perfectly hardy on the seacoast as far north as southern British Columbia, but is not reliably hardy in the colder interior valleys; and in any case it is not too happy away from the seacoast. It forms an attractive tree eventually as much as 100 ft. high with thick, sturdy branches forming a broad, irregular head. Like other trees of rapid growth, it is not long lived, attaining its full size in from 80–100 years, and seldom living to be older than 150 years. The shiny, dark brown, egg-shaped cones, 4–6 in. long, are carried in clusters and remain on the branches for many years; it is occasionally possible to count as many as 22 sets of cones studding the branches, back into the interior of the tree. The grayish white new buds are quite conspicuous.

P. sabiniána (VII), the Digger Pine, is a native of most of California except the extreme south. It is rather sparsely furnished with long, pale grayish green needles in threes, and produces enormous cones, with thick, hooked cone scales. It makes an interesting, medium-sized tree for dry sunny locations, lacy in aspect, and giving only thin shade. Trunks are often forked. Surprisingly, it has done very well in Seattle.

P. stróbus (II), Eastern White Pine, is the smaller counterpart of *P. monticola* from western North America, and is a more useful tree for gardens, since it reaches only about 70–80 ft. It has soft, bluish green foliage, similar to that of *P. monticola,* with the needles also in fives. Like that species it is subject to blister rust. Cones are shorter and more slender. Several clonal selections are offered by nurseries:

'Fastigiata' is narrowly columnar with ascending branches, to an ultimate height of 70 ft.

'Pendula', the weeping form, needs its leader trained upward when young in order to display the long-sweeping branches to best effect.

'Pumila', a bushy, rounded dwarf, to about 3 ft. each way, is one of a number of low-growing forms.

'Nana' forms a loose, rounded bush, quite glaucous, with little pinkish brown, pitchy cones, ½ in. by 2 in., at only 2 ft. tall.

P. sylvéstris (II), Scots Pine, is found from Scotland across northern Europe, where it is an important timber tree, to the Russian Far East. It can grow to a height of 120 ft., and is an ornamental 2-needled pine with dark bluish green or glaucous foliage, scaling orange-red bark, and attractive, small brown cones about 2 in. long. The type forms a broadly pyramidal crown, eventually irregular and often picturesque, and is a favorite small pine for Northwest gardens. A great many geographical varieties have been described in the wild, and this species has been in cultivation long enough to have produced many cultivars differing in size, shape and foliage color.

'Argentea Compacta' is a densely branched dwarf with silvery gray needles.

'Aurea' is a slow-growing form of rounded, compact habit, with needles golden in winter.

'Hillside Creeper' makes a fluffy horizontal growth to 15 in.

'Watereri' is a slow-growing form to eventually 20 ft. tall and wide in which the main branches curve outward and upward, the glaucous leaves also being curved and twisted.

There are many other dwarf forms on the market under such names as 'Nana', 'Pygmaea' and 'Compacta', 'Globosa', etc., some of these also with foliage variants.

'Fastigiata' is a narrow, dense form to 20 ft., with upright branches.

'Pendula' has weeping, broadly spreading branches.

A dwarf form of the Scots pine (*Pinus sylvestris* 'Watereri'). Photo by Brian Mulligan.

P. thunbérgii (V), the Japanese Black Pine, can grow to 80–100 ft. It is a vigorous 2-needled pine with dark, deeply furrowed bark. It is quite distinctive, with its silvery white buds against the darker green foliage, and is one of the handsomest of the larger pines for gardens here. It is often trained into irregular shapes in Japanese gardens, and is useful for seaside plantings. The cones are eggshaped, about 2 in. long, and are sometimes borne in very large clusters.

P. wallichiána (P. excélsa, P. griffíthii) (V–VI), the Himalayan or Bhutan Pine, is a broadly pyramidal 150 ft. tree, somewhat resembling *P. monticola* and attaining a spread of 40–50 ft. It grows very rapidly when young and soon makes a handsome lawn specimen, with its branches drooping to the ground. The gray-green needles, 5–6 in. long, in clusters of five, are drooping; the 6–10 in. pendulous cones are obviously stalked, but otherwise quite similar to those of *P. monticola.* 'Zebrina' has needles cross-banded with yellow, giving branchlets a ringed effect. This species is said to be resistant to blister rust.

PODOCÁRPUS, the Plum Yews, are a group of evergreen trees or shrubs mainly from the Southern Hemisphere, but extending to the Himalayas and Japan. They are for the most part too tender for us, but a few species have been grown successfully outdoors at the Washington Park Arboretum in Seattle for a number of years. They seem to grow well in loam to clay-loam soils and enjoy full sun although they will tolerate partial shade.

P. alpínus (V–VI), from Tasmania and the mountains of New South Wales, is a low, evergreen shrub 2–3 ft. high or larger in time, with a dense mass of drooping branches and very small, 2-ranked needles. It produces a bright red, plumlike fruit about ¼ in. across.

P. andínus (VII), native to the Chilean Andes, is a rare tree to 40–50 ft, or a large shrub of very dense habit, somewhat yewlike in appearance. Its fruits are plumlike and edible. It is slow-growing and needs a sheltered location.

P. macrophýllus (VII), Yew Pine, native in Japan and southern China, can be a tree to 60 ft., but with us is usually an erect, shrubby plant. Its leaves are large, up to 4 in. long and ¼ in. wide, bright green, thick and leathery. The fruits consist of a small seed set on a purple receptacle. This species requires a warm situation to do its best, but may be grown in any well-sheltered location, preferably in a well-drained, sandy soil. It makes a popular container plant for entryways in commercial buildings. Var. *máki* is the shrubby form usually seen.

P. nivális (V–VI), Alpine or Snow Totara, from both islands of New Zealand, is a low evergreen shrub 1–3 ft. high and wide, with upturned shoots and stiff olive green leaves, suitable for the rock garden. The fruits, rarely seen here since it is dioeceous, are bright red. This species is fully hardy in Seattle, being a mountain plant in its native habitat.

PSEUDOLÁRIX *amábilis (P. kaémpferi)* (V), the Golden Larch, is a native of eastern China. Deciduous like *Larix,* it reaches an ultimate size of 100 ft. or more with a trunk 2–3 ft. in diameter. Its needles are clustered as in larches, but are somewhat coarser and yellowish green, turning a rich golden yellow in the fall, hence the common name. A rare, slow-growing, but hardy tree, it is amenable to most garden conditions, but dislikes lime.

PSEUDOTSÚGA menzíesii (VI), the Douglas Fir, is the primary lumber tree of the Pacific Northwest, with an ultimate height of 200–300 ft., and 8–10 ft. through. It is thus far too large a tree for the average garden, fast enough growing to require removal for safety reasons at around 50 years. Nevertheless, its fluffy medium green needles, jaunty, upswept branches, and pendent, trident-bracted cones make it a most attractive background plant for the time that it remains in scale for the usual city lot. It is an extremely variable tree, plants with conspicuously weeping habit, and others with needles as blue as Blue Spruce being among the occasionally seen or planted forms.

'Densa' is a dwarf spreading form with very short needles. 'Compacta' may be the same plant.

'Fletcheri', a dwarf, rounded, slow-growing form to 6 ft., has needles green above, but glaucous beneath, an attractive plant.

'Idaho Gem' is the dwarfest selection.

'Rogers Weeping' grows flat on the ground, but weeps gracefully if its leader is staked.

Var. *glaúca* (IV), the Rocky Mountain form, is hardier and slower growing than the West Coast trees. The leaves are often more glaucous and the cones smaller.

SCIADÓPITYS verticilláta (V), the Japanese Umbrella Pine, is a most distinctive conifer of very ancient origin. A slow-growing tree retaining its lower branches to form a narrow, conical head, it is said to reach a height of 100–120 ft. in Japan. Specimens planted in gardens here under ideal conditions of rich, light, well-drained soil have not exceeded 35 ft. in 50–60 years. The broad, glossy, bronzy green needles, each composed of two, united to appear as one, are arranged in whorls up the stem. Those at the tips of the twigs are larger than the leaves of most conifers, and look like the ribs of an umbrella, hence the common name. The foliage pattern of the tree as a whole is coarse textured, but striking. The cones, 2–3 in. long have broad, reflexed margins to their scales, and require two years to mature. It prefers a sunny, well-drained situation.

SEQUÓIA sempervírens (VII), the Coastal Redwood, is found in the coastal fog belt of northern California and extreme southwestern Oregon. It is distinguished from *Sequoiadendron* by its yewlike foliage and small, woody cones about 1 in. long. Its colossal proportions—well over 300 ft. in the wild, and 25 ft. in diameter—are enough to discourage its use in gardens, although it is an attractive tree when young, with lacy foliage and stringy, red-brown bark. Plenty of year-around moisture is its chief cultural requirement. It is not quite as hardy as *Sequoiadendron giganteum*, having been damaged by the exceptional November 1955 freeze in Seattle.

In the cultivar 'Adpressa' ('Albospica') the new growth tips are creamy white. It can be maintained as a dwarf if leaders are cut out as they appear. It is more cold sensitive than the type.

'Aptos Blue' has dense blue-green foliage on weeping branchlets from nearly horizontal branches. Along with 'Santa Cruz' and 'Soquel', this plant is of California origin.

'Prostrata' ('Cantab') has semiprostrate habit, with unusually wide needles. It originated at Cambridge, England, as a bud mutation.

'Santa Cruz' is a large tree with pyramidal habit, and pale green foliage.

'Soquel' is a small pyramidal tree with dark green needles, blue on the underside.

SEQUOIADÉNDRON gigantéum (VI), the Big Tree of the western slope of the Sierras, is a truly gigantic tree capable of achieving a height of 250–300 ft., and a diameter of 30 ft., and living 3,000–4,000 years. Heavily massed, cordlike foliage distinguishes it from the Redwoods (*Sequoia*). The

Young trees of the giant Sequoia (*Sequoiadendron giganteum*) in Seattle. Photo by Jean Witt.

thick, squat cones, 2–3 in. long, take two years to ripen. It needs a deep, rich soil and plenty of moisture throughout the year. This is a stately tree for park or avenue planting. Probably the only form that can be considered as a garden tree is the weeping form, 'Pendulum', which has an erect leader, and forms a tall, narrow column, with the pendent branches swooping down, more bizarre than beautiful.

TAXÓDIUM distichum (IV), the Bald Cypress of eastern United States as far north as Delaware and hardy to New York and Illinois is the ideal conifer for wet places, though it will also thrive in ordinary good soil if watered through the summer. However, since it can reach a height of 150 ft. with a base 4–6 ft. in diameter, it is better suited to parks than to the average garden. As the tree matures, the tapered trunk becomes strongly buttressed at the base and the roots may send up the curious woody structures aptly dubbed "cypress knees," particularly if they stand in water in the wintertime. Pyramidal in outline when young, with a striking winter branch pattern, the Bald Cypress has airy foliage, and the dainty green needles turn a beautiful russet brown in autumn just before the twiglets drop. Male flowers are borne in pendent catkins; female cones are about 1 in. across. A position in full sun suits it best. A grove of them stands in the swamp on the east side of the Washington Park Arboretum in Seattle.

TÁXUS. The Yews are slow-growing trees or shrubs with rich, dark green foliage. Although classified as conifers, they do not have cones, but small red berries, with seeds surrounded by a fleshy red cup or aril, attractive to birds (and to small children—a hazard, since the seeds are poisonous). Yews are among the best of all hedge materials, able to withstand even the closest clipping. Needing rich, moist, well-drained soil, which may vary from peaty to quite alkaline, they may be grown in full sun, but are tolerant of deep shade. The three species mentioned here are very closely related, and are considered by some authorities to be merely geographical varieties of a single species. Individual plants are either male or female (dioecious), and thus not all produce fruits.

T. baccáta (VI), the English Yew, is perhaps the handsomest of the group, and is well known as an ornamental evergreen tree or shrub with a great many distinct growth forms and color variants. The type, a tree occasionally reaching 60–75 ft. with a rounded or wide-spreading outline and a huge, thick trunk, is less often planted than its shrubby variations. Seeds and other plant parts are poisonous—the red aril apparently is not. The cultivated forms must be propagated vegetatively.

'Adpressa' is a dense, wide-spreading shrub with much smaller leaves than the normal type, a female clone to an eventual height of 30 ft.

'Adpressa Aurea', of somewhat smaller proportions, has golden foliage. In 'Adpressa Variegata' the leaves are paler yellow with a central green vein.

'Dovastoniana', a male clone, is a multistemmed shrub or small tree, with widespreading branches and pendulous new growth.

A weeping form of *Taxus baccata*, perhaps 'Dovastoniana', draped over a wall. Photo by Don Normark.

'Dovastoniana Aurea' has golden yellow branchlets with yellow-margined leaves, particularly good in summer, and is also male:

'Fastigiata', the Irish Yew, a female clone, is stiffly columnar in outline, with one or more leaders, ultimately 40–50 ft. in height. Foliage is deep green, almost black in winter. Fruits may be produced and often result in fastigiate plants.

'Fastigiata Aurea', the Golden Irish Yew, has golden foliage, varying somewhat from one source to the next.

'Gracilis Pendula' is a weeping form, very graceful.

'Standishii' is considered the best of the fastigiate golden forms—it is very slow growing, and its color is especially good in the winter.

'Repandens', an attractive, almost prostrate form 15–20 ft. across, has loose, soft, widely spreading branches and dark green, curved leaves. It is a female form.

'Nana' is a dwarf with open and irregular form to about 3 ft., needles smaller and darker green and very glossy.

'Pygmaea' is only 15 in. high, a dense dwarf with very small needles.

T. brevifólia (IV), our native yew, is an understory tree in Northwest forests, and thus of use in heavily shaded situations—a tree to keep if it comes with one's property, but with no great horticultural merit. Reaching 50–60 ft. with spreading and sometimes pendulous branches, it is rather sparsely clothed with yellowish green foliage. The rich reddish bark of mature trunks is perhaps its best feature. It is somewhat gawky as a young tree; larger specimens do not transplant well.

T. cuspidáta (IV), the Japanese Yew, is very widely grown in northeastern United States, both as a hedge plant and as individual specimens, being hardier than the English Yew, but it is equally suitable for Northwest gardens. It can be a tree to 40–50 ft. in Japan; however, in cultivation it is usually a spreading shrub. Over a hundred cultivars have been described, but they seem to be less common in West Coast nurseries than the hybrid, *T.* × *média.* Its needles are slightly wider than those of *T. baccata,* and yellowish beneath. 'Minima' is very dwarf, not more than 1 ft. high; it is especially valuable for planting in shady portions of the rock garden. 'Nana', though not as small as its name would imply, is slow growing to a height of 10 ft, but may attain a spread of 15–20 ft.

'Thayerae', fast growing and flat topped, much wider than tall, is a female clone.

× *média* (VII) covers a group of hybrids intermediate in foliage color and texture—and also in hardiness—between *T. baccata* and *T. cuspidata.* Among the hybrid varieties offered are:

'Hatfieldii', a male plant, broadly columnar or pyramidal to 15 × 12 ft. in time.

'Hicksii' resembling an Irish Yew in habit but with larger, glossy, spine-tipped leaves, very free fruiting.

THUJA, the Arborvitaes, native to Asia and America, are pyramidal trees with scalelike leaves, fibrous, stringy bark, and tiny, oblong cones consisting of only a few scales. Some species are valued for their lumber, but they have also produced a great variety of excellent horticultural forms. They need a rich, moist soil for their best development, and may be grown in full sun, but are also tolerant of shade.

T. occidentális (II), American Arborvitae or White Cedar, native to eastern Canada and northeastern United States, is a slow-growing, pyramidal tree to 40–50 ft. with deep yellow-green foliage turning russet brown in winter. The type is not often grown, but there are a great many distinct horticultural forms.

'Buchananii', is narrowly conical to about 15–20 ft., very graceful, with whiplike branches.

'Fastigiata' makes a slender, dense column, 3–4 ft. through and 25–30 ft. tall. It is excellent for low-maintenance hedges when planted close enough together to fuse the foliage.

'Pyramidalis Compacta' is a tall, conical form, to about 30 ft.

Among the innumerable dwarf and juvenile forms suitable for the rock garden are 'Tom Thumb' and 'Little Gem', which form small, compact balls less than 2 ft. high.

'Caespitosa' is a low, flat cushion, less than a foot high, with an 18 in. spread.

'Ericoides', with juvenile foliage soft green in summer and brown in winter is moderately dwarf to about 10 ft. high by 6 ft. wide.

'Hetz Midget' with dark blue-green foliage is perhaps the slowest

A group of the American Arbor-vitae (*Thuja occidentalis*) in a native stand. Photo by Brian Mulligan.

growing of all Thujas, a compact globe with a vertical branching system.

In 'Cristata' the branches are crested, and in 'Filiformis' they are long and threadlike.

'Lutea' and 'Rheingold' are two of a number of cultivars with golden foliage.

'Wareana' of dense, pyramidal habit 8–10 ft. tall, has bright green leaves.

'Woodwardii' is a green, globose dwarf, to about 8 ft. after several decades.

T. orientális (V–VI), the Oriental Arborvitae of northern and western China can be distinguished from other Thujas at a glance by its upright branchlets with foliage sprays set vertically. The cones are larger and more glaucous than those of other species. A shrub or small tree, to 30–40 ft. in height, with a long history of cultivation in China and Japan, it is represented in our gardens by fewer forms than the preceding species. The most popular of these are the golden-leaved forms, listed collectively as 'Aurea', with closely massed branches in candle-flame shape and bright yellow early spring color, slowly reaching a height of 8–10 ft.

'Aurea Nana' is very dwarf, not more than 2 ft. high, with foliage bright yellow in spring, gradually turning yellow-green as the season advances. In U. S. nurseries it is often confused with 'Berckman', which is a taller form.

'Blue Cone' has conical habit and blue-green foliage, with many 1-in. hook-tipped oval cones at a young age.

'Juniperoides' is a compact 3–4 ft. tall shrub, with awl-shaped juvenile foliage, gray-green in summer, and purplish in winter. It is less hardy than other juvenile forms.

'Rosedalis' or 'Rosedalis Compacta' is very dwarf, also with nearly heatherlike very soft juvenile leaves, which begin as a creamy yellow, progressing to light green, turning plum-purple in winter.

All varieties with juvenile foliage will benefit from a sheltered planting site, as they are definitely less hardy than the species.

T. plicáta (V), Western Red Cedar or Giant Arborvitae, with its massive, tapered boles and fragrant wood and foliage, needs no introduction. Though ultimately an enormous tree, suitable only for parks and estate gardens, it is nevertheless widely grown and has produced a number of cultivars. It is both versatile and highly ornamental in the garden. Closely spaced trees can be sheared into tall hedges, or with only the leaders topped, will make a beautiful background screen. Specimen trees retain their lower branches well, with foliage clear to the ground. Voracious roots make cultivating under them difficult.

'Hogan' is a particularly fastigiate form from the Kelso-Woodland area of southwestern Washington and the Portland area of Oregon.

A compact, pyramidal form of the western red cedar, *Thuja plicata* 'Hogan', from southwestern Washington and northern Oregon. Photo by Brian Mulligan.

'Rogersii' is a slow-growing, golden-leafed dwarf of conical habit to 3 ft. tall which turns bronzy gold in winter.

'Cuprea', another dense, slow-growing form, has coppery yellow shoots in spring.

'Zebrina', the Gold Spot Arborvitae, has yellow patches dappling the usual green shoots, producing a golden green effect the year around, but especially valuable in winter.

THUJÓPSIS dolabráta (VI–VII), from Japan, has coarse foliage something like *Thuja*, but with wider, flatter branchlets and larger, thicker scale leaves. It makes a pyramidal tree to 40–50 ft., and presents a boldly textured pattern of foliage, bright green above, whitish beneath, the branchlets all in the same flat plane. The cones of this tree are almost globose like those of *Chamaecyparis* and not elongated like *Thuja*, and are hard and woody. It grows well in moist soil, in full sun or partial shade. Good examples can be seen outside the entrance to the Japanese garden in the Washington Park Arboretum in Seattle.

'Variegata' has patches of creamy white scattered over the dark green foliage and must be propagated from the variegated shoots to maintain the pattern.

'Nana' is a dwarf form, dense and bushy, to about 3 ft.

TÓRREYA. The Torreyas are divided between North America and Asia, and are distinctive for their very large, typical conifer needles, and for their solid, oval fruits.

T. califórnica (VII), California Nutmeg, is widespread but not common in the forests of California both in the Coast Ranges and the foothills of the Sierra Nevada, a broadly pyramidal tree to 50–75 ft., with horizontal branches and drooping branchlets. Its extra-large, stiff, spine-tipped needles, up to 3 in. long and 1/8 in. wide are a dark, glossy green and aromatic, borne in wide, flat sprays. Bark is orange-brown. Instead of cones this tree bears large plumlike fruits 1½ in. long, olive green streaked with purple, with thin flesh over a hard seed. This is a very handsome plant which could well see more use in Northwest gardens. An understory tree, it will grow in the shade, and with its oversized needles, makes a rather dramatic effect in the landscape. There is a good specimen in the Hoyt Arboretum in Portland.

T. nucífera (VII) from Japan is a shrub or small tree in cultivation, to about 10 feet, though much larger in the wild. Its sharply tipped needles are about half the length of those of the preceding species, and very aromatic when crushed. The green, elliptical fruits are also somewhat smaller. It prefers a moist, shady site.

TSÚGA. The Hemlocks are graceful trees with feathery outlines, dark green foliage and small cones. They require plenty of moisture for their best growth, and are shade tolerant, though thriving in full sun as well.

T. canadénsis (IV), the Eastern or Canadian Hemlock, native to northeastern United States and eastern Canada, is an ornamental tree with reddish brown bark, occasionally reaching 100 ft. or more in its native habitat. Its foliage seems somewhat sparse and pale compared with *T. heterophylla*, but it is a more suitable tree for garden use because of its smaller size. Many mutant forms are found in commerce, usually propagated vegetatively, with dwarf types being especially numerous.

'Albospica' is a slow-growing conical form, with white new growth, best in midsummer.

'Cole's Prostrate' or 'Cole' is a dripping pancake with small needles, to about 1 ft. high in 20 years but much wider. It can be staked to form a weeper.

'Gable Weeping' is especially attractive, of broadly pendulous form to 5–6 ft.

'Golden Splendor' is upright in habit, with golden foliage.

'Gracilis' is low growing, gracefully drooping with tiny needles.

'Hussii' is an upright form to 10–15 ft. with very short needles, whitish beneath.

'Jeddeloh', a recent introduction from northwestern Germany, is dwarf, with a swirled pattern of branches, hollow in the center.

'Minima', 'Bennett's Minima' or 'Bennett' is a spreading shrub, broader than high, the branches arching at the tips.

'Ruggs Washington Dwarf' is densely globose, with bronzy yellow foliage, especially in the spring.

'Stockman's Dwarf' is a slow-growing dwarf of conical shape, with short, thick, densely crowded needles.

T. caroliniána (IV), Carolina Hemlock, native to southeastern United States, is a compact, pyramidal tree to 80 ft. in the wild, distinguished from other American hemlocks by its hairy, reddish brown or golden brown new shoots. It makes a pleasing specimen tree and is also useful for hedges. It is said to be pollution tolerant.

T. heteróphylla (V), Western Hemlock, is a major forest tree to 250 ft., of elegant habit, usually somewhat spirelike. The pendent tips of its leaders, more delicate foliage, and much smaller cones easily distinguish it from Douglas Fir. Adapted to shade, but growing well in full sun, it makes excellent hedge material if carefully trained when young. It transplants easily when small but with difficulty when larger.

'Iron Springs' is a very slow-growing dwarf form from coastal Washington.

T. mertensiána (IV), Mountain Hemlock, as it grows in our mountains, is one of the most fascinating of all the timberline trees. Up to 100 ft. in the wild, it is usually not more than 20–30 ft. in gardens. It can be distinguished from Western Hemlock because of the way its needles are arranged radially around the twigs, while those of *T. heterophylla* lie in an almost flat spray. The cones, often purple when young, may be up to 3 in. long. This species does well in lowland gardens, in full sun if the soil is not too dry. Collected seedlings soon make rapid growth under lowland conditions; a very few retain their stunted mountain form and are ideal for the rock garden. Blue forms—some of them as blue as Colorado Blue Spruce—are occasionally available. 'Elizabeth' is a charming dwarf form from Washington.

T. siebóldii (V–VI), Japanese Hemlock or Siebold's Hemlock from Japan, can grow to a height of 100 ft., but with us is a relatively slow-growing small tree rarely seen, but valuable for its shining green foliage.

CHAPTER XV

Trees for Street and Park Planting

Public parks and spaces, and areas along streets called planting strips, tree lawns or parkways, represent gardens in public space. Here the scale of design and the conditions for planting and growth are unlike those in private gardens off the street.

A primary difference is that of scale. Most parks and most street rights-of-way offer a larger scale than do many home properties. Trees that would be oversized for a small home may be appropriate for these larger spaces. In gardens, trees may dwarf buildings. Conversely, office towers can intimidate rows of flowering plums as surely as towering firs and Deodar Cedars dwarf a small house on a city lot.

Another important difference is that of duration of use. Streets and parks occupy the same position for perhaps centuries. Residences and their occupants come and go more quickly. (By the 1980s the average duration of property occupancy in the United States had dropped to about five years.) This duration-of-use factor, coupled with the one of scale, means that the largest trees, which sometimes are the slowest to mature, are proper choices for streets and parks more often than for small residential gardens. There is the place to plant the grand oaks, larger maples, beeches, elms, plane (sycamore) trees, ginkgos, tulip poplars, chestnuts and the like,—and in some places the larger conifers. This chapter will discuss these tree uses, giving more attention to street than to park conditions because of their more limited nature.

STREET CONDITIONS, AT AND BELOW GROUND

Street conditions are not chosen with soils as a primary consideration. The accident of grid pattern on a plat map is the usual determinant, sometimes modified by topography. If soils in the area are ideal for trees, those along the streets are likely to be the same. In much of the Pacific

Northwest the general soils are poor glacial gravels or heavy clays, and streetside soils can be expected to be no better.

Drainage is frequently inadequate. Streets make effective dams that can cause areas of wet, poorly aerated soil. Both the street's activities and those on bordering areas, as well as the construction of the roadway itself, result in soils being more compacted. Top layers are squeezed down, diminishing the amounts of air that can enter the soil; such conditions are difficult to reverse or counter. Such negative influences reduce the supply of soil organisms from levels normal in a healthy soil. Road salts, soil pollutants, alkaline rubble from walls or buildings, solvents, herbicides, and toxic spills all influence the environment above and below ground. Underground are water, sewer and various other utility lines, occasional gas leaks, perhaps steam heating lines, building foundations and physical obstructions. At ground level, curbs and pavements restrict and redirect the area and configuration of tree root systems.

Confronted with these formidable challenges street trees frequently grow poorly. Vehicles leaving the roadway may injure them, driving over or parking upon their root systems. They may suffer vandalism by broken branches or damaged stems, and often carelessness when constructing new buildings, sidewalks or street widening. Streetside trees must endure the gray mud-mist that splashes in wintertime from the roadway, coating any stems or foliage with the same greasy film that appears on auto windshields. This is a major killer of evergreen shrubs along streets in Pacific Northwest cities. To a large extent deciduous trees escape it, and this is one of several reasons why they are usually a better choice for street trees than evergreens.

STREET CONDITIONS ABOVE GROUND

Air pollution has been an increasing problem the past 40 years and is greatest along streets. Pollutants arising from automobile exhaust systems affect different trees with different impact; many conifers such as most pine species and native forest trees (Douglas Firs and hemlocks) seem very susceptible to injury. The planner must choose trees for a street with great care in this respect. Some species which survive the lesser pollutant levels on residential streets cannot live next to busy intersections or main arterials.

Tall buildings flanking a street create and intensify wind problems to sometimes critical levels, and the canyons between such buildings are in some cases permanently shaded. In the nursery, trees are grown in sunny fields, and no street tree likes such shade. Radiant heat from buildings, reflected heat and light from building faces, and retained heat released at night from those buildings, all affect the street environment for trees. Dust and soot and other particulates in the air drop on to leaves, often carrying chemicals from cleaning windows, scouring building faces, or other industrial pollutants.

Overhead on streets there may be numerous wires carrying power or telephone lines; many require clearance distances from tree limbs, thus creating problems both as to the choice of trees for planting and the methods of pruning to maintain those clearances. Street lights designed to illuminate sidewalks and street surfaces are handicapped by tree canopies. Low-limbed trees may cause problems by hiding intersections, driveways, very sharp turns or even traffic signals. They may interfere with building canopies, commercial or other street signs. As solar energy gains acceptance as an electrical source there will be increasing conflicts between large trees and solar receptors.

Trees in parks and along streets in many cities can block valuable views, so the designer must weigh the choice of trees between recreational, artistic or street uses, and the wish to preserve those views. Certain genera and species of trees are more prone to blowing down or losing branches in windstorms than others. This is a critical safety factor along city streets or in public squares or parks, more so than in private gardens. Trees that cause excessive litter or a heavy drop of fruits, (e.g., Horsechestnuts or Mountain Ashes) would be objectionable on a street but acceptable in a park or garden.

The width of sidewalk area alongside multistory buildings and the width of the planting strip are often critical factors in the choice of an appropriate tree. Large trees crowded into narrow sidewalks alongside tall buildings will lean out over the street. Because tall vans moving along the street may be up to 14 feet in height, low-limbed trees or those with horizontal branching, such as Pin Oaks, would be poor choices for such situations. However, the same species might be perfectly acceptable for wider strips on residential streets.

The growth potential of the tree itself is often forgotten in the haste to install something green. Large-growing trees with notably powerful but shallow root systems may be poor choices to be squeezed into small spaces surrounded by concrete, when compared with others which may grow slower but have less invasive roots. The quicker effect of the former type will certainly be lost in a decade or two when the tree must inevitably be removed, with the added cost of repairing the damaged sidewalk and installing a more suitable substitute. Since even city trees have the potential for many decades of growth, such a quick effect and then replace pattern is short-sighted and wasteful.

PLANTING FOR SURVIVAL

Sometimes the planter or designer is confronted with a very hostile urban environment where trees are desired but where they may have real difficulty in surviving. The common practice of choosing a tree first for its decorative attributives in this extreme but not unusual situation fails to address reality. No matter how beautiful or desirable a particular tree may seem, if it is dying or dead in five years or less, it is a failure. From the following list of some of the toughest urban survivor trees one might select a species with the best combination of desirable attributes for any given situation. This selection is based on ability to survive, with the most durable listed first. Many might rate low on a desirability scale where the planter had a wider range of choices, but they will rate high in the critical requirement—ability to survive.

A DOZEN TOUGH BROAD-LEAVED TREES FOR CITY CONDITIONS*

1. *AILANTHUS altissima* (IV), Tree of Heaven. To 60 feet. "Grows better under city conditions in this country than any other tree, native or exotic" (Donald Wyman). Sexes on separate trees; avoid male trees when possible because of the foul-smelling flowers. Grow from seeds or root cuttings. Tolerates a wide variety of soil moisture conditions; not particular about pH. No serious disease or insect pests. Can withstand root submergence in salt water. Bold-textured, coarse compound leaves give a semitropical look; female trees have showy coppery red fruits. Fast growing, to a rounded top, but wood can be weak in storms.

2. *PLATANUS* × *acerifolia* (V), London Plane or Sycamore. To 100 feet. A tough hybrid between *P. orientalis* from southeastern Europe and western Asia and the American *P. occidentalis*. Seedlings apparently arose in more than one place. In cultivation in Britain by mid- 18th century. Survives really bad city conditions well, except poor drainage. Some susceptibility to auto-exhaust pollution, mildew in some areas, anthracnose fungus in climates with wet, cool springs. Strong root system is no problem in areas with fertile soils but can badly damage pavements on shallow soils. Hairs from maplelike leaves in spring may cause allergies in some people.

3. *POPULUS-SALIX* Complex, Poplars and Willows. Best known are the cottonwoods, *P. trichocarpa* (IV) from the West, *P. deltoides* (II) from eastern North America. Both can grow 150–200 ft. in height. Tolerant of extremely poor and often dry soils, these trees grow readily in moist or even soggy soils. Some willows will tolerate standing water part of the year. Both genera tend to have brittle wood and can pose safety hazards in wind or ice storms, so should be used only in sites where this is not a problem.

4. *ACER.* The maples. Toughest is probably the Norway Maple, *A. platanoides,* (III), to 90 ft., followed by the native Big-leaf Maple, *A. macrophyllum,* (VI), also to 90 ft. tall, and the Red Maple, *A. rubrum,* (III), to 120 ft.,

---

*Selected by the late Marvin Black, City Arborist, Seattle, in 1984.

tolerant of poorly drained soils. Large leaves in the two former species, varying autumn-colored foliage, golden in *A. macrophyllum,* red in *A. rubrum.* Many cultivars of *A. platanoides* and of *A. rubrum* available.

5. *TILIA* spp., Lindens. The best is probably the Little-leaf Linden, *T. cordata,* (III), to 90 ft. but usually less; *T.* × *euchlora,* the Crimean Linden, (IV), to 60 ft.; and *T. tomentosa,* (IV), the Silver Linden, to 75 ft. Avoid the last-named in dusty or sooty areas as the leaves collect dust. These are very tough, durable trees but subject to summer attacks by leaf-feeding insects, not fatal but annoying and disfiguring. Clusters of pale green flowers in summer, often sweet scented. Several clones of *T. cordata* now available, usually of more compact habit.

6. *AESCULUS hippocastanum* (III), the Horse-chestnut, to 100 or more ft. Fast-growing, with bold, palmately compound leaves, trusses of white flowers in May, but messy large fruits in fall. Subject to leaf diseases in some areas but less so in the Northwest. Heavy limbs are said to break in windstorms, but rarely in this region. Wyman doesn't like it, but Bean (for the U.K.) says, "at once the best-known and most beautiful of flowering trees of the largest size." Durable in poor city soils. The doubleflowered cultivar 'Baumannii' is seedless.

7. *GINKGO biloba* (IV), the Maidenhair tree. To 75 feet or more. Here is a long-lived tree that needs no spraying, very little pruning, has handsome leaves that turn golden in fall, has notable pollution tolerance, and yet is not much planted. Why? Because it becomes quite large, (through narrow, fastigiate forms are available), seedlings may bloom after 20 or more years, and female trees produce ill-smelling fruits. However, male trees can be propagated by cuttings, and female trees can be sprayed to abort the fruits, as is done in Washington, D.C. The tree is gaunt during its first decade until it begins to fill out, and is somewhat more difficult to handle in nurseries than most trees.

8. *ROBINIA pseudoacacia* (III), the Black Locust. (60–70 ft.), and *GLEDITSIA triacanthos* (III), the Honey Locust, 50–70 ft. Both trees are quick growing, with fine, feathery foliage; both are tolerant of poor soils, including alkaline types, winter road salts, and some coastal salt spray. The Black Locust has, in particular, fragrant white flowers in May, and is one of the toughest of all trees in harsh, dry climates. Both species, however, can be weedy and may seed and sucker freely, and both have several insect pests and diseases which may need controlling, though few in this region. The Honey Locust, in particular, has experienced dieback diseases in cities during the past decade. Both kinds are intolerant of poor drainage.

9. *QUERCUS,* Oaks. Species tolerant of poorly drained sites include *Q. palustris,* the Pin Oak (IV), 60–80 ft.; *Q. phellos,* the Willow Oak (V), to 75 ft.; and two non-swamp species, the Red Oak, *Q. rubra* (III), and *Q. shumardii,* the Texas Red Oak (V), to 75 ft. All make rounded or upright-oval trees, all have sturdy wood, most have bright autumn color, though for the first 10 years they may be awkward in appearance. The Willow Oak

grows especially quickly, up to 2 ft. annually.

10. *CARPINUS betulus* (IV), the European Hornbeam, most often seen in its egg-shaped cultivar, 'Fastigiata', the pyramidal hornbeam of the nursery trade, which in time reaches about 30 ft. Very dense and twiggy, this is a neat and formal tree, tolerant of clay soils but disliking gravelly or very wet conditions. Few pests bother it. Can be sheared into hedge form if needed.

11. *ULMUS parvifolia* (IV), the Chinese or Lacebark Elm, 45–50 ft. Only this one notably superior species is included here, since most other elms have too many problems to recommend any of them. This is the true Chinese Elm; the name is in disrepute because nurserymen have so frequently offered the inferior Siberian Elm, *U. pumila*, as the Chinese species. It can be distinguished from the latter by its very small buds, (those of *U. pumila* are large and fat), by its flowering in autumn, and the peeling bark in older trees. It is somewhat resistant to Dutch elm disease and to the elm leaf beetle, has excellent tolerance of dry, poor soils and a wide range of soil pH.

12. *MAGNOLIA kobus* (V), from Japan; to 50 ft. Variable in habit when grown from seeds but usually more or less pyramidal in outline with upright-spreading branches. Quantities of showy white flowers, each with 6–9 tepals, decorate them in April before the leaves develop, which are oblong and fairly large, turning pale yellow in fall. Fruits are seldom formed and not a problem. This species tolerates street conditions well and should be used more than it has been, particularly the clone 'Wada's Memory',* with its larger flowers. *M. denudata (M. heptapeta)* (V), the Yulan of China, to 30 ft., is even more showy than *M. kobus* when in bloom, but slower to form a good tree; it is also more subject to vandalism when in bloom, which must be considered before planting it.

---

*Now determined to be form of *M. salicifolia.*

A clone of the Sycamore maple, *Acer pseudo-platanus,* used as a street tree in Holland, underplanted with the rose 'Grootendorst'. Photo by Brian Mulligan.

A row of Pin oaks on Madison Street in Seattle. Photo Campus Studios, University of Washington.

Native birch trees (*Betula papyrifera* var. *commutata*) near Bellingham, Washington. Photo by Marvin Black.

Fastigiate hornbeams (*Carpinus betulus* 'Fastigiata') planted along a street. Photo by Marvin Black.

Japanese cherries 'Kwanzan' flowering along a street in Vancouver, B.C. Photo by Marvin Black.

CHAPTER XVI

The Garden Month by Month

This chapter is a thumbnail sketch of some outstanding garden pictures which can be created each month by the imaginative use of plant materials described in the body of the book. It is also a simple outline of garden operations in chronological order throughout the year.

In writing this chapter we were again impressed by the very small amount of work that a shrub planting actually requires each month once it is established under ideal cultural conditions. Herbaceous perennials and bulbs, which give the planting a finishing touch, require more work than all the woody plants put together. It was with the greatest difficulty that we refrained from mentioning herbaceous plants in painting the seasonal pictures. There are now good books on this subject, so we need not deal with them here.

This chapter is, therefore, a recapitulation of what has gone before, reiterating some of the information presented in the body of the book. At the same time, it suggests the possibilities of garden design based upon a practical knowledge of the plants themselves. There is no attempt to elaborate on details or explain the procedures mentioned. The practical points that are touched upon lightly can be found fully discussed under their respective headings.

JANUARY

January need not be a dreary month in the well-planted garden in the Pacific Northwest. There may be comparatively little to be seen or done in the worst years, when a prolonged cold spell strikes around New Year's Day, but the garden need not lack interest even then. Many broad-leaved evergreens achieve their richest hues only in cold weather. There is a surprising amount of color in the twigs, bark and fruits of deciduous shrubs and trees.

When the cold spell is past, or if the season is mild, several jobs are awaiting the gardener by the middle of the month. The garden should be cleaned up thoroughly if this has not already been done. Fallen leaves, debris from herbaceous material, and so forth should be collected and put on the compost pile. Tender plants or young plants in cold frames may be covered with cut fir boughs for protection, as long as these are not left on too long after the freeze is over. Use a good dormant spray on all deciduous trees and shrubs and do any necessary winter pruning of flowering, fruit, and shade trees. Spraying should always be done while the weather is mild—neither frosty nor windy.

The branches of many winter-blooming trees and shrubs can be brought into the house and forced into bloom. Avoid bringing them in during a frost. Many of the flowering plums, especially the purple-leaved *Prunus cerasifera* 'Atropurpurea' ('Pissardii') and its improved varieties such as 'Thundercloud' and 'Vesuvius', are beautiful when forced; the flowers open almost a pure white, making a shimmering cloud against the dark branches. *P.* × *blireiana,* with purple leaves and double pink flowers, will also open indoors, although its flowers will be much paler pink, turning to lavender as they fade.

Mahonia 'Arthur Menzies' is already setting off its whorls of bold foliage with spikes of bright yellow flowers, ready to cater to Anna's hummingbird.

Early-flowering varieties of *Chaenomeles,* the Japanese Quince, are already showing color in the garden in a mild season. From December onward the bright yellow flowers of the Winter Jasmine, *Jasminum nudiflorum,* twinkle on the slender branches cascading down a sunny slope or over a wall or fence. Though individual flowers are easily spoiled by frost, there is always a reserve of undamaged buds, and at every mild spell of weather they open undaunted. Both the jasmine and the quince can be brought into the house successfully, and the jasmine is particularly good, since a number of buds open at one time, turning the twigs into a shower of golden stars. The winter-flowering cherry, *Prunus subhirtella* 'Autumnalis', behaves very much like the jasmine, opening its little pink blooms from a surprising reserve of waiting buds. *Hamamelis mollis,* the Chinese Witch-hazel, and its hybrids are outstanding now, especially if planted where its bare branches and spidery golden flowers stand out against a dark green background. It fills the air with a rich, sweet perfume on a warm winter's day, though it gives off little fragrance when the weather is cold. Small branches can be cut to keep the pattern of the shrub open. They last well in water and are doubly welcome for their exquisite form and sweet aroma.

Pernettya mucronata loses its berries in a severe winter, but it they have escaped the frost, their masses of fruits—white, silvery rose-pink, crimson, or maroon—add glowing life to shrub groupings, augmenting and combining perfectly with the flowers of the winter-blooming heathers. The vigorous Mediterranean Heather, *Erica* × *darleyensis,* flowers cheerfully from November to April, as does *E. carnea* 'Eileen Porter', and they are especially welcome this month when most of the varieties of *E. carnea* are not yet in full bloom. The brilliant scarlet berries of *Cotoneaster horizontalis* are much more enduring than those of the pernettyas, and remain throughout the winter (unless the birds become too hungry). Avoid planting it with the lavender-pink of *Erica × darleyensis,* for the two colors clash badly! One more note of color which may be added to the heather and pernettya grouping is the pink to magenta *Rhododendron mucronulatum* which opens its first few blooms this month. Another purple-flowering shrub that holds its color through the darkest days is the short, stiff *Daphne mezereum,* with small, intensely fragrant flowers tightly clustered around upright stems. The creamy white albino form is recommended for the gardener who cannot stand magenta purple even in the dead of winter. In a shady corner the berries of *Skimmia japonica* have changed to the bright red which they hold all through the spring and on into summer. The white-berried *Skimmia* is exquite now, especially in combination with the pearly white flowers of the Christmas Rose, *Helleborus niger.* The yellow-berried forms of English Holly contribute a bright and cheerful note in the midst of all the scarlet fruited plants, while *Pyracantha* berries offer a full range from clear yellow to red-orange. The shiny black fruits of *Sarcococca confusa* are conspicuous on their branches, just before the flowers open.

Variegated hollies, trimmed in silver or gold, help to brighten the garden at this time of year, as do the golden or silvery blue conifers, some of which, such as *Chamaecyparis obtusa* 'Crippsii', *C. pisifera* 'Filifera', *Juniperus scopulorum* forms, and *Chamaecyparis lawsoniana* 'Stewartii', are at their most colorful in midwinter.

There really can be a great deal of color at this season if one plans for it. The sparkling white of birch trunks, the burnished red-brown of *Prunus serrula,* and the striped bark of maples such as *Acer davidii* and *A. hersii,* show off best at this time of year; nor should we forget the beauty of the branching patterns of deciduous trees in the winter garden. The delicate tracery of the fine twigs of a birch, or the gnarled and twisted branches of an oak, or the upward surging lines of a Lombardy Poplar etched against the winter sky—these are the most dramatic elements in the garden scene, each in its own way.

FEBRUARY

Most of the chores which could have been done in January are left, as a rule, until February, and by the end of the month there is a rush to complete the dormant spraying and the winter pruning before the first buds burst. Climbing roses which have made an uncontrollable tangle can be thinned out and pruned lightly at this time. Leaving this job until later jeopardizes the tender new shoots. The deciduous climbing honeysuckles such as *Lonicera periclymenum*, the English Woodbine, are among the first plants in the garden to break into leaf, and especially in a mild season, must be pruned and trained this month.

If the frost is out of the ground, February is an ideal time for the preparation of planting areas; it is not, however, a good thing to bury 4–5 in. of frozen soil beneath the surface. This is also the month for sowing seeds in frames equipped with bottom heat. Cuttings wintering in frames should be kept well on the dry side until danger of severe frost is past, then they should be thoroughly watered.

Deciduous trees and shrubs should be moved before they start into growth, and depending on the season, February will be a good time, even after a long, cold winter. However, it is necessary to wait until the frost is out of the ground.

A heavy fall of wet snow occasionally occurs during this month, which may break down the branches of brittle evergreen shrubs such as *Camellias* and *Cistus*. The snow should be shaken off as quickly as possible before its weight can damage these and other broad-leaved evergreens.

The deciduous *Rhododendron mucronulatum*, with its vivid rose to magenta flowers, carries over from January and is followed by its hybrid, the semi-evergreen × *R. praecox*, which is similar though slightly paler in color. *Rhododendron* 'Christmas Cheer' and 'Rosamundi' also appear this month. All of these make a pleasing combination planted among the named forms of the winter-flowering heather, *Erica herbacea (carnea)*, such as 'King George', 'Ruby Glow', and 'Springwood White', which are just reaching their prime. Grouped behind them, the foliage of *Mahonia aquifolium*, the tall Oregon Grape, which turns to deep bronze-purple after the frosts of January, supports this color scheme. The earliest of the camellias, which may have had occasional scattered blossoms since January if the weather has been mild, double their efforts this month and can make quite a showing. The white *C. japonica* 'Nobilissima' is outstanding among these, as is 'Daikagura', striped rose and white.

Prunus cerasifera 'Atropurpurea' is coming into bloom by the end of the month in the mildest sections and is fully out in warm years. 'Thundercloud' and 'Vesuvius' are dependable performers. Pussy Willows, native as well as the garden forms of *Salix caprea*, and *Corylus*, the filberts, are expanding their catkins, and the black and red ones of *Salix gracilistyla* are out in force. Two early fragrant bush honeysuckles are *Lonicera fragrantissima* and *L. standishii*, both excellent for cutting and bringing indoors.

February also opens the season for fertilizing rhododendrons and other early-flowering shrubs and trees, such as magnolias, although rain will be needed to wash the materials into the soil.

MARCH

March is a busy month in the garden and an important one, too. It is a month of prelude to the full pageantry of spring. Trees and shrubs that have flowered sparingly earlier, now come into full bloom and are joined by others. The first of the spiraeas, *S. thunbergii,* and the forsythias, *F. × intermedia* and 'Spectabilis', tell us that spring is really on the way and winter is past. All of these can be cut for decoration, either in bud for forcing, or in full flower. As soon as the bloom is spent, the flowering wood should be cut away.

The pruning of shrub roses begins in late March, and at this time the pruning of climbing roses other than ramblers should be completed, and the shoots trained and tied into position, if they were not dealt with last fall. Many gardeners want to get at this job before now, but the experienced ones know that it is wiser to wait.

The large-flowered Clematis such as *C. × jackmanii* should be cut back, as should deciduous shrubs which bloomed in late summer, such as *Fuchsia, Buddleia, Hydrangea, Tamarix,* and vines like *Polygonum baldschuanicum, Vitis* spp., *Clematis tangutica, C. paniculata, C. vitalba,* and others of the same type.

March is a good time for the spring transplanting of evergreens, both broad-leaved and coniferous—just as they are starting into active growth—if this was not done the previous fall. A few shrubs, such as the photinias, which start into growth before the others, should be transplanted correspondingly earlier. Choose showery weather for this work if possible or else keep the root ball covered when moving plants.

Pieris japonica has partially opened its flowers. Like a number of shrubs which flower early, such as *Viburnum tinus,* this one is particularly noteworthy for its long season of bloom. A few of the tight green buds in grapelike clusters show pearly white as early as late January in mild season; from then on until it reaches its climax in April, this splendid shrub is a constant joy.

A number of appleblossom pink rhododendrons make a fine succession this month, including *R. fargesii* and *R. oreodoxa,* the hybrids 'Tina' and 'P.J.M.', with pale yellow 'Bo Peep' for contrast. The species *R. lutescens,* one of the parents of 'Bo Peep', flowers for 2–3 weeks at this season. The so-called winter-flowering heathers, varieties and hybrids of *Erica herbacea (carnea),* now reach their peak although their blooming period extends from January to April, 'Vivellii' being the latest.

In an early season *Osmanthus delavayi* can bloom late this month, but usually reaches its peak in April. *Viburnum × burkwoodii,* several weeks ahead of its parent *V. carlesii,* keeps the *Osmanthus* company; both have deliciously fragrant flowers. The Williamsii hybrid camellias such as 'J. C. Williams', 'Donation' and 'Mary Christian' are likely to be opening flowers by the middle or end of the month, though a good percentage of them do not bloom until April. The pale yellow bells of *Corylopsis spicata* and *C. pauciflora* provide a different color in the woodland. Another woodlander, *Magnolia stellata,* is the first of that genus to open, and a very worthy standard bearer it is.

The popular *Prunus* × *blireana* is in its prime. The breathtaking Yoshino Cherry, *P. yedoensis,* especially the form 'Akebono', is a diaphanous cloud of white or palest pink, as are also most of the single Japanese spring cherries, varieties or clones of *Prunus subhirtella,* 'Rosea' ('Whitcombei'), var. *pendula,* and 'Stellata'. Indeed, the pace of springtime quickens all through the month—one event following another with increasing rapidity until finally we are plunged into the full splendor of the spring garden in April.

APRIL

April is a gala month for trees and shrubs in the Pacific Northwest. The early plums and cherries still hang on if the weather is cool as a multitude of later ones hurry into bloom. The first of the large-flowered Japanese cherries is 'Shirotae' ('Mt. Fuji') fully 10 days ahead of the others, followed by 'Ojochin' and 'Tai-haku'. As they go over the double Japanese cherries come on with a rush—the pale yellow 'Ukon', the popular pink 'Sekiyama' ('Kwanzan'), the very pale pink 'Shogetsu' and many others.

In the meantime a score of rhododendron species have come into bloom, including the beautiful violet-blue *R. augustinii,* pink *R. davidsonianum* and *R. yunnanense,* representatives of the subsection *Triflora.* Many of the *Lapponica* subsection including *R. impeditum,* grace the rock garden, along with the hybrids such as white 'Dora Amateis', pale yellow 'Cream Crest', and 'Blue Tit' and 'Blue Diamond' for blue tones, the pink *R. cilpinense,* and bright red 'Unknown Warrior'. Camellias, both *C. japonica* forms with single and double flowers in all shades from white to red, and the later *C.* × *williamsii* hybrids are in their prime; also the Chinese *C. reticulata* and its hybrids where they can be grown. It is advisable to thin out the buds of the *C. japonica* kinds when they are heavily budded.

Berberis darwinii is aglow with orange flowers. Some forms of its hybrid, *B.* × *stenophylla,* flower at the same time and others come a little later, but are generally not as spectacular. The native *Mahonia aquifolium* is lovely while it lasts, with soft fluffy spikes of clear yellow. The native dogwood, *Cornus nuttallii,* with its large white flowers, can hold its own with any of the exotics. Azaleas, both deciduous and evergreen, are coming into bloom. The delicate *R. schlippenbachii,* a worthy representative of the deciduous Azaleas, is clothed in shimmering pink. Of the evergreen kinds, the gaudy 'Hinodegiri', 'Arnoldiana', and some of the other Kurumes are a riot of color. Most of the rest will reach their peak in May.

Magnolia × *soulangeana* and its many varieties are in their glory during the latter half of this month. *Clematis armandii,* one of the most desirable of evergreen vines, makes its own dark background of leathery leaves for the waxy, ivory white flowers. Many of the spiraeas, such as *S. thunbergii* and *S. prunifolia,* cascade with wreaths of snowy white flowers. The orange yellow of *Kerria Japonica* is better known in the double-flowered form than in the more refined single form with its arching wands of rose-like blossoms. The many *Chaenomeles* hybrids which have been blooming tentatively ever since February now burst forth into masses of color.

This is a satisfying month in the garden with plenty of work to be done, a time of continuous interest and sustained pleasure. Prune deciduous shrubs such as forsythias and spiraeas promptly as they go over. Any evergreen shrubs which were not pruned last fall, or which flowered in September or October, should be cut back now as they start into active growth. These include the various heathers—*Calluna vulgaris, Erica vagans* and *E. tetralix, Daboecia cantabrica, Lavandula* (lavenders), *Abelia, Ceanothus* 'Gloire de Versailles', and so on. English Ivy, as a groundcover under trees or draping over a wall, should be cut back hard to keep it neat and within bounds.

The middle of April in a normal year should be considered the deadline for the planting and transplanting of most evergreen material, both broad-leaved and coniferous. Container-grown plants are an exception.

Frequently April brings with it a dry spell, many a gardener is caught unawares, and the growth of his shrubs is checked at the most critical period. Be attuned to weather changes and water if rainfall is inadequate.

This is the month for fertilizing and topdressing many rhododendrons and other ericaceous shrubs that are in bloom or coming into bloom. Keep them thoroughly soaked before and after the application of fertilizer.

MAY

May brings the climax of the spring and early-summer flowering shrubs. Large numbers of hybrid rhododendrons are masses of bloom—white, pink, and red, lavender and purple. The lovely new yellows such as 'Idealist', 'Full Moon', and 'Crest' add a note of distinction and a contrast in color. The native *Rhododendron macrophyllum* is a beautiful sight on the Olympic Peninsula and down the coast in Oregon. The Chinese species, *R. fortunei,* with its fragrant pink blooms, is at its peak this month. 'Faggetter's Favorite' is a fine hybrid from it.

This is the month when rhododendrons need their heaviest watering. It is almost impossible to give them too much. Give those which bloomed in April a second application of fertilizer, along with a heavy fertilization for those just coming into bloom. Remove the faded flower heads from rhododendrons, azaleas and similar plants as soon as possible. Disbudding of the rhododendron hybrids should not be overlooked if you want to improve the display. The discriminating gardener usually prefers quality to quantity of bloom.

A great number of hybrid deciduous azaleas centering around *Rhododendron japonicum* are in full bloom by the middle of the month, ranging in hue from rosy apricot and flame to orange and yellow. Although they thrive under the same conditions, they are better kept apart from their kin the evergreen rhododendrons with bright rose or pink flowers because the colors clash. Hybrids of the native azalea, *R. occidentale,* such as 'Graciosa' and 'Exquisita', come a little later, many of them in softer colors which combine readily with the pink rhododendrons. Some of the other species which flower early in May are delightful, delicate plants for the edge of thin woodland. Pink *R. vaseyi,* following closely on the heels of *R. schlippenbachii,* is a shrub of great charm. *R. calendulaceum,* the Flame Azalea, makes a brilliant display in late May and early June.

The race of hybrids known as the Ghent Azaleas also blooms at this time with a color range similar to though wider than the Mollis group. The popular 'Aurea Grandiflora' ('Altaclarense') is one of the best known of these, with rich orange flowers marked in deep bronze. Any of the orange and flame azaleas are particularly pleasing placed in front of broad-leaved evergreen shrubs with bronzy new foliage, just as the native azalea on the Oregon coast mingles with the evergreen Huckleberry, the rich pink buds of the former glowing above the bronze or crimson of the latter's new shoots. Any of the hybrids interplanted with evergreen Huckleberry, or combined with *Photinia glabra,* present a rich and satisfying grouping. Some of the Glenn Dale Hybrids with their wide range of habit and flower colors are most useful in our local gardens. *R. mucronatum* has large, snowy white flowers, or sometimes a soft pinkish lavender in 'Amethystinum'.

Deutzia, Philadelphus and *Weigela* shrubs all begin to bloom this month, although their main show is in June. Any of them that finish flowering in May, together with any forsythias and spiraeas which were not pruned in April, should have all the spent flowering wood removed now. Pines that are to be given special character should have their "candles" nipped back to half their length or else pinched out before the new needles are put forth.

A number of broad-leaved evergreens which make energetic growth at this season may have the tips of their shoots pinched out or even cut well back to keep them from making long, straggly growth. These include *Photinia glabra* and *P. serrulata, Stranvaesia davidiana, Mahonia aquifolium, Abelia grandiflora,* and many others. This type of pruning is especially necessary when the shrubs are young, and will be advisable for the majority of broad-leaved evergreen shrubs for the first 3–4 years.

May is the month for Lilacs. Common *Syringa vulgaris* still holds its own. The innumerable garden varieties, mostly hybrids of French origin, but some from the U.S.A., attract increasing attention. The older dark wine-colored 'Ludwig Spaeth' and the double white 'Mme. Lemoine' are fairly well known. The coastal Northwest with its acid soil is not as good lilac country as areas east of the Cascades. The dainty Persian Lilac arches out with showers of fragrant bloom. Lilacs may be grouped happily at the back of a well-limed herbaceous border or perhaps used to form a background for groups of hybrid peonies or tall bearded irises. Clip off the withered flower heads of lilacs as soon as they fade to insure the best bloom for next year, and fertilize the plants well. Cut the blooms sparingly for decoration and water heavily at this critical period.

The spring-flowering *Tamarix*, *T. tetrandra*, spreads out over a steep bank, its branches clothed with deep crimson buds quickly followed by fluffy pink flowers among the soft gray-green foliage. It should be cut back hard after flowering. It, too, is a fine foil for the vigorous bearded irises. Other shrubs not to be forgotten for a similar situation are the beautiful, single-flowered species roses. The gorgeous orange of 'Austrian Copper', the rich blood red of the Chinese *Rosa moyesii*, and the delicate pale yellow of the spiny *R. hugonis* all have gracefully arching branches that display the dainty flowers to good advantage.

Two outstanding large vines in bloom this month are the beautiful *Clematis montana*, especially its pink-flowered form 'Rubens', and the wisterias. Both these vines require careful pruning, but in entirely different ways. The *Clematis* flowers on the new wood and so is cut back immediately after flowering; *Wisteria* demands more attention. As soon as it starts into growth, which occurs simultaneously with its blooming, the new shoots must be curtailed by regular pruning which should be continued throughout the summer. The Chinese Wisteria, *W. sinensis*, with its short, broad panicles, comes a little ahead of the more graceful Japanese *W. floribunda*, which hangs its curtains of long, slender panicles well into June. The unbelievable 'Longissima Alba' with pure white panicles 4 ft. long, the rich coloring of the well-named 'Royal Purple', the delicate flesh pink of 'Carnea' are the sort of wisterias which make the bother of constant summer pruning worth the effort.

The large-flowered hybrid *Clematis* such as 'Jackmanii', Ramona', 'Nellie Moser', etc. which were cut back earlier should now be growing apace. They can be given an application of fungicide solution as a precautionary measure against the disease which sometimes affects them. Other vines which are making active growth at this season should be carefully trained and tied into place to prevent unmanageable tangles later.

Many of the flowering trees have come and gone in April, but this month gives its name to the Hawthorn, the May Tree of English literature. This long-suffering tree is sometimes clipped unmercifully into dense heads that scarcely bloom, but as a free-grown specimen with branching pattern enhanced by judicious pruning, the May Tree, with its single or double white, pink or crimson flowers, is a magnificent sight, and from a distance possessed of a pleasingly sweet fragrance which does not improve, however, upon closer acquaintance! The laburnums are in bloom with their drooping clusters of pea-shaped blossoms. A few of the many flowering crabs still remain. The small, shrubby Sargent's Crab ushers in the month, and at its close the upright Bechtel's Crab, *M.* × *ioensis* 'Plena', bears large pink flowers that have a sweet, musky fragrance.

Paeonia suffruticosa, the Chinese Tree Peony, and its exotic-looking hybrids are in their prime. These plants are gross feeders. They should be fertilized and watered heavily after flowering and enjoy an annual mulch containing plenty of humus. Pruning is seldom necessary.

Low-growing shrubs in the rock garden, such as *Daphne cneorum,* gaultherias, *Leiophyllum buxifolium,* and some of the heathers should be top-dressed with peat or compost before the weather becomes warm and dry.

The early part of May is one of the most deceptive periods in the garden. Not only can it be a season of unexpected drought, but all shrubs need a maximum of water when they are making their new growth. If rainfall is not adequate, be prepared to augment it with the hose.

JUNE

While May is the month of grand climax for the flowering shrubs, the parade continues into June. Roses now have their day, both species and hybrids. At the beginning of the month almost everything in the garden is making maximum new growth, a fact of which the ants with their herds of aphids are well aware. Spray as soon as they appear. Do not wait for the foliage to become curled and unsightly.

The June-blooming hybrid and species rhododendrons are especially noteworthy. Fragrant white to pale pink *R. decorum* flowers during the month, preceded by 'Azor', one of the loveliest of the tall, salmon-pink hybrids, and the various forms of 'Fabia' in shades of coppery orange. The showy, large-flowered, low-growing *R. indicum* makes a bold splash of red that lasts well through the month. There are now many fine hybrids derived from it. The double pink 'Balsaminiflorum' is a form of it excellent for rock gardens.

The dark green *Cistus laurifolius* covers itself in a shower of single, snowy-white "roses" at the end of June. The hybrids 'Doris Hibberson', 'Cyprius', and 'Purpureus' are equally floriferous and flower over a longer period, carrying on well into July.

The earliest of the large-flowered *Clematis* such as 'Barbara Jackman', 'Dr. Ruppel', 'Nellie Moser', and 'Henryi' begin in June, if they have not been pruned in the spring; but the majority of them flower in July. Selected forms or hybrids of the native *Rhododendron occidentale,* the Oregon Azalea, will still be in bloom, along with some of the later eastern azaleas such as *R. viscosum,* the Swamp Honeysuckle, and *R. arborescens,* both very fragrant.

This is the month for many of the deciduous shrubs. The weigelas are in their prime—the crimson-flowered 'Eva Supreme', the vigorous, pale pink *W. rosea,* and the hybrids 'Newport Red', 'Bristol Snowflake', and 'Pink Princess'. *Kolkwitzia amabilis,* the Beauty Bush, related to the weigelas, requires a sunny situation. *Deutzia scabra (D. crenata)* is a shower of white or pale pink flowers. The deservedly popular *Philadelphus* cultivars hold their semidouble, fragrant white flowers most of the month, and our own *P. lewisii* is much in evidence. Some of the single varieties like 'Atlas', 'Belle Etoile' or 'Norma' are exquisitely beautiful, though less fragrant and more fleeting. 'Virginale' is the well-known tall, double, white-flowering plant. All of these deciduous shrubs and any others remaining from May should be pruned as soon as possible after flowering; or of course they can be cut for decoration in the home.

Many of the shrubs which will bloom later in the summer begin in June, for example the varieties of *Hydrangea macrophylla* (Hortensias) in varying hues from white and pale pink to deep red, and from purple to blue, but mostly blue. If the color of the flowers needs intensifying, aluminum sulphate can be applied, preferably in the fall. The sturdy escallonias with their shining leaves make a fine display in pink or crimson. The hybrid 'E. C. F. Ball' is a good intermittent bloomer throughout the summer, with large, bright red flowers. 'Apple Blossom' has pink bell-shaped blooms, the habit more compact.

Summer pruning, which began in May with the Flowering Quince and wisterias, continues this month with many trees added to the list, including most of the *Prunus, Pyrus* and *Malus.* In fact, all except the peaches and almonds need some attention while they are young in order to form a pleasing, clean, open structure and at the same time produce a maximum of flowers or fruit. Espaliered fruit trees are trained by means of intensive summer pruning. Watch for watersprouts on any of the trees that have been heavily pruned the previous year. These should be pulled off as soon as they appear. Keep a diligent lookout for suckers from the rootstock of grafted or budded plants. Do not wait for them to grow large before removing them. Rhododendrons, lilacs, tree peonies, and *Hamamelis* especially, need this watching when young.

A final application of fertilizer, either for rhododendrons or other woody plants, should be given this month. Watering of newly planted shrubs and trees should continue unabated, but for most plants that are thoroughly established, watering can begin to taper off by the end of the month.

The middle of June is the beginning of the season for taking summer cuttings. Any material which has half-ripened wood is ready to be taken. *Cytisus* and *Genista, Cistus, Forsythia, Spiraea, Deutzia, Philadelphus* and many other shrubs which tend to ripen their growth early in the season should be taken as soon as possible.

Broad-leaved evergreen shrubs like the photinias should be cut back a second time about the middle of the month if necessary, and any shrubs which are being trained against a wall, such as *Camellia sasanqua, Pyracantha,* and evergreen *Ceanothus,* require pruning and training.

JULY AND AUGUST

July marks a slackening of the pace in the care of trees and shrubs. Watering should be gradually tapered off in August so as to harden and ripen all growth before fall. The business of taking summer cuttings begun in June gets into full swing in July, especially for heathers and many of the small-leaved evergreens including helianthemums, *Penstemon, Arctostaphylos, Euonymus* and *Hebe.* Those of the larger-leaved rhododendrons which can be rooted successfully are usually taken by the end of July.

Although these months reputedly have a dearth of flowering shrubs, with proper planning it is possible to have a considerable number. Many of those which started in June continue unabated. The fragrant yellow Spanish Broom, *Spartium junceum,* a typical example of these, should be lightly pruned as the flowers go over, if it has not been persistently cut for decoration. Broad-leaved evergreen shrubs such as lavender and some of the heathers (*Erica* and *Calluna*) which bloom in July and August can be cut back immediately after flowering. Lavender blooms which are to be gathered to dry should be cut as soon as the first flowers open, and then the bushes pruned immediately if necessary.

The hybrid *Ceanothus,* of which the popular pale powder blue 'Gloire de Versailles' is typical, are in bloom continuously from the beginning of July until the end of August. Those that are kept lightly cut over often bloom again in a warm October. A worthy companion for any of these blue *Ceanothus* is the floriferous *Abelia × grandiflora,* with its glossy bronze foliage, small, tubular, soft lilac-pink flowers, and accumulating pinkish-bronze bracts. Properly grown, it is one of the finest summer shrubs and makes and excellent hedge. The less well known *A. schumannii* and its hybrid 'Edward Goucher' are also good and help to swell this list. *Fuchsia magellanica,* the hardiest of the genus, and available in a pink-tinted white form as well well as red-purple, gives a good account of itself and is especially luxuriant in cool, coastal gardens.

On warm sunny banks rolling drifts of the Ling (*Calluna vulgaris*) or heather of the Scottish moors, are swept with hues of pale, soft purple, silvery pink, or snowy white by the middle of July. Some are out of bloom by the end of August and should then be cut back immediately so that they will make bushy new growth which can ripen before winter. Others flower on into the fall, and these should not be cut until just as they start into growth in April. The Cornish Heath, *Erica vagans,* and its fine selected forms, the dwarf salmon pink 'St. Keverne', the darker flowered, more robust 'Mrs. D. F. Maxwell', and the equally vigorous white 'Lyonesse', are a mass of bloom by the middle of August. A group of the light violet-purple *Crocus speciosus* showing through a drift of *Erica* 'St. Keverne' is one of the best combinations this month has to offer. *Erica cinerea* clones and *Daboecia cantabrica* and the hybrid *D.* × *scotica* will also be in bloom at this time.

The many color forms of *Potentilla fruticosa* such as the bright yellow 'Goldfinger', canary yellow 'Moonlight', and orange-colored 'Tangerine' are most useful and add variety at this season.

The best forms of *Buddleia davidii,* grown on a rough, dry bank among other energetic neighbors, produce their long, pointed panicles of purple, pink or white flowers in endless succession, as though they never tire of attracting butterflies. Among the lesser-known gray-foliaged shrubs of somewhat similar appearance and usefulness is *Caryopteris,* sometimes known as Blue Spiraea, with its gray foliage and blue inflorescences. The summer-flowering *Tamarix ramosissima (T. pentandra),* with its feathery plumes of soft sage green foliage, terminates in equally feathery panicles of soft, fluffy pink flowers. Although the sterile, ball-headed blue *Hydrangea macrophylla* is commonly grown, the flat-topped, fertile form—the Lacecaps—are more rarely seen, and are perhaps even more desirable plants in the garden scene. Another species, *H. quercifolia,* is likewise uncommon but deserving, with loose, open, almost pendent trusses of both sterile and fertile flowers in a delicate greenish ivory above distinctive, slightly gray-green oaklike foliage, as its name implies. It needs a moist situation.

Besides the *Cistus* already mentioned in June, the small-leaved species and hybrids such as *C. florentinus, C. monspeliensis* and *C.* × *hybridus* belong especially to late summer.

Clematis 'Jackmanii' and its kin, draped over doorways or fences, or even up into trees, make a gorgeous splash of color in July. The beautiful lavender-blue 'Ramona' and the soft pink 'Comtesse de Bouchaud' are especially good in combination with the climbing rose 'Mermaid'. In fact, many happy color combinations and successions of bloom may be had by combining one or more of these late-summer *Clematis* with the everblooming climbing roses. Shrubs, too, may be draped with them, whenever color is wanted at this season. Loniceras, especially 'Heckrottii' and *L. japonica* are also prominent in the late summer garden, as are the Trumpet Vines, *Campsis grandiflora* and *C. radicans* and the hybrid 'Mme. Galen.'

Yuccas hold forth in creamy splendor, while certain individuals of *Cornus nuttallii* may be almost as filled with second bloom as they were at their spring flowering. The hybrid *Senecio* 'Sunshine' is covered with bright yellow daisies, overtopping its gray foliage.

Few trees flower in August, but *Albizia julibrissin,* the Silk Tree, is eyecatching and exotic looking, its wide-spreading crown topped with pompoms of pink stamens, borne in large clusters.

By August the berries are coloring up rapidly on many shrubs. *Berberis thunbergii* and its varieties are sprinkled with masses of scarlet fruits, whereas in *B. darwinii* they hang in purple bunches. *Euonymus* and *Sambucus* are beginning to color up their fruits as well.

One of the more spectacular small trees is *Clerodendron trichotomum,* the Harlequin Glorybower, with its bright blue fruits centered in pointed collars of crimson. The white or pink spikes of *Clethra alnifolia* can accent the rear of the perennial border.

For months usually thought of as having few blooming shrubs, July and August can actually produce a good display for the gardener who knows which ones to choose and has the space to grow them.

SEPTEMBER

September gives the first hint of change toward the glow of autumn. The heat and dryness of summer is usually broken by the first fall rains. Once some rain comes, there is a great deal that may be done in the garden. It is not too late to take summer cuttings of partially ripened wood, although a smaller percentage may strike than of those taken earlier; such cuttings should stay in the cold frame all winter.

The well-planned garden can be rich in color of flowers, foliage and fruit during September. A number of rampant vines running into tree tops make showers of bloom or seedpods. *Polygonum baldschuanicum* and *P. aubertii,* the Fleece Vines, have covered themselves with filmy panicles of white or faintest silvery pink. *Clematis maximowicziana* is transformed into a bank of creamy old ivory by the myriads of tiny, fragrant flowers which quickly change to fluffy seeds that glint in the afternoon sunlight. However, first place for its striking seedheads must be given to *C. tangutica.* The beauty of its rich yellow campanula-like bells, so freely produced in July and August, and lingering into September, is almost upstaged by the seed-tails covered with glistening silky buff and amber hairs. On an old rail fence where such a tangle seems at home this clematis makes a charming combination with one of the purple-leaved grapes. It is lovely, too, growing up through the native blue elderberry—the combination of buff and powdery blue is as pleasing in pattern and texture as in color. The silvery seedheads of Traveler's Joy, *Clematis vitalba,* and our native *C. ligusticifolia* draped through evergreen trees, make a pleasing contrast with the reds and crimson of fall color.

Virginia Creeper, *Parthenocissus quinquefolia,* trained up into tree tops, flashes with crimson as some of its foliage begins to change. Many of the shrubs which have been blooming all summer, or that pause in late

August, now renew their efforts—*Abelia, Ceanothus,* Hydrangeas, and several heathers, to name a few. *Hibiscus syriacus,* the Rose of Sharon, is in full bloom in September. Its musty purple color forms are difficult to combine in the garden scene, but the whites and clear pinks can be most attractive. *Vitex agnus-castus* puts up stiff little lavender-blue spikes, like those of a *Buddleia.*

The fascinating color schemes of *Euonymus* species, the Spindleberry—Japanese, American, and European—are suddenly evident, as the magenta or crimson pods begin to split, showing the vivid orange seeds. Pyracanthas, their branches bowed down under the weight of the fruit, are beginning to color a fiery orange-red, scarlet or yellow. The deciduous *Cotoneaster frigidus* rivals even the Mountain Ash, *Sorbus aucuparia,* in the brilliance of its fruit, which are perfectly contrasted with the cool blue-green foliage.

OCTOBER

October is the month of autumn color, though the change from summer hues is first noticeable in September, particularly in a dry year, in such shrubs as *Viburnum opulus.* Fall color in our native trees and shrubs is not as spectacular as that of the eastern hardwood forests, but Vine Maples, Huckleberries and Mountain Ashes light up the mountains, along with the gold of larches; and Bigleaf Maples, Oregon Ash and poplars are orange and yellow in the lowlands. Northwest gardens, however, can have outstanding fall color displays, if trees and shrubs are selected with this in mind. Sumacs, the common snowball, oaks, maples, sourwoods, azaleas and witch-hazels will all perform brilliantly in most years, particularly if they have been kept on the dry side during August and September. Moisture-loving trees, such as the Sweetgums, color at the touch of frost even when it is not preceded by a drought.

Several ericaceous shrubs besides the deciduous azaleas are brightly colored this month. The slender, upright *Enkianthus campanulatus,* rising from a bank of heather becomes a blaze of crimson or gold, the small, neat leaves holding their color for several seeks. *Oxydendrum arboreum,* the Sourwood Tree, behind a drift of deciduous Azaleas, vies with the brightest of them, its leathery, glossy leaves, which during the summer give a suggestion of being evergreen, now turn quickly to reds and red-oranges. *Euonymus alatus* and *Cornus florida* turn to different shades of red, while the purple-leaved forms of *Cotinus coggygria* brighten to burnished orange, and the *Stewartias* fire up with orange and red-bronze.

Flowers and foliage have reversed their positions in the spectrum at this season. At other times of year, foliage, with its myriad variants of green, supplies the cool sequences of color, while flowers provide most of the warm colors with the cooler flower colors being used largely for contrast. Now with foliage dominating the warm end of the color scale, blue, lavender, and violet flowers come into prominence. *Ceanothus* blues seem better at this time of year, and Michaelmas Daisies are the flower of choice with autumn foliage.

The flowering of the graceful *Camellia sasanqua* is the big event of the month—long, arching branches of single or semidouble flowers, varying in color from white and palest appleblossom pink to deep rose-pink. The double 'White Doves' with its almost trailing branches, either trained against a wall or spreading over the ground, forms a mat of glossy, dark green foliage with the exquisite flowers festooning every branch and twig. The pink and white 'Apple Blossom', with its drooping habit is lovely, though fleeting; the dainty 'Briar Rose', which forms a compact, twiggy shrub, lasts much longer in bloom. Semidouble pink 'Jean May' is another desirable clone, usually lasting a month or more in bloom.

The Strawberry Tree, *Arbutus unedo,* which is now starting to bloom, is one of those shrubs which carries its flowers and its fruits at the same time. The large, red fruits contrast strikingly with the pale green *Pieris*-like flowers.

This is a great month for the gardener who wants to move plants. It is the principal fall transplanting season when the majority of evergreens, both broad-leaved and coniferous, are readily moved, provided the ground is sufficiently moist. Some deciduous material may be handled by the end of the month, but generally it is better left until it is completely dormant. Fall cuttings of ripened shoots of deciduous shrubs may be taken now, including roses. Pruning can be done from now on.

NOVEMBER

November is clean-up month in the garden. As the brilliance of the autumn foliage fades and the leaves start coming down, the garden should be put to bed for the winter. Any foliage or growth that has been attacked by disease or that is likely to harbor the eggs of insect pests should be gathered and burned. The great bulk of leaves and herbaceous material should be saved for the compost pile. Partially rotted compost can be spread around shrubs as a winter mulch if it is necessary to clear it out to make room for the incoming supply of leaves. Compost of barnyard manure will also prove beneficial dug lightly into stiff clay soils. Such ground can be handled more readily next spring if plenty of humus is dug in now, leaving the surface rough to absorb the winter rains. Recently set-out small plants can be protected somewhat from frost heaving later if given a mulch now.

The color of berries and fruits is increasingly welcome as the flower and leaf colors fade. The leathery, dark green foliage of the Carriere Thorn hangs on all month almost as though it were an evergreen. Clusters of large orange-scarlet fruits make this one of the showiest of all the haw-thorns in fruit; and when the leaves finally drop after a sharp frost, the vivid color is even more noticeable against the vigorous pattern of its twiggy, spiny branches. Laurustinus begins to bloom this month; its pink-tinted flowers and metallic blue berries combine to make a very attractive show. Planting more than one clone will improve berry set. The lavender-pink Mediterranean hybrid heather, *Erica × darleyensis*, is already showing color, blending harmoniously with the berries of *Pernettya*, which range in color from white through silvery pink to crimson and maroon. After the first sharp frost, the silver-variegated form of *Euonymus radicans* turns to a rosy bronze, making it another acceptable companion for the Laurustinus.

DECEMBER

Many of November's chores can be allowed to carry over into December in a mild season. Hardy deciduous material can be trans-planted at any time during its dormant period, providing there is no frost in the ground. The owner of a frame equipped with bottom heat can put in cuttings at this time, especially leaf (bud) cuttings of Camellias. As winter comes on the gardener can relax with most of his work in the garden done.

English Holly is perhaps the most famous of all the berried shrubs or trees which add color to the winter garden. The silver-variegated forms are particularly pleasing. The yellow-fruited form is equally cheerful and deserves to be better known. *Skimmia japonica* is another red-berried shrub which makes a good display to brighten a shady corner. The large berries of *Aucuba* are still a pale green and will not turn to vivid red until after Christmas. The ivory white stems and flower heads of *Fatsia japonica* are startlingly beautiful for decoration now. *Cotoneaster lacteus* holds its fruits until after Christmas, as does the yellow-fruited *C. × rothschildianus.*

Bold clumps of yellow-barked willow and Red Osier Dogwood which have been cut back each spring, present masses of bright young twigs to enliven the winter landscape. Golden- and silver-needled forms of small conifers, such as Junipers, *Chamaecyparis*, and *Thuja*, are also useful for brightening the winter garden scene. Dwarf conifers are fine accents for the rock garden, dwarf pines braving the windswept ridges, and small spruces nestled in the sheltered valleys. They set the scale for the planting, lending character to the scene.

The great range of color in the foliage of broad-leaved evergreens becomes especially apparent at this time of year. The vivid yellow-green of Mexican Orange, *Choisya ternata*, and the variegated forms of *Euonymus japonicus* contrast markedly with the gray-greens of the drought-resistant shrubs such as lavender, rosemary and *Cistus*. The strong, dark tones of Laurustinus are highlighted here and there with cluster-heads of reddish flower stalks and pink buds opening white. The deep green of many leaves is enriched as they change color at the touch of frost. Oregon Grape, *Mahonia,* and the Evergreen Huckleberry, *Vaccinium ovatum, Euonymus radicans* forms, and golden-variegated forms of *Elaeagnus pungens* show subtly blended hues from pinky bronze to dusky crimson and wine purple. The polished leaves of *Aucuba, Skimmia* and *Pachysandra* are a cool, lush green. All these and almost every intermediate hue combine to paint a picture that brightens the winter gloom. Where broad-leaved evergreen shrubs have been wisely used the garden scene is never dull nor lacking in interest and vitality. Indeed, there is never a "dead" season in the gardens of the Pacific Northwest. Each month has its own individual charms and attractions.

CHAPTER XVII

Lists of Trees and Shrubs for Special Purposes

The lists which follow have been devised to assist the gardener with his choice of plant materials for a variety of purposes and special garden conditions.

Twelve Good Flowering Trees

Albizia julibrissin

Cornus kousa

Cornus 'Eddie's White Wonder'

Halesia tetraptera

Magnolia denudata

Magnolia salicifolia 'Wada's Memory'

Oxydendrum arboreum

Prunus × yedoensis 'Akebono'

Prunus sargentii

Prunus serrulata 'Shirofugen'

Stewartia pseudocamellia

Styrax japonica

Twelve Broad-leaved Evergreen Shrubs for Hot, Dry Conditions

Arbutus unedo

Arctostaphylos columbiana

Artemisia spp.

Ceanothus spp. and hybrids

Choisya ternata

Cistus spp.

Phillyrea spp.

Lavandula angustifolia

Penstemon fruticosus

Rosmarinus officinalis

Salvia officinalis

Santolina chamaecyparissus

Twelve Broad-leaved Evergreen Shrubs for Full Sun

Abelia × grandiflora

Buxus spp.

Carpenteria californica

Choisya ternata

Cotoneaster spp.

Escallonia spp.

Garrya spp.

Mahonia aquifolium

Photinia glabra

Pyracantha spp.

Raphiolepis spp.

Viburnum tinus

Twelve Deciduous Shrubs for Partial Shade

Callicarpa japonica
Enkianthus campanulatus
Fothergilla major
Hydrangea quercifolia
Hamamelis spp.
Magnolia stellata

Rhododendron schlippenbachii
Ribes sanguineum
Viburnum carlesii
Viburnum plicatum
Vaccinium parvifolium
Weigela spp.

Twelve Deciduous Shrubs for Full Sun

Chaenomeles spp. and vars.
Euonymus alatus
Forsythia spp.
Kolkwitzia amabilis
Philadelphus spp. and hybrids
Potentilla fruticosa and cvs.

Rhododendron luteum
Rhododendron molle
Rhododendron occidentale
Rosa spp.
Spiraea × vanhouttei
Syringa spp. and vars.

Twelve Broad-leaved Evergreen Shrubs for Partial Shade

Camellia spp. and cvs.
Gaultheria shallon
Ilex crenata forms
Leucothoe fontanesiana
Mahonia nervosa
Pachistima myrsinites

Rhododendron spp.
Sarcococca spp.
Skimmia japonica
Stranvaesia davidiana
Vaccinium ovatum
Viburnum cinnamomifolium

Twelve Good Groundcovers

Arctostaphylos uva-ursi
Ceanothus gloriosus
Cotoneaster dammeri
Erica herbacea cvs.
Gaultheria procumbens
Genista pilosa

Hedera helix 'Green Feather'
Iberis sempervirens
Pachysandra terminalis
Rubus calycinoides
Vaccinium vitis-idaea
Vinca minor

Trees and Shrubs for Wet Places

Acer rubrum
Betula glandulosa
Cornus alba, C. stolonifera
Kalmia polifolia
Larix decidua
Metasequoia glyptostroboides

Myrica spp.
Nyssa sylvatica
Populus spp.
Rhododendron viscosum
Salix spp.
Taxodium distichum

Evergreen Vines
Akebia quinata (semi)
Bignonia capreolata
Clematis armandii
Clematis cirrhosa var. balearica
Euonymus radicans
Hedera canariensis
Hedera colchica
Hedera helix and vars.
Jasminum officinale (semi)
Lonicera etrusca (semi)
Lonicera japonica 'Halliana'
  (semi)
Pileostegia viburnoides
Solanum crispum
Solanum jasminoides
Stauntonia hexaphylla

Showy Deciduous Vines
Akebia trifoliata (fl., fr.)
Ampelopsis brevipedunculata
  (fr.)
Campsis grandiflora, radicans,
  × tagliabuana (fl.)
Celastrus orbiculatus, scandens
  (fr.)
Clematis species and hybrids (fl.,
  fr.)
Hydrangea anomala ssp.
  petiolaris (fl.)
Jasminum nudiflorum,
  × stephanense (fl.)
Lonicera brownii, ciliosa,
  × heckrottii, periclymenum,
  × tellmanniana (fl.)
Muehlenbeckia complexa
Rosa banksiae, brunonii, filipes,
  hybrids (fl.)
Schizophragma hydrangeoides
  (fl.)
Vitis coignetiae, davidii, vinifera
  'Purpurea' (fall color)
Wisteria floribunda, sinensis,
  venusta (fl.)

Quick-Growing Vines for Cover
Actinidia chinensis
Actinidia arguta
Aristolochia macrophylla
Clematis flammula, ligusticifolia,
  maximowicziana, vitalba
Parthenocissus quinquefolia
  (fall color)
Parthenocissus tricuspidata
  (fall color)
Polygonum aubertii,
  baldschuanicum
Vitis californica, coignetiae

Vines with Fragrant Flowers
Akebia quinata
Clematis armandii, flammula,
  maximowicziana, montana,
  rehderiana, vitalba
Hydrangea anomala ssp.
  petiolaris
Jasminum spp.
Lonicera etrusca, japonica,
  periclymenum
Polygonum aubertii
Rosa, some hybrids and species
Wisteria spp.

Fragrant Flowering Trees
Arbutus menziesii, unedo.
Aesculus californica
Cladrastis lutea
Crataegus monogyna
Elaeagnus angustifolia
Laurus nobilis
Magnolia fraseri, kobus, macro-
  phylla, salicifolia, virginiana,
  wilsonii
Malus baccata, ioensis, others
Oxydendrum arboreum
Paulownia tomentosa
Prunus mume, padus, 'Shirotae',
  × yedoensis
Pterostyrax hispidus
Pyrus spp.

Robinia pseudoacacia
Sophora japonica
Styrax japonica, obassia
Syringa reticulata
Tilia cordata, × euchlora,
    europaea, tomentosa

Fragrant Flowering Shrubs
Azara microphylla
Buddleia spp.
Calycanthus floridus,
    occidentalis
Camellia sasanqua, some clones
Carpenteria californica
Chimonanthus praecox
Clerodendron bungei,
    trichotomum
Choisya ternata
Clethra alnifolia and others
Corylopsis pauciflora, sinensis,
    spicata
Cytisus × praecox
Daphne spp.
Elaeagnus spp.
Fothergilla gardenii, major
Hamamelis spp. and hybrids
Itea virginica
Lonicera fragrantissima,
    standishii
Magnolia spp. and hybrids
Mahonia aquifolium
Malus sargentii
Osmanthus spp.
Philadelphus, most spp. and
    hybrids
Pittosporum tobira
Poncirus trifoliata
Prunus tomentosa
Raphiolepis umbellata
Rhododendron atlanticum,
    arborescens, auriculatum,
    canescens, decorum, for-
    tunei, × loderi, prinophyllum,
    serrulatum, viscosum, others
Ribes aureum

Rosa nutkana, rugosa, hybrids
Rosmarinus officinalis
Sarcococca ruscifolia, confusa
Symplocos paniculata
Syringa spp. and varieties
Ulex europaeus
Viburnum × bodnantense, burk-
    woodii, × carlcephalum,
    carlesii, farreri
Vitex agnus-castus

Plants with Fragrant Foliage
Betula lenta
Cedrus spp.
Comptonia peregrina
Eucalyptus spp.
Juniperus spp.
Laurus nobilis
Lavandula spp.
Lindera benzoin
Myrica spp.
Populus balsamifera
Rhododendron spp. (in
    Subsections Glauca,
    Lapponica, Saluenensia and
    others)
Rhus aromatica
Rosa eglanteria
Rosmarinus officinalis
Salvia officinalis
Santolina spp.
Thymus vulgaris and others
Umbellularia californica

Trees for Fall Color
Acer circinatum, ginnala,
    palmatum forms, platanoides,
    rubrum, saccharum, others
Amelanchier spp.
Betula spp.
Carya ovata
Cercidiphyllum japonicum
Cornus florida, kousa, nuttallii
Crataegus phaenopyrum
Fagus sylvatica

Franklinia alatamaha
Fraxinus latifolia (oregana),
    oxycarpa 'Raywood'
Ginkgo biloba
Larix spp.
Liriodendron tulipifera
Liquidambar formosana,
    styraciflua
Nyssa sylvatica
Oxydendrum arboreum
Parrotia persica
Populus tremuloides, others
Prunus spp.
Pyrus calleryana clones
Quercus coccinea, palustris,
    rubra, others
Sassafras albidum
Sorbus aucuparia, others
Stewartia monadelpha,
    pseudocamellia
Zelkova carpinifolia

Shrubs for Fall Color
Berberis koreana, thunbergii
Clethra spp.
Corylopsis spp.
Disanthus cercidifolius
Enkianthus spp.
Euonymus alatus, sieboldianus
Fothergilla major
Hamamelis spp. and hybrids
Hydrangea quercifolia
Photinia villosa
Rhus, all spp.
Rhododendron luteum, occi-
    dentale, schlippenbachii
Rosa nitida, rugosa, virginiana
Spiraea bumalda, prunifolia,
    thunbergii
Stephanandra spp.
Vaccinium corymbosum,
    virgatum, other deciduous
    spp.
Viburnum opulus, plicatum and
    vars., prunifolium.

**Plants Flowering in
July and August**
Abelia grandiflora
Aesculus parviflora
Albizia julibrissin
Aralia chinensis, elata
Buddleia davidii and vars.
Calluna vulgaris and vars.
Campsis radicans, × tagliabuana
Caryopteris incana
Catalpa bignonioides
Ceanothus 'Gloire de Versailles'
Ceratostigma willmottianum
Clematis large-flowered
    hybrids, maximowicziana,
    paniculata, tangutica
Clethra spp.
Cornus nuttallii, some
    individuals
Daboecia cantabrica
Erica cinerea and vars., stricta,
    tetralix, vagans
Eucryphia glutinosa,
    × intermedia
Fuchsia magellanica and hybrids
Hebe × andersonii, 'Patty's
    Purple'
Hibiscus syriacus and cvs
Hydrangea macrophylla and
    cvs., quercifolia
Hypericum × 'Hidcote', others
Itea virginica, ilicifolia
Lavandula angustifolia and
    hybrids
Leycesteria formosa
Lonicera etrusca, × heckrottii,
    japonica
Magnolia grandiflora, virginiana
Olearia × haastii
Polygonum aubertii,
    baldschuanicum
Potentilla fruticosa cvs. and
    hybrids
Rhododendron arborescens,
    auriculatum, discolor,

prunifolium, serrulatum, viscosum
Rosa hybrids, 'Mermaid'
Senecio × 'Sunshine'
Solanum crispum
Sophora japonica
Sorbaria arborea, sorbifolia
Spartium junceum
Stewartia spp.
Syringa reticulata
Tilia cordata, × euchlora
Yucca spp. and vars.

Plants Flowering in September, October, November
Arbutus unedo
Camellia sasanqua
Calluna spp. and vars.
Clematis 'Bill McKenzie', flammula, maximowiczii, tangutica
Erica × darleyensis, tetralix, vagans
Fatsia japonica
× Fatshedera lizei
Hamamelis virginiana
Hedera helix
Hydrangea quercifolia
Osmanthus armatus, heterophyllus
Pileostegia viburnoides
Prunus subhirtella 'Autumnalis'
Viburnum × bodnantense, tinus

Plants Flowering in December, January, February
Arbutus unedo
Alnus spp.
Camellia japonica 'Daikagura', sasanqua and cvs.
Chimonanthus praecox
Cornus mas
Corylus spp.
Erica herbacea and × darleyensis
Garrya elliptica, × issaquahensis

Lonicera fragrantissima, standishii
Mahonia 'Arthur Menzies', bealei, japonica
Oemleria cerasiformis
Prunus subhirtella 'Autumnalis'
Rhododendron dauricum, moupinense and hybrids, mucronulatum, × nobleanum, × praecox
Sarcococca hookeriana and vars., ruscifolia
Salix cinerea, gracilistyla var. melanostachys, hookeriana
Viburnum × bodnantense, farreri (fragrans), tinus

Trees and Shrubs for Seaside Planting
Acer pseudoplatanus
Arbutus menziesii, unedo
Arctostaphylos columbiana
Atriplex spp.
Baccharis pilularis
Buddleia spp.
Calluna vulgaris
Caragana arborescens
Ceanothus spp. and hybrids
Cistus spp. and hybrids
Colutea arborescens
Cotoneaster spp.
Crataegus pinnatifida, others
Cytisus, most spp. and hybrids
Elaeagnus angustifolia
Erica arborea var. alpina
Escallonia, all
Euonymus japonicus, patens, radicans and vars.
Fraxinus angustifolia, excelsior
Fuchsia magellanica and hybrids
Hebe, most kinds
Helianthemum spp. and hybrids
Hippophae rhamnoides
Hydrangea macrophylla
Ilex aquifolium, glabra, opaca

Juniperus, most
Laurus nobilis
Lavandula spp.
Lonicera japonica, 'Halliana',
  nitida, tatarica
Mahonia aquifolium
Myrica californica
Myrtus communis
Olearia haastii, others
Phormium tenax
Photinia × fraseri, glabra,
  serrulata
Picea abies and vars., sitchensis
Pinus contorta, radiata,
  thunbergii
Pittosporum tobira
Platanus × acerifolia
Prunus spinosa
Populus alba
Potentilla fruticosa and cvs.
Pyracantha, all
Quercus garryana, marilandica,
  robur, virginiana
Rosmarinus officinalis
Rosa nutkana, rugosa,
  pimpinellifolia, wichuraiana
Salix, many
Sambucus racemosa
Santolina spp.
Sorbus aucuparia
Spiraea douglasii
Symphoricarpus, all
Tamarix spp.
Ulmus parvifolia
Ulex europaeus
Vaccinium ovatum
Viburnum dentatum, opulus,
  tinus

Plants with Showy Fruits

Ailanthus altissima
Aralia elata
Arbutus menziesii, unedo
Berberis thunbergii, other spp.
Callicarpa japonica, others
Celastrus spp.
Cornus kousa, stolonifera,
  others
Cotoneaster dielsianus,
  henryanus, horizontalis,
  salicifolius, others
Crataegus crus-galli, laciniata,
  laevigata, × lavallei,
  phaenopyrum, others
Elaeagnus umbellata
Euonymus europaeus,
  sieboldianus
Gaultheria spp.
Hippophae rhamnoides,
  salicifolia
Koelreuteria paniculata
Leycesteria formosa
Lonicera maackii, tatarica,
  xylosteum, others
Malus baccata and vars., 'Dolgo',
  'Zumi', others
Pernettya mucronata
Rosa glauca, moyesii, rugosa,
  others
Pyracantha spp. and hybrids
Sambucus caerulea, racemosa
Skimmia japonica, reevesiana
Sorbus aucuparia, others
Stranvaesia davidiana
Symphoricarpos spp.
Viburnum davidii, dilatatum,
  opulus, tinus

Root Weevil Resistant Species Rhododendrons*
burmanicum
dauricum
desquamatum
ferrugineum
heliolepis
hemsleyanum
impeditum
intricatum
minus
scintillans

Root Weevil Resistant Hybrid Rhododenrons*
Cilpinense
Cowslip
Exbury Naomi
Jock
Lucky Strike
P. J. Messitt (P. J. M.)
Pride of Leonardslee
    (Luscombei)
Rose Elf
Sapphire
Virginia Richards

---

*from Cooperative Extension publication "How to Identify Rhododendron and Azalea Problems," Washington State University, Pullman, Washington, 1987.

Glossary

Adventitious—plant parts arising from an abnormal site
Alternate—leaves arranged one to a node rather than opposite
Anther—the part of a stamen which bears the pollen
Arborescent—treelike
Ascending—growing obliquely upward
Axil—the angle formed by the union of a leaf stalk with the stem
Berry—a fruit with seeds set in the pulp and surrounded by a skin
Bisexual—having both stamens and pistils
Bole—stem of a tree
Bract—a leaflike or sometimes petal-like organ beneath the true flower
Calyx—the outer set of perianth segments or floral envelope, usually green in color and smaller than the petals; sepals, collectively
Campanulate—bell shaped
Capsule—a dry, dehiscent fruit of two or more cells
Catkin—a slender, usually pendulous inflorescence with scaly bracts enclosing the flowers
Ciliate—with a fringe of marginal hairs
Clone—a group of identical plants originating from a single plant by vegetative propagation
Compound leaf—a leaf made up of two or more parts
Coniferous—cone bearing
Cordate—heart shaped, referring to leaf bases
Coriaceous—leathery in texture
Corolla—the inner whorl or floral envelope, often colored, inside the calyx; the petals, collectively
Crenate—applied to leaf margins with rounded teeth
Culm—stem of grass or bamboo
Cultivar—vegetatively propagated or true-breeding lines of plants of clearly distinguishable character
Cuneate—wedge shaped
Dentate—with wide spreading, pointed teeth

421

Dioecious—producing male and female flowers on separate plants of the same species.

Dissected—deeply and often repeatedly divided into small, slender segments

Endemic—confined to a small geographical area

Entire—not toothed or lobed

Espalier—to train a plant flat against a framework or wall

Fastigiate—of close, erect growth, as in Lombardy Poplar

Fruit—the ripened ovary with surrounding parts

Genus—a group of species possessing traits in common, but differing in lesser characteristics; collectively, genera

Glabrous—smooth; without hairs

Glaucous—covered with a white or blue-white, waxy bloom

Habit—general aspect or manner of growth

Hybrid—plant resulting from a cross between two genetically dissimilar plants

Indumentum—a hairy covering, as of leaves

Inflorescence—arrangement of flowers on the axis; the flower cluster of a plant

Lanceolate—lance-shaped leaves

Legume—dry fruit of the Pea Family, usually splitting down both sides

Lepidote—covered with scurfy scales, as on the undersides of the leaves of certain Rhododendrons

Linear—leaves several times longer than wide, with parallel margins, as in grasses

Monoecious—with separate male and female flowers on the same individual plant

Mucronate—with a small, sharp point

Mutation—a sudden visible genetic change in some character of a plant; a sport

Node—joint of a stem bearing a leaf or bud

Obovate—inversely egg shaped, the broadest part above the middle of a leaf or petal

Opposite—two at a node, as of leaves

Ovate—egg shaped in outline

Palmate—with veins or segments radiating from a common point

Panicle—a branched inflorescence, as distinct from a narrow raceme or spike

Perfoliate—with the leaf blade surrounding the stem

Perianth—calyx and corolla taken together or either of them if only one is present

Petiole—the stalk of a leaf

Pinnate—of leaves, leaflets on either side of a common stalk, featherlike

Pistillate—female flowers having no functional stamens

Pubescence—a general term for hairiness

Raceme—an elongate inflorescence with stalked flowers, opening from base to apex

Reticulate—veins forming a network

Rhizome—an underground stem

Scabrous—rough or gritty to the touch

Scandent—climbing

Scion—a small portion of a plant used in vegetative propagation

Sepal—one unit of the calyx, often green

Serrate—having a saw-toothed edge

Sessile—without a stalk

Solitary—occurring alone, not clustered

Species—a natural group of plants composed of similar individuals, the first subdivision of a genus

Sport—a sudden change in one or more plant characteristics; a mutation

Staminate—male flowers having stamens but no pistil

Stellate—starlike hairs with radiating branches

Stipules—basal appendages of a petiole or leaf stalk

Stoloniferous—with a horizontal, rooting stem

Sucker—a shoot arising from beneath the surface of the ground

Tendril—a modified stem or leaf that twines about a support

Tepal—a segment of a perianth not differentiated into calyx and corolla, as in some Magnolias

Trifoliate—having three leaflets

Variety—subdivision of a species, varying from the type in one or more characteristics

Whorl—parts borne in a circle around an axis

Bibliography

Arno, Stephen F., and Ramona P. Hammerly. (1977), *Northwest Trees;* The Mountaineers, Seattle, Washington.

Bean, W. J. (8th edition 1970–1980), *Trees and Shrubs Hardy in the British Isles;* John Murray Ltd., London. vols I–IV.

Den Ouden, P., and B. K. Boom. (1965), *Manual of Cultivated Conifers;* Martinus Nijhoff, The Hague, Netherlands.

Dirr, Michael A. (1983, 3rd. ed.), *Manual of Woody Landscape Plants;* Stipes Publishing Company, 10–12 Chester Street, Champaign, Illinois.

Galle, Fred C. (1985), *Azaleas;* Timber Press, Portland, Oregon.

Harrison, Charles R. (1975), *Ornamental Conifers;* Hafner Press, Macmillan Co., Inc., New York.

Hitchcock, C. Leo, and Arthur Cronquist. (1973), *Flora of the Pacific Northwest;* University of Washington Press, Seattle and London.

Hitchcock, C. Leo., Arthur Cronquist, Marion Ownbey, and J. W. Thompson. (1955–1969), *Vascular Plants of the Pacific Northwest,* parts 1–5; University of Washington Press, Seattle and London.

Kruckeberg, Arthur R. (1982), *Gardening with Native Plants of the Pacific Northwest;* University of Washington Press, Seattle and London.

Krüssman, Gerd. (1976–1978), *Manual of Cultivated Broad-leaved Trees and Shrubs,* vols. I, II, III, translated by M. E. Epp; Timber Press, Portland, Oregon.

Krüssman, Gerd. (1985), *Manual of Cultivated Conifers,* translated by M. E. Epp; Timber Press, Portland, Oregon.

Krüssman, Gerd. (1982), *Pocket Guide to Choosing Woody Ornamentals,* translated by M. E. Epp; Timber Press, Portland, Oregon.

Lloyd, Christopher. (1965), *Clematis;* Country Life Limited, London.

McClintock, Elizabeth, and Andrew T. Leiser. (1979), *An Annotated Checklist of Woody Ornamental Plants of California, Oregon, and Washington;* University of California, Berkeley, California.

New Western Garden Book (4th ed. 1979), Editors of Sunset Books and Sunset Magazine, Lane Publishing Co., Menlo Park, California.

Rehder, Alfred. (2nd. ed. 1940), *Manual of Cultivated Trees and Shrubs;* Macmillan Co., New York.

Rhododendron Handbook (1980), Part I, *Rhododendron Species in Cultivation;* compiler, Alan Leslie, Royal Horticultural Society, London.

Rhododendron Handbook (1964), Part II, *Rhododendron Hybrids;* Editors P. M. Synge and J. W. Platt, Royal Horticultural Society, London.

Smith, Geoffrey. (1973), *Shrubs and Small Trees for Your Garden;* Collingridge Books, London.

Swartley, John G. (1984), *The Cultivated Hemlocks;* Timber Press, Portland, Oregon.

Thomas, G. S. (new ed. 1983), *Climbing Roses Old and New;* J. M. Dent & Sons Ltd., London, Melbourne, Toronto.

Thomas, G. S. (1957;1983), *The Old Shrub Roses;* J. M. Dent & Sons Ltd., London, Melbourne, Toronto.

Thomas, G. S. (1980 ed.), *Shrub Roses of Today;* J. M. Dent & Sons Ltd., London, Melbourne, Toronto.

Welch, H. J. (1979), *Manual of Dwarf Conifers;* Theophrastus Publishers/Garland Publishing, Inc., New York, New York.

Wyman, Donald. (1971), *Wyman's Gardening Encyclopedia;* Macmillan Co., New York; Collier-Macmillan Ltd., London.

Wyman, Donald. (1965), *Trees for American Gardens,* revised edition; Macmillan Co., New York; Collier-MacMillan Ltd., London.

Woody Plants in the University of Washington Arboretum Washington Park (1977), Compiled by Brian O. Mulligan, University of Washington, College of Forest Resources, Seattle, Washington.

Index to Botanical Names

Index to Common Names

Index to Illustrations